DATE DUE

NO 2 0 02			

DEMCO 38-296

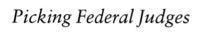

Picking Federal Judges

SHELDON GOLDMAN

Picking Federal Judges

LOWER COURT SELECTION FROM ROOSEVELT THROUGH REAGAN

Yale University Press
New Haven &
London

Set in Sabon type by Keystone Typesetting, Inc.
Printed in the United States of America.

Library of Congress Cataloging-in-Publication Data
Goldman, Sheldon.
    Picking federal judges : lower court selection from Roosevelt
  through Reagan / Sheldon Goldman.
        p.   cm.
    Includes bibliographical references and index.
    ISBN 0-300-06962-6 (cl : alk. paper)
      1. Judges — Selection and appointment — United States — History.
    2. District courts — Officials and employees — Selection and
    appointment — United States — History.   I. Title.
    KF8776.G65   1997
    347.73'234 — dc21   97-7129
                                                                      CIP

A catalogue record for this book is available from the British Library.

The paper in this book meets the guidelines for permanence and durability of the
Committee on Production Guidelines for Book Longevity of the Council on Library Resources.

10 9 8 7 6 5 4 3 2 1

For my children

Contents

Preface

This book tells the story of the selection of lower federal court judges from the administration of Franklin D. Roosevelt through that of Ronald Reagan. I aim to describe the judicial selection process used by each administration, the changes that have occurred over the years, and the impact of those changes on the profile of those selected. To what extent was each president personally involved in the selection process? Did each administration have an agenda that was affected by the actions of the courts, and to what extent did each administration seek to place philosophically compatible people on the bench? How did administrations deal with senators, party organizations, the American Bar Association, and other players in the process? How did administrations respond to calls for the diversification of the bench in terms of gender and race?

The judges whose selection and backgrounds are examined in this book are the lifetime (Article III) appointees to lower federal courts of general jurisdiction. This means that the territorial courts whose judges serve specified terms and the courts of specialized jurisdiction are not included in the statistics and generally are not discussed in terms of selection politics. This choice of focus reflects the fact that Article III courts of general jurisdiction hear cases raising the major constitutional and statutory questions and are considered the most important of the federal courts. Their decisions are more likely to be relevant to the policy concerns of an administration. Selection politics are geographically based in the district courts and courts of appeals.

The selection of Supreme Court justices is not within the purview of this work; it would require a book of its own. Moreover, there are a number of fine studies devoted to Supreme Court selection, whereas lower-court selection has received much less attention. Presidential involvement in Supreme Court selection politics is more intense and, it can be argued, qualitatively different. Nevertheless, there will be occasions within this narrative when Supreme Court appointments will command our attention.

A variety of sources was used to gather material and data, including the presidential papers of the nine presidents examined in this book, personal interviews with key participants in the process, unpublished as well as published Senate Judiciary Committee hearings and documents, materials at the Federal Judicial Center, newspaper accounts from papers across the country, various biographical directories, and the annual editions of the *Martindale-Hubbell Law Directory*. I have drawn upon data I have collected since 1964.

The United States of 1933, when this narrative of lower-court judicial selection begins, was a far different country than the United States of 1989, when we end our story. In those fifty-six years, the population grew from 125 million to 248 million people. America in 1933 was a country mired in the greatest economic depression of the nation's history; in 1989 it was a country in which most people enjoyed prosperity.

This half-century witnessed major economic, technological, and social changes. It also saw African Americans and then women emerge from second-class citizenship and stultifying racism and sexism to the status of full legal equality and unparalleled progress toward economic and occupational opportunity. The struggle to bring blacks and women into the federal judiciary is recounted in this book.

The size, functions, responsibilities, and expenditures of the federal government in 1933 pale by comparison with the government of 1989. The history of the fifty-six-year period covered in this book is one of massive governmental expansion brought on by the New Deal response to the Great Depression. The Second World War accelerated the growth of big government, as did the Great Society programs of the 1960s, which continued to enlarge in the 1970s and beyond. Americans now looked to the federal government to handle economic and social problems, including regulation of industry and business, the defense of civil rights, the provision of social welfare, and the alleviation of the miseries of poverty and crime. The Cold War and arms race produced a vast military-industrial complex that also contributed to a mushrooming bureaucracy.

This change in the role of government led to enormous increases in the caseloads of the federal courts. The Supreme Court itself played a part in the federalization of law, particularly with respect to criminal law. The explosion of litigation in the federal courts produced continuing pressure by the Judicial Conference of the United States to expand the federal judiciary. The various omnibus judgeship acts that passed Congress added judicial appointment opportunities for every administration with the exception of Ford's. The number of lower federal court judgeships quadrupled from 1933 to 1989. Judicial selection by 1989 required a bureaucratic apparatus of its own, and we shall see the growth of that apparatus.

Just as the courts and their business grew, so did the legal profession, whose proportionate increase was even greater than that of the federal bench. There was more than a fourfold increase from 1948 to 1989 in the number of lawyers practicing in the United States. Vast changes in the practice of law took place as well over the fifty-six-year period. Whereas solo practice was the dominant mode of legal practice in 1933, by 1989 a significant proportion of lawyers were members of law firms. Law firms grew to keep pace with expanding litigation, and the large law firms, as we shall see, were a significant source of judicial candidates.

One final note is in order. This book was written with two audiences in mind—general and specialized, and I have tried to meet the needs of each without neglecting the other. I ask the forbearance of each audience if in the course of the narrative I assume too much or too little.

Acknowledgments

Many judges, government officials, lawyers, archivists, librarians, journalists, and academic colleagues have been of invaluable help in my quest for understanding selection processes and politics as well as in data collection. I am grateful to all of them and hope this work will be seen as justifying their time and efforts on my behalf.

I wish to thank the Harry S. Truman Library Institute, the Lyndon Baines Johnson Foundation, and the Gerald R. Ford Library for grants that facilitated extended visits to examine their collections. The University of Massachusetts at Amherst has been wonderfully supportive of my research by way of a Joseph P. Healey Endowment Grant and also a Faculty Fellowship, which permitted me to devote the entire calendar year of 1989 to this project. I am also deeply grateful to the Department of Political Science for providing ongoing support and a scholar-friendly environment.

I also wish to thank the staffs who oversee the presidential papers and the archivists that worked with me. They were helpful and courteous and made my research visits pleasant experiences. In particular, I would like to thank William R. Emerson of the Franklin D. Roosevelt Library at Hyde Park, New York; Philip D. Lagerquist of the Harry S. Truman Library at Independence, Missouri; Dr. James W. Leyerzapf of the Dwight D. Eisenhower Library at Abilene, Kansas; William Johnson of the John F. Kennedy Library at Boston,

Massachusetts; Claudia Anderson of the Lyndon Baines Johnson Library at Austin, Texas; Dr. Byron D. Parham, of the Nixon Presidential Materials Project now located at College Park, Maryland; Dr. Helmie Raaska of the Gerald R. Ford Library at Ann Arbor, Michigan; Garry M. Faulk of the Jimmy Carter Library at Atlanta, Georgia; and Diane Barrie of the Ronald Reagan Library at Simi Valley, California.

Robert Lipshutz was generous in giving me his time as well as access to his personal files. I am deeply grateful for his ongoing interest in this project. Griffin Bell was also gracious in talking with me about judicial selection, and I thank the American Enterprise Institute for bringing us together in June 1981 for a panel on affirmative action for the judiciary. Years earlier, Judge Bell had consented to an extensive interview that included his experience with judicial selection.

In the spring of 1964, Joseph Dolan, then assistant deputy attorney general, and Nicholas Katzenbach, then deputy attorney general, were extraordinarily kind to a young graduate student, offering me the benefit of their candid insights into the selection process and allowing me access to the Justice Department files (with the exception, of course, of the FBI files) of all sitting judges. At that time, the focus of my research was on the courts of appeals, and in the course of several visits to the Justice Department I was able to review and take extensive notes on all active and senior appeals court judges serving in 1964. I have used the data and insights from this research gold mine in a number of published works and also in this book. In 1964, I also benefited from an interview with Lawrence Walsh, who discussed judicial selection during the Eisenhower administration when he served as deputy attorney general. In subsequent years, I received valuable assistance from various Justice Department officials, including John Duffner, Philip Modlin, and Jane Swift. Especially helpful during the Reagan presidency was Stephen J. Markman, who was quite generous with his time and whose cooperation as well as interest in my research will not be forgotten. Over the years I have been aided by Sheila Joy, and I am happy to acknowledge my debt to her.

Twenty-seven appeals court judges were generous and gracious in allowing me to interview them in 1964, and their insights into the appointment process have been a source for this book: Judges Bailey Aldrich, Stanley N. Barnes, Griffin B. Bell, Jean S. Breitenstein, James R. Browning, Richard H. Chambers, John A. Danaher, Henry J. Friendly, J. Cullen Ganey, Clement F. Haynsworth, Jr., Paul R. Hays, Roger J. Kiley, M. Oliver Koelsch, Joseph E. Lumbard, Jr., Marion C. Matthes, Carl E. McGowan, Charles M. Merrill, Harry Phillips, Albert A. Ridge, Elmer J. Schnackenberg, Oliver Seth, Simon E. Sobeloff, Luther M. Swygert, Elbert P. Tuttle, Paul C. Weick, John M. Wisdom, and J. Skelly Wright. More recently, a number of district and appeals judges responded to my confidential inquiries to fill in the gaps in their biographical profiles. To all the members of the third branch who have helped me I offer my profound gratitude.

Thanks are due to the Federal Judicial History Office, which continues to play an important role in gathering data on and from the federal judiciary so that there is a continuing historical record of the people who have served or continue to serve on the federal bench. Peter Wonders was particularly helpful, and I also wish to thank Dr. Bruce Ragsdale. Dr. Russell Wheeler of the Federal Judicial Center has been of ongoing help, as has Dr. Steven Schlesinger of the Administrative Office of the United States Courts. Rodney A. Ross of the National Archives aided in tracking down the ABA ratings of some Eisenhower appointees.

Senate Judiciary Committee staff over the years have earned my gratitude, including Philip Shipman, who was extraordinarily helpful and considerate. It was a great joy to work with my friend and former student Kenneth R. Feinberg when he served as Senator Edward Kennedy's administrative assistant. There are many other staff from the Senate Judiciary Committee who were unfailingly courteous and helpful, among them Mark Gitenstein, Chip Reid, Christine Phillips, Reginald C. Govan, Steve Metalitz, and Harriet Grant.

I have been fortunate to have received the help of various former officials as well as staff of the American Bar Association, including Bernard G. Segal, Robert W. Meserve, Ralph I. Lancaster, Jr., Irene Emsellem, and Stephen Goldspiel.

When I began my study of judicial selection and backgrounds in the 1960s, I was fortunate to be befriended by Professor Harold W. Chase, who offered invaluable guidance, as did Professors Ralph A. Straetz, V. O. Key, Jr., Robert G. McCloskey, and Arthur Sutherland. Other colleagues over the years have been supportive of my endeavors, and I am grateful to them all. I would like to give special mention to Professor Elliot Slotnick for help with the Carter appointees, Professor Peter Fish for sharing his insights and materials on the Carter judicial nomination commissions, and Professors Gerard Gryski, Deborah Barrow, and Gary Zuk for their generosity in sharing data and for sending me a copy of the page proofs of their important book *The Federal Judiciary and Institutional Change* (University of Michigan Press, 1996). The anonymous readers of an earlier version of this book gave it careful scrutiny and offered helpful suggestions.

My thanks also go to Paul Brace, Christine Harrington, and Gary King for inviting me to deliver the James Phelps Stokes Lecture at New York University on April 23, 1987. That lecture, "Judicial Appointments and the Presidential

Agenda," subsequently published in their edited book *The Presidency in American Politics* (New York University Press, 1989), provided the stimulus for my thinking on the linkages between appointments and agendas. I am especially grateful to Christine Harrington for her suggestions.

David Richert, editor of *Judicature*, encouraged me to undertake biennial assessments of judicial appointments, starting with my first article in 1978 on the first two years of Carter appointments. His ongoing interest and enthusiasm and the positive responses from peer reviewers have been deeply appreciated.

My departmental chairs, colleagues, and secretaries over the past thirty years all deserve my thanks, as do students who have aided me in my research. The chairs, who were a constant source of encouragement and support, included William C. Havard, Glen Gordon, Loren P. Beth, Lewis C. Mainzer, George T. Sulzner, and Eric Einhorn. Secretaries who at various times did work connected with this project include Beverly Labbee, Donna Dove, and Vera Smith. Students who have helped me include Jennifer Kates, Phyllis Farley Rippey, Jennifer Kosmelo, Marsha Marotta, Alan Gaitenby, Jeanne Sheehan Zaino, Doug Telling, Tyler Gannon, Matthew Saronson, Diego Figueroa, and Jennifer Houde. My departmental public law colleagues, Dean Alfange and John Brigham, have my gratitude for their long-standing friendship and support. The government documents and law materials staff at the University of Massachusetts Library are consummate professionals who have aided my research over the years. In particular I wish to acknowledge Bill Thompson and Jeanne Kocsis. William C. Ramsey and Joseph M. Kimmel helped with the proofreading.

A special note of thanks is reserved for John Covell, senior editor at Yale University Press, for his friendship, patience, and belief in this project. His encouragement is deeply appreciated, as was the care and attention given my manuscript by the editorial and production staff, especially Richard Miller and Lawrence Kenney.

My three children, Ellen, Jeremy, and Sara, at various times helped type in the data base. My wife Marcia has been a constant source of help and good cheer. Needless to say, all those acknowledged here are not responsible for errors of fact and interpretation. That burden is mine alone.

Picking Federal Judges

Judicial Selection in Theoretical and Historical Perspective

The selection of a Supreme Court justice is front-page news. At times, it may dominate the headlines for days or weeks, as occurred with Lyndon Johnson's ill-fated attempt to elevate Associate Justice Abe Fortas to chief justice, Ronald Reagan's equally ill-fated struggle to place Robert H. Bork on the Supreme Court, and George Bush's ultimately successful fight to win confirmation for Clarence Thomas. Going back further in American history for examples we find similar prolonged public attention to Andrew Jackson's efforts to put Roger B. Taney on the Court and Woodrow Wilson's to appoint Louis D. Brandeis.[1] But throughout American history we find little such national attention given to the selection of lower federal court judges.

In part, this lack of interest may be attributed to the fact that the lower federal judiciary is organized regionally and locally. The metropolitan New York media, for example, have little interest in who is nominated for a U.S. district court judgeship in Iowa or who is being named to the Ninth Circuit on the West Coast. In part, at least until the late 1960s, inattention could also be attributed to the lack of appreciation by the media and the general public of the work of the lower courts and their impact — both in individual cases and cumulatively — on the course of public policy. At most, a local newspaper might have picked up on the politicking by state and local party leaders surrounding an appointment.

As a result of what might be considered public indifference, judicial selection during much of the period covered in this book largely took place shielded from public view.[a] This had the effect of perpetuating public ignorance of the lower courts and the anonymity of the judges who served on them. Because little of consequence was perceived as happening in the selection process, the media generally treated federal judicial selection as an uninteresting event. What occurred behind the scenes, however, was often rich in drama and harbored significance for public policy. Indeed, we can view judicial selection by the president of the United States as an exercise of policymaking furthering a presidential agenda.

While the selection of lower-court judges is rarely a subject of national interest,[2] the decisions of those judges have commanded some attention. In the 1970s and 1980s the federal courts' policymaking activity in civil liberties and civil rights led the courts themselves to become a political issue. The successful election campaign of Ronald Reagan in 1980 focused on the so-called social issues of abortion, prayer in the public schools, busing for the purpose of school desegregation, affirmative action at the workplace, and the rights of criminal defendants, issues defined by court rulings.[b]

When Ronald Reagan took office, his administration perceived the federal courts as being so activist as to have created an imbalance in the federal system that threatened state powers and expanded federal judicial policymaking beyond the competence and capacity of the courts.[3] The Reagan administration saw judicial appointments as intimately linked to the success of the president's domestic-affairs agenda.

By late 1994, another facet of lower-court selection commanded national attention. The administration of Bill Clinton was the subject of media stories noting its historic naming of women and minorities to a majority of its judicial appointments.[4] The struggle for women and minorities to be taken seriously as

a. It can be argued that this was less the case during the Reagan administration, when some media attention was devoted to the administration's ideological/philosophical screening of judicial candidates. Chapter 8 discusses this screening process.

b. During the 1996 presidential election year, Republicans sought to make judicial appointments to the lower courts a campaign issue. President Clinton was portrayed as appointing soft-on-crime liberals. See Senate Judiciary Committee chairman Orrin G. Hatch's speech on the Senate floor as reported in *New York Times,* March 26, 1996, B9. Senator Bob Dole extended this to a full-scale attack on Clinton's lower-court appointments, warning that more Clinton appointees would mean "More Federal intrusion in the lives of average Americans. More centralized power in Washington. Less freedom of religious expression. More rights for criminals. And more arrogant disregard of the rights of law-abiding citizens." *New York Times,* April 20, 1996, p. 1.

federal judicial candidates has been long and difficult, as the selection process was affected by pervasive racism and sexism. The story of how each administration handled the candidacies of women and African Americans shows the excruciatingly slow pace of diversification of the federal bench over the fifty-six-year period encompassed by this book. We will see how integrating the bench by gender and race came to be a policy concern commanding presidential attention.

Presidential Agendas

To understand judicial selection, it is useful to make a distinction between a president's policy agenda, partisan agenda, and personal agenda.[5] By *policy agenda,* I mean the substantive policy goals of an administration, including its legislative and administrative objectives. By *partisan agenda,* I mean the use of presidential power to shore up political support for the president or for the party. By *personal agenda,* I mean the use of the president's discretion to favor a personal friend or associate.

Although the policy agenda, the partisan agenda, and even the personal agenda may all be furthered at the same time, what distinguishes one from the others is presidential motivation. If the principal concern is, for example, to help party leaders, to maintain a good relationship with a senator, to resolve a party rift, to reward individual party supporters, to cater to a particular constituency group, or to enhance the president's reputation and appeal, then presidential action can be seen as promoting a partisan agenda even if there are also policy consequences. If the president is primarily concerned with the policy consequences of his action, the action may be considered part of the policy agenda. If the president's concern is to exercise personal patronage by rewarding a friend or associate, that action may be considered part of a personal agenda.

There are, to be sure, problems with this conceptual scheme. Motivation can be elusive to document. The motivations of administration officials and members of Congress in making recommendations may be different from those of the president. Presidential motives may be mixed, and it may be difficult to be reasonably certain which motive was responsible for presidential behavior. The data sources used in this book are limited in these regards. We thus must, at times, make reasonable inferences based on the available evidence.

When an administration's judicial appointments are essentially partisan-agenda or personal-agenda actions, the policymaking activity of the courts is not seen as related to administration goals. Judicial appointments then are a species of political patronage dependent more on partisan or personal political reasons, including considerations of enhancing the president's appeal, than the appointees' ideology or judicial philosophy. In contrast, an administration whose judicial appointments are driven by its policy agenda will view the courts as likely to affect the success or failure of its policy goals. Hence changes in court policy may be necessary, and an administration can be expected to use the selection process to appoint those who share its ideology.[c]

Assuming the validity of these concepts, can we specify the conditions that lead to the use of judicial appointments to further a policy agenda? I believe we can. As I have written elsewhere, "when the party system is in flux, the constitutional policies of the federal courts will tend to be seen as out of step with the emerging new party system, resulting in policy agenda considerations dominating judicial appointments."[6] Along these lines I have suggested, following the work of scholars of American political parties, that certain presidential elections have signaled the breakup of the old party system and the emergence of a new political order.[7] These elections include Thomas Jefferson's prevailing in 1800, Andrew Jackson's victory in 1828, the election of Abraham Lincoln in 1860, the success of William McKinley in 1896, Franklin Roosevelt's triumph in 1932, and Richard Nixon's elections in 1968 and 1972 reinforced by Ronald Reagan's win in 1980. Judicial selection during a period of party-system stability can be expected to follow a partisan agenda even when a deviating presidential election has temporarily placed in power the party that does not ordinarily dominate that political period.[8] Personal-agenda selection can occur during any period but may be more frequent during a period of party-system stability. The accounts in this book will have relevance for these propositions as we explore judicial selection over the fifty-six years from 1933 to 1989. But first I examine briefly the history of judicial selection from the debates of the Constitutional Convention to the administration of Franklin Roosevelt. This provides a context that furthers understanding of the development of the selection process.

c. There is also the expectation that the president and his administration will ordinarily choose persons who have the education, experience, temperament, and reputation of legal acumen and integrity requisite for judicial office. It would be self-defeating, given that the federal government is the principal litigant in the federal courts, for the Justice Department to help place on the bench mediocre or incompetent individuals. Likewise, it would do no administration good to appoint rogues who could bring disrepute to the office and in the process discredit the appointing administration. In contrast, it may be good politics, furthering the partisan agenda, for an administration to appoint to the courts those who are seen as of high quality. Bar associations and editorial writers approve such appointments, and a quality judiciary may be a legacy important to a president.

Historical Perspectives on Selection

The Constitutional Convention may not have devoted great attention to judicial selection, but it did not ignore the subject. There was a difference of view between supporters of legislative supremacy and those advocating a strong executive. The Virginia Plan included a provision that "a National Judiciary be established . . . to be chosen by the National Legislature." The executive would not be involved in the selection of judges; rather, both houses of the legislature would do the selecting. On June 5, 1787, this aspect of the Virginia Plan was debated, and a consensus soon emerged that selection by the entire legislature would be unwieldy. James Wilson suggested as an alternative that the executive be given exclusive appointment power. The New Jersey Plan also provided for executive appointment of the judiciary. But there was little support for this solution. John Rutledge's views probably reflected the inclinations of many of the delegates that he "was by no means disposed to grant [such] a power to any single person." James Madison suggested that he was "inclined to give [power of judicial selection] to the Senatorial branch," an institution "sufficiently stable and independent" to make "deliberate judgments."[9]

On June 13, Madison proposed that judicial selection be an exclusive power of the Senate, and the convention adopted the motion, apparently without objection. But on July 18, when the matter was reconsidered, James Wilson again proposed "that the Judges be appointed by the Executive." This motion was defeated by a vote of six states to two. A much closer vote came on a compromise motion to have judges appointed by the executive "by and with the advice and consent" of the Senate, but the vote was a tie and the motion failed. Three days later, the convention discussed involvement of the executive in the appointment process, and delegate George Mason stated his view that appointment by the executive was a "dangerous prerogative" that "might even give [the executive] an influence over the Judiciary department itself." The convention reaffirmed the Senate's exclusive power of judicial appointment by a vote of six states to three.[10]

On August 6, 1787, the Committee on Detail presented its draft of the Constitution, which specified in Article IX, Section 1, that the Senate shall have the power to appoint Supreme Court justices. This provision was neither discussed nor acted upon. Ultimately, on September 4, the Special Committee on Postponed Matters turned to the proposal that had previously failed on a tie vote, that "The President . . . shall nominate and by and with the advice and consent of the Senate shall appoint . . . Judges of the supreme Court, and all other officers of the U.S. whose appointments are not otherwise herein provided for." The "all other officers" included any lower-court judgeships that might be created. On September 7, the Convention discussed this provision. Gouverneur Morris from Pennsylvania argued in its favor: "as the President was to nominate, there would be responsibility, and as the Senate was to concur, there would be security." The Convention unanimously approved the provision for the appointment of judges to the Supreme Court, and by a vote of nine states to two it agreed to the "all other officers" clause.[11]

Clearly, the founders conceived of a major role for the Senate in the selection process. During debate on these provisions, however, the delegates also approved an amendment that allowed appointments when Congress is in recess to be made by the president. In the spirit of compromise with supporters of executive authority, the president was to receive important appointment powers.

What finally emerged in the Constitution was the placement of judicial selection in Article II, which is devoted to the powers of the president. In Article II, Section 2, the Constitution states that the president "shall nominate, and by and with the Advice and Consent of the Senate, shall appoint . . . Judges of the supreme Court, and all other Officers of the United States." The provision for recess appointments, in paragraph 3, states that the president has the authority "to fill up all Vacancies that may happen during the Recess of the Senate, by granting Commissions which shall expire at the End of their next Session." Thus the placement of the power of judicial selection with the powers of the president rather than those of Congress suggests that the executive branch is a principal player in the appointment process.[12]

The *Federalist Papers* offer some insight into the intent of the framers. In *Federalist 76*, Alexander Hamilton pointed out that the president has sole responsibility for nominations and that the Senate cannot name the appointee. Hamilton observed that it is "not very probable that [the president's] nomination would often be overruled." Yet "the necessity of [the Senate's] concurrence . . . would be an excellent check upon a spirit of favoritism in the President, and would tend greatly to preventing the appointment of unfit characters."[13]

Whatever the intent of the framers may have been, judicial selection began a life of its own with the first administration of George Washington. The Judiciary Act of 1789 established the structure of the federal court system and provided for five associate justices of the Supreme Court, one chief justice, and thirteen district court judges.[14] Responsibility for judicial selection was placed in the office of the secretary of state and remained there until 1853, when President Franklin Pierce, heeding the advice of his attorney general, Caleb Cushing, shifted responsibility for handling judicial nominations to the attorney general in the Department of Justice.

The first two presidents, Washington and John Adams, appointed fellow Federalists to the federal courts. When Adams was defeated for reelection in 1800 by the Democratic-Republican Thomas Jefferson, the lame duck Federalist Congress enacted the Judiciary Act of 1801, which created new federal court positions including separate circuit court judgeships.[d] Thomas Jefferson recognized the policy implications of Federalist judges dominating the federal judiciary and noted in a letter to James Madison, "The Federalists . . . have retired into the judiciary as a stronghold . . . and from that battery all the works of Republicanism are to be beaten down and erased."[15] Kermit Hall, in his study of nineteenth-century lower-court judicial appointments, found that kinship ties (either by blood or by marriage) to leading Jeffersonian Republican congressmen played a major role in the selection of the several dozen lower-court judges during the first party system, under Presidents Jefferson, Madison, James Monroe, and John Quincy Adams.[16]

Andrew Jackson's presidency ushered in the second party system, with the new Democratic Party wearing the mantle of champion of democracy for the lower classes and enemy of privilege and wealth. Jackson's administration was sympathetic to the states setting economic and social-welfare policy. The property-oriented and federal-supremacy-minded Supreme Court of Chief Justice John Marshall was not in tune with the song of Jacksonian democracy. Jackson, however, used his power of appointment to name to the Supreme Court five men, including Chief Justice Roger B. Taney, whose policy views were in harmony with those of the administration. So, too, with Jackson's seventeen district judge appointments. Hall noted that Jackson "appreciated that judicial decision making often reflected a judge's values" and consequently was determined to name as judges only those (in Jackson's words) whose "principles of the Constitution are sound, and well fixed."[17]

Once the new party system was established, judicial appointments by Jackson's successor, Martin Van Buren, became "more party directed than it had been during Jackson's administration."[18] Van Buren made seventeen lower-court nominations. Unlike Jackson's, Van Buren's nominees (with only one exception) met no opposition in the Senate.

Van Buren was defeated for reelection by the Whig Party ticket of William Henry Harrison and John Tyler, the first deviating election within a stable party system.[e] Harrison died one month into his term and Tyler succeeded to

d. The intermediate level of the federal court system that we know today, the United States Courts of Appeals, was not established until 1891.

e. A deviating election occurs when short-term events stimulate the election of the party that is not ordinarily in control of the White House. The party balance does not shift significantly, and in four or eight years there is a return to the majority party.

the presidency. Hall found that Tyler's twenty-two lower-court nominations were calculated to provide support for his reelection as a third-party candidate. The Democrat James Polk succeeded Tyler in 1845, and his eight district court nominations, according to Hall, were guided by the Democrats in Congress.[19]

In 1848, another deviating presidential election sent the Whig candidate Zachary Taylor to the White House. Taylor, in making his ten lower-court appointments, "wielded . . . judicial patronage in an outwardly party-directed fashion."[20] His successor, Millard Fillmore, assuming the presidency after Taylor's death in office, also used judicial appointments for partisan purposes.

Democrat Franklin Pierce was elected president in 1852, when the North-South conflict was threatening to destroy the Democratic Party, if not the nation. The evidence suggests that Pierce tried to accommodate both the northern and southern wings of the party, and in his judicial appointments he generally deferred to Democrats in Congress. With the election of Democrat James Buchanan and the emergence of the new Republican Party, the party system that had been in place since Andrew Jackson was coming apart. Buchanan wanted to appoint judges with a conservative view but generally felt obliged to defer to Democratic senators loyal to him. Nevertheless, he was more concerned with ideology than had been any president since Jackson.[21]

The split within the Democratic Party, the demise of the Whig Party, the emergence of the new Republican Party, the election of Republican Abraham Lincoln in 1860, and the onset of the Civil War brought about the third party system. President Lincoln's judicial appointments, including his four to the Supreme Court, helped further his policy agenda.[22] After the Civil War, the Republican Party dominated a relatively stable party system. Democrat Grover Cleveland won election in 1884 and 1892, but these can be seen as deviating elections. Cleveland did not view the federal courts as fostering policy in conflict with his own policy agenda. Indeed, Cleveland's four appointments to the Supreme Court were Democrats who shared conservative economic views. There is no evidence that they and Cleveland's thirty-four lower-court appointments (all Democrats) were intended to produce major policy shifts. Rather, traditional political patronage considerations within the partisan agenda dominated judicial selection.

In the 1896 presidential election, the Democratic Party and the Populists joined forces, transforming American politics and producing the fourth party system, which lasted until the Great Depression. The Republican Party's victory in 1896 marked a new dominance over a changed party system. The progressive wing of the party viewed the courts as hostile to efforts by government to regulate the excesses of capitalism. When Theodore Roosevelt became

president in September 1901, following the assassination of William McKinley, the Progressive movement became fully integrated within the Republican
Party, and policy agenda considerations began to influence court appointments. Roosevelt's successor, William Howard Taft, took an interest in judicial selection beyond that of his predecessors. Three of his appointees to the
Supreme Court were Democrats, as were five of his thirty-nine lower-court
judicial appointments. Taft screened his appointments to assure that they
shared his "real politics."[23]

Judicial selection in the administrations of Woodrow Wilson, whose elections can be considered deviating elections, appear to have been primarily
partisan agenda appointments. The return to Republican domination in the
1920s was a return to selection as usual. There is no evidence that Presidents
Harding, Coolidge, or Hoover sought to change court policy or saw appointments to the federal courts as a vehicle for furthering their policy agendas.
However, Herbert Hoover, with the aid of his attorney general, William Mitchell, attempted to break the grip that Republican senators had on lower-court
appointments in order to improve the quality of the appointees. This resulted
in several battles with Republican senators and ultimately in an administration retreat.[24]

The Mechanics of Judicial Selection

The mechanics of judicial selection as practiced by the administration of
Franklin Roosevelt remained intact for much of the next fifty-six years. These
procedures and practices were concisely summarized for the incoming Nixon
administration in late November 1968 by Warren Christopher, deputy attorney general in the Johnson administration, in a "Memorandum to My
Successor."[25][f]

Christopher began by noting that the deputy attorney general traditionally
assisted the attorney general "by advising on and processing judicial appointments."[26] The presidential appointment unit was housed in the deputy's office
under the supervision of an assistant to the deputy.

Christopher pointed out that judicial vacancies typically arise from death,
resignation, retirement, disability, or legislation creating new judicial posi-

---

f. More than twenty-four years later, Warren Christopher was appointed secretary of
state in the Clinton administration serving during Clinton's first term. The identity of
Christopher as the author of the memorandum was revealed by Larry Temple, of the
Johnson White House staff, in his Oral History interview with Joe B. Frantz, on August 11, 1970. Transcript of Tape 7, pp. 45–46. LBJ Library.

tions.ᵍ Candidates for judicial office come from many sources, including state and local judiciaries, the federal district bench (for positions on the appeals courts), private practice, law school faculties, and state and federal official-dom. Similarly, suggestions to fill judicial vacancies may come from the president and his staff in the White House, officials in the Department of Justice, senators, representatives, governors, state and local party leaders, state and local bar associations, individuals who want to be considered for judgeships, and individuals who recommend others.[27]

Each week, the assistant to the deputy attorney general prepares and distributes on a confidential, need-to-know basis lists containing the name of each candidate for a judicial position on a specific court, the sponsors and endorsers of the candidate, and the status of the investigation. Files are begun on all potential judicial candidates, and they are first screened in the deputy's office. Christopher observed that "every effort is, of course, made throughout the process to be attuned" to the president's "wishes," and he highlighted the role of senators: "Recommendations of a Senator of the President's Party from the state where a vacancy exists are very important. Moreover, the views of any Senator, whatever his Party, from the state where the vacancy exists cannot be ignored, for Senate tradition gives them a virtual right of veto."[28]

Personal data questionnaires are sent to candidates who survive the initial screening, and they return the completed copies to the Justice Department and, since the 1950s, to the chair of the American Bar Association Standing Committee on Federal Judiciary. The ABA committee is asked to make a confidential, informal evaluation based upon responses to the questionnaire "and discreet inquiries made by the Chairman of the Committee and the ABA representative from the candidate's area." The "informal" evaluation "can perhaps best be described as a prediction as [to] what the ABA's formal inquiry will find."[29] The ABA ratings in use from the latter part of the Eisenhower presidency until the Bush administration were "exceptionally well qualified," "well qualified," "qualified," and "not qualified."ʰ

If the ABA's informal evaluation is favorable, the Federal Bureau of Investigation then investigates the candidate. As Christopher explained, "In this process, agents interview Federal and state judges, attorneys, associates, government officials, business and civic leaders, religious and civil rights leaders, neighbors and personal physician. National agency, police and credit checks

g. A vacancy can also be created through the rarely used provisions of impeachment by the House and removal after conviction by the Senate.

h. The "exceptionally well qualified" rating was dropped at the start of the Bush administration.

are made. An Internal Revenue Service report is obtained. Concurrently a formal report of the ABA is requested. The formal report will reflect a vote by all members of the ABA Committee."[30]

Assuming that both the FBI and ABA reports are favorable and the Justice Department decides to proceed,[i] the next step is the preparation of papers of recommendation to be transmitted to the attorney general. These papers include:

1. A letter from the attorney general to the president formally recommending the nomination;
2. A memorandum from the deputy attorney general to a "designated" White House assistant "touching on matters not in the attorney general's formal letter" (typically who recommended the candidate and what political clearances were obtained);
3. The candidate's resume or biographical sketch;
4. A summary of the FBI Report along with the complete report itself;
5. All other file material on the candidate including the responses to the personal data questionnaire.[31]

When the attorney general signs the letter of recommendation to the president, the deputy attorney general's office then sends that letter, the deputy's memorandum, the biographical sketch of the nominee, and the formal nomination document to the designated official in the White House. Christopher advised "never to reveal that papers have been sent to the White House. Generally preliminary discussions take place between the Attorney General and the President, the Attorney General and the Deputy Attorney General, and the Deputy Attorney General and the White House staff before papers are finally sent to the White House. If the President approves, the nomination is signed and sent to the Senate."[32]

When the Senate receives the nomination, it is referred to the Senate Judiciary Committee. At the time the nomination goes to the Senate, a copy of the biographical sketch is sent to the Office of Public Information in the Department of Justice. The White House Press Office is also apprised of the nomination.

---

i. The locus of the decision to proceed began to change during the Carter administration, when the Office of White House Counsel became increasingly involved in the selection process. The Reagan administration created a joint White House–Justice Department committee chaired by the White House counsel to oversee the selection process. Presidents Bush and Clinton retained the committee concept, and this bureaucratic structure now appears to be a permanent part of the selection process. The implications of this change are discussed in chapters 7 and 8.

At the Senate Judiciary Committee, the counsel for the committee sends out "blue slips" to the two senators from the nominee's state. Christopher noted that if a blue slip is returned marked "objection" by either senator "regardless of party," "the custom is that no hearing will be scheduled."ʲ But if the blue slips are returned marked "no objection," "counsel, with approval of Chairman, places notice in Congressional Record scheduling hearing on the nomination, usually not less than seven days hence."[33]

Christopher pointed out that the committee depends upon the Justice Department officials to notify the nominee to be present at the hearing. One Justice Department official has the responsibility for briefing the nominee on the hearing and providing guidance in answering questions. A Justice Department official usually accompanies the nominee to the hearing and remains with the nominee. At the hearing itself, it is traditional for both senators from the nominee's home state to introduce the nominee to the nominations committee or subcommittee. As Christopher observed, "Unless controversial, hearings last only a few minutes."[34] Assuming a favorable subcommittee recommendation, the nomination is considered at the next executive session of the full Judiciary Committee. If the full committee votes in favor, it then sends the nomination to the Senate with a formal recommendation to confirm.

The nomination is typically not acted upon by the Senate for a twenty-four-hour period; however, if unanimous consent is given, the nomination can be brought up the same day for consideration. The Senate generally votes by voice vote; roll-call votes on judicial nominations occur only when there is controversy. If a nomination is not acted upon, it dies at the end of the session unless there is a motion to carry it over to the next session. If a carry-over motion is not made and approved, the president must renominate the candidate. All nominations die at the end of a Congress.

Once the Senate gives its advice and consent, the president must sign the judicial commission officially appointing the individual. The appointee's seniority on the bench dates from the day the commission is signed. The signed commission is returned to the Justice Department for engraving the date of appointment (determined by the actual day the president signs the commission) and for the signature of the attorney general and the placing of the Justice Department seal. The deputy attorney general then sends the commission by

j. In Christopher's time, if a senator withheld the blue slip, the head of the Senate Judiciary Committee, James O. Eastland, likewise refused to schedule a hearing. In 1979, the new Senate Judiciary Committee head, Edward Kennedy, announced that the withholding of a blue slip would not necessarily mean the demise of a nomination. Kennedy said he would refer the nomination to the full committee to determine a course of action.

registered mail to the appointee, along with the oath of office and a photocopy of the confirmation document from the Senate.

Each of the next seven chapters explores one or two presidencies, starting with that of Franklin D. Roosevelt and continuing in chronological order. Each chapter opens with a brief historical overview and is followed by an examination of the evidence of presidential involvement in judicial selection within the context of the overall political landscape. This opens a window on presidential motives and the extent to which policy, partisan, and personal agendas dominated the judicial selection process of each presidency. The emphasis is on detail in order to try to capture the flavor of the appointment process within each administration. Appointments to the federal district bench, which typically are dominated by senators of the president's party, are differentiated from appointments to the federal appeals (or circuit) courts, which span several states and traditionally offer an administration more leeway in choosing nominees.[k]

k. For those unfamiliar with the structure of the federal court system some explanation is in order. The principal federal trial courts are the United States district courts. Each state has at least one federal district court, and some have as many as four. Where states contain more than one district, each district court is confined to specific geographic boundaries. For example, the state of Pennsylvania is divided into three geographic regions where the district courts are located: Pennsylvania Eastern, Pennsylvania Middle, and Pennsylvania Western. There are eighty-nine federal district courts in the states. There is also one federal district for the District of Columbia and one for Puerto Rico. These federal district courts, which total ninety-one, are courts of general jurisdiction and are composed of judges who have lifetime tenure. There are currently 645 judgeship positions on these courts. In addition, there are federal district courts in the federal territories of Guam, the Virgin Islands, and the Northern Mariana Islands whose judges do not have lifetime tenure (their terms of office are for ten years) and whose courts deal with both federal and local concerns. These territorial courts as well as federal trial courts of specialized jurisdiction such as what once was the Customs Court but is now the Court of International Trade are not covered in this book.

Federal district courts of general jurisdiction may hear cases that raise questions of federal statutory law (acts of Congress), federal constitutional law (concerning a provision of the United States Constitution), a federal treaty, or disputes under admiralty or maritime law. Furthermore, federal courts have diversity of citizenship jurisdiction whereby a citizen of one state can sue a citizen of another state in a federal district court situated in either state provided that the amount at issue meets the congressionally set minimum (currently it is $50,000).

When a case has been tried by a federal district court, the losing party may take an appeal to one of the United States courts of appeals (also called circuit courts). There are currently eleven numbered regional circuits, each encompassing at least five district

I next focus on the president's policy agenda and the extent to which it had an impact on judicial selection. I then consider the role of senators in the process. Examples focusing on senators help us to form a view of the selection process of each administration and the extent to which administrations have defined the partisan agenda in terms of senatorial patronage.

In each chapter I look at numerous other influences on the appointment process, including the extensiveness of partisan considerations. We will see over the years, for example, the gradual waning of the influence of the national party organizations on the selection process and the lessening to some extent of the dispensing of judgeships as political patronage. Geographic considerations are explored not only with respect to the regional appeals courts but also concerning the state-based district courts. We also view the role of the attorney general, other key administration and political figures, and, from the Eisenhower administration forward, the American Bar Association.

An important issue throughout the book is the role of gender and race in the selection process. The chapters that follow document the barriers and biases that women and African Americans faced in being taken seriously for judgeships and trace the slow process of diversification of the bench.

The final section of each chapter paints a composite portrait of the judiciary appointed by each president. And the concluding chapter contains an overview of demographic trends among judicial appointees over the nine presidential administrations.

---

courts and at least three states. The twelfth circuit is the United States Court of Appeals for the District of Columbia, which hears appeals not only from the federal district court for the District of Columbia but also involving administrative agencies and other boards or commissions based in Washington, D.C. The United States Court of Appeals for the Federal Circuit is a specialized court hearing claims, customs, patent, copyright, and trademark appeals. Only the appeals courts of general jurisdiction are considered in this book. Currently there are 167 judgeships on those courts. Appeals courts hear cases in panels of three judges (occasionally a case is reheard by the entire membership of the court).

The Supreme Court of the United States is at the head of the federal judicial system. Unlike the trial and appeals courts, which are obliged to hear cases that meet jurisdictional and other technical requirements, the Supreme Court for the most part can choose which cases to hear. Every president considered in this book with the exception of Carter was able to fill at least one of the nine positions on the Supreme Court.

2

Roosevelt Remakes the Courts

The presidency of Franklin D. Roosevelt was shaped by the twin national traumas of the Great Depression and the Second World War.[1] The extraordinary events were matched by an extraordinary politician — the quintessential hands-on president to whom subsequent presidents have inevitably been compared. Roosevelt's New Deal inaugurated the welfare state and the regulated economy, which were among the great legacies of his administration. So too was the transformation of the federal courts and the constitutional law they expounded.

In 1932, the Republican president Herbert Hoover was running for reelection as the country was experiencing its severest economic crisis. He was opposed by the Democratic Party candidate, New York governor Franklin Roosevelt, who blamed the Depression on Hoover and the Republicans. The voters not only elected Roosevelt by a landslide, they also carried into office an overwhelmingly Democratic Congress — Democrats outnumbered Republicans in the House by 313 to 117 and in the Senate by 59 to 36.[2]

Roosevelt offered Americans a "new deal," and during his first one hundred days in office he acted dramatically. His agenda was designed to restore public confidence in the economy, ameliorate the harsh effects of the Depression, and institute fundamental economic and social-welfare reform. In so doing, the federal government expanded its role with the assumption of many new responsibilities. This had a profound effect on the work of the federal courts, whose judges were now asked to interpret federal laws and administrative actions of unprecedented reach. As the power of the federal government increased, so did the power of the federal judiciary, thereby making federal judicial selection a process with profound implications for administration policy.

During the first hundred days Roosevelt sponsored legislation that provided for federal regulation of the banking industry and created the Federal Deposit Insurance Corporation to protect depositors. The Securities Act of 1933 sought to shield investors and established federal government regulation of the stock market and the investment industry. The Agricultural Adjustment Act was aimed at rescuing farmers and inaugurated a system of agricultural financial support and regulation. The National Industrial Recovery Act created a program designed to help business and labor. The United States went off the gold standard, and clauses in public and private contracts requiring payment in gold-backed currency were voided by an act of Congress. The Federal Emergency Relief Administration provided emergency aid directly to state and local governments, including federally created jobs for those able to work and money payments to those who could not. The Tennessee Valley Authority offered inexpensive public hydroelectric power and helped to rehabilitate a seven-state region. These and other New Deal programs fundamentally redefined the task of the federal government.

In the congressional elections of 1934, Democrats gained nine seats in the House and ten in the Senate, and these results were widely seen as a vote of confidence in Roosevelt and the New Deal. But the country still faced serious economic difficulties. During early 1935, there was much labor unrest and many Americans demanded more fundamental reform of American institutions. The New Deal responded by taking a sharp left turn. Roosevelt introduced such measures as a Wealth Tax, the Social Security Administration, the Works Progress Administration (WPA) program that would build public works and support Americans in a wide variety of occupations, legislation ending holding companies, and the National Labor Relations Act, which recognized and protected labor's right to unionize.

As the New Deal turned leftward, the federal courts, especially the Supreme Court, turned obstructionist. Over the sixteen months beginning in January 1935, the Supreme Court heard ten major cases concerning New Deal measures and in eight of them struck down legislation as unconstitutional. But the American people spoke once again in the presidential election of 1936, returning Roosevelt to office with 60.8 percent of the vote (a record that would last until Lyndon Johnson's election in 1964). Roosevelt would be returned to office twice more — in 1940 and 1944 by comfortable popular margins.

After the election of 1936, Roosevelt introduced a court reform proposal that was designed to pressure the Supreme Court to stop blocking the New Deal. Under this prodding by the president, later buttressed by eight associate justice appointments to the Supreme Court, the high Court effectuated a constitutional revolution, legitimating the legal basis for the New Deal and the new role of the federal government in assuming responsibility for the nation's economic and social welfare. At the same time, the United States entered a new political era in which the Democratic Party dominated the institutions of national government for most of the next several decades.

When we examine in greater detail the Roosevelt administration's selection process of lower federal court judges, we find a complex reality not unlike judicial selection in previous administrations. Yet we can also discern distinctive elements of judicial selection that lend support to the policy-agenda hypothesis suggested in the first chapter. To be sure, however, judicial selection was to evolve in the shadow of traditionally understood senatorial and party politics.

To best understand judicial selection under Roosevelt, it is necessary to appreciate the president's personal involvement in the process, an involvement that continued through the tense and wearying years of the Second World War.

Presidential Involvement in Selection

Franklin D. Roosevelt was a president who enjoyed politics, political problem solving, and micromanagement. His administrative style frequently defied the clear lines of an organizational chart. He took an interest in all aspects of his administration and embraced being at the center of the selection of lower-court judges. Indeed, over the twelve years of his presidency, Roosevelt filled 133 lifetime lower-court judgeships to the district courts and fifty to the appeals bench. Filling these judgeships apparently did not consume an unreasonable amount of time, and the dispensing of these relatively scarce and valuable political resources was an activity that Roosevelt apparently relished.

Roosevelt's personal interest and involvement appear with some frequency in his presidential papers. For example, on May 2, 1934, Roosevelt proposed a solution to a patronage dispute in South Carolina: "Here is a suggested slate to cover the whole South Carolina problem. Will you talk with Jim Farley [Chairman of the Democratic National Committee and Postmaster General] about it and you two might then have a conference with [South Carolina] Senators

Byrnes and Smith." Roosevelt then offered a five-point package, including the appointment of a district judge. "Myers for District Judge from Charleston. This is [Senator] Jim Byrnes' recommendation." Other elements of the package included two federal marshals, one United States attorney, and the collector of customs for South Carolina.³ Myers was named to the federal district bench the following month.

When Missouri Democratic senator Bennett Champ Clark wanted his former campaign manager, George H. Moore, to receive a federal district judgeship, Roosevelt agreed. The *St. Louis Post-Dispatch*, however, responded with an editorial attacking Moore as an undistinguished political hack. Roosevelt shot back a memo on March 19, 1935, to Attorney General Homer Cummings: "Send for Chas. Ross and see if Post Dispatch will stop attacks on Moore if he made Judge. Do it on ground that we have gone over every charge and they do not hold water."⁴ Moore was appointed even though the editorial attacks continued.

Roosevelt's papers reveal occasional instances of the president's explicit use of a judicial appointment to further his personal agenda. For example, in a memo to Cummings on August 15, 1935, Roosevelt wrote: "I understand that Judge Edward R. Meek of the northern district of Texas will retire this Autumn. I should personally much like to have you consider former Lieutenant Governor T. W. Davidson, an old friend and supporter of ours and, incidentally, I think both the Senators would approve."

Davidson was checked out by the Justice Department and then formally recommended. However, Texas senator Tom Connally was not pleased with the appointment. On January 21, 1936, the day before the nomination was sent to the Senate, Roosevelt wrote to Connally explaining why he was nominating Davidson and suggested to Connally that "this could be called a personal appointment on my part."⁵ Davidson was subsequently confirmed.

The president's personal involvement in judicial selection can also be seen in the communications from the attorney general to the president. Cummings wrote to Roosevelt on March 25, 1935:

> I received through Miss LeHand [Roosevelt's personal secretary] your message relative to the United States Judge in Rhode Island. I told Miss LeHand that I had but lately received a letter from Senator [Peter G.] Gerry in which he recommended John Mahoney. I have since contacted Senator Gerry and he feels pretty strongly that John Mahoney should have the place. . . . Mr. Gerry speaks very highly of the other leading candidates; namely Mr. Hartigan, the present Attorney General, and Mr. George Hurley, the one you mentioned. He says they are very able men, but no abler than Mahoney, and do not stand any higher, and have not had as much experience in Federal practice. . . . I

shall have all of the candidates carefully checked up. . . . Perhaps I ought to add that Judge Letts [Federal District Judge Ira L. Letts, whose resignation created the vacancy] telephoned in to this office and volunteered the information that he thought either Hartigan or Hurley stood higher at the bar than Mahoney, although he spoke very well of Mahoney.

On the top of the page Roosevelt scrawled to his appointments secretary, Marvin H. ("Mac") McIntyre: "Take up appointment with me."[6]

The above also gives some hint of the variety of participants in the process. But the story continues. Roosevelt then had Thomas Corcoran, a close political associate and administration official, survey the situation. Corcoran wrote back: "Have checked Rhode Island judgeship . . . Gerry's choice Mahoney, Governor [Theodore Francis] Green's choice Hartigan. Probable second choice of both George Hurley, recommended by [Harvard law professor] Zechariah Chafee and Felix [Frankfurter, also a Harvard law professor and later a Roosevelt appointee to the Supreme Court]. In order of general legal ability, Hurley clearly ranks way ahead of others — then Mahoney . . . and last Hartigan."[7] Roosevelt selected Mahoney, whose nomination was sent to the Senate the following month. When a vacancy on the First Circuit opened up in September 1939, former governor and now senator Green pushed for the elevation of Mahoney and the selection of Hartigan to fill the district judgeship that Mahoney would vacate. Roosevelt wrote a memo to Attorney General Frank Murphy (who replaced Cummings in the beginning of 1939) on November 1: "Theo. Green insists. Shall we?"[8] Although there were other candidates for the First Circuit position with political backing, Roosevelt went along with Senator Green's package, and the names of Judge Mahoney and John Hartigan were sent to the Senate on January 11, 1940. (Hartigan himself would later be elevated to the First Circuit by President Harry S. Truman.)

After his landslide reelection victory in 1936, Roosevelt confronted the constitutional crisis that had begun brewing about two years earlier when the federal courts began enjoining and then striking down a series of New Deal measures. The Supreme Court was the focus of attention with Roosevelt's court reform plan, introduced on February 5, 1937, that soon became known as the "court packing" plan. The plan would have allowed the president to appoint an additional justice for every justice over the age of seventy who did not voluntarily retire (with a maximum of six new appointments). Had the plan been enacted by Congress, Roosevelt would have been able immediately to name enough new justices to give the New Deal a majority on the Court.[9]

Presidential involvement in the selection of lower-court judges increasingly reflected a new concern with the policy agenda. For example, on January 16, 1937, some three weeks before the court reform plan was announced, Roosevelt wrote to McIntyre concerning the candidacy of Sidney C. Mize (who was strongly backed by one of the Mississippi senators) for a district judgeship in Mississippi: "I want more information on the man as to whether he is a liberal or a reactionary, what sort of fellow he is."[10] McIntyre contacted Joseph B. Keenan, the assistant to the attorney general in charge of judgeship matters, and on January 25 Keenan replied, enclosing a letter from William Green, the president of the American Federation of Labor, endorsing Mize. Keenan also noted that he looked carefully "into this matter . . . and I am convinced that Mr. Mize is a man of liberal views and sound legal learning and would measure up in all respects to the expectations of the President."[a]

Roosevelt was considering appointing Claude McColloch, the state chairman of the Democratic Party in Oregon and a Roosevelt supporter, to the federal district court in Oregon. The attorney general submitted the formal recommendation for nomination on June 17, 1937. But Roosevelt was told that McColloch was too friendly with private utility interests, and this so alarmed Roosevelt that he personally asked Keenan to look into it. (It was typical of Roosevelt to go outside of channels to lower-level officials, who would report back directly to Roosevelt with the information they had gathered.)[11] The next day Keenan sent a five-page memo to Roosevelt which disputed the allegations against McColloch: "I know how important it is that you be in possession of all the facts particularly on matters which affect so vitally one of the major objectives of the Administration."[12] Roosevelt, however, held onto the nomination and allowed the opposition to the nomination to be articulated. Indeed, in a letter dated July 15, Secretary of the Interior Harold Ickes wrote to Roosevelt opposing McColloch because of alleged ties to private power interests. Nevertheless, Roosevelt apparently felt comfortable going ahead with the nomination, which was sent to the Senate on August 5.

Although policy-agenda considerations became more deliberately a part of the selection process, the president's typical involvement indicated a pragmatic, partisan-agenda approach to lower-court selection. For example, there were two leading candidates for a district judgeship in New York, James Duffy, a congressman from New York, and the well-connected Rochester corporation counsel Harold P. Burke. In a memo to Cummings on February 19, 1937, Roosevelt asked: "Will you look into this personally? I do not know anything about either Burke or Duffy except that Burke is the organization choice. I have felt all along that Bernard Ryan might be a good compromise. Ryan is now a member of the State Court of Claims in Albany." Ryan's can-

a. Years later, Victor Navasky characterized Mize as "a diehard segregationist judge." *Kennedy Justice* (New York: Atheneum, 1971), 265.

didacy, however, did not get off the ground. After receiving reports on the leading candidates, Roosevelt wrote to both Cummings and Jim Farley on March 1 that "Jim Duffy of Rochester [is] much better than Burke who is 'small town.'" The matter was resolved, however, when Duffy was appointed by the governor of New York to a New York State Supreme Court judgeship. Roosevelt sent Burke's name to the Senate on April 27.[13]

Another example offers some insight into Roosevelt's selection calculus. In a memo to Cummings on February 20, 1937, Roosevelt wrote: "Will you give consideration to Judge Philip J. Finnegan of the Cook County Circuit Court for one of the [U.S. Seventh] Circuit Court vacancies? He is a brother of Dick Finnegan of the Chicago Times. Please also look into the qualifications of Charles P. Schwartz of Chicago — Jewish immigrant from Poland in his boyhood, brilliant record at the University of Chicago, Secretary to [federal circuit] Judge Julian Mack, advisor and personal attorney to [social-work pioneer] Jane Addams."[14] Roosevelt here paid keen attention to press connections and ethnic background. However, nothing came of Roosevelt's suggestions. More than a decade later, in 1949, Philip Finnegan was appointed by President Truman to the U.S. Court of Appeals for the Seventh Circuit.

In these examples we see Roosevelt maintaining an active interest in who goes on the bench, even though his preferences did not necessarily translate into judicial appointments. There were, however, occasions when the president's wish was indeed a command. Roosevelt sent a memo to Attorney General Robert Jackson (who replaced Frank Murphy in 1940 after Murphy was appointed to the Supreme Court) conveying his wishes concerning two vacancies in California: "Why not put in Jefty [James F. T.] O'Connor for one place and let the other go until after election?"[15] O'Connor, a personal friend who managed Roosevelt's primary campaign in California in 1932, served as comptroller of the currency from 1933 to 1938 and at Roosevelt's request ran for governor of California in 1938 but was defeated. His nomination was sent to the Senate about three weeks later, and the second seat was not filled until after the 1940 presidential election.

In 1943, Attorney General Francis Biddle (who succeeded Jackson when Jackson was appointed to the Supreme Court in 1941), on the basis of a highly negative FBI report, strongly opposed naming Richard M. Duncan to a federal district court position in Missouri. Duncan, a Democratic congressman defeated for reelection in 1942, was strongly backed by Missouri senator Harry S. Truman. Roosevelt, in a memo to Biddle on June 17, 1943, noted: "Duncan cannot be as impossible as you think, for he has the affection and sincere recommendation of practically everybody who has ever known him." In reply, Biddle detailed the basis of his negative assessment of Duncan: "My judgment is based on an FBI investigation. This shows that almost all of the lawyers who knew Duncan consider him an inexperienced and mediocre lawyer. His local Bar Association refused to endorse him by a vote of 23 to 1. The one was a former law partner. . . . I strongly advise against the appointment of Duncan." Five days later Roosevelt responded in a memo to the attorney general:

> I have your memorandum about Duncan of Missouri. This is one — I think the first — occasion where I cannot agree.[b] I have done a good deal of checking and, in spite of what you say about his legal ability, I have a hunch that he has as much legal ability as at least half of the people we put on the District bench! What you need on the District bench is old fashioned, homespun common sense. This is more important than being able to teach at the Harvard Law School!. . . . Please tell Truman that if [Missouri Senator Bennett Champ] Clark will go along with it I will send Duncan's name up and I think Truman will be perfectly willing to let the other Judgeship [there were two vacancies at this time] go to the southeastern part of the State.

Biddle swallowed hard and obeyed orders. On July 9, 1943, he submitted his official letter from the attorney general enclosing the formal nomination document and noted: "Mr. Duncan is a lawyer of ability and, I believe, is qualified to perform the duties of a United States District Judge. . . . I recommend the nomination." Duncan was promptly confirmed by the Senate. Years later, in his autobiography, Biddle wrote: "I am told by those in position to know that he [Duncan] has made a pretty good judge."[16]

The Duncan appointment occurred in the midst of the Second World War. One would think that Roosevelt would have had little time and patience for judicial-selection politics with the nation in all-out war, but the evidence suggests that he continued to be personally involved with judgeships. Even in the immediate aftermath of Pearl Harbor, which plunged a traumatized nation into war, Roosevelt was involved in a thorny tangle over a vacancy in the federal district court in New Jersey caused by the resignation of Thomas G. Walker, whom Roosevelt had appointed just two years earlier. Walker was a protégé of New Jersey Democratic Party boss Frank Hague. Hague wanted to replace Walker with Thomas F. Meaney, and New Jersey's Democratic senator went along with this recommendation. Hague was insistent that Roosevelt name Meaney. But his support elicited a vigorous protest from New Jersey

b. Roosevelt apparently forgot Justice Department opposition just six months earlier to another Democratic politician who had lost an election, the former governor of Idaho, Chase A. Clark, for a federal district judgeship in Idaho. Roosevelt nevertheless went ahead with the Clark appointment. OF 208 uu Idaho 1941–1943, Roosevelt Library.

governor Charles Edison, a former secretary of the Navy in the Roosevelt administration and a reform-minded governor who was engaged in a bitter intraparty fight with Hague.

Governor Edison, in a letter to Roosevelt of January 5, 1942, chronicled Hague's use of Walker and Meaney as pawns "being moved around on the chessboard of New Jersey politics" in order to make a place on New Jersey's highest court for Hague's thirty-four-year-old son, Frank Hague, Jr. Some two years earlier, in 1939, Meaney, who was then sitting as a state trial judge, was induced by Hague to resign to become a special counsel to the New Jersey banking and insurance commissioner in a bankruptcy proceeding that would produce lucrative fees for Meaney. Hague's legal adviser had made the announcement of Meaney's appointment before Meaney had even made public his intent to leave the state court. Governor Edison, in his letter, recounted that after Meaney's resignation, Walker resigned *his* seat on New Jersey's highest court and was promptly given the lower-state-court post vacated by Meaney. Then, Frank Hague, Jr., was appointed by Governor Edison's predecessor, Harry Moore, to take Walker's place on the New Jersey high court. Hague, Jr., had been a member of the bar for just two years and five months at the time of his appointment. (When naming Hague, Governor Moore stated: "I know this appointment will make his dad happy.")[17] As Governor Edison wrote to Roosevelt: "This appointment of Hague's son to a place on New Jersey's court of last resort shocked a great many people in the state as you may remember."

Walker, however, soon reaped his reward for faithful service to Boss Hague when he was named to the federal judgeship. But Walker held this position for only about two years before resigning to make way for Meaney. In his letter of resignation to Roosevelt, Walker elliptically gave as his reason that "an opportunity has presented itself and it seems advisable to accept it." Did Hague see to it that Walker had an offer he could not refuse? Walker resigned to become general counsel for the New Jersey Bell Telephone Company.[18]

Roosevelt apparently was well aware of this sorry situation before the governor's letter arrived. The previous December 22, only two weeks after Pearl Harbor, in a memo Roosevelt asked Attorney General Biddle for his view of Catesby L. Jones as a possibility for the New Jersey vacancy. Biddle, after some checking, reported in a memo of January 29, 1942, that Jones was worthy of selection. Biddle's memo contained some biographical information on Jones, including the fact that he practiced law in New York but had never practiced in New Jersey. Roosevelt responded in a memo of February 9: "This is not a bad idea in relation to Catesby Jones. My principal hesitation comes from the fact that he does not practice law in New Jersey. I do not know how much difference that would make in Federal court. Please talk to me about this later."

Apparently Roosevelt became convinced that Jones could not receive the necessary political clearance and on March 17, 1942, wrote to Biddle: "How about our making a decision in favor of Meaney for the district judgeship? From all I hear, though he is undoubtedly a Hague man, he is about the best timber we have." The Meaney nomination was sent to the Senate on May 4. Eleanor Roosevelt became aware of the Meaney affair and urged her husband to look further into the matter. In a memo dated May 19, 1942, Roosevelt explained to his wife: "The fact remains that the person selected seemed to be the best qualified person from the point of view of qualifications for judge in the whole list of candidates proposed. None of the others measured up to him in ability."

About the same time that the New Jersey vacancy was a source of conflict, another vacancy, in upstate New York, occupied the president's time. Many candidates for this position were brought to the president's attention. Both the Democratic State Committee and the Democratic National Committee backed Stephen W. Brennan, a Utica attorney, and Attorney General Biddle formally recommended him to Roosevelt on February 28, 1942. However, the runner-up, James J. Butler, was the cousin of Marguerite ("Missy") LeHand, Roosevelt's private secretary. LeHand may have said something to her boss that spurred him to ask Biddle how the selection process resulted in the recommendation of Brennan. In a memorandum for the president of March 6, 1942, Biddle noted that New York senator James M. Mead had put forward the names of eight men, including Brennan and Butler. Biddle continued:

> Mr. Justice Jackson, [when Attorney General] had spoken highly in behalf of Mathias P. Poersch. You had indicated some interest in him and Mr. Lee. The usual investigations were conducted by the FBI on the candidates. When these reports were completed, a conference was held with Senator Mead, as a result of which he submitted three names, *any of which* [emphasis in the original] selected by the Department would be acceptable to him. These were Boyle, Brennan, and Butler. At the same time the Democratic State Committee of New York . . . recommended the appointment of any one of the three above named men. Likewise, [Democratic National Committee chairman] Edward Flynn joined in the recommendation and left the matter to this Department to make a selection. By consent, the name of Mathias P. Poersch was added to the three so that the selection would be from four. Thereafter, the Department asked the FBI to interview Federal and State Judges, Bar Association officials, and prominent lawyers in the Northern District of New York to ascertain which, in their opinion, would make the best Federal judge.

Brennan received the most support from judges, bar association leaders, and lawyers in the district. Biddle's chronology continued:

> Thereafter, both Mr. Brennan and Mr. Butler were requested to call at this Department. I must admit that Mr. Butler made a very good impression with everyone in the Department who talked with him. The Bureau report on him is most excellent. Also he was not well known among the judges and lawyers. In the final analysis, Mr. Brennan was chosen because of the overwhelming majority of the judges and members of the Bar of that State having felt that he would make the best judge.[19]

Apparently this still did not satisfy Roosevelt, and Biddle wrote an even more detailed memo dated March 26, 1942, outlining all the endorsements of the leading candidates. He also noted that according to Senator Mead, Brennan always supported Roosevelt and served as Oneida county chairman of the Democratic Party at the request of the Roosevelt faction. Butler, on the other hand, voted for Jim Farley at the 1940 Democratic convention. Biddle reported, however, that Harry L. Hopkins, then an adviser to Roosevelt and the former secretary of commerce, had heard that none of the three candidates "were real Roosevelt men." But the bottom line was that, in Biddle's opinion, "Brennan is the outstanding candidate from a legal point of view." Brennan's appointment soon followed.

An interesting point to note, aside from the political intrigue surrounding the nomination, was the use of the FBI to gather professional assessments of the leading candidates. Years later this is what the American Bar Association Standing Committee on Federal Judiciary would be doing.

Thus far we have examined Roosevelt's personal involvement in appointments to the federal *district* courts. Although Democratic senators had great impact on the selection process in that they had to approve, if not acquiesce in, appointments in their states, the senators did not necessarily dictate who would be the nominees. The president and the Justice Department were active participants in selection. Appointments to the federal circuit courts of appeals, however, have been understood to give an administration more leeway than with the district bench because each of the numbered circuits spans at least three states. It is relevant to examine evidence of Roosevelt's involvement with these judgeships.

Early in his administration, Roosevelt selected a Republican federal district court judge serving in Nevada, Frank H. Norcross, for elevation to the U.S. Court of Appeals for the Ninth Circuit. Norcross's elevation would allow a deserving Democrat to fill the seat Norcross would vacate. Roosevelt gave Norcross a recess appointment on September 25, 1933, and the following January forwarded the nomination to the Senate. There Norcross ran into trouble when certain allegations were made concerning his handling of two bankruptcy cases.[20] The fact that he was a Republican probably did not help. The nomination was stalled in the Senate even though Norcross was sitting as a circuit judge because of his recess appointment. It was clear to Roosevelt that he would have to name another person to the post, and in a memo of October 10, 1934, to Cummings he wrote: "Will you speak to me about Denman for Circuit Judge in California?"[21] William Denman, a friend and supporter of Roosevelt's, had the reputation of being a New Deal progressive. On January 1, 1935, Judge Norcross formally requested that his name be withdrawn. (He returned to the district bench, where he served until his retirement in 1945.) Ten days later Denman's nomination was sent to the Senate, and he was promptly confirmed.[c]

Another Ninth Circuit position was to be filled in 1935, this one a newly created judgeship. The attorney general submitted to Roosevelt two names, and Roosevelt had to choose between Samuel V. Stewart, a sixty-three-year-old justice on the Montana Supreme court and former governor of Montana, and Bert E. Haney, a fifty-six-year-old former United States attorney and a strong New Dealer from Oregon. Roosevelt picked Haney, who was quickly confirmed. In a thank-you letter to Roosevelt, Haney referred to himself "as one who has always considered himself to be a Liberal, and . . . who has tried to understand law as a progressive science."[22]

Roosevelt recognized the policy-agenda implications of his circuit court appointments, particularly after 1935, and actively sought to recruit appropriate judges. He had his eye on the liberal dean of the Yale Law School, Charles E. Clark, and waged a personal campaign to recruit him. Roosevelt wanted Clark for an opening on the Court of Appeals for the District of Columbia and offered him the post in the summer of 1937. Clark turned him down. Roosevelt persisted with a cablegram to London, where Clark was visiting Harold Laski. In the cable of August 19, 1937, Roosevelt pointedly noted that the D.C. circuit "has taken on a wholly new importance in the last few years — is now easily the second most important Federal Court in the country."[23] Clark did not accept, but less than a year and a half later he agreed to be named to the

c. Once on the bench Denman upheld New Deal legislation; see, for example, *Edwards* v. *United States,* 91 F.2d 767 (1937). In 1943, Denman gained attention with his dissent from the Ninth Circuit decision upholding the curfew and exclusion of Japanese Americans on the West Coast, published in 140 F.2d 300 (1943). That case, *Hirabayashi* v. *United States,* went to the Supreme Court, which upheld the federal government; the justices ignored Denman's stirring defense of civil liberties. Denman's courageous stand took its personal and professional toll, and he lost standing within the administration. See Memorandum for the President from the Attorney General, September 30, 1943, OF 209 i 9th Circuit 1940–1945.

Court of Appeals for the Second Circuit, where he established himself as a leading liberal jurist.[24]

Another vacancy on the U.S. Court of Appeals for the District of Columbia became official with a formal letter of retirement from Judge Charles H. Robb. Cummings wrote to Roosevelt on November 3, 1937, that the letter of retirement "clears the way for a disposition of the matter along the lines we originally discussed. I would be glad to talk with you about the situation as soon as you may find it convenient. Perhaps if there is to be a Cabinet Meeting on Friday, I could get a few moments with you then."[25] The "disposition" that Cummings referred to was a package that included the elevation of the liberal Republican Lawrence Groner from an associate judgeship to the vacant chief justiceship of the Court of Appeals for the District of Columbia,[d] the appointment of the Cornell law professor and noted liberal Henry White Edgerton to the associate judgeship being vacated by Judge Groner,[e] and the appointment of the New Deal congressman (and later chief justice of the U.S. Supreme Court) Fred Vinson to replace Judge Robb. The nominations of Groner, Edgerton, and Vinson were sent to the Senate on November 26, 1937, and were quickly confirmed.

One of the most fascinating examples of Roosevelt's personal involvement in selection to the federal appeals court bench concerned the appointment of Francis Biddle, a friend and classmate of Roosevelt's at Groton.[26] Biddle had served in the administration in various capacities, including as chairman of the National Labor Relations Board, before returning to a lucrative private law practice in Philadelphia. But he did not want a judgeship. In fact, in the fall of 1938 a major campaign was being waged, in part by organized labor, to place the liberal Pennsylvania state court judge Michael A. Musmanno on the Third Circuit. The Democratic U.S. senator from Pennsylvania, Joseph F. Guffey, strongly backed Musmanno and was most anxious for speedy action. Guffey wrote to Roosevelt's appointments secretary, on December 13, 1938:

> If the President will send [Musmanno's nomination] during the first two or three days of the session and I am able to have the Judiciary Committee and

---

d. Since 1955, the chief judge has been determined by seniority and held up to the age of seventy. Before 1955, it was a separate presidential appointment that had life tenure.

e. In 1962, the *Washington Post* legal-affairs writer John P. MacKenzie noted that "Judge Edgerton in cases ranging from local criminal appeals to major national cases involving rights of free speech, employment, privacy, and equality of opportunity, established himself as the leader of the liberal wing of the court." *Washington Post*, March 22, 1962, B1. Judge Edgerton's position as a liberal judge is empirically supported by the analysis of voting behavior reported in Sheldon Goldman, "Conflict and Consensus in the United States Courts of Appeals," *Wisconsin Law Review*, 1968: 468, 473.

the Senate confirm it by not later than January 15th, our present Democratic Governor will appoint Judge Musmanno's successor to the Common Pleas Bench of Allegheny County. If the nomination should not be sent up and confirmed until after that date, the incoming Republican Governor would appoint his successor. We would not want the latter to happen, of course. Won't you kindly advise the President of this?[27]

Roosevelt, however, delayed, and two weeks later directed Mac to "call up Joe Guffey and ask him whether he wants Musmanno appointed or Mr. [Charles Alvin] Jones, the late unsuccessful [Democratic] candidate for Governor, appointed." On the bottom of the memo Roosevelt hand-wrote the answer he received: "Guffey backing MM."[f]

But Roosevelt did not name Musmanno. Instead, early the following February, he named Biddle, who did not want the job, had personally told Senator Guffey that he did not want it, and had so written to Attorney General Frank Murphy. But Biddle agreed after Roosevelt made a personal plea that included a promise that the appeals court position would only be temporary, because Roosevelt planned to name him solicitor general within a year or two (a position Biddle coveted). This extraordinary arrangement is recounted by Biddle in his memoirs, in which he recalled the phone call from the president. The president said "Francis . . . I want you . . . to go on the Third Circuit Court." Biddle balked at the idea: "It's like becoming a priest, taking the veil." He recalled Roosevelt chuckling and "sounding as if he were repeating what I had said to someone else." "But it won't be for long," Roosevelt continued. "Frank Murphy wants to be Secretary of War, why God only knows. But it will take a little time to persuade Harry Woodring [who was then secretary of war] to resign, perhaps five or six months. When he does go I'll put Frank in his place, make Bob Jackson Attorney General, and you Solicitor General. What do you say? Bob Jackson and Felix Frankfurter are sitting here next to me and they are witnesses to the plot."

A stunned Biddle replied that he needed time to think about it. He asked Roosevelt whether he needed an immediate answer. Biddle recalled Roosevelt's response: "Yes, he did, he might announce my appointment the next day, he was moving Robert Patterson [a liberal Republican] from the District Court in New York to the Second Circuit. . . . I'd be in good company."[28]

The day after the phone call, Biddle and his wife took the train to Florida for a vacation. Biddle wrote to Roosevelt on February 6, 1939:

> On our way to Florida today Senator Guffey got on the train to talk to me. He said you had not spoken to him about my appointment, and seemed rather

f. Within six months, Jones was named to another position on the U.S. Court of Appeals for the Third Circuit.

upset. He wanted to know why I had changed my mind, and I told him of our talk yesterday. I think this was due to the stories in the Philadelphia afternoon papers (I don't know who gave them out). The story in the *Bulletin*, for instance, might have given the impression that I had been named over Guffey's head, without his being consulted. He indicated, however, that he would not oppose me.

Until you spoke with me yesterday, I had made up my mind against accepting, and had so written the Attorney General on Saturday. Joe [Guffey] had spoken to me about it when I was in Washington Thursday, and I told him I did not want to be a judge. When you called me I did not think of mentioning this.

I have always been on excellent terms with Joe; representing him now, as a matter of fact, in the Annenberg libel suit. He seemed hurt. I am sure that a word from you would help.

I am proud that you want me, and by no means insensible of the honor.[29]

Biddle's nomination was sent to the Senate on February 9, 1939. He was confirmed within a month and took his judicial oath of office on March 31, 1939. On January 22, 1940, less than a year later, he resigned his judgeship to become solicitor general of the United States when Frank Murphy was named to the U.S. Supreme Court and Robert Jackson moved from solicitor general to attorney general. The next year, when Jackson went on the Supreme Court, Biddle became Roosevelt's attorney general.

The question, of course, is why Roosevelt resisted naming Musmanno and insisted on Biddle for the Third Circuit, knowing that Biddle's tenure would be temporary. The answer apparently is not that Musmanno was personally or politically incompatible with Roosevelt or that his appointment would be inconsistent with Roosevelt's policy agenda.[g] But it may lie in an understand-

---

g. In fact, Roosevelt replied to a letter from United Mine Workers of America president John L. Lewis expressing alarm that "our tried and true friend, Judge Musmanno" would not receive the appointment with the following:

> Dear John:
> You are right about Judge Musmanno being a real friend. If it had been the District Court there could have been no question. Perhaps there will be a vacancy very soon.
> You will find that Biddle is not only a brilliant scholar but that he is just as liberal and progressive as the Judge, and I know you will be happy when you see him at work.
> > As ever yours,
> > FDR

John L. Lewis to Roosevelt, February 7, 1939; Roosevelt to John L. Lewis, February 13, 1939, in OF 209 c 3rd Circuit Oct.–Dec. 1938. Musmanno never did receive a federal

ing of the broader political context of Roosevelt's relationship with Democratic senators. In 1938, Roosevelt's attempt in Democratic primaries to "purge" the party of anti–New Deal Democratic members of Congress was largely unsuccessful.[30] And earlier in the week of Biddle's confirmation (before Roosevelt's phone call) the Senate Judiciary Committee rejected the nomination of the New Dealer Floyd Roberts to a Virginia district court position. The Virginia Democratic senators invoked senatorial courtesy to scuttle the appointment. It would appear that Roosevelt wanted to reassert authority over Democratic senators, even friendly New Dealers like Senator Guffey; hence the deliberate leak to the papers that Biddle was being named over Guffey's head. Additional credibility is given to this explanation from Dean Acheson in his memoirs that Roosevelt personally called him around this time to try to persuade him to accept a judgeship on the District of Columbia Court of Appeals: "The President then explained to me that he was in a row with the Senate about a judicial nomination in Virginia which he had submitted without prior consultation with the Virginia senators. To make his point he wanted to submit three nominations without consultations which the Senate would have to confirm. They were to be Robert Patterson for the United States Court of Appeals in New York; Francis Biddle for the Court in Philadelphia; and myself for the one in Washington. I could not, he urged, break the symmetry of this plan."[31]

Acheson turned Roosevelt down. Biddle and Patterson did not. The vacancy Roosevelt wanted Acheson to fill was soon filled by another professionally impeccable, personal selection of Roosevelt's, the dean of the University of Iowa Law School, the liberal New Dealer Wiley B. Rutledge, whom Roosevelt would subsequently elevate to the Supreme Court.

The Policy Agenda and Selection

When Roosevelt took office in March 1933, the federal judiciary was not seen as an obstacle to administration policies, and there was no overriding imperative to change the direction of judicial decisionmaking. Judicial selection focused primarily on more traditional partisan-agenda and even personal-agenda considerations. But beginning about one to two years after the start of Roosevelt's presidency, lower-court decisions (and then Supreme Court decisions) struck down various actions and programs of the New Deal. More than

---

judgeship, but ten years later he was elected to the Pennsylvania Supreme Court, where he established himself as a charismatic liberal jurist. See Henry R. Glick, *Supreme Courts in State Politics* (New York: Basic Books, 1971), 128–29.

one-third of the lower-court federal judiciary during 1935 and 1936 issued a total of about sixteen hundred injunctions to prevent the enforcement of various New Deal measures. Not insignificantly, almost three-fourths of lower-court federal judges were Republicans.[32]

Roosevelt was of course aware that primarily it was Republican judges who were placing legal obstacles in the way of his programs. For example, Roosevelt chose to keep in his files a short newspaper editorial sent to him by Jim Farley in September 1935 that noted two recent appeals court decisions from the First and Sixth circuits striking down New Deal programs by votes of 2 to 1. In both cases the opponents of the New Deal were Republican judges and the supporters were Democrats. The editorial asked: "Who runs the government, anyway?"[33] Acknowledgement of the ideological or policy outlook of judicial candidates and nominees became more frequent and commonplace, although more traditional party considerations always permeated judicial selection.

Evidence of concern and interest in the candidate's compatibility with Roosevelt's economic and social-welfare policy agenda can be seen in both district court and appeals court appointments. Even as early as 1933, senators were recommending people to Roosevelt for the district courts by praising them as liberal or progressive.[h] In their letter recommending Congressman Heartsill Ragon for a federal district court position in Arkansas, the Democratic Arkansas senators noted: "Mr. Ragon takes a progressive and sound view of public questions."[34] Eight days later Ragon's name was sent by the White House to the Senate, and Ragon was confirmed the same day.

By 1935, references to candidates being liberal became more frequent. On May 3, the New Deal senator Burton Wheeler, from Montana, recommended his former law partner and then United States attorney for Montana, James H. Baldwin, for a district judgeship, describing him in a letter to Roosevelt as "a liberal Democrat." Two weeks later, Baldwin's nomination was sent to the Senate.[35]

In December, Attorney General Cummings wrote to Roosevelt recommending David J. Davis, a former law partner of Alabama senator Hugo Black, for a federal district judgeship. In addition to praising Davis's "high personal integrity," Cummings made of point of noting that "he would be rated as a Progressive or Liberal Judge."[36] Davis received the judgeship.

Albert B. Maris was nominated to a vacancy on the federal district court in

---

h. Candidates were referred to as "liberal" or "progressive" according to their views of the need for government to regulate the economy in the public interest and to provide for social welfare — in short, economic liberalism.

Philadelphia in June 1936. In letters of recommendation to Roosevelt he was described as "liberal." Upon his nomination he wrote to the president: "It will be my highest object[ive] to so administer my office as to reflect the greatest credit upon you and upon the great liberal Democratic party of which we are members."[37] Maris was elevated two years later to a Third Circuit judgeship.

In late 1936, Ninth Circuit judge William Denman, a Roosevelt appointee, wrote to the president emphasizing the importance of naming district and circuit judges sympathetic to the administration's policy agenda. Denman put the point bluntly: "The New Deal needs more Federal judges." Roosevelt forwarded the letter to the attorney general with the notation, "Speak to me about this when I get back."[38]

In 1937, the administration was considering Ralph E. Jenney for a district judgeship in southern California. Assistant Attorney General Keenan reported that he had had a personal interview with Jenney. Keenan noted in his memo that he found Jenney to be "a forward-looking liberal-minded . . . lawyer." Jenney's name was forwarded to the Senate five days later.[39]

Roosevelt occasionally received memos pointing out the pro–New Deal decisions of his appointees. In a 1937 memo, Secretary of Agriculture Henry Wallace wrote to Roosevelt that John W. Holland, whom the president had appointed the previous year to a district court in Florida, found constitutional the marketing provisions of the Agricultural Adjustment Act while Holland's colleague, a Republican Hoover appointee had voted to strike down the provisions.[40]

By 1938, letters from Democratic members of Congress to Roosevelt recommending candidates for district judgeships almost routinely touted their candidates' liberalism. One letter praised a candidate for a Washington State federal district judgeship, Lloyd L. Black (later appointed), as "a young and vigorous progressive." Another Washington candidate, himself a member of Congress, was applauded by then Speaker of the House W. B. Bankhead as "a man of liberal views . . . a consistent sponsor of New Deal legislation."[i] Arkansas senator John Miller, a candidate for an Arkansas judgeship (and soon appointed), was praised by a House colleague for his "liberal and progressive convictions."[41]

When a state has no senators from the president's party, the administration has the greatest leeway in selecting judgeships. This is an opportunity for the president's policy agenda to drive the process. In December 1940, two princi-

---

i. That individual, Charles H. Leavey, did not receive that particular judgeship, which went to the New Deal senator Lewis B. Schwellenbach, but he filled the next vacancy, which occurred in 1941.

pal candidates emerged for a North Dakota judgeship: the United States attorney Powless Lanier, for whom an active campaign was waged, and Charles J. Vogel, the Democratic national committeeman for North Dakota and unsuccessful Democratic candidate for the United States Senate in 1940. Governor John Moses wrote to Roosevelt on December 12, 1940, praising Vogel as "liberal and progressive in his thinking." As the campaign intensified, Secretary of Agriculture Claude R. Wickard wrote to Roosevelt, backing Vogel and stating, "I know he is a firm believer in the principles of the present administration."[42] Three months later, Vogel's name was sent to the Senate and he was soon confirmed, thus launching a judicial career that would include his elevation in 1954 by President Eisenhower to the Eighth Circuit.

Policy-agenda considerations did not necessarily take the highest priority, however. When the political backing was exceptionally strong and there were questions raised as to the candidate's fidelity to the New Deal, the benefit of the doubt was often given to the candidate. For example, the Senate majority leader, Kentucky senator Alben W. Barkley, championed Shackelford Miller, Jr., for a district court position. Miller had been Barkley's state campaign manager and was the head of the Democratic organization in Louisville. He also had impeccable professional credentials. But the Kentucky Federation of Labor opposed Miller, calling him "anti-New Deal in practice and opposed to organized labor." A memo from a special assistant to Attorney General Frank Murphy noted that "we have had a considerable number of protests, particularly from organized labor and labor groups against Mr. Miller's appointment. On the other hand, there have been many labor groups who have endorsed Mr. Miller." The memo also noted that the FBI investigation showed Miller (and three other men whose names were given to the Justice Department by the Kentucky senators) to be "qualified" for the appointment. The FBI had been instructed to contact a number of Louisville lawyers about Miller's qualifications. The senators, in their letter to the attorney general, had said that Miller "is a profound student of the law and believes in its liberal interpretation and application. If appointed to this position, his services will, in our judgement, be entirely satisfactory to the Government and to the people as a whole."[43] Miller received the appointment, and in 1946 he was elevated by President Truman to the Sixth Circuit.

While active opponents of the New Deal were not seriously considered for judgeships by the Roosevelt administration, being too left-wing could likewise be cause for rejection. In 1941, Roosevelt rejected one candidate for a California judgeship as too "radical."[44] In this instance the president appeared to be voicing his own antipathy to what he perceived to be left-wing extremism.

The examples given thus far all concern district judgeships and at the least suggest that policy-agenda considerations played some role in the selection process, although as a criterion it was not a systematically applied one. The selection of appeals court judgeships, however, is generally recognized as allowing an administration more discretion, and so we would expect to find policy-agenda considerations more evident. When we turn to the evidence we find some support for this view.

In 1934, for example, the administration was considering the elevation of Federal District Judge Charles B. Faris to the Eighth Circuit. Faris's age, seventy, may have given Roosevelt pause. But Faris was strongly backed by Missouri senator Bennett Champ Clark, to make way for Clark's choice to fill the federal district court position Faris would vacate. Clark pitched Faris to Roosevelt on policy-agenda grounds, emphasizing a Faris decision upholding New Deal legislation and sending along Faris's judicial opinion to Roosevelt.[45] Faris was subsequently appointed (but retired only ten months later).

By 1937, it had become routine for policy-agenda considerations to play a part in circuit court appointments. In October of that year, Roosevelt asked Cummings to check on an associate judge on the U.S. Court of Appeals for the District of Columbia, D. Lawrence Groner, for possible elevation to chief justice of that court. Cummings responded that Groner "may be rated as a Liberal Republican."[46]

There were two vacancies in 1937 on the Court of Appeals for the Ninth Circuit. A Montana attorney in the Justice Department, Walter L. Pope, waged a campaign for one of the slots and enlisted the aid of Montana senator James Murray, who wrote to Roosevelt praising Pope as "an able and aggressive New Dealer." James Roosevelt, serving as an assistant to his father, subsequently wrote in a memo to Roosevelt: "Just a note to let you know this [Ninth Circuit nomination document] is still being held up at your request. You wanted to get some additional information about a man named Pope."[47] Pope, however, did not get one of the positions. (They went to candidates from Idaho and California.) But two months later, he thought he had a chance at a judgeship on the Court of Appeals for the District of Columbia and wrote to Senator Murray: "I know that the administration would want a liberal on this court which passes on so much New Deal legislation. My entire file on the other application is still here, and I would think that if the President were reminded by you of his former wish that a judicial position could be found for me, then he might possibly approve."[48] Pope did not receive this appointment either. (The New Dealer and Cornell law professor Henry Edgerton did.) Pope stayed on at the Justice Department until 1941 and then returned to Montana, where he resumed the practice of law. In 1949 he realized his life's ambition when he was named by Harry Truman as the first Montanan to serve on the Ninth Circuit.

John Biggs, Jr., who had impeccable professional and political credentials — he had served as chairman of the State Democratic Committee for Delaware and delivered the Delaware delegates for Roosevelt at the 1932 national convention — was named to the Third Circuit Court of Appeals in 1937. Biggs had been thoroughly checked out by the Justice Department, because he had served as counsel for the Duponts. But the departmental investigation showed that his legal work was only on minor matters and noted that Biggs "is very much in sympathy with all that the Administration does." After his appointment Biggs wrote to Roosevelt: "It is our pride [referring to himself and his wife] to have been your supporters and followers in Delaware."[49]

Policy-agenda considerations clearly took centerstage in the appointment process after Roosevelt introduced his court reform plan in February 1937. The plan had been presented as having been designed to bring new, young blood to the judiciary. Early the next month, however, Cummings sent to the White House the nomination of sixty-eight-year-old Robert L. Williams, then a federal district judge in Oklahoma, for elevation to a seat on the Court of Appeals for the Tenth Circuit. Roosevelt's appointments secretary alerted his boss: "You will note that Judge Williams is 68 yrs old. Do you want to hold this up a little bit because psychologically it should not go out at this time unless publicity shows that it is a temporary appointment." Roosevelt responded: "Send this back to Cummings and get something from Judge Williams so that we can — or somebody can — announce that he will retire when he is seventy."[50]

Mac turned this task over to an assistant, who noted in a memo the next day, "Phoned Asst. Atty-Gen'l Keenan — who said he would get desired statement and asked that nomination be held here [in the White House]." The assistant subsequently informed Mac that the attorney general "advises that he has the desired letter from Judge Williams and that he will telephone the President about it." In that letter Williams wrote: "I understand that you are considering me for promotion to the Tenth Circuit Court of Appeals. . . . It is agreeable to me in event of such promotion to retire at age 70. . . . This would be in harmony with the President's judicial program and court plan, which I endorse and approve."

Williams was opposed by the Tulsa branch of the National Association for the Advancement of Colored People (NAACP) and by other African American groups, because twenty-three years earlier, when he was chief justice of the Oklahoma Supreme Court, he had upheld a grandfather clause in a statute making it more difficult for blacks to vote. That decision was overturned and the Oklahoma law struck down by the U.S. Supreme Court in 1915.[51] But the Oklahoma New Deal senator Josh Lee, who backed Williams, assured Cummings that Williams was "liberal."

The appointment went through, and true to his word Judge Williams retired two years later. His successor on the Tenth Circuit, Kansas governor Walter A. Huxman, was praised in the official letter of recommendation from Attorney General Frank Murphy to Roosevelt as "an able lawyer, a man of broad experience, liberal in his attitude toward our social and economic problems."[52] Many other examples of the ascendance of policy-agenda considerations can be drawn from the circuit appointments.[j]

When there was uncertainty as to a leading candidate's compatibility with the policy agenda, the Justice Department attempted to find out. When Gerald McLaughlin was being considered for the Third Circuit, Attorney General Biddle noted that McLaughlin "has not taken any very active part in politics; was recently asked to be chairman of the Washington Day dinner, but refused on the ground that he was rather out of active politics. I have asked John Biggs [a Third Circuit Judge and Biddle's former colleague] to make a very discreet inquiry."[53] Evidently, the word on McLaughlin was positive, for he received the appointment.

One First Circuit vacancy had many candidates, including the son of a retired First Circuit judge. That judge, George Bingham of New Hampshire, had retired the previous year after he indirectly received word from Attorney General Murphy that his son Robert would be appointed in his place. Mur-

j. For example, Tennessee senator McKellar, in a three-and-a-half-page, single-spaced letter to Roosevelt recommending the elevation of U.S. District Judge John D. Martin, Sr., to the Sixth Circuit, noted a number of pro–New Deal decisions handed down by Martin since Roosevelt placed him on the district bench in 1935. McKellar to Roosevelt, October 17, 1938, OF 209 f 6th Circuit 1934–1938. Martin received a Sixth Circuit appointment. In Attorney General Frank Murphy's official letter recommending Calvert Magruder for the First Circuit, he described Magruder as "a scholar of liberal outlook." OF 209 a 1st Circuit 1935–1939. Magruder's Justice Department file contains an analysis of an article published two years earlier in the *Harvard Law Review* sympathetic to collective bargaining. The analysis noted that the article "shows not only a great knowledge of law but an understanding of and sympathy with social growth." In the official letter to the president from the attorney general concerning the recommendation of Senator Homer T. Bone to the Ninth Circuit, he noted that Bone "is highly regarded as to character and integrity, is a lawyer of ability, broad and liberal in his viewpoint, and a man possessed of judicial temperament." OF 209 i 9th Circuit 1940–1945. The governor of Nebraska, in letters to the Justice Department, praised Harvey M. Johnsen (later appointed to the Eighth Circuit) as "a liberal Roosevelt Democrat through and through." Justice Department file of Harvey M. Johnsen. Herbert F. Goodrich was recommended to Roosevelt by then Third Circuit judge Francis Biddle for the position that Biddle would soon be vacating in order to become solicitor general. Biddle wrote that Goodrich "is a sound liberal with vision and imagination, and very loyal to your administration." Biddle to Roosevelt, December 12, 1939, OF 209 c 3rd Circuit 1939.

phy, however, recommended Calvert Magruder but indicated that he would be favorably disposed to name Robert Bingham for the next vacancy.[54] That vacancy, however, was filled by Rhode Island senator Green's candidate, U.S. District Judge John Mahoney, whose elevation made room on the district bench for Green's close political ally John Hartigan.

Still another vacancy opened up on the First Circuit, for which Robert Bingham was in competition with candidates from Massachusetts and Maine. The candidate from Maine, Harold Dubord, was a Democratic national committeeman and former Democratic candidate for senator, governor, and Congress. Roosevelt sent a memo to Murphy: "Dubord in place of Bingham for CCA 1st Dist.?"[55] Murphy, however, soon left to take his seat on the Supreme Court, and Robert Jackson became attorney general.

Bingham's name was dropped from active consideration, and another from New Hampshire took his place, Peter Woodbury, an associate justice on the New Hampshire Supreme Court who was also the son of a former colleague of Roosevelt's from the Wilson administration. But Woodbury proved to be controversial, for he was charged with being anti-labor. In April 1940, Secretary of Labor Frances Perkins wrote to Jackson enclosing a decision of the New Hampshire Supreme Court in which Woodbury participated and observed: "I feel that Judge Woodbury's attitude, as shown by this opinion, is entirely out of harmony with what I have understood to be the attitude of the New Deal toward labor."[56] The day after Jackson received the letter, a Justice Department lawyer, Alexander Holtzoff (later himself to be appointed a federal district judge in the District of Columbia), sent a memo to Assistant Attorney General Matthew McGuire (also a future colleague of Holtzoff's on the D.C. bench) analyzing the opinion: "Clearly, the opinion does not display any liberal tendencies. I am not ready to conclude, however, on the basis of a single opinion, confined very largely to a discussion of the authorities, and without the benefit of argument by counsel, that a judge's concurring in such an opinion is reactionary or is tinged with an anti-labor bias. . . . It would be advisable to make a study of Judge Woodbury's opinions in the New Hampshire Reports before reaching a definite conclusion as to his qualifications for appointment to the Federal Bench."[57]

Five days later, another Justice Department lawyer presented an analysis of Woodbury's thirty-one economic and labor decisions, finding that in sixteen cases he held against the individual or employee and in favor of the railroad, insurance company, or manufacturer. The memo included brief analyses of the individual cases and questioned whether Woodbury was "a true liberal." In early May, there was a newspaper story that Woodbury was out of the running because he was anti-labor. This, in turn, produced a flurry of pro-Woodbury letters and telegrams to the Justice Department. The Brotherhood of Railroad

Trainmen of Nashua, New Hampshire, wired that Woodbury "has always been a friend of labor." The chairman of the Manchester Democratic City Committee wrote that Woodbury "has always been a hard worker for the cause." The Democratic national committeeman for New Hampshire asserted, "He is definitely favorable to labor."

But the protest letters continued to arrive, and Secretary Perkins continued to forward telegrams from various labor unions opposed to Woodbury. Eventually, on December 26, 1940, Roosevelt received word that the New Hampshire State Federation of Labor had endorsed Woodbury.[58] On January 31, 1941, Woodbury's nomination was sent to the Senate, and he was confirmed within several weeks.

From the presidential papers and also Justice Department files for some of the appointees, it appears that twenty-four of Roosevelt's fifty appointments to the courts of appeals were policy-agenda appointments. Of these, twenty (over 80 percent) occurred between 1935 and 1940, precisely when the actions of the judiciary spelled life or death for the New Deal. During this time, there were also thirteen partisan-agenda and two personal-agenda appointments. Fifty-seven percent of the 1935–1940 appointments were of the policy-agenda type.[k]

Senators and Selection

It is a truism that during the Roosevelt administration Democratic senators were particularly sensitive about their prerogatives when it came to recommending federal district judges. Illustrating this point is an angry letter from New Jersey Democratic senator William H. Smathers to Assistant Attorney General Joseph Keenan: "I want to say to you that I will not stand for any interference from the Department of Justice which in any way attempts to interfere with my right and prerogative in recommending to the President my choice of appointees in the State of New Jersey. . . . I tried for four or five days to reach you in Washington to tell you that I had heard you were sympathetic to an effort to defeat my choice for the U.S. District Court, and that I would not brook any interference from you or anyone else in this respect."[59][l]

---

k. No policy-agenda appointments could be identified in 1933 and 1934. Indeed, the five appointments in those two years appeared to be of the partisan-agenda kind. Of the ten appointments made from 1941 to 1945, four were policy-agenda, five were partisan-agenda, and one was a personal-agenda appointment.

l. Because of the feud between Smathers and Boss Hague's New Jersey Democratic organization, the federal district court position remained vacant for close to a year and a

When there were two Democratic senators who preferred different candidates, the administration had more room to maneuver, but it also may have had to fashion a political compromise between the senators. An example of this occurred with the senators from Ohio. On December 3, 1938, Attorney General Cummings sent a memo notifying Roosevelt that Ohio's Democratic senators Robert J. Bulkley and Vic Donahey endorsed Carl Friebolin for a district court judgeship. Although Friebolin was distinguished, he was over sixty. Age had become an issue with Roosevelt's failed court-reform bill the year before. The United States attorney in the district, Emerich B. Freed, was almost twenty years younger than Friebolin, very well qualified, and actually the preferred choice of Senator Bulkley. As Cummings put it, "If you should pass over Mr. Friebolin on the ground of age, Senator Bulkley would welcome the appointment of Mr. Freed, and very gladly indeed. Senator Donahey would acquiesce. . . . [But] Senator Donahey says that Friebolin is his first and only choice." Cummings also pointed out that if Freed were promoted, "his leading assistant would be well qualified for promotion to his place." If Friebolin were appointed, the post of referee in bankruptcy would become vacant and Friebolin's successor, chosen by Republican judges, would likely appoint someone "who was not in sympathy with your administration." The attorney general also pointed out that Freed openly supported Roosevelt's court reform bill, while Friebolin took no public position.[60]

About two weeks later, Friebolin withdrew his name for health reasons. Cummings prepared a recess commission for Freed, noting that he "has been strongly endorsed by Senator Bulkley." But Senator Donahey was clearly unhappy. Donahey claimed in a letter to Mac (with the likely intent that Mac would inform Roosevelt), "I think the new Attorney General of the United States [Frank Murphy] should be told that I have not had a single appointment. I was promised equal patronage with Bulkley by Joe Keenan, and never received any."[61] Roosevelt also got word that the International Ladies Garment Workers Union opposed Freed. The president decided not to sign the

---

half. The man Smathers favored did not get the appointment, because the Justice Department found him to be less qualified professionally than Hague's candidate, Thomas G. Walker. But the judgeship was not filled until a deal was worked out with the feuding New Jersey Democrats, by which Walker received the judgeship and the Hague organization supported the creation of a new judgeship so that the next appointment would go to someone Smathers backed. A new federal district judgeship in New Jersey was filled by a Smathers candidate, William F. Smith, in 1941. Ironically, Attorney General Cummings had thought of Smith three years earlier, but the Hague organization had stood fast for their candidate, Walker, and at that time Smathers had insisted on his original choice.

recess commission for Freed. About five months later, Attorney General Murphy recommended Robert N. Wilkin, who was backed by Senator Donahey, but Roosevelt hesitated. The attorney general asked White House staffer James Rowe, Jr., what the reason was for not signing the nomination, and Rowe in turn asked LeHand. The handwritten reply was: "The President is doing a little checking on him." Wilkin, however, received the appointment, and two years later, when another vacancy opened up, Freed received that judgeship. Thus both senators Bulkley and Donahey were eventually satisfied. Clearly, the administration did not wish to unnecessarily antagonize Democratic senators whose support for the president's programs was needed in the Senate.

One of the grounds for passing over Carl Friebolin was his advanced age, yet in another instance, three years later, age did not prove an obstacle to appointment. In December 1941, Roosevelt responded to Texas senator Tom Connally's desire to secure a judgeship for a sixty-eight-year-old political ally, Walter A. Keeling: "Tom Connally wants Keeling for Judge. Has been Atty. Gen. of Texas. Just over age — Can we do."[62] Keeling was appointed, and died on the bench three years later.

The Ohio appointment discussed earlier demonstrates that it was important for the administration to know which Democratic senator was actually behind a candidate for purposes of dividing patronage. When John Caskie Collet was recommended for a district judgeship in Missouri, the attorney general sent a handwritten note pointing out that Judge Collet, then a justice on the Supreme Court of Missouri, "is the choice of Sen. Truman. It is his first choice - and 100% - He is very much interested. Sen. [Bennett Champ] Clark is merely going along."[63] The nomination was promptly submitted to the Senate and confirmed. In 1947, Collet's personal friend Truman, now president, promoted him to the Eighth Circuit.

A senator sometimes wants the administration to place a close relative on the federal bench. In such an event the senator must tread carefully, lest there be a negative public reaction and charge of nepotism. The administration therefore must carry the ball if the appointment is going to go through. For example, Roosevelt easily accommodated Georgia senator Richard Russell by appointing Russell's thirty-nine-year-old brother, Robert L. Russell, to the federal district bench in Georgia in 1940. (Nine years later, Harry Truman was equally accommodating in promoting Russell to the Fifth Circuit.) But Roosevelt felt he could not be so obliging when Senator Tom Connally wanted his thirty-two-year-old son Ben to receive a federal judgeship. Roosevelt, in a memo to Mac, wrote: "Tell Tom Connally — I do not want to put it in writing — that I am most anxious to appoint Ben to the Judgeship but that I think it would be terribly embarrassing for Ben himself in view of his age and not at all a good thing for him personally. Ask Tom if he will let me have four or five names of other people so that I can appoint someone soon."[64]

Senator Connally complied with Roosevelt's wishes, submitting a list of five names but calling Mac to tell him (and Roosevelt) the two candidates he really favored.[65] One of the two received the nomination just three days later. Ben Connally, the senator's son, eventually received a federal district judgeship from Harry Truman, in 1949.

When selecting judges, Roosevelt took into consideration what impact his decision would have on a senator's support for the administration. In explaining to Harry Hopkins why Archibald Lovett received a Georgia judgeship in September 1941, James Rowe, Jr., pointed out that "[Georgia] Senator [Walter] George *while* Chairman of [the Senate Committee on] Foreign Affairs, was extremely active on behalf of Lovett. *Res ipsa loquitor* [the thing speaks for itself]." In this crucial time before America's entry into the Second World War, Roosevelt badly needed the support of the chairman of the Senate Committee on Foreign Relations.[66] The other Georgia senator, Richard Russell, had wanted the judgeship to go to his former campaign manager, Frank M. Scarlett. But Roosevelt apparently felt he had to accommodate Senator George, and after all, Russell's brother had received a judgeship the previous year. Scarlett, however, was to get his judgeship from Harry Truman in September 1945.

Another example of the relationship between judicial appointments and senators' votes can be seen in a personal and confidential memorandum to the president from the attorney general on April 2, 1943. Biddle urged the elevation of Louisiana U.S. District Judge Benjamin C. Dawkins to the Fifth Circuit but noted that while the Louisiana senators "have publicly recommended him," they "dislike Dawkins and have told me so privately because he was the presiding judge in the Huey Long trials." Naming Dawkins "will not make the Louisiana Senators very happy. From the point of view of the judiciary this is immaterial. In view of world considerations, the question is not only how important their two votes may become to the Administration's program and to the nation and the future happiness of the world, but also whether the appointment of their candidate would have any appreciable influence on the way they exercise their votes in world affairs. That of course is a matter for your judgment, not mine."[67] Dawkins did not receive the Fifth Circuit position. The preferred candidate of the Louisiana senators, Elmo Pearce Lee, Sr., was Roosevelt's choice.

The decision to fill the Fifth Circuit appeals court judgeship with a Louisianan came after a defeat in the Senate Judiciary Committee of a nominee from Texas for that position. That nominee was James V. Allred, a former governor of Texas, who was placed on the federal district bench by Roosevelt in 1938. In May 1942, Allred had resigned from the bench to run in the Democratic primary for a U.S. Senate seat but had lost to Pappy O'Daniel. Allred's friends, including Justice William O. Douglas and Congressman Lyndon Johnson, successfully persuaded Roosevelt to name Allred to the appellate vacancy on the Fifth Circuit. The nomination was sent to the Senate on February 18, 1943, but ran into trouble in the Judiciary Committee, because the newly elected O'Daniel was not about to let his rival win a patronage plum. Even though the senior senator from Texas, Tom Connally, supported Allred, the committee by a vote of 9 to 9 refused to recommend Allred. Attorney General Biddle reported on the stalemate to Roosevelt: "I had a long talk with Senator Connally Monday morning about the situation. He suggests and I agree that we should make no move for the next few weeks. At that time, if agreeable to you, I will suggest to Jimmy Allred that he write to you pointing out that the vote of the Committee shows his nomination is being considered on purely political partisan lines, without regard to the merits, and that therefore he is asking you to withdraw his name. I feel Allred will do this in a few weeks, but I am sure he will not do it now."[68] The next month, Allred asked Roosevelt to withdraw his name and Biddle suggested that the vacancy go to someone from Louisiana. Allred was eventually reappointed to the federal district bench in Texas in 1949 by Truman — after O'Daniel was no longer in the Senate.

The most publicized clash between Roosevelt and senators over a judgeship occurred in 1938 and early 1939 over the nomination of a fifty-nine-year-old Virginia state judge and New Deal supporter, Floyd Roberts. The Virginia Democratic senators, Carter Glass and Harry Byrd, were conservative opponents of Roosevelt. Glass and Byrd recommended two men for the opening on the federal district bench, both of whom resided in the district of the pro–New Deal representative John W. Flannagan, Jr., an opponent of the Byrd organization.[69] Flannagan backed Roberts and was joined in this recommendation by Virginia governor James H. Price and three former Virginia governors. In a memo to Roosevelt on June 2, 1938, Mac reported on a phone call he had received from a Price ally, State Senator C. J. Harkrader, who was also the publisher of two of the only three daily newspapers in Virginia supporting the New Deal. In the memo Mac reported that Harkrader had said: "Judge Roberts is an original Roosevelt man and highly qualified. Senator Glass and Senator Byrd will oppose anybody who is an out and out New Dealer as is Judge Roberts. . . . The matter is of vital concern to the President because in Virginia his friends have been making a great fight for the New Deal, which Glass and Byrd oppose."[70]

On July 5, Roosevelt gave Roberts a recess appointment as United States district judge for the Western District of Virginia. The president also informed the Virginia senators of his action. Senator Glass replied by telegram that he and Senator Byrd would oppose the nomination and invoke senatorial courtesy. Representative Flannagan, in contrast, wrote to Roosevelt praising the appointment and noting that Judge Roberts "is a progressive by principle and he has really and truly been in sympathy with your program."

When the Senate reconvened in January 1939, Roosevelt sent Roberts's name to the Senate for confirmation. By this time Senator Glass was taking the position that he was affronted by the manner in which the nomination had been made. In a letter to Mac on January 7, 1939, Harkrader wrote: "I have an idea that if the President could have a personal talk with Glass that he could be smoothed over and the confirmation go through without opposition. . . . He tells everybody his feelings are injured, so I believe the President could give him an explanation that would do him good." On top of the letter (which Mac gave to Roosevelt) Roosevelt wrote "Mac — Do you think I should have Carter Glass down?" Mac apparently agreed; a meeting was scheduled for January 24, but nothing came of it.

The Senate Judiciary Committee held a hearing on the nomination, and Senator Glass spelled out his objections. In an argument that resonated well with fellow senators in light of Roosevelt's attempt the previous year to purge congressional opponents, Glass claimed that Roosevelt was trying to rebuke the Virginia senators for their independent views on administration policy. He also charged that "Mr. Cummings never had the slightest idea of giving consideration to the recommendations of the two Virginia Senators because the Governor of Virginia had been promised the right of veto on nominations that they made." (Roosevelt would later publicly declare: "Neither of these statements is true.") The Virginia senators pronounced the Roberts nomination to be "personally obnoxious," the language used to invoke senatorial courtesy. The Senate Judiciary Committee, on February 1, 1939, voted 15 to 3 against confirmation, and the full Senate rejected the nomination five days later by a vote of 72 to 9. Judge Roberts, who had resigned his state judgeship to take the recess appointment, was now out of a job, and the administration was seen as having suffered a stunning political defeat.

But Roosevelt was not going to bow to the Virginia senators. On his own, during a visit to his son, Franklin, Jr., who was a law student at the University of Virginia, Roosevelt approached the highly respected dean of the law school, Armistead M. Dobie, and offered him the Virginia judgeship. Dean Dobie accepted, and Roosevelt allowed the Virginia senators to claim that Dobie was selected only after consultation with them. The nomination was sent to the Senate, and nine days later Dobie was confirmed. In a congratulatory letter to

Dean Dobie, Roosevelt wrote: "I am delighted confirmation went through all right—even though your two Senators let it appear that I had carefully consulted them before sending your name to the Senate! However, that is part and parcel of an outmoded system."[71] Less than eight months later, Roosevelt promoted Dobie to the Court of Appeals for the Fourth Circuit, where he served for fifteen years before retiring.

Other Considerations in the Appointment Process

Thus far, we have seen that judicial selection for the lower courts during the Roosevelt administration was characterized by the president's personal interest and frequent involvement in the process. We have seen the saliency of policy-agenda considerations, particularly between 1935 and 1940. Senatorial prerogatives continued, namely, the expectation that senators of the president's party from the state where there was a judicial vacancy would continue to play an important role in choosing the nominee. But we have also seen that the Justice Department was far from being a rubber stamp of senatorial preferences.

Purely partisan-agenda considerations were also a part of the process. James Farley, as chairman of the Democratic National Committee (he was also Roosevelt's postmaster general),discussed judicial appointments with the president, usually in personal meetings.[72] Farley's successor in 1940 was Ed Flynn, and he too was usually contacted, although by memo or by telephone. For example, on the formal letter from the attorney general to Roosevelt recommending Archibald B. Lovett to the federal district bench in Georgia, there was a handwritten notation: "Jim Rowe says Mr. Flynn O.K.'s." Another example is found in a memo for Mac from Rowe, noting, "The following names have been cleared with the Democratic National Committee," and the name of a judgeship candidate who was a member of Congress was included.[73]

Opposition from the Democratic National Committee chairman seems to have derailed at least two nominations. One would have been Roosevelt's first and only appointment of a woman, Marion Harron, to the federal district court bench.[m] The other concerned the nomination of Nathan Ross Margold for a position on the federal district bench for the District of Columbia, sent to the Senate on January 22, 1945. Just six days earlier, however, Flynn's successor as chairman of the Democratic National Committee, Robert E. Hannegan, had warned Roosevelt that he would not clear Margold because "in 1925

m. Marion Harron is discussed later in this chapter, as is Florence Allen, Roosevelt's only female lifetime judicial appointee, named to the Sixth Circuit in 1934.

Margold was appointed to the attorney general's staff as a Republican and a member of a Republican organization," and that in the 1944 presidential campaign "he was not active directly or indirectly, financially or otherwise." Margold, however, was a New Dealer, had served as solicitor for the Department of the Interior, and had the strong backing of Interior secretary Harold Ickes. Since 1942 he had been serving on the Municipal Court for the District of Columbia, having been given a term appointment by Roosevelt. As a member of the judiciary, it was not unreasonable for him to have not participated in the 1944 campaign. Hannegan, in his letter, also noted that "there is considerable opposition to [Margold's] appointment in the District."[74] The nomination went nowhere in the Senate Judiciary Committee, and when Truman succeeded to the presidency after Roosevelt's death the following April, he soon withdrew Margold's name.

Partisan-agenda considerations were also prominent in the twenty-three judicial appointments out of 183 (12.6 percent) that went to Democratic members of Congress who were either currently serving, recently defeated, or, in at least one instance, gerrymandered out of a seat. The gerrymandered member of Congress was Arthur Healey of Massachusetts, the subject of a September 1941 memo for the president from James Rowe, Jr.:

> Some time ago I spoke to you about Congressman Arthur Healey whose District in Massachusetts has been gerrymandered in such a way that he has no chance to be re-elected. At that time, Healey wanted to be appointed to the Democratic vacancy on the Customs Court of New York. Since then you have received the resignation of two District Court judges in Massachusetts. Healey would be perfectly happy to receive any one of the appointments. As I pointed out to you before, I doubt whether there is any other Congressman this Administration owes so much to as Healey. He has always shown great courage in fighting for the Administration on issues quite unpopular with his constituents. . . . He voted for the extension of Selective Service, being one of very few Irishmen who dared to do it. The appointment would be politically pleasing. I do not pretend to pass on the legal ability of Healey, since I know nothing about it. I have heard favorable comment.[75]

Healey, with the strong backing from Massachusetts Democratic officials and officeholders, received the district court judgeship.

Another consideration in the selection process, particularly for the courts of appeals, was geography. In February 1941, Michigan Democratic senator Prentiss M. Brown wrote to Roosevelt concerning a vacancy in the Sixth Circuit: "I think Michigan is entitled to this place. Ohio has had two judges — both Democratic appointments. . . . Tennessee has two, Kentucky has one and Michigan one. Kentucky's Judge Hamilton was a Democratic appointment.

Michigan has one Republican. We are the second State [in the Sixth Circuit] in size. We are the only one without a Democratic appointment." In an accompanying personal note to Roosevelt, Senator Brown added:

> On two occasions you personally asked my help — on the reciprocal trade agreements and the reorganization bills. In each instance I went with you. I believe I can truthfully say the aid I gave was vital.
>
> We in Michigan badly need your assistance now. Working this matter out may mean the election or defeat of our Highway Commissioner [and lucrative state contracts to be awarded].
>
> We need either the elevation of [Federal District] Judges Lederle or Picard. I shall be delighted to go along with your suggestion of Justice McAllister, but would like it coupled with the appointment of Koscinski to the District of Columbia bench.
>
> Of course you know I am loyal to you. Then too, Tom McAllister is one of my best friends as I told you the other day. I will be glad to see him elevated if you want him and even if you do not give us the Washington district judgeship, I will bow, but will feel a bit bad over the Koscinski angle.[76]

This letter reveals not only Roosevelt's personal involvement in selection but also the preference of senators for package deals whereby a federal district judge from the state is elevated to the appeals court (hence the claim for geographic representation) and the senator then has a hand in filling the district court vacancy. In this case, Michigan "received" the appointment to the Sixth Circuit, but the judgeship went to Roosevelt's choice, Thomas F. McAllister, then a forty-five-year-old associate justice on the Michigan Supreme Court, an unsuccessful Democratic candidate for Congress, and the husband of the former director of women's activities for the Democratic National Committee. There was no package deal, and Arthur Koscinski, who for the previous two years had been strongly pushed by Polish groups, did not receive a judgeship from Roosevelt. (In 1945 he was appointed by Harry Truman.)[n]

Another example of geographic representation at work is illuminated in a letter from Arkansas senator Hattie Caraway's secretary to Mac, who was an old friend, with the intent that it be shown to Roosevelt. The letter noted that

n. Polish ethnic groups had been pushing to have someone of Polish ancestry appointed to the bench. Finally, in 1944, the first federal district judge of Polish ancestry was appointed. As Attorney General Biddle had put it the previous October in a memo for the president, "Ed Kelley [the Democratic boss of Chicago] wants a Pole nominated from Chicago. We are now making an investigation of two of his suggestions. Kelley spoke to you about this sometime ago." The judgeship went to Walter La Buy, who was appointed to the U.S. District Court for the Northern District of Illinois. Biddle to Roosevelt, October 22, 1943, OF 208 e Illinois 1933–1945.

Senator Caraway "has been trying to get Judge Walter G. Riddick of Little Rock, or two other Arkansans" appointed to the vacancy on the Eighth Circuit Court of Appeals, but to no avail. "Our state has never had a major appointment by any Democratic Administration." The secretary noted that the absence of an Arkansas appointment "has resulted in our being injured in Arkansas because they say that Senator Caraway has not enough influence with the Administration to even get a Judge's appointment." The letter ended by noting, "As you know, the Senator has been loyal to the Administration, voting with it despite the pressure used against her."[77] Riddick received the nomination some six weeks later and was speedily confirmed.

Geographical representation also could give the administration an excuse to shift the appointment from one state to another when the Democratic powerhouses in the first state were at loggerheads over a prospective appointment. For example, Attorney General Cummings wrote to Roosevelt:

> The vacancy in the Court of Appeals for the Seventh Circuit has been pending a long time and, in view of opinion that seems to exist in Illinois with reference to this matter, I have been wondering whether it would not be feasible to go to Indiana for an appointee.
>
> . . . It rather strikes me that you would be justified in appointing the new Judge from Indiana. This would at least have the merit of cutting the Gordian knot and would be an act of poetic justice in view of the mess that Chicago has made of the matter.[78]

The attorney general recommended the Democratic senator from Indiana, Sherman Minton, but Minton himself supported Indiana Supreme Court justice Walter E. Treanor. Cummings noted that he had had a personal interview with Judge Treanor, "arranged, as you suggested, through Senator Minton." Cummings lavished praise on Treanor, calling him "very high-class" and observing that Treanor's appointment would be "an eminently satisfactory and desirable solution of a rather vexing business." Treanor's name was sent to the Senate four days later, and confirmation followed rapidly. When Treanor died three years later, White House aide James Rowe, Jr., informed Roosevelt that "Minton is very anxious to be put on the Circuit bench." He reminded the president of his long-standing intention to appoint Minton to a vacancy on the circuit court, adding that "Minton would be replacing an Indianan." Minton by this time was serving as a White House aide, having been defeated the previous November for reelection to the Senate. On the bottom of Rowe's memo, Roosevelt scribbled, "Can we do right away?"[79] The following week Minton was named to succeed Treanor.

As we see, geographic considerations can reinforce a pronounced leaning toward a particular candidate. But they can also be seen to be rationally and fairly taken into account by the administration. For example, Cummings once recommended to Roosevelt: "You will recall mentioning the vacancy in the Sixth Circuit. There are four states in that Circuit; namely, Kentucky, Michigan, Ohio and Tennessee. . . . On the theory of rotation . . . the next appointee should come from Tennessee. On the theory of the amount of business transacted, it would no doubt be claimed that Ohio should be favored."[80] The immediate vacancy went to Ohio; the next went to Tennessee.

Geographical considerations can also play a part in district court appointments when a state is divided into two or more districts. One example from the Roosevelt administration is the exception that proves the rule. In 1938, attorney general Biddle recommended Charles H. Leavey, a member of Congress from eastern Washington state, for a judgeship in the western district. Biddle wrote to Roosevelt: "Because of geographical considerations, [Democratic] Senator Bone has not endorsed Mr. Leavey. I am advised, however, that the Senator has the greatest respect and admiration for Mr. Leavey's ability and will interpose no objection to his nomination."[81]

Representative Leavey's name was sent to the Senate, but the smooth sailing predicted by Biddle did not prevail. In fact, Senator Bone held up confirmation for several months before permitting the nomination to be confirmed. Although there is no evidence in the presidential papers of a deal, Bone himself was named to the next vacancy on the Court of Appeals for the Ninth Circuit some two years later.

The attorney general as we have seen, has some discretion and influence in the selection process. One unusual episode points up the potential influence of an attorney general and specifically how Attorney General Francis Biddle used his power to frustrate the ambitions of William Clark. Some background is needed.

William Clark, a liberal New Jersey Republican, was an old friend of Roosevelt's. In 1925, Clark had been appointed by Calvin Coolidge to the federal district bench in New Jersey, and Roosevelt named Clark to the Court of Appeals for the Third Circuit in 1938. The next year, Francis Biddle joined Clark as a colleague on the court. Clark at first was enthusiastic about Biddle, but Clark and Biddle had a serious personality clash. Biddle, in his autobiography, wrote that Clark "had the instability of an advanced egocentric" and was "cantankerous by nature."[82]

Clark and Biddle had served together only ten months when Roosevelt named Biddle solicitor general; then, in August 1941, he asked Biddle to be attorney general. Before Biddle was appointed to the latter post, Clark wrote to Roosevelt: "You will remember that I rather favored our friend Francis' appointment to our Court. I was, however, thoroughly disappointed by his work. He seemed to me superficial and spent most of his time lobbying for further advancement. More than that, he evinced a rather unstable and opportunistic radicalism. My impression is that he is not well regarded generally."[83]

Roosevelt did not wish to answer this allegation personally, but he dictated a reply to his aide General Edwin M. Watson to be sent under Watson's name to Clark. That reply mentioned that the president "hopes to see you in Washington very soon," and also that the president "remarked that he thought you did not quite realize what a really grand record Biddle has made in Washington."[84]

After the Japanese attacked Pearl Harbor, Clark, who was fifty-one years old, desperately wanted to enlist. He was able to negotiate a commission as lieutenant colonel in the Army. On March 24, 1942, wearing his army uniform, he went to see Roosevelt. He had with him a letter of resignation but asked the president to consider the resignation a leave of absence without pay so that he could return to the bench after the war. Roosevelt responded generously and dumped the letter in the wastebasket. Roosevelt's press secretary, Stephen T. Early, was present at the meeting. The story of the judge who enlisted to fight for his country had captured the attention of the media, and Early was expected to offer the press a recap of the meeting between the president and the courageous judge.[85]

After Clark left Roosevelt's office, Early rescued the letter of resignation from the wastebasket, and Biddle was informed of what had transpired.[86] The next day, Biddle wrote to Roosevelt that he was "informed that Judge Clark suggested to you that he take leave of absence without pay so as to retain his position when he left the Army." Biddle claimed that "this would be directly contrary to the statute which provides that no person who holds office, the salary attached to which amounts to the sum of $2,500 or more, shall be appointed to hold any other office to which compensation is attached." Of course, Clark would be going on leave without pay. Nevertheless, Biddle argued, "There is grave legal doubt whether Clark could take leave of absence even without a salary to go into the Army." If Clark were to do this, Biddle stressed, "his office as a Judge would be vacated." Then Biddle went for the jugular: "The feeling both on his court and at the bar in his circuit is so strong against him that I think it would be unwise to approve any arrangement under which he would return. In case you indicated to Clark that some such arrangement might be made, that could be handled by your writing him that you have been advised by me that it cannot be done under the law."[87]

Roosevelt, however, delayed taking action until he was finally persuaded that Clark's seat had to be filled. On August 5, 1942, the Justice Department announced that the president had formally accepted Clark's resignation, effective the previous March, when Clark joined the Army. Clark's seat was filled by another New Jersey native, Gerald McLaughlin. In late 1944, however, when Clark was due to leave the Army,° Roosevelt asked Biddle to speak to him about appointing Clark to one of two vacancies on the Third Circuit. Again the attorney general mounted a strong case against appointing Clark. In one memo Biddle pointed out: "As to Willie Clark, New Jersey is entitled to not more than one Judge on the Court, relative to the amount of business. His vacancy has already been filled by an excellent Judge, McLaughlin from New Jersey. Pennsylvania should have the two other judges." But Roosevelt persisted, and in a second memo Biddle laid it on the line. "The appointment of a New Jersey judge would result in vigorous opposition from the two Pennsylvania Senators. Clark's appointment would also have the vigorous opposition of the New Jersey Bar and of the Democratic organization of that State. Congressman Hart, Chairman of the Democratic State Committee, has already expressed opposition."[88]

Clark did not receive his old seat back. When Roosevelt died in April 1945 and Harry Truman became president, Biddle continued as attorney general for several months. Clark, feeling deeply wronged and convinced that he had been on leave without pay and entitled to his judgeship back, pursued his grievance with the Truman administration and then before the Court of Claims, but to no avail. However, in 1948, Clark was given a judicial position in Europe as chief justice of the Court of Appeals of the Allied High Commission for Germany.ᵖ Ironically, his old nemesis, Francis Biddle, also served in Germany, as a member of the International Military Tribunal in Nuremberg.

o. Apparently Clark's army career was less than successful. The Army delicately put it "that no position was available nor in prospect commensurate with Col. Clark's grade and qualifications." None of the other major commands wanted him. Clark spent a month in Washington "negotiating with various officials in the War Department in order to secure a new position in the European Theater of Operations." But according to a War Department official, "some concern has been expressed about the possibility of Colonel Clark's being returned overseas. . . . However, he apparently has not met with success and existing orders call for the termination of his active duty status." It seems that during the time he spent in Washington he was technically AWOL (absent without official leave), but the Army papered this over. See the memoranda for General Watson, January 4 and January 8, 1945, in P.P.F. Box 575–600 PPF 576 Clark, William.

p. Once again, Judge Clark proved to be troublesome. In 1953, he was notified by the State Department that he would not be reappointed, but he refused to accept that decision. Finally, the State Department dismissed Clark, seized his diplomatic passport, and ordered him back to the United States. See *New York Times*, October 11, 1957, p. 27.

Women and Judgeships

From the perspective of the last decade of the twentieth century, the almost total exclusion of women and African Americans from serious consideration by the Roosevelt administration for lifetime federal judgeships is a major indictment of Roosevelt's judicial selection process. From the standpoint of the 1930s, however, the Roosevelt administration was responsible for a historic breakthrough for women and at least showed good intentions regarding blacks.

The breakthrough was the selection of Ohio Supreme Court justice Florence Allen for a position on the Court of Appeals for the Sixth Circuit in March 1934. Judge Allen was the first woman in the history of the United States to receive a lifetime federal judgeship on a court of general jurisdiction.[q] The tenacity of sexism in the selection process is underscored by the fact that it took more than thirty years before another woman received an appeals court appointment. A happy convergence of favorable factors led to Judge Allen's selection. She had outstanding professional credentials, having served as an elected Ohio jurist for the preceding thirteen years, including service on the state's highest court. She had experience as a county prosecutor. But most important, she had been politically active and was able to muster the necessary political backing from Ohio Democrats. Furthermore, Mary Dewson, head of the Women's Division of the Democratic National Committee, as well as the president's wife, Eleanor Roosevelt, strongly backed Allen and helped coordinate a campaign on her behalf. Roosevelt was well aware of the political importance of his women supporters and was happy to go along. Allen was confirmed within two weeks after the Senate received the nomination.[89][r]

As important as the Allen appointment was, it stood alone. During the entire Roosevelt administration there was only one other time when a woman was seriously considered for an appeals court position. In October 1943, an Oregon congressman, Walter M. Pierce, wrote to Roosevelt recommending Celia Galvin for a vacancy on the Ninth Circuit Court. In a note, Roosevelt

q. Genevieve Rose Cline was the first woman appointed to a lifetime federal judgeship. She was appointed to the Customs Court by Calvin Coolidge in 1928.

r. Judge Allen reported in her autobiography that after she was sworn in, a group of women attorneys in Washington, D.C., hosted a luncheon for her at which invited speaker Attorney General Cummings noted: "Florence Allen was not appointed because she was a woman. All we did was to see that she was not rejected because she was a woman." Florence Ellinwood Allen, *To Do Justly* (Cleveland: Press of Western Reserve University, 1965), 95.

asked Mac: "Will you thank [Pierce] and take up with the attorney general? I do not think it is a bad idea."[90] But nothing came of it, and six months later, Washington's Democratic senator Bone was named to fill the vacancy.

Very few women initiated a candidacy for the appeals courts. One who did was Kathryn Van Leuven, who was legal counsel for the Oklahoma Unemployment Compensation Division and had been the first woman to be an Oklahoma state's attorney (a position equivalent to district attorney in many states). She wrote to Mac in 1937 asking to be considered for a vacancy on the Tenth Circuit. But she was never seriously in the running.

More women were candidates for federal district court judgeships. One, Marion J. Harron of California, was actually on the verge of having her nomination to the Southern District of California sent to the Senate when the chairman of the Democratic National Committee, Ed Flynn, the old-line boss of the Bronx, refused to clear her. In the formal nomination letter accompanying the nomination document for Harron, dated January 14, 1942, Attorney General Biddle noted her many accomplishments, including legal research positions at Columbia and Johns Hopkins, four years as a general practitioner in New York City, assistant code attorney and later special attorney in the National Recovery Administration, attorney with the Resettlement Administration, and, beginning in 1936, a member of the United States Board of Tax Appeals. Biddle wrote that Harron "is endorsed for this appointment by prominent members of the Bench and Bar, and I am advised that [Democratic] Senator [Sheridan] Downey will interpose no objection."[91] At the top of the letter is the poignant notation, "Nomination not sent in."

What had happened is explained in a memo to Roosevelt from Mac, dated January 19, 1942: "I am holding up the nomination of Marion Harron because Jim Matthews (Dem. Com.) cannot clear it and the only report I can get from Flynn's office is that he cannot be reached."[92] Flynn preferred a male for the position, but Flynn's candidate did not receive the nomination.[s] One can only wonder whether Roosevelt might have been more firm with Ed Flynn had his mind not been on more pressing matters, such as the conduct of the war, in the months after Pearl Harbor. Whatever the reason, Roosevelt chose not to defy the chairman of the Democratic National Committee and did not go ahead with a nomination the chairman refused to clear. Flynn thus succeeded in blocking the only woman during Roosevelt's twelve years in office who had almost made it through the district judge selection process.

s. Roosevelt instead sent to the Senate the nomination of a former member of the administration, Pierson Hall, who had been appointed a United States attorney during Roosevelt's first term. Hall was cleared by Flynn.

There were two other women candidates for judgeships in California, in 1938 and 1939. Letters came to the White House and Justice Department backing Ida May Adams and Dorothy M. Williams (none, however, from important Democratic party leaders). But the candidacies were not taken seriously by the administration.[93]

In contrast, in the fall of 1941, a strong campaign was mounted for Massachusetts judge Golda Richmond Walters. She had the backing of the chairman of the Democratic State Committee and of former governor (and former mayor of Boston) James M. Curley, who was also a Democratic national committeeman. There were two vacancies at the time. New Deal congressman Arthur Healey had the inside track for one of them, but the other provided an ideal opportunity to name such a well-qualified woman as Judge Walters. Another candidate for the second vacancy was the wunderkind (and member of the administration) Charles E. Wyzanski, Jr. The thirty-five-year-old Wyzanski was a former law clerk to both Augustus Hand and Learned Hand of the U.S. Court of Appeals for the Second Circuit, both of whom enthusiastically wrote on his behalf. In a memo to James Rowe, Jr., the president attached the letter from Representative Healey asking to be considered for one of the vacancies and wrote: "Will you take this up with Francis Biddle? I would be inclined to appoint Healey and Wyzanski to the District Court vacancies in Massachusetts."[94] This is precisely what occurred.

Another seemingly viable candidacy of a woman was that of Mary Connor Myers, a lawyer for the Agricultural Adjustment Administration. Myers was backed by Secretary of Agriculture Henry Wallace and also by Jerome Frank, chairman of the Securities and Exchange Commission, for a vacancy on the federal district bench in the District of Columbia in the fall of 1939. The administration had great leeway with such appointments, because the District of Columbia had no senators with whom to deal. Nevertheless, Frank Murphy, who as attorney general was committed to finding (in his words) the "best qualified *man*," disregarded Myers and recommended David A. Pines, who was serving as United States Attorney for the District of Columbia, and Roosevelt went along. Roosevelt himself on several occasions told reporters that "the federal judiciary should be filled by *men* under 60 years of age."[95]

In 1938, Susan Brandeis, the daughter of revered Supreme Court justice Louis D. Brandeis, was a candidate for a newly created district court position in New York. A campaign was mounted on her behalf by prominent lawyers, judges, and politicians. But despite the torrent of letters to the White House and Justice Department, there is no evidence that anyone in the administration gave her special consideration, and the record is curiously silent on Roosevelt's view of her candidacy. She was not appointed to that vacancy. Two years later, when another new judgeship was created in New York, Brandeis, then an assistant United States attorney, again wished to be considered. But she then withdrew her name, for reasons that remain unclear. Perhaps she had been disappointed by the results of her previous campaign for a district judgeship and decided against what likely would have been a quixotic enterprise, given the biases against women. Some months later, a woman less well connected than Brandeis was a candidate. The position, however, went to the former law partner of Democratic senator Robert F. Wagner, Simon H. Rifkind, who went on to an illustrious career on the bench and, after resigning from the bench, a noted career in private practice.[96]

Active candidacies by women for the federal bench were rare during the Roosevelt years. However, given the success of Ohio's Florence Allen, it is perhaps understandable that two other Ohio women attorneys made an attempt at winning a federal judgeship. In February 1937, there was a campaign for Eva Epstein Shaw for a federal district court position, but Congressman Frank LeBlond Kloeb received the nomination.[97] In 1938, State Judge Lillian M. Westropp campaigned for a vacancy. The Cleveland Bar Association ignored her candidacy and recommended five males. Although the Cleveland Bar Association carried no particular weight with the administration, its apparent bias against women serving on the federal bench reflected an obstacle to the advancement of women lawyers that was not confined to Cleveland. The administration, in filling this vacancy, was more concerned with the feelings of the Democratic senators, particularly Senator Vic Donahey, who complained that he was not receiving "equal patronage." Donahey's *man* received the judgeship.

The odds against women becoming federal judges were overwhelming. In 1939, Harriet S. Daggett, a professor of law at Louisiana State University, was a candidate for a federal district judgeship. Daggett had earned a doctorate in law from Yale, was the author of four books, and was listed in *Who's Who in America*. She had some political and professional backing. But the Louisiana senators recommended three men for the judgeship, and the administration chose one of them.

African Americans and Judgeships

Although women encountered repeated frustration in their attempts to gain federal judgeships, there was at least the breakthrough appointment of Florence Allen to an appeals court. For African Americans, there were similar obstacles, biases, and frustrations, but no comparable breakthrough. No African Americans were appointed by Roosevelt to lifetime federal judgeships.

The administration did, however, name William H. Hastie in 1937 to a term appointment on the territorial federal district bench in the Virgin Islands.

William Hastie was extraordinary by any measure. He was a brilliant student at Amherst College, where he was elected in his third year to Phi Beta Kappa. He graduated first in his class. He went on to Harvard Law School, where he was a member of the editorial board of the *Harvard Law Review,* and he was graduated cum laude in 1930. Hastie joined the faculty of the law school at Howard University and in 1933 became an assistant solicitor in the Department of Interior, where he gained the attention of Secretary Harold Ickes. Hastie worked on Virgin Islands cases (the Virgin Islands came under the supervision of the Department of Interior), and when a vacancy arose on the district bench there, Secretary Ickes recommended him. Hastie was the first African American appointed to a federal judgeship. He served for two years before resigning to become dean of the Howard law school.

In his letter of resignation to Roosevelt of February 14, 1939, Judge Hastie observed:

> I hope that my term of office here may have helped to demonstrate that the Negro lawyer of today can serve on the Federal bench competently, effectively, and with the good will of the community. I am confident that the people of the Virgin Islands and the people of most communities in the continental United States as well, will welcome and respect a competent and impartial judicial officer whatever his race may be.
>
> If in years to come my term as United States Judge in the Virgin Islands can be viewed in retrospect, not as an isolated incident, but as the beginning of a continuing tradition of the Negro on the Federal bench, I believe something of consequence for our democracy will have been accomplished.[98]

Hastie's successor on the Virgin Islands court, Herman E. Moore of Illinois, was also black. As for Hastie himself, in late 1944 a delegation from the predominantly black National Lawyers Guild met with Attorney General Biddle to recommend him for a vacancy on the U.S. District Court for the District of Columbia. Biddle told them that Roosevelt already had someone in mind. Biddle then wrote to the president telling him of the visit and noting: "You will remember that I suggested to you some time ago that you should appoint a Negro to a Court in the District. Washington is an excellent place to make the appointment. If [District of Columbia Municipal Court judge Nathan] Margold is put on the [federal] District Court that would leave a vacancy on the Municipal Court. I think you should give serious consideration to putting Hastie in Margold's place."[99]

Biddle pointed out that "Hastie is a man of great ability." Chief Justice Harlan Fiske Stone had told Biddle that Hastie's oral argument before the

Supreme Court in *Smith* v. *Allwright,* the case that challenged the Texas primary election for whites only, "was one of the best that he had heard during
the term." Roosevelt replied: "I think this suggestion about Hastie is an excellent one. Will you speak to me about it on my return?"[100]

Margold was indeed nominated for the federal district bench, but his nomi-
nation went nowhere because of opposition from the Democratic National
Committee. Hastie remained dean at Howard until appointed in 1946 by
President Truman to be governor of the Virgin Islands. Hastie served in that
capacity for three years, until Truman made the landmark appointment of
Hastie to the United States Court of Appeals for the Third Circuit.

Even before the push for Hastie for a district court judgeship, Hastie's
colleague and vice-dean at Howard, Dr. Leon A. Ranson, was a candidate for
a vacancy. So eventually was another black lawyer in the District of Columbia,
George E. C. Hayes, who along with Ranson earned recommendations from
the Washington Bar Association. Hayes had been an honors graduate from
Brown University and received his law degree from Harvard. There is no
evidence, however, that Ranson and Hayes were seriously considered. Earlier,
in 1939, Hayes had also been a candidate for a vacancy. At that time, still
another brilliant black Harvard Law School graduate, Charles Houston, was
mentioned for a District of Columbia judgeship. White males, of course, filled
the positions.[101]

There were far fewer black candidates than even the small number of
women candidates for federal judgeships, and the very few there were emerged
after Judge Hastie had been appointed to the Virgin Islands in 1937. In 1940,
there was a campaign waged on behalf of New York City tax commissioner
Hubert T. Delaney for a vacancy on the federal district bench in New York.
The great singer Marian Anderson wrote to Eleanor Roosevelt recommending
Delaney "in the event the President is considering the appointment of a
Negro." That letter was turned over by the president to Attorney General
Robert Jackson with the cover notation "For Your Information." Also, in
1940, the Chicago branch of the NAACP proposed to Roosevelt that he name
Hastie's successor on the Virgin Islands court, Herman E. Moore, to a vacancy
on the federal district bench in Illinois, but this was not part of any extensive
campaign on Moore's behalf. So, too, in 1940, both the Baptist Ministers'
Conference and the Pennsylvania State Baptists Convention wrote to ask that
a black be named to a vacancy on the federal bench in Philadelphia.[102]

In Massachusetts, in 1941, there were major campaigns by African Americans for two vacancies on the federal district bench. One of the candidates was
a Boston attorney, Julian Rainey, who had served as director of the "Colored
Division" of the Democratic National Committee. One might think his impor-

tant role in maintaining the Democratic Party coalition would have resulted in his candidacy being taken seriously by the administration, but there is no evidence that it was. It also appears that the campaign was waged after Roosevelt had settled on naming Healey and Wyzanski. But even had the campaign been pressed before Roosevelt had made a decision, there is no evidence that the president or any of his four attorneys general was prepared to name an African American, no matter how brilliantly qualified, to a lifetime judgeship.

The Demographic Profile of Roosevelt's Judges

Table 2.1 presents the statistics concerning several background variables of Roosevelt's lifetime appointees to the district and appeals court benches.[1] It permits us to examine variations from term to term and to determine, for example, if the second term appointees, whose selection was the most driven by the policy agenda, differed in pronounced ways from the more partisan-agenda-driven appointees of the first term.

AGE

In his second term, Roosevelt turned to younger candidates to fill court vacancies. This is not unexpected, considering that at the start of the second term he introduced his court reform bill, which on its surface focused on the age of the justices (and their alleged inability to keep up with their workload). Although Roosevelt was really concerned with the anti-New Deal decisions of the federal courts, age nevertheless became a more prominent part of the selection process. The drop in the average age of lower-court nominees during the second term and beyond suggests that the concern with age was not a passing political gesture but signaled a change in the criteria used for considering potential nominees. It could also be argued that during Roosevelt's first term the Democrats, so long out of national power, had longstanding political debts to pay and that necessarily they tended to be paid through judgeships to

1. Note that these figures do not include the four nominations, including two recess appointments (one district and one appeals), that were unsuccessful. They also do not include the one nominee, William Baxter Lee of Tennessee, who was confirmed but died before taking office, or the elevation of Lawrence Groner to chief judge of the Court of Appeals for the District of Columbia. Groner was already on the appeals court as an associate justice, thus his "elevation" to an administrative task is not considered to have been a judicial appointment in the sense that an appointment to the court in the first place would be so considered. The figures *do* include Roger T. Foley of Nebraska, who was confirmed April 10, 1945, two days before Roosevelt's death, but whose judicial commission was subsequently signed by Harry Truman.

Table 2.1. *Selected Backgrounds of Lifetime Roosevelt Appointees to the Federal District and Appeals Courts of General Jurisdiction*

	District Court Appointees			Appeals Court Appointees		
	First Term	*Second Term*	*Third+ Term*	*First Term*	*Second Term*	*Third+ Term*
Average age at time of appointment	51.6	48.4	50.3	57.3	51.1	52.4
Undergraduate Education						
Public	22.9% (8)	29.1% (16)	32.6% (14)	33.3% (4)	32.1% (9)	40.0% (4)
Private not Ivy	34.3% (12)	34.5% (19)	34.9% (15)	41.7% (5)	32.1% (9)	30.0% (3)
Ivy League	2.9% (1)	5.5% (3)	9.3% (4)	8.3% (1)	21.4% (6)	20.0% (2)
None	40.0% (14)	30.9% (17)	23.3% (10)	16.7% (2)	14.3% (4)	10.0% (1)
Law School Education						
Public	17.1% (6)	40.0% (22)	32.6% (14)	25.0% (3)	21.4% (6)	30.0% (3)
Private not Ivy	57.1% (20)	30.9% (17)	44.2% (19)	25.0% (3)	32.1% (9)	30.0% (3)
Ivy League	8.6% (3)	16.4% (9)	9.3% (4)	16.7% (2)	42.9% (12)	30.0% (3)
None	17.1% (6)	12.7% (7)	13.9% (6)	33.3% (4)	3.6% (1)	10.0% (1)
Experience						
Judicial	34.3% (12)	34.5% (19)	41.9% (18)	58.3% (7)	60.7% (17)	30.0% (3)
Prosecutorial	45.7% (16)	50.9% (28)	48.8% (21)	58.3% (7)	32.1% (9)	40.0% (4)
Neither	37.1% (13)	32.7% (18)	30.2% (13)	8.3% (1)	21.4% (6)	40.0% (4)
Occupation						
Politics — Government	20.0% (7)	12.7% (7)	25.6% (11)	16.7% (2)	17.9% (5)	30.0% (3)
Government Lawyer	20.0% (7)	21.8% (12)	23.3% (10)	8.3% (1)	3.6% (1)	10.0% (1)
Judiciary	25.7% (9)	20.0% (11)	16.3% (7)	41.7% (5)	50.0% (14)	30.0% (3)

Table 2.1. Continued

	District Court Appointees			Appeals Court Appointees		
	First Term	Second Term	Third+ Term	First Term	Second Term	Third+ Term
Large Law Firm*	2.9% (1)	—	2.3% (1)	—	—	10.0% (1)
Medium-Size Law Firm†	2.9% (1)	5.5% (3)	13.9% (6)	—	7.1% (2)	10.0% (1)
Small Law Firm‡	20.0% (7)	25.5% (14)	13.9% (6)	33.3% (4)	3.6% (1)	10.0% (1)
Solo Practice	8.6% (3)	12.7% (7)	4.7% (2)	—	—	—
Law Professor	—	1.8% (1)	—	—	17.9% (5)	—
Party						
Democratic	94.3% (33)	100.0% (55)	100.0% (43)	100.0% (12)	92.9% (26)	100.0% (10)
Republican	5.7% (2)	—	—	—	7.1% (2)	—
Prominent Party Activism						
	60.0% (21)	67.3% (37)	55.8% (24)	66.7% (8)	64.3% (18)	70.0% (7)
Prior or Current Members of Congress						
	14.3% (5)	9.1% (5)	16.3% (7)	16.7% (2)	7.1% (2)	20.0% (2)
Religion						
Protestant	68.6% (24)	69.1% (38)	58.1% (25)	83.3% (10)	92.9% (26)	70.0% (7)
Catholic	28.6% (10)	29.1% (16)	32.6% (14)	16.7% (2)	7.1% (2)	20.0% (2)
Jewish	2.9% (1)	1.8% (1)	9.3% (4)	—	—	10.0% (1)
Total Number of Appointees						
	35	55	43	12	28	10

* A large law firm was defined as consisting of ten or more partners and associates.

† A medium-size law firm was defined as consisting of from five to nine partners and associates.

‡ A small law firm was defined as consisting of from two to four partners and associates.

those who had waited the longest and were therefore the oldest. This conjecture can be tested in part by examining the proportion of prior or current members of Congress appointed to the bench. However, when we examine these data we find little support for the more-political-debts-to-pay hypothesis as tied to age. In the first term, they comprised about 14 percent of appointees (to the district courts) and over 12 percent of appointees in the second term and beyond. The court reform/packing episode most likely brought about an awareness of age and a desire to appoint younger judges.

EDUCATION

A large proportion of first-term district court appointees had no undergraduate college education (40 percent), as compared to about 31 percent of second-term and about 23 percent of third-term appointees. There was a smaller gap between appointees of the first and second/third terms of those without a *law school* education. Those without formal law school training studied law as apprentices in law offices.

The profile of the education of the appeals court appointees was somewhat different from that of the district court appointees. There were smaller proportions without an undergraduate education and for the first term (but not the other terms) a larger proportion without law school training. Appeals court judges were more likely than district judges to have attended an Ivy League school (whether as undergraduates or as law students). This is most noticeable during the second term, when over 40 percent of Roosevelt's appeals court appointees had been graduated from among the most prestigious law schools. It is possible that the appeals courts appointees tended to be of a higher caliber intellectually, professionally, and perhaps even economically than the district court appointees on the whole.

Only small proportions of district court appointees attended the Ivy League colleges and law schools. Public-supported undergraduate colleges accounted for an increasing proportion of appointees during the Roosevelt years, and this seemed to hold true for public-supported law schools as well. Only a minority of district and appeals court appointees had a private school undergraduate education. For the most part, however, a majority of appointees went to private law schools.

EXPERIENCE

Almost half of Roosevelt's district court appointees had experience as prosecutors, while only about one-third had served as judges. About one-third had neither judicial nor prosecutorial experience. (Some appointees had both.) It would seem that professional credentials were of some import in the selection process.

For appeals court appointees, during the second term almost twice as many appointees had judicial experience as had prosecutorial experience. Again, this is consistent with what we would expect from a policy-agenda-driven selection process. Those with judicial experience had track records that indicated to the Roosevelt administration that they were likely to be New Deal supporters.

OCCUPATION

At least one out of five district court appointees served as a government lawyer, typically in the United States Attorney's office, when chosen for the federal bench. Twice the proportion of appeals court appointees than district court appointees were serving in the judiciary at the time of appointment, with seventeen elevated from the federal district courts. (Five were serving on state supreme courts.) There were far fewer appeals court judges who came to the bench from serving as a government lawyer, and generally somewhat fewer holding other elective or appointive office.

Those who were appointed from law practice for the most part came from small law firms or solo practices. Only two district court judges and one appeals court judge came from a large law firm. These findings are consistent with the class-based differences between the constituencies of the Democratic and Republican parties and suggest that these differences extended from the rank and file to include the party elites.

Only one law professor was appointed to the district bench, and only five were placed on the appeals bench. But the figure for the appeals courts is somewhat misleading, because a law professor such as Calvert Magruder, who left Harvard to join the administration, is not counted in the figures for law professor; neither is Thurmond Arnold, who was professor of law at Yale before his government service. Walter Treanor was a law professor at Indiana University until he was elected to the Indiana Supreme Court in 1930, whence he was selected in 1937 for the U.S. Court of Appeals for the Seventh Circuit. Treanor is also not counted in the statistics as a law professor. If these three are counted, the proportion of law professors chosen for the appeals bench is 16 percent overall and 25 percent during the second term. This one-in-four rate during the second term makes sense in policy-agenda terms. These law professors could articulate a judicial philosophy that would favor the New Deal and provide intellectual leadership on their courts supporting economic liberalism.

PARTY

Only two nominal Republicans were appointed to the district bench during the entirety of Roosevelt's presidency. One, Michael Roche, began classifying himself as a Democrat several years after going on the bench. Two Republicans were appointed to the appeals bench, both of whom were political liberals and friends of Roosevelt. Roughly two out of three district and appeals court appointees had a history of prominent party activity or a close political relationship with Roosevelt or a Democratic senator. Close to 13 percent of the district court appointees and 12 percent of the appeals court appointees had been members of Congress. This level of partisanship in appointments likely is due not only to the Democrats' having been out of power for twelve years before Roosevelt's victory in 1932 but also to concern with making policy-agenda appointments.

RELIGIOUS ORIGIN OR AFFILIATION

Catholics accounted for a substantial proportion of district court appointments but a noticeably lower proportion for the appeals courts. The largest discrepancy occurred during the second term, when four times as many Catholics were named to the district courts (proportionally) as to the appeals courts. Clearly, at the district court level Catholics were generously recognized, perhaps a reflection of the influence of Catholic participation in the ranks of the Democratic party and the prominence of Catholics at the head of local party organizations. On the other hand, Jewish appointees were few and far between on both the district and appeals courts.

There is evidence that during his second term Roosevelt became increasingly aware of the religion of his judicial nominees and sensitive to the charge that he was appointing a disproportionate number of Catholics. On August 1, 1939, Roosevelt wrote a memo to New York senator Robert Wagner which was attached to a letter the president had received from a friend asking to be considered for a judgeship in the Southern District of New York. Roosevelt wrote: "What do you think? Doubtless you have known him, as I have, for many years and he is a fine citizen. It is perfectly true that I am distinctly embarrassed by the fact that I have appointed to the District Court for the Southern District one Jew and four Catholics, and to the Brooklyn Court, first one Catholic and a week ago another."[103][u] On another occasion Attorney General Biddle wrote a memo to Roosevelt concerning a vacancy in the district court for Nebraska:

u. The applicant, Adolphus Ragan, did not receive the judgeship.

You asked me to see [Nebraska] Senator Norris . . . to suggest to him the advisability of appointing [John W.] Delehant, a Catholic, to the Court in accordance with the recommendations of Jim Lawrence, Quigley, and Ed Flynn. He had previously expressed his belief that a Protestant should be appointed. . . .

You will remember that the choice boiled down to Delehant and Paul F. Good (Protestant), both are excellent lawyers. . . . [Senator Norris] will not oppose anybody you appoint on the District Court in Nebraska, but is still definitely of the opinion that it would be a mistake to appoint a Catholic.[104]

Roosevelt had filled the previous vacancy in Nebraska with a Catholic. Nevertheless, Delehant was appointed.

The following year, a special assistant to the attorney general undertook a major research project that determined the religion of United States judges appointed by the Roosevelt administration from 1933 through much of 1942 compared to judges appointed by Republican administrations from 1922 to 1933. Each judge and the judge's religion were listed and summary tables prepared highlighting the percentage of Catholics in the population of each state and the percentage of Catholic Roosevelt appointments from each state. For the entire United States, the statistics showed that "the percentage of Catholic appointments to federal judgeships . . . is 23.8 as against a Catholic population percentage of 16.9."[105] They also showed that Roosevelt appointed more than four times the proportion of Catholics as had his Republican predecessors but that the proportion of Jewish appointees remained the same (under 5 percent). There was no recommendation that fewer Catholics should be appointed, and in fact for the balance of the Roosevelt administration an even higher proportion of Catholics received judicial appointments.

Roosevelt's judges were drawn from among the Democratic Party elite, and in religion and economic background they more or less mirrored the party's rank and file. But appointees did *not* reflect the party's constituency in gender and race. With one exception, all of Roosevelt's lifetime appointees were male, and all were white. Roosevelt took a hands-on approach to judicial selection even during the Second World War; and while he tried to accommodate party leaders, including Democratic senators, he also showed a strong interest in appointing New Deal supporters and those who had the necessary professional qualifications, particularly for appeals court appointments. The policy agenda seemed to have the greatest play starting in 1935 and particularly during the second term, once the administration began to focus on the federal courts in an effort to appoint supporters of the New Deal. The partisan agenda was always important, but less so from 1935 to 1940. Personal-agenda appointments occurred rarely.

The 1930s permanently altered the political and governmental landscape of the United States. The party system was transformed, with the party of Roosevelt capturing the allegiance of a majority of the electorate, an allegiance that would produce Democratic Party domination of the federal government for decades. The New Deal programs that cemented the new alliance between the voters and the Democrats transformed the scope and nature of government. The national government assumed new responsibilities for the economic and social welfare of the American people and in so doing created a much enlarged federal bureaucracy.

The federal courts also underwent a concomitant change in the 1930s. Law became increasingly federalized, as federal programs, standards, and regulations were imposed on the states. The business of the federal courts grew and also shifted so that public law disputes as well as federal criminal prosecutions began to dominate the circuits.[106] The courts expanded: new judgeships were created during all but four years of Roosevelt's presidency. At the time of Roosevelt's death, there were 193 lifetime positions on the district bench and fifty-nine on the appeals bench, a growth since 1933 in excess of 25 percent. Clearly, federal judgeships became increasingly significant as governmental positions having an impact on public policy.

3

Truman Carries On

With Franklin Roosevelt's unexpected death on April 12, 1945, Vice President Harry S. Truman became president. A shocked and stunned nation knew relatively little about Truman. He had achieved some degree of national attention when as a senator in 1941 he chaired what became known as the Truman Committee — the Senate Committee to Investigate the National Defense Program — which exposed waste, inefficiency, and mismanagement in defense spending, in particular the building of army camps. After Pearl Harbor and America's entry into the Second World War, the Truman Committee oversaw the war effort, and press accounts portrayed Truman as a powerful senator. But the fact remains that Truman was more a political insider than a widely known figure.[1] Picked by the Democratic National Convention to be Roosevelt's running mate in 1944, Truman became vice president as Roosevelt won an unprecedented fourth term. In his almost three months as vice president, Truman was almost invisible to the general public.

By 1945, the New Deal political coalition had achieved some degree of stability. New Deal programs had become a fixed part of America's economic and social structure. Ideological warfare was conducted on the margins of domestic policy, although to be sure many Republicans had dreams of undoing the New Deal.

The big issues for Truman were bringing the war to a close, planning for the postwar conversion to a peacetime economy, and laying the foundation for an active role for the United States in rebuilding Europe and securing international stability. Truman was immediately concerned with assuring the American public that he would provide the necessary leadership both domestically and internationally.

By 1946, the country was no longer at war, and most of the massive controls on the wartime economy had been lifted. The immediate result was a dramatic rise in the rate of inflation.[2] Organized labor, free from wartime restraints, conducted a series of strikes in 1946. The strikes in the mines and railroads threatened to paralyze the country, and Truman ordered the federal government to seize these industries. Such presidential actions helped stimulate labor and management to reach settlements. Nevertheless, inflation, strikes, and even occasional food shortages damaged the Democratic Party in the 1946 congressional elections. Republicans gained control of both houses of Congress for the first time since 1930 (with a 56 seat gain in the House and a 13 seat gain in the Senate). Yet Republican control did not undo the New Deal; indeed, most Republicans at least implicitly accepted the major reforms and programs that by 1947 were well established. A Republican Congress also meant that the Senate Judiciary Committee, and the judicial confirmation process, came under the control of Republicans. Republicans won impressive gubernatorial victories in every region, with the exception of the still solidly Democratic south. Truman's popularity plunged, and Republicans eagerly anticipated winning the 1948 presidential election.

Not only did Truman have political problems on the domestic front; he also faced an expansionist Soviet Union. Indeed, the worldwide spread of Soviet-style communism was considered as severe a threat to the United States and the western democracies as the fascists had been. The Truman administration undertook a number of major aid programs and established the military alliance of the western democracies, the North Atlantic Treaty Organization (NATO). But despite Truman's programs and their many successes, frustration mounted in the United States over the direction of world events. The anxiety, even paranoia, about alleged communist infiltration and subversion of American government was exploited by many politicians.

Fueling the fears was Russia's development of atomic weapons, a result Americans believed came about by the work of communist spies within and outside of government who stole nuclear secrets and delivered them to the Soviets. Truman reacted by establishing a loyalty program to prevent communist sympathizers from being employed by the federal government and by ordering the Justice Department to examine the activities of the American Communist Party with an eye toward prosecution.

Truman confronted the long-festering problem of the denial of basic civil rights to African Americans. He unilaterally desegregated the armed forces. On February 2, 1948, he presented Congress with a comprehensive civil rights program—which promptly died in a Congress dominated by segregationists. Five months later, when the Democratic National Convention adopted a strong civil rights plank for the party platform, most of the southern delegates walked out of the convention. The rebellious southern Democrats formed the new States' Rights Party and nominated South Carolina governor Strom Thurmond as its presidential candidate. (Thurmond, some thirty-three years later as a Republican senator, would assume the chairmanship of the Senate Judiciary Committee and remain in that position during the first six years of Ronald Reagan's presidency, when Republicans controlled the Senate.)

With both the left and right wings of the Democratic Party abandoning him and running third-party presidential candidates, Truman entered the presidential election campaign of 1948 a decided underdog. The Republicans nominated New York governor Thomas E. Dewey and, as his running mate, California governor Earl Warren. Dewey conducted an overconfident and bland campaign buoyed by public opinion polls predicting a Republican landslide. But Truman, refusing to concede defeat, waged a vigorous and aggressive campaign that resulted in the most stunning upset in American political history. Not only was Truman reelected by a comfortable margin (Truman's popular vote exceeded Dewey's by more than two million), but Democrats gained seventy-five seats in the House and nine in the Senate to regain control of Congress. In his second term, Truman promoted a wide-ranging program he called the "Fair Deal," which included national health insurance, major programs of aid to education, increased public health benefits, other social welfare legislation, a new program of aid to farmers, and new civil rights legislation. Conservative Democrats controlled key congressional committees, and they and their Republican allies managed to kill most of the Fair Deal proposals.

The issue of "subversives" in government gained new life when the civil war in China was won by the Communists at the end of 1949 and when Wisconsin Republican senator Joseph McCarthy, in a speech on February 11, 1950, charged that fifty-seven communists were working in the State Department. The intense media interest was fueled by McCarthy's wildly escalating allegations of communist infiltration of American public life. The invasion of South Korea on June 25, 1950, by Communist North Korea and the ensuing involvement of the United States in the Korean War fed the anticommunist hysteria. In 1950, Republicans made substantial congressional gains, increasing their membership in the House by twenty-eight seats and coming within two seats of controlling the Senate.

Within this context, necessarily an encapsulization of momentous and complex events, we begin to examine the Truman administration and appointments to the lower federal courts.

Presidential Involvement in Selection

Truman and Roosevelt were a study in contrasts. Whereas Roosevelt came from a patrician background, Truman was proud of his common roots and a self-made man. Roosevelt was a charismatic personality who could charm, cajole, and convince politicians one on one as well as millions of people with his speeches and "fireside chats." Truman was anything but charismatic. With the exception of his Give-em-hell-Harry election campaign performance in 1948, which led to his surprise victory, he was an earnest but uninspiring speaker. Roosevelt immensely enjoyed a complex game of politics, policy, and manipulation of people and events, often playing it close to the vest; Truman, although a master politician, seemed to be playing a more simple and straightforward game. Roosevelt was revered, loved, even lionized by much of the nation. Truman eventually won grudging respect for his gutsiness, plain speaking, and hard work, but his presidency never assumed the aura of Roosevelt's and at some points achieved a nadir never approached by his predecessor.

As a former senator Truman was appreciative of senatorial prerogatives. But as president he was at times a stubborn defender of the prerogatives of his office. As we shall see in this chapter, both traits came into play in the many dramas surrounding judicial selection in his administration. Truman, although priding himself as an effective administrator, did not micromanage judicial selection as Roosevelt did. But that does not mean that he was indifferent to judicial selection. At the most basic level of judgeships as political patronage Truman was usually personally involved.

The judiciary inherited by Truman was a New Deal Democratic judiciary. The great constitutional issues that had put the New Deal on trial were long since resolved by the time Truman became president, yet, as we shall also see, he remained aware of the policy implications of judicial appointments.

Roosevelt's death threw off balance behind-the-scenes maneuvering to obtain judgeships for particular individuals. These nominations had to await either renegotiation or encouragement from the new president. For example, on April 18, just six days after taking office, Truman received a letter from the North Carolina senators requesting a meeting to discuss a district court vacancy. At the meeting on April 20, the senators urged the selection of Donnell Gilliam, and in a follow-up letter to Truman they emphasized Gilliam's service to the Democratic Party.[3] Gilliam's nomination was sent to the Senate on May 3.

Truman maintained close friendships with former colleagues in the Senate, especially those who served with him on the Truman Committee. One such close colleague, Republican senator Joseph H. Ball of Minnesota, wrote to Truman on May 15, 1945, concerning a district judgeship, urging that Truman not choose two particular individuals "both of whom appear to me completely unqualified." Ball then provided an annotated list of three men who "would be acceptable to me." One, he noted, had backing from the Teamsters. Another was "probably the best legal mind of the lot . . . [but] age is against him." The third, Dennis Donovan, was "tops as a lawyer . . . a lifelong Democrat . . . has the endorsement of labor." On May 18, Truman replied: "I certainly did appreciate very much your note of the fifteenth, and I shall recommend one of the men on your list."[4] Despite some opposition from Minnesota Democratic Party officials and from some labor groups, Donovan's nomination was sent to the Senate the following June 1, less than two weeks after Truman's promise to his former Republican colleague.

In August, Truman named fellow Missourian Bennett Champ Clark, who in 1944 had lost his fight for reelection to the Senate, to a judgeship on the Court of Appeals for the District of Columbia. F. Ryan Duffy was a former senatorial friend of Truman's who, after losing his bid for reelection in 1938, was rewarded by Roosevelt for his loyalty as a New Dealer with a federal district judgeship. Truman elevated his friend to the Seventh Circuit some ten years later. Another former Senate colleague, Republican Ernest W. Gibson of Vermont, was personally chosen by Truman for a Vermont federal district judgeship, although Truman's attorney general had sent over the papers of another aspirant (a Democrat) and Democratic Party leaders in Vermont claimed that naming Gibson would "wreck the organization." But Truman had been reelected in 1948, Vermont had never been a Democratic stronghold or crucial to the national party's fortunes, and Truman was happy to accommodate his friend Vermont Republican senator George D. Aiken, who backed Gibson. A show of bipartisanship also was helpful in dealings with Republican senators on the Judiciary Committee.[5]

When it came to judgeships, Truman was loyal to his Missouri friends. Roy W. Harper, Democratic state chairman and a political ally of Truman's, was named in 1947 to a federal district judgeship. Truman's longtime friend Caskie Collet, whom Roosevelt named to a federal district judgeship on the urging of Truman, was elevated by Truman to the Court of Appeals for the Eighth Circuit. A non-Missouri friend, Richmond B. Keech, who served as an administrative assistant to Truman, was appointed to the federal district bench for the District of Columbia in late 1946. Keech continued playing poker on occasion with Truman after his appointment. Fred Vinson, Harold Burton,

Tom Clark, and Sherman Minton, tapped by Truman for the Supreme Court, were personal agenda appointments.[6]

Although the evidence suggests that Truman was less concerned with judicial selection than was Roosevelt, he nevertheless was personally involved on a number of occasions and like Roosevelt, he insisted on making the final selection. For example, there was a federal district judgeship to be filled in Kansas. Carl Rice, the Democratic national committeeman from Kansas, had been a candidate but then bowed out. Two remaining candidates for the position were Arthur J. Mellott, a judge on the Tax Court of the United States, and Edgar C. Bennett, a Kansas state judge, both of whom had numerous supporters. Attorney General Tom Clark's memo of November 9, 1945, to Truman outlined the situation: "Carl Rice is endorsing Judge Mellott. He has withdrawn his candidacy. Judge Helvering [R. L. Helvering, chairman of the Democratic county central committee] says either Bennett or Mellott." Truman chose Mellott.[7]

When a seat on the district bench in Virginia came open in 1947, Truman noted in a memo to Clark: "Byrd [head of the Democratic organization in Virginia] and his colleagues have recommended five or six people for Judge in Virginia. I am informed that Albert Bryan of Alexandria is about the best of the lot. I'll appreciate it if you will look him up."[8] Truman appointed Bryan, and fourteen years later John F. Kennedy elevated him to the Fourth Circuit.

When there was no Democratic senator from a state with a judicial vacancy, presidential involvement in selection was even more likely. Early in 1949, a judicial vacancy on the district court in Wisconsin was created by the elevation of F. Ryan Duffy to the Seventh Circuit. There were three leading candidates, Carl R. Becker, Robert E. Tehan, and Thad F. Wasielewski. Becker, Duffy's referee in bankruptcy and a former assistant United States attorney, had the support of Judge Duffy. Becker was supported by much of the local bar. The former Justice Department official Joseph Keenan told the White House staff that "Carl R. Becker is 100% okay." He had political support as well, although in a telegram to Truman the editor and publisher of the *Capital Times* of Madison, Wisconsin, asserted that Becker's support came "from reactionaries in the Democratic Party. . . . [His appointment would have] ruinous effect . . . on hope for uniting liberals and progressives of this state for a successful campaign in 1950."[9]

Wasielewski, a former member of Congress, was backed by many congressional colleagues, who wrote to Truman. Wisconsin congressman Clement J. Zablocki in particular urged Wasielewski's appointment because of his appeal to Polish-American Democrats.[10] Polish-Americans wrote the White House urging that it was time to appoint a judge with a Polish background.

Tehan, a former state senator, a lawyer in private practice, and a Democratic national committeeman, had the backing of organized labor and Wisconsin liberals. Fearing that the White House was tilting toward Becker, Minnesota senator Hubert H. Humphrey wrote to Matthew J. Connelly, Truman's appointments secretary, supporting Tehan and warning, "To have anyone who was less active in the party caucuses rewarded by such an important appointment would literally undermine the efforts of the political leadership of Wisconsin." But there was division among Truman's advisers. Harry H. Vaughan suggested to Donald Dawson, Truman's administrative assistant for personnel, that Tehan was a party hack.[11]

On April 5, Truman met with two key Wisconsin Democratic congressmen, Zablocki and Andrew J. Biemiller, who both recommended Tehan. (Just six days earlier, Zablocki had written to Truman urging the appointment of Wasielewski!) Truman apparently had been leaning toward Tehan, who had vigorously supported the president's uphill reelection campaign. Indeed, the paperwork nominating Tehan had already been prepared. With the recommendation and go-ahead from the Wisconsin congressmen, the White House forwarded Tehan's nomination to the Senate that same day. Eight days later, Representative Zablocki wrote to Truman thanking him for naming Tehan, "a loyal Party man."[12]

Truman's personal involvement sometimes resulted in an unintended clash with senators, which was surprising given Truman's senatorial background and what had been his sensitivity to senatorial prerogatives. Three prominent examples of such conflict occurred after his reelection in 1948.

A vacancy on the federal district bench in Georgia was created by the elevation to the Fifth Circuit of Judge Robert L. Russell. Judge Russell was the brother of Senator Richard Russell, and Truman believed that the senator should have been pleased by his brother's elevation. To fill the vacancy, Truman picked M. Neil Andrews, a former United States attorney and an active supporter of Truman's reelection when many southern Democrats were deserting the party to back Strom Thurmond. Andrews was known as a liberal and had the support of blacks and labor. To fill another vacancy, which was actually a new position, Truman named Frank A. Hooper, who was supported by both Georgia senators, Russell and Walter George. Both nominations were sent to the Senate on October 15, 1949. But Senator Russell had committed himself to William Boyd Sloan for the vacancy created by his brother's elevation. Senator George also backed Sloan but was willing to accept Andrews. But Russell was not willing to compromise with the president, and he blackballed Andrews.[13]

Truman was committed to Andrews, and when the Senate failed to act on his nomination by the time it adjourned, the president gave Andrews a recess appointment. He resubmitted Andrews's name at the start of the next session of Congress. Russell, however, continued his opposition and declared the Andrews nomination "personally obnoxious," thus invoking senatorial courtesy, the practice of the Senate deferring to the wishes of a home-state senator opposing a nominee from that state. When the Judiciary Committee voted on the nomination on August 1, 1950, it turned down Andrews but sent the nomination to the full Senate. On August 10, the Senate rejected Andrews, thus delivering Truman a stinging rebuke.[a] On October 31, Judge Andrews resigned his recess commission. Truman, undoubtedly annoyed with Russell, was in no rush to fill the Georgia vacancy. Finally, on February 15, 1951, he met with Russell and agreed to name Russell's candidate, Sloan, whose name was sent to the Senate four days later and who was quickly confirmed.

Another example of presidential involvement and an irksome relationship between the president and a Democratic senator occurred in California in 1949 and 1950. But in this instance Truman was trying to play peacemaker between the warring factions of the California Democratic Party. Two new positions on the federal district court were created for the Northern District of California. Democratic senator Sheridan Downey backed two California state judges, Edward P. Murphy and S. Victor Wagler. Murphy, in addition, had connections to the Democratic National Committee. But the Democratic party organization in California favored two other men, Samuel P. Finley and Everett C. McKeage. In a letter to Truman, Oliver Carter, who had directed the president's reelection campaign in California and had been state chairman of the California Democratic Party, gave the political reasons for the organization's opposition to Murphy and Wagler.[14] Senator Downey refused to budge, and Truman was reluctant to oppose his loyal California friends. Moreover, there were other viable candidates for the positions, including Matthew Tobriner, who would later go on the California Supreme Court and have a distinguished career on that bench.

There was stalemate for almost a year. The Democratic national committeewoman for California wrote to Truman in early 1950 suggesting a solution to the impasse and recommending that Oliver Carter and Matthew Tobriner be named.[15] But eventually Truman fashioned a tentative compromise: he would pick one of Downey's favorites (Wagler) and one of the organization's (McKeage). But that was apparently unsatisfactory to Downey. Truman then

---

a. At the same time, the Senate also turned down another Truman nominee, Carroll O. Switzer, to the federal district court of Iowa. Iowa Democratic senator Guy M. Gillette opposed Switzer. See *New York Times,* August 10, 1950, p. 1.

decided to name Oliver Carter to one of the positions, and Carter's nomination was sent to the Senate on September 1. For the second position Truman named another Downey candidate, Murphy, and his nomination was sent to the Senate on December 4. By this time, however, Senator Downey was no longer a political force to be reckoned with, as illness had forced him to retire. Both Carter and Murphy were eventually confirmed.

The most famous example of Truman's involvement reveals his concern with presidential prerogatives. Three judicial positions were to be filled in the Northern District of Illinois, which includes Chicago. Two were newly created by Congress in 1950 thanks to the efforts of Illinois congressman Adolph J. Sabath, the powerful head of the House Rules Committee. Sabath wanted one of the new judgeships to go to his nephew, Joseph J. Drucker, who was a Chicago municipal court judge. Sabath had previously told Truman of his strong desire that his nephew receive a federal judgeship. Now he asked Speaker of the House Sam Rayburn to take the matter up with the president, and Rayburn agreed, forwarding a copy of Drucker's biographical sketch. On August 15, Truman wrote on the bottom of the sketch: "Cong. Sabath's nephew. He wants him made a federal judge. It should be done." The annotated resume was given to Truman's assistant, Matt Connelly. Truman informed Sabath of his commitment to naming Drucker. There is no evidence, however, that Truman cleared this with the two Democratic senators from Illinois, Scott Lucas, who was majority leader, and Paul Douglas. In November 1950 Senator Lucas was defeated for reelection, thus leaving Douglas as the principal senatorial player.[16]

There was a scramble over these new judgeships. Some people urged the president to name an African American, and others pushed for a woman to fill one of the vacancies. For the second of the new judgeships, the White House settled on Cornelius J. Harrington, a Cook County circuit court judge. For the third judgeship, the president nominated Joseph S. Perry, a former state representative and Democratic county chairman, who was serving as public administrator of Dupage County. Perry was actively supported by Senator Douglas and had widespread political backing.[b] The three prospective administration nominees made a "balanced" ethnic ticket. Drucker was Jewish, Harrington was Catholic, and Perry was Protestant.

b. In an amusing and candid recital of how he became a federal judge, Perry told how he had aspired to a judgeship seven years earlier but had insufficient senatorial backing. He learned from that experience. He also had the good luck of actively supporting Paul Douglas in his successful bid for a Senate seat, in 1948. See Joseph Samuel Perry, "How I Got to Be a Federal Judge," in *Courts, Judges, and Politics,* 4th ed., ed. Walter F. Murphy and C. Herman Pritchett (New York: Random House, 1986), 151–53.

Senator Douglas, apparently aware of the administration's inclinations, made his choices known on January 26, 1951. Douglas, too, had a "balanced" ticket. Perry was Douglas's Protestant. But instead of Drucker, Douglas insisted on Cook County circuit court judge Benjamin Epstein, who was also Jewish. In place of the Roman Catholic Harrington, Douglas recommended another Roman Catholic, William H. King, Jr., a Winnetka attorney. Both Epstein and King had the approval of the leader of the Chicago Democratic Party organization, Jacob (Jake) M. Arvey.[17]

An impasse followed. Why did the administration decide to flout senatorial prerogatives? An answer can be found in a news item that Connelly planted with a friendly *Chicago Sun Times* columnist: "According to a White House intimate [Connelly], one reason President Truman is so determined to go all-out in backing his federal judgeship nominees, Cornelius J. Harrington and Joseph J. Drucker, is this: The President feels he has been generous in cooperating with Sen. Douglas and the Cook County Democratic organization in dispensing federal patronage; and that he thus was entitled to name the federal judges without incurring opposition from within his own party."[18c]

But before the rift with Douglas escalated into a public dispute, an attempt was made by Congressman Sabath to compromise. What happened is recounted in a memorandum for the file written by the White House patronage secretary, Donald Dawson, on April 26, 1951:

> Congressman Sabath called me today advising that he had heretofore agreed to withdraw the candidacy of his nephew, Drucker, for District Judge in Illinois. As a result of an agreement reached with Senator Douglas, [Jake] Arvey and others, Drucker would be placed on the ticket to succeed Judge Epstein [on the Cook County Circuit Court] who [then] would be nominated for the District Judge vacancy. The Congressman said this was done in order that the President might be relieved from an embarrassing situation. He went on to say that yesterday the new Chairman [of the Cook County Democratic Committee] by the name of [Joseph L.] Gill, had refused to agree to Drucker's nomination for the Epstein place and that the deal was off.[19]

Dawson noted in his memorandum that Sabath claimed that Gill was opposed to Epstein going on the federal bench, because Epstein had been a lawyer for the gangster Al Capone and allegedly had thrown legal business from his court to Arvey's law firm. Gill was apparently concerned that if the newspapers printed this, the Democratic Party would be damaged.

---

c. A copy of the column was sent with a cover letter to Matthew Connelly: "Dear Matt, Here's the column for Sunday, Aug. 13, in which I used the judgeship item. Please keep me posted on any new developments." OF 208 t Northern District.

With a deal out of the question, the president finally went ahead and, on July 13, sent the nominations of Drucker, Harrington, and Perry to the Senate. Four days later, Senator Douglas, a respected liberal and supporter of Truman's legislative agenda, announced that while he believed Drucker and Harrington to be "worthy," his choices of Epstein and King were superior and he would ask the Chicago Bar Association to poll its members. Such a poll was unusual, but evidently Senator Douglas was confident that the outcome would favor his candidates. The president of the Chicago Bar Association sent the results to Truman at the end of July: they showed that 3,656 lawyers preferred Epstein and 3,003 preferred King (the senator's candidates), whereas only 1,310 favored Harrington and 553 Drucker (the president's nominees). More than three-quarters of the Northern District residents of the Illinois Bar Association said Drucker was not qualified to be a federal district judge. The American Bar Association urged the Senate to reject Drucker but took no position on Harrington.[20]

Senator Douglas openly opposed Drucker and Harrington. When he appeared before the Senate Judiciary Committee, he said that while Drucker and Harrington themselves were not personally obnoxious to him, the process by which the president selected them *was* personally obnoxious. On September 17, the committee sided with Douglas but sent the disputed nominations to the Senate floor, where on October 9 both Drucker and Harrington were rejected.[21]

Truman did not take kindly to this defeat, and the administration made no move to fill the two new judgeships. The fall of 1951 was clearly a low point for the Truman presidency. The Korean War, which had been ongoing for almost sixteen months, was stalemated, and as casualties mounted, the war grew unpopular. The White House was under continued attack from Senator Joseph McCarthy, who charged that the administration harbored communist sympathizers and spies. The administration was also being attacked for influence peddling and corruption, including a scandal involving the Internal Revenue Service. It was in this broader context, in which the fate of two Illinois judgeships may not have seemed so important, that Jake Arvey labored to find a compromise. Senator Douglas would support any of seven Jewish men instead of Epstein (the names given to Truman included Superior Court judge A. L. Marovitz, a former state senator, and Edward Levi, dean of the University of Chicago Law School who over two decades later would become attorney general under President Gerald Ford), but the other nomination would go to William King. Arvey did note that the Cook County Democratic Committee endorsed King and Marovitz.[22]

Truman, however, took no action until the last months of the administration, when the attorney general prepared recess commissions for King and Marovitz. But the commissions were never sent; they were destroyed at the White House.[d] The two new judgeships were filled in 1953 by Truman's Republican successor, Dwight D. Eisenhower. The saying "cut off your nose to spite your face" is most applicable to the behavior of the Democrats. Truman's personal involvement in selection and then the rift with Douglas and the Chicago Democratic organization resulted in the "loss" of two judgeships.

The Policy Agenda and Selection

In response to a letter of appreciation from a man he had recently named to the federal district court bench in California, Truman noted: "The appointment of Federal judges is the most important thing I do. They will long outlast my tenure of office and if they do the right thing the people benefit by it."[23]

Did Truman really believe that? He certainly repeated those sentiments on a number of occasions. But Truman and his administration primarily treated judgeships as patronage, in the service of the partisan agenda. By 1945, the federal courts were no longer the battleground for executive and legislative supremacy over the nation's economic and social-welfare policy. Roosevelt's appointments now dominated the lower courts, and the Supreme Court had made a constitutional about-face in support of New Deal programs. Truman's policy agenda, the Fair Deal, was hardly in contention in the courts. Indeed, most of his proposals were never enacted into law, having been bottled up by conservatives who controlled key committees in Congress. The one time that Truman was rebuffed by the Supreme Court, when he ordered the steel mills taken over by the government to prevent a disruption of the Korean War effort, the Court had struck down the executive branch's actions because they were not authorized by Congress.[24] Thus the courts were not seen during Truman's presidency as crucial for the success of the president's policy agenda. Hence judicial selection was largely based on Truman's partisan and personal agendas. Nevertheless, on a few occasions the ideological orientation of the candidate may have had a subtle influence on the process.

When the indefatigable William Clark, who in 1942 had left his position on the Court of Appeals for the Third Circuit to take a commission in the Army, asked for his old job back, he was rebuffed by Attorney General Francis Biddle, with whom he had feuded. And Clark was unable to get the full attention of his longtime friend Franklin Roosevelt, who was preoccupied by

d. Marovitz was eventually named by Kennedy in 1963 to a district judgeship.

the conduct of the war and was in failing health. When Roosevelt died, Clark renewed his efforts and finally had a personal meeting with a presidential assistant, General Harry H. Vaughan, on September 5, 1945. Vaughan gave Clark a sympathetic hearing and reported to President Truman. In a memorandum for Attorney General Tom Clark (no relation to William), Harry Vaughan wrote: "The President would appreciate a statement from some member of your staff giving the judicial record of Col. William M. Clark, formerly a Judge of the Circuit Court of Appeals in Philadelphia."[25]

Clark's Justice Department file, including several hostile memos written by Biddle, was sent to the White House. The coup de grace for Clark's ambition to return to the federal bench was a phone conversation that Matt Connelly had with Richard Nacy, the executive vice chairman of the Democratic National Committee, with whom Clark had been in contact. Nacy told Connelly: "You probably know more about Clark than I—but I doubt if you know the War Dept. story, which Col. Davenport could tell if you wanted to hear. He is definitely bughouse, besides being a Groton-Harvard Republican."[26] The William Clark story, of course, involves much more than ideology. But the administration clearly considered Clark out of tune with its policy agenda—probably an unfair assessment, as Clark's judicial reputation was as a liberal.[e]

There are few policy-agenda references in the files of Truman's judicial candidates, in marked contrast to the files of judicial candidates during the Roosevelt administration. One early exception concerned the candidacy of Detroit lawyer Theodore Levin to a federal district judgeship in Michigan in 1946. There were several other candidates, including a Democratic member of Congress. Both senators were Republican, so the administration had more leeway than would otherwise be the case. Levin was the administration's preferred candidate, and he was backed by the Democratic national committeeman and committeewoman from Michigan. But someone had spread the charge that Levin was a Republican. The national committeeman, in a letter to Truman, assured the president that Levin was "an outstanding lawyer, a liberal, and . . . has actively supported our ticket."[27] Levin was appointed.

e. Clark unsuccessfully sued in the U.S. Court of Claims. See *New York Times*, July 8, 1947, p. 4. In January 1948, he joined the legal staff of General Lucius Clay, who commanded the occupation forces in Germany. In August 1948, Clark was named chief justice of the Allied Appeals Court in Nuremberg. In 1953, he was notified that he would not be reappointed chief justice and was ordered home. Clark made a futile effort to be appointed by the Eisenhower administration to the New Jersey federal district court bench. He died four years later, at the age of sixty-six. See the obituary in *New York Times*, October 11, 1957, p. 27.

The presidential election of 1948 brought Truman's policy agenda to the forefront. In the campaign Truman sought to sharpen the policy differences between Democrats and Republicans. Not surprisingly, after his upset victory there would be several instances in 1949 where policy-agenda considerations came into play. For example, in the formal letter accompanying the nomination papers for Thomas P. Thornton to a federal district judgeship in the Eastern District of Michigan, Attorney General Tom Clark noted that Thornton "is considered an able and sound lawyer of liberal outlook."[28]

Another 1949 nominee was Gus J. Solomon, for a position on the federal district court in Oregon. Solomon was backed by Monroe Sweetland, the Democratic national committeeman from Oregon, who pointed out that Solomon had been the treasurer of the Re-Elect Truman Committee in Oregon and had been active in party affairs. Solomon was under attack by conservative Democrats for being "leftist." He was active in the Oregon chapter of the American Civil Liberties Union and had been its treasurer in 1937. A newspaper editor wrote to Truman in support of Solomon, noting that he had backed Truman's policy agenda, including national health insurance and civil rights. Solomon was eventually confirmed. Still another 1949 nominee, Willis W. Ritter (to the federal district bench in Utah), was attacked for being "pink."[29]

In 1949, Illinois governor Adlai Stevenson recommended Charles Fahy for a circuit judgeship. "My respect for him," Stevenson wrote to Truman, "both as a lawyer and as an incisive, sensible, liberal thinker has grown with the years and the maturity of our acquaintance."[30] Fahy, who had been solicitor general from 1941 to 1945, was named by Truman to a position on the Court of Appeals for the District of Columbia.

From Truman's presidential papers it appears that Judge Fahy's appointment is the only one to an appeals court that was likely made on the basis of policy-agenda concerns. It is plausible, however, that the appointments of Assistant Attorney General David L. Bazelon and Assistant Solicitor General George T. Washington also to the District of Columbia circuit were policy-agenda appointments designed to assure that that circuit, which considers cases involving federal agencies, would remain friendly to the legacy of the New Deal. But this is an inference drawn from their having been selected from within the administration. At best, then, three of the twenty-six circuit court appointments were based on policy-agenda considerations (11.5 percent).

Another three of these appointments appear to have been personal-agenda appointments. The remaining twenty (77 percent) seem to qualify as partisan-agenda placements. There simply is no evidence that the federal courts were of concern to the administration in terms of Truman's Fair Deal policy agenda.

Senators and Selection

Truman sometimes got into tangles with senators over judicial appointments, as we saw when he failed to consult Senator Russell of Georgia and Senator Douglas of Illinois. In both instances, Truman had thought he had more than accommodated the senators—elevating Russell's brother to the circuit court, bowing to Douglas's wishes on previous appointments. Truman was only trying to claim for himself the right to name a few judges! But in both instances he suffered embarrassing defeats and was reminded of the power of senators of the president's party, who claim their birthright to name federal district judges in their states.

Another variation of this lesson occurred with Truman's attempt to fill an Iowa judgeship with the candidate of his choosing, a political ally backed by the state party but not the state's Democratic senator. Just one week after being sworn in for his second term after his stunning win the preceding November, Truman received a letter from Iowa district judge Charles Dewey conveying his intention to retire from active service effective March 1. The administration decided to nominate as his replacement Carroll O. Switzer, a forty-year-old Des Moines lawyer, who had been the unsuccessful Democratic candidate for governor in 1948 and a strong backer of Truman's reelection. Switzer had the endorsement of the state party, and the chairman of the Democratic state central committee, Jake Moore, claimed that he had obtained a verbal commitment from Democratic senator Guy M. Gillette not to oppose Switzer, even though Gillette considered him unqualified. Switzer's name was sent to the Senate on June 7, but four days later Senator Gillette issued a public statement protesting Switzer's nomination, asserting that Truman's choice of Switzer "came as a great and unpleasant surprise to me." Gillette charged that "long established senatorial courtesy" was violated by the White House in not filling the judgeship with one of the two men (William F. Riley and Ed Halbach) he had recommended.[31]

On June 25, Gillette announced that he would fight the Switzer nomination. The chairman of the Senate Judiciary Committee, Pat McCarran, sided with Gillette. The Iowa State Bar Association opposed Switzer. Matters came to a standstill until Switzer, under the impression that he was respecting Truman's wishes, sent a telegram on August 4 offering to withdraw. On August 10, the *New York Times* claimed that the president was going to withdraw Switzer's name. Truman, however, responded to Switzer's telegram: "I've never hinted that I wanted you to withdraw from the Judgeship controversy and I am still debating whether to follow through on your telegram or not." Truman decided to fight for his nominee, and on September 8 he announced that he would not withdraw Switzer's name. On October 21, when the Senate was in recess, Switzer received a recess appointment to the bench.[32]

Truman resubmitted Switzer's name on January 5, 1950, but Gillette persisted in his opposition. The following August 1, Switzer was rejected by the Judiciary Committee (as was M. Neil Andrews from Georgia). On August 9, 1950, the full Senate rejected Switzer (and Andrews), thus honoring senatorial courtesy.[33] Three months later, Truman deferred to Gillette and nominated William F. Riley, a sixty-six-year-old Des Moines lawyer. Switzer resigned from the bench.

When both of a state's senators belong to the president's party but are in disagreement over judicial nominations, the administration is caught in the middle. Texas senator Tom Connally, Truman's old friend and former colleague on the Truman Committee, recommended Joe B. Dooley for a judgeship in the northern district, and the administration submitted the nomination at the beginning of 1947. Dooley, an Amarillo attorney, was a former president of the Texas Bar Association. But the junior senator from Texas, W. Lee ("Pappy") O'Daniel, angry that he was not receiving patronage, opposed the nomination and delayed it for six months. At a showdown meeting of the Judiciary Committee, the vote was 8 to 4 to approve Dooley. The full Senate voted to confirm by a vote of 48 to 36.

O'Daniel did not run for reelection in 1948. His successor was Lyndon B. Johnson. In 1949, James V. Allred was named to a district judgeship in the southern district. O'Daniel had blocked a previous Allred appointment, because Allred had run against him in the senatorial primary in 1942. Also named to a district court judgeship, with Johnson's backing, was Senator Connally's son, Ben.

The Allred and Connally nominations highlight the typical pattern during the Truman administration: the president accommodated senators. When Montana senator James Murray wanted his son to be a federal district court judge, Truman was happy to oblige, submitting the nomination in April 1949.

Even with circuit court judgeships the administration was often willing to defer to senators. For example, Senate Judiciary Committee chairman Pat McCarran of Nevada wanted a Nevadan, William E. Orr, chief justice of the Nevada Supreme Court, to fill a vacancy on the Ninth Circuit. Attorney General Clark advised Truman in a memo: "As you know, the Judiciary Committee of the Senate can be most helpful to us in the administration of our duties in the Department and I believe the nomination of Judge Orr would be of great benefit in this regard. Senator McCarran is most anxious that the nomination come up before the planned recess of the Senate."[34] The nomination was sent to the Senate, where Orr was quickly confirmed.

For two of the almost eight years that Truman was president, Congress was controlled by the Republicans (the Eightieth Congress, elected in 1946). This meant that the Senate Judiciary Committee was headed by Republican Alexander Wiley of Wisconsin. Wiley announced even before he assumed the chairmanship that the Republican controlled Senate would not confirm nominees who were "leftists." Early in the first session, he stated that he wanted a political balance in appointments, specifically the appointment of Republicans. He also proclaimed that he would oppose any further appointments of New Dealers.[35] The committee under Wiley held up nominations, and the number of confirmations of lifetime appointments to the federal district and appeals courts dropped from sixteen in 1946 to ten in 1947.[f] In 1948, with Republicans anticipating the recapture of the White House, confirmations ground to a virtual halt: only two lifetime federal district court nominees and one appeals court nominee were confirmed. After the Democrats regained control of Congress and Truman was reelected in 1948, the Eighty-first Congress confirmed sixty-three district and appeals court nominees. This was a new record, facilitated by the creation of twenty-seven new judgeships in 1949 and seven in 1950.

But even in friendly Democratic hands, the Senate Judiciary Committee could go its own way. On April 26, 1949, the administration submitted to the Senate the nomination of Representative Herman P. Eberharter for a district judgeship in Pennsylvania. The Judiciary Committee held hearings, where allegations of drunkenness and misbehavior were made against Eberharter. The committee decided to take no action on the nomination, and Eberharter eventually withdrew his name.[36]

Other Considerations in the Appointment Process

Local party leaders often have strong views about who should be named to a federal district judgeship. Taking them into account may prolong the selection process. If the administration prefers someone else, it cannot act quickly lest the local leaders think their preferences were not even considered at all. In 1950, when New Jersey Democrats were split over whom to back for

f. The *New York Times,* July 1, 1947, p. 14, observed that the Republican-controlled Senate Judiciary Committee "has built a reputation for making full and often lengthy investigations into the backgrounds of judicial and legal nominees."

a federal district judgeship, the Democratic chairman for the city of Elizabeth and the county chairman sought a meeting with the president to discuss their recommendation for the post. William M. Boyle, Jr., the chairman of the Democratic National Committee, was contacted about this request and advised Matt Connelly that if the president met with individual county chairmen on such matters, he "would be setting a precedent that might lead to endless requests of a similar nature in the future."[37] Connelly politely turned down the request, citing the president's heavy schedule. Because of the split in the New Jersey Democratic Party (both senators at that time were Republican), it took the administration about a year before it was politically possible to send a nomination to the Senate.

The administration on occasion used a judgeship to avert party strife in a particular state. In Colorado in 1950, Democratic governor William Lee Knous was gearing up to enter the senatorial primary, where he would be facing the popular member of Congress John Carroll. A fight was prevented, however, when Knous was nominated to fill a vacancy on the Colorado federal district bench.[38] Knous, it should be noted, had served for ten years on the Colorado Supreme Court before being elected governor and had the professional credentials for the position to which he was appointed.

Another governor, Luther W. Youngdahl of Minnesota, also received a judgeship. But Youngdahl was a Republican, and the judgeship he received, on the district bench of the District of Columbia, helped Minnesota Democrats by removing a popular Republican political figure from state politics. Minnesota Democratic senator Hubert H. Humphrey strongly supported the Youngdahl appointment, reportedly so that Youngdahl would not challenge Humphrey in 1954 when Humphrey would be up for reelection.[39]

The Democratic National Committee (DNC) continued to play a role in selection. Clearing nominations with the DNC was typically pro forma.[g] But on occasion, the chairman of the DNC took a more active role. On January 22, 1945, President Roosevelt nominated Nathan Ross Margold for a federal district judgeship in the District of Columbia over the objections of DNC chairman Robert E. Hannegan. After Roosevelt's death, Hannegan urged Truman to withdraw Margold's name, pointing out that the Margold nomination was going nowhere in the Senate Judiciary Committee. Truman replied: "Your

g. The notation "cleared by the DNC" is often found on the appointment papers of judges. See, for example, the appointment letter for Edward S. Kampf, OF 208 i Northern District. Sometimes a letter from the DNC was attached to the nominating papers. See, for example, the letter from the vice-chairman of the DNC, Oscar R. Ewing, noting that the nomination of Edward M. Curran to a judgeship in the District of Columbia was "satisfactory" to the DNC. OF 41 g District Court of the U.S. for the District of Columbia.

note of the eighteenth [of May] in regard to Margold read with a lot of interest. I think I explained the situation to you when we discussed it."[40] After the Senate adjourned for its summer recess on August 1 without having taken action on the nomination, Truman quietly abandoned Margold. When the Senate reconvened in September, he submitted the name of Alexander Holtzoff for the vacancy. Holtzoff was a member of the administration, serving as executive assistant to the attorney general.

In 1951 a district court judgeship opened up in Pennsylvania, where both senators were Republican. The chairman of the DNC wrote to Peyton Ford, the deputy attorney general, suggesting Democrat William Alvah Stewart for the position.[41] Stewart received the judgeship. Other examples of the influence of the DNC are evident from the memo quoted at length at the end of this section.

The Truman administration seems to have made some effort to appoint Republicans to a few positions — perhaps to rebut Republican charges of undue partisanship, but also perhaps as a reflection of Truman's own views. In a letter to a Democratic representative concerning a vacancy on a circuit court of appeals, Truman wrote: "I really don't think Courts of Appeals should be made of one political party, no matter how judicially minded they are."[42] Although in this particular instance a Democrat was appointed, in three other instances Republicans received appeals court positions: Walter C. Lindley, Wayne G. Borah, and James M. Proctor.

The Lindley appointment reflects a number of considerations that were spelled out in a letter to Truman from his old senatorial friend Sherman Minton, who was then serving on the Court of Appeals for the Seventh Circuit. Minton announced at the outset, "I am authorized to speak for the Court." He noted that there were two vacancies on the five-member appeals court. The first came about because of the death of Judge Evan A. Evans, a Wisconsin native. The second arose from the retirement of Judge William M. Sparks, from Indiana, "the last Republican left out here." For the first vacancy, Minton recommended the elevation of federal district judge F. Ryan Duffy ("one of our best District Judges"), a Democrat who had served in the Senate with Truman and, like Evans, hailed from Wisconsin. For the second vacancy, Minton urged Truman to name Lindley. Minton called him "one of the least partisan [persons] I have ever known" and "one of the ablest District Judges in the country." Minton went on:

> If Judge Lindley were appointed to our Court, it would create a vacancy in the
> District Court which [U.S. Senator] Scott Lucas has been wanting for years to
> fill with a friend of his. Scottie wants to appoint Lindley because the District
> Court appointment is worth more organization-wise than an appointment

here. The Cook County [Chicago] organization has a half-dozen candidates now and it will grow and there will be a terrific fight in Illinois for the Sparks vacancy. Indiana will be claiming the appointment as its own. A quick appointment of Lindley will reward a faithful Judge, avoid a fight in Illinois, take Scott Lucas off the spot and give him a more desirable appointment, and will give this Court its much needed help. The Judicial Conference has authorized an additional judge for our Court. We are sure it will be granted by you and Congress and that appointment can go to Indiana. My plea is for action in the best interests of the Court and a wise move for the Party.[43]

Truman sent a copy of Minton's letter to his assistant in charge of presidential appointments, Donald Dawson, with a notation that Minton's "judgment is good, I think."[44] Not only was Duffy elevated to the Seventh Circuit, but Lindley too was tapped for that circuit when Truman elevated Minton to the Supreme Court in 1949. The Sparks vacancy went to Philip J. Finnegan of Illinois,[h] and the newly created Seventh Circuit position was filled by an Indianan. When Lindley left his district court position, Senator Lucas's friend Casper Platt, an Illinois state judge, was named to the vacancy. All the pieces fit into place, but it is clear that the appointment of a Republican in this instance was part of an overall package satisfying party and senatorial needs.

Another Republican appointed by Truman to an appeals court was Wayne G. Borah of Louisiana. Borah, the nephew of the late Republican senator William E. Borah of Idaho,[i] was serving as a federal district judge. The Louisiana senators were able to choose Borah's successor on the bench, J. Skelly Wright.[45][j]

There was a third Republican appointed by Truman to an appeals court, James M. Proctor, elevated from a district judgeship in the District of Columbia to the court of appeals. Proctor was sixty-five years old at the time of his nomination on February 2, 1948, and his elevation was linked with the nomination of Democrat Edward A. Tamm to fill the district court position Proctor

---

h. Finnegan, a state court judge, publicly attributed his appointment to the efforts of Chicago mayor Martin H. Kennelly: "It was through Mayor Kennelly's efforts that I was appointed by the President." *New York Times,* August 13, 1949, p. 9.

i. Senator Borah, who died in 1940, had befriended Truman when Truman first came to the Senate. See David M. McCullough, *Truman* (New York: Simon and Schuster, 1992), p. 214.

j. Wright was to become a leading liberal, first on the district bench, as a strong supporter of school desegregation after *Brown* v. *Board of Education,* and later as an appeals court judge on the U.S. Court of Appeals for the District of Columbia, a post to which he was appointed by President Kennedy.

would be vacating. The Republican-controlled Senate was quick to confirm Proctor.

To the district bench Truman named the Republican governor of Vermont, Ernest W. Gibson, whose father had served in the Senate with Truman, as had Gibson himself for a brief time. Democratic party leaders in Vermont were dismayed. So, too, in New Jersey, Truman bucked the party, which was badly split and could not agree on a candidate, by naming Republican Richard Hartshorne to the federal bench. Hartshorne, a state judge, apparently first came to Truman's attention in a letter from the president's old friend, Judge John Caskie Collet of the Eighth Circuit. Chief Justice Vinson backed Hartshorne, and New Jersey's Republican senators gave their approval. After the nomination was sent to the Senate, several editorials appeared praising the Hartshorne nomination. Attorney General J. Howard McGrath sent copies to the president's secretary, who gave them to Truman. In a memo to the attorney general Truman wrote: "I think we did the right thing in making that [the Hartshorne] appointment."[46]

Vermont and New Jersey did not have Democratic senators, thereby giving Truman some leeway in appointing Republicans. Similarly, appointments to the federal district bench of the District of Columbia, which has no senators, afforded the president more latitude than usual. To that court Truman named three Republicans, James R. Kirkland, Walter M. Bastian, and Luther W. Youngdahl.

There is one instance in which Truman was thinking seriously of naming a close friend from World War One, Ed Felker, a Republican who had once practiced law in Ohio. Truman wrote to Ohio Republican senator Robert A. Taft: "If you have no serious objection to his appointment, I would like to consider him seriously for the Federal judge vacancy in Ohio."[47] Taft responded by noting that he did not personally know Felker, that as far as he could determine Felker had only practiced law in Ohio for about seven years and since the end of the Second World War had been practicing law in the District of Columbia. Taft pointedly added: "I am inclined to think that in a district containing so many good lawyers, Democratic and Republican, it would be unwise to appoint one who has had so little practice in the District. I am fairly certain that the Bar Associations of northern Ohio would consider him a kind of carpet-bagger. This might lead to rather a strenuous opposition and I would not like to commit myself not to oppose him, although he certainly would be in no way personally objectionable to me."[48] Felker dropped out of consideration, and a good Democrat eventually got the position. For all the rhetoric of Republican senators that more Republicans should receive judgeships, in this instance parochial considerations were more important for a leading Republican senator than the appointment of someone from his own party.

During the Truman administration a new player in the federal judicial appointment process emerged, the American Bar Association (ABA). In 1946, the ABA created the Standing Committee on Federal Judiciary to assess the suitability of federal judicial nominees. In early 1947, the new chairman of the Senate Judiciary Committee, Republican senator Alexander Wiley, announced that the committee would consider the views "of respected legal groups" when screening presidential nominees. The following July, the Judiciary Committee delayed its consideration of the nomination of Leo F. Rayfiel to a district judgeship in New York so that the ABA committee and the Federal Bar Association could complete their investigations. Rayfiel, a former member of Congress, was backed by Democratic senator Robert Wagner, but some lawyers in New York opposed Rayfiel as not qualified for the judgeship. Although the ABA committee and the New York State Bar Association opposed the nomination, the Judiciary Committee nevertheless approved Rayfiel.[49][k]

The ABA committee spoke out on other occasions. In early 1948, it voiced its opposition to the nomination of Edward A. Tamm to the federal district bench in the District of Columbia. The Republican-controlled Senate took no action on Tamm, but the following year, after the Democrats regained control, Tamm was confirmed. The ABA committee, however, also began working behind the scenes trying to influence nominations. Its members realized that once a nomination is made, it is difficult to defeat it. The best opportunity for influencing judicial selection is at the pre-nomination stage.

In late 1949, the Ohio Democratic leader and former mayor of Cleveland Ray T. Miller wanted his brother, United States attorney Donald C. Miller, to be named to a vacancy on the district court bench.[l] Ray Miller insisted that he would veto any other nomination. Joseph B. Keenan, who had once handled judicial selection in the Justice Department and was originally from Ohio, wrote to Truman that Miller "lacks the experience" for the judgeship and that "were he appointed the public would regard it as an appointment due to his brother." Keenan highly recommended an Ohio state judge, Charles Mc-

k. The Federal Bar Association and the Brooklyn Bar Association approved Rayfiel. Senator McCarran told the ABA committee and New York state bar representatives: "To my mind you have presented nothing to show this man is unqualified." *New York Times,* July 16, 1947, p. 16.

l. This was the vacancy that Truman had written to Senator Taft about when Truman wanted to consider his Republican friend Ed Felker.

Namee, as being exceptionally capable and having a fine reputation. Truman thanked Keenan for his views, but complained that "it is really a pain in the neck to get that situation [of the Ohio judgeship] ironed out." He attached Keenan's letter to a memo to his assistant Donald Dawson, saying: "I'll talk with you about it at the first opportunity."[50]

Meanwhile, Howard F. Burns, who had a law practice in Cleveland and was chairman of the ABA committee, came to see Dawson at the White House about the Ohio vacancy. Burns brought with him a list of men the committee was recommending for consideration. Judge McNamee was on that list. Over the course of 1950, Burns spoke from time to time with Dawson about the Ohio judgeship. Finally, on February 8, 1951, the White House sent McNamee's nomination to the Senate. Burns then wrote to Dawson praising the nomination and noting that it "is regarded as an outstanding one" and that the "Committee is deeply gratified that one of the nominees recommended by our Committee was selected by the President."[51]

Another notable example of ABA committee involvement before nomination occurred in 1952 with a vacancy in South Carolina. Burns, searching for a more institutionalized role for the ABA in the process, wrote to the attorney general, J. Howard McGrath, recommending four men. At the top of the list was L. Mendel Rivers, a member of Congress and an opponent of Truman's program. Burns, however, noted that if someone other than the four on the list was under consideration, "it will be regarded as a favor if the views of the [American Bar] Association with regard to the qualifications of such men are requested."[52] There already was a heavy campaign for Mendel Rivers.[m] But Rivers eventually withdrew his candidacy, and Truman nominated someone not on the ABA list, a Democrat who had supported Truman in the 1948 presidential election—Ashton H. Williams, one of the last Truman judges confirmed by the Senate.

In 1951, the ABA committee publicly opposed two judicial nominees who subsequently were denied judgeships. While its opposition was not the main reason that the nominees were defeated, it was undoubtedly a contributing factor. One of the nominees was the second woman ever nominated for a federal district judgeship, Frieda B. Hennock. The ABA committee asserted that she was "totally unqualified." The other nominee was Joseph J. Drucker,

---

m. Truman attached to a memo to Donald Dawson a letter from five South Carolina congressmen recommending Rivers. Truman wrote: "Get Mendel Rivers' record for me. Also find out if [he] has made bitter speeches"—a reference to the allegation that Rivers made personal attacks on Truman. Truman to Donald Dawson, February 12, 1952, OF 208 mm Endorsements of Eastern District A–V.

who was also opposed by Senator Douglas for an Illinois judgeship. The ABA committee took no position on Cornelius J. Harrington, the other disputed Illinois nominee. After Drucker was voted down by the full Senate and the Hennock nomination died in committee, a testy Truman remarked that it was not the job of bar associations to make appointments.[53]

Yet events unfolded that brought the ABA committee into the judicial selection process to an unprecedented extent. Troubles in the Justice Department led Truman to fire Attorney General McGrath on April 3, 1952, and replace him with U.S. District Judge James P. McGranery. McGranery recruited New Mexico attorney Ross Malone, a lawyer of impeccable reputation and outstanding credentials, to serve as deputy attorney general. Malone was long active in the ABA and was serving on the ABA's Board of Governors at the time he joined the Justice Department. Malone, with the approval of the attorney general, established a procedure whereby the names of the leading candidates for judicial vacancies would be submitted to the ABA committee for its evaluation. The Justice Department would make no final nominating decisions before considering the committee's views.[54] But by the time this arrangement was agreed to, the administration was in its waning months and no judicial nominations were forthcoming. This arrangement was accepted, however, by the Eisenhower administration, and the ABA committee became an active partner in the selection process.

The ABA committee's raison d'etre is to foster a high-quality federal judiciary. But determinations of quality are of course subjective, and there were quite marked differences in evaluations of candidates, particularly when they were nontraditional with respect to gender and race. In general, however, the qualifications of nominees also were of concern to the Truman administration and at times overshadowed purely political considerations. In the case of the judgeship in Ohio and the appointment of McNamee, as well as in the appointment of New Jersey Republican Hartshorne, Truman went with the person the administration believed to be best qualified. Another example when considerations of quality seemed to come to the fore concerned a vacancy in Maine. Because there were no Democratic senators from Maine, the administration had more flexibility. F. Harold Dubord, the state's Democratic national committeeman, was a candidate for the judgeship, and he was backed by the state party organization. Retiring U.S. District Judge John A. Peters, however, thought longtime United States Attorney John D. Clifford to be the most qualified of all the candidates. Truman went with Clifford.[55]

At the appeals court level the president usually has more leeway. Republican Robert P. Patterson, a former administration official and friend of Truman's, was at the heart of the legal establishment in New York City. When there was a vacancy on the Second Circuit, Patterson wrote to Attorney General McGrath (but gave the letter to Truman to give to McGrath) highly recommending the elevation of U.S. District Judge Harold Medina as the best qualified for the post. Patterson also noted that Medina was approved by the Judiciary Committee of the Association of the Bar of the City of New York. Some six weeks later, Paul Fitzpatrick, chairman of the Democratic State Committee, submitted to Donald Dawson six names for consideration for the Second Circuit vacancy. Among them were five judges, including Medina and, coincidentally, Patterson, who had previously served on the circuit but resigned at the request of Roosevelt to serve in the wartime administration. Fitzpatrick noted: "All of the above named gentlemen are outstanding men and have received the approval and endorsement of the County, City and State Bar Associations, as qualified to fill this position. The Honorable Edward J. Flynn of New York [Democratic leader of Bronx County] joins me in recommending them." Medina's name was sent to the Senate on June 11, 1951, with confirmation following soon thereafter.[56]

Geography also played a part in the appointment process, particularly at the court of appeals level but even occasionally with district court appointments. In 1945, there was a vacancy on the Southern District of California bench, and San Diego lawyers and politicians wanted a San Diegan for the position. They supported Jacob Weinberger, but the judgeship went to a Los Angeles lawyer and former president of the California Bar Association, William C. Mathes. The next vacancy in the district, however, went to Weinberger — with Democratic senator Downey's support.[57]

Consideration of geography was most frequent when a small state overshadowed by larger states in the circuit was involved. In 1949, the entire Democratic Party establishment in Montana successfully exhorted Truman to name Montanan Walter Pope to a vacancy on the California-dominated Ninth Circuit, which had seven seats covering seven states and Alaska and Hawaii. In a handwritten appeal to Truman, Congressman Mike Mansfield wrote: "You know what this appointment means to [Senator] Murray and me and to the Democratic party in Montana so — I plead with you to give this appointment to this man."[58]

Thus far we have seen the appointment process during the Truman administration largely from the perspective of the White House. But the routine processing, the investigations, and most of the initial recommendations came from the Justice Department. On occasion, White House staff would meet with Justice officials to make recommendations to fill vacancies. For example, on July 26, 1949, administration officials met in the office of Peyton Ford, the assistant to the attorney general, to discuss filling the twenty-seven new judgeships that were contained in a bill that was expected to clear Congress momentarily.[n] Among the officials, aside from Ford, were the soon-to-be-announced attorney general, J. Howard McGrath,[o] and Donald Dawson from the White House.

The notes on the conference reveal that aside from mentioning specific individuals, the group was concerned with which senators and Democratic Party leaders should be consulted. They did, however, agree on a tentative list of individuals to fill the new positions on the U.S. Court of Appeals for the District of Columbia and on the U.S. District Court for the District of Columbia. For the three additional judgeships on the D.C. appeals court the memo recommended, in order, "George T. Washington, Bolitha Laws or Matthew F. McGuire, Charles Fahy, William E. Leahy or William J. Hughes, Jr. [and] Walter M. Bastian."[59] For the three new judgeships on the D.C. district bench the memo put forward, in order, "David Bazelon, James R. Kirkland, [and] Julien G. Sourwine."

In the end, three current or former Justice Department officials — Assistant Solicitor General Washington, former Solicitor General Fahy, and Assistant Attorney General Bazelon — received the court of appeals positions. Bastian, a Republican, received a subsequent vacancy on the district bench in 1950 (and was elevated to the appeals bench by Eisenhower in 1954). Kirkland, also a Republican, got one of the new district judgeships. The two other new judgeships went to Burnita Shelton Matthews, the first woman federal district court judge and Truman's personal choice, and to former Nebraska congressman Charles F. McLaughlin.

The group went on to consider filling the new judgeship on the Court of Appeals for the Third Circuit: "Senator McGrath [attorney general designate] will talk with [Pennsylvania Democratic] Senator Myers with reference to: 1. Appointment of a colored man, and 2. Of a candidate outside District." The African American William Henry Hastie, who was living outside the Third Circuit in the District of Columbia, received the historic appointment, and he was officially designated an appointment from Pennsylvania.

n. On August 3, Truman signed the new judgeships bill into law.

o. McGrath was a senator from Rhode Island and also was serving as chairman of the Democratic National Committee. He had succeeded Robert E. Hannegan on the DNC in 1947. McGrath had managed Truman's successful 1948 campaign. Interestingly, at a news conference on July 28, Truman claimed that he had just that day offered the vacancy on the Supreme Court to Attorney General Tom Clark and that the attorney general's slot would go to McGrath. Truman claimed that Clark and McGrath were so taken by surprise that they requested a few days to consider. *New York Times,* July 29, 1949, p. 1. Truman's claims are inconsistent with the fact that McGrath but not Clark participated in the crucial July 26 meeting that mapped the strategy for filling the new judgeships.

For the new judgeship on the Seventh Circuit, the notes read: "Senator McGrath will talk over the matter with [Executive Vice Chairman of the Democratic National Committee and Chairman heir apparent] Bill Boyle[p] with reference to Senatorial contest in Indiana." (Indiana had no Democratic senators). Indiana Democrat H. Nathan Swaim received the judgeship with strong backing from Indiana Democrats.

For the new judgeship on the Tenth Circuit: "Name of John C. Pickett, United States Attorney, Wyoming, tentatively selected. Mr. [Peyton] Ford to discuss with Senators Kerr and Thomas." Pickett received the appointment. Senators Robert Kerr and Elmer Thomas were from Oklahoma, and Ford sought to get their approval for giving the judgeship to Wyoming, which had never been represented on the Tenth Circuit. Oklahoma already had a "representative." Pickett, long active in the Democratic Party, was championed by the Wyoming senators.

The balance of the memo dealt with the newly created district judgeships. For the two new judgeships in the Northern District of California, the group agreed that "Mr. Boyle to talk with Bill Malone concerning candidates." These judgeships were the subject of a rift between Senator Downey and the Democratic Party organization that took over a year to be filled. For the two new vacancies in the Southern District of California, the memo noted: "The names of James M. Carter and Harry C. Westover were tentatively selected. Mr. Boyle to check regarding Westover." Carter and Westover were backed by the California Democratic congressional delegation, and they received nominations about four weeks after the July 26 meeting.

For the new judgeship in Georgia, the group noted: "Mr. Ford to check with Senator Russell." This new judgeship was filled by Senator Russell's choice, Frank A. Hooper.[q] For the additional judgeship in Florida: "Mr. Ford to check with [Florida Democratic] Senators Pepper and Holland." For the new Kansas judgeship: "The name of former United States Attorney Randolph Carpenter was tentatively agreed upon. Mr. Dawson to check." Carpenter was the unsuccessful Democratic candidate for governor in 1948. But he had a fatal political flaw in his background: he had backed Henry Wallace and not Truman for vice president in 1944. The judgeship went to Delmas C. Hill, the Kansas Democratic state chairman.

p. William M. Boyle, Jr., was expected to take over as chairman of the DNC. On August 24, 1949, he was formally elected chairman. See *New York Times*, August 25, 1949, p. 1.

q. The administration also elevated Russell's brother to the Fifth Circuit. Truman then named his choice of M. Neil Andrews to fill the district judgeship vacated by Russell's brother, but the nomination died after Russell claimed senatorial courtesy and insisted on naming another. See the earlier discussion.

For the additional New Jersey judgeship: "Mr. Ford to discuss with Mr. Boyle regarding candidate — re Isaiah Matlack." What actually happened was that the Justice Department eventually sent over the nomination papers for Matlack, but at the last moment they were withdrawn probably because of the bad split in the Democratic Party in New Jersey, where the different factions backed different candidates. After more than a year, Truman named United States Attorney Alfred E. Modarelli.

For the four new judgeships in the Southern District of New York, the memo simply stated: "Mr. Ford to discuss with [Chairman of the New York State Democratic Committee] Mr. Paul Fitzpatrick." Actually, Fitzpatrick had a personal meeting with Truman the following day to discuss the New York judgeships. Although there was pressure on the administration to name a woman or a black to one of these positions, the administration went along with Fitzpatrick's choices: Irving R. Kaufman, Gregory F. Noonan, John F. X. McGohey, and Sidney Sugarman. Fitzpatrick had consulted the Judiciary Committee of the Association of the Bar of the City of New York and had given the committee the opportunity to determine whether prospective candidates were "qualified." The four men Fitzpatrick recommended were approved by that bar group.[60]

For the Oregon judgeship: "Mr. Ford to discuss with Mr. Boyle." Since Oregon had no Democratic senators, the party organization carried great weight. Boyle spoke with the Democratic national committeeman from Oregon, Monroe Sweetland, who vigorously pushed for Gus Solomon, who ultimately received the appointment.

For the three new Pennsylvania judgeships: "Mr. Ford to discuss with [Pennsylvania Democratic] Senator Myers and Mr. Boyle." And for the two additional judgeships for the Southern District of Texas, the memo said: "F.B.I. reports have been initiated on Ben Connally, James V. Allred, and B. Dudley Tarlton." Connally and Allred received the judgeships.

Attached to the memo of the conference meeting were lists of the names of the candidates for each of the vacancies, their dates of birth, the date (if any) of FBI reports, and a "Remarks" column that included, by the names of the few African American candidates, the notation "colored."

Women and Judgeships

During Truman's presidency, little changed from the Roosevelt era concerning the appointment of women to the federal judiciary. Sexism and sexist attitudes posed obstacles that few women could surmount. It has been reported that Truman himself said he would not have a woman in the cabinet.[61]

How sympathetic could he have been, then, to women who aspired to federal judgeships?

Whereas in the New Deal era the promise of securing equal rights for women was personified in the active role of First Lady Eleanor Roosevelt, the Truman era lacked such symbolism. Although Franklin Roosevelt's appointment of Florence Allen to the Sixth Circuit in 1934 encouraged other women to be candidates for judgeships, when the final accounting was done, Allen stood as the lone woman appointed by Roosevelt to a major federal court. It should come as no surprise, then, that when Truman became president there were few women willing to pursue what undoubtedly appeared to be the quixotic quest for a federal judgeship. Judgeships were referred to by Truman and other men in and outside the administration as belonging to men. For example, in a letter to Colorado senator Edwin Johnson concerning a vacancy on the district bench, Truman stated that he would select "the *man* I think is best fitted for the job." In a letter released to the public, Truman wrote: "It has always been my policy to be very careful in the selection of *men* who sit on the Federal bench."[62] Nevertheless, there were some women who made the attempt—one who almost succeeded and one who did succeed.

Among the women who tried but failed to win a judgeship was the daughter of Justice Louis Brandeis, Susan Brandeis. Influential supporters called her to Truman's attention in connection with a district court vacancy in New York. Brandeis had been a candidate before, during the Roosevelt administration. Despite a successful legal career, however, she was unable to muster the support of the Judiciary Committee of the Association of the Bar of the City of New York, which strongly backed a vice-president and former chairman of the association's executive committee, a highly regarded lawyer and professor, Harold R. Medina. When Medina was chosen, editorial writers gushed over the selection, which they pronounced had been made on merit and not politics. Interestingly, two other women lawyers, Florence P. Shientag and Anna M. Kross, aspired to the vacancy, and their supporters had contacted the administration.[63]

The Massachusetts Association of Women's Clubs recommended that four women be considered for a Massachusetts district court vacancy in 1948. Three of the four were state judges.[64] None, however, was seriously considered. The district judgeship went to United States Attorney William T. McCarthy, who was championed by Congressman John McCormack.

In April 1949, while a new judgeships bill was working its way through Congress, the National Association of Women Lawyers sent a resolution to the president recommending that outstanding women members of the bar be considered for district and appeals court positions. In 1949, there were several strong candidacies of women for judicial office. Anna X. Alpern, the Pittsburgh city solicitor, tried to win a district bench vacancy, and she gathered much support. At the White House, Donald Dawson backed her and wrote, in a memorandum for the president:

> India Edwards [Vice Chairman of the Democratic National Committee and Director of the Women's Division] is *greatly* interested in women in the government, as you so well know. She feels it would be greatly to your credit, and a number of us agree, if you could now appoint a woman to some important judgeship.
>
> Mrs. Edwards has an admirable candidate in Anna X. Alpern of Pittsburgh. She is City Solicitor and President of the National Institute of Municipal Law Offices, an organization composed of city attorneys in over 500 cities. Attorney General Clark approves her and Dave Lawrence [mayor of Pittsburgh and Democratic Party leader] thinks she is "tops" but has not indicated his approval of her appointment.
>
> It might be that you would think it advisable to mention her name in your conversation with Dave Lawrence this morning as there will be a vacancy shortly on the District Court.[65]

Eleanor Roosevelt wrote to Truman in support of Anna Alpern.[66] But Truman was leaning toward giving the judgeship to U.S. Representative Herman P. Eberharter. As Truman explained to Mrs. Roosevelt in response to her letter:

> There has been a great deal of pressure from the Mayor of Pittsburgh and the Chairman of the County Commissioners of Allegheny County for the appointment of Miss Alpern as Federal Judge.
>
> I haven't made up my mind what to do about that appointment. There is a Congressman [Eberharter] who is very anxious to get it. He is a very able gentleman and has always been on our side of the fence.[67]

Eberharter received the nomination, but he ran into trouble in the Senate Judiciary Committee because of allegations of drunkenness and misbehavior. After Eberharter withdrew his name, Alpern was again passed over in favor of another white male, forty-four-year-old Rabe Ferguson Marsh, Jr., an assistant district attorney.[r]

---

r. India Edwards, who was vice-chairman of the DNC, claimed that Mayor David Lawrence vetoed Alpern and told Edwards his reasons: "Why should she have a lifetime appointment as a federal judge that pays $15,000 a year, which would mean that she would be making more than her husband does? She now makes $7,500 as city solicitor and I think that is enough for any woman to be paid. I do not approve of women making

Two new judgeships were created for the Southern District of California in 1949. A state judge, Ida May Adams, aspired to one of the positions, and a campaign was waged on her behalf, but it was unsuccessful. The Democratic establishment rallied around James M. Carter and Harry C. Westover, who received the nominations.

The Southern District of New York received four new judgeships in 1949. Anna Kross was again a candidate, and letters on her behalf came to the administration. So, too, was Assistant United States Attorney Florence P. Shientag, who won the endorsement of the New York Women's Bar Association as well as the backing of Representative Emanuel Celler, who personally called on Truman to convince him to name Shientag. The mayor of New York, William O'Dwyer, wrote to Truman urging that of the four new judgeships "you designate at least one woman and one Negro." O'Dwyer noted that women "have amply demonstrated their fitness and ability . . . and many of them have served with distinction in the minor courts — [but] they have been denied the opportunity to serve as Judges in our higher courts." O'Dwyer released his letter to the press at about the time it arrived at the White House.[68]

It is difficult to discern whether O'Dwyer's publication of the letter increased the pressure on the administration or came across as political grandstanding. During this period, however, the Democratic state chairman was making recommendations after consultation with the Association of the Bar of the City of New York. Women candidates did not stand a chance. But the pressure to name a woman to a judgeship in New York City was not lost on the administration. Two years later, Truman nominated Frieda B. Hennock, who had been appointed by Truman to the Federal Communications Commission after twenty-one years in legal practice in New York, to a vacancy on the New York federal district bench.

Hennock had many supporters who wrote to the administration on her behalf. Among her noted backers was Second Circuit judge Jerome Frank, who strongly endorsed Hennock in a personal letter to the president. Truman decided to name Hennock, and her nomination was sent to the Senate on June 11, 1951. But the legal establishment in New York was not ready for a woman federal judge. One day after the nomination was sent to the Senate, the Asso-

---

more than their husbands. So, I will not endorse her. That is final." India Edwards, *Pulling No Punches: Memoirs of a Woman in Politics* (New York: Putnam, 1977), 260. When Lawrence was governor of Pennsylvania, however, he named Anna Alpern in 1961 to the Pennsylvania Supreme Court to fill a vacancy until the next election. Alpern ran, but she lost the election. She subsequently won a seat on the Allegheny County Court.

ciation of the Bar of the City of New York announced its opposition to Hennock, charging that she was unqualified.[s] The Standing Committee on Federal Judiciary of the American Bar Association soon added its own opposition. Truman refused to back down and insisted that the bar groups were wrong. Women's groups rallied to support Hennock. At her Senate confirmation hearings, the male bar groups attacked Hennock's qualifications while the women's bar associations supported her nomination. The predominantly male Federal Bar Association of New York, New Jersey, and Connecticut, however, endorsed Hennock. Attorney General McGrath appeared before the Senate committee in closed session supporting Hennock, as did others, but there were powerful sexist forces at work against her. Chief Judge John Knox of the U.S. District Court for the Southern District of New York wrote to the Judiciary Committee questioning whether Hennock had the "capacity to perform the bench duties for which she has been nominated." According to India Edwards, an affair Hennock had had with a prominent married judge in New York was used against her behind closed hearings doors. The ABA committee representatives alleged past professional misconduct. Although the charges were rebutted, Senator Pat McCarran, the conservative Democrat who chaired the Judiciary Committee, decided to kill the nomination, and the committee took no action on it. Frieda Hennock wrote to the president declining a recess appointment. Thus ended what would have been a breakthrough appointment on the New York bench.[t] It would take another fifteen years before a woman would become a federal judge in New York.[69]

Two new judgeships plus a vacancy in an existing judgeship were up for grabs in Illinois in 1951. These were the judgeships that led to a confrontation between Truman and Senator Douglas as described earlier. A woman lawyer, Helen M. Cirese, past president of the West Suburban Bar Association of Illinois, was a candidate, and she was promoted by India Edwards, the indefatigable champion of women on the Democratic National Committee.[70] Other letters came to the administration as well, but there is no evidence that Cirese was ever seriously considered.

The one triumph for women was the historic appointment in 1949 of Bur-

s. The Association had never found a woman to be qualified for a federal district judgeship.

t. After her term as commissioner on the FCC ended in 1955, Hennock returned to private practice, remaining in Washington, D.C. She died at the age of fifty-five on June 20, 1960. She had come a long way from Kovel, Poland, where she was born, and New York City, where she grew up in a poor immigrant family. She attended City College and worked her way through Brooklyn Law School. She climbed the professional ladder, but a federal judgeship was denied her because of sexism.

nita Shelton Matthews to the federal district bench in the District of Columbia. The evidence suggests that she was a last minute choice of Truman, who substituted her for Walter Bastian, a Republican, who had been slated for one of three new positions on the District of Columbia court. Much pressure was placed on the administration by women's groups and others to name women to some of the new judgeships. Truman, no doubt, was aware that Roosevelt had appointed a woman to a high judicial post. Could Truman do no less? The District of Columbia judgeships always offer an administration the greatest leeway in appointments, thus with a little prodding Truman seized the opportunity.[71]

Matthews had been practicing law for twenty-nine years. She and her supporters were wise to the ways of Washington, and she had been a judicial candidate before. Now her backers waged a letter-writing campaign on her behalf, starting in March 1949. Because Matthews originally came from Mississippi, southern senators were enlisted to promote her candidacy. Mississippi senators John C. Stennis and James O. Eastland wrote separate letters to Truman recommending Matthews, as did Tennessee senator Estes Kefauver and both Arkansas senators, John McClellan and J. William Fulbright. Iowa senator Gillette also wrote in support of Matthews.[72]

In October 1949, India Edwards wrote to Truman "begging that one woman be included in the twenty-seven new judges whom you will nominate soon. . . . I do feel that there will be a bad reaction to the naming of so many new judges and not one woman among them." Edwards then brought up Matthews, noting that she was endorsed by the District of Columbia Bar Association. "If there is any chance," she concluded, "that Mrs. Matthews could be included in your list of nominations for the U.S. District Court for the District of Columbia, I am sure she would do credit to you, to our party, and to my sex." When the letter reached the White House, Donald Dawson on instructions from Truman called Edwards and asked her to bring Matthews to the White House for an interview.[73] Truman decided to name her and included Matthews's nomination in the batch sent to the Senate on October 17. When the Senate adjourned shortly thereafter, Truman gave Matthews (and the other nominees whose nominations the Senate had not had an opportunity to act upon) a recess appointment. Her name was resubmitted in January 1950, and she was confirmed later that year. Matthews was fifty-three years old when she went on the bench. She served for more than three decades.[u]

u. Matthews faced sexism on the district bench. While her nomination was before the Senate, a judge on the district court, T. Alan Goldsborough, stated publicly that although Matthews was capable, there was "just one thing wrong: she's a woman." When she

African Americans and Judgeships

Early in his administration Truman named an African American, Chicago lawyer Irvin C. Mollison, to a lifetime federal judgeship — the first African American so named.[v] The court to which Mollison was appointed, however, was a court of specialized jurisdiction, the U.S. Customs Court sitting in New York.[74] Mollison's appointment certainly had symbolic significance, but it was only a token — a meager one at that, given the importance of the black vote for the Democratic Party coalition.

Just as with the Roosevelt administration, there was pressure on Truman to appoint blacks to federal judgeships. In 1945, after Nathan Margold's nomination to the federal district bench in the District of Columbia ran into trouble and the Senate adjourned without taking action, the president of the National Bar Association (the nationwide bar association of black lawyers) wrote to Truman urging him to name William Henry Hastie to the post. A group of black Virginia lawyers sent a telegram to Truman promoting the brilliant black attorney Charles H. Houston.[75] But the judgeship went to a white Justice Department lawyer, Alexander Holtzoff.[w]

In late 1946, there was a vacancy on the bench of the Southern District of New York. Black leaders waged a campaign for the appointment of a black, and there were encouraging signs. The *New York Times* reported that the administration, with the support of state Democratic leaders, was set to appoint a black to the judgeship. The New York City Democratic Party organization, Tammany Hall, with the approval of Democratic State Chairman Fitzpatrick, submitted a list of three black city judges and a fourth black attorney, who was a collector of internal revenue.[76] The next day, the president of the Association of the Bar of the City of New York, Harrison Tweed, fired off a telegram to Truman which dramatically demonstrates the obstacles that blacks faced in attaining federal judgeships:

---

joined the district bench, her male colleagues gave her a cool reception, and she was at first handed the dullest, least rewarding assignments. But Matthews remained steadfast. She also always hired women to be her law clerks. See *New York Times,* April 28, 1988, D27. Matthews was in active service from 1949 to 1968 and served as a senior judge hearing cases from 1968 to 1983. She stopped presiding as a judge at the age of eighty-eight and died at age ninety-three on April 25, 1988.

v. Note that the two African Americans named by Roosevelt to the federal district court in the Virgin Islands, William Henry Hastie and Herman E. Moore, were named to nonlifetime judgeships. The term of office has a limit of ten years.

w. The following year, however, Truman named Hastie governor of the Virgin Islands, a first for an African American. Three years after that, as we shall discuss shortly, Truman appointed Hastie to a circuit judgeship.

> We have seen it reported in the press that one of several named persons, all of whom are Negroes have been urged for selection as district judge for the southern district of New York and that this is done solely on political grounds and apparently without regard to qualifications. The Association of the Bar of the City of New York vigorously opposes a selection on any other basis than qualifications for judicial office without regard to race, color, or creed.[77]

Tweed need not have worried, as a later *New York Times* story revealed that the earlier story was incorrect. The administration had no intention of naming an African American.[78]

Furthermore, Republicans had won control of Congress in the 1946 elections, and the new chairman of the Senate Judiciary Committee, Alexander Wiley of Wisconsin, announced two days after Tweed's telegram the committee's intent to consider bar association opinions in its deliberations. The Association of the Bar of the City of New York ultimately claimed a victory when its candidate, association activist Harold R. Medina, received the nomination.[79]

Truman's reelection victory in 1948 would have been impossible without the firm support of the black vote. To be sure, Truman came out in favor of civil rights for blacks, had a civil rights program, and earlier in 1948 had issued executive orders desegregating the armed forces and ordering an end to discrimination in the civil service. But black leaders also expected that blacks would be named to high governmental positions, including judgeships. The National Bar Association, at its annual convention, urged the president to name blacks to federal district judgeships. Truman, in his message to the association, acknowledged that "we Americans have a long way to go to reach our goal of equal rights and equal opportunities for all, but we are making progress."[80] The NAACP also urged the administration to name qualified black lawyers to some of the twenty-seven new judgeships created by Congress. Again, attention focused on the Southern District of New York, which was slated for four new judgeships.

Among those named on the list of candidates that was appended to the notes of the important July 26, 1949, meeting at the Justice Department (discussed earlier) was Thurgood Marshall, then counsel for the NAACP. Under "remarks" was written "colored."[81]

On August 12, Mayor O'Dwyer wrote to Truman urging that he name one woman and one black to the New York district bench. If it was imperative to appoint a woman, O'Dwyer observed,

> The reasons and urgency for the appointment of a Negro as a Federal Judge are even more compelling.
>
> During your campaign and after your election, the American people were imbued with the fond hope that they were at last to embark on a program to

end the shameful discrimination against minorities in our country. The obstruction and the opposition that your program has encountered in Congress has caused keen disappointment. That disappointment should not be permitted to turn into despair.

The suggested appointments would be well within the spirit of your great Civil Rights Program.[82]

Four days after the letter was sent, the mayor's brother, Paul O'Dwyer, and Philip Watson, the president of the Harlem Lawyers Association, went to Washington and met with White House staffer David K. Niles, urging that the president name a black to a New York vacancy. But the administration was also pressured by the Liberal Party in New York (which backed Truman in 1948) to pick from its list of choices.[83] In the end, Truman went with Fitzpatrick's candidates, who were white males approved by the bar associations and the party organizations. However, Truman sent the New York nominations to the Senate on the same day that he sent the Hastie nomination, thus providing an appointments package that included naming an African American to the second highest court in the land.

Two new federal judgeships were created in Philadelphia in 1949. Here, too, Truman was asked to appoint an African American. Representative William A. Barrett urged Truman to consider a number of well-qualified "Negro Philadelphia attorneys who have been loyal Democrats for many years." One was the distinguished attorney Raymond Pace Alexander, a graduate of the University of Pennsylvania and Harvard Law School. Some prominent people wrote to Truman on his behalf, including David E. Lilienthal, chairman of the Atomic Energy Commission. Alexander himself wrote to David Niles urging that Hastie be considered for a judgeship where he lived, in the District of Columbia, and not in the district court in Philadelphia or the Third Circuit. Furthermore, Alexander noted that "qualified Negro lawyers at our [Philadelphia] bar . . . have striven and given of their time, their energy, their money and services in every way to the Democratic party over the years." Alexander made it clear that *he* wanted to be considered for a district or circuit judgeship. He pointed out that if, as reported, Pennsylvania Democratic senator Francis Myers wanted to reward a black with a judicial appointment, the appointment should go to a Philadelphian and not to an outsider like Hastie. Myers, Alexander noted, would need the active support of Philadelphia blacks in his re-election campaign in 1950.[84] But Alexander's federal judicial ambitions were thwarted, and Hastie received the Third Circuit appointment.[x]

x. Coincidentally, Senator Myers, who was also the Democratic whip in the Senate, was defeated for reelection in 1950. Raymond Pace Alexander entered elective politics

William Henry Hastie was the first African American appointed to a circuit judgeship. Hastie was an extraordinary man who had excelled at Amherst College, at Harvard Law School, and at every position he held in his career. He was the first black named to a federal judgeship (a term appointment by Roosevelt to the district court in the Virgin Islands) and the first black governor of a federal territory (the Virgin Islands, named by Truman in 1946). Hastie had been dean of the Law School at Howard University. During the 1948 elections, Hastie campaigned for Truman across the country. Former attorney general Francis Biddle wrote to Truman after Biddle read that Hastie was under consideration for a Third Circuit vacancy: "I hope you will appoint him." He noted that he had known Hastie for some years and that "I admire his judgement and high intelligence and liberal outlook." Truman responded, "I think very highly of the Governor [Hastie]."[85] Hastie was nominated on October 15, 1949, and received a recess appointment on October 21. His name was resubmitted on January 5, 1950.

Confirmation did not proceed smoothly. Opposition mounted against Hastie ostensibly because he belonged to alleged Communist-front organizations. The White House responded with copies of Hastie's speeches and writings "indicating his vigorously anti-Communist views." The Senate Judiciary Committee held lengthy hearings that were closed to the public. The committee finally approved Hastie on July 17, 1950, but Senator McCarran refused to disclose the vote. The full Senate voted unanimously to confirm on July 19. Black leaders applauded the appointment, and so did Third Circuit judge John Biggs, Jr., who wrote Truman praising the president's "courage and wisdom" in naming Hastie and noting pointedly, "We are most pleased to have him."[86] Hastie remained the only African American on the circuit bench until President John F. Kennedy named Thurgood Marshall to the Second Circuit twelve years later. No African American was named by Truman to a lifetime appointment on the federal district bench. That, too, would have to wait for Kennedy's presidency.

The Demographic Profile of Truman's Judges

One might expect some differences in the profiles of Truman's appointees to the federal judiciary in his first and second terms, because during the second term the president's own party controlled Congress, whereas during the last

---

when he won a seat on the Philadelphia City Council from 1952 to 1958. In 1959, he became a judge on the Common Pleas Court in Philadelphia, a post he occupied until his death at age seventy-six in 1974.

two years of the first term he faced a Republican Congress and Republican-led Judiciary Committee in the Senate. Also, after his victory in the presidential election of 1948 Truman might have felt he had greater latitude with judicial appointments, particularly to the courts of appeals. But these suppositions are not supported by the evidence, presented in table 3.1.[y]

AGE

The Roosevelt administration's concern with age did not carry over into the Truman administration. During Truman's first term, the average age of district court appointees jumped more than two years compared to that of Roosevelt's third-term appointees and more than four years compared to that of Roosevelt's second-term district court appointees. In Truman's second term, however, the average age of district court appointees dropped by two years. The average age of Truman's appeals court appointees in both terms was greater than that of Roosevelt's second-and third-term appointees.

These findings suggest that the Truman administration paid no particular attention to age. Interestingly, in the papers of White House staffer Martin L. Friedman, who was the assistant to Donald Dawson, there is a listing of all federal judges appointed by Truman and their ages at the time of appointment.[87] The listing was dated July 26, 1951. Someone — Friedman or Dawson, or possibly Truman — was curious about the ages of appointees in the early twilight of the Truman presidency.

EDUCATION

Truman's first-term district court appointees differed from his second-term appointees in their undergraduate and law school education. More than one-third of the first-term appointees had no undergraduate education as compared to one-fifth of the second-term appointees. About three in ten first-term appointees attended a private undergraduate college or university as compared to about one in two second-term appointees. Very few first- and second-term appointees had no formal legal education. But three in five

y. Table 3.1 contains findings only for those judges who were nominated by Truman and confirmed by the Senate. Not included are the eight nominees to the federal district courts who were not confirmed by the Senate, including three recess appointees. Also not included is the elevation of Associate Judge Harold M. Stephens of the District of Columbia Circuit to be chief judge, an administrative position that since 1955 has gone automatically to the judge on the circuit with the most seniority under the age of seventy. Also not included in these figures is U.S. District Judge Roger T. Foley of Nebraska, who was nominated by Roosevelt and confirmed by the Senate two days before Roosevelt's death, but whose judicial commission was signed by Truman.

second-term appointees had attended a private law school as compared to two in five first-term appointees. These data hint that the first-term appointees may have tended to come from less affluent families than the second-term appointees.

As for appeals court appointees, a much higher proportion had no formal law school education than was the case for district court appointees. But among those who attended law school, a much higher percentage went to an Ivy League school. These comparisons must, however, be treated with caution because of the relatively small numbers of first- and second-term appeals court appointees. On the whole, there do not appear to be significant differences in education between the first- and second-term appeals court appointees, although none of the first-term appointees had a public law school education.

EXPERIENCE

The professional experience of the district court appointees in both terms was similar, and the findings for the Truman appointees are strikingly similar to those we saw in the last chapter for the Roosevelt appointees. There were larger proportions of those with prosecutorial experience than judicial experience. About one-third of the district court appointees had been judges, but about half had been prosecutors. (Some, of course, had been both.) About one-third had neither judicial nor prosecutorial experience. Clearly, professional credentials played a part in the selection process.

With the appeals court appointees, about three in five had judicial experience but only about three in ten had prosecutorial experience. This was closer to the Roosevelt record for his second-term appointees than for his first- and third-term appointees. Judicial experience and a judicial track record may have subtly played into the appointment process calculus. Like the district court appointees, however, about one-third had neither judicial nor prosecutorial experience.

OCCUPATION

About one in five first- and second-term district court appointees held political office (elected or appointed) at the time of their judicial nominations. A somewhat smaller proportion were government lawyers, typically United States attorneys or district attorneys. Twice the proportion of first-term as compared to second-term appointees were members of the judiciary (almost all on the state bench) at the time of appointment. More than twice the proportion of appeals court appointees as compared to district court appointees were serving as judges. Of the thirteen appointed to the appeals courts who were judges at the time of their appointment, eleven were federal district court

Table 3.1. Selected Backgrounds of Lifetime Truman Appointees to the Federal District and Appeals Courts of General Jurisdiction

	District Court Appointees		Appeals Court Appointees	
	First Term	Second Term	First Term	Second Term
Average age at time of appointment	52.6	50.6	54.7	55.3
Undergraduate Education				
Public	23.7%	22.0%	33.3%	23.5%
	(9)	(13)	(3)	(4)
Private not Ivy	31.6%	49.2%	33.3%	35.3%
	(12)	(29)	(3)	(6)
Ivy League	7.9%	8.5%	11.1%	17.6%
	(3)	(5)	(1)	(3)
None	36.8%	20.3%	22.2%	23.5%
	(14)	(12)	(2)	(4)
Law School Education				
Public	42.1%	22.0%	—	23.5%
	(16)	(13)		(4)
Private not Ivy	42.1%	61.0%	44.4%	41.2%
	(16)	(36)	(4)	(7)
Ivy League	13.2%	13.6%	22.2%	23.5%
	(5)	(8)	(2)	(4)
None	2.6%	3.4%	33.3%	11.8%
	(1)	(2)	(3)	(2)
Experience				
Judicial	36.8%	33.9%	66.7%	58.8%
	(14)	(20)	(6)	(10)
Prosecutorial	50.0%	47.5%	44.4%	35.3%
	(19)	(28)	(4)	(6)
Neither	34.2%	32.2%	33.3%	23.5%
	(13)	(19)	(3)	(4)
Occupation				
Politics — Government	21.1%	20.3%	11.1%	11.8%
	(8)	(12)	(1)	(2)
Government Lawyer	18.4%	15.2%	—	11.8%
	(7)	(9)		(2)
Judiciary	26.3%	13.6%	55.6%	47.1%
	(10)	(8)	(5)	(8)
Large Law Firm*	—	1.7%	—	—
		(1)		
Medium-Size Law Firm†	10.5%	8.5%	11.1%	5.9%
	(4)	(5)	(1)	(1)

Table 3.1. Continued

	District Court Appointees		Appeals Court Appointees	
	First Term	Second Term	First Term	Second Term
Small Law Firm‡	13.2%	18.6%	11.1%	17.6%
	(5)	(11)	(1)	(3)
Solo Practice	2.6%	18.6%	11.1%	5.9%
	(1)	(11)	(1)	(1)
Law Professor	2.6%	1.7%	—	—
	(1)	(1)		
Other	5.3%	1.7%	—	—
	(2)	(1)		
Party				
Democratic	97.4%	91.5%	88.9%	88.2%
	(37)	(54)	(8)	(15)
Republican	2.6%	8.5%	11.1%	11.8%
	(1)	(5)	(1)	(2)
Prominent Party Activism				
	55.3%	61.0%	66.7%	58.8%
	(21)	(36)	(6)	(10)
Prior or Current Members of Congress				
	7.9%	6.8%	11.1%	5.9%
	(3)	(4)	(1)	(1)
Religion				
Protestant	52.6%	54.2%	77.8%	64.7%
	(20)	(32)	(7)	(11)
Catholic	34.2%	32.2%	11.1%	29.4%
	(13)	(19)	(1)	(5)
Jewish	13.2%	10.2%	11.1%	5.9%
	(5)	(6)	(1)	(1)
Other§	—	3.4%	—	—
	—	(2)	—	—
Total Number of Appointees				
	38	59	9	17

* A large law firm was defined as consisting of ten or more partners and associates.

† A medium-size law firm was defined as consisting of from five to nine partners and associates.

‡ A small law firm was defined as consisting of from two to four partners and associates.

§ Two Christian Scientists were appointed.

judges, one was on a state supreme court, and one was on a lower state bench. Half of all Truman's appeals court appointees were judges at the time of their elevation to the appeals bench. Far fewer appeals court appointees were government lawyers or held other (nonjudicial) governmental positions at the time of their appointment.

Of those in law practice, only one came from a large law firm. Most came from small firms or practiced solo (almost one in five second-term district court appointees were solo law practitioners). This trend was consistent with that for the Roosevelt appointees. It also, to some extent, mirrored the practice of law in the United States.

Unlike the Roosevelt administration, the Truman administration did not look to the law schools for appointments to the appeals bench. Two district court appointees, however, were law professors at the time of appointment.

PARTY

Although about nine out of ten Truman appointees were Democrats, the proportion (and number) of Republicans appointed was considerably larger than in the Roosevelt administration. Roosevelt appointed two Republicans out of a total of 133 district court appointments. Truman appointed six Republicans out of a total of ninety-seven (with five of the six coming during the second term). He appointed three Republicans (out of twenty-six appointments) to the appeals bench. Roosevelt appointed two Republicans (out of fifty appointments). Truman's Republicans were not known as political liberals; Roosevelt's were. Three of Truman's six Republican district court appointments were to the District Court for the District of Columbia. One of the three Republican appeals court appointments was to the Court of Appeals for the District of Columbia. It would seem that the Truman administration deliberately used the greater discretion it had with appointments to the District of Columbia bench to appoint Republicans. Appointments of Republicans to both court levels, although small in number, were perhaps aimed at administration critics who decried the overwhelming partisan imbalance on the bench. Truman himself did not appear to link party affiliation to judicial decisionmaking.

About three in five Truman appointees to both court levels had records of prominent party activity or a close political relationship with Truman or a Democratic senator. About 7 percent of all appointees were either current or former members of Congress — close to half the proportion of the Roosevelt appointees. Judicial appointments did not constitute sinecures that were routinely given to members of Congress. Neither did they reflect policy-agenda concerns on the part of the administration.

RELIGIOUS ORIGIN OR AFFILIATION

Truman's proportion of Catholic appointees exceeded Roosevelt's. A larger proportion of Catholics was appointed by Truman to the district bench (33 percent) than to the appeals bench (23 percent), but the proportion of Catholics appointed to both court levels was unprecedented. Curiously, when Truman replaced the one Catholic on the Supreme Court (Frank Murphy, who died in 1949) with a non-Catholic (Tom Clark), he was criticized for abandoning the "Catholic seat." The next vacancy on the Court went to Truman's friend Sherman Minton, whose wife and children were Catholic. The administration may have been sensitive to Catholics when it came to appeals court appointments in particular. Truman's proportion of Catholic appeals court appointees was almost double that of Roosevelt's.

Truman's proportion of Jewish appointees was considerably greater than Roosevelt's. More than 11 percent of Truman's district court appointees were Jewish; the figure for Roosevelt was only 4.5 percent. Truman's proportion of Jewish appointees to the appeals bench was 7.7 percent; Roosevelt's was 2 percent. It would seem that religious barriers to advancement in the judiciary were lowered for both Catholics and Jews during the Truman administration. Given the importance of Catholics and Jews in the Democratic coalition, this was a logical development.

Truman's appointees were in many respects representative of the Democratic Party coalition, but decidedly not in terms of gender and race. Only two women were nominated, and one of those nominations was derailed by the white male bar establishment. Only one African American was a lifetime Truman judicial appointee to a court of general jurisdiction. Yet even those token appointments were welcomed, as they were unprecedented and offered the promise of shattered barriers (a promise not fully realized until the Carter administration).

Although Roosevelt was the quintessential hands-on president when it came to judicial appointments, Truman was far from indifferent. The record of Truman's involvement in selection demonstrates an interest in and grasp of the politics of selection, if somewhat less micromanagement of the process. But Truman in some ways was even more assertive than Roosevelt when he felt justified in exercising presidential prerogatives in naming judges. However, Truman suffered more senatorial defeats than did Roosevelt.

Unlike in the 1930s, the federal courts by the 1940s were not bastions of opposition to the federal government's social and economic policies. The New Deal was won, and ideology was not on the front burner of American politics, at least as far as the courts were concerned. Truman's judicial selection process reflected this new reality. Yet his administration was a continuation of Roosevelt's and sought to consolidate the accomplishments of the New Deal and attend to some of the unfinished business, in particular in civil rights. Truman's presidential style, although different from Roosevelt's creative administrative chaos, was also hands-on. Roosevelt's appointments showed a mixture of policy-agenda and partisan-agenda considerations, with an occasional selection based on his personal agenda. Truman's appointments largely reflected a partisan agenda, although there were some personal-agenda and occasional policy-agenda appointments.

The presidency and the nation were to experience a sharp shift with the election of Republican Dwight David Eisenhower to the presidency in 1952. Twenty years of Democratic rule came abruptly to a halt. A partisan imbalance on the federal bench due to twenty years of Democratic appointments was expected to (and in fact did) end in the Eisenhower administration. A popular general, who never held elective office until winning the highest office in the nation, was now charged with making appointments to the nation's courts.

Eisenhower Takes Charge

Dwight David Eisenhower was a war hero who was widely admired and beloved for his leadership during the Second World War. His postwar career as president of Columbia University and then Supreme Commander of the Allied Powers in Europe kept him in the public eye.[1] There was much speculation that General Eisenhower would enter politics, although his political orientation was unknown. Democrats and Republicans alike hoped that he would join their respective parties and be their candidate for president. When he decided to seek the Republican nomination in 1952, he did not have the free ride that he might have expected. Yet a victorious Eisenhower and his supporters brought new life to the Republican Party, and the term *Eisenhower Democrat* was seen as symbolic of the undoing of the New Deal electoral coalition.

The Republican victory in 1952 was a landslide. Eisenhower received 55.1 percent of the popular vote and 83 percent of the vote in the electoral college. The Republicans gained twenty-two seats in the House and one seat in the Senate, giving them control of both houses of Congress. Yet Republican leadership of the federal government in 1953 and 1954 did not result in the repeal of the New Deal but rather in its essential acceptance. The president's agenda did not include dismantling the welfare state.

Barely nine months after Eisenhower assumed the presidency, he had to name a new chief justice of the United States Supreme Court. Eisenhower chose Earl Warren, who would lead the Court to the unanimous decision in *Brown* v. *Board of Education* that can be said to have ushered in the civil rights revolution. Civil rights moved from a muted issue of public policy to one that was trumpeted on the front pages of newspapers and over the broadcast media. Litigation mounted, southern states were defiant, controversy and violence ensued, and more and more demands were made by those seeking an end to all forms of racial discrimination as well as the redress of historic wrongs. The implementation of court-ordered school desegregation in Little Rock, Arkansas, provided a dramatic confrontation between state and federal authority. It reached a climax when President Eisenhower ordered federal troops to enforce the court order in Central High School. Congress, too, felt the pressure of the civil rights revolution and in 1957, for the first time since 1875, enacted a civil rights bill. The legislation, modest in scope, established a Civil Rights Commission with investigatory powers and also empowered the attorney general to seek injunctions when citizens were denied the right to vote.

Democrats recaptured control of Congress in 1954, regaining nineteen seats in the House and one in the Senate. But this had no effect on Eisenhower's reelection bid two years later. The country liked "Ike," reelecting him with 57.4 percent of the popular vote. But the Democrats had only a two-vote margin in the Senate and a thirty-three-vote majority in the House. As a practical matter, this meant that conservative Republicans and conservative southern Democrats still controlled Congress. In 1958, however, the country was hit hard by an economic downturn that had significant political implications for the November congressional elections. Democrats won an additional forty-nine seats in the House and seventeen in the Senate. Most of the congressional newcomers were liberals. This new liberal strength enabled passage of the Civil Rights Act of 1960, which strengthened the powers of the Civil Rights Commission and also the role of the attorney general in redressing illegal restrictions on the right to vote.

Eisenhower's victory in the 1952 presidential election and his reelection in 1956 had a stunning effect on American politics. The New Deal coalition seemed to come apart, most noticeably in the realm of presidential politics, with the collapse of the one-party Democratic South. Eisenhower captured the growing suburban vote in major metropolitan areas, as scores of upwardly mobile Democrats left the central cities and their Democratic Party heritage.

Eisenhower was faced with major problems when he assumed office. The unpopular Korean War was in stalemate, and during the campaign Eisenhower promised to end it. The Cold War with the Soviet Union and the accompanying arms race demanded immediate attention. The fear of communist subversion at home continued to be exploited by demagogues like Wisconsin

Republican senator Joseph McCarthy and other politicians in both major political parties. Just below the surface was the simmering issue of civil rights for African Americans, which was before the United States Supreme Court in *Brown*. And Eisenhower was expected to turn his personal political victory into more permanent gains for the Republicans. This is the general political context within which the Eisenhower administration undertook its task of appointing federal judges.

Presidential Involvement in Selection

Eisenhower brought a leadership style to the presidency far different from Roosevelt's or Truman's. Eisenhower, however, had a winning personality and, much like Roosevelt, evoked strong feelings of personal loyalty and admiration from his supporters and, as his presidency progressed, derision from his opponents. To his supporters, Eisenhower was a benign father-figure who, standing above petty partisan politics, competently and wisely steered the ship of state. To his critics, Eisenhower was a figurehead president, weak, indecisive, easily manipulated by Republican politicos in his administration, who spent more time on the golf course with his industrialist friends than in the Oval Office running the federal government. Insofar as judicial selection is concerned, the truth falls somewhere between these extreme versions of Eisenhower's presidency.

Eisenhower's leadership style was shaped by his military training and experience. In the armed forces, a superior's orders are obeyed without question by inferior officers and enlisted personnel. Micromanagement is foreign to this style of leadership. But in the Oval Office, the military command style had its perils. As Truman observed in 1952 about what would happen were Eisenhower to become president, "He'll sit here and he'll say, 'Do this! Do that!' *And nothing will happen.* Poor Ike—it won't be a bit like the Army. He'll find it very frustrating."[2] Eisenhower indeed was sometimes frustrated with judicial selection. The chain-of-command military style of leadership often did not work and left the president out of the decision-making loop. But, also, as we shall see, Eisenhower learned on the job and sought to improve his effectiveness in the process.

If in appeal Eisenhower was more like Roosevelt than Truman, he was more like Truman in his modest background. Like Roosevelt, Eisenhower had health problems while in office, but unlike Roosevelt's, Eisenhower's problems were very public. His heart attack on September 24, 1955, his operation for ileitis on June 8, 1956, and his minor stroke on November 25, 1957, were closely followed by the nation. Eisenhower, like Truman, was not as manip-

ulative as Roosevelt, although there is some evidence that he was more involved with the politics of judicial selection than he let on in public, although
his involvement cannot be characterized as manifesting a hidden-hand presidential style of leadership.[3] The evidence, however, suggests that the above-
politics image that Eisenhower cultivated as his public persona bore little
resemblance to how he actually behaved on the job. This was a president who
showed his concern about the future of the Republican Party by his record of
judicial selection.

When Eisenhower took office, the federal judiciary was in a state of acute
political imbalance, brought about by twenty years of Democratic appointments. About four out of five federal judges were Democrats.[a] Clearly, Republicans were an endangered species on the courts. Yet, just as with Truman,
the federal courts were not seen as central to the president's policy agenda. The
issue of school desegregation following *Brown* v. *Board of Education* resulted
in the activities of the federal courts becoming more controversial, but the
Eisenhower administration, for the most part, did not link judicial appointments to policy concerns. As will become evident later in this chapter, the
president himself did not fully appreciate the workings of courts and their
potential importance for promoting or frustrating a policy agenda.

In a meeting with Republican legislative leaders in January 1956, Eisenhower noted that he had taken judicial nominations "under his own eye."[4] To
some extent the evidence seems to back up this statement insofar as the process of selection, the criteria for selection, and some specific instances were
concerned.

Eisenhower described the process of selection in a letter to former governor
Edward F. Arn of Kansas, who was angling for a federal judgeship. "We go
through a very thorough system of investigation and of balancing ... considerations before anyone is appointed to a Federal Court. This process holds
largely to the responsibility of the Attorney General who enlists the help of the
American Bar Association and others. Normally he puts in some weeks at this
kind of work before making any recommendation to me."[5]

---

a. The proportion of Republicans serving in lifetime positions on the federal district
bench when Eisenhower took office was 19.2 percent, Democrats 77.5 percent; there
were seven vacancies. The proportion of Republicans on the appeals bench was 16.9
percent, Democrats 80.0 percent; with two vacancies. On the Supreme Court, eight of the
nine justices were Democrats. For all three court levels, Republicans comprised 18.5
percent, Democrats 78.4 percent. These figures are based on Justice Department documents, *Active Republican Life-Time Judges Sitting,* August 21, 1952, and *Active Democrat Life-Time Judges Sitting,* August 22, 1952, found in William Rogers Papers, Box 49,
Judgeships file, Dwight David Eisenhower Presidential Library, Abilene, Kansas. The
"active" refers to the judges' status as full time judges in active service.

Eisenhower, early in his first term, directed that judicial nominations be cleared through the chairman of the Republican National Committee. He insisted that the selection process should go through channels — that is, the Justice Department — and not be negotiated from the White House. In 1955, in his third year as president, Eisenhower wrote to his principal assistant, former New Hampshire governor Sherman Adams: "Please refer to the Attorney General all recommendations for appointment as District Judges. Replies from this office should be rather pro forma, merely stating that we are delighted to have the writer's opinion and noting that the recommendation has been transmitted to the Attorney General."[6]

But Eisenhower discovered that simply going through channels did not suit the political dynamics of the selection process. The president needed to know what was happening long before he received a formal recommendation from the attorney general.[b] Finally, in 1958, Eisenhower asked Attorney General William Rogers to place the president in the decision-making loop: "I have always taken a deep personal interest in the appointment of Federal Judges. For this reason I should like that, before you submit a formal nomination for signature, you drop in to confer with me about the matter; if the time element is important, you can call me on the telephone. It has been my habit to look over such nominations very carefully before we have committed ourselves to making them."[7]

Apparently this memo did not produce the results Eisenhower desired. Eleven months later, midway in his second presidential term, in a letter bursting with presidential frustration, Eisenhower wrote to Rogers:

> From my viewpoint there are a few disturbing flaws in the procedures that we are using in selecting individuals for appointment to the Federal judiciary. . . . Primarily, of course, I depend upon the Attorney General to assist me in this work and, indeed, to take the initiative in mobilizing pertinent facts upon which I can base a decision. Your findings, involving such factors as character, experience and ability, are of necessity practically conclusive. But the White House has a very direct interest in other considerations, an interest that must often express itself long before the time has arrived for a final decision.
>
> Too often the White House, by which I mean my two principal assistants as well as myself, is uninformed as to vacancies, prospective vacancies, and possible candidates for some judicial position until it is far too late to have any

---

b. Eisenhower's first attorney general was Herbert Brownell. Brownell's deputy attorney general was William P. Rogers. In 1957, Brownell stepped down and Rogers became attorney general. Rogers's deputy was Lawrence E. Walsh, who resigned from the federal district court bench to go to the Justice Department. Rogers later became secretary of state in the Nixon administration, and Walsh achieved fame in the late 1980s and early 1990s as the special counsel (prosecutor) in the Iran-Contra investigation.

flexibility in choice. It is more than embarrassing to find, for example, that I have approved a man's name for appointment, and later to discover that a number of highly respected citizens and political associates were vigorously sponsoring another individual, but without full White House knowledge of the situation. . . .

I expect my staff to give me timely information provided by you and by outside individuals as to pertinent facts in these cases so that I may have adequate freedom of choice before any appointment, direct or indirect, has been made on my behalf. In turn my staff will keep you informed as to facts presented directly to the White House by others. . . .

I request that you follow the simple procedure below outlined:

(1). Either personally, or by *confidential* memorandum sent to me (through either General Persons or Mr. Morgan) you will please, at the earliest practicable moment, notify me of what vacancies are expected to occur or have actually occurred.

(2). In the same or a later *confidential* memorandum to me, list the names of the individuals who have been recommended to you and those who are being considered by your office, together with the names of principal sponsors, particularly where these include the Governor, Senators, or members of the Congress from any given state. (Note: If either item 1 or 2 is carried out through personal conversation between you and me, please leave with me a short memorandum of pertinent facts).

(3). When you believe that the accumulated information warrants a decision, please confer with me as soon as convenient in order that I can personally discuss with you the matter and give final approval.

(4). Thereafter the final papers should be processed as promptly as practicable.

In the past I have always tried to keep these matters almost wholly on a verbal basis, particularly because of the importance of avoiding leakage while the process of selection goes on. However, I have found that not only is my memory far from infallible, but it is also important that in certain considerations applying to the appointing process I need the counsel and advice of my own principal staff officers.[8]

Eisenhower met with the attorney general on February 12, 1959, and outlined the new procedures he wanted followed, but he did not give Rogers the letter. It was sent later, and Eisenhower asked for Rogers's comments. There is no record of a formal reply from Rogers in the presidential papers.[9] This suggests that as late as six years into his presidency Eisenhower still was not in full control of judicial selection.

In his memoirs, Eisenhower recounted that at the outset of his administration he provided Attorney General Herbert Brownell with criteria for the appointment of judges. Eisenhower told Brownell "that I would appoint no one who did not have the approval of the American Bar Association" and that age was an important qualification. Eisenhower wrote that he "finally fixed sixty-two as the upper age limit for initial appointment to the federal courts," but was willing to be flexible within a year or so "if other qualifications were unusually impressive." Eisenhower was concerned with "the general health of the person proposed." Lastly, he wrote that he was concerned with appointing people with "solid common sense" and that he wanted excluded from consideration "candidates known to hold extreme legal or philosophical views." Eisenhower wanted to appoint "judges who commanded the respect, confidence, and pride of the population."[10] There is some evidence that during his administration Eisenhower indeed sought to promote these standards.

For example, on several occasions he made clear that he was only interested in nominees "of the highest professional standing and unimpeachable character." Eisenhower wanted the ABA's evaluation of judicial candidates, and in 1956 the ABA rating of each nominee began to be included in the formal letter from the attorney general to the president recommending the nomination. Eisenhower considered judicial experience valuable and indeed a prerequisite for appointment as an associate justice of the Supreme Court. He made it clear that he would use an appeals court appointment as a stepping stone to the Supreme Court. In his diary, Eisenhower recounted that he spoke with Attorney General Brownell about appointing Brownell to the Supreme Court: "I told [Brownell] that if he had any ambitions to go on the Court, that we should appoint him immediately to the vacancy now existing on the Appellate Court in New York and then when and if another vacancy occurred on the Supreme Court, I could appoint him to it."[11] Brownell turned Eisenhower down.[c] Of the four associate-justice appointments made by Eisenhower, three went to appeals court judges he had originally appointed — John M. Harlan, Charles Whittaker, and Potter Stewart.[d]

Eisenhower demonstrated concern with the age of his nominees. In February 1959, the two Kentucky Republican senators met with Eisenhower and recommended a man who was sixty-five years old for a position on the Court of Appeals for the Sixth Circuit. The following week, Eisenhower wrote to Senator John Sherman Cooper concerning this candidate: "I have given a great deal of thought to this matter, and have concluded that I cannot make an

c. Eisenhower nevertheless considered appointing Brownell in 1958, despite his lack of judicial experience, but wound up appointing Potter Stewart. Eisenhower to Rogers, September 17, 1958, Rogers Papers, Pres. Eisenhower, May 1958–Dec. 1958.

d. The fourth appointment to an associate justiceship went to William J. Brennan, who was serving on the New Jersey Supreme Court at the time of appointment.

exception in the age limitation in this case. I have decided to go ahead and submit the nomination of Judge Cecil. While Judge Cecil is about the same age as Mr. Park, Judge Cecil is being promoted from the District bench to the Circuit Court of Appeals, and promotions have never been considered as coming within the age rules."[12]

There is evidence that Eisenhower was alert to the politics of judicial selection. For a vacancy on the Seventh Circuit in 1956, the Indiana Republican senators Homer Capehart and William Jenner could not agree on judicial patronage. Capehart backed John S. Hastings, an Indiana lawyer and West Point graduate who also had been chairman of the Citizens Committee for Capehart. The Justice Department favored Hastings, and his nomination was sent to Eisenhower. The president signed the nomination paper but "was hesitant . . . apparently because of the feeling that this might be the man about whom there was some difference of opinion in Indiana. He did so, however, but instructed that it be rechecked with him personally after clearance and before submission to the Senate."[13] The nomination was sent to the Senate later that same day and, after months of delay, Hastings was confirmed.

Another example occurred with the filling of a Third Circuit vacancy in 1958. Democratic governor Robert B. Meyner of New Jersey wrote to Eisenhower recommending the elevation of District Judge Phillip Forman, a Republican. On the letter Eisenhower handwrote the following: "Send to Bill Rogers — This *looks* good — especially because we have a Democrat recommending a Republican."[14]

Eisenhower was also aware of the importance of wooing traditionally Democratic Roman Catholics to the Republican Party. In a remarkable letter of March 8, 1955, to Attorney General Brownell, Eisenhower wrote:

> In going over the list of members of the United States Commission for the Celebration of the Two Hundredth Anniversary of the Birth of John Marshall, I find there is not a single Catholic in the group. In view of all the efforts we have made to appoint a few Catholics to the bench, I think we have really overlooked a chance to make a bow in their direction. [Eisenhower then mentions some well-known Catholics he wants to invite to the luncheon.] In addition, I still want the name of some fine, prominent Catholic to nominate to the bench.[15e]

Eisenhower, on occasion, was involved in the filling of specific appointments. He might pass on suggestions from others to the attorney general or occasionally make a suggestion of his own, and in several instances he met with Republican senators.

e. This last reference is probably to the Supreme Court. The next Supreme Court appointment went to William J. Brennan, a Democrat and a Roman Catholic.

Within two weeks of taking office, Eisenhower was visited by a clergyman whose brother, a former Republican governor of Minnesota, was on the federal district bench in the District of Columbia. Eisenhower related in a memo to Attorney General Brownell: "Reverend Youngdahl says that there will probably soon occur, in Minnesota, a vacancy in the Circuit Court of Appeals. He thinks that his brother would be the best qualified appointee we could find. I merely promised Reverend Youngdahl to pass the above on to you."[16][f] Eisenhower displayed somewhat more active involvement in selection in this memo to the attorney general in December 1954: "Two people, who are not only friends of mine but people of high character and dedicated Americanism, recommend to me that Judge M. M. McGown, of Jackson, Mississippi, be appointed to a vacancy, which they say exists, in the Fifth Circuit Court of Appeals. Undoubtedly he has always been a registered Democrat, but we should appoint an occasional Democrat even though our ration from that party is already overwhelming. I understand that he is an anti–New Deal individual. In any event, please consider his record very carefully."[17] It is remarkable that Eisenhower either was not told or did not recall that a vacancy existed in the Fifth Circuit following the retirement of Judge Edwin R. Holmes. Given the Supreme Court's decision in *Brown* v. *Board of Education*, any appointment to the southern Fifth Circuit would be of great importance. In the end, the vacancy went to a Mississippi Republican, Benjamin F. Cameron, whose subsequent judicial record on the appeals court became one of opposition to desegregation.[18] The memo also contains a rare acknowledgment of Eisenhower's awareness of ideological orientation, although it is unclear whether the president was merely neutral or was signaling his desire to appoint "anti–New Deal" people.

On June 22, 1954, Eisenhower met with Senators Capehart and Jenner to discuss judicial appointments in Indiana. Both senators strongly backed former Republican state chairman Cale Holder for one of two vacancies on the federal district bench. Capehart supported former Republican congressman Robert Grant for the other vacancy and urged that Lynn Parkinson, the favorite of the Indiana congressman Charles Halleck, who was the Republican majority leader in the House, be given the next vacancy on the Seventh Circuit. Jenner, however, suggested that Parkinson be given the second district court position and that Grant wait for the next circuit vacancy. According to an account of the meeting by White House assistant I. Jack Martin, "Capehart replied that he didn't want to stand in the way and if that would satisfy

---

f. Youngdahl was mistaken. The Eighth Circuit judge from Minnesota, John B. Sanborn, although seventy years of age in 1953, remained on the bench until June 30, 1959. His successor was Harry A. Blackmun, the future Supreme Court justice.

everybody it was all right with him. . . . The President said he would take another look at the matter and let them know his decision shortly. The President also stated the one thing that he thinks is most important for the Republican Party is that they get the best men to fill all vacancies, especially in the Judicial Branch, and he feels it is his duty to appoint only such men to office."[19g]

Eisenhower's administrative style, as suggested earlier, was undoubtedly influenced by his military experience, and this meant in practice that the Justice Department (in particular the attorney general and the deputy attorney general) had responsibility for judicial selection with little interference from the White House. Justice Department officials were aggressive in selecting people they believed to be the best available, even if it meant going against the wishes of Republican senators. The president became involved only at the last minute, and then typically to give his imprimatur to whatever his attorney general was recommending.

In 1953, for example, the Pennsylvania Republican senators James H. Duff and Edward Martin recommended three people for district court judgeships, John L. Miller (a law partner of Duff's), John W. Lord, Jr. (a former Republican state senator whose wife was president of the Republican Women of Pennsylvania), and an individual who was a Republican county chairman but who did not meet Justice Department standards. The Philadelphia Bar Association recommended seven people, one of whom was Francis L. Van Dusen. About the same time, Van Dusen's brother wrote to his friend Bernard Shanley, acting special counsel to the president, recommending Van Dusen for a judgeship, and Shanley contacted Attorney General Brownell on Van Dusen's behalf. Van Dusen's law partner was the southeastern Pennsylvania chairman of Citizens for Eisenhower. Van Dusen had impeccable professional credentials — he was a former editor of the *Harvard Law Review* and a member of a prestigious Philadelphia law firm. Brownell and his deputy, William Rogers, decided to recommend Miller, Lord, and Van Dusen. The Republican senators cleared Miller and Lord but refused to clear Van Dusen. Leonard Hall, the

---

g. Holder and Parkinson received the district court positions. When a vacancy occurred on the Seventh Circuit in 1956, Capehart pushed for his close political ally John Hastings, Jenner backed Lloyd Hartzler, and Halleck supported the elevation of Parkinson. Former U.S. Representative Robert Grant, who lost out in 1954, got the backing of eight Indiana Republican representatives to fill the district court judgeship that would become vacant with Parkinson's elevation. After a year, the logjam was broken when another vacancy materialized on the Seventh Circuit. Hastings and then Parkinson were named to the Seventh Circuit, and Grant received the district court position vacated by Parkinson. See the account in the *Chicago Tribune*, March 15, 1957, p. 17.

chairman of the Republican National Committee, cleared all three. When the nomination papers came to the White House, an assistant to Sherman Adams wrote a cover memo for Adams and handwrote on the bottom that the attorney general had called: "he had told Pres. whole story and Pres. said that as long as Len Hall says O.K. to go ahead [with Van Dusen] and take our chances."[20] Five days later, all three nominations were sent to the Senate, where Miller and Lord were confirmed. Van Dusen's nomination, however, languished to the end of the session and died because of the opposition by the Republican senators.

The following November, the Justice Department proposed renominating Van Dusen and sent his name to the White House, but Sherman Adams said to take no action on it. In January 1955, the attorney general asked that the nomination be sent to the president. The White House ascertained that Van Dusen was still cleared by the Republican National Committee. Finally, the Justice Department made a deal with the Pennsylvania senators over two new judgeships in Pennsylvania,[21] whereby Herbert P. Sorg, a former speaker of the Pennsylvania House of Representatives rated "not qualified" by the ABA but pushed by Senators Duff and Martin, and John W. McIlvaine, the United States attorney for the western district of Pennsylvania, were nominated along with the resubmission of Van Dusen on May 20, 1955. With the Pennsylvania senators having dropped their opposition to Van Dusen, all three nominations were confirmed. Twelve years later, Van Dusen was elevated to the Third Circuit.

The Van Dusen example suggests that Eisenhower was only peripherally involved in decisions concerning judicial selection. Nonetheless, it is reasonable to assume that the Justice Department and Eisenhower's assistants, in making key screening decisions, were acting in tune with Eisenhower's wishes.

There are other instances of the president's involvement in selecting federal judges. In January 1955, Eisenhower wrote to the attorney general: "Next time I see you, will you please bring up the matter of the appointment to the Federal judgeship for the Southern District of Florida." At the bottom of the letter Eisenhower handwrote: "I have a sheaf of letters favoring a man named Anderson."[22] The appointment, however, went to Joseph P. Lieb.

When a recess commission for J. Smith Henley to be a United States district judge for Arkansas came to the president, he signed it but asked that his assistant, General Wilton B. Persons, telephone the attorney general to make sure that this was the right thing to do. An aide wrote Eisenhower: "Pursuant to your direction, General Persons phoned the Department of Justice and was assured by the Deputy Attorney General that they have thoroughly checked into the matter of a recess appointment . . . and renew their recommendation that it be done at this time. . . . I am holding the signed Commission. Unless you wish otherwise, the appointment in the normal course will be announced at [presidential press secretary] Hagerty's next conference with the Press." At the bottom of the memo Eisenhower handwrote "OK."[23]

Charles M. Metzner was the assistant campaign manager for Eisenhower in New York State in 1952. Following the election he went to Washington, where he served as executive assistant to Attorney General Brownell for two years before returning to his native New York City to resume the practice of law. In 1958, he was executive director of Nelson Rockefeller's successful campaign for governor of New York. Metzner had the full backing of the New York Republican organization when he made a bid for a federal district judgeship. His former colleague at the Justice Department, William Rogers, offered him a position on the District of Columbia bench, but Metzner said he wanted the vacancy on the Southern District of New York. The problem was that Lloyd F. MacMahon, who was national head of Citizens for Eisenhower, wanted to fill that vacancy. An aide to Eisenhower outlined in a memo to the president the reasons why MacMahon should receive the appointment. He noted that those in Citizens for Eisenhower had not received patronage and observed: "At this point some of the New York lawyers who helped MacMahon are wondering if in serving Citizens they were actually harming their political future." The aide further argued: "Metzner has a secure berth as a partner in a law firm and can comfortably await another opening. With MacMahon it is a different story, having sacrificed his law practice . . . and having held himself available for this appointment since the election last year."[24] Both Metzner and MacMahon were rated "qualified" by the ABA. In the end, Eisenhower selected Mac-Mahon for the vacancy,[h] and about five weeks later Metzner was nominated for a position that had come open in the interim.

In early 1960, Jack Porter, who had led the Eisenhower forces in Texas and played an important role in Eisenhower's 1952 campaign, recommended John Q. Adams for a federal judgeship in Texas. Eisenhower responded to Porter's letter: "I have been assured by the Attorney General that Mr. Adams is receiving the most careful consideration. I understand also that [Republican National Committee chairman] Thruston Morton has discussed the matter at length with you. Therefore I assume that you are thoroughly familiar with the problem involved and the earnest efforts the Attorney General is making to surmount the obstacles." The "problem" was that Adams was sixty-one, over the age limit of sixty imposed by the ABA but under Eisenhower's preferred

h. In a "Dear Lloyd" letter, Eisenhower wrote that he was "delighted to be able to send your nomination." March 12, 1959, OF 100 c New York Southern.

limit of sixty-two. Apparently Attorney General Rogers and his deputy, Lawrence Walsh, were unable to persuade the ABA committee to relax its age rule and were preparing to send the name of Everton Kennerly, whom Jack Porter claimed had bolted the Texas precinct convention in 1952 when it went for Eisenhower. Porter wrote to Eisenhower: "I will consider it a personal favor if you will intervene and insist on the appointment of Mr. Adams."[25] There is no record of the president's reply. But the position remained unfilled when John F. Kennedy took office the next year.

In a letter of October 14, 1959, Frank McCarthy, a wartime associate of Eisenhower's, recommended another World War II colleague, H. Merrill Pasco, for a judgeship in the eastern district of Virginia. McCarthy wrote of Pasco's high qualifications — he was graduated third in his law school class at the University of Virginia and was a senior partner in a prestigious Richmond law firm — and his political and financial support of Eisenhower's presidential campaigns. At the bottom of the letter Eisenhower wrote: "Send to [General] Persons [assistant to the president] and Atty. Gen."[26] On March 21, 1960, however, Eisenhower nominated Oren R. Lewis for the position. Lewis was a Republican Party activist and had been a delegate to the Republican National Convention in 1952. That same day, Eisenhower wrote to McCarthy explaining why Pasco was not chosen:

> Frankly and privately, I had this situation very carefully weighed by the Justice Department, to which I look for primary recommendations on judgeships. Pasco, after a check with the State Bar, looked like a splendid appointment; but so did another person [Lewis] with whom conversations had proceeded quite a distance before your letter arrived.
>
> Informally, a check was made with Pasco through my own Staff channels. I found that he was evidently of a mixed mind about this, and definitely was not willing to make any sort of an open struggle for this appointment, whereas the other candidate [Lewis] was eagerly interested.
>
> Finally, weighing the two degrees of interest, weighing also the fact that both men were very well qualified, and measuring just a bit the fact that one of the candidates was avidly striving for the appointment while the other seemed interested but not greatly so, I concluded to select Pasco's competitor.[27]

Once, however, Eisenhower did actively try to place a personal and political friend on the bench, but he was unsuccessful. Edward F. Arn was governor of Kansas when Eisenhower first approached him about service on the federal judiciary. As Governor Arn recounted in his letter to Eisenhower of November 15, 1954: "As you departed Abilene last Thursday you suggested that I write you as to whether I would have a desire to serve the Federal Judiciary if and when such an opportunity may arise. . . . I must say . . . that I have had such a desire and ambition. . . . I would like very much to serve upon our Federal Court." Eisenhower immediately passed the note on to the attorney general: "Herewith a letter that was sent to me at my request. Will you please hold against the possibility that an appropriate vacancy at the District Judge level might arise? If it does, would you have the usual and exhaustive examination made of Governor Arn's qualifications. He seems to me like a very nice type or, of course, I would not be making this suggestion to you."[28]

Arn had once been attorney general of Kansas, had served as a justice on the Kansas Supreme Court, and was completing his second four-year term as governor. He was forty-eight years old at the time he was approached by Eisenhower. But there was no vacancy on the Kansas federal district bench until three years later, in 1957. Before that vacancy arose, however, the seat on the Tenth Circuit occupied by a Kansan came open, and Arn wrote to Eisenhower about filling that position. Eisenhower replied: "Of course from the personal viewpoint I feel a very strong interest in your candidacy, but I am sure you will understand that a number of States in the Tenth Circuit will undoubtedly lay claim to consideration in the selection of a man to fill this vacancy. . . . [The attorney general] knows of your interest in the vacancy and I assure you that the consideration he gives it will be both exhaustive and sympathetic."[29]

Several weeks later, Eisenhower met with Senator Gordon Allott, who pushed for Colorado's claim to the seat and the elevation of Colorado district judge Jean Sala Breitenstein. Colorado had been unrepresented on the Tenth Circuit since 1940. Republican senators from Wyoming and Utah, states also in the Tenth Circuit, endorsed Colorado's claim and Allott's candidate. So did the Republican national committeeman from New Mexico.[30] Judge Breitenstein was appointed to the Tenth Circuit.

In August 1957, Eisenhower was informed that there would be a vacancy on the federal district bench of Kansas, and he wrote to Acting Attorney General Rogers: "I would like to have Governor Arn seriously considered for this particular spot. I am assuming, of course, that his appointment would have the approval of the American Bar Association."[31]

But Arn did not receive the nomination. Apparently the Justice Department was not enthusiastic. (There is no mention in the presidential papers of the position taken by the ABA.) In a January 1958 letter, Eisenhower hinted to Arn that he would not likely be chosen: "The matter of filling the vacancy . . . is under serious consideration in the Department of Justice, and your application and recommendations are in the hands of the people involved. As I think you know, I must be guided by the Department in the final decision (which I understand may be detained, because of some details, for some time). Nonetheless, I am glad you brought this matter to my personal attention."[32]

The judgeship went to Arthur J. Stanley, Jr., a Kansas City lawyer who was five years older than Arn, with no judicial experience and much less political experience. But Stanley had a "well qualified" rating from the ABA. Presumably Arn did not. Had Eisenhower been insistent, he could have secured a judgeship for Arn.[i]

Why did Eisenhower have a tendency to be deferential in the selection process? Perhaps the answer lies in Eisenhower's uncertainty about the functioning of courts. He may also have been self-conscious about his unfamiliarity with law and so chose to defer to the "experts" in the Justice Department. At a private function, Eisenhower was once overheard expressing what was interpreted to have been anger over the decisions of the Supreme Court. This found its way into a newspaper story that was brought to the president's attention. He at once sent an apologetic letter to Chief Justice Warren:

> I have no doubt that in private conversation someone did hear me express amazement about one decision, but I have never even hinted at a feeling such as anger. To do so would imply not only that I knew the law but questioned motives. Neither of these things is true. So while resolving that even in private conversations I shall be more careful of my language, I do want you to know that if any such story appeared, it was a distortion.[33][j]

Furthermore, Eisenhower's deference to the Justice Department was consistent with his chain-of-command administrative style. He set the guiding principles for the selection of judges, and it was up to his people in the Justice Department to follow through. Bucking the department's recommendations would have been at odds with Eisenhower's management philosophy.

i. This is not to suggest that Eisenhower's suggestions were not heeded. A former administration official, who later was appointed to the Fifth Circuit, suggested that Eisenhower initiated the appointment of Charles E. Whittaker, of Kansas City, Missouri. Eisenhower's brother Arthur recommended Whittaker to the president. Interview with Judge Elbert Tuttle, July 14, 1964. Also see Henry J. Abraham, *Justices and Presidents,* 2d ed. (New York: Oxford, 1985), 266–67. This, then, is an atypical example of Eisenhower initiating a successful appointment. Whittaker was appointed to the district bench in 1954, elevated to the Eighth Circuit two years later, and one year after that was appointed to the Supreme Court where he served five years before resigning to return to private practice.

j. The decision that apparently exasperated Eisenhower was *Reid* v. *Covert,* 354 U.S. 1 (1957), in which the Court denied court-martial jurisdiction over American dependents of overseas military personnel who commit crimes on foreign soil. The Court ruled that civilians cannot be denied their due process rights, including trial by jury, even when trial by court-martial was provided for in an agreement with the foreign power (in this case, Japan). Eisenhower, as a former military man, no doubt had a special interest in this ruling.

The Policy Agenda and Selection

Just as with Truman, Eisenhower did not see judicial appointments as affecting the policy agenda of his administration. When Eisenhower had to fill a Supreme Court vacancy in 1958, he told his attorney general that he was interested in seriously considering only those whose views "reflect a middle-of-the-road political and governmental philosophy." This was also Eisenhower's goal in filling lower-court positions. In his memoirs, Eisenhower wrote that at the start of his presidency he instructed Attorney General Brownell to exclude from judicial appointments "candidates known to hold extreme legal or philosophical views."[34] This also meant that the administration checked out prospective appointees when there was concern that they might be too liberal.

When Democrat J. Joseph Smith, a federal district judge in Connecticut, was first under consideration by the Justice Department to fill a "Connecticut" seat on the Second Circuit, Deputy Attorney General Walsh asked Second Circuit judge Joseph E. Lumbard, Jr., to check out Smith. Lumbard made some discreet inquiries and reported back that "[Smith's] views are not those of CEC [Charles E. Clark, a noted liberal serving on the Second Circuit] and are quite different."[35] Smith received the appointment.

Occasionally letters from influential politicians to Justice Department officials referred to the policy outlook of candidates. One letter from a former senator and Eisenhower supporter to the attorney general on behalf of Clement F. Haynsworth, Jr., for a position on the Fourth Circuit noted that Haynsworth "is conservative in politics and one who would not have radical social theories that would influence his interpretations of the Constitution." Republican senator Ralph E. Flanders of Vermont wrote to Deputy Attorney General Rogers endorsing Sterry R. Waterman for a Second Circuit position. Flanders wrote that "[Waterman's] Republicanism is beyond reproach."[36] Both Haynsworth and Waterman were appointed.

An Eisenhower appointee to the Fifth Circuit who had close ties to Justice Department officials summed up his impressions of the administration's concern with the policy views of candidates. "There is no cataloguing of biases or prejudices taken by the Department of Justice," said Judge John Minor Wisdom. "Instead, what is of concern is whether the man is a qualified lawyer, knowledgeable, has community standing and judicial temperament. If a man has been a judge, the Justice Department will look at the man's judicial record as part of the screening process."[37]

There was one occasion that had the potential for changing Eisenhower's perception that the federal courts were not linked to his policy concerns. In a letter to Attorney General Rogers dated May 12, 1958, the president admitted to uncertainty about the role of the courts:

> I have a considerable curiosity concerning several phases of the arguments that now center around the functioning of the Supreme Court. In order to obtain specific information on some of the points bothering me, I wonder whether it would be possible for someone in your office to prepare me a succinct study — in layman's language — to guide my own thinking in certain of these matters.
>
> There are several things that I think would be helpful to me:
>
> (a). A very short summation of certain recent decisions of the Court that have attracted considerable editorial comment, and, from some quarters, some resentment. For example, the case denying the States the right to prosecute Communists; the Mallory case; . . . and other cases which do not come immediately to mind but I am sure that you well know which the more important ones are.
>
> (b). The arguments centering around the so-called "legislation" by the Court. Who determines whether the Court is legislating or whether it is merely making a decision and issuing the necessary orders therewith? . . .
>
> (c). What are the main purposes of the two pieces of legislation that have been introduced in the Congress and, in one case, report[ed] favorably out of a Senate Committee?
>
> (d). While I understand that you have reported adversely against these particular bills [the Justice Department formally opposed them], is there any necessity for any kind of additional legislation respecting the functioning of our Courts, especially the Supreme Court?
>
> (e). I believe that the Constitution accords to the Congress the right to pass certain laws affecting the Courts. Does this right extend to the passing of laws affecting the functioning of the Courts and the kinds of cases they may properly decide? I realize that the foregoing covers a lot of ground, but I repeat that what I need is a series of statements, rather than legal arguments. Seemingly I get more confused every time the Court delivers another opinion.[38]

Two weeks later, the attorney general responded in a seven-page, single-spaced letter that explained the functioning of the Supreme Court and the controversies to which the president alluded. The letter essentially defended the Court:

> You inquired about the decision denying the States the right to prosecute Communists (*Pennsylvania* v. *Nelson*). . . . The *Nelson* case does not hold that the states may not prosecute Communists. It merely holds that Congress did not make clear that it intended the states to prosecute Communists. . . . The case of *Mallory* v. *United States* concerned the use in federal criminal trials of confessions obtained from the accused. . . . The Supreme Court reversed the

conviction on the ground that the confession should not have been admitted into evidence since Mallory was not taken before a magistrate as the rule required "without unnecessary delay." . . . There are several bills before the Congress seeking to clarify the decision. The FBI has had no difficulty with the case and therefore we have taken no position on the legislation. . . .

Those who criti[ci]ze the Supreme Court on the ground that it is "legislating" usually mean that, in their view, the Justices are playing too expansive a role; that they are injecting too much personal philosophy into their decisions; and that they are thus determining what they think the law ought to be, instead of giving effect to the statutes enacted by Congress in the way Congress intended. Sometimes the complaint that judges are "legislating" is a careless charge made primarily because the critic does not find particular court decisions to his liking. In other instances, the criticism, though made sincerely and without bias, stems from a grossly over-simplified notion of "law."

The law in many areas is bound to lack certainty for words do not have fixed and unvarying meanings as applied to the million varied factual situations which arise. Constitutional phrases such as . . . "equal protection of the laws" and "due process of law" are broad and flexible, and they can be given specific meaning only as applied to concrete factual situations. The same is often true when courts are interpreting statutes. . . .

I opposed this bill taking away jurisdiction from the Supreme Court because it represents a retaliatory approach of the same general character as the court-packing plan of 1937 . . . and because this type of legislation threatens the independence of the Judiciary. . . . Our legal system requires one final arbiter. Only once — after the Civil War — has Congress limited the jurisdiction of the Court, and this was soon recognized as a mistake and corrected. . . .

The essential features of our constitutional form of government . . . have imposed special and heavy responsibilities upon the Supreme Court. . . . Many of the significant — and what today are regarded as some of the wisest and most profound — decisions of the Court were very unpopular at the time they were made. Of course, there have been many unwise decisions by the Court. . . . [But] despite errors made in particular decisions, [the overwhelming consensus of public opinion is that] the independence and integrity of the Court must be preserved. . . .[39]

Significantly, Rogers did not link changing the course of court decisions to the appointment process. Also, it appears that Brownell, Rogers, and other Justice Department officials were more liberal than the president, which would have made it awkward, to say the least, to use judicial selection as an engine of public policy. Officials were, however, alert to the policy views of candidates on issues of criminal procedure,[40] and there was also concern with candidates' views on racial segregation following the Supreme Court's desegregation rulings.

In the fall of 1958, New Jersey federal district court judge Philip Forman, a Republican, was being supported by various state politicians for promotion to the Third Circuit to replace a retiring judge, Albert B. Maris. White House aide Bernard M. Shanley, who came from New Jersey, wrote to the Justice Department endorsing Forman. Deputy Attorney General Walsh asked one of his assistants to examine Judge Forman's judicial record, particularly in criminal cases, and Walsh received the following reply:

> [Judge Forman's] decisions uniformly manifest respect for legal precedent, appreciation of the problems of law enforcement and awareness of the rights of the accused. There is nothing in his decisions that would indicate an anti-prosecution bias; where concern for the rights of individuals is shown, it is more than justified by the evidence he adduces in support of his decisions. . . . The five opinions which resulted in the dismissal of criminal charges all seem well grounded and do not indicate a predilection against the enforcement of any particular statute or class of statutes. . . . Nor do Judge Forman's dispositions of petitions for habeas corpus from accused or convicted criminals support a conclusion that he is reticent to enforce the criminal law. . . .
>
> Lastly it should be noted that Judge Forman most decidedly has not shown any anti-government bias in civil cases involving the government.[41]

Another Walsh assistant searched for any statement, speech, or action by Judge Forman that would indicate antipathy toward the federal government or any enforcement agency but could find nothing in the public record.[42] Forman was appointed but served less than two years before retiring.

The issue of racial segregation was a particularly troubling one for the administration after *Brown* v. *Board of Education*. Eisenhower privately expressed the view that "I personally think the decision was wrong." While president, he never publicly indicated approval (or disapproval) of *Brown* and went so far as to remove from a draft of the Republican Party platform in 1956 any reference to his administration's supporting the Supreme Court's decision.[43] On the other hand, Justice Department officials who had come from the Republican Party's eastern liberal wing were supportive of *Brown* and efforts to end segregation. Though Eisenhower disapproved of *Brown*, he nevertheless believed it was his duty to carry out the Court's rulings, and in this there was compatibility with the Justice Department.[k] The administration's southern appointments to the lower federal courts, however, took on special

---

k. In his memoirs, however, Eisenhower wrote that "there can be no question that the judgment of the Court was right." See Eisenhower, *Mandate for Change*, 230. But this was not Eisenhower's view during his presidency. See Ambrose, *Eisenhower: The President*, 190–92, 303–7, 327–28, 337–38, 498.

significance to the extent that compliance to *Brown* was considered by administration officials to be a policy-agenda item.

Eisenhower named twenty-four southerners to federal district court positions. Of these, nineteen were Republicans, and most of them had been party activists. Five Democrats were named, and three of them had been active Eisenhower Democrats. A study by Jack Peltason of how southern federal judges implemented *Brown* found only five Eisenhower appointees worthy of praise: Frank M. Johnson of Alabama (later elevated by Jimmy Carter to the Fifth Circuit), William A. Bootle of Georgia, William E. Miller of Tennessee (later elevated by Richard Nixon to the Sixth Circuit), Henry L. Brooks of Kentucky (also elevated by Nixon to the Sixth Circuit), and Walter E. Hoffman of Virginia. Peltason criticized five Eisenhower-appointed district judges for their pro-segregation rulings, including Harlan H. Grooms of Alabama, J. Smith Henley of Arkansas, Emmett C. Choate of Florida, Ben C. Dawkins, Jr., of Louisiana, and Joe E. Estes of Texas.[44] The nomination of Henley in 1958 illustrates the conflicting pressures on the Justice Department.

The Arkansas vacancy was of particular importance because of the national attention on Arkansas that had followed the drama at Central High School in Little Rock in September 1957, when Eisenhower called out federal troops to enforce the district court's desegregation order. Arkansas Democratic senator John L. McClellan, a segregationist, was reported to be backing a Democratic segregationist for the position. There was also some support for Richard Butler, who was attorney for the Little Rock School Board and who reportedly supported the attorney general's and the president's position on desegregation. But there was even greater support from Arkansas Republicans for the United States attorney in Little Rock, Osro Cobb, who represented the federal government in the clash with Arkansas governor Orval Faubus. Cobb had been Arkansas Republican state chairman and had served in the state House of Representatives. A letter from a Republican Little Rock attorney to the Republican National Committee pointed out that "great gains have been made in bringing Negro citizens back into the Republican party. If a segregationist Democrat is named district judge at Little Rock, it will destroy those gains and make it virtually impossible for the Republican party to win in 1960." Cobb, however, had been rated "not qualified" by the ABA in a preliminary report from ABA committee chairman Bernard G. Segal to the deputy attorney general.[45] But the ABA had based its rating on consultations with the legal establishment in Little Rock, which was not known for its sympathy for desegregation. The appointment eventually went to Republican J. Smith Henley, whose brother was the state chairman of the Arkansas Republican Party. Henley was serving in the Justice Department at the time of his appointment. He received a "qualified" rating from the ABA. (Henley was elevated to the Eighth Circuit in 1975 by President Gerald Ford).

The Eisenhower administration named eight men to the southern Fourth and Fifth Circuits. Only one of them, Benjamin F. Cameron, was an "ultra segregationist."[46] Cameron, from Mississippi, was rated "exceptionally well qualified" by the ABA. He was an active Republican and was sixty-four years old when appointed. A telegram from a labor leader in Mississippi, found in Cameron's Justice Department file, asserted that "he is trusted by all classes and races." That may not necessarily have been so; nevertheless, Cameron's political and professional credentials resulted in his appointment despite his favoring segregation. He was the "best" that the Justice Department could find to appoint from Mississippi.

On the other hand, the administration also named to the Fifth Circuit Elbert P. Tuttle, John R. Brown, and John Minor Wisdom, all three of whom became prominent supporters of desegregation. Tuttle had been general counsel for the Treasury Department and was well known to Justice Department officials. He had led the Republican Party in Georgia, was a known southern liberal, and had been an early Eisenhower supporter. He received an "exceptionally well qualified" rating from the ABA. Brown was a Republican activist in Texas and was an Eisenhower delegate to the Republican National Convention in 1952. He, too, was rated by the ABA "exceptionally well qualified." But there is no indication that Justice Department officials were aware of his liberal views. John Minor Wisdom, a Republican leader in Louisiana and an early Eisenhower supporter, was rated "well qualified." He was the Republican national committeeman from Louisiana and worked with the administration in dispensing patronage in his state. In an interview he characterized himself as "a liberal Republican," and his record on the Fifth Circuit certainly reflected his liberalism.[47l]

Attorney General Rogers revealed in an interview that the Justice Department checked out prospective candidates for southern judgeships to make sure that they were not members of "rabid segregationist organizations" nor had made outrageous racist statements. For example, when Warren L. Jones of Florida was being considered for a position on the Fifth Circuit, Attorney General Brownell approached Fifth Circuit judge Elbert Tuttle at a dinner and

l. Judges Wisdom, Tuttle, and Brown were members of the liberal bloc on the Fifth Circuit. See Sheldon Goldman, "Conflict and Consensus in the United States Courts of Appeals," *Wisconsin Law Review* (1968): 466–72, and "Conflict on the U.S. Courts of Appeals 1965–1971: A Quantitative Analysis," *University of Cincinnati Law Review* 42 (1973): 648, 650.

asked if he would check on Jones. Tuttle wrote back to Brownell: "I have made inquiries of members of the Jacksonville bar in as discreet a manner as possible, and of people in Jacksonville with whom I have close personal relationships but who are not lawyers."[48] Tuttle heard good reports, and Jones was subsequently appointed.[m] Jones received the "exceptionally well qualified" rating from the ABA.

Just how touchy race was for Eisenhower's southern judicial appointments is illustrated by the nomination in 1956 of Solicitor General Simon Sobeloff, a supporter of the *Brown* decision, to the Fourth Circuit. Sobeloff, a resident of Maryland, was to take a seat to which South Carolina laid claim. In a letter to the president, former South Carolina governor James F. Byrnes,[n] an Eisenhower Democrat, urged the appointment of someone from his state. Byrnes further asserted that Warren Burger, then a Justice Department official, had told a mutual friend of Byrnes and Eisenhower "that no lawyer would be appointed who had participated in any way in the effort to continue segregated schools." Byrnes continued, "I hope this statement is not correct." And he argued that it would be wrong to disqualify from judicial office those who supported the Constitution as it had been interpreted until *Brown*. The president answered Byrnes immediately and sent a copy of the letter to the Justice Department. Attorney General Brownell telephoned Byrnes and assured him that Warren Burger had not made such a statement and that in any event its sentiments did not reflect the view of the attorney general or the president.[49] The next appointment to the Fourth Circuit went to Eisenhower Democrat Clement Haynsworth of South Carolina, who in 1969 would be nominated by Richard Nixon for an associate justiceship on the Supreme Court only to be rejected by the Senate.

Justice Department files for thirty-eight of the forty-five appointees to appeals courts,[50] as well as documents from the presidential papers on all forty-five, suggest that policy-agenda considerations were prominent in only five instances (11.1 percent). There were no personal-agenda appointments. Forty (88.9 percent) were primarily partisan-agenda appointments. No doubt Justice Department officials were familiar with the views of appointees who had

m. Jones also proved to be an "inconsistent" supporter of desegregation, according to the editors of the *Yale Law Journal* in their study "Judicial Performance in the Fifth Circuit," *Yale Law Journal* 73 (1963): 121n156.

n. Byrnes had served on the U.S. Supreme Court during 1941–1942, resigning to become a high-level assistant to Roosevelt in managing domestic affairs during the Second World War. He later served as Truman's secretary of state before returning to South Carolina politics.

served or were serving in the administration at the time of appointment. And of course administration officials were aware of the southern appointees' views on segregation. Yet the clear domination of the partisan agenda over the policy agenda° is consistent with expectations, if we assume that the elections of 1952 and 1956 were not realigning elections.

Senators and Selection

Roosevelt was willing to do business with senators and other party leaders and even name some members of Congress to the judiciary. But Roosevelt also had his eye on his policy agenda. Truman also negotiated with senators but on a few occasions he insisted on naming his own choices, disregarding those of Democratic senators. Eisenhower, however, delegated authority to the Justice Department; and although on occasion he personally met with Republican senators, there is no evidence that he did more than listen to them.

There is no record of Eisenhower's negotiating with senators or other party leaders over judgeships. General Wilton B. Persons, Eisenhower's White House aide and liaison to Congress, as well as Sherman Adams, and other White House staff would run interference with senators so as to insulate the president from political pressures. One former Justice Department official (later appointed by Eisenhower to the circuit bench) said of Eisenhower in an interview, "He wasn't a politician." Perhaps a more accurate representation of Eisenhower is that while he was a very successful politician in many senses of that term he was not as skilled as Roosevelt and Truman in negotiating with senators and party leaders over judgeships. Nonetheless, the evidence suggests that the Justice Department was the locus of dealings with members of Congress, and it appears that William Rogers and Lawrence Walsh were willing at times to stand their ground.[51] Of course, Rogers and Walsh would consider recommendations from the senators and from other party people. If none of

---

o. A number of appointees on both the district and appeals court benches strongly backed by the administration were thought to be of superior quality professionally. Appointment of high-quality judges *was* good politics, enhancing the administration's reputation and thus in the broadest sense serving the partisan agenda. Eisenhower himself had suggested as much when he said that he thought it "most important for the Republican Party that they get the best men to fill all vacancies, especially in the Judicial Branch." Memorandum for Mrs. Ann C. Whitman from I. Jack Martin, July 7, 1954, Ann Whitman Diary Series, July 1954 (5). This does not suggest that the president or Justice Department officials were cynical. On the contrary, administration officials were undoubtedly sincere in their efforts to appoint those they believed were the best possible persons within understood political parameters.

the recommendations met the standards set by the Justice Department, officials there would then take the initiative to find a suitable candidate. In their dealings with members of Congress they were sometimes successful, sometimes not.

In the early months of the Eisenhower administration, there was a vacancy to be filled in the state of Washington. Both Washington senators were Democrats, so the Justice Department could bypass them and consult with the Republican governor and the state's Republican congressional delegation. The governor recommended George H. Boldt, who had once successfully handled legal challenges to his first election. The Republican members of Congress were backing a colleague, Representative Thor Tollefson. Justice Department officials determined that Boldt was the superior candidate, and accordingly Attorney General Brownell recommended him. A White House staffer briefed General Persons that the six Republican members of the state's congressional delegation opposed Boldt and that if the name were sent to the Senate, the two Democratic senators "will object and they will be joined by a Republican Senator on the Judiciary Committee who has agreed to fight Boldt."[52] The administration, however, stood firm, and the Republican-controlled Senate confirmed Boldt.

In 1956, Justice Department officials determined that Frederick van Pelt Bryan should fill a vacancy on the bench of the Southern District of New York. Bryan was highly qualified professionally and in 1952 had been chairman of the New York State Eisenhower clubs. He was not, however, backed by Republican senator Irving M. Ives (the other New York senator was a Democrat). When the nomination was at the White House a cover memorandum noted: "Although Senator Ives has no personal objection to Bryan, he does not wish to go on record as having endorsed him. At the request of Governor [Sherman] Adams we are going ahead on this basis."[53]

In 1957, Justice Department officials were considering filling a Second Circuit post and had to contend with a strong campaign to elevate federal district judge Irving R. Kaufman, a Democrat. Republican senator Jacob Javits, elected in 1956, endorsed Kaufman, but Justice Department officials decided on Republican Leonard P. Moore, who had the backing of New York's senior Republican senator. Administration officials held firm but did talk with Javits, who agreed not to object to Moore. The president did not get personally involved.[54]

Another example of the Justice Department's persistence but also willingness to compromise was the nomination of Francis Van Dusen to a seat on the federal district bench in Pennsylvania (discussed earlier). Ultimately the Justice Department had to settle for a package deal that included a nominee rated "not qualified" by the ABA. But more typically the department used a negative ABA rating as the coup de grace to a nomination they wanted to scuttle. For example, in 1957 the two Republican senators from Maine backed different candidates to fill a federal district judgeship.[55] Both candidates were rated "not qualified" by the ABA. Deputy Attorney General Rogers persuaded the senators to send more names, which they did. One of them, Edward T. Gignoux, received a "well qualified" rating. Gignoux received the appointment.

Illinois senator Everett Dirksen, a Republican leader in the Senate during Eisenhower's second term, could be an obstacle to Justice Department officials because he supported Republican senatorial prerogatives in the selection process. For example, when Henry J. Friendly, a distinguished New York lawyer, was nominated for a position on the Second Circuit in 1959 in the face of another campaign to elevate Judge Kaufman, Senator Dirksen (then the minority leader) withheld his approval because New York's Republican senators had not been asked for *their* approval. Although the Friendly nomination was held up in the Senate for several months, Friendly was so clearly an outstanding nominee and the organized bar so strongly backed him that he was eventually confirmed. Also at about this time, the Justice Department recommended John R. Bartels, a Brooklyn lawyer, for a federal district judgeship in the Eastern District of New York. An internal memo in the White House noted: "Senator Dirksen withholds approval because the New York Senators have not as yet given their approval. Senator Dirksen reports that both Senators Javits and Keating say that to date the [Republican] New York State Committee has not approved the nomination of John Bartels and they are withholding their approval until action by the State Committee."[56] The White House staff held up the nomination for about five weeks until the necessary political clearances came through, and then the nomination was sent to the Senate.

Once, Senator Dirksen was able to kill a nomination that the attorney general had sent to the White House. In 1960, the Justice Department recommended Democrat Jon Wiig of Hawaii to fill a new lifetime position on the federal district court in that state. (Hawaii had become a state in August 1959.) Dirksen, however, opposed Wiig because Republican senator Hiram Fong did not approve. In an internal White House memorandum there is the notation: "Dirksen says do not send up."[57] The nomination was never sent.

The power of the Senate was dramatically demonstrated to the Eisenhower administration in 1959. Lyndon B. Johnson, the Senate majority leader (Democrats had regained control of Congress in the 1954 elections), felt he was entitled to name at least one judge for the federal district bench in Texas. His candidate for a vacancy was Joe J. Fisher, who was closely associated politically with Johnson and who since 1956 had been serving as a state judge. The Justice Department ignored Johnson and recommended John G. Tucker, who was rated "exceptionally well qualified" by the ABA. Johnson retaliated by putting a halt to consideration of *all* judicial nominations by the Senate. In the interim, Tucker asked the administration to withdraw his nomination because of the delay. The Texas Republican state committee recommended another individual, but the ABA committee "declined to submit a favorable report"[58] and the Justice Department decided to face reality. Attorney General Rogers, in his letter to the president accompanying the formal nomination papers for Fisher, wrote: "The Committee on Federal Judiciary of the American Bar Association has submitted a favorable report in Judge Fisher's behalf. He bears a satisfactory reputation as to character and integrity. Although there is a division of opinion as to his professional qualifications it is believed that he will be able to perform the duties of his office — and in view of the position of the Senate Majority Leader his nomination is the only alternative to a long continuing vacancy in this district."[59]

What Rogers undoubtedly knew was that Fisher was the only alternative to stalemate of all judicial nominations. Fisher's nomination was sent to the Senate on September 7 and approved by the Senate Judiciary Committee the next day. On September 9 Fisher and twelve other judicial nominees were confirmed by the full Senate, and the bottleneck was broken. Fisher's nomination was sent to the Senate and confirmed within three days![p]

Other Considerations in the Appointment Process

PARTY ORGANIZATIONS

Republican state party organizations played some role in the selection process in the Eisenhower years. When both senators were Democrats, those recommended by the state party would have the inside track, provided they met Justice Department and ABA standards. In 1959, Sixth Circuit judge Florence E. Allen, who occupied an Ohio seat, retired. To replace the only woman on the circuit bench, Clarence J. Brown, who was a member of Congress as well as Republican national committeeman from Ohio and chairman of the Ohio Republican patronage committee, recommended that U.S. District

p. White House officials sought to control damage among Texas Republicans. White House counsel David W. Kendall sent a telegram to Texas Republican leader H. J. Porter (the Republican national committeeman from Texas): "Nomination Joe J. Fisher Eastern District sent up today. Tried reaching you by telephone. Only possible solution as I believe Morton [chairman of the Republican National Committee] has advised you but have appreciated interest and concern." GF 4 d Texas.

Judge Paul C. Weick (appointed by Eisenhower three years earlier) be promoted to the Sixth Circuit. To replace Weick on the bench, the patronage committee recommended common pleas court judge Girard Edward Kalbfleisch.[60] The ABA rated Weick "well qualified" and Kalbfleisch "exceptionally well qualified." Both men were appointed.

When a state's senators were Democrats and the state party was split, the Justice Department had more leeway. The Rhode Island Republican state committee was badly split over whom to recommend to fill a federal district judgeship. The committee voted 12 to 9 to recommend the Republican Rhode Island national committeeman. But one of the dissenters telephoned White House special counsel Bernard M. Shanley and emphatically stated that the person recommended "is neither qualified by character or legal experience for the post."[61] The person recommended by the state committee did not receive the judgeship.

In the south, which had no Republican senators in the 1950s, Republican Party organization leaders exerted influence, as did Democratic party officeholders who were Democrats for Eisenhower. In a 1953 memorandum to Sherman Adams, Bernard Shanley noted: "I talked with John [Minor] Wisdom today relative to the appointment of the Federal District Court Judges in Louisiana. Wisdom is to receive the appointment of Mr. Dawkins and Governor Kennon [an Eisenhower Democrat] is to receive the appointment of Mr. Nackmann. Wisdom indicated that Governor Kennon will be very unhappy over the former appointment. He told me that the Governor had told him that you had committed yourself to the appointment of both of Governor Kennon's candidates."[62] John Minor Wisdom was the Republican national committeeman from Louisiana and had handled patronage until 1957, when he was appointed to the Fifth Circuit.[63] Governor Robert F. Kennon's choice did not receive a federal district judgeship, but Ben C. Dawkins, Jr., did.[q] And Sherman Adams appears, at least at the outset of the Eisenhower administration, to have wheeled and dealed judgeships, perhaps prompting the directive quoted earlier in this chapter from Eisenhower to let the Justice Department handle judicial appointments.

Eisenhower wanted the Republican National Committee to clear judicial nominees, but there is no evidence that the national committee or its chairman played the kind of active role that the chairman of the Democratic National Committee had during the Truman administration. However, evidence sug-

---

q. Dawkins, an active Eisenhower Democrat, was characterized by Jack Peltason as "among the more ardent segregationists serving on the federal bench." *Fifty-eight Lonely Men,* 133.

gests that the national committee may have carried more weight than an individual state committee. On a paper accompanying the nomination of Walter H. Hodge, a sixty-three-year-old justice on the Alaska Supreme Court, to fill a new lifetime position on the federal district bench of Alaska, there was the notation: "Reluctantly cleared by Chairman Morton. *Not* cleared by the Republican Party of Alaska." On the other hand, there was the appointment to the federal district bench in Wisconsin of Kenneth P. Grubb, which was not cleared by the Republican National Committee but was approved by the state's Republican senators.[64]

STATE REPRESENTATION

At the circuit court level, party leaders and senators expect that their state will be represented on the bench by a citizen of that state. Larger states feel entitled to more than one seat on their circuit. Smaller states in circuits in which there are not enough seats to go around expect that they will have a turn at representation.

Typically, when a state's only member on the appeals court retires or dies, the senators of the president's party are quick to reclaim that position. For example, Vermont senator Ralph E. Flanders wrote to the deputy attorney general: "I assume that the position made vacant by Judge [Harrie B.] Chase's retirement will be filled by a Vermont appointment. . . . I might also say that I have received indications from many of the Vermont lawyers who are anxious that Vermont continues to be represented on the second circuit court of appeals."[65] A Vermonter, Sterry R. Waterman, was appointed.

Among senators and leaders of both parties there is a sense of entitlement to representation on the circuit courts. When there was a vacancy on the Eighth Circuit, Democratic senators from Arkansas and Missouri argued that the late judge Caskie Collet, who came from Missouri, should be replaced by someone from Missouri. Arkansas senator John McClellan recognized that the majority of the circuit's business originated in Missouri, and Missouri senator Tom Hennings threatened to delay consideration of a nominee from any other state. Hennings championed the elevation of Republican U.S. District Judge Charles Whittaker, whose promotion was actually initiated by Attorney General Brownell.[66] Whittaker was promoted in 1956 and one year later was elevated to the Supreme Court.

When Justice Department officials could not find a candidate who met their standards and also received the necessary political clearance, they were prepared to bypass that state for appointment. With no legal requirement of state representation on appeals courts, senatorial courtesy cannot be readily invoked solely on the ground that the nominee is a citizen of a different state.

However, the political firestorm likely to arise in the bypassed state is something no administration would relish provoking. For example, a seat on the Ninth Circuit came open by the retirement of William Healy on November 30, 1958. Healy had been appointed from Idaho, and Idaho politicians, including Republican senator Henry C. Dworshak, recommended eight men, all of whom were unsatisfactory to Justice Department officials. An internal Justice Department working paper listed all eight candidates and their drawbacks. One, who was sixty-two years old and a state judge, had after his name: "Informal Bar check shows him to be mediocre and, therefore, out on account of age." Another, a federal district court judge, was the subject of informal checks with Ninth Circuit judges, who said he "is a well meaning but unskilled judge. This is borne out by other comments by members of the Bar." Still another: "Lacks judicial temperament." For one candidate the comment was, "Conflicting reports as to legal ability." Others were ruled out on account of age.

The memo noted that there were excellent possible appointments from other states in the circuit. For Nevada, the memo referred to Charles M. Merrill, chief justice of the Nevada Supreme Court: "Informal check by the [American] Bar Association group indicates that he would be reported 'exceptionally well qualified.' At present, Nevada, like Idaho, has no judge on the Court of Appeals. Unfortunately, Nevada does not have a Republican senator."[67]

The Justice Department wanted to go with Merrill, but Idaho senator Dworshak and Idaho Republicans were resisting. For months, the Merrill nomination languished in the Justice Department. Meanwhile, the Idaho Bar Association stepped into the picture and recommended state district judge M. Oliver Koelsch. The association conducted a campaign to generate support for Koelsch, who until then was not known to Justice Department officials. At that moment of stalemate, fate intervened, when Ninth Circuit judge James Alger Fee of Oregon died. Two days later, Merrill's nomination was sent to the Senate to fill the Idaho seat. And about two weeks after that, Koelsch was nominated to fill the Oregon seat after the ABA cleared him with a "well qualified" rating.[68] Both men were confirmed. These were the last Eisenhower appointments to the Ninth Circuit.

THE AMERICAN BAR ASSOCIATION

During the Eisenhower administration the American Bar Association Standing Committee on Federal Judiciary came to play an institutionalized role in the selection process. This role had been worked out in the last months of the Truman administration, but there had been no occasion in which to implement it.[69] The original architect of the arrangement whereby the committee would be asked its views on leading candidates for specific judicial nominations was Ross Malone, a member of the ABA Board of Governors, who had become deputy attorney general in August 1952. After Eisenhower won the election, Malone met with Brownell and Rogers, who would soon be taking over the Justice Department, and briefed them on what had been agreed. Brownell and Rogers were willing to implement the arrangement, although they insisted that the committee not promote its own candidates.

It was not until June 1956, however, that the ABA ratings were included in the letter transmitting the nomination to the president. This came about after Eisenhower specifically asked for the committee's recommendation concerning a nomination sent to him. As White House assistant Robert Gray then related, "I talked with Bill Rogers. . . . He sees no objection to the reference [to the committee rating] in future correspondence."[70]

The ABA committee had a good working relationship with the Justice Department. In practice this meant that the deputy attorney general and the chairman of the committee were in frequent contact, usually by telephone. In 1956, Bernard Segal became chairman, and he served in that capacity for six years. In 1957, Lawrence Walsh became deputy attorney general, and by Walsh's own account they developed an exceptionally close association. Speaking before the House of Delegates of the ABA in 1959, Walsh stated, referring to Segal, "Your chairman has become, next to the Attorney General himself, I think, my most intimate associate in Washington. I work with him and spend more time with him than anybody else in the Department."[71]

In his memoirs Eisenhower wrote that at the outset of his administration he told the attorney general that "I would appoint no one who did not have the approval of the American Bar Association." But in fact there were exceptions. During Eisenhower's first term, seven out of ninety-four appointments (about 7.5 percent) received the "not qualified" rating, and some others went unrated. In February 1953, the committee report on Elmer J. Schnackenberg, a candidate for the Seventh Circuit, noted that "he was qualified by training and experience but because of age and a demonstrated lack of judicial temperament he should not be appointed." The Chicago Bar Association, however, was willing to go along with the nomination, and despite Schnackenberg's age (sixty-four) his name was sent to the Senate. Given the position of the Chicago Bar Association, the committee decided not to oppose Schnackenberg actively.[72]

Some Eisenhower nominees were rated "not qualified because of age." In one instance, the nomination of Edwin R. Hicklin to the federal district bench in Iowa, the committee also based its opposition on the nominee's health. The administration, however, ignored the ABA. Hicklin went on the bench and within two years suffered a disabling stroke. He retired from office shortly thereafter. In other instances, those rated "not qualified" in terms of their professional qualifications received appointments. None of these, however, occurred during the tenure of Lawrence Walsh as deputy attorney general.

For the most part, the Eisenhower Justice Department took the committee ratings seriously and eliminated numerous candidates for judgeships because of adverse committee reports. Committee chairman Segal worked with Walsh behind the scenes to promote the candidacies of persons they thought to be of high quality. One example is the appointment of Harry A. Blackmun to the Eighth Circuit.

A vacancy on the Eighth was created by the retirement in 1959 of Judge John B. Sanborn of Minnesota. The Justice Department determined that the position would be filled by someone from Minnesota, whose senators were both Democrats. Five men were under consideration. An internal Justice Department memo indicated that four people were consulted as to their views: Judge Sanborn, District of Columbia Circuit Judge Warren Burger (the future Chief Justice of the Supreme Court and former Justice Department official who came from Minnesota), Minnesota Republican congressman Walter Judd, and former Minnesota Republican senator Edward Thye. Heading the list was Harry A. Blackmun. He was fifty years old, general counsel of the Mayo Clinic, and was "said to be brilliant student, lawyer and teacher. Recommended by Judge Sanborn, Judge Burger. Satisfactory to Congressman Judd. Former Senator Thye says 'best you've got.' "[73]

Another candidate was U.S. District Judge Edward J. Devitt, who had been appointed by Eisenhower in late 1954. Devitt was a former member of Congress and had backing from Republican Party leaders. "Well liked — not scholarly," was the comment. The memorandum indicated that all four advisers approved of Devitt, but Sanborn, Burger, and Thye preferred Blackmun.

A third candidate was Oscar T. Knutson, who was a justice on the Minnesota Supreme Court — "said to be ablest State Justice." Sanborn, Burger, and Judd found him acceptable, but not Thye. A fourth candidate, found satisfactory by all four, was a state district court judge, but the memo reported that Burger said "he is fine but not in a class with Blackmun." The fifth candidate was a former secretary to Senator Thye and was recommended only by him.[74]

Blackmun had not been politically active. Devitt, on the other hand, seemed to have the most political support. The ABA committee gave Blackmun a tentative rating of "well qualified." Walsh determined that Blackmun was the superior candidate and so informed committee chairman Segal, who responded in a handwritten memo: "I am hopeful I can raise him to an 'exceptionally well qualified' status." Segal subsequently sent a letter to a member of the committee, a copy of which he sent to Walsh. In the letter Segal suggested that Blackmun be accorded the highest ABA rating, giving as justification that the ABA should encourage this type of nomination. Segal noted that Blackmun had not been active in the party and that since there was so much politicking over the judgeship, the top man should receive the top rating.[75]

Blackmun's nomination was sent to the Senate in August 1959, provoking opposition from Republican Party activists in Minnesota. Democratic senator Eugene McCarthy told Walsh that pressure on behalf of Blackmun would be helpful, and Walsh enlisted Segal's aid. In a letter to Walsh, Segal reported that he had spoken with the editor of a leading Minneapolis newspaper, who was "most cooperative, showed a keen appreciation of the problem, demonstrated a willingness to be guided as to what should appear in the editorial." Segal informed Blackmun that he had spoken with more than a dozen individuals in Minnesota "in the all-out-effort to blast your nomination loose and to have the Senate act on it." He noted that those who responded enthusiastically "included lawyers, bankers, newspaper editors, and businessmen." Segal also credited Walsh, "who led the battle, alerted me to the need for immediate action, and never relinquished his effort until the desired result was achieved."[76]

Reform of the judicial selection process was high on the agenda of the ABA. On August 26, 1958, the ABA's House of Delegates adopted a resolution urging that "judicial appointments should be completely removed from the area of political patronage and made only from those lawyers and judges, irrespective of party affiliation and political consideration, who possess the highest qualifications." Toward that end the resolution pressed the establishment of "an independent commission established as an agency of the President, to advise with the President on appointments, and to receive from outside sources and from all segments of the organized Bar, suggestions of names of persons deemed highly qualified for appointment as judges in their respective jurisdictions." The resolution further recommended that "to make the courts truly non-partisan or bi-partisan, . . . a substantial percentage of the members of any Federal Court should be from the ranks of a party other than that of the President."

The resolution, along with a brief justifying the recommendations, were sent to Eisenhower in 1959. Rogers wrote to the president that the commission concept "is unrealistic and of no practical value." But Rogers did agree with the ABA and Eisenhower "that a serious effort should be made to effectuate an agreement between the two major parties to prevent a partisan imbalance from occurring in the federal judiciary." The commission concept, however, did not die; it was adopted by President Jimmy Carter eighteen years later. The concept of bipartisan appointments, on the other hand, was promoted by the Eisenhower administration as an incentive for the Democratic Congress to enact a new judgeships bill. On August 27, 1959, Rogers promised that if Congress created new judgeships, half of the new positions would be filled by Democrats. But Congress moved slowly, and on May 30, 1960, Rogers added another incentive to enacting a bill — that not only would half of any new appointments go to Democrats, but the judgeships would go only to Democrats approved by the Democratic leaders of Congress.[77][r] The new judgeships bill was enacted in 1961, after Eisenhower had left office — a Democratic Congress's gift to a new Democratic president of seventy-three new judgeships.[s] The ABA attempt to change the selection process may have come too late in the Eisenhower presidency to have been effective.

Women and Judgeships

Stephen Ambrose, in his comprehensive biography, writes that Eisenhower "had no women as close friends, had never worked with any woman on a regular or equal basis, and had sharply limited ideas on what women were capable of accomplishing." A record of a briefing of the president before a press conference on April 25, 1956, contains the following revealing item: "*Equal rights for women* came up, but nobody seemed to know exactly what was meant. Jack Martin [White House aide] thought it was that state laws were different in different states as far as working time and conditions for women were concerned."[78] The president and his men had not a clue about women's rights.

Although Eisenhower had a woman in his cabinet (Oveta Culp Hobby, secretary of health, education, and welfare), there is no evidence that at any time during his administration he or the top Justice Department officials seriously considered a woman for a lifetime federal judgeship on a court of general jurisdiction. Unlike Roosevelt and Truman, who responded positively to the pressure for a token appointment of a woman to a major constitutional court, the best Eisenhower and his men could do was one appointment to the Customs Court.

r. Richard Nixon, as the Republican presidential candidate in 1960, committed himself to appointing equal numbers of judges from the two major parties. John F. Kennedy, during the campaign, while not accepting the concept of bipartisan appointments, nevertheless urged less stress on party affiliation in making appointments. *New York Times,* August 31, 1960, p. 14.

s. Kennedy primarily appointed Democrats. When Nixon was elected in 1968, he rejected the concept of bipartisan appointments.

Eisenhower and Justice officials spoke and wrote of appointing *men* to judicial office. Rogers wrote in a letter, "The President is dedicated to the proposition that appointments to the federal courts should be limited to *men* of the highest qualifications." Eisenhower wrote to the president of the ABA in 1954 of his "desire to select *men* of the highest efficiency, ability and integrity for our bench and law-enforcement agencies."[79]

Despite this lack of receptivity to appointing women as federal judges, there were occasionally some women candidates whose names wound up in Justice Department or White House files. Sometimes these women had the backing of important political figures. In 1954, the governor of Oklahoma recommended Nellie S. Hayse for a federal district judgeship in Kentucky. A file was started on her — not under her own name, but as "Mrs. Joseph M. Hayse." The dean of her law school sent Eisenhower a transcript of her "outstanding record."[80] But aside from starting a file on her, there is no evidence that she was seriously considered by the Justice Department.

In 1956, Illinois representative Sid Simpson and others recommended Lillian E. Schlagenhauf for a district judgeship. Schlagenhauf was a Republican state senator, had received her law degree from the University of Illinois, and for eight years had been an assistant attorney general in the Illinois attorney general's office. Her candidacy went nowhere. The same fate awaited Helen Munsert, who was recommended by the Alliance of Business and Professional Women of Chicago and in support of whom a number of letters had been sent. Robert Gray, a White House special assistant, sent a memo to Clive Palmer, special assistant to the deputy attorney general, noting: "The President has received 66 letters from various branches of the Illinois Federation of Business and Professional Womens' Clubs suggesting that a woman be appointed to the United States District Court for the Northern District of Illinois."[81] The administration went ahead and named men to fill two vacancies.

In 1954, the president of the Westchester Women's Bar Association wrote to Eisenhower urging the appointment of a woman to one of the New York vacancies on the federal district bench. The Joint Committee of Women's Bar Associations sent a letter recommending two women (Mary H. Donlon and Ruth Kessler Toch) for a vacancy in the Southern District of New York, but they received no serious consideration.[82]

The only woman on the circuit bench, Florence Allen, retired in 1959, and no effort was made to search for a suitable woman to replace her. (Paul C. Weick was promoted from the district bench to fill the slot.) The only other woman candidate for a circuit position was a state judge, Leonore Underwood, who was recommended to the administration to fill a Ninth Circuit slot. Again, nothing happened.[83]

Although Mary Donlon had been passed over for a federal district judge-ship, despite the recommendation of the New York county Republican com-mittee,[84] the administration did pick her for a less important judgeship on the U.S. Customs Court. Donlon was a member of the New York State Republi-can executive committee, former chair of the New York State Workmen's Compensation Board, and a successful lawyer. The vacancy Donlon filled was created by the retirement of the first woman on the federal bench, Judge Genevieve Cline. Donlon's confirmation went smoothly, and on August 10, 1955, she took the oath of office. Fifth Circuit judge Elbert Tuttle, a classmate of Donlon's at Cornell Law School, came up from Atlanta to administer the oath. Donlon was the fourth woman in the history of the United States to occupy a lifetime federal judgeship.

The attitudes towards women on the bench held by Eisenhower and the top Justice Department officials were shared by much of the organized bar and the American public.[t] Moreover, women seemed to have less clout within the Republican president's party than they had had with the Democrats under Roosevelt and Truman. Thus Eisenhower was able to finish his eight years in office having made only one token appointment of a woman to a lifetime federal judgeship — to a court less prestigious than that to which his two pre-decessors had named token women.

African Americans and Judgeships

The civil rights revolution of the 1950s was spurred on by the historic Supreme Court decision in *Brown* v. *Board of Education* in 1954. The Eisen-hower administration was responsible for the first civil rights acts since 1875 — the acts of 1957 and 1960. Although these acts pale besides the historic Civil Rights Act of 1964, they were important at least symbolically. The rights of African Americans were now on the front burner of American politics.

Given these developments, it would be reasonable to expect that the admin-istration would have made an effort to place at least one black on a federal court. In an interview with Eisenhower in 1964, the political scientist Harold Chase asked about the appointment of blacks to the courts. According to Chase, Eisenhower responded "by saying that as president he instructed those about him to seek the appointment of the very best people without regard to

t. Stories about the appointment of Mary Donlon to the Customs Court appeared on the woman's page in the *New York Times,* along with fashion news and engagement announcements. See *New York Times,* May 27, 1955, p. 27, and *New York Times,* July 29, 1955, p. 10.

religion, the national background of their forebears, or their color, and that he never urged that they seek someone for appointment on that basis either."[85] Clearly, affirmative action was an unknown concept. In at least one instance, however, it appears that the Justice Department actively sought to place an African American on a federal district court.

On July 13, 1956, Attorney General Brownell, apparently at his own initiative, sent a memorandum to Sherman Adams:

> I would like to recommend to the President the appointment of Honorable Scovel Richardson as United States District Judge for the Eastern District of Missouri (St. Louis). If the President approves I will get up the formal papers of recommendation so that the nomination may go forward to the Senate early next week.
>
> You will remember that the President appointed Scovel Richardson in 1953 as Chairman of the Parole Board and he was the first Negro to hold that high office, and has served very acceptably. In private life he was a practicing attorney and dean of a Negro law school in St. Louis. His reappointment to the Parole Board by the President was confirmed by the Senate during the past few days.[86][u]

Richardson did not get the judgeship. As reported in the *St. Louis Globe-Democrat* some months later, although Brownell was prepared to recommend Richardson's appointment, overwhelming opposition from the Missouri Republican Party and others resulted in an administration retreat. Many racist letters opposing the appointment were sent to the White House and the Justice Department.[87] Although the administration backed down, in early 1957 Richardson was named to a lifetime position on the U.S. Customs Court. No African American, however, was appointed by Eisenhower to a lifetime position on a federal court of general jurisdiction.

Blacks were candidates for several federal judgeships and some had important political endorsements. For example, Republican senator John Sherman Cooper wrote to Eisenhower recommending "one of the outstanding negro attorneys in Kentucky and the south," Charles W. Anderson, Jr., of Louisville. Anderson had served as an assistant commonwealth attorney in Louisville and also as a member of the Kentucky House of Representatives. Senator Cooper lauded Anderson as "an outstanding man in every way" and recommended

u. Richardson received his B.A. degree from the University of Illinois and his law degree from Howard University. He was dean of the School of Law of Lincoln University in St. Louis when he was picked to be chairman of the United States Board of Parole. Richardson was a Republican and had been active in Eisenhower's 1952 campaign. He was the first black lawyer in Missouri to be admitted to the American Bar Association. See *New York Times,* October 5, 1956, p. 8, and March 5, 1957, p. 1.

"his appointment to a judicial position in the Government, such as the Court of Claims or the Court of Customs and Patent Appeals."[88] But Cooper had not recommended Anderson for the federal district bench in Kentucky when there had been a vacancy four years earlier. Anderson was not appointed to the federal courts Cooper mentioned in his letter.

The Ohio Republican patronage committee favored Chester K. Gillespie "for a possible appointment to the U.S. Court of Claims or to any other Federal Court position in the District of Columbia." The writer of the letter, Representative Clarence J. Brown, was chairman of the committee and also a member of the Republican National Committee. He praised Gillespie as "one of the outstanding colored leaders and Republicans of Ohio . . . [who] has served his city and state in many capacities and is exceptionally well qualified for a judicial appointment."[89] Just as Cooper did, Brown was in effect recommending a qualified African American for a judicial appointment any place but here. Nothing came of Gillespie's candidacy.

Those with much less political clout on occasion recommended African Americans. An African American Republican attorney in Philadelphia wrote to Bernard Shanley at the White House recommending a fellow Republican and African American, local judge Theodore O. Spaulding, for the federal district bench in Philadelphia. The handwritten notation at the top of the letter perhaps reveals an unwillingness to pursue black candidates; it said simply, "no reply necessary."[90]

In early 1954, there were four vacancies on the federal district bench in New York City. Democratic congressman Adam Clayton Powell, the most outspoken African American politician in the United States, called on the Eisenhower administration to name a black to one of the judgeships. There were several prominent black attorneys mentioned in letters to the administration, including New York City Court judge Francis E. Rivers, Hubert T. Delaney, and Harold A. Stevens. Later that year, when Supreme Court justice Robert Jackson died, the chief judge of the Ninth Circuit, William Denman, recommended as Jackson's replacement the only African American on the circuit courts, the distinguished Third Circuit jurist William Henry Hastie. When a vacancy occurred on the Supreme Court in 1956, Judge Denman again recommended Judge Hastie.[91] There is no evidence that Hastie was even remotely considered by anyone in the administration.

A campaign was launched in 1954 for George E. C. Hayes, a black attorney in Washington, D.C., to fill a vacancy on the Circuit Court for the District of Columbia. Walter White, the executive director of the NAACP, sent a telegram to Eisenhower urging him to name a qualified black.[92] Nothing came of these efforts.

Scovel Richardson was Eisenhower's token African American judicial appointee, and the token position was on a relatively minor court. In this sense, the Eisenhower administration took a step backward from the Truman administration, which had chosen an African American to fill a seat on a U.S. Court of Appeals.

The Demographic Profile of Eisenhower's Judges

Eisenhower's first-term appointments were a result of the recommendations of Attorney General Herbert Brownell and Deputy Attorney General William Rogers. During much of the second term, Rogers was attorney general and Lawrence Walsh was deputy attorney general. The differences between first-and second-term appointees, although minor, likely reflect the change in leadership at the Justice Department and the closer relationship with Bernard Segal, chairman of the ABA's Standing Committee on Federal Judiciary, who emphasized professional accomplishments. Table 4.1 presents the background statistics for the Eisenhower lifetime appointees to courts of general jurisdiction.[v]

AGE

Eisenhower was opposed to the appointment of elderly judges. But he apparently had no special concern about appointing young judges. The average age of the second-term judges was higher than that of the first-term judges. Second-term appointees also had more professional accomplishments. The profile of the second-term appointees was closer to the profile preferred by the ABA committee than was that of the first-term appointees. With the exception of Eisenhower's first-term district judges, the average age of the Eisenhower appointees was higher than that of the Truman appointees.

EDUCATION

Only one in seven first-term and one in ten second-term district court appointees had no undergraduate education—significantly lower rates than under Truman. Eisenhower's district court judges tended to have better legal

v. The figures do not include the district court nominations of Thomas E. Kennerly, C. Nils Tavares, John Feikens, and Andrew Caffrey, who were not confirmed when Eisenhower was in office. President Kennedy subsequently resubmitted the names of Caffrey, Feikens, and Tavares as a goodwill gesture toward the Republicans in the early days of his presidency. Caffrey and Tavares were confirmed and are counted with the Kennedy appointees. The figures also do not include the nomination of J. C. Tucker to a Texas judgeship. Tucker withdrew his name after the long Senate delay on nominations in 1959.

Table 4.1. Selected Backgrounds of Lifetime Eisenhower Appointees to the Federal District and Appeals Courts of General Jurisdiction

	District Court Appointees		Appeals Court Appointees	
	First Term	Second Term	First Term	Second Term
Average age at time of appointment	51.6	53.1	55.3	56.5
Undergraduate Education				
Public	39.4%	29.1%	30.4%	27.3%
	(28)	(16)	(7)	(6)
Private not Ivy	28.2%	43.6%	17.4%	18.2%
	(20)	(24)	(4)	(4)
Ivy League	18.3%	16.4%	30.4%	18.2%
	(13)	(9)	(7)	(4)
None	14.1%	10.9%	21.7%	36.4%
	(10)	(6)	(5)	(8)
Law School Education				
Public	40.8%	38.2%	34.8%	27.3%
	(29)	(21)	(8)	(6)
Private not Ivy	36.6%	34.5%	39.1%	36.4%
	(26)	(19)	(9)	(8)
Ivy League	19.7%	27.3%	26.1%	31.8%
	(14)	(15)	(6)	(7)
None	2.8%	—	—	4.5%
	(2)	—	—	(1)
Experience				
Judicial	29.6%	36.4%	56.5%	72.7%
	(21)	(20)	(13)	(16)
Prosecutorial	46.5%	60.0%	30.4%	45.5%
	(33)	(33)	(7)	(10)
Neither	40.8%	30.9%	21.7%	22.7%
	(29)	(17)	(5)	(5)
Occupation				
Politics — Government	5.6%	3.6%	8.7%	4.5%
	(4)	(2)	(2)	(1)
Government Lawyer	2.8%	16.4%	13.0%	4.5%
	(2)	(9)	(3)	(1)
Judiciary	19.7%	23.6%	43.5%	68.2%
	(14)	(13)	(10)	(15)

continued

Table 4.1. Continued

	District Court Appointees		Appeals Court Appointees	
	First Term	Second Term	First Term	Second Term
Large Law Firm*	12.7% (9)	12.7% (7)	13.0% (3)	9.1% (2)
Medium-Size Law Firm†	11.3% (8)	16.4% (9)	4.3% (1)	4.5% (1)
Small Law Firm‡	30.9% (22)	20.0% (11)	13.0% (3)	4.5% (1)
Solo Practice	16.9% (12)	7.3% (4)	4.3% (1)	— —
Other	— —	— —	— —	4.5% (1)
ABA Rating				
Exceptionally Well Qualified	8.4% (6)	9.1% (5)	34.8% (8)	36.4% (8)
Well Qualified	45.1% (32)	40.0% (22)	39.1% (9)	45.5% (10)
Qualified	28.2% (20)	43.6% (24)	17.4% (4)	13.6% (3)
Not Qualified	8.4% (6)	3.6% (2)	4.3% (1)	— —
Unknown/Not Rated	9.9% (7)	3.6% (2)	4.3% (1)	4.5% (1)
Party				
Democratic	2.8% (2)	7.3% (4)	4.3% (1)	9.1% (2)
Republican	97.2% (69)	92.7% (51)	95.7% (22)	90.9% (20)
Prominent Party Activism	54.9% (39)	72.7% (40)	73.9% (17)	63.6% (14)
Prior or Current Members of Congress	2.8% (2)	1.8% (1)	4.3% (1)	4.5% (1)
Religion				
Protestant	74.7% (53)	70.9% (39)	86.9% (20)	68.2% (15)

Table 4.1. Continued

	District Court Appointees		Appeals Court Appointees	
	First Term	Second Term	First Term	Second Term
Catholic	18.3%	20.0%	8.7%	18.2%
	(13)	(11)	(2)	(4)
Jewish	4.2%	9.1%	4.3%	9.1%
	(3)	(5)	(1)	(2)
Other§	2.8%	—	—	4.5%
	(2)	—	—	(1)
Total Number of Appointees				
	71	55	23	22

* A large law firm was defined as consisting of ten or more partners and associates.

† A medium-size law firm was defined as consisting of from five to nine partners and associates.

‡ A small law firm was defined as consisting of from two to four partners and associates.

§ Includes one Mormon and one Christian Scientist to the district bench and the elevation of the Christian Scientist to the appeals court.

education. About one in five first-term and more than one in four (second-term) appointees attended Ivy League law schools.

A comparison of the first-term appeals court appointees to the second-term appointees reveals few differences, except that one in five first-term and more than one in three second-term appointees had no undergraduate education. Over one-fourth of both first- and second-term appointees attended an Ivy League law school.

EXPERIENCE

About four in ten first-term district court appointees had neither judicial nor prosecutorial experience. In the second term, that proportion dropped to three in ten. There were more appointees during the second term who had judicial and especially prosecutorial experience. For the appeals court appointees in both terms, only about one in five had neither judicial nor prosecutorial experience. There was a marked increase in second-term appeals court appointees with both judicial and prosecutorial experience. This may have reflected a preference of the Justice Department officials, shared by the

ABA committee, for those with a well-rounded professional background. During the second term, appeals court appointees with judicial experience were primarily those who were sitting on the federal district bench at the time of their promotion.

OCCUPATION

Because they had been out of power for twenty years, Republicans had not had opportunities to serve as United States attorneys or hold other federal government positions from which to be promoted to the federal bench. Only two first-term district court appointees were United States attorneys at the time of appointment — less than 3 percent of the appointees. In contrast, during Eisenhower's second term nine appointees were government lawyers (eight were United States attorneys and one worked for the Justice Department) — about 16 percent of the second-term appointees.

Over 70 percent of the first-term district court appointees came from private practice. This contrasts with about 26 percent of Truman's first-term district court appointees. During Eisenhower's second term, about 56 percent of the appointees came from private practice. About one-third of those in private practice during the first term and about half of those in private practice during the second term came from large or medium-sized law firms.[w] In contrast, none of Truman's first-term district court appointees came from a large law firm, and during Truman's second term only about 20 percent of those in private practice came from large or medium-sized law firms. The Eisenhower appointees tended to come from the more prominent law firms.

About one in five first- and second-term district court appointees were judges at the time of their appointments, and all but one were serving on state courts. The one exception was a municipal court judge for the District of Columbia (technically a federal judgeship).

About one-third of the first-term appeals court appointees were in private practice at the time of their appointment to the circuit bench. For the second-term appointees, only about one-sixth were in private practice. The biggest difference was among those who were serving as judges at the time of appoint-

w. The Eisenhower appointees from private practice were not representative of how law was practiced. In 1948, 61 percent of lawyers were practicing solo. By 1966, that proportion was down to 40 percent. In 1948, 28 percent of lawyers were partners or associates in a law firm, a proportion that would rise to 36 percent by 1970. Bette H. Sikes, Clara N. Carson, and Patricia Gorai, eds., *The 1971 Lawyer Statistical Report* (Chicago: American Bar Foundation, 1972), table 5.

ment. About four in ten first-term appointees but seven in ten second-term appointees were on the bench when elevated. During the first term, 60 percent of those whose occupation at time of appointment was the judiciary were serving as federal district court judges (six judges, only one of whom was first appointed by Eisenhower). During the second term, that figure was 80 percent —twelve of the fifteen judges. Ten of those twelve were first appointed by Eisenhower.

Eisenhower appointed no law professors to either the district or the appeals courts. Justice Department officials apparently shared with the ABA a bias against recruiting judges from law schools.

AMERICAN BAR ASSOCIATION RATINGS

During Eisenhower's second term, over half of the district court appointees and over 75 percent of the appeals court appointees received the two highest ratings from the ABA Standing Committee on Federal Judiciary. The high ratings for the appeals court appointees reflect not only the broad discretion the administration had in these appointments but also the close working relationship between Chairman Segal and Deputy Attorney General Walsh. That over 6 percent of the district court appointees during Eisenhower's eight years in office were rated "not qualified" shows that the ABA did not have absolute veto power.

PARTY

Although more than 90 percent of Eisenhower appointees to the district and appeals courts were Republican, the proportion of Democrats more than doubled from the first term to the second. The six Democrats appointed by Eisenhower to the district courts were, with one exception, from the south and tended to be Eisenhower Democrats. Of the three Democrats appointed to the courts of appeals only one was a southern Eisenhower Democrat. One of the other two appeals court appointees was from North Dakota, and the other was from Connecticut. Eisenhower named the same number of Democrats to district and appeals courts as Truman named Republicans.

About three in five appointees had records of prominent party activism, about the same level as Truman's appointees had. But under 3 percent of all appointees had previously served in Congress. This was less than half the proportion of the Truman appointees and slightly less than one-fourth the proportion of Roosevelt's appointees. No sitting member of Congress was named by Eisenhower to the federal bench. This was a deliberate policy of the Justice Department.[93]

RELIGIOUS ORIGIN OR AFFILIATION

Eisenhower, as we saw earlier, was interested in naming Catholics to the courts as a way of strengthening the Republican Party. Somewhat less than one in five appointees were Catholic. That proportion, however, was less than the proportion of Catholics named by Truman. But Eisenhower was responsible for "restoring" the Catholic seat on the Supreme Court with the naming of Justice William Brennan in 1956, just prior to the presidential election.

Eisenhower's proportion of Jewish appointees to the district courts (over 6 percent) was greater than Roosevelt's (4.5 percent) but smaller than Truman's (over 11 percent). His proportion of Jewish appointees to the appeals courts (also over 6 percent) was also less than Truman's (close to 8 percent) but more than Roosevelt's (2 percent). The trend over these three administrations seemed to be for the appointment of Catholics and Jews to become more commonplace.

Eisenhower, like his two immediate predecessors, did not appoint a cross-section of America to the federal bench. For women and African Americans, Eisenhower's judicial legacy represented a step backward. Unlike Roosevelt and Truman, Eisenhower did not name even one woman or black to a lifetime judgeship on a court of general jurisdiction. One woman and one black were named to the Customs Court, and this was blatant tokenism.

Eisenhower's administrative style was markedly different from Roosevelt's and Truman's. He delegated virtual authority for appointments to the Justice Department, although he made some attempts during his second term to establish more control over the process. He was not a hands-on president with respect to judicial appointments, but he was not indifferent either. He maintained a general interest in the judiciary (on several occasions even an interest in filling a particular vacancy), and was concerned that his appointees be of high quality and meet the approval of the ABA. He never directly challenged the Senate, however, and unlike Roosevelt and Truman, none of his nominees were rejected by a vote of the full Senate.

Eisenhower's presidency was generally a time of economic prosperity, although the recession of 1958 was troublesome. The nation was at peace, although Cold War tensions were ever present. Eisenhower, representing the moderate wing of the Republican Party, did not dismantle the New Deal, but he did not add to it either. Civil rights for African Americans became a burning issue, and although Eisenhower acted in the desegregation crisis in Little Rock, he was criticized by civil rights forces for not speaking out about the evils of racial segregation. *Brown* v. *Board of Education* notwithstanding,

Eisenhower did not consider the federal courts germane to his presidential agenda and his administration. With only a few exceptions in the south with the civil rights issue, for the most part the administration did not use ideological criteria in the appointment process. To be sure, primarily Republicans were appointed, but that meant that at the end of Eisenhower's presidency the courts were about evenly balanced between Democrats and Republicans. Appointments, on the whole, furthered the partisan agenda.

Eisenhower was the nation's oldest president when he left office, a record only exceeded by Ronald Reagan. Eisenhower's successor, John F. Kennedy, was the nation's youngest elected president. Kennedy promised a new vitality and dynamic, hands-on leadership. After Kennedy's tragic assassination some three years into his term, Vice President Lyndon B. Johnson assumed the nation's highest office and gave a new meaning to the hands-on presidency. We turn our attention in the next chapter to Kennedy-Johnson's era and how they handled judicial selection.

The New Frontier/Great Society Judiciary

John F. Kennedy seemed to suddenly burst upon the national stage in 1960. He had been elected to the U.S. House of Representatives from Massachusetts in 1946 and to the Senate in 1952, the year Eisenhower headed the victorious Republican ticket. Kennedy was overwhelmingly reelected in 1958, but he was not a particularly well known senator nationally, despite a run for the vice-presidential nomination in 1956. He had few legislative accomplishments to his name. Perhaps his biggest claim to national attention was his Pulitzer Prize–winning book, *Profiles in Courage,*[1] which recounted key crises in American history and the men who put their careers and reputations on the line on behalf of principle.[a]

Through meticulous planning and behind-the-scenes gathering of delegates as well as waging a vigorous campaign in the presidential primaries, Kennedy secured the presidential nomination at the 1960 Democratic National Con-

a. Some saw an irony in the fact that the author of such a book was nearly invisible during the biggest domestic crisis of the early 1950s, when the demagoguery of Senator Joseph McCarthy of Wisconsin and the "witch hunt" for communists in government and key sectors of American life undermined American civil liberties. Of course, Kennedy had shown his personal courage during wartime and was an authentic war hero.

vention.[2] He picked as his running mate Lyndon B. Johnson, the powerful Senate majority leader who had presidential ambitions of his own.

In the general election Kennedy triumphed over Richard Nixon by an exceedingly slim 49.7 percent of the popular vote — becoming the first Catholic and youngest person ever elected president. But by his dynamic and charismatic personality and his inspiring, idealistic rhetoric, he struck a responsive chord in the nation. He articulated a vision of meeting new challenges in science and space and tackling the problems of peace and war, poverty and prejudice, what he called the New Frontier. He also faced a Congress dominated by elderly conservative southern Democrats, who through their seniority captured most of the important chairmanships, including the Senate Judiciary Committee, through which Kennedy and later Johnson's judicial nominees had to pass. Kennedy's assassination on November 22, 1963, tends to overshadow consideration of his presidency.[3] The heartbreaking events of that period are imbedded in the American psyche and even revelations years later of alleged romantic liaisons in the White House and that he suffered from Addison's disease but concealed that fact from the public have not diminished the luster of his reputation and the continuing national sense of loss from his death.[4]

During the Kennedy and Johnson years, the Cold War was the central fact of foreign policy, precipitating the Cuban missile crisis in 1962 and American involvement in the civil war in Vietnam.[5] On the domestic front, civil rights for African Americans commanded the attention of both presidents, as sit-ins, boycotts, freedom marches, mass demonstrations, and urban riots punctuated the struggle. Many Americans were appalled by the massive resistance by segregationists to the implementation of *Brown* v. *Board of Education*, as well as the shocking violence directed at civil rights workers by some southern law enforcement officials and individual racists. In 1963, President Kennedy submitted to Congress new civil rights legislation, including a section prohibiting racial discrimination in public accommodations. On August 29, 1963, at the climax of a series of nationwide protests, more than two hundred thousand people rallied in Washington, D.C., where they heard the Reverend Martin Luther King, Jr., and other civil rights leaders urge an end to racism in all areas of life, including employment, public accommodations, and housing.

After Kennedy's assassination, Lyndon B. Johnson assumed the presidency and successfully pushed for the enactment of the civil rights bill. The Civil Rights Act of 1964 was the strongest and most sweeping civil rights legislation in almost ninety years. Among its many provisions was one empowering the Civil Rights Commission to investigate deprivations of equal protection of the law. The reports of the commission sharply illustrated the fact that African Americans, especially in rural parts of the South, were still being denied voting rights. Martin Luther King led a series of marches during the first part of 1965 to dramatize the need for strong legislation to protect the right to vote. The march on Selma, Alabama, attracted nationwide attention, as did the murders of white civil rights workers from the North who had joined Dr. King's campaign. President Johnson, building on the momentum of the demonstrations and the outrage at the murders, guided the passage of the Voting Rights Act of 1965, which provided for federal supervision of elections in states violating the Fifteenth Amendment and the elimination of tests used to discriminate on the basis of race. Johnson similarly won passage of the Civil Rights Act of 1968 following the assassination of Dr. King. The 1968 legislation, among other provisions, prohibited racial and religious discrimination in the sale and rental of housing.

Johnson won election to the presidency in 1964 with an historic 61.1 percent of the popular vote. He accomplished the most comprehensive domestic policy program since Roosevelt's New Deal, which he called the Great Society. That agenda included not only civil rights legislation but the creation of Medicare and the War on Poverty programs. But the 1960s were years of intense social ferment. In the summers of 1964 and 1965 there were urban riots in many of the black ghettos. As the Vietnam War intensified, opponents conducted marches and engaged in civil disobedience. The threat of anarchy seemed to loom, with growing black militancy, the spread of the drug culture and drug-related crimes, the sharp increase in violent crime, and the rise of the hippie and counterculture movements that displayed contempt for private property and traditional values.

The decade of the 1960s was one in which a liberal activist majority on the Supreme Court, led by Chief Justice Earl Warren, was handing down major and often controversial rulings expanding the rights of the accused, outlawing prayer rituals in the public schools, liberalizing political free speech and obscenity law, establishing a right to privacy, mandating "one person, one vote" as the principle for legislative districting, and striking down racial discrimination. The Supreme Court as well as liberal Democrats were being blamed increasingly by conservative politicians for the social chaos. In the 1966 congressional elections, the Republicans gained forty-seven House seats and three Senate seats, though the Democrats retained control of Congress by a comfortable margin.

In the summer of 1967, there were devastating riots in the ghettos of Newark and Detroit. By 1968, the country was in turmoil over the Vietnam War. Johnson, whose popularity had sunk, announced he would not run for reelection. In April, Dr. King was assassinated, setting off rioting, burning, and looting in the black areas of more than one hundred cities. On June 5, Senator Robert F. Kennedy, who had emerged as a contender for the Democratic presidential nomination and assumed leadership of antiwar and liberal party forces, was murdered after he won the important California primary. Against this backdrop of dynamic and turbulent change, as well as a series of traumatic national events, John F. Kennedy and Lyndon B. Johnson selected judges.

Presidential Involvement in Selection

On the surface, Kennedy and Johnson were more similar than dissimilar in many important ways.[6] Of course there were the superficial differences in that Kennedy was born into a wealthy family and received the privileges that come with wealth. He had the breeding, grace, style, and wit that characterize the best of America's moneyed aristocracy. In contrast, Johnson came from more modest circumstances (his father was a farmer and state representative and usually in debt), was educated not in private schools and at Harvard, as was Kennedy, but in public schools and a state teacher's college. Johnson was loud, at times coarse and crude, with rough edges that over the years were somewhat smoothed. He was the southwestern frontiersman to Kennedy's New England patrician. But in terms of leadership style there were marked similarities. Both were seen as activist, hands-on presidents. Both understood the workings of government and what had to be done to accomplish their agendas. Both were charismatic leaders who appealed to the nation's idealism and sought to inspire its youth to public service. Both, as senators, were political moderates but, once in the White House, became more liberal.

Kennedy inherited a federal judiciary that was evenly split between Democrats and Republicans.[b] The partisan imbalance that Eisenhower faced when he had taken office had been corrected. The American Bar Association pushed the new administration hard for bipartisan appointments but met with little success, except to make Attorney General Robert Kennedy and his Democratic successors in office self-consciously seek to name a handful of Republicans to judgeships.

Kennedy undoubtedly had an interest in judicial selection. His brother Rob-

b. The Department of Justice reported that there were 163 Democratic and 163 Republican federal judges when Eisenhower left office. *St. Louis Post Dispatch,* January 10, 1962, 1C. This is confirmed in Deborah J. Barrow, Gary Zuk, and Gerard S. Gryski, *The Federal Judiciary and Institutional Change* (Ann Arbor: University of Michigan Press, 1996), 62.

ert was attorney general, and the deputy attorney general, Byron P. White, was a close friend who had helped him win the presidency. They were in continuous, informal contact with the president. When Kennedy appointed White to the Supreme Court, Nicholas deB. Katzenbach became deputy attorney general. Although he was not as close to Kennedy as was White, he nevertheless had a good working relationship with both Kennedys. There are, however, no memos, letters, and miscellaneous notes by Kennedy in his presidential papers that document his personal involvement with selection. The late Professor Harold W. Chase, who had the unique opportunity for about two months in the fall of 1962 to observe firsthand the workings of judicial selection in the Justice Department, wrote that the fact that Robert Kennedy, White, Katzenbach, and Assistant Deputy Attorney General Joseph F. Dolan had close personal ties among themselves and with Kennedy and his key White House staff meant that "there was little resort to formalities and written memoranda. Consultation about judgeships between White House and Justice officials took place over the phone, at lunch, or during quick office visits and was frequently just one item of business sandwiched among many others."[7] Kennedy's personal concern is revealed for the most part by other evidence.

Joseph F. Dolan as assistant deputy attorney general worked full-time on judicial selection in the Kennedy administration. In an interview Dolan noted, "I'm almost sure that almost all of [Kennedy's] personal involvements [in judicial selection] were in conversations with Bob [Robert Kennedy]. . . . [Kennedy's] dealings with the Justice Department were, I think, in person principally with his brother, the Attorney General, the Deputy Attorney General, Byron White, and with Burke Marshall [head of the Civil Rights Division]. Those dealings were incessant." Dolan also noted that he would frequently talk with Kennedy assistant Kenneth O'Donnell, who would want to know details about judicial selection and would suggest that Kennedy wanted to know about a nomination or why his team at the Justice Department was not doing this or that about filling a judicial vacancy. But sometimes O'Donnell would want to know who is being considered for a position "without indicating it was for the President." Dolan assumed that O'Donnell would bring the matter up with Kennedy, perhaps in anticipation of what O'Donnell knew was of interest to the president.[8]

Unlike Eisenhower, who dealt directly with his attorney general and not lesser Justice Department officials or who relied on his staff to obtain information he wanted about judicial selection, Kennedy would sometimes speak directly to Dolan. As Dolan recounted, Kennedy would call him when the attorney general and the deputy attorney general were unavailable: "Joe, what about So-and-So? I remember once he said, Senator So-and-So is coming through the door. Why can't I appoint his man?" As Dolan remembered, "Usually it was the question of the status of a vacancy on a judgeship—what should be done about a nomination that was pending where there was opposition. Should we stay with it or not?"[9] There was at least one instance when Kennedy wished to offer a highly valued member of his administration a district judgeship: "I hope he turns it down, but offer it to him."[10]

Robert Kennedy claimed that for the most part the president left judicial selection up to him and the deputy attorney general, "except where we wouldn't appoint somebody, and the senator or congressman wanted him appointed, and they raised a fuss about it. Then he got into it. Otherwise he didn't get into it." He estimated that the president got actively involved in about a half dozen such situations.[11]

One instance in which President Kennedy intervened and overrode his brother's judgment concerned a district judgeship in Oklahoma. Senator Robert Kerr from Oklahoma was the second-ranking Democrat on the Senate Finance Committee, and he wanted Luther L. Bohanon to fill the vacancy. Justice Department officials were convinced that Bohanon was not qualified—and so was the ABA. When it became clear that Kennedy's tax program would not be enacted unless Kerr's man received the judgeship, the president insisted that Bohanon be nominated.[12][c]

When Robert Kennedy spoke with Arthur Goldberg about his serving as secretary of labor, Goldberg said that his ambition was to become a judge and that he would like to be appointed to the Court of Appeals for the Seventh Circuit. "The president said fine," reported the attorney general, "without any absolute commitment, but the understanding was that he would get that position."[13] Goldberg accepted the labor post, and about eighteen months later Kennedy chose him to replace Felix Frankfurter on the Supreme Court.

Early in the Kennedy administration, Terry Sanford, governor of North Carolina and a strong Kennedy supporter, was pushing for the appointment of State Senator J. Spencer Bell, a liberal and also a Kennedy backer, to a vacancy on the Fourth Circuit. One North Carolina Democratic senator was backing a state judge, and the other was neutral. A Washington newspaper then ran a

c. Robert Kennedy recalled that "the judge in Oklahoma [Bohanon] that we were so concerned about has turned out very good." Robert F. Kennedy, recorded interview by Anthony Lewis, December 4, 1964, p. 407, John F. Kennedy Oral History Program of the John F. Kennedy Library. According to Victor S. Navasky, Bohanon "turned out to be a strong pro–civil rights judge." *Kennedy Justice* (New York: Atheneum, 1971), 253.

story with the headline, "N.C. Senators Tell JFK — You Pick Our Judge." Kennedy sent the article to Byron White with a handwritten note over the headline: "Byron have you seen this?"[14d]

Kennedy's interest in judicial appointments comes across in a 1962 memorandum from one White House staffer to another: "The President asked me to remind him he wanted to discuss Arkansas judgeships with [Congressman James W.] Trimble off a brief conversation he had with Trimble in the Mansion. You will recall this is an over-aged Judge that Tom Harper and others have been pleading for promotion."[15]

In the sphere of judicial selection, Johnson operated somewhat differently from Kennedy. He did not have his brother serving as attorney general. He did have his protégé and fellow Texan, Ramsey Clark, serve in the Justice Department first as an assistant attorney general and later as attorney general. But as close as Johnson may have been to Clark, Johnson did not delegate judicial selection to him to the extent that Kennedy did with brother Robert. Indeed, Johnson's presidential papers, unlike Kennedy's but similar to Roosevelt's, portray a president who micromanaged judicial selection, even while under the heavy burden of conducting a war. Unlike Roosevelt's experience, however, Johnson fought an increasingly unpopular and divisive war that resulted in a dramatic fall from public favor over the four-year period from his election in 1964. As Johnson became more enmeshed in controversy, he insisted that his appointees, including those to the federal bench, be loyal — which meant at least approving of Johnson's conduct of his presidency and having no record of criticism of his war policies.

After his election in 1964, Johnson asked John W. Macy, Jr., the chairman of the Civil Service Commission, to take responsibility for the recruitment and screening of high-level executive appointments. This included judgeships and

---

d. Sanford warned Robert Kennedy that if Bell were not named, this "would damage seriously the Kennedy forces in North Carolina. Bell was openly for Kennedy before L.A. [the Democratic National Convention in Los Angeles] and stood strong and voted there. He is one of my closest friends. He is an excellent lawyer — and on the merits alone, better qualified than Judge Pless. The Senators will give you no trouble, but we have put this on the line in public, and if Bell is not appointed it will be a mortal blow." Sanford to Robert Kennedy, May 20, 1961, Justice Department file of J. Spencer Bell. Bell received the appointment and went on to become a leading liberal on the Fourth Circuit. See Sheldon Goldman, "Conflict and Consensus in the United States Courts of Appeals," *Wisconsin Law Review* (1968): 467, 471, and Sheldon Goldman, "Conflict on the U.S. Courts of Appeals 1965–1971: A Quantitative Analysis," *University of Cincinnati Law Review*, 42 (1973): 647, 650, 655.

meant evaluating credentials on the basis of merit. Macy's efforts concerning the judiciary duplicated what was being done in the Justice Department and by White House staff; toward the end of Johnson's presidency they were discontinued. Nevertheless, Macy was in a position to see Johnson in action: "[Johnson] followed the appointment operations with the closest care, was very much involved personally in every selection."[16]

Until his election, Johnson had kept the Kennedy team in the Justice Department, and there is little evidence of micromanagement in the presidential papers of that period. But in September 1964, Robert Kennedy resigned the attorney generalship to run for the Senate. Nicholas Katzenbach was moved from deputy to acting attorney general, and Ramsey Clark was designated deputy attorney general. The February following the presidential election, Katzenbach assured Johnson that Clark would take prime responsibility for judicial appointments and would report directly to Johnson and to John Macy in the White House.[e] Johnson was apparently more confident of Clark's personal loyalty to him than Katzenbach's, who, after all, was originally a Kennedy man. Johnson also relied on Macy, with whom he discussed judgeships.[17]

An example of Johnson's micromanagement occurred with the filling of a vacancy on the Second Circuit that came about with the departure of Thurgood Marshall to become solicitor general. Senator Robert Kennedy and Katzenbach preferred U.S. District Judge Edward Weinfeld, a highly regarded, scholarly jurist, while Johnson favored a younger district judge, Wilfred Feinberg, whose brother Abraham was a wealthy political ally. The *New York Times* ran an editorial that portrayed Judge Feinberg in an unflattering and inaccurate fashion. The editorial indicated a preference for Weinfeld. Myer Feldman (former Kennedy White House special counsel who also had served as Johnson's White House counsel), at Johnson's request, compiled a list of Feinberg's accomplishments including his graduating Phi Beta Kappa from Columbia College and becoming editor-in-chief of the *Columbia Law Review* and the fact that his rulings as a federal district judge had *never* been reversed. When Johnson saw the list he ordered: "Get this to Lee White and tell him to tell Myer Feldman or someone to write the NY Times Editor in reply to the editorial—the facts on Feinberg."[18]

Ramsey Clark kept Johnson apprised of his options when a vacancy arose.

e. Katzenbach also noted: "You may rely on the fact that all his recommendations will have been discussed with me and are mine as well." Memo, Katzenbach to Johnson, February 3, 1965, FG 500 The Judicial Branch 11/23/63–3/16/67 WHCF, Johnson Library.

When a seat came open on the Eighth Circuit, Clark presented a menu of leading candidates with a "yes/no" check-off. (In this instance, Johnson checked the "no" boxes.) Sometimes Johnson became impatient and wanted to be informed sooner. For example, when former senator Joseph Hickey of Wyoming wrote to Johnson expressing interest in a Tenth Circuit vacancy, Johnson handwrote on the letter: "Marvin [Watson, Johnson's appointments secretary] — Talk to Ramsey C and let me know who is being considered." Watson followed through and reported in a memo dated January 20, 1966, that Wyoming senator Gale W. McGee recommended two people, including Hickey. Watson asked Johnson, "Do you want Mr. Hickey to receive first consideration if we can get unanimous support?" to which Johnson replied, "By all means and hurry!"[19]

Johnson followed the selection process closely. He often jotted notes on memoranda regarding appointments:

> "Let's send it up with a half dozen other judges. Hurry up Ramsey."[20][f]
>
> "Ask [Ramsey Clark] to talk to Minn. Senators."[21][g]
>
> "Yes, I would sure like call to Ramsey and Barefoot [Sanders] and ask them what they think about this [selecting Donald Russell to fill a Fourth Circuit vacancy] . . . and tell them this is who I would like to appoint."[22][h]
>
> "Let's watch this carefully — ask Mike Manatos to help also and remind me."[23][i]

f. The nomination to be sent up was that of Robert A. Ainsworth, Jr., a southerner who had generated some opposition from civil rights groups, to the U.S. Court of Appeals for the Fifth Circuit. Ainsworth was confirmed and went on to become a conservative on the bench. See Goldman, "Conflict on the U.S. Courts of Appeals," 648, 650, 655.

g. Attached to the memo was a letter from Orville Freeman, the secretary of agriculture, recommending for an Eighth Circuit judgeship Gerald Heaney, a Duluth, Minnesota, lawyer. Freeman in his letter to Johnson noted that Heaney was a close personal friend, had served as a Democratic national committeeman from Minnesota, was an excellent lawyer, and a supporter of Johnson's Great Society program. Freeman to Johnson, May 27, 1966, CF FG 505 Circuit Court of Appeals, WHCF, Johnson Library. Watson in his memo of the same date asked Johnson, "Do you want us to have Ramsey Clark check out Mr. Gerald Heaney of D[u]luth, Minnesota?" to which Johnson replied. Heaney was nominated and confirmed. He became a core member of the liberal bloc on the Circuit. Goldman, "Conflict on the U.S. Courts of Appeals," 648.

h. Donald S. Russell, a former governor of South Carolina and U.S. senator, had just been appointed by Johnson to the district bench in South Carolina. He did not receive the appeals court position on the Fourth Circuit. In 1971, however, he was elevated to that circuit by Richard Nixon.

i. Watson had reported in a memo that seniority on the bench is determined by the date when the judicial commission is signed by the president. Johnson had two commissions to

"Marvin — be sure Governor wants this and they will follow us at convention."[24]j

Johnson cherished personal loyalty. As his presidency became mired in the disastrous Vietnam War, as his popularity faded, and as he faced increased opposition within the Democratic Party, he became more insistent that appointments by his administration go to his political supporters. Judicial selection, traditionally handled in the Justice Department with only minimal intervention by the White House, now became more of a White House enterprise. By 1968, the deputy attorney general, Warren Christopher, sought White House guidance in filling specific vacancies.[25]

Kennedy, we have seen, had some interest in the judiciary but only occasionally was personally involved in judicial selection. He tended to defer to his brother Robert's judgment. By contrast, Johnson not only had an active interest in judicial selection but on numerous occasions micromanaged the process, involving the White House to an extent not seen since Roosevelt.

The Policy Agenda and Selection

"Judicial philosophy is important," Nicholas Katzenbach, who became deputy attorney general when Byron White went on the Supreme Court, noted in an interview. Right-wing conservatives simply would not be considered by the Kennedy administration, which preferred to appoint "a judge who is a careful liberal, a good technician, liberal yet cautious." Yet Justice Department officials did not ordinarily look at the decisions of those who had a judicial record, and "there was no saliva test for liberalism," according to Joseph Dolan.[26]

Letters to Justice Department officials sometimes praised not only a candidate's legal qualifications and political credentials but also that individual's overall policy orientation. For example, U.S. District Judge Willis W. Ritter of

---

sign and wanted Andrew Hauk to have seniority over William Gray. Watson wrote Johnson, "We will, therefore, make special effort to assure that Judge Hauk's commission leaves the White House prior to that of Judge William Gray." Johnson's notation was written on the memo in response to it.

j. Presidential aide Larry Temple wrote Johnson that the Democratic state chairman for Delaware, William Potter, recommended James L. Latchum, Potter's law partner, for a federal district judgeship. Potter told Temple that Latchum was a strong Johnson supporter and had been so as a delegate to the Democratic national convention in 1960, and also that Delaware governor Charles Terry strongly supported him. Latchum received the judgeship.

Utah, a Democrat, wrote to Robert Kennedy urging the elevation of U.S. District Judge Delmas C. Hill of Kansas to fill a vacancy on the Tenth Circuit: "He is our kind of Democrat. He and I were appointed on the same day by President Truman in October 1949 and I am well acquainted with his views for we have had many occasions upon which to exchange them."[27][k]

An example of an appointment in which ideological considerations seemed to have prevailed concerned the filling of a vacancy on the Ninth Circuit. Judge Walter L. Pope of Montana retired from that court and, following custom, it was understood that his replacement would also be from Montana. Montana's two Democratic senators, Mike Mansfield and Lee Metcalf, sent a letter in which they recommended three individuals for consideration. First on their list was James R. Browning, who was born, raised, and educated in Montana but for the previous twenty years had lived in Washington, D.C., working for the Justice Department, subsequently engaging in private practice, and for three years previous serving as clerk of the United States Supreme Court. Senator Metcalf in particular, favored Browning and so informed the deputy attorney general.[28] The second name on the list was that of Missoula, Montana, attorney Russell E. Smith. (The third name was soon eliminated from consideration.) Justice William O. Douglas, a longtime friend of the Kennedy family, strongly supported Browning. So did James Rowe, a Justice Department official during the Roosevelt administration and a leading liberal Washington attorney with ties to the Kennedys.

Rowe, who originally came from Montana, wrote to Robert Kennedy about Browning and Smith. He observed that both men would make competent judges but that Browning was superior to Smith for the circuit bench because of his service with the Supreme Court. Rowe went on:

> Assuming that I exaggerate and that these two men are actually comparable in competence and judicial temperament, there are I think the intangibles which weigh more heavily in favor of Browning than of Smith. I must tread softly here for, by definition, intangibles are hard to weigh. Nonetheless, I submit

---

k. Hill received the circuit judgeship, but not for ideological reasons. The administration wanted to appoint some Republicans to district judgeships. There already was a district court vacancy in Kansas. By elevating Hill, another vacancy on the Kansas district bench was created, thus making it politically possible for the administration to name a Republican to one of the vacancies. Interview with Joseph Dolan, February 18, 1964. See the more detailed account later in this chapter of the Hill appointment as part of a package deal. Hill turned out to be conservative in his voting behavior. See Goldman, "Conflict on the U.S. Courts of Appeals," 649.

the trend as toward Browning and against Smith: First, not only is the Ninth Circuit a weak bench, it is a conservative bench quite out of step with the premises of the New Frontier and almost all of us understand those premises. In the great run of cases it does not much matter whether a judge is liberal or conservative if he is a good judge. There are a handful of cases, however, — and, Heaven knows, they always seem to be the important ones! — where the judicial mind can go either way, with probity, with honor, self-discipline and even with precedent. This is where the "liberal" cast of mind (we all know it, few of us can define it) can move this nation forward, just as the conservative mind can and does hold it back. This is intangible truth, but every lawyer knows it as reality! Browning would go forward, Smith would hold back.[29]

Rowe went on to point out that "the political point of view of a candidate deserves weight when other things are equal, or almost equal." He also noted Browning's "devotion" in contributing "vast amounts of time and money to good Democrats." But Smith was not a good Democrat, and in the 1950s he had been for Eisenhower. Rowe wrote, "I do not think it is unduly partisan of me if I feel a good man cannot and should not live in both worlds!" In conclusion Rowe urged the appointment of Browning as "the more competent, the more liberal, the consistent Democrat."

Rowe attached a note to the letter, urging Robert Kennedy's secretary to call it to his attention. Rowe told Browning, "I knew there were 100 judgeships he had to consider but that my letter was so brilliantly written it was part of his education to read it." When Rowe wrote to Browning, he attached a copy of the handwritten reply from Robert Kennedy: "Dear Jim, I did see it. Your friend, Bob. I greatly enjoyed your note to Angie [Kennedy's personal secretary]. Call me on Friday if you have a chance."[30]

Complicating matters was that the ABA rated Browning "not qualified." In a memorandum to the president prior to the submission of the formal nomination papers to the White House, the attorney general summed up the situation. He noted that the Justice Department "feels that Mr. Browning, who has been recommended by Senators Mansfield and Metcalf, is qualified for the Court of Appeals for the Ninth Circuit." He added that "Justice Douglas also strongly recommends his appointment." The memo continued:

> However, the Judiciary Committee of the American Bar Association, from whom we regularly get opinions, has found him to be unqualified. Their opinion is based to a great extent upon the reactions of Western judges and lawyers. Mr. Browning, who hails from Montana, has not spent much, if any, of his legal career in the West and it seems to us that those people giving adverse opinions are somewhat unfamiliar with his development. It is antici-

pated that this appointment, if made, will draw considerable criticism from the Bar Association and conservative press. . . . The Senators and Mr. Browning prefer to go ahead, as does the Department.[31]

Browning was appointed and confirmed without difficulty.[l] Five years later, Russell Smith received a federal district court appointment from Johnson.

When the Kennedy administration had its first vacancy to fill on the Supreme Court, the Kennedy brothers thought that "it would make a helluva impact around the world" if a black person were appointed. They seriously considered elevating Judge William Henry Hastie, the first and at that time one of only two African Americans on the federal circuit bench.[m] Robert Kennedy had Justice Department lawyers analyze Hastie's decisions. He concluded that "if you were going to consider the five or six best judges of the circuit court, you'd put him [Hastie] up there." But many of the president's White House aides were opposed and, according to Robert Kennedy, so was Chief Justice Earl Warren and Justice William O. Douglas. As Robert Kennedy recalled: "I went to see Warren about [Hastie] who was very much against having him on. . . . [H]e wasn't liberal enough and so he didn't want him on. . . . Bill Douglas didn't want him on because he said he wasn't liberal enough."[32]

Thus ideology, in part, torpedoed what would have been an historic appointment. Ironically, the seat on the Court went to Byron White, who did not join the Warren-Douglas wing but rather became a generally conservative justice.[n]

Had Kennedy appointed Hastie, it is unlikely that the administration would have received such harsh criticism for its appointment of segregationists to the lower federal courts.[o] President Kennedy's southern appointments were in-

l. Browning became a leading liberal on the Ninth Circuit. See Goldman, "Conflict and Consensus," 467, 472, and Goldman, "Conflict on the U.S. Courts of Appeals," 649, 651, 655. He won the praise of Chief Justice William Rehnquist for his innovative leadership as chief judge of the Ninth Circuit. See William H. Rehnquist, foreword to Arthur D. Hellman, ed., *Restructuring Justice* (Ithaca, N.Y.: Cornell University Press, 1990), xi.

m. Hastie was extraordinarily gifted and had been appointed to the Third Circuit by President Truman. Robert Kennedy recalled that Hastie "was about the only good one, really, that we could come up with." Robert F. Kennedy, recorded interview by John Barlow Martin, April 13, 1964, p. 135, John F. Kennedy Oral History Program of the John F. Kennedy Library. The other African American on the circuit bench was Thurgood Marshall, who had been nominated by Kennedy to the Second Circuit and was serving a recess appointment while awaiting confirmation by the Senate.

n. Another irony is that Hastie's record on the Third Circuit became more decidedly liberal in the mid- to late 1960s. See Goldman, "Conflict on the U.S. Courts of Appeals," 647.

o. See, for example, the charge by Governor Nelson Rockefeller in the *New York*

deed a sore point, all the more so because neither of the Kennedys wanted to appoint racists; indeed, that would have been counter to the administration's civil rights policy agenda. Yet President Kennedy appointed segregationist judges.

The most notorious racist he appointed was William Harold Cox, to the federal district bench in Mississippi. In his courtroom, Cox would refer to blacks seeking the right to vote as "a bunch of niggers ... acting like a bunch of chimpanzees." In the formal letter to the president from the attorney general accompanying the nomination, Robert Kennedy noted that Cox "bears an excellent reputation as to character and integrity, has judicial temperament, and is well qualified, I believe, to be a United States District Judge."[33] What led Robert Kennedy to recommend Cox?

Cox was strongly promoted by Mississippi senator James Eastland, the chairman of the Senate Judiciary Committee. Cox received the ABA committee's highest rating, "exceptionally well qualified." He was not associated with the White Citizens Council or other racist groups, and there was no public record of racist speeches or activity. Cox was interviewed at the Justice Department and assured officials, including the attorney general, that he would follow the Supreme Court's interpretation of the Constitution, including its civil rights rulings. As Robert Kennedy recounted, "I had the conversation with him; I was convinced he was honest with me, and he wasn't."[34]

Unlike Cox, who did not have a public record of racism, J. Robert Elliot, who was placed on the federal district bench in Georgia, was on record as having made racist statements while serving in the Georgia legislature. Georgia Democratic senator Herman Talmadge pushed heavily for the appointment of Elliot. Robert Kennedy spoke with Fifth Circuit judge Elbert Tuttle and asked him to find out if Elliot would be o.k. on civil rights. According to Robert Kennedy and Burke Marshall (the assistant attorney general who headed the Civil Rights Division), Tuttle reported that he thought Elliot would be all right. According to Robert Kennedy, so did Kennedy Fifth Circuit appointee and future attorney general (in the Carter administration) Griffin B. Bell. But Elliot turned out to be hostile to civil rights.[35]

Southern Democrats, because of their seniority, had a lock on key committee chairmanships in Congress. They had the power to kill the president's agenda and so had to be cultivated by the administration. If the administration

Times, March 6, 1963, p. 4, and Kennedy's denial at a news conference reported in *New York Times,* March 7, 1963, p. 1. Robert Kennedy publicly defended the administration's southern appointments; see *New York Times,* April 27, 1963, p. 9. A scathing and detailed critique of Kennedy's southern appointments is presented in Navasky, *Kennedy Justice,* 243–76.

tended to give the benefit of the doubt to those recommended for the district bench by powerful southern Democratic senators, they were, however, more resolute when it came to circuit court appointments. It was the determined policy not to appoint segregationists to the Fourth and Fifth circuits. If there were doubts about a candidate, Dolan did not move that candidate forward. There were two Kennedy appointments to the Fourth Circuit and two to the Fifth. There was also one Kennedy appointment from Tennessee, in the Sixth Circuit, and one from Arkansas, in the Eighth Circuit. In every instance the administration sought to discover the candidate's views on racial segregation, and in only one instance, the candidate from Arkansas, did the administration knowingly appoint a segregationist.[36]

The segregationist appointee was Pat Mehaffy, who was a Democratic national committeeman, personal counsel to Governor Faubus, whose actions had precipitated the Little Rock crisis in 1957, and drafter of segregationist legislation. He was actively supported by Arkansas Democratic senator John McClellan and was also backed by Senator J. William Fulbright. When Kennedy was inaugurated, the Arkansas seat on the Eighth Circuit was vacant, and McClellan began pushing Mehaffy. The Justice Department resisted, but McClellan kept on insisting and indicated that he would block anyone else. After a two-and-a-half-year stalemate, the administration relented. In a July 2, 1963, memo to Joseph Dolan, an assistant summarized the negative information on Mehaffy concerning civil rights: "Mehaffy has been close to Governor Faubus for some years, and Messrs. Ed Wright and Joe Barrett believe that Mehaffy's views on integration are the same as those of the Governor. The President of the Arkansas State Bar Association also thinks that Mehaffy believes in segregation."[37]

Furthermore, the assistant told Dolan that the chief judge of the U.S. District Court for the Eastern District of Arkansas, J. Smith Henley, did not think that Mehaffy was qualified for appointment. The ABA committee, however, unanimously rated Mehaffy "qualified." The nominee was swiftly confirmed.[p]

Harry Phillips of Nashville was named to the U.S. Court of Appeals for the Sixth Circuit. Phillips had been recommended by Tennessee senator Albert Gore (father of the future senator and vice president). Phillips had served as Gore's campaign manager, was active politically, and had twice been elected to the state legislature. Before his nomination there was an intensive effort to find out about Phillips's political views, particularly on civil rights. Various attorneys in the Justice Department were asked to contact their law school

---

p. Mehaffy's voting record on the circuit turned out to be conservative on matters of civil liberties. See Goldman, "Conflict on the U.S. Courts of Appeals," 648.

classmates from Tennessee.[q] A former administration official, John Seigen-thaler, who returned to Nashville to take over the editorship of the city's leading newspaper (the *Nashville Tennessean*), was contacted by Dolan, who reported directly to Robert Kennedy that "John Seigenthaler says that he has no doubt whatever that Phillips will be all right on civil rights questions." Dolan also reported the results of his talk with Phillips himself. "Phillips . . . volunteered that he has no feelings of racial bias or prejudice whatever, and that if appointed he would apply the law in the civil rights field as laid down by the Supreme Court without any hesitation, and would feel quite comfortable about it."[38][r]

The administration took a gamble with the appointment of Alabama at-torney Walter P. Gewin to the Fifth Circuit. To be sure, Gewin was rated "exceptionally well qualified" by the ABA and had been president of the Ala-bama Bar Association. He had wide support among lawyers, judges, and the dean of the University of Alabama Law School. Gewin was a former state representative and member of the Alabama State Democratic executive com-mittee. Senators Lister Hill and John J. Sparkman actively backed Gewin, a fact Byron White communicated to Kennedy. But when Gewin was on the Fifth Circuit, he was unsympathetic to civil rights claims and joined the con-servatives on the bench. Among his decisions was one striking down the public accommodations section of the Civil Rights Act of 1964, a decision unan-imously overturned by the Supreme Court. Griffin Bell, also appointed to the Fifth Circuit, considered himself a moderate on civil rights and sought to find a middle ground between the liberals and conservatives on the court. His voting record, however, placed him in the conservative wing.[39][s]

The two appointments to the Fourth Circuit, J. Spencer Bell and Albert V. Bryan, were a study in contrasts—the former a known liberal, the latter a more conservative jurist. (Bryan was a federal district judge.) On the bench

q. For example, Phillips's Justice Department file contains a copy of a memo sent to Justice Department attorney Oliver Lofton that began: "The following is a list of Ten-nessee attorneys who attended George Washington University during the years you were there." The file contains copies of other memos to Justice Department lawyers who were Harvard and Yale law graduates.

r. Phillips's subsequent record on the appeals court was mixed. He was an economic liberal but tended to be conservative on civil liberties issues. See Goldman, "Conflict on the U.S. Courts of Appeals," 648.

s. When Bell became attorney general in the Carter administration, however, he imple-mented the Carter policy of opening up the judiciary to women, African Americans, and other ethnic minorities. Historic numbers of these groups were appointed to the federal courts.

Bell joined the liberals, Bryan the conservatives.[40] Having satisfied themselves that Gewin, Griffin Bell, J. S. Bell, and Bryan would not espouse segregationist positions on the circuits, Kennedy's Justice Department officials went ahead with the appointments, notwithstanding the candidates' overall ideological orientation.

President Johnson, starting in mid-1966, insisted on knowing the civil rights view of candidates for the judiciary. "How is he on civil rights?" Johnson asked about one candidate. He then instructed his aide, Marvin Watson: "Ask Ramsey [Clark] to thoroughly explore background—prior associations in cases etc. and give me memo before I act. Want this on every judge."[41] On another southern candidate Johnson instructed Watson: "Call Ramsey. Check to be sure he is all right on the Civil Rights question. I'll approve him if he is."[42]

Johnson's presidential papers contain numerous memos that show that his concern with the civil rights views of nominees was followed through by his administration. For example, Ramsey Clark noted in a memo about C. Clyde Atkins for a district judgeship in Florida that Atkins was a "strong supporter of civil rights." Clark spoke with the liberal Fifth Circuit judge John Minor Wisdom about the possible elevation of U.S. District Judge Robert Ainsworth to the Fifth Circuit and reported that Wisdom deemed Ainsworth "completely trustworthy on civil rights."[t] Clark recommended Charles R. Scott for a federal district judgeship in Florida and noted that he had checked with civil rights leaders, including the Florida NAACP president, who "affirms Scott's good reputation." John Macy reported that James A. Comiskey, recommended for the federal district bench in New Orleans, "is regarded as a moderate on civil rights matters." About U.S. District Judge Claude F. Clayton, a candidate for a vacancy on the Fifth Circuit, an aide reported to Johnson that "Ramsey has checked carefully to determine his attitude on civil rights and has concluded that he has been fair and just."[43] Clayton was appointed.

In recommending Frederick J. R. Heebe for the New Orleans district bench, Ramsey Clark reported that on civil rights "we believe him to be a liberal who will follow the law." Dan M. Russell, Jr., appointed to a Mississippi judgeship, had been found to have a "quite satisfactory" position on civil rights that was acceptable to local and national civil rights leaders. Also "endorsed by local civil rights leaders" for a Mississippi judgeship was William C. Keady. Orma R. Smith, still another Mississippi appointment, was described by Deputy Attorney General Warren Christopher as "moderate on race relations," but

---

t. Ainsworth was appointed. However, he joined the conservative bloc on the Fifth Circuit. See Goldman, "Conflict on the U.S. Courts of Appeals," 648, 655.

the Mississippi civil rights leader Charles Evers sent a telegram to Johnson protesting Smith's nomination and calling Smith "a racist."[44]

Smith was not the only southerner to receive a judicial appointment from Johnson without a consensus as to his commitment to civil rights. Earlier, Johnson had decided to proceed with the nomination of former Mississippi governor James Coleman to the Fifth Circuit and instructed Marvin Watson to "ask Nick [Katzenbach] to clear this and get praise from all civil rights groups." This was easier said than done. The Coleman nomination produced great opposition from civil rights leaders. Vice President Hubert Humphrey sent a memo to Johnson alerting him to growing opposition, but it was too late in the game. Johnson stayed with Coleman, who was eventually confirmed.[45 u]

Another troublesome southern nominee was Woodrow Wilson Jones, to the North Carolina federal district bench. The *Charlotte Observer* noted that Jones "is a conservative and an admitted segregationist." Jones, who had been a member of Congress, had signed the Southern Manifesto pledging opposition to desegregation and was "strongly opposed" by the North Carolina NAACP — but actively pushed by North Carolina Democratic senators Sam Ervin and B. Everett Jordan. White House aide Barefoot Sanders advised Johnson that "Jones needs a good talking to on civil rights." The administration rushed and successfully got Jones confirmed before the NAACP's annual convention.[46 v]

The nomination of Alexander Lawrence to a Georgia judgeship in 1968 proved to be extremely troublesome. Lawrence was recommended by Ralph McGill, publisher of the *Atlanta Constitution,* as a fair-minded person who was also "an old-time segregationist." Ramsey Clark was opposed to Lawrence, who was the choice of Senator Richard Russell. Clark tried to prevent the nomination. The ABA committee, however, unanimously gave Lawrence a "well qualified" rating. And Lawrence wrote a letter in which he explained his views in detail and declared his commitment to uphold civil rights laws were he to serve on the bench. That letter was sent to a banker friend of Lawrence's, who gave it to Ralph McGill, who in turn sent it on to the White House. At

u. Coleman became one of the most conservative judges on the Fifth Circuit bench. See Goldman, "Conflict on the U.S. Courts of Appeals," 648, 655.

v. The appointment of Jones seems to contradict Johnson's concern with his civil rights agenda. Johnson apparently believed that it was unwise to defy two powerful senators. The political costs outweighed the benefits of deferring to the NAACP. Johnson no doubt felt he could do this because just about two weeks earlier, on June 13, 1967, he had named Thurgood Marshall to the Supreme Court.

Johnson's request Justice Abe Fortas read the letter. Fortas responded by saying, "This is conclusive to me. I think we should go ahead on this now for sure." Johnson nominated Lawrence, but the delay had brought about a rupture in the relationship between Johnson and Lawrence's sponsor Senator Russell. Russell had been expected to support Johnson's nomination of Fortas for chief justice of the Supreme Court and to bring with him other southern Democrats. But Russell did not support Fortas; instead he joined with a group of Republican senators to doom the nomination. Lawrence, however, was confirmed, and once on the bench he enforced desegregation.[47]

As the Vietnam War came to dominate Johnson's presidency and opposition to Johnson became increasingly vocal, Johnson wanted to make sure that those he appointed were his supporters. As he put it in a note to Watson concerning the nomination of Robert McRae to a Tennessee district judgeship: "Will he be an all out J-man?" In evaluating candidates for a Wisconsin judgeship, Johnson was told that Myron Gordon "is clearly the Johnson man." A cover memo with the nomination papers for John T. Curtin for a New York judgeship deemed him "loyal to the Administration." Watson also commented that according to New York Democratic leader Ed Weisl, Sr., Curtin and another nominee for a New York judgeship, Morris E. Lasker, "believe in the principles of President Johnson's program and believe in the President personally." Presidential aide Larry Temple, in a memo to Johnson concerning prospective appointees in 1968, suggested: "Barefoot [Sanders] and I can meet with both of them and be sure of their loyalty before their appointments are announced." Johnson gave the go-ahead, and five days later Temple reported that "both possess the ability and loyalty requirements."[48] These appointments clearly point up Johnson's personal-agenda concerns.

When the available evidence concerning appointments to the courts of appeals is evaluated, it appears that Kennedy made three appointments (15 percent) where policy-agenda considerations were prominent, sixteen appointments (80 percent) that were dominated by partisan-agenda concerns, and possibly one personal-agenda appointment. Johnson made three (7 percent) where the policy agenda was noticeable, thirty-five (85 percent) that could be characterized as partisan-agenda appointments, and three (7 percent) that were personal-agenda appointments. With the exception of civil rights, neither Kennedy nor Johnson appeared to view the courts as vehicles of public policy relevant to their agendas. It is therefore not surprising to find that the policy agenda played a relatively minor role in judicial selection. On the other hand, Johnson's style of micromanagement, which Kennedy shared to a large degree, extended to judicial selection at a level beyond that shown by Kennedy. This perhaps explains the fact that Johnson had more personal-agenda appointments than did Kennedy.

Senators and Selection

During the Kennedy and Johnson administrations, senators of the president's party continued to exert great influence on the selection of lower federal court judges. When a senator's candidate was professionally qualified according to the standards applied by the Justice Department, the department typically was accommodating. In Robert Kennedy's estimate, however, about one in five recommendations from Democratic senators was unacceptable, and the result was a struggle with senators to secure a nominee measuring up to the administration's standards.[49]

Johnson was insistent that no judicial nominations go forward unless the Democratic senator or senators from the nominee's state approved. Johnson, after all, had been Senate majority leader and himself had insisted on picking a federal district judge in Texas even though a Republican (Eisenhower) was in the White House. Johnson was certainly sympathetic to senatorial sensibilities and was not about to defy, if at all possible, his former colleagues and allies. For example, before acting on Ramsey Clark's recommendation for a Wisconsin appointment that was not Democratic senator William Proxmire's first choice, Johnson noted on a memo, "Tell Ramsey I must see Proxmire first." When White House assistant Bill Moyers sent Johnson a note passing on a suggestion for the federal district court in Ohio, Johnson succinctly noted, "Senators make the choice." Concerning two prospective nominations, Johnson instructed Watson to proceed "if both sitting senators can and will confirm." Johnson even sought to accommodate the Senate Republican minority leader, Everett Dirksen, by naming a Dirksen man to a judgeship. As Johnson explained to an aide, "We want to get Dirksen's help on the tax bill."[50]

Other Considerations in the Appointment Process

PARTY ORGANIZATIONS

When the Democrats recaptured the White House in 1960 after eight years out of office, the Democratic National Committee did not have the clout it had had in previous Democratic administrations. Kennedy had put together his own team in his successful run for the nomination, and he relied primarily on his organization to win the White House.[51] Once in office, Kennedy's administration placed much less reliance on the DNC in clearing nominees for public office. Indeed, there is no evidence that the DNC played any special role in judicial selection. In the oral histories of Robert Kennedy and Joseph Dolan there is no mention of the DNC in connection with judicial selection; neither is there mention in Kennedy's presidential papers or Justice Department files on judges.

Johnson, however, seemed somewhat more accommodating to the DNC. Concerning the nomination of Howard Bratton to a district judgeship in New Mexico, a White House memo contained the notation, "Democratic National Committee has been advised." A memo concerning two nominees to New York judgeships noted that "their appointments have been approved by the Democratic National Committee."[52]

Local and state party organization leaders attempted to promote their candidates for judicial office, and both the Kennedy and Johnson administrations were receptive. The Democratic governor of New Jersey, Robert B. Meyner, wrote to Kennedy endorsing the elevation of a federal district judge to the Third Circuit: "All the [party] leaders have united in recommending . . . the promotion of Judge William F. Smith."[w] Smith was appointed. After Democratic Party leader and Chicago mayor Richard Daley wrote to Robert Kennedy promoting the candidacy of Illinois judge Roger J. Kiley to the Seventh Circuit, Kiley received the job. (Of course, he had met Justice Department and ABA standards).[x] Johnson, like Kennedy, was respectful of local party leaders and organizations, and there are examples of this attitude in the presidential papers.[53]

Party organizations and leaders had to be dealt with when the Kennedy administration attempted to appoint Republicans to judgeships. As Robert Kennedy recounted, "I wanted to appoint some Republicans and so we appointed some Republicans—not a great number, but we appointed some—and that didn't go over very well [with the party organizations]." Republicans tended to be appointed from states with Republican senators. President Kennedy, however, resubmitted the names of three Republicans who had received recess appointments before Eisenhower left office. The three were Andrew Caffrey from Massachusetts, C. Nils Tavares from Hawaii, and John Feikens from Michigan. The first two were confirmed, but the strongly cohesive Michigan Democratic Party bitterly opposed the naming of a Republican, and the

w. Smith's subsequent voting record on the Third Circuit was that of a moderate, falling between the liberal and conservative blocs. See Goldman, "Conflict and Consensus," 467, and Goldman, "Conflict on the U.S. Courts of Appeals," 647, 654.

x. Kiley went on to become a member of the liberal wing on the Seventh Circuit. See Goldman, "Conflict on the U.S. Courts of Appeals," 648.

Michigan Democratic senators successfully blocked Feikens (who was subsequently appointed by Nixon, in 1970).[54]

It was easier for the Kennedy administration to name a Republican to a judgeship when that was part of a package arrangement that included one or more Democratic appointments. That way the party organization received at least some recognition. For example, the Kansas Democratic Party organization pushed for the elevation of U.S. District Judge Delmas C. Hill, himself a former chairman of the Kansas State Democratic Party, to a position on the Tenth Circuit. Democratic member of Congress J. Floyd Breeding was especially active in the campaign, and it was successful. The administration was looking for a Republican to fill the vacancy on the district bench created by the elevation of Hill. But that did not please the Kansas Democrats. Congressman Breeding sent a telegram to Robert Kennedy advising that the Kansas State Democratic Party opposed the appointment of a Republican and recommended two worthy Democrats, including Wesley E. Brown. The Justice Department began looking into the leading candidates and soon settled on Republican George Templar. As Joe Dolan put it in a letter to Kennedy assistant Kenneth O'Donnell: "Brown is Breeding's recommendation. Templar was recommended through [Republican minority leader] Senator Dirksen by [Kansas Republican] Senator [Frank] Carlson and the late [Kansas Republican] Senator [Andrew F.] Schoeppel. Both are "Well Qualified" by the American Bar Association formal opinion. . . . Templar was [Democratic leader Frank G.] Theis's preference in the event a Republican had to be appointed." Shortly after Templar was nominated, Deputy Attorney General Byron White, responding to criticism from the ABA of a partisan imbalance in appointments, stated with a straight face that appointments were made on the basis of legal ability and not party affiliation.[55]

Dolan, knowing Robert Kennedy's desire to make appointments to Republicans, and knowing that such appointments would deflect criticism of partisanship in appointments, came up with suggestions for a package arrangement that would permit a Republican appointment. When there was a vacancy on the Sixth Circuit that was to be filled by someone from Michigan and the leading candidate, George C. Edwards, Jr., sparked some negative reaction from Senate Judiciary Committee chairman James Eastland, Dolan suggested that Michigan district judge Talbot Smith, whom he noted "liberals would like," be elevated, and that a Republican be appointed to the district bench. The deputy attorney general responded, "Let's discuss."[56] Evidently, recalling the doomed attempt to place Republican John Feikens on the federal bench in Michigan and recognizing the united support of the Michigan Democratic Party behind George Edwards, the administration went along with Edwards, who was confirmed in December 1963.

Like Kennedy, Johnson ran into obstacles when it came to appointing Republicans. In fact, the proportion of Johnson district court appointees who were Republican was about half that of Kennedy's (although Johnson appointed two Republicans to the appeals courts and Kennedy appointed none). In at least one instance Johnson had told his staff "that if a more qualified Republican were available," he "preferred to nominate him." Johnson had wanted to appoint liberal Republican senator Thomas Kuchel of California to a new Ninth Circuit judgeship after Kuchel was defeated for renomination in the California primary in 1968. But he discovered that because the judgeship was created when Kuchel was in the Senate, Kuchel could not constitutionally be appointed during the balance of his senatorial term.[57]

Some of Johnson's Republican appointments came about after Republican senators put pressure on the administration. Pennsylvania Republican Senator Hugh Scott, a member of the Judiciary Committee, claimed that he had been promised a Republican judgeship. Scott wanted E. Mac Troutman to be appointed to the federal district bench. But earlier, David L. Lawrence, former governor of Pennsylvania and a member of the Democratic National Committee, bitterly opposed naming Republicans to federal judgeships in Pennsylvania and had warned of severe adverse political consequences. Johnson nevertheless decided to elevate a Pennsylvania Republican, U.S. District Judge Francis Van Dusen, to the Third Circuit, but he held off on Scott's choice of Troutman for the district bench.[y] Senator Scott, however, still insisted that his man Troutman be appointed. To demonstrate his determination, Scott held up the nomination of a Democrat, Thomas A. Masterson, to the Pennsylvania federal district bench. Masterson was sponsored by Pennsylvania's other senator, Democrat Joseph Clark, who retaliated by withholding approval of Van Dusen to the Third Circuit. At that point the administration went ahead with Troutman, and as White House assistant Barefoot Sanders put it in a memo to Johnson, that "will break the deadlock." Sanders also noted that "Troutman is acceptable to Senator Clark."[58]

Another example of such pressure from a determined Republican senator

y. When he was attorney general, Robert Kennedy was interested in naming to the Third Circuit another Pennsylvania Republican, Bernard G. Segal, chairman of the ABA Standing Committee on Federal Judiciary. Democratic Senator Joseph Clark, however, vetoed that appointment. Katzenbach to O'Donnell, December 27, 1963, FG 505/FG 216, WHCF, Johnson Library.

occurred with the filling of several vacancies on the federal district bench in New York. Republican senator Jacob Javits insisted that a Republican be named to one of the vacancies, and to drive home his determination he placed a hold on the nomination of Democrat Morris Lasker. Johnson, whose presidency had been weakened by 1968, was vulnerable to this sort of pressure. He subsequently nominated Republican Orrin Judd to fill one vacancy. Deputy Attorney General Warren Christopher observed that "the Judd nomination should clear the way for Senate confirmation of Mr. Lasker."[59]

STATE REPRESENTATION

Considerations of state representation came into play for appointments to the courts of appeals. Griffin Bell, who had served in 1960 as Georgia co-chairman of the Kennedy-Johnson campaign, wanted one of the two new judgeships slated for the Fifth Circuit. Bell wrote a personal letter to Robert Kennedy indicating that the Georgia senators would support him. He also noted, "I was gratified by the attitude of the Senators, not only for their assurances of support, but because they indicated rather strongly that they thought Georgia, based on population, commerce, and loyalty should have one of the judgeships. Incidentally, each state in the Circuit, Florida, Georgia, Alabama, Mississippi, and Louisiana has one judgeship now with Texas having two."[z] Johnson's men in the White House and Justice Department were also sensitive to claims of state representation and geographic considerations for determining which states would receive the new circuit judgeships.[60]

THE AMERICAN BAR ASSOCIATION

Less than two weeks before John F. Kennedy was sworn into office, Robert Kennedy met with the president of the American Bar Association, Whitney North Seymour, and the chairman of the ABA's Standing Committee on Federal Judiciary, Bernard G. Segal, and agreed to continue the relationship the Eisenhower administration had with the ABA committee. But relations between the Kennedy administration and the ABA committee, though close, did have their points of tension. Segal continued to push for bipartisan selection. Justice Department officials responded by saying that Republicans would be appointed to judgeships, but they refused to commit the administration to a

z. In a March 17, 1961, letter to Attorney General Kennedy, the Georgia senators, Talmadge and Russell, suggested the names of three men including Bell, "either of which we feel would serve with distinction if selected." Justice Department file of Griffin B. Bell. Bell was appointed.

particular percentage. In August 1961 Kennedy thanked the ABA for evaluating judicial candidates, and Segal praised Kennedy's appointments but again urged the administration to adopt bipartisanship in the selection process.[61]

During Kennedy's first year in office, eighty-two out of eighty-five judicial appointees were Democrats, prompting the ABA to decry partisan "imbalance." Although the ABA was unhappy when the administration appointed those rated "not qualified," Segal pointed out that during his tenure as ABA chairman from the start of the Kennedy administration until July 1962, there were 150 individuals rated "not qualified" who did *not* receive nominations.[62]

The ABA mounted all-out fights over one Kennedy nominee and one Johnson nominee rated "not qualified." Irving Ben Cooper, Kennedy's nominee to a federal district judgeship in New York, had the strong backing of House Judiciary Committee chairman Emanuel Celler and the Democratic Party establishment, including Eleanor Roosevelt and Robert F. Wagner. The New York Criminal and Civil Courts Bar Association also endorsed Cooper. But the ABA claimed that he lacked judicial temperament, and the president of the New York City Bar Association called Cooper "emotionally unstable." Cooper received a recess appointment and, after a Senate hearing in which the detractors and defenders of Cooper were heard, he was confirmed by the Senate.[63]

The Johnson nominee was Francis X. Morrissey. Shortly before Robert Kennedy resigned from the attorney general's office, he recommended to Johnson that Morrissey be appointed to the federal bench in Massachusetts. Not much transpired with the Morrissey candidacy until one year later, when Robert Kennedy's successor, Nicholas Katzenbach, warned Johnson about opposition to Morrissey from much of the legal profession.[aa] Johnson assistant Marvin Watson suggested to the president that Senator Edward Kennedy should explicitly ask that Morrissey be nominated before Johnson proceed.[64]

Morrissey was nominated, and the ABA vigorously opposed him at his Senate confirmation hearing. Although the Senate Judiciary Committee by a divided vote sent Morrissey's nomination to the Senate floor with a favorable recommendation, there was continuing controversy as the press latched onto the nomination and made embarrassing revelations about Morrissey. Edward Kennedy moved to send the nomination back to committee to consider the

aa. "I agree with the American Bar Association that Judge Morrissey does not come up to the standards in terms of experience and legal competence which would ordinarily lead us to recommend him to you for appointment." Katzenbach also noted that "there is nothing in the FBI file which reflects [adversely] on Judge Morrissey's character, integrity, or judicial temperament." Katzenbach to Johnson, September 2, 1965, Ex FG 530/ST 15/A–ST 21/A, WHCF, Johnson Library.

new allegations, but the effect was to kill the nomination. A short time later, Morrissey formally requested that Johnson withdraw his name.[65]

The ABA emerged the victor from the fight over the Morrissey nomination. When the dust settled some months later, Johnson met with the ABA committee, and the relationship between the administration and the ABA improved markedly. At the end of Johnson's term, the chairman of the ABA committee commended the president for his "outstanding" record of judicial appointments.[66]

RELIGION AND ETHNICITY

Would the nation's first Roman Catholic president take religion and ethnicity into account in the selection of judges? Assistant Deputy Attorney General Joe Dolan answered both yes and no: "We never considered religion. Perhaps we were somewhat sensitive about it due to the fact that this was the Administration of the first Catholic president." But then Dolan made this acknowledgment:

> Ethnic composition is a consideration in gross. . . . [I]t does seem unbelievable that you could have four years without appointing any Irish-American to the judiciary, or any Italian name, or Jewish, or if you didn't appoint a single Negro, I think it would be regarded as somewhat remarkable. People wouldn't believe you if you said it was just a coincidence, if you said it just happened that way. So in my opinion you can't let it happen. You have to look and you have to be alert to the possibilities. Let's say Polish-Americans — there aren't too many Polish lawyers in the United States. . . . So you bet we look for a Pole. At the same time you maintain your standards.[67]

Robert Kennedy told about Arthur Goldberg's selection to the Supreme Court to replace retiring justice Felix Frankfurter, a Jew. He noted that the president "just decided on Goldberg. First, I think it basically was going to come to a Jew. . . . If you were going to appoint a Jewish lawyer, certainly Arthur Goldberg is awful smart, and there wasn't any reason to try in some other direction. I think even if the Jewish aspect of it hadn't been involved, Arthur Goldberg would have been high on the list of lawyers . . . considered."[68]

Johnson and his officials also were sensitive to the need to recognize ethnic groups, particularly Italian-Americans. For example, Katzenbach saw the political importance of seeking someone of Italian heritage for a district court vacancy in Connecticut. White House assistant Jack Valenti stressed to Johnson the need to appoint those of Italian and Polish ancestry. When Robert Belloni was appointed to the federal bench in Oregon, White House assistant Joseph Califano informed Johnson that Belloni was not an Italian-American and should not be cited by Johnson as an Italian-American appointment. There is other evidence of efforts to appoint Italian-Americans. There is also evidence that the administration was aware of Jewish candidates for judgeships and of the significance of appointing only the second hispanic to a lifetime judgeship.[69]

Women and Judgeships

Congress enacted a new judgeships bill within the first months after Kennedy took office. Upon signing the bill creating seventy-three new positions, Kennedy pledged to appoint "men and women of unquestioned ability." This was the first time a president of the United States had ever publicly promised to appoint women to the federal judiciary. As expected, just as had occurred with his three immediate predecessors, Kennedy was asked by women's groups to appoint women to the federal judiciary. Congressman Emanuel Celler, chairman of the House Judiciary Committee, urged Kennedy to appoint women, and Kennedy's assistant Lawrence O'Brien responded on the president's behalf: "Your belief that well qualified women should be considered for these appointments is shared by the President and the Attorney General, who welcome your comments and suggestions."[70]

However good the intentions, Kennedy appointed only one woman to a lifetime federal judgeship, Sarah T. Hughes to the Northern District of Texas. She was rated "not qualified" by the ABA because of her age (she was sixty-five years old when appointed). There is no evidence that women were given serious consideration either by Democratic senators or by the president's men in the administration. Perhaps the administration decided to spend its political capital on securing federal judgeships for African Americans. Whatever the reason, Kennedy's record on women appointments was as poor as his three immediate predecessors'.

In 1966, a bill was enacted creating forty-five new judgeships. In 1968, nine new appeals court positions were established. Thus Johnson, like Kennedy, had an opportunity to expand the opportunities of women to be federal judges. Johnson's record of appointing women to judgeships, however, while better than any of his predecessors', still has the look of tokenism. Nevertheless, there is evidence that Johnson and his administration were more activist than was the Kennedy administration in trying to recruit women. By 1967, however, Johnson had appointed only one woman to a lifetime judgeship, although this was the first appointment of an African American woman to the federal bench. The appointee, Constance Baker Motley, had been recommended to Johnson by New York senator Robert Kennedy.

In 1964, Johnson approached Carol Agger, the wife of Abe Fortas and herself a prominent Washington attorney, to determine if she were interested in an appointment to the U.S. Court of Appeals for the District of Columbia. She was not. In general, according to Johnson's personnel director John Macy, Johnson "was very strong on trying to bring more women into the administration." Macy recalled that he had lists of "negroes, mexican-americans, women," and that "it was a matter each time of seeing if we couldn't find somebody from the list." Yet when it came to judgeships, all too often the mind-set was to appoint men. White House assistant Larry Temple recalled that the administration would encourage a senator to accept its preferred candidate "if we had an exceptionally talented *guy*." In considering filling a position on the Eighth Circuit, Johnson wrote in 1965, "Why not a good man from Mo.?"[71]

In 1967, when the Democratic Party activist India Edwards wrote to Johnson that "we have fallen behind in the appointment of women to the bench," Johnson responded that "this matter has my personal and continuing attention." Shortly after this exchange, Marvin Watson sent a memo informing Johnson that Mary Goode Rogan was a candidate for a California federal district court position and asking whether he wanted her to be "checked out by Justice" Johnson marked the "yes" box. However, nothing came of it.[72]

By 1968, it was clear that few women had received judgeships. In recommending to Johnson several people for local judgeships in the District of Columbia, Ramsey Clark noted that the list included "two women lawyers, a category in which your appointments have been very very few."[73] The administration also decided to appoint a woman, June Green, to the federal district bench in the District of Columbia. Larry Temple explained that decision in a memo to Johnson: "It may be that a man could be found who is a little better qualified than Mrs. Green. However, one of the three vacancies on the U.S. District Court was created by the retirement of a woman, Judge Burnita Matthews. Moreover, in the over four years of your Presidency, only one woman has been named to a lifetime federal judicial post—Constance Motley in New York. [Justice Abe] Fortas, [James] Rowe, [Judge Gerhard] Gesell, [Deputy Attorney General Warren] Christopher, and I all agree that it would be advisable to name a woman to one of these Judgeships in light of all of these circumstances."[74] Green received the judgeship, becoming one of only two Johnson appointments of women to lifetime federal district court positions, which nevertheless remained the historic record until the Carter administration.

But the big push in 1968 for a woman on the federal bench occurred with the filling of one of the positions on the Ninth Circuit created by the Judgeships Act of 1968. In a memo to Johnson, Clark mentioned a highly regarded California judge, Shirley Hufstedler, as a candidate for the position and added,

"More women should be appointed to the bench, and I am not aware of any woman lawyer who has better credentials than Mrs. Hufstedler." The administration focused on Hufstedler and on Mildred Lillie, also a California judge who before going on the bench was active in the Democratic Party and whose husband continued to be a party activist.[bb] Johnson was told, however, that if either Hufstedler or Lillie were named to the Ninth Circuit, "the boys won't like it" because it would give Republican governor Ronald Reagan the opportunity to make a judicial appointment. The deputy attorney general recommended Hufstedler as the better qualified candidate, and she was nominated and confirmed, one of the last of Johnson's judicial appointments.[75][cc]

Kennedy and Johnson established their record of women appointments just as the women's movement was gaining momentum through the 1960s. Betty Friedan's *The Feminine Mystique* had helped to raise the consciousness of millions of readers about the stifling sexism that reduced career opportunities and prevented most women from achieving their full potential. The Civil Rights Act of 1964 had prohibited discrimination on the basis not only of race but also of gender. As the decade progressed, it became clearer that the 1960s had launched women's rights much as the 1950s had launched civil rights. But as we have seen, there were few gains for women on the federal bench even though there were over six thousand women practicing law in 1950 who by the 1960s would likely have had the necessary experience to be professionally qualified for appointment. Women were yet to be in a position to provide effective political pressure to integrate the bench by gender.[76]

African Americans and Judgeships

In March 1961, Kennedy, in a letter to the president of the predominantly black National Bar Association, recalled his meeting with the group's judiciary committee in the summer before the presidential election of 1960. He wrote: "I can assure you that the objective of this Administration is the fair and equitable representation on the basis of the merit of all our people in all the branches of our government including the Judiciary. You should give your specific suggestions to the Attorney General or the Deputy Attorney General."[77]

bb. Mildred Lillie was reportedly President Richard Nixon's choice to fill one of two vacancies on the Supreme Court in 1971. The ABA committee, however, rated her "not qualified," and the nomination was never made. See Donald Dale Jackson, *Judges* (New York: Atheneum, 1974), 352–53.

cc. By John Macy's count, Johnson appointed twenty-five women to executive and judicial positions, including three women to lifetime judgeships. John W. Macy, Jr., transcript of oral history, interviewed by David McComb, April 26, 1969, p. 12.

The creation of new federal judgeships in 1961, 1966, and 1968, provided Kennedy and Johnson with opportunities to appoint African Americans. When six new judges were to be appointed in the Southern District of New York and three to the Second Circuit in 1961, the chairman of the House Judiciary Committee, Democrat Emanuel Celler, had especial clout with the administration because New York's two senators were Republicans. Celler submitted to the attorney general the names of "several of the Negro race. I do this advisedly because President Kennedy is strongly of the opinion that a Negro should occupy one of the available posts in New York." Among these candidates was Thurgood Marshall, whom Celler noted was a Democrat and "the best qualified of all Negro applicants."[78] Also on the list was Robert L. Carter, an attorney for the NAACP in New York City. But when Kennedy decided to name Marshall to the Second Circuit, Carter was passed over for an appointment. Marshall was then chief counsel of the NAACP Legal Defense and Educational Fund, and the administration did not want to name two NAACP lawyers.[79] (Carter later received a district judgeship from Nixon, in 1972).

At first, the Justice Department had hoped to name Marshall to a district judgeship, but Marshall said he would only accept an appeals court appointment. Marshall's nomination in September 1961 garnered numerous endorsements from many individuals and groups, including various branches of the NAACP. The deans of the nation's major law schools supported the nomination, and the ABA rated him "well qualified." But there was also considerable racist opposition.[80]

Kennedy gave Marshall a recess appointment after the Senate adjourned in the late fall without having acted on the nomination. The chairman of the Senate Judiciary Committee, Mississippi Democrat James O. Eastland, held up Marshall's nomination in the Senate but had privately informed Robert Kennedy that eventually he would put Marshall through. Eastland was true to his word, although he himself voted against Marshall in the committee (which recommended Marshall by a vote of 11 to 4) and on the Senate floor. Marshall was confirmed on September 11, 1962, about one year after he was first nominated, by a vote of 54 to 16. Although Senator Eastland delayed Senate confirmation of the handful of Kennedy's black judicial appointees, according to Robert Kennedy "he never caused us any trouble."[81]

In 1961, President Kennedy named the first African American to a lifetime federal district court position. He appointed James B. Parsons to the Northern District of Illinois, which includes Chicago. Kennedy also selected Wade H. McCree, Jr., for the Eastern District of Michigan, which includes Detroit. Black groups exerted some pressure on the administration to name a black to the federal bench in Philadelphia.[82] Kennedy responded in part by naming black attorney A. Leon Higginbotham to the Federal Trade Commission in 1962. About two months before his assassination, Kennedy nominated Higginbotham for the Philadelphia federal district court.[dd]

Kennedy's fifth black nominee to a lifetime judicial position was Spottswood W. Robinson, whom the president had previously named to the Civil Rights Commission. Robinson, was a resident of Virginia when Kennedy was set to nominate him for a seat on the District of Columbia district court. But the two Democratic senators from Virginia would not approve the appointment of a black from their state. The senators agreed, however, that if Robinson moved his residence to the District of Columbia "this will not be offensive to them," as Deputy Attorney General Katzenbach put it in a memo to Kennedy's assistant Kenneth O'Donnell: "We would expect that the nomination would now be sent down showing Robinson from Virginia, that he would not be confirmed at this session, and that he would be given a recess appointment. His nomination would be resubmitted at the next session showing his new residence in the District of Columbia, and this would avoid the senatorial problem. Mike [Manatos, White House congressional liaison] discussed this with both senators and neither indicated that he would oppose. I have discussed this with Robinson and he is amenable."[83]

Katzenbach went on to note that when Robinson was nominated he would resign from the Civil Rights Commission. He then observed: "That is his only political liability (apart from being a Negro, of course)". Katzenbach put in writing the reality of the legacy of racism that the administration faced when making an unprecedented number of judicial appointments to African Americans. Being a member of the Civil Rights Commission was a political liability, and "of course" so was "being a Negro." Katzenbach concluded by noting that the ABA found Robinson to be "well qualified" and that "he is highly regarded by white lawyers in both the District of Columbia and Virginia."[ee]

Robert Kennedy's serious consideration of William Hastie to fill a Supreme Court vacancy (recounted earlier) represented the first time in American his-

dd. Johnson gave Higginbotham a recess appointment and resubmitted his nomination in 1964. He was confirmed later that year. In 1977 President Carter elevated him to the U.S. Court of Appeals for the Third Circuit.

ee. Johnson gave Robinson a recess appointment and resubmitted the nomination in 1964 after Robinson had moved from Virginia to the District of Columbia "in accordance with an informal understanding arrived at with the Virginia Senators." Katzenbach to Hopkins, January 9, 1964, Ex FG 530/FG 216/A, WHCF, Johnson Library. Robinson was subsequently confirmed. Two years later Johnson elevated him to the U.S. Court of Appeals for the District of Columbia.

tory that an African American was an actual contender for the high court. But even had Chief Justice Warren and Justice Douglas been enthusiastic, it is uncertain whether President Kennedy would have been willing to make the tremendous political effort it would have taken to secure confirmation.

In all, Kennedy's administration was the first to move beyond a mere token appointment of an African American. The administration worked hard to achieve this historic breakthrough. Johnson continued the momentum and exceeded Kennedy's record. His efforts culminated in the landmark appointment of Thurgood Marshall to the Supreme Court in 1967.

Johnson and his administration actively recruited African American judges. William T. Coleman, Jr., a well-known and highly regarded African American lawyer practicing in Philadelphia (and a Republican), was suggested to the administration by Democratic senator Joseph Clark, but Philadelphia congressman Bill Green strenuously objected. After Green's death, Ramsey Clark recommended that a Third Circuit vacancy be filled by either Coleman or former ABA committee chairman Bernard Segal. Johnson directed him to proceed with Coleman — "if OK with both senators." The senators agreed. Johnson personally approached Coleman, but Coleman declined the nomination.[84] (Coleman was later to serve in the cabinet of President Gerald Ford as secretary of the Department of Transportation.)

The Justice Department wanted to promote Leon Higginbotham in 1968 to one of the vacancies on the Third Circuit, but Senator Clark believed it important for an Italian-American to be appointed and was backing Ruggiero Aldisert. The Democratic mayor of Pittsburgh backed David Stahl, a Jewish candidate. Johnson appointed Aldisert and Stahl. (President Jimmy Carter promoted Higginbotham nine years later.)

Johnson was determined to appoint an African American to the Supreme Court. Although it is assumed that Thurgood Marshall was being groomed for the position, having resigned his lifetime judgeship on the Second Circuit to become Johnson's solicitor general, there is evidence that Johnson briefly considered William Hastie. Johnson did not hesitate to promote his record of African American appointments, and at one point he ordered, "Find out how many Negro judges I have named. Have a planted question [at press conferences] — each time one is announced."[85]

Johnson wanted to achieve another breakthrough — naming the first African American to a federal judgeship in the South. But this was to prove too difficult. Not that there were no highly qualified candidates. Vice President Hubert Humphrey urged Johnson to elevate Spottswood Robinson to the southern Fourth Circuit.[86] Recall that Robinson went on the federal district bench in the District of Columbia in 1964 after he moved his residence from

Virginia to the District. Robinson, a former dean of Howard Law School, was widely admired for his brilliance. However, Johnson would have found it impossible to get approval from Virginia's senators, who just two years earlier would not accept Robinson for the Virginia federal district court bench. Furthermore, having moved his residence from Virginia to the District of Columbia, Robinson no long resided within the Fourth Circuit. Johnson instead elevated Robinson to the Court of Appeals for the District of Columbia.

On April 8, 1967, a delegation of forty African American attorneys from the Fourth Circuit visited the Justice Department and urged the appointment of a black to their circuit. They met with John Duffner, an assistant to the deputy attorney general, and representatives of the group met with Ramsey Clark. They left a list of candidates with Duffner.[87] There is no evidence that any action was taken on that list.

Georgia senator Herman Talmadge recommended an African American attorney from Atlanta, Donald Hollowell, for the Fifth Circuit, and an assistant told Johnson that the editor of the Atlanta Constitution "would go along" if the appointment were made. When the administration pursued the suggestion, Larry Temple informed Talmadge, it encountered "a slight amount of difficulty with the Bar." Talmadge responded: "Hollowell is the best qualified Negro in my state and possibly one of the best in the Fifth Circuit. I recommend him because I thought the President might want to appoint a Negro to one of the Fifth Circuit vacancies. Of course, I won't insist upon his appointment if the Bar objects; [b]ut I think he is qualified." Temple told the president that Warren Christopher would try to expedite ABA clearance and that the necessary FBI investigation of Hollowell was about to get under way.[88]

Hollowell was not appointed, and it is not clear from the presidential papers why. But it seems likely that some form of racism, whether from the bar or from senators in the Fifth Circuit, made it impossible for the administration to follow through. An added factor may be that Johnson was a lame duck president nearing the end of his term, and he was marshalling his political clout to get Abe Fortas confirmed as chief justice. Republican senators preferred to keep judgeships vacant in anticipation that a Republican would be elected president in November who would then get to fill those positions. Thus Johnson was not in a strong position to battle for Hollowell.[ff]

John Macy in his oral history pointed out that "a total of 50 Negroes have

---

ff. Johnson did name an African American, James L. Watson, to a lifetime judgeship on the Customs Court. Watson was assigned by the chief judge of that court in 1966 to sit in the southern states of Georgia, Florida, and Texas. Thus, it can be argued that at least indirectly Johnson named a black to serve on a federal court in the South.

been appointed to major executive and judicial posts, including the first Negro in the Cabinet [Robert Weaver, the first Secretary of the Department of Housing and Urban Development] and the Supreme Court."[89]

The Demographic Portrait of the Kennedy-Johnson Judges

The statistics concerning lifetime judicial appointees of Presidents Kennedy and Johnson are contained in Table 5.1. The Kennedy appointees are those who were confirmed before Kennedy's assassination on November 22, 1963.[gg] Five Kennedy nominees were confirmed under Johnson . Two of the five (Charles Tenney and George Edwards) were confirmed in December 1963. Johnson gave the remaining three (John M. Davis, A. Leon Higginbotham, and Spottswood Robinson) recess appointments in January 1964 and then resubmitted their nominations when the new session of Congress convened. The statistics do not include failed nominations.[hh]

gg. One judge, Homer Thornberry, was confirmed before the assassination, but his judicial commission was signed by Johnson. The signing of a commission of a duly nominated and confirmed judge can be considered a nondiscretionary act of the president. Thornberry is therefore classified as a Kennedy appointee. The reason Kennedy did not immediately sign Thornberry's commission after the Senate confirmed him on July 15, 1963, was that Thornberry, then serving in the U.S. House of Representatives and a member of the powerful House Rules Committee, was needed to help pass Kennedy's legislative program and had thus submitted his resignation from Congress to be effective December 20. See *New York Times,* September 28, 1963, p. 8. All Kennedy nominees who were not confirmed by November 22 but were confirmed afterwards are classified as Johnson appointees because Johnson could have withdrawn the nominations at any time before confirmation.

hh. Kennedy's one failed nomination was that of Republican John Feikens to the Michigan district bench. Michigan's Democratic senators refused to accept him, and the nomination died in the Senate. David Rabinovitz (Wisconsin), was also a Kennedy nominee but his nomination failed during Johnson's presidency. Rabinovitz, rated "not qualified" by the ABA, was opposed by Wisconsin's Democratic senators, and his nomination lapsed at the end of the 88th Congress. Johnson chose not to fight the senators. Johnson not only had the failed nomination of Francis X. Morrissey, but in his last year in office four lifetime judicial nominations lapsed when the 90th Congress adjourned. The nominees included Barefoot Sanders to the D.C. Circuit and, to district judgeships, David Bress (District of Columbia), Cecil Poole (California), and William M. Byrne (California). After Richard Nixon was elected president but before Johnson left office, Johnson renominated all four, along with a territorial judge nominee, after being led to believe that Nixon approved. See the discussion in Neil D. McFeeley, *Appointment of Judges: The Johnson Presidency* (Austin: University of Texas Press, 1987), 126–32. When Nixon assumed office, however, he withdrew the nominations but subsequently resubmitted

The Kennedy judicial selection team in the Justice Department was gradually replaced by Johnson people, but there was continuity in the standards used to evaluate candidates. There were more similarities than differences between the Kennedy and Johnson judicial appointees.

AGE

The youthful administration of Kennedy showed no particular inclination to appoint younger judges. The average age of Kennedy's district court judges was slightly higher than that of Eisenhower's first-term district judge appointees but a full two years younger than Eisenhower's second-term appointees. On average, Johnson's district judges were slightly younger than Kennedy's, and Johnson's appeals judges were two years younger than Kennedy's, but Kennedy and Johnson's appeals court judges were younger than Eisenhower's.

EDUCATION

Kennedy's and Johnson's district judge appointees had similar undergraduate educational backgrounds. But about twice the proportion of Johnson's appointees attended an Ivy League school. Their law school educational backgrounds were similar in that about two in five were graduated from a publicly supported law school, as were about one in five from an Ivy League law school. There were proportionately more Kennedy district court appointees who had attended private, non-Ivy law schools. All of the Kennedy district court appointees and almost all of the Johnson district court appointees had a law school education.

Roughly the same proportion of Kennedy and Johnson appeals court appointees attended an Ivy League college as undergraduates. But a higher proportion of Johnson's appointees went to a public college or university, and more of Kennedy's appointees were without an undergraduate education (one in five). About the same proportion of Kennedy and Johnson appeals court appointees were graduated from a publicly supported law school, but more of Johnson's appointees had an Ivy League law school education (over one in four) and proportionally less private, non–Ivy League law school training.

EXPERIENCE

About one in three Kennedy and Johnson district court appointees had neither judicial nor prosecutorial experience. Unlike the Roosevelt, Truman,

---

William M. Byrne's name. Poole, an African American, was named to the federal district bench in 1976 by President Ford. Sanders was eventually named to the Texas district bench in 1979 by President Carter.

Table 5.1. Selected Backgrounds of Lifetime Kennedy and Johnson Appointees to Federal District and Appeals Courts of General Jurisdiction

| | District Court Appointees | | Appeals Court Appointees | |
	JFK Appointees	LBJ Appointees	JFK Appointees	LBJ Appointees
Average age at time of appointment	51.8	51.1	54.0	52.0
Undergraduate Education				
Public	43.7%	42.9%	15.0%	41.5%
	(45)	(54)	(3)	(17)
Private not Ivy	36.9%	34.9%	50.0%	34.2%
	(38)	(44)	(10)	(14)
Ivy League	7.8%	17.5%	15.0%	17.1%
	(8)	(22)	(3)	(7)
None	11.7%	4.8%	20.0%	7.3%
	(12)	(6)	(4)	(3)
Law School Education				
Public	38.8%	42.1%	40.0%	39.0%
	(40)	(53)	(8)	(16)
Private not Ivy	42.7%	34.1%	40.0%	34.2%
	(44)	(43)	(8)	(14)
Ivy League	18.4%	22.2%	20.0%	26.8%
	(19)	(28)	(4)	(11)
None	—	1.6%	—	—
	—	(2)	—	—
Experience				
Judicial	42.7%	38.9%	50.0%	65.9%
	(44)	(49)	(10)	(27)
Prosecutorial	39.8%	42.9%	50.0%	31.7%
	(41)	(54)	(10)	(13)
Neither	35.9%	32.5%	35.0%	24.4%
	(37)	(41)	(7)	(10)
Occupation				
Politics — Government	10.7%	9.5%	5.0%	9.8%
	(11)	(12)	(1)	(4)
Government Lawyer	1.9%	12.7%	5.0%	2.4%
	(2)	(16)	(1)	(1)
Judiciary	33.0%	30.2%	50.0%	56.1%
	(34)	(38)	(10)	(23)
Large Law Firm*	3.9%	3.2%	5.0%	4.9%
	(4)	(4)	(1)	(2)

continued

Table 5.1. Continued

	District Court Appointees		Appeals Court Appointees	
	JFK Appointees	*LBJ Appointees*	*JFK Appointees*	*LBJ Appointees*
Medium-Size Law Firm†	28.2%	23.0%	25.0%	17.1%
	(29)	(29)	(5)	(7)
Small Law Firm‡	19.4%	16.7%	—	2.4%
	(20)	(21)	—	(1)
Solo Practice	2.9%	0.8%	—	7.3%
	(3)	(1)	—	(3)
Professor of Law	—	4.0%	5.0%	—
	—	(5)	(1)	—
Other	—	—	5.0%	—
	—	—	(1)	—
ABA Rating				
Exceptionally Well Qualified	13.6%	7.1%	20.0%	26.8%
	(14)	(9)	(4)	(11)
Well Qualified	48.5%	43.7%	45.0%	46.3%
	(50)	(55)	(9)	(19)
Qualified	30.1%	46.8%	30.0%	22.0%
	(31)	(59)	(6)	(9)
Not Qualified	6.8%	2.4%	5.0%	2.4%
	(7)	(3)	(1)	(1)
Unknown/Not Rated	1.0%	—	—	2.4%
	(1)	—	—	(1)
Party				
Democratic	89.3%	94.4%	95.0%	95.1%
	(92)	(119)	(19)	(39)
Republican	10.7%	5.6%	—	4.9%
	(11)	(7)	—	(2)
Other	—	—	5.0%	—
	—	—	(1)	—
Prominent Party Activism				
	57.3%	57.1%	85.0%	63.4%
	(59)	(72)	(17)	(26)
Prior or Current Members of Congress				
	1.9%	4.0%	—	7.3%
	(2)	(5)	—	(3)
Religion				
Protestant	60.2%	60.3%	70.0%	61.0%
	(62)	(76)	(14)	(25)

Table 5.1. Continued

| | District Court Appointees | | Appeals Court Appointees | |
| | *JFK* | *LBJ* | *JFK* | *LBJ* |
	Appointees	*Appointees*	*Appointees*	*Appointees*
Catholic	27.2%	27.0%	25.0%	24.4%
	(28)	(34)	(5)	(10)
Jewish	9.7%	10.3%	5.0%	14.6%
	(10)	(13)	(1)	(6)
Other§	1.9%	—	—	—
	(2)	—	—	—
None	—	0.8%	—	—
	—	(1)	—	—
Unknown	1.0%	1.6%	—	—
	(1)	(2)	—	—
Gender				
Male	99.0%	98.4%	100.0%	97.6%
	(102)	(124)	(20)	(40)
Female	1.0%	1.6%	—	2.4%
	(1)	(2)	—	(1)
Ethnicity/race				
White	96.1%	92.1%	95.0%	95.1%
	(99)	(116)	(19)	(39)
Black	1.9%	5.6%	5.0%	4.9%
	(2)	(7)	(1)	(2)
Hispanic	1.0%	2.4%	—	—
	(1)	(3)	—	—
Asian	1.0%	—	—	—
	(1)	—	—	—
Total Number of Appointees				
	103	126	20	41

* A large law firm was defined as consisting of twenty-five or more partners and associates.

† A medium-size law firm was defined as consisting of from five to twenty-four partners and associates.

‡ A small law firm was defined as consisting of from two to four partners and associates.

§ Includes one Mormon and one Christian Scientist.

and Eisenhower appointees, there was a larger proportion of Kennedy appointees with judicial experience than with prosecutorial experience. Johnson's appointees, however, reverted to the more typical pattern of a larger proportion with prosecutorial over judicial experience.

Appeals court appointees, by contrast, traditionally have had more judicial than prosecutorial experience. The proportions of those with judicial and prosecutorial experience, however, were the same for the Kennedy appointees, with over one-third having neither judicial nor prosecutorial experience. Johnson's appeals court appointees showed the traditional edge to judicial experience over prosecutorial experience, with about two-thirds having had judicial experience and less than one-third having had prosecutorial experience. Many judges had both judicial and prosecutorial experience, but about one in four Johnson appointees had neither judicial nor prosecutorial backgrounds. Most of the Kennedy and Johnson appeals court appointees with judicial backgrounds were serving as federal district court judges.

OCCUPATION

The United States attorney's office, typically a source of federal district judge recruitment, was largely unavailable to Kennedy because Eisenhower's Republicans had staffed those positions. Kennedy appointed only two of his United States attorneys (less than 2 percent of his appointees) to the district bench. Kennedy's United States attorneys, however, provided Johnson with fourteen of his district court appointments. Johnson also promoted two of his own United States attorney appointees to district court positions. In total, one in eight Johnson district court appointees were United States attorneys at the time of appointment.

Politics and other government service provided about 10 percent of the district court appointments of Kennedy and Johnson. Among those selected by Kennedy were five state senators, two members of Congress, one federal executive-branch official, and three state or local officials. Among those selected by Johnson were three members of Congress, one governor, six state or local officials, and two federal government officials.

Politics and government service were the source of four (about 10 percent) of Johnson's appeals court appointments. Those chosen included the secretary of health, education, and welfare (Anthony J. Celebrezze), the governor of Illinois (Otto Kerner), a foreign aid official (Frank M. Coffin), and the Detroit police commissioner (George Edwards, who was actually nominated by Kennedy). Kennedy, however, selected only one person holding political office, North Carolina state senator J. Spencer Bell. The United States attorney's office provided no recruits for Kennedy's or Johnson's appellate courts.

The judiciary was a fertile ground for recruitment to the district and appeals courts. Close to one-third of the Kennedy and Johnson district court appointments and at least one half of the appeals court appointments went to those who were members of the judiciary. Of Kennedy's district court appointments, there were two federal bankruptcy referees and two federal judges, Andrew A. Caffrey and C. Nils Tavares to whom Eisenhower had given recess appointments to the federal district bench in 1960. All other Kennedy district court appointees with a judicial occupation were on the state bench. Similarly all but one of Johnson's appointees to the federal district bench were serving on the state bench at the time of appointment.

As one would expect, the federal district bench provided a recruiting ground for the Kennedy and Johnson appeals court appointments. Eight out of ten appointees who were serving as judges at the time of appointment were on the federal district bench. All of Kennedy's elevations from the district bench went to Democrats originally appointed by Roosevelt or Truman. Johnson promoted only one of his own district judge appointees (Spottswood Robinson). About two-thirds of Johnson's elevations from the district bench had originally been appointed by Kennedy.

Private law practice was the major source of recruitment for the district courts. About 55 percent of Kennedy's and about 48 percent of Johnson's district court appointees were in private practice at the time of appointment. This compares to over 70 percent of Eisenhower's first-term district court appointees and about 56 percent of his second-term appointees. The proportion of Kennedy and Johnson appointees in private practice who came from large or medium-size law firms was about three in five.[ii] This exceeded the proportion of Eisenhower appointees in private practice who came from large or medium-size firms (from one-third during Eisenhower's first term to one-half during his second) and far exceeded the Truman proportion. (In Truman's second term only about one in five of those in private practice were from large or medium-size law firms.) These findings reflect in part the significant changes in the practice of law that accelerated in the 1950s and 1960s. Those selected from private law practice were not representative of lawyers in private practice. Only 1.7 percent of the Kennedy and Johnson appointees were solo practitioners, whereas at least 35 percent of the nation's lawyers during the 1960s practiced individually.[90]

Private law practice was a source of recruitment for the appeals courts for

ii. Note a change in the definitions of large and medium-size law firms in table 5.1. This reflects trends in law practice and the growth of law firms in the 1960s. See, for example, Joseph C. Goulden, *The Superlawyers* (New York: Weybright and Talley, 1971).

about three in ten Kennedy and Johnson appointments. Of those in private practice, most were associated with large or medium-size law firms.

The law schools were, to some extent, a source of judges for the Roosevelt administration. The Truman administration appointed only two law professors, and Eisenhower appointed none. Kennedy appointed one (Paul Hays of Columbia Law School) to a circuit court, and Johnson appointed five law professors (or 4 percent of his appointees) to the district bench.

AMERICAN BAR ASSOCIATION RATINGS

Over 60 percent of Kennedy's district court appointees and more than half of Johnson's district court appointees were given one of the two highest ratings by the ABA. These were higher proportions than that achieved by the Eisenhower administration. The proportion of Kennedy district court appointees with the highest two ratings was the highest given by the ABA to any group of presidential district court appointees through the Bush presidency.[91] At the same time, the proportion, although small, of Kennedy appointees receiving the "not qualified" rating was the highest of any group of presidential appointees. Kennedy's Justice Department officials, while working closely with the ABA Standing Committee on Federal Judiciary, nevertheless felt free on occasion to go ahead with a nomination despite a "not qualified" rating. Kennedy even overrode his own brother's judgment and insisted on appointing Luther Bohanon despite a negative rating.

Johnson's few "not qualified" appointments came in 1964 and 1965. After the failed Morrissey nomination in the fall of 1965 and a subsequent meeting between ABA officials and Johnson, the administration never again named someone with a "not qualified" rating.

The ABA ratings of the Kennedy and Johnson appeals court appointees were roughly comparable. The proportion receiving the highest two ratings was lower than that of the Eisenhower appointees but was nevertheless in excess of about two-thirds of the appointees.

PARTY

Slightly more than one in ten of Kennedy's district court appointees was a Republican, a tribute to the efforts of the Kennedy Justice Department to achieve some partisan balance. Unlike Eisenhower's Democratic appointees, almost all of whom were southern Eisenhower supporters, Kennedy's Republicans were regionally distributed: four were from the East, three from the West, and four from the Midwest. (The South, still primarily Democratic, did not yield a Republican appointee.) Johnson had half Kennedy's proportion of Republicans appointed to the district bench but, unlike Kennedy, he appointed

Republicans (two) to the appeals bench. Seven of Johnson's nine Republican appointees were from the East, one from the Midwest, and one from the West. In absolute numbers, Kennedy and Johnson together named more than twice the number of Republicans to district and appeals courts as Eisenhower named Democrats.

More than half of Kennedy's and Johnson's district court appointees had records of prominent political activity, and more than eight in ten Kennedy appeals court appointees had previously been involved in politics. About two-thirds of Johnson's appeals court appointees had similar records of partisan activism. Johnson appointed the largest proportion of current or previous members of Congress since Truman.

RELIGIOUS ORIGIN OR AFFILIATION

More than one in four Kennedy and Johnson appointees to the district courts were Catholic. This was higher than Eisenhower's proportion of Catholic district court appointees (19.0 percent) but lower than Roosevelt's (30.1 percent) and Truman's (33.0 percent). About one in four Kennedy and Johnson appeals court appointees were Catholics, substantially above the level under Roosevelt (12.0 percent), and Eisenhower (13.3 percent).

Close to 10 percent of Kennedy and Johnson district court appointees were Jewish. This was higher than Roosevelt's (4.5 percent) and Eisenhower's (6.4 percent) proportions but slightly lower than Truman's (11.3 percent). Only one of Kennedy's appeals courts appointees was Jewish, but Kennedy appointed a Jew, Arthur Goldberg, to the Supreme Court, thus maintaining "the Jewish seat" on the Court when Felix Frankfurter retired. Johnson's proportion of Jewish appointments to the appeals courts was almost three times Kennedy's, and Johnson replaced Arthur Goldberg with Abe Fortas, also of Jewish heritage. Of all five presidents, Johnson appointed the highest proportion of Jews to the appeals courts and Roosevelt the lowest.

Although these figures do not definitively prove the presence or absence of subtle religious biases within the judicial selection process, it appears that whatever biases had existed were no longer at work in most parts of the country by the late 1960s.

GENDER, RACE, AND ETHNICITY

Kennedy's and Johnson's appointments of women were clearly tokenism. Women made up only 1 percent of Kennedy's district court appointments and 1.8 percent of all of Johnson's lifetime judicial appointments.

Kennedy and Johnson had more impressive records of appointing African Americans. Kennedy added three to the lifetime federal judiciary, and two other blacks were nominated by Kennedy but confirmed under Johnson. Johnson named eight blacks to the district bench, but one, Cecil Poole of California, was blocked by Republicans in 1968 as part of election year maneuvering. Overall, close to 5 percent of all of Johnson's judicial appointments went to African Americans.[jj] Clearly, both Kennedy and Johnson heralded the beginning of meaningful opportunity for talented black lawyers within the federal judiciary, and they and their administrations were responsible for pathbreaking appointments.

Kennedy was also responsible for the appointment of the first publicly acknowledged hispanic to a lifetime federal judgeship—Reynaldo B. Garza, a Mexican-American from Texas.[kk] Johnson named another hispanic, Manuel L. Real, also a Mexican-American, to a judgeship in California, and he named two Puerto Ricans to the first two lifetime judgeships in Puerto Rico.[92]

Before Eisenhower left office he had nominated C. Nils Tavares to a Hawaiian district judgeship. Tavares's mother was a native Hawaiian. Kennedy resubmitted the nomination, and Tavares became the first person of Asian ancestry to occupy a lifetime federal judgeship.

Kennedy and Johnson changed the demographic and political complexion of the federal judiciary, but in different ways. Kennedy, although interested in the judiciary, delegated responsibility to his brother Robert, who as attorney general had unusual leeway and access to the president. The federal courts were not seen as particularly relevant to the president's policy agenda, with the important exception of civil rights. In the course of furthering the partisan agenda, the Kennedy administration strived to make quality appointments and, with the exception of some southern appointments, largely succeeded. Johnson, too, saw the federal judiciary as important to the administration largely in terms of civil rights. But unlike Kennedy, Johnson furthered his personal agenda and personally oversaw judicial selection. Kennedy was not necessarily less interested in the judiciary than was Johnson, but he could trust his brother to take care of the details. As far as presidential involvement in judicial selection was concerned, Johnson was more like Roosevelt and Kennedy was more like Eisenhower. Yet Kennedy and Johnson aimed to appoint

---

jj. These figures do not include James L. Watson's appointment to the Customs Court.

kk. Truman named Harold Medina to the federal district bench and later promoted him to the U.S. Court of Appeals for the Second Circuit. Although Medina's father was Mexican American, Medina was not raised as a latino, did not present himself as latino, and was not considered by the public and the Truman administration as having hispanic origins. Even Medina's obituary in the *New York Times* failed to mention Medina's hispanic roots. See *New York Times,* March 16, 1990, B7.

similar kinds of judges, and both administrations shied away from public battle with Democratic senators (in contrast to Roosevelt and Truman). None of the few failed nominations to the lower courts ever came to a vote in the Senate.

The 1960s were years of turbulent change. Kennedy had promised to get America moving again and indeed America moved, albeit not altogether in the sense that Kennedy had meant. During Kennedy's presidency, despite or because of a series of racial crises in the South, the nation lurched toward the goal of ending racism. The assassination of Kennedy was followed by America's growing involvement in the bloody and controversial Vietnam War. The war mobilized and divided millions of Americans and accelerated the pace of social change. It also altered the face of American politics, as did the summers of racial riots and the assassinations in 1968 of Martin Luther King, Jr., and Robert Kennedy.

The Democratic presidential convention in the summer of 1968 was a tumultuous one, climaxed by rioting outside the convention hall at about the time that Vice-President Hubert Humphrey, the quintessential Democratic Party liberal, won the Democratic presidential nomination with Johnson's blessing. Alabama governor George Wallace mounted a third-party challenge and threatened to siphon off white lower-class votes from the Democrats. Richard Nixon, defeated for the presidency in 1960 and for the governorship of California in 1962, mounted a remarkable political comeback and won the Republican nomination.

In the fall of 1968 the federal courts became a campaign issue. Both Wallace and Nixon attacked the courts for being soft on crime and for being too liberal. With his election by a plurality of 43.4 percent of the popular vote, Nixon was given the opportunity to reshape the federal bench.

6

Picking Judges in the Shadow of Watergate

In the 1968 presidential election campaign, Richard Nixon attacked the Warren Court's judicial activism along with its criminal procedures decisions.[1] Nixon promised to name "strict constructionists" and implied that he would use the power of judicial selection to change the balance on the courts from liberal activism to conservative law and order.[2] On May 21, 1969, President Nixon named District of Columbia Court of Appeals judge Warren E. Burger, an opponent of the Warren Court's liberal criminal procedures decisions, to the chief justiceship, replacing the retiring Earl Warren. Prior to naming Burger, the Nixon administration also stage-managed (by strategic leaks to the media and innuendoes of wrongdoing) the resignation of the liberal justice Abe Fortas, thus creating another vacancy to be filled.[3] It was easier to pressure Fortas into resigning, however, than it was to fill the vacancy.

At first Nixon nominated a southern, conservative appeals court judge, Clement Haynsworth, but he was rejected by the Senate after organized labor and civil rights groups mounted a campaign against him and liberal Democratic senators uncovered what they claimed were conflicts of interest. Nixon tried again with another southern conservative, the federal appellate judge G. Harrold Carswell, who, unlike the scholarly, Harvard law-trained Haynsworth, was seen as a mediocre jurist. Again, opponents came up with damaging background information, and Carswell was defeated on the floor of the

Senate. Finally, a conservative midwestern appeals court judge, Harry Blackmun, was approved, and the seat on the Court that had been vacant for more
than a year was filled. These events placed the selection process of Supreme
Court justices—and Supreme Court policymaking—on the front burner of
American politics. The effect of the Burger and Blackmun appointments was
to destroy the liberal activist majority on the Court, although years later
Blackmun would move to the Court's liberal wing, becoming at the end of his
judicial career its mainstay.

Although Nixon had won the 1968 election, he did not bring a Republican
Congress with him. The Democrats were in firm control, with only four fewer
House seats and five fewer Senate seats than they had had in the previous
Congress. President Nixon made a strenuous effort in the 1970 off-year elections, but the results were mixed—a three-seat gain in the Senate but a twelve-
seat loss in the House. In 1971, controversy over the continuing Vietnam War
heated up with the publication of the Pentagon Papers, and public opinion
polls showed a sharp drop in the president's popularity. Indeed, at the start of
1972, most polls indicated that Maine senator Edmund Muskie, the front
runner for the Democratic nomination, would defeat Nixon. It was then that
plans and strategies were put in place by Nixon operatives that were designed
to reelect the president. Those plans included surveillance activities such as the
infamous break-in on June 17 at Democratic Party headquarters at the Watergate complex in Washington and harassment of the Muskie campaign that
eventually brought down Muskie's candidacy.

After the break-in, Nixon and his close aides, along with various other
officials, engaged in a coverup to limit the political and legal damage stemming
from the arrests of the Watergate burglars. At first they were successful, and
the Nixon reelection effort gained momentum, particularly as the Democratic
National Convention was taken over by the political left, choosing as its
nominee the antiwar South Dakota senator George McGovern. Nixon and his
vice president, Spiro Agnew, were reelected by a landslide 60.7 percent of the
popular vote, rivaling Roosevelt's 1936 victory and coming close to Johnson's
modern popular vote record of 61.1 percent. This stunning electoral victory
did not result in the election of a Republican Congress, although Republicans
gained thirteen seats in the House (but had a net loss of two in the Senate).

The Nixon presidency began unraveling in 1973 as the Watergate-related
crimes became public and Nixon's authority and administration were undermined. The grand jury that considered the Watergate burglary and the subsequent coverup of the crime (which itself constituted the crime of obstruction
of justice) eventually named Nixon himself as an unindicted co-conspirator.
But even before then, under political and public pressure, the administration

named a special prosecutor to investigate the crimes arising from the 1972 presidential election. The Senate began hearings on Watergate in May 1973, which continued through the summer. One sensational revelation followed the next. When one witness revealed the existence of recordings of Oval Office conversations, the special prosecutor sought possession of the tapes, and the administration resisted turning them over. The scandal-plagued administration was thrown into deeper disgrace when, in October 1973, Vice President Spiro Agnew resigned from office after pleading no contest to income tax evasion for not reporting the bribes he had received as income. Nixon replaced Agnew with the popular House Republican minority leader, Gerald Ford.[5]

When the Supreme Court ruled that Nixon was obliged to turn over key tapes to the special prosecutor,[6] the game was over. Facing impeachment, on August 9, 1974, Nixon resigned the presidency, and Gerald Ford became president of the United States.[7]

Barely a month passed before the new president extended a blanket pardon to Nixon for any crimes for which he might otherwise have been convicted. Public reaction against the pardon undercut the widely favorable view the public had of the new president. In the November 1974 congressional elections the Democrats picked up forty-three seats in the House and four in the Senate. Against the backdrop of these tumultuous political events Richard Nixon and then Gerald Ford selected federal judges.

Presidential Involvement in Selection

Unlike fellow member of the bar Franklin D. Roosevelt, Richard M. Nixon did not seem to have much interest in lower-court judgeships or the politics surrounding them. To be sure, he wanted lower-court appointees to share his judicial philosophy. But there are only few instances where Nixon's hand can be seen in selection. This is true for both Nixon's first term (pre-Watergate) and second term (post-Watergate). The conclusion is inescapable that judicial selection below the Supreme Court level held little interest for him. As his biographers amply demonstrate, plotting grand political strategy and conducting foreign policy were activities that challenged him intellectually. Evidently, lower-court selection held less fascination, although very late in his presidency Nixon sought more White House involvement in selection.

An example of personal involvement by Nixon is suggested by a 1969 memorandum from White House assistant Harry Dent about former New Mexico senator Ed Mechem, who was subsequently appointed to the federal district bench. Dent wrote:

On Tuesday I was asked by the President what has been done for Ed Mechem of New Mexico. I checked with Peter Flanigan and Dick Kleindienst. I found that Senator Mechem wants to be a Federal District Judge and is expecting to be appointed to the new judgeship to be created when the omnibus judgeship bill is finally passed by the Congress, perhaps this year. I talked with Senator Mechem to let him know of the President's interest in him and he was most grateful. Dick Kleindienst knows of the President's interest and will follow through on this nomination at the appropriate time.[8]

Nixon also got involved in filling a vacancy in Minnesota for which a brother of former aide Clark MacGregor was a candidate. MacGregor's brother was not the choice of Minnesota Republican representative Ancher Nelsen. Nelsen backed Donald Alsop, who headed Nelsen's reelection committee in 1972 and was also a Nixon delegate to the 1968 Republican National Convention. In his letter to MacGregor, Nixon noted: "As you know, the competition for this seat is intense, but you can be sure your brother's candidacy will not be overlooked during the selection process."[9] What in fact happened, however, was that Alsop was nominated on Nixon's last full day in office.

One of the most controversial nominations of Nixon's presidency was that of Republican Connecticut governor Thomas Meskill to the U. S. Court of Appeals for the Second Circuit. This nomination was helpful politically to the Republican Party in Connecticut, given Meskill's outspoken support for Nixon and likely difficulty in being reelected in 1974. But the ABA strenuously objected to Meskill as "not qualified." Nevertheless, on June 24, 1974, when his presidency was in its terminal stage, Nixon wrote to Meskill: "I understand Dave Wimer [of the White House Counsel's Office] has been talking with you during my absence. You may be sure he will keep in touch with you and make every effort to work this situation out to your satisfaction."[10] Meskill was also nominated on Nixon's last working day in the White House.

Just about one month before his resignation, Nixon wrote to Attorney General William Saxbe[a] hinting at a gulf between the White House and the

---

a. Nixon's first two attorneys general, John Mitchell and Richard Kleindienst, were tarnished by scandal, and his third, Elliot Richardson, was fired in the "Saturday Night Massacre," when he refused to dismiss Watergate special prosecutor Archibald Cox. Mitchell was convicted of a felony in connection with Watergate and went to prison. Kleindienst pleaded guilty to a non-Watergate-related misdemeanor (refusing to answer accurately and fully questions of a congressional committee), and was given one month's unsupervised probation. See Kleindienst's account in Richard G. Kleindienst, *Justice: The*

Justice Department over judicial selection: "In order to insure that I have a range of suitable options for all future appointments to the Federal bench, henceforth please submit for my consideration at least three qualified candidates for each judicial vacancy. I will, of course, continue to expect your recommendation as to the most qualified potential nominee."[11]

John Ehrlichman, assistant to the president for domestic affairs, played a special role in judicial selection, particularly for Ehrlichman's home state of Washington. But Ehrlichman also took an interest in some other judgeships, and it appears that Nixon simply delegated responsibility to him and took little personal interest in these matters. For example, in a memo to Deputy Attorney General Kleindienst, Ehrlichman highly recommended Peter Fay, "who was our Nixon-Agnew Chairman in Miami" and "is completely loyal to the President." Ehrlichman praised Fay as "professionally outstanding, morally impeccable and politically loyal." He closed his memo by asking: "Would you please put him at the top of your list for the northern district of Florida and permit me to do whatever is necessary to assist in assuring his appointment?"[12] Fay was indeed appointed.

In other instances, Ehrlichman was not quite so pushy. For example, he told the attorney general that he "had an inquiry about the prospects of Robert Macey Taylor for appointment to the Federal District bench in Alabama" and that he "would appreciate both a political rundown and your estimate of whether he will receive your favorable recommendation and, if so, when."[13] Taylor did not receive an appointment.

With appointments from the state of Washington, Ehrlichman clearly picked the judges. For example, a week before Nixon's first inauguration, Eugene A. Wright, a Seattle lawyer and close friend of Ehrlichman's, wrote of his interest in one of four newly created Ninth Circuit positions. Wright asked Ehrlichman for his "recommendation as to what, if anything, I should be doing." Ehrlichman handwrote on the top of the letter "Discuss w/ Kleindienst" and subsequently replied to Wright, asking for "a full resume of your life and career so that I can place it in the hands of the Deputy Attorney General at the soonest possible minute." Ehrlichman added, "I can't think of anyone I would rather recommend for a judicial post than you." Wright eventually received the appointment. Because of Ehrlichman's personal interest and intervention, Wright's commission was dated one day earlier than two other Ninth Circuit appointees whose commissions were sent to the White House, in order to give Wright seniority.[14]

Memoirs of Attorney General Richard Kleindienst (Ottawa, Ill.: Jameson Books, 1985), 90–109, 175–97.

Another indicator of Ehrlichman's activism in selecting federal court nomi- nees for the state of Washington is revealed by a memorandum for the record written by Ehrlichman's administrative assistant, Tod R. Hullin. Hullin wrote: "Ehrlichman plans to appoint [Walter T.] McGovern to the Federal District Court and the Governor will appoint Judge Mo [Morrell E.] Sharp to the Supreme Court of the State of Washington and Gordon Clinton to a Superior Court position." Ehrlichman also engineered Sharp's eventual appointment to the federal district bench in Washington. Sharp acknowledged Ehrlichman's role in his advancement when he wrote to Ehrlichman, "Thanks to you, I will be sworn in tomorrow morning."[15]

When Judge Charles L. Powell of the Eastern District of Washington in- formed the Justice Department of his planned retirement, Kleindienst wrote to Ehrlichman, "Please call me at your convenience . . . so that we can begin to program a replacement." U.S. district judge Walter T. McGovern wrote a letter to Ehrlichman recommending Marshall A. Neill as "a high caliber guy and a credit to the bench, bar and Republican Party."[16] Neill was appointed to replace Powell.

Earlier, Ehrlichman had a correspondence with his friend C. Robert Ogden, who was interested in the judgeship that went to Neill. In a letter to Ehrlich- man, Ogden wrote that he had met with Kleindienst, who said "there was no objection to me from the standpoint of the Justice Department. . . . He indi- cated, however, that appointments from the State of Washington are in your hands." Ogden asked Ehrlichman for his "approval for appointment as Judge of the United States District Court for the Eastern District of Washington." Ehrlichman wrote back to Ogden: "The suggestion that judicial appointments from the State of Washington are in my hands is somewhat overstating the case, I am afraid. I will certainly talk with Dick [Kleindienst] about your strong interest in this appointment and doubtless you will be hearing from him about it."[17] That same day Ehrlichman wrote to Kleindienst: "Here is a letter from Bob Ogden of Spokane. I'll call your attention particularly to the second paragraph in which he says that appointments from the State of Washington are in your hands, meaning me. I have no doubt that you are more discreet than to have said that and I've written him the enclosed letter to try and set matters straight as to where the real power lies."[18]

During the Ford administration, there was no one person on the White House staff with Ehrlichman's clout in matters of judicial selection, although White House Counsel Philip Buchen at times played a leading role. Ford him- self was somewhat more involved in judicial selection than was Nixon. Along with the White House Counsel's Office, the director of the Presidential Person- nel Office was concerned with selection. The staff obtained Ford's approval of a nomination before a formal letter of recommendation, along with the nomination documents, was sent by the attorney general to the president.[19]

Ford chose as his attorney general the president of the University of Chicago, Edward Levi, a noted legal scholar and a man of impeccable reputation.[b] Levi's deputy attorney general was U.S. district judge Harold Tyler, who resigned his judgeship upon joining the Justice Department in April 1975. These blue-chip appointments were designed to restore the reputation of the Justice Department, which was badly damaged by the Watergate scandals. Ford's relationship with Levi and Tyler, however, tended to be formal; indeed, there is no evidence in the presidential papers of any interchange concerning judicial selection between Tyler and the president. There is also little evidence of informal interchange between Levi and Ford over lower-court judgeships.

The formality of the relationship between Ford and his attorney general is suggested by the briefing paper that White House aide James E. Connor prepared for the president in anticipation of Ford's first private meeting with the attorney general. The paper opened with a background section:

> You previously saw him at the last Cabinet meeting on February 21st, and you were present at his swearing-in at the Justice Department on February 7th. This is the first of a series of meetings with your new Cabinet officers. It is intended to enable you and the Attorney General to get to know one another better, and to enable each of you to indicate general policy areas and approaches you consider important.

Connor briefed the president on the issues to be discussed and concluded with several "Talking Points":

> 1. Ed, this is the first of a series of meetings I intend to have with my new Cabinet officers. I want to focus on broad policy questions to get your views and to let you know my own.

b. Some twenty-three years earlier, Francis Biddle, attorney general under Roosevelt and Truman, had recommended Levi for an Illinois judgeship. Levi was then dean of the law school of the University of Chicago. Biddle wrote: "Levi is a liberal Democrat, and has the endorsement of the Americans for Democratic Action." Biddle to Truman, January 23, 1952, OF 208T Northern District End. Miscel., Harry S. Truman Presidential Library. But Levi assumed a more nonpartisan stance, particularly when he became president of the University of Chicago. At his confirmation hearing, he noted that he was a political independent and had not registered with any political party for a number of years. See U.S. Senate, *Hearings on the Nomination of Edward H. Levi to be Attorney General, before the Committee on the Judiciary,* 94th Cong., 1st Sess. (Washington, D.C.: Government Printing Office, 1975), 7, as cited by Nancy V. Baker, "Rebuilding Confidence: Ford's Choice of Attorney General," in Bernard J. Firestone and Alexej Ugrinsky, eds., *Gerald R. Ford and the Politics of Post-Watergate America* (Westport, Conn.: Greenwood, 1993), 1:85.

2. I understand that there were several areas you wanted to raise. Let's start with them. . . .

6. I want you to know that you will have access to me when you need it. I've asked Jim Connor to meet with you regularly. If you need quick answers or want to see me, let him know.[20]

Other meetings with the attorney general were similarly scripted.[21]

When Ford had his own suggestions for judgeships, he apparently did not communicate directly with Levi or Tyler. Instead he wrote to his staff, typically the director of the Presidential Personnel Office. In a note to William N. Walker, who was director until June 12, 1975, Ford handwrote: "Sen. Marlow Cook indicated to me his interest in a Federal Judicial apptmt. Extremely well qualified. CCA [circuit court of appeals] would be excellent. Anything in prospect." Cook, however, did not receive a judgeship. In a note to Walker's successor, Douglas Bennett, Ford handwrote: "Judge Peter Fay—for CCA. *Good man.*"[22] There was a happier ending for the candidate in this instance: Fay was appointed by Ford to the Fifth Circuit in 1976.

In approving the nomination of J. Blaine Anderson to a judgeship on the Court of Appeals for the Ninth Circuit, Ford asked, "Was Judge James Battin considered? Let me know."[23] Battin had previously been a congressman, and Ford maintained an interest in his former colleagues. Indeed, he liked to know who the nominee's member of Congress was, and this information was included in the cover memo to the president with the official nominating documents.

Periodically, a "judicial status report" was circulated in the White House reporting on judicial vacancies, those for whom an informal ABA recommendation was sought or already obtained, and those for whom the formal FBI and ABA reports were in progress or completed. On one such status report, in February 1976, Ford wrote, "We must *move* on those in Justice and elsewhere."[24] He was undoubtedly aware that during a presidential election year it was essential to act quickly to fill vacancies because Democrats, in control of the Senate, would be reluctant to confirm judgeships until after the election. Ford was right: as it turned out, ten nominations for lifetime judgeships to the district and appeals courts died with the Ford presidency.

The Policy Agenda and Selection

Although it was unusual for Nixon to be involved in specific judicial nominations, he had a broader interest in judicial selection and its implications for his policy agenda. Early in his first term, a young White House staffer, Tom Charles Huston, wrote a seven-page memorandum to the president concerning judicial selection. Huston began by noting, "Perhaps the least considered aspect of Presidential power is the authority to make appointments to the federal bench — not merely to the Supreme Court, but to the Circuit and District benches as well. Through his judicial appointments, a President has the opportunity to influence the course of national affairs for a quarter of a century after he leaves office."

Huston went on to observe that in a recent Gallup survey 75 percent of those polled expressed dissatisfaction with the courts and that

> growing popular disillusionment with the courts can most likely be traced to recent Supreme Court rulings on crime and segregation. The man in the street believes the courts are soft on criminals and blacks. To the thoughtful critic of the courts, however, the problem is more fundamental: the courts have opted for active combat in the political arena and judges have thereby forfeited their claim to impartiality and detachment.[25]

Huston continued, emphasizing, *"In approaching the bench, it is necessary to remember that the decision as to who will make the decisions affects what decisions will be made.* That is, the role the judiciary will play in different historical eras depends as much on the type of men who become judges as it does on the constitutional rules which appear to set at least the outer limits of judicial action."[26]

Huston noted that there are several ways in which the president can select judges. The president can appoint those who are best qualified professionally, as determined by the ABA "consistent with practical political considerations." Or the president can consider judicial appointments "essentially a patronage problem to be worked out with the interested political parties." Or the president "can take an active personal interest in appointments to all judicial vacancies." The final possibility, which Huston advocated, "is for the President to establish precise guidelines as to the type of man he wishes to appoint — his professional competence, his political disposition, his understanding of the judicial function — and establish a White House review procedure to assure that each prospective nominee recommended by the Attorney General meets the guidelines."[27]

Huston concluded by observing that if the President "establishes *his* criteria and establishes *his* machinery for insuring that the criteria are met, the appointments he makes will be *his,* in fact, as in theory."[28]

Huston submitted the memo to H. R. Haldeman, who gave it to John Ehrlichman, who turned it over to the staff secretary to place in the president's reading matter. Nixon not only read the memo carefully, but he directed it to Deputy Attorney General Kleindienst with a handwritten notation: "RN *agrees* — Have this analysis in mind in making judicial nominations."[29]

There is no evidence, however, that a formal White House review procedure, as Huston advocated, was ever put in place — that would not occur until the presidency of Ronald Reagan. Ehrlichman, it seems, handled judicial appointments and occasionally reported to Nixon. For example, in a memo to the president, Ehrlichman praised two court of appeals candidates as "a good Republican" (Roger Robb) and "your friend in Minnesota" (George MacKinnon).[30]

There is one instance, early in the first term, suggesting Nixon's concern with the policy views of a judicial candidate for a circuit judgeship. The candidate was U.S. district judge William E. Miller of Tennessee. Bryce Harlow, a close Nixon aide, wrote to the president: "Senator Robert Griffin [Michigan Republican] telephoned May 23 to report to you, as promised, his check on Judge Bill Miller of Tennessee. . . . Griffin states that Judge Miller's civil rights attitudes are still unknown as far as Griffin is concerned, and he believes this should be carefully checked. But otherwise, he regards Miller on the conservative side philosophically, a good Republican, but not immoderately conservative."[31] There is no evidence, however, that Miller's civil rights record was checked or that the administration was concerned about candidates' views on civil rights.

Typically, letters to the president and his assistants supporting candidacies for judgeships emphasized the candidates' conservative views. For example, a letter to Nixon recommending William Erickson for the Colorado federal district bench praised Erickson (who did not receive an appointment) as "hard lined and a real strict constructionist." A letter to Alexander M. Haig, Jr., when he was assistant to the president in 1974, praised John L. Coffey, an unsuccessful candidate for the federal district bench in Milwaukee who was then serving on the state bench, as "an extremely tough conservative law and order judge."[32] (Eight years later, Coffey would be appointed by Ronald Reagan to the Seventh Circuit.)

One Nixon nominee to the Seventh Circuit, Charles A. Bane, ran into trouble in the Senate Judiciary Committee over allegations of antisemitism.[33] The nomination was withdrawn on October 22, 1969, and eleven months later Nixon named John Paul Stevens to that vacancy, thus launching a judicial career that six years later would take Stevens to the Supreme Court.

Richard Nixon liked the idea of a constitutional amendment requiring reconfirmation of federal judges after a ten-year term. Undoubtedly this was tied to policy concerns. But Nixon proceeded cautiously, as revealed by this memo from Ehrlichman to White House legislative liaison William Timmons: "The President feels the best way to proceed with this idea is to have a friendly Senator introduce it early in the session to give the President an opportunity to react at a press conference or in some other forum in a favorable fashion. Will you please cause a bill to be prepared and introduced without any commitment for or by the President and without his auspices?"[34]

In the heady days after Nixon's landslide reelection, anything seemed possible, even the radical alteration of the judicial branch of government. But Watergate derailed any plans to rewrite Article III of the Constitution.

Given Nixon's rhetoric about law and order, it is surprising to find so little concern about the issue in presidential papers regarding specific appointments. Of course, mostly conservative Republican senators were making recommendations of primarily conservative Republican lawyers. There surely would be no appointments of known liberal activists, yet the lack of evidence of careful policy-agenda screening might lead one to conclude that for Nixon law and order was more a potent campaign issue than a high-priority agenda item for judicial selection.

The Ford administration showed little concern with ideology. There was, however, an instance when one staffer suggested holding off on liberal New York Republican senator Jacob Javits's choice for the New York federal district bench until after the senatorial election. If the Conservative Party candidate, James Buckley, were to win a Senate seat, the staffer noted, "a Buckley choice would be much closer to the President's philosophy than a Javits choice."[35]

The only instance to be found in the Ford presidential papers of his concern with the policy views of specific individuals occurred with the nomination of John Paul Stevens to the Supreme Court. Attorney General Levi described Stevens as "a moderate conservative" and discussed his voting record as a circuit judge on criminal justice issues. The president himself "asked what Judge Stevens' views were on environmental questions."[36] The Ford administration made a great effort to recover from the Watergate scandal, and part of that effort was a judicial selection process that sought quality appointments with apparently little concern for the impact of judicial selection on the president's policy agenda.

There is hardly any evidence in the Nixon and Ford presidential papers of policy-agenda concerns in appeals court appointments. For only one Nixon appointee is there evidence of stated policy concerns; there is no evidence of policy-agenda screening for the Ford appointees. Yet we know that liberal Democratic activists were not chosen. What seems apparent is that there were no specific policy-agenda concerns that drove the appointment process. Rather, the papers reveal more traditional partisan concerns in both the patronage and the broader good-appointments-are-good-politics sense. There is no evidence of personal-agenda appointments by either president.

Senators and Selection

The Nixon administration, as expected, showed deference to senators of the president's party when it came to filling federal district judgeships. The administration tried to exercise more independence from Republican senators when it came to filling circuit court judgeships. For example, Hawaii Republican senator Hiram Fong wanted a Hawaiian (he suggested U.S. district judge C. Nils Tavares) to be appointed to one of the three new positions on the Ninth Circuit. When the administration said no, Fong held up appointments to the circuit. The administration apparently struck a deal with Fong, because he stopped obstructing nominations and the next vacancy on the Ninth Circuit went to a Hawaiian.[c]

The Nixon administration treated powerful opposition senators respectfully, particularly because Democrats maintained control of the Senate. For example, the deputy assistant to the president wrote to West Virginia Democratic senator Robert C. Byrd, who was majority whip:

> The President has asked me to thank you and Senator [Jennings] Randolph for your joint letter regarding the elevation of the Honorable John A. Field, Jr. to the Fourth Circuit Court of Appeals and also recommending [Democrats] Robert B. Bailey, William T. Brotherton and K. K. Hall for consideration to fill the vacancy created in the District Court for the Southern District of West Virginia. All three men appear to be very fine candidates and I am certain all would make fine Federal judges. Unfortunately only one will be selected and we will ask the Justice Department to start the selection process immediately.[37]

Field, a Republican, was promoted to the Fourth Circuit, and Democrat Kenneth K. Hall was named to replace him on the federal bench in West Virginia.

Another example involved the two Democratic senators from the state of Washington. The administration was set to name Morrell Sharp to a district court position. Ehrlichman's administrative assistant wrote to Kleindienst: "John [Ehrlichman] feels he cannot approach Senators [Henry M.] Jackson and [Warren] Magnuson on the appointment of Mo Sharp to this position. He feels they would 'try to take a bite out of him' and that it would be much less complicated if somebody from the Justice Department approached them on Sharp's appointment. Incidentally, Judge Boldt has indicated that each of the Senators will wholeheartedly support the appointment of Sharp."[38]

---

c. Herbert Y. C. Choy was appointed. Senator Fong's initial delaying tactics were reported in the *Wall Street Journal*, August 21, 1969.

On another occasion, Ehrlichman was counseled that "if Senator Jackson were advised that by some agreement one position might go to a Democrat, it might be possible to move ahead on any suggested openings that are coming." Ehrlichman responded to this advice: "I appreciate your bringing this situation to my attention. I will talk with the Attorney General about it as soon as possible."[39] A Democrat, Donald S. Voorhees, was appointed in 1974.

The Ford administration had one major problem with a Republican senator and learned the hard way to respect senatorial courtesy. The senator that caused the headaches was William Scott of Virginia. Ford later wrote in his memoirs that Scott was "inflexible" and "very disagreeable." Scott "vigorously" backed the appointment of Glen M. Williams to fill a vacancy on the Virginia federal district court bench. Ford, however, preferred William B. Poff, who was strongly backed by Congressman Caldwell Butler. Poff was rated "qualified" by the ABA and despite Scott's insistence on Williams, Poff was nominated. Scott, however, invoked senatorial courtesy, and the Senate Judiciary Committee tabled the Poff nomination. In a letter to the president, Poff asked that his nomination be withdrawn because of Senator Scott's "invocation of the doctrine of senatorial courtesy," and on June 3, 1976, it was.[40]

Once it was clear that the Poff nomination was dead, U.S. district judge Ted Dalton, a former Republican leader in Virginia, urged the administration to name Glen Williams. Dalton noted that Williams "is very capable" and "had no part in Scott's opposition to Poff and . . . was an innocent bystander." But the administration did not move to fill the Virginia judgeship during the summer of 1976. Ford was preparing for the Republican National Convention, and he faced a challenge from Ronald Reagan (whom Senator Scott backed). Judge Dalton wrote to Ford on August 23, asking for an appointment to discuss the judgeship, but White House Counsel Buchen vetoed that idea as "not proper." Key administration advisers met on September 2 and recommended that Ford nominate Tom Wilson for the judgeship. Ford approved, but Wilson's nomination was blocked by Senator Scott. The administration then relented and named Williams, who won quick confirmation.[41]

Florida Democratic senators Richard Stone and Lawton Chiles established a Judicial Selection Commission consisting of nine commissioners, including three appointed by the Board of Governors of the Florida Bar and three by each senator. The commission was to screen judicial candidates and name the five who were best qualified. The senators would then select one of the five to recommend to the president. The senators said they would withhold their endorsement of candidates who did not come through this process. This put them on a collision course with the administration. The administration defied the Florida senators by naming Elizabeth Kovachevich, who was rated "qualified" by the ABA, to fill a Florida vacancy, although she was not on the commission's list. The Democratic senators opposed her nomination, and she was not confirmed.[d] Two months later, the Democratic senators recommended Democrat Sydney Aronowitz, although the administration's preferred Republican candidate received a higher ABA rating ("well qualified") than did Aronowitz ("qualified"). The administration went with Aronowitz, who was confirmed.[42]

The Ford administration nominated Donald Walter to a Louisiana judgeship, but Senator Russell Long was opposed.[43] The Walter nomination was one of ten that failed to win approval in late 1976 at the end of the Ford presidency.

Other Appointment Process Considerations

PARTY ORGANIZATION INVOLVEMENT

In the Nixon and Ford administrations strong party organizations carried great weight in the absence of Republican senators. For example, the Republican leadership in Georgia agreed on four candidates for four newly created district judgeships in their state. Florence Cauble, the Georgia national committeewoman, wrote to Nixon recommending William C. O'Kelley, Charles A. Moye, Richard C. Freeman, and Anthony A. Alaimo. Harry S. Dent, special counsel to the president, replied: "Your letter to the President recommending candidates for the Federal Judgeships for Georgia has been received. I am personally giving this to the Attorney General at the President's request."[44] All four received appointments.

Party organization considerations came into play concerning a vacancy in Pennsylvania. Republican governor Ray Shafer was unpopular, and the Republican Party organization feared that he would lose at the next election. Harry Dent, in a memo to Ehrlichman, raised the possibility that Governor Shafer might be interested in a federal judgeship, although it was unclear then whether Pennsylvania Republican Hugh Scott, the Senate minority leader, would back Shafer for the federal bench. Peter M. Flanigan, assistant to the president, subsequently wrote to Attorney General John N. Mitchell recom-

d. Kovachevich received a federal judgeship from Ronald Reagan in 1982. John Moore, another Florida Republican nominated by Ford but not backed by the Florida senators, also failed to win confirmation. He, too, was subsequently placed on the bench by Reagan (in 1981).

mending that Shafer be considered, although he noted that "the one key interested party" — a reference to Senator Scott — did not back the idea.[45e]

Ford's administration, like Nixon's, was respectful of party organizations. As a matter of routine, the names of judicial nominees were submitted to the Republican National Committee for clearance before the nominations were sent to the Senate. When there were no Republican senators from the state with the judicial vacancy, the most important state party leader was consulted. For example, in West Virginia, Republican governor Arch Moore made the recommendations; in Wisconsin, the Republican national committeeman; and in California, Governor Ronald Reagan. One of Reagan's recommendations to fill a vacancy on the Court of Appeals for the Ninth Circuit was Anthony M. Kennedy, who would later be appointed to the Supreme Court when Ronald Reagan was president. Kennedy's nomination was made despite the fact that within the White House Counsel's Office there was the belief that there was "inadequate evidence of quality."[46f]

The appointment of a member of the opposition party ordinarily causes anxiety on the part of party organizations. For example, a South Carolina Republican leader sent a telegram to Nixon to protest the impending appointment of a Democrat. Harry Dent reassured the leader that "no one who supported Hubert Humphrey in South Carolina in 1968 will be appointed to a judgeship in 1971." Dent also noted: "At the present time there is only one vacancy in South Carolina and if we wind up with only one that will go to a Republican. If another vacancy is created, the nominee for this position will also come from the list submitted by Senator [Strom] Thurmond. As you may know, the Senator has stated that he submitted Republicans and Democrats. I know, however, that no one who supported Humphrey is going to be a judge in South Carolina."[47] Two federal district judges were appointed in 1971, Republican Robert F. Chapman and Democrat Solomon Blatt.

There was one instance in which the Nixon administration flirted with the idea of giving a federal judgeship to a Democrat to serve a more important

e. Shafer was not appointed to the federal bench. He did not run for reelection in 1970 and returned to private practice. From 1975 to 1977 he served as counselor to Vice President Nelson Rockefeller.

f. Philip Arreda of the counsel's office, on leave from a professorship at Harvard Law School, had noted on a memo from the presidential personnel office to the counsel's office: "If appointed this man will be on the bench for more than 30 years. The President should require more evidence of quality than appears here. Maybe Kennedy is qualified, but neither ABA view [Kennedy was rated "qualified"] nor this memo shows it." January 24, 1975, Appointments — Judges, Attorneys, Marshalls (1), Schmults collection, Ford Library.

political objective. Philip Elman, a Democrat and member of the Federal Trade Commission, had impeccable legal credentials and was considered for a judgeship because "If such an appointment could be brought about, it would assist us greatly in gaining control of the Federal Trade Commission" by naming Elman's replacement.[48] But Elman remained on the commission.

More than one-fifth of the Ford administration's district court appointees were Democrats. There is little to suggest that this result was deliberate, although Attorney General Levi and Deputy Tyler believed that high professional quality was a more important criterion for selection than partisanship. Some of the Democrats appointed by Ford were forced on the administration, like Judge Aronowitz of Florida. Others were somewhat reluctantly nominated after strong Republican senatorial sponsorship. For example, New Jersey Republican senator Clifford Case recommended a Democrat, New Jersey superior court judge John F. Gerry, for a New Jersey district judgeship. As Senator Case explained in an October 23, 1974, letter to Donald Rumsfeld, assistant to the president, "Of a total of 14 judges recommended by me, he is the first Democrat."[49] Case noted that the ABA found Gerry "well qualified" and that the Republican member of Congress from Gerry's district "has formally endorsed him." He pointed out that the attorney general recommended Gerry and sent the nomination papers to the White House on August 5, 1974, where the nomination "has languished ever since." That letter seemed to have shaken things up, because Gerry's nomination was subsequently sent to the Senate.

New York senator James Buckley supported Democrat Vincent L. Broderick for a Manhattan judgeship, and that nomination was made. Alaska Republican senator Ted Stevens backed Alaska supreme court judge James Fitzgerald, a Democrat, for a federal district judgeship, and Fitzgerald was appointed. Another Democrat, Kenneth K. Hall, was promoted to the Court of Appeals for the Fourth Circuit as part of a package deal that called for Hall's replacement on the district bench to be Republican John T. Copenhaver, Jr.[50][g]

THE AMERICAN BAR ASSOCIATION

Early in Nixon's first term, Deputy Attorney General Richard Kleindienst announced that it was the policy of the administration not to nominate anyone to the lower federal courts found unqualified by the ABA. This was the first time that any administration publicly gave the ABA veto power in the

g. In addition to Aronowitz, Gerry, Broderick, and Fitzgerald, Ford named eight other Democrats. Of these eight, two were African American, two were Asian American, and one was Hispanic.

selection process. Kleindienst's public revelation followed a behind-the-scenes meeting between Kleindienst, Attorney General Mitchell, and the ABA committee. Cloyd Laporte, acting chairman of the committee, wrote to the attorney general on June 5, 1969, restating "the basic principles which were discussed and agreed upon at our meeting."[51] The administration and the ABA agreed that

1. An individual sixty years of age or over should not receive a lifetime federal judgeship unless "he" (the assumption being that males would be appointed) received a rating of "well qualified" or "exceptionally well qualified" and was "in excellent health." In no instance would someone be considered eligible for appointment after the age of sixty-four.
2. The age standard also would apply to promotions of federal district judges to courts of appeals with the exception that a federal district judge over the age of sixty-four but under sixty-eight and "in excellent health" who received an "exceptionally well qualified" rating would be eligible for promotion.
3. A prospective judicial appointee would be expected to have been a member of the Bar for at least fifteen years and have had "a substantial amount" of trial experience. However, "in exceptional cases" prospective appeals court appointees, but not district court appointees, "might be approved [by the ABA] without trial experience."
4. Political activity on the part of judicial candidates would not pose any obstacle to ABA approval, but political activity would not be a "substitute" for the practice of law.

Two weeks later, Attorney General Mitchell responded:

Your letter accurately and adequately sets forth those basic principles which were discussed and agreed upon. You can rest assured that the Department of Justice will do its part in the implementation of these principles, just as I am sure that the American Bar Association will do its part. I am sure that you will agree with me that by this mutual cooperative effort the standards of judicial selection will be raised to and maintained at a high level and thereby the administration of our laws and justice will be better served.[52]

Why did Mitchell (and Nixon) agree to this arrangement with the ABA? The presidential papers offer no clues, but we can speculate that Mitchell and Nixon valued the approbation of the establishment bar, which the ABA committee represented. Mitchell came to the Justice Department from a prestigious law firm (Mudge, Rose, Guthrie and Alexander), which had also served as the base for Richard Nixon when he was planning his run for the presidency. (Nixon also practiced law for the firm.) ABA establishment lawyers likely had served as a reference group for Mitchell during his professional life. He could well have seen them as sharing his conservative values — Wall Street lawyers were typically Republican — and in any event their seal of approval on the administration's judicial appointees could not help but be professionally and politically useful to Mitchell and the administration. The "mutual cooperative effort" that Mitchell referred to could also help the administration in its negotiations with senators. After all, it was less than a decade since the Eisenhower administration and the ABA committee had worked closely to shape the selection of blue-chip conservative Republicans. Nixon, of course, had been Eisenhower's vice president and was pals with Eisenhower's attorney general, William Rogers, thus it is reasonable to infer that Nixon had learned from his executive-branch experience and contacts that a good relationship with the ABA would in the broadest sense help further his agendas.

Whatever the motivation, the administration's commitment was soon put to the test when Senate minority leader Hugh Scott promoted the candidacy of Lee Donaldson, the Republican leader of the Pennsylvania state house, for a federal district judgeship. The ABA found Donaldson to be "not qualified" because of insufficient trial experience, and the Justice Department so notified Senator Scott, who protested that "[t]he rule which seeks to thwart Lee Donaldson's appointment is totally ill-conceived."[53] This was particularly touchy for the administration because it was in the midst of the confirmation fight over Clement Haynsworth to fill the Supreme Court vacancy created by the resignation of Abe Fortas, and Scott's assistance was vital. But Donaldson was not nominated.

After the debacle of Senate rejection of the Haynsworth and Carswell nominations, the administration agreed that for future Supreme Court vacancies it would submit the names of leading candidates to the ABA for evaluation. The implication was that no Supreme Court nomination would go to any individual found "not qualified."[54]

This new procedure was implemented in the early fall of 1971 when Justices Hugo Black and John Marshall Harlan retired. The administration submitted a list of six names and asked the ABA to focus on two, Herschel H. Friday, a Little Rock municipal bond lawyer, and Mildred L. Lillie, a California state appeals court judge who had been in the running during the Johnson administration for the Ninth Circuit vacancy filled in 1968 by Shirley Hufstedler. All six names were leaked to the press, and mounting opposition focused on Friday and Lillie. The ABA Standing Committee on Federal Judiciary found Lillie unqualified by a vote of 11 to 1, and Friday received a split vote, with half voting "not qualified" and half "not opposed." Nixon dropped Friday and Lillie but also was upset with the leaks, which the administration claimed came from the ABA. The administration abruptly ended the procedure of advance submissions of names to the ABA, and ABA committee members were as surprised as the rest of the nation when Nixon announced the nominations of Lewis Powell, a former president of the ABA, and William Rehnquist, a Justice Department official, to fill the vacancies.[55]

Although the ABA was understood to have a veto power with lower-court appointments, that power became tenuous by late 1973. Acting Attorney General Robert H. Bork formally submitted the nomination of Thomas E. Stagg, Jr., for a Louisiana federal district judgeship on November 29, 1973. In the letter accompanying the nomination papers, Bork noted:

> The Standing Committee on Federal Judiciary of the American Bar Association has submitted a report in which they state their opinion that Thomas E. Stagg, Jr., is not qualified for appointment to this post. The exact vote of their Committee was three votes "qualified" and nine votes "not qualified." Based on our review of a full field FBI investigation of his background, I have determined that he bears an excellent reputation as to character, integrity, and has the professional qualifications for appointment as a United States District Judge.[56]

The nomination sat in the White House awaiting the confirmation of William B. Saxbe as attorney general. As Saxbe subsequently noted in a letter to Nixon, "On January 31, 1974, after reconsideration, the [ABA] Committee has reported that, in their opinion, Mr. Stagg is qualified for appointment. . . . I recommend the nomination."[57] The nomination was then sent to the Senate. The ABA committee evidently realized that it was better to give the administration the benefit of the doubt and retain the "veto" rather than risk a rupture in the relationship.

On August 8, Nixon's last full working day in office, he sent to the Senate the nomination of Connecticut governor Thomas J. Meskill for a judicial position on the Court of Appeals for the Second Circuit despite the ABA committee's unanimously rating Meskill "not qualified." Meskill was actively supported by Connecticut Republican senator Lowell Weicker. When Meskill agreed to be nominated for the Second Circuit, he had announced he would not run for reelection.

Gerald Ford, as vice president, had supported Meskill's bid for the appeals court. Ford had served together with Meskill in the House of Representatives. Second Circuit judge William H. Timbers wrote Ford strongly supporting Meskill despite ABA opposition. Ford responded: "I wholeheartedly agree with you that he [Meskill] is well qualified to serve as a member of the Court of Appeals, and you may be sure he will have my full support."[58]

Upon assuming the presidency, Ford endorsed the Nixon nominations then pending, including Meskill's.[h] Opposition to Meskill strengthened, however. Leading law professors from Yale and the University of Connecticut publicly opposed Meskill, as did the *New York Times*.[59] In addition, Meskill was accused by political opponents in Connecticut of improper behavior as governor.

Senator Weicker took on the ABA and accused the committee of being "snooty" in rejecting Meskill, who, after all, was a former member of Congress and an incumbent governor.[60] Meskill also had the support of Democratic senator Abraham A. Ribicoff, himself a former governor of Connecticut.

In a memo to Ford, an assistant wrote that Governor Meskill had telephoned at the suggestion of Senate minority leader Scott and Senator Weicker to let the president know that "he still wanted to see the confirmation process through."[61] Meskill also noted that the Connecticut legislature's inquiry into the charges of misconduct had cleared him of any wrongdoing. He hoped that the president would "stick with we" and would resubmit his name to the next Congress. On top of the memo Ford wrote, "I will resubmit," and in January 1975 he did so.

The ABA lobbied against the nomination, and the major issue was Meskill's competence to serve on the prestigious Second Circuit. Two days before the Senate Judiciary Committee was scheduled to vote on the nomination, White House staffer Ken Lazarus wrote a memo for White House Counsel Philip Buchen. Lazarus noted that he had reviewed the entire FBI report on Meskill, which was submitted to the attorney general in response to inquiries from the Senate Judiciary Committee, and that "there is nothing contained in this report which should preclude the appointment of Meskill to the Second Circuit."[62] He continued, however, that in his opinion "this nomination should not have been made at the outset . . . because the current system which in effect requires ABA endorsement has elevated the level of the federal judiciary." The nomination having been made, there were two reasons why the administration should continue to support Meskill: "First, he has become a pawn in an ABA power play and at this point in time his personal integrity is on the line. Second, if the President is defeated on this nomination it will become an unfortunate political item to be used against him in the next election."

On March 21, the Senate Judiciary Committee approved the nomination by a vote of 8 to 6. The full Senate voted on the nomination on April 22, and by a

h. In a letter from Thomas J. Korologos of the White House congressional liaison office to Senate Democratic leader Mike Mansfield, dated September 10, 1974, Korologos said that President Ford had reviewed the list (including Meskill) and "approves and reaffirms" the nominations and hoped for their prompt confirmation. *New York Times*, September 19, 1974, p. 23.

vote of 54 to 36 Meskill was confirmed.[63] Although the ABA lost the battle, it won the war: no other person rated "not qualified" was named by the Ford administration to the federal bench.

Indeed, the Ford administration was so sensitive about deferring to the ABA that in the summer of 1976 it agonized over whether to make a nomination until the formal ABA report, which had been expected to be favorable, was received. What had happened was that U.S. district judge Harry Wellford was backed for elevation to the Sixth Circuit by Tennessee Republican senator Howard Baker, who called the White House on July 26. According to the account of the call, "The Senator is urging us to send this forward to the Senate without formal ABA approval. I understand informal approval has been obtained." Ken Lazarus reported back to White House legislative liaison Jack Marsh: "I have discussed this matter with [Deputy Attorney General] Judge Tyler who is, of course, willing to accept our direction, but suggests that it would be in the best interests of all concerned (including Judge Wellford) to await formal approval of the ABA which should be forthcoming within a period of two weeks. . . . To bypass formal ABA approval . . . could raise unnecessary friction and suspicions."[64] One week later, Wellford's nomination was sent to the Senate.[i]

ETHNICITY

Nixon nominated the first Asian American to the appeals court bench. Herbert Y. C. Choy, of Korean ancestry, was born in Makaweli, Hawaii, had served as state attorney general, and practiced law in Honolulu. He was a Republican, was rated "qualified" by the ABA, and was nominated for a seat on the Ninth Circuit on April 7, 1971. Choy was rapidly confirmed. Interestingly, there is no evidence in the presidential papers of the administration making much of this or recognizing that this was a breakthrough appointment.

Politically, the Asian American vote was likely seen as too diffuse and too small to be of major importance for the Republican Party. This was not the case with Hispanic Americans. In particular, there is evidence that within the White House there was special interest in recruiting Mexican American judges. White House aide Frederic V. Malek sought to recruit a hispanic for a

---

i. The Senate Judiciary Committee held a hearing on Wellford on September 1, 1976, in which considerable opposition was voiced by civil rights groups. The controversy surrounding the nomination led the Senate Judiciary Committee to take no action, and the nomination died with the election of Democrat Jimmy Carter as president. In 1982, President Ronald Reagan nominated Wellford for elevation to the Sixth Circuit, and the Republican-controlled Senate Judiciary Committee and then the full Senate approved.

California judgeship and wrote to the attorney general about Arthur L. Alarcon: "Attached is a resume on an outstanding Mexican-American Republican Judge who I believe deserves consideration for a Federal appointment. It is my understanding that there are no Federal Mexican-American Judges in the United States[j] and that an appointment of this type would be very well received. Members of my staff have interviewed Judge Alarcon and have been extremely impressed with his capabilities. Please let me know any steps that I might take in obtaining further references on him or arranging interviews as appropriate."[65] The Nixon Justice Department, for reasons not revealed in the presidential papers, did not follow through. Eight years later, Democrat Jimmy Carter appointed the Republican Alarcon to the Ninth Circuit.

The president himself seems to have been interested in appointing a Mexican American. In a memo to Malek, presidential aide Gordon Strachan asserted: "The President feels that Edward J. Guirado, currently a judge in the Superior Court of California, would make an excellent appointment to the District Court with his qualifications as a Mexican/American and the fact that he is a strong lawyer, etc."[66] On the memo Malek asked: "Do you know about him? Do you agree? Please provide background if possible." Malek learned that Guirado, a graduate of President Nixon's alma mater, Whittier College, was sixty-eight, far too old to be named to the federal bench under the ABA criteria to which the administration adhered.

Malek continued the pressure to appoint hispanics. He wrote to Kleindienst:

> Attached is a letter and biographical material on Richard Ibanez, a candidate for a Federal judicial appointment. I would appreciate your handling the response to this. Also this is but the latest of a number of our qualified Mexican-Americans who could be candidates for Federal Judgeships. As you know, we feel it is extremely important to make every effort to appoint a Mexican-American to the Federal Bench during the coming year. Of course, you may not have any opportunities in California. If not, Ibanez may not be possible.[67]

Malek followed up with another memorandum: "Attached are some additional recommendations on Richard Ibanez. I recognize that there are probably no vacancies in California at this point. However, should one arise, I

---

j. Malek was wrong. Kennedy appointee Reynaldo Garza and Johnson appointee Manuel Real were the first two acknowledged Mexican American judges, and they were sitting on the federal bench during the Nixon presidency. Also sitting on the federal bench was Harold Medina, whose father was Mexican American but whose hispanic roots were unknown by the administration that appointed him and by the public.

would think that Ibanez — or someone else of Mexican descent — could be an outstanding choice."[68] Although the administration went on to make three appointments to the California federal district bench, none of the appointees were hispanic. There is no evidence that the Justice Department shared the White House's desire to find a suitable hispanic appointee, or that Nixon articulated a preference to the attorney general or the deputy attorney general.

Although the presidential papers do not show the Ford administration to have been concerned with ethnicity in appointments to the federal bench, such a concern may be inferred from the administration's record as discussed later in this chapter.

Women and Judgeships

Richard Nixon named only one woman, Cornelia G. Kennedy, to a federal judgeship, in the Eastern District of Michigan in 1970. As we saw earlier, however, Nixon apparently was willing to consider Mildred Lillie for the Supreme Court and presumably would have nominated her had she met with ABA approval. Nevertheless, the Nixon record of only one judicial appointment to a woman was a setback for gender integration of the judiciary. There is little evidence that the Nixon administration sought to promote sexual equality in judicial selection, although in 1973 an African American woman, Jewell LaFontant, was appointed deputy solicitor general and in early 1974 Carla A. Hills was appointed assistant attorney general in charge of the Civil Division of the Justice Department.[k]

The women's rights movement gained momentum in the early 1970s. Like the civil rights movement, it pressed its agenda in the courts and also before the executive and legislative branches. The National Women's Political Caucus urged the administration to consider women for judicial positions, and the deputy attorney general expressed his willingness to meet with representatives from the group. Within the White House, Jane Hruska talked up Elizabeth Kovachevich, a Florida state judge, as a prospect for a federal judgeship. The Nixon administration did not act on Kovachevich, but she was later nomi-

---

k. John Ehrlichman reported that Nixon was intrigued with the idea of placing Jewell LaFontant on the Supreme Court. See John Ehrlichman, *Witness to Power* (New York: Simon & Schuster, 1982), 239. A Nixon friend, U.S. district judge A. Andrew Hauk, wrote to Nixon praising Carla Hills as "a most outstanding lawyer and surely one whom you would want to keep in mind when you take up consideration of appointing a *lady* judge." Emphasis in original. Hauk to Nixon, February 15, 1974, Ex FG 53/ST 1–ST 15 1/1/73–[8-9-74], WHCF, Nixon Materials Project.

nated by Ford. Her nomination, however, lapsed at the end of the Ford administration when Florida's Democratic senators blocked her because she had not been screened by their judicial selection commission. Kovachevich was rated "qualified" by the ABA, and administration officials believed the Florida senators used their power "to defeat judicial nominees solely on the basis of political affiliation."[69] Ford had hoped to challenge the Democratic senators' commission by bypassing its recommendations and naming a woman deemed qualified by the American Bar Association. It would take some six years before another Republican president, this time successfully, would name her to the federal bench.

The Office of Women's Programs was organized in the White House in 1973, and Anne Armstrong was placed in charge with the title counselor to the president. Counselor Armstrong planned a meeting of women who were serving in high-level policy positions to discuss ways of bringing more women into government. These activities had no impact on judicial selection. There were a few instances of women being recommended to fill particular judgeships, but there is little evidence that the women mentioned were given serious consideration.[70]

Only because it appears that a woman was seriously considered for a Supreme Court position can the Nixon administration be seen as a slight improvement over the Kennedy administration. But when the dust settled, both the Kennedy and the Nixon administrations appointed only one woman. The same was true for Ford, although the Ford administration tried to do better. Counselor Armstrong, in a note to Deputy Solicitor General Jewel LaFontant, praised President Ford's "commitment to advance women's roles in Government."[71] Ford successfully named one woman, Mary Ann Richey, to a federal district judgeship in Arizona.

The Ford administration was set to name another woman, Mariana R. Pfaelzer, to a federal district court position in California. She received ABA approval but was not nominated. The judicial status report had the notation "doesn't want app't" next to her name.[72] Pfaelzer, a Democrat, was appointed to the federal district court two years later by Jimmy Carter.

Several women were suggested for the Supreme Court to replace Justice Douglas, whose ill health had forced him to retire. Sandra Day O'Connor was among those mentioned.[73] Senator Jesse Helms wrote in support of Susie Sharp, the chief judge of the North Carolina Supreme Court. But the shorter list only included two women — Judge Cornelia Kennedy and Carla Hills. The list was further narrowed, and Seventh Circuit judge John Paul Stevens emerged as Ford's first choice and was easily confirmed.

African Americans and Judgeships

With little fanfare, the Nixon administration named six African Americans to lifetime positions on the federal district bench — a total of 3.4 percent of its district court appointments.[1] This was a breakthrough for a Republican administration. An exchange of letters between California superior court judge David W. Williams to H. R. Haldeman in 1969 suggests the sequence of events that eventually led to Williams' appointment, the first of an African American by a Republican president to the federal district bench. Williams had met Haldeman some three years earlier and used that as the opening gambit in his letter. He then came to the point:

> I am interested in being considered for nomination to a vacancy on the U.S. District Court, Central District. Upon learning of my interest, [Republican] Senator George Murphy invited me to have lunch with him in January and after interviewing me, indicated that he would forward my name to President Nixon with his recommendations. Chief Judge Thurmond Clarke [of the federal district court] called me when he learned of my desire for this elevation and thereafter sent a letter to Senator Murphy urging him to support me for nomination.
>
> I am a Negro, a life-long Republican and possessed of 14 years judicial experience.[74]

Haldeman responded warmly and told Judge Williams: "Your letter and resume are being referred to Mr. George Revercomb [Associate Deputy Attorney General] in the Justice Department for his attention. I am certain that you will be hearing from him in the near future. My best wishes in your attainment of this nomination."[75]

Whitney M. Young, Jr., executive director of the National Urban League, lobbied both the president and the attorney general for the appointment of Clarence Clyde Ferguson, who was then serving as ambassador to Uganda, to replace Judge William H. Hastie, who had retired from the Third Circuit. Young wrote to the attorney general that Hastie's replacement was of great concern to the black community. He pointed out that Ferguson, a former dean of the Howard University Law School and on leave from a professorship at Rutgers University Law School, "is a life-long Republican, with a voting residence in New Jersey. It is my understanding that [Republican] Senator [Clif-

---

1. Almeric Christian, an African American and a Democrat, was given a term appointment on the federal district bench for the Virgin Islands. Richard Kleindienst wrote that Nixon named thirteen blacks to the local courts in the District of Columbia. See Kleindienst, *Justice*, 130.

ford] Case has already recommended him to you, and I am certain clearance can be had from the other appropriate Senators." Young also recommended Revius O. Ortique, Jr., "a highly respected and distinguished black attorney" for the federal district bench in New Orleans. But nothing came of either suggestion.[76]

Ferguson was indeed pushed by Senator Case, but he was rejected, reportedly for being too liberal. Ortique was considered by the Ford administration, but he did not win ABA approval and was dropped, despite the backing of both Louisiana senators.[77]

John Ehrlichman received a recommendation from black acquaintances of his late uncle, who wrote recommending King County superior court judge Charles Z. Smith, an African American and a Republican. Ehrlichman replied, "I know Charley well and consider him very qualified."[78] But Morrell Sharp received the appointment.

There was some activity in the Nixon administration that, had it been successful, would have led to the naming of the first African American — who was also a woman — to a southern federal judgeship. Elreta Alexander was a Republican and an elected state judge in a North Carolina county that was 75 percent white. Bob Brown of the White House staff called her to the attention of White House assistants Dent and Malek. Both wrote memos to Justice Department officials. Dent urged the attorney general to name Judge Alexander, noting that "her credentials are very good." He suggested three alternatives:

> (1) Name her to succeed Middle District Judge Stanley who just died. The State GOP would prefer a white from among several already jockeying for the vacancy.
>
> (2) Put her in the vacancy now existing on the Fourth Circuit. . . . Later, Judge Alexander might succeed Thurgood Marshall as a Black and woman.
>
> (3) To sweeten the pot for the North Carolina GOP, we could promote one of two North Carolina Judges to the Fourth Circuit and put her in the existing District vacancy and let the North Carolina GOP put their choice in the other vacancy created by the promotion. This would be the best politically.

Dent also emphasized that the people he had asked to check on Judge Alexander's acceptability among whites had all "come back with glowing reports." Even the head of the North Carolina Republican Party said, "She's okay." Dent recommended option three.[79]

Malek wrote to Haldeman about Judge Alexander:

> The Attorney General is rather reluctant because of his concern as to the political backlash among whites in North Carolina and perhaps elsewhere in

the South. Her nomination would receive considerable national public attention. [Bob] Brown knows her and Dent has had several people check on her.
They both are convinced she is a reasonable, able, and deserving person. They
agree there would be some adverse repercussions, perhaps mostly from North
Carolina Republicans. However, quite a few people have written letters in her
behalf, and her credentials cannot be successfully challenged. Kleindienst is
now having the ABA give a preliminary check as to whether she would be
deemed qualified.[80]

Malek went on to argue that "Brown and Dent feel that this nomination
would be very helpful to the president politically with blacks and young people across the country" and that it would be worth the risk of political back-
lash in North Carolina. At the bottom of the memo a handwritten notation
summarized Kleindienst's position on the Alexander candidacy:

   1. Possibilities but also problems
   2. If Sen. Ervin & Jordan have no prob., cleared thru Sen. Eastland, & party
      people don't object, then it would make sense.
   3. He is enthusiastic about it.[81]

Kleindienst's qualifiers and reluctance to commit himself to promoting
the candidacy suggest that he was less than enthusiastic. Attorney General
Mitchell's misgivings were more in line with his southern political strategy to
win back whites who had voted for Alabama governor George Wallace in the
1968 presidential election, particularly in the south and border states. Appointment of a black woman in the south, no matter how deserving, would be
inconsistent with Mitchell's southern strategy.

Malek, Dent, and other White House staff had very different views from
Mitchell of the potential political effect of a southern black appointment.
Malek tried once more in a memo: "It would be extremely helpful to make at
least one judicial appointment in the South a black. I have discussed in the past
with Kleindienst the possibility of appointing Elreta Alexander, of North Carolina, to a North Carolina District Court vacancy. I would appreciate your
following up on this and working with Justice to attempt to gain the appointment of at least one black."[82] Neither Alexander nor any other African American, however, was named to the federal bench in the south by either Nixon or
Ford, although Ford considered an African American for a New Orleans
judgeship. Judge Alexander served on the state district bench until her retirement in 1981.

The Nixon administration tried to obtain an appeals court judgeship for
Deputy Solicitor General Jewell LaFontant. It would have been an historic
appointment—the first African American woman named to an appeals court.
But the ABA Committee on Federal Judiciary found her unqualified, despite

her being a graduate of the University of Chicago Law School and having a professional career of distinction.[m] The administration dropped her from consideration.

Massachusetts Republican senator Edward Brooke, the Senate's only African American, strongly recommended an African American attorney, Herbert Tucker, to the federal district court bench in Massachusetts. The ABA committee, however, opposed Tucker because of insufficient federal court experience, and the Nixon administration refused to nominate him.[83] Senator Brooke was unable to obtain a judgeship for an African American despite his position as a Republican Senator. Tucker was subsequently appointed to the state judiciary in 1973 and served until his retirement in 1985.

The Louisiana senators, Democrats Long and Johnston, informed Ford on May 19, 1975, that U.S. district judge James A. Comiskey had announced his intention to resign from the bench. They wrote, "We strongly urge that you nominate a black lawyer from our state to fill his vacancy." Long and Johnston continued, somewhat disingenuously, given Louisiana's racial history:

> The population of the parishes comprising the Eastern District of Louisiana is 45–50 per cent black. Presently, all nine of the Federal District Court judges sitting in Louisiana are white. And coupled with this is the great anomaly that there are no black federal judges sitting in any of the Deep South states. The picture is clear: black lawyers have not been considered for federal judgeships in the South. This opportunity should be taken to correct this situation. . . . There are many able black lawyers in the South who, if appointed to the federal bench, would bring credit upon themselves, upon the federal judiciary and upon this nation. . . . We take no position on the question of which black lawyer should be nominated. . . . We urge only that this judge be black.[84]

Nothing much happened. On February 24, 1976, some nine months later, Long and Johnston again wrote to Ford urging him to appoint "a qualified black lawyer" for the Eastern District of Louisiana.[85] Finally, in a letter to Ford one week later, the Louisiana senators suggested the names of four blacks: Robert Collins[n], Nils R. Douglas, Ernest N. Morial[o], and Revius O. Ortique, Jr. Ortique was considered until the ABA vetoed him.

In total, Ford named three African Americans, 5.8 percent of his district

m. *Washington Post*, February 2, 1974, A3. LaFontant left government service in 1975. In 1989, President George Bush named her as U.S. coordinator for refugee affairs, with the rank of ambassador-at-large.

n. Collins was appointed by Carter to the federal district bench in 1978. In 1991, Collins was convicted of taking a bribe in exchange for imposing a lighter sentence on a convicted drug smuggler. Collins resigned from the bench on August 6, 1993.

o. Ernest Morial was elected mayor of New Orleans and served from 1978 to 1986.

court appointments. In addition, he appointed Matthew J. Perry, Jr., a South Carolina Democrat, to fill the remainder of a term on the Court of Military Appeals. Perry was later named by Carter to the federal district bench of South Carolina.

The Demographic Portrait of the Nixon-Ford Judges

In table 6.1, the Nixon appointees are those who were nominated and confirmed before August 9, 1974, the day Nixon left office. The statistics for the Ford appointees include four nominations made by Nixon before he resigned the presidency that had not been confirmed when he left office. Two of those nominees were for positions on the Second Circuit, and two were to fill district judgeships. Three of those four nominations were submitted to the Senate on Nixon's last full day in office, August 8, 1974. Gerald Ford could have withdrawn them but he did not. Only one was controversial—the nomination of Thomas J. Meskill to the Second Circuit. Failed nominations are not included in the statistics.[p]

Ford sought to restore public confidence in the Justice Department by placing its leadership in the hands of a brilliant legal scholar (Levi) and a respected federal judge (Tyler). Although there are many similarities in the demographic portrait of the Nixon and Ford appointees, they differ in professional experience and party affiliation, perhaps a result of the different caliber of leadership in the Justice Department and White House. Note that because Ford appointed only twelve appeals court judges (compared to Nixon's forty-five) percentage differences between the Ford and Nixon appointees must be treated cautiously.

AGE

The average age of the Nixon and Ford district court appointees was almost identical, about two years younger than the Kennedy and Johnson appointees. For the appeals court, the average age of the Ford appointees was a year and a half younger than that of the Nixon appointees and about the same average age as the Johnson appointees. There is no evidence, however, that either the Nixon or Ford administrations considered age when making appointments.

p. Nixon made one nomination that he later withdrew, that of Charles A. Bane to the Court of Appeals for the Seventh Circuit. Ford withdrew one nomination, that of William B. Poff to a district judgeship, after Senator William Scott exercised senatorial courtesy. Also there were ten nominations that were held up in the Senate pending the outcome of the presidential election. Ford lost and the nominations died. Four of the ten later received appointments from President Reagan.

Table 6.1. Selected Backgrounds of Lifetime Nixon and Ford Appointees to the Federal District and Appeals Courts of General Jurisdiction

	District Court Appointees		Appeals Court Appointees	
	Nixon Appointees	Ford Appointees	Nixon Appointees	Ford Appointees
Average age at time of appointment	49.1	49.2	53.7	52.2
Undergraduate Education				
Public	41.9%	46.2%	40.0%	41.7%
	(75)	(24)	(18)	(5)
Private not Ivy	39.1%	36.5%	35.6%	50.0%
	(70)	(19)	(16)	(6)
Ivy League	19.0%	17.3%	20.0%	8.3%
	(34)	(9)	(9)	(1)
None	—	—	4.4%	—
	—	—	(2)	—
Law School Education				
Public	43.0%	44.2%	37.8%	50.0%
	(77)	(23)	(17)	(6)
Private not Ivy	35.8%	38.5%	26.7%	25.0%
	(64)	(20)	(12)	(3)
Ivy League	21.2%	17.3%	35.6%	25.0%
	(38)	(9)	(16)	(3)
Experience				
Judicial	35.2%	44.2%	57.8%	75.0%
	(63)	(23)	(26)	(9)
Prosecutorial	39.7%	51.9%	28.9%	25.0%
	(71)	(27)	(13)	(3)
Neither	39.7%	28.8%	28.9%	25.0%
	(71)	(15)	(13)	(3)
Occupation				
Politics — Government	3.9%	5.8%	4.4%	8.3%
	(7)	(3)	(2)	(1)
Government Lawyer	7.3%	15.4%	—	—
	(13)	(8)	—	—
Judiciary	29.6%	34.6%	53.3%	75.0%
	(53)	(18)	(24)	(9)
Large Law Firm*	11.2%	9.6%	4.4%	8.3%
	(20)	(5)	(2)	(1)
Medium-Size Law Firm†	27.4%	25.0%	22.2%	8.3%
	(49)	(13)	(10)	(1)

continued

Table 6.1. Continued

	District Court Appointees		Appeals Court Appointees	
	Nixon Appointees	Ford Appointees	Nixon Appointees	Ford Appointees
Small Law Firm‡	12.8%	7.7%	6.7%	—
	(23)	(4)	(3)	—
Solo Practice	5.6%	1.9%	—	—
	(10)	(1)	—	—
Professor of Law	2.2%	—	2.2%	—
	(4)	—	(1)	—
Other	—	—	6.7%	—
	—	—	(3)	—
ABA Rating				
Exceptionally Well	3.4%	—	15.6%	16.7%
Qualified	(6)	—	(7)	(2)
Well Qualified	39.7%	48.1%	57.8%	41.7%
	(71)	(25)	(26)	(5)
Qualified	57.0%	51.9%	26.7%	33.3%
	(102)	(27)	(12)	(4)
Not Qualified	—	—	—	8.1%
	—	—	—	(1)
Party				
Democratic	6.1%	23.1%	6.7%	8.3%
	(11)	(12)	(3)	(1)
Republican	93.9%	75.0%	93.3%	91.7%
	(168)	(39)	(42)	(11)
None	—	1.9%	—	—
	—	(1)	—	—
Prominent Party Activism				
	55.3%	55.8%	62.2%	50.0%
	(99)	(29)	(28)	(6)
Prior or Current Members of Congress				
	2.2%	—	4.4%	8.3%
	(4)	—	(2)	(1)
Religion				
Protestant	68.7%	63.5%	71.1%	58.3%
	(123)	(33)	(32)	(7)
Catholic	17.3%	13.5%	15.6%	33.3%
	(31)	(7)	(7)	(4)

Table 6.1. Continued

| | District Court Appointees | | Appeals Court Appointees | |
	Nixon Appointees	Ford Appointees	Nixon Appointees	Ford Appointees
Jewish	7.3%	9.6%	8.9%	8.3%
	(13)	(5)	(4)	(1)
Other§	2.8%	3.8%	4.4%	—
	(5)	(2)	(2)	—
None	0.6%	1.9%	—	—
	(1)	(1)	—	—
Unknown	3.3%	7.7%	—	—
	(6)	(4)	—	—
Gender				
Male	99.4%	98.1%	100.0%	100.0%
	(178)	(51)	(45)	(12)
Female	0.6%	1.9%	—	—
	(1)	(1)	—	—
Ethnicity/race				
White	95.5%	88.5%	97.8%	100.0%
	(171)	(46)	(44)	(12)
Black	3.4%	5.8%	—	—
	(6)	(3)	—	—
Hispanic	1.1%	1.9%	—	—
	(2)	(1)	—	—
Asian	—	3.8%	2.2%	—
	—	(2)	(1)	—
Total Number of Appointees				
	179	52	45	12

* A large law firm was defined as consisting of twenty-five or more partners and associates.

† A medium-size law firm was defined as consisting of from five to twenty-four partners and associates.

‡ A small law firm was defined as consisting of from two to four partners and associates.

§ District court appointees included two Mormons appointed by Nixon and one by Ford, two persons affiliated with the Greek Orthodox church (one appointed by Nixon and one by Ford), and two who were Christian Scientists. The appeals court appointees were elevations of a Nixon-appointed Mormon and Christian Scientist.

EDUCATION

The undergraduate educational backgrounds of the Nixon and Ford district court appointees were similar, but there were marginally more Ford appointees from public undergraduate institutions and marginally fewer Ford appointees from Ivy League schools. The same held true for the Nixon and Ford appeals court appointees.

All the Nixon and Ford appointees to the district and appeals courts had a law school education. There were proportionally more Nixon than Ford appointees that attended Ivy League law schools.

EXPERIENCE

About four in ten Nixon appointees to the district courts had neither judicial nor prosecutorial experience. But less than three in ten Ford district court appointees were without both types of professional experience. This is consistent with the view that Ford's Justice Department placed more emphasis on professional credentials than did Nixon's. For both the Nixon and Ford appointees there was a larger proportion with prosecutorial experience than with judicial experience.

For the Nixon and Ford appeals court appointees, there was a larger proportion with judicial experience than with prosecutorial experience. Although there were relatively few Ford appeals court appointees, the larger proportion of those with judicial experience as compared with the Nixon appointees appears to represent a genuine difference between the two administrations. For both groups, fewer than three in ten appointees had neither judicial nor prosecutorial experience.

OCCUPATION

Only a small proportion (under 6 percent) of the Nixon and Ford district court appointees held political or governmental office (excluding judges and government lawyers) at the time of appointment to the bench. More than twice the proportion of Ford than Nixon district court appointees were government lawyers. All of the Ford appointees and all but three of the Nixon appointees who were government lawyers at the time of their judicial appointments were serving in the offices of United States attorneys, and all but one of the United States attorneys had first been appointed by either Nixon or Ford.

The judiciary accounted for more than one-third of the Ford and just under 30 percent of the Nixon district court appointees. The Ford proportion was higher than that of the Kennedy and Johnson administrations. None of the Nixon appointees were U.S. magistrates at the time of appointment, but three

Ford appointees (about 6 percent) held that position at the time of appointment to the district court bench. The Nixon and Ford administrations each appointed one person who was a referee in bankruptcy.

For the district bench, close to three out of five Nixon appointees and more than two out of five Ford appointees were in private practice at the time of their judicial appointments. About the same proportion of Nixon and Ford appointees came from large and medium-size firms, but a larger proportion of Nixon than Ford appointees came from small law firms or practiced solo. (But the proportion in individual practice was dramatically lower than the national figure, approximately one-third of the bar.) The Ford administration may have had somewhat more of a tendency to recruit from the more established law firms than did the Nixon administration. Nixon, but not Ford, named law professors to the bench (about 2 percent of the district court appointees).

Three out of four appeals court appointees of Ford but only slightly more than half the Nixon appeals court appointees were sitting on the bench at the time of their appointments. Of those elevated by Nixon, all but two were federal district judges, about half of whom Nixon had originally appointed. All the Ford elevations were from the federal district bench (seven of the nine had been Nixon appointments). About one-third of Nixon's appeals court appointments were recruited from private practice, with medium-size law firms the principal source. Nixon appointed one law professor, Ford none.

AMERICAN BAR ASSOCIATION RATINGS

Insofar as appointments to the district bench were concerned, the Nixon administration stood by its 1969 agreement with the ABA not to name anyone rated "not qualified" by the ABA, and the Ford administration honored that commitment. But both administrations apparently were not as aggressive in pushing for the highest-rated appointees. Whereas 62 percent of Kennedy's district court appointees and 51 percent of Johnson's received the two highest ABA ratings, only 43 percent of Nixon's and 48 percent of Ford's received such ratings.

The Nixon administration broke its agreement with the ABA to nominate Thomas Meskill, rated "not qualified," to an appeals court position. Because Ford embraced the nomination and Meskill was confirmed during the Ford administration, the Ford administration is credited with naming one "not qualified" person to the circuit bench. Otherwise, the ratings of the Nixon and Ford appeals court appointees are close. Approximately three out of four Nixon appeals court appointees received the two highest ratings, the same proportion received by the Johnson appeals court appointees.

PARTY

The most pronounced difference between the Nixon and Ford district court appointees was in party affiliation. Almost one in four Ford district court appointees was not affiliated with the president's party. This is the largest proportion of all the administrations from Franklin Roosevelt through Bill Clinton. This result may not have been deliberate, but it shows that the administration was more willing to name an individual associated with the opposition party than predecessor administrations had been. Furthermore, over 40 percent of the Democrats chosen by Ford were from ethnic minorities — two African Americans, two Asian Americans, and one hispanic. The largest number of Ford Democratic appointees was from the western states (four) and the fewest from the south (two). There was, however, little difference in party affiliation between the Nixon and Ford appeals court appointees. More than nine out of ten appeals court appointees were Republicans.

Over half the Nixon and Ford appointees to the district and appeals courts had records of prominent party activism. These proportions are similar to those of previous presidential appointees to the lower courts. Of the 288 Nixon and Ford appointees to the district and appeals courts, seven (2.4 percent) had served in Congress. Of the 290 Kennedy and Johnson appointees, ten had congressional backgrounds (3.4 percent). All four presidents had been in Congress, but Johnson appointed more than half of those with congressional backgrounds (eight of the seventeen appointed by all four administrations). Ford appointed only one person with a congressional background (Meskill), which is probably a reflection of Ford's lower profile than Johnson's in the judicial selection process.

RELIGIOUS ORIGIN OR AFFILIATION

Slightly more than one in six Nixon and Ford appointees to the lower federal courts was Catholic. This was close to the Eisenhower proportion but less than the one-in-four rate for Kennedy and Johnson appointees. The religious gap between Democrats and Republicans would remain until the Reagan years. The Nixon proportion of Catholic appointees to the district bench was larger than the Ford proportion. The reverse was true for appeals court appointments.

The proportion of Jewish appointees of the Nixon and Ford administrations overall was about half the proportion of Catholic appointees. About one in fourteen Nixon and Ford appointees was Jewish, compared to one in ten Kennedy and Johnson appointees. These differences no doubt largely reflected the religious composition of the population of Republicans and Democrats likely to be considered for the bench. However, the continuous line of Jewish justices on the Supreme Court, begun with the appointment of Louis Brandeis in 1916, was broken in 1969 with the resignation of Abe Fortas and his replacement by a non-Jew (Harry Blackmun). None of the five Nixon-Ford Supreme Court appointees was Jewish. There is no evidence, however, that this was deliberate. Twenty-four years later, President Bill Clinton named Ruth Bader Ginsburg and, the next year, Stephen Breyer, both Jewish, to the Court. No longer does it appear in appointments that religion is the factor it once was.[86]

GENDER, RACE, AND ETHNICITY

Nixon and Ford each appointed one woman to the federal district bench. They appointed two women and 286 men to lifetime judgeships on the district and appeals courts. Kennedy and Johnson had named four women (including one to an appeals court) and 286 men to these courts. Even the tokenism of Kennedy and Johnson was reduced by Nixon and Ford, although the Ford administration made attempts to appoint more women, and both the Nixon and Ford administrations had considered briefly the idea of putting a woman on the Supreme Court.

The Nixon and Ford records were better for the appointment of ethnic minorities. Over 3 percent of the Nixon and Ford appointees were African Americans, all appointed to the district bench. Nine African American men were added to the ranks of the federal judiciary. They included three to the federal bench in New York City (Robert L. Carter and Lawrence W. Pierce, appointed by Nixon to the Southern District, and Henry Bramwell, appointed by Ford to the Eastern District), one to the federal bench in Philadelphia (Clifford S. Green, appointed by Nixon to the Eastern District of Pennsylvania), one to the District of Columbia bench (Nixon appointee Barrington D. Parker), one to the Ohio bench (Nixon appointee Robert M. Duncan, to the Southern District), one to the federal bench in Chicago (Ford appointee George N. Leighton, to the Northern District of Illinois), and two appointed to the California federal bench (Nixon appointee David W. Williams, to the Central District, and Ford appointee Cecil F. Poole, to the Northern District). While this record was formidable compared to the lack of even one African American appointee to the district bench by the last Republican administration (Eisenhower's), it fell short of the Kennedy-Johnson record of nine African Americans to the district bench (including one woman), three to the appeals bench, and one to the Supreme Court.

Nixon and Ford appointed three hispanics to the federal district court of Puerto Rico. By contrast, Kennedy and Johnson named four, of which two were to the Puerto Rico district bench. Ford named two Asian Americans to the district courts, and Nixon named one to an appeals court[q], whereas only one Asian American was named by Kennedy (to a district court) and none by Johnson.

Gender, race, and ethnicity were gradually becoming more salient in American politics and the politics of judicial selection. For the Nixon and Ford administrations, the greatest headway was in the selection of African Americans and, to a more modest degree, Asian Americans. Affirmative action in judicial selection was not to fully flower until Ford's successor, Jimmy Carter, took office.

When at the outset of Nixon's first term the administration agreed to a de facto veto of persons the ABA found to be unqualified, the competency of appointees appeared to be reasonably assured, although subject to the possible biases of local legal establishments that provided the bases for ABA evaluations. No judicial appointee confirmed during the presidency of Richard Nixon was found to be unqualified by the ABA. With the exception of the Meskill appointment, the same was true for the Ford administration. As a consequence, one would expect a similar demographic portrait of the Nixon and Ford appointees. Yet we know that Watergate dominated the Nixon administration's second term and that after Nixon resigned, Ford sought to rehabilitate the Justice Department by naming to its leadership nonpartisan establishment appointees with unassailable legal pedigrees and reputations for personal integrity. The evidence suggests, however, that with the important exception of party affiliation of district court appointees, there were few demographic differences between the Nixon and Ford appointees. In a few instances, the ABA was responsible for vetoing blacks and women, and arguably the rigidity of the standards and possibly subtle traces of racism and sexism may have helped to perpetuate a largely white male judiciary. Neither the Nixon nor the Ford administration undertook to persuade the ABA committee of the need for a more diverse federal bench and the importance of greater flexibility in the evaluation process.

Although there was great sentiment early in the Nixon administration to use judicial selection to further the policy agenda, there is no evidence of systematic follow-through both before and after Watergate, and the partisan agenda appears to have predominated. On the campaign trail in 1972, Nixon promised to continue appointing "strict constructionists," and he did appoint primarily Republicans, most of whom were generally conservative. But in that respect he was no different from his political godfather, Dwight Eisenhower.

q. Nixon also named an Asian American to a position on the U.S. Court of Claims.

The Ford administration did not appear to use judicial selection for policy-agenda purposes; to the extent that an agenda was furthered, it was the partisan agenda. Nixon inherited a judiciary in which just over 70 percent of the judges were Democrats. When Ford left office, the Nixon-Ford appointments had shifted the partisan balance so that over half the judiciary consisted of Republicans.[87]

American politics was transfixed and dominated by the Watergate-related scandals and the disgrace and resignation of President Richard Nixon and several members of his Cabinet and White House staff. Gerald Ford appeared to offer hope that, in his own words, "our long national nightmare is over."[88] But the promising beginning of Ford's presidency was aborted when he issued a pardon to Richard Nixon for all crimes he committed while president. Ford did not emphasize in his public statement that Nixon's acceptance of the pardon was an admission of guilt. There was widespread suspicion that a deal between Nixon and Ford had been made before Nixon had resigned, although there was no supporting evidence for that suspicion and Ford vigorously denied any deal. Although Ford performed well for the remainder of his presidency, he was unable to recapture the widespread approval he had achieved in his first few weeks in office.

The Republican Party suffered large losses in the congressional elections of 1974, and its right wing sought to take over the party. Led by former California governor Ronald Reagan, the right attempted to snatch from Ford the 1976 Republican presidential nomination. Ford fought hard for the nomination, shed Vice President Nelson Rockefeller for a new running mate, Senator Bob Dole, and overcame a large deficit in the polls to come within striking distance of winning the presidential election. But Jimmy Carter won, and his victory had tremendous implications for the selection of judges.

7

Carter Reforms Judicial Selection

James Earl Carter, Jr., or Jimmy Carter, as he preferred to be called, was a different sort of politician than other presidents.[1] He described himself not as a professional politician but as a peanut farmer who had entered politics as a civic obligation. He ran for president as the outsider who campaigned against the insiders who ran the country. He advocated high professional standards in the conduct of government and favored opening up positions of power to women and minorities. He opposed patronage as the main criterion for appointment to high office. Carter presented himself to the American people as a born-again, highly moral Christian who was also open-minded and tolerant of others. His personal honesty and integrity were seen to contrast with the political cynicism and moral ambiguities of Washington power brokers. Carter clearly tapped into public disillusionment and dissatisfaction with American national politics following the Watergate scandals, the Nixon resignation, and then the Nixon pardon. The economic downturn of 1975–76 coupled with rising inflation fueled public discontent.

Carter emerged from the Democratic National Convention in July 1976 with a 33-percentage-point lead over Gerald Ford in the Gallup Poll.[2] Ford was saddled with a contentious battle for the nomination, fighting off the right wing of the Republican Party that had rallied around Ronald Reagan. Yet Ford managed to overcome much of Carter's lead in the polls, and when the votes were tallied on election day Jimmy Carter had won with 50.1 percent of the popular vote to Ford's 48.0 percent. Carter's electoral college vote total was 297 to Ford's 240. The Democrats retained control of Congress.

The years of Carter's presidency were relatively peaceful ones both at home and abroad. Yet the energy shortage, the high price of oil, budget deficits, and wage and price spiralling, produced double-digit inflation that alarmed much of America. Indeed in public opinion polls inflation was considered America's number-one problem, and the administration seemed incapable of dealing with it. Carter came across as a moralistic taskmaster exhorting Americans to turn down their thermostats in winter and up in summer and to shake off their "malaise."[3] The administration seemed not to be in control of the domestic economy. And despite several foreign policy successes, including the historic Camp David peace accords between Israel and Egypt, the strategic arms limitation treaty with the Soviet Union (SALT II), and the Panama Canal Treaty, the administration was perceived as being uneven in the conduct of foreign affairs.

When the Shah of Iran was deposed, he was granted admission to the United States for medical treatment on October 20, 1979. This enraged the Iranian revolutionaries, who on November 4 overran the American embassy in Tehran and seized American diplomatic and embassy personnel as hostages. The captors demanded the return of the Shah and his wealth. So began a fourteen-month ordeal for the hostages, their families, and the Carter administration which lasted until Carter's final day in office. It was questioned why there was such lax security for the American embassy given the turmoil in Iran and why the embassy personnel had not been evacuated when the unrest began. Some challenged the wisdom of admitting the Shah to the United States and not having recognized that such an action would be a provocation in a highly volatile situation. A disastrous rescue attempt by the military in April 1980 only compounded the frustration. Ironically, the issue of competency in the management of government affairs, which Carter had raised when running for the presidency in 1976, was thrown back at him by the Republicans and by an increasing number of Democrats, including Senator Edward Kennedy.

Kennedy decided to try to wrest the nomination from Carter, having been convinced that Carter could not win reelection. Carter's many accomplishments were not given the recognition they deserved, and the Republicans and the Kennedy Democrats questioned Carter's leadership ability. Although Carter won renomination and in the general election was opposed by someone whom Democrats viewed as a right-wing extremist opponent, the affable former Hollywood movie star and two-term California governor Ronald Reagan, Carter faced an uphill battle. Ultimately image triumphed over substance. And the Ayatollahs of Iran in effect manipulated the hostage crisis that doomed Carter on election day.

Against this backdrop, the Carter administration attempted serious reform of judicial selection. By the end of his term, Jimmy Carter had appointed close to 40 percent of the federal bench, had changed judicial selection procedures, and had opened the judiciary to unprecedented numbers of women and minorities.

Presidential Involvement in Selection

Carter took a personal interest in reforming the process of judicial selection. As a candidate, he promised that if elected president he would not use political patronage as the basis for appointing judges but rather would select judges on the basis of professional qualifications. To that end, he suggested establishing merit selection commissions that would recommend a slate of qualified persons for each judicial vacancy. On December 13, 1976, before taking office, Carter and his attorney general designate, Griffin Bell, met with Mississippi Democratic senator James O. Eastland, chairman of the Senate Judiciary Committee, to negotiate a change in the method of judicial selection. Senator Eastland insisted on continued senatorial prerogatives in the selection of district court judges, although he said he would "help the president persuade senators to establish judicial selection commissions in their states." He agreed, however, to Carter's proposal to establish a judicial selection commission to screen and recommend judges for the courts of appeals, thus presumably removing senators from active participation in choosing appellate judges.[4]

On February 14, four weeks after taking office, President Carter issued Executive Order 11972 creating the United States Circuit Judge Nominating Commission. The commission consisted of thirteen eleven-member panels appointed by the president (one for each judicial circuit, with the exception of the large Fifth and Ninth circuits which were split geographically with eastern and western Fifth Circuit panels and northern and southern Ninth Circuit panels). The executive order specified that "[e]ach panel shall include members of both sexes, members of minority groups, and approximately equal numbers of lawyers and nonlawyers." Each panel would be charged with preparing a confidential report for the president within sixty days after being notified of a judicial vacancy, the report to include the panel's recommendations of the five persons "best qualified" to fill the judgeship. Panels were to extend a wide net by advertising the vacancy and soliciting suggestions of potential candidates.

The executive order, however, failed to mention affirmative action. Six panels established in 1977 and early 1978 failed to find even one woman to recommend on their slates submitted to the president, and five panels failed to recommend a member of a racial minority. These results were unexpected, because 45 percent of the panelists were women and 24 percent were from racial minorities.[5] Of even more concern to those in the White House counsel's office was that none of the first twelve appeals court nominees were women, although three were African Americans. Eventually Carter issued a revised executive order (12059, issued on May 11, 1978) that encouraged panels "to make special efforts to seek out and identify well qualified women and members of minority groups as potential nominees."

White House counsel Robert J. Lipshutz and the attorneys working directly under him, Margaret McKenna and Douglas Huron, became impatient with the Justice Department over the pace of achieving affirmative action. In July 1977, McKenna went to a conference in Chicago in which panel chairmen were in attendance. (The first five panels had been established on May 7, 1977.) In speaking to the chairmen, she stressed the need for panels to actively recruit women and racial minorities. To her surprise, she was told that Justice Department officials had never discussed affirmative action with them.[6]

In the fall of 1978, the nominating panels for the Fifth and Sixth circuits made their recommendations, and on each list was a woman. The Sixth Circuit commission also included on its recommended list an African American male. Attorney General Bell, however, ranked two white males at the top — U.S. district judges Albert Henderson of Georgia and Thomas Lambros of Ohio — and recommended their appointments. In his rankings, however, Bell placed Georgia state judge Phyllis Kravitch as his second choice for the Fifth Circuit slot and African American Nathaniel Jones as his second choice for the Sixth Circuit position. White House counsel Lipshutz, along with White House aides Tim Kraft and Frank Moore, sent a memo to Carter:

> The most severe criticisms to date of this Administration's judicial appointments have come from women's groups, who are distressed that *none* of the 12 circuit judges nominated to date have been women. In part, this has been caused by the failure of many nominating panels to include women on the list of candidates submitted to us. In this case, however, both the panels have included women among their nominees. The 5th Circuit panel nominated Phyllis Kravitch, and Ann McManamon was named by the Sixth. We believe it imperative to select a woman, and we agree with Justice that Kravitch is the better of the two. She should be nominated for the Georgia vacancy.[7]

As for the Sixth Circuit vacancy, the memo revealed a split among Carter's advisers. Lipshutz and Moore recommended Nathaniel Jones, noting that "Jones is black and for the last 9 years served as General Counsel to the NAACP. He is one of the ablest black lawyers in the country and he is supported by all civil rights groups as well as by the AFL-CIO." Kraft favored Thomas Lambros, whom he said was "more strongly supported by the Democratic Party leadership in Ohio as well as by the Greek-American community." But all three Carter advisers agreed that "both of them are well qualified to serve in this position." The president was informed that Democratic senators Glenn and Metzenbaum had agreed to go along with any of the five on the panel's list. The memo concluded with an appeal to Carter to further the partisan agenda: "We believe that these two appointments should be announced simultaneously and that they can be politically beneficial by emphasizing your commitment to increase the number of well qualified minority and women judges."[8] At the bottom of the memo Carter checked the "approve" boxes for Kravitch and Jones, and at the top of the memo he handwrote: "Frank [Moore, congressional liaison] & Jody [Powell, press secretary]. Handle p.r. & Senate relations with care."[9]

The next day, October 11, Lipshutz was asked to notify the attorney general of the decision. Even so, about a month later, Lipshutz's assistant, Douglas Huron, complained that Justice Department officials had not notified Kravitch and Jones and that "the Attorney General (and Charles Kirbo)[a] have been lobbying to get the president to reverse the Kravitch decision." Bell, in the account of his tenure in office, told of his despair over losing sole control of judicial selection.[10] He was, however, able to delay the Kravitch nomination for about three months and the Jones nomination for about ten months. Finally Kravitch was nominated on January 19, 1979, and Jones was nominated the following August 28. Albert Henderson was nominated four months after Kravitch to fill another vacancy on the Fifth. Thomas Lambros remained on the federal district bench.

Many months earlier, Lipshutz's staffers had urged coordinated White House involvement with judicial selection in order to achieve the appointment of more women and minorities. During Carter's first year in office, Lipshutz was willing to let Griffin Bell and Michael J. Egan, the associate attorney general in charge of day-to-day matters concerning judicial selection, implement affirmative action for the judiciary. When results were disappointing, particularly regarding the appointment of women, Lipshutz, McKenna, and Huron became more aggressive in promoting affirmative action candidacies.[11][b]

a. Carter described Kirbo, a Georgia lawyer, as "my closest friend" and an advisor of long standing. Jimmy Carter, *Keeping Faith: Memoirs of a President* (New York: Bantam, 1982), pp. 49, 128.

b. Lipshutz believed that Bell wanted Carter to fire Margaret McKenna. Lipshutz notes on Griffin Bell's book, Lipshutz personal files. Bell's barely contained animus against McKenna is evident in his reference to her in his memoirs. Griffin B. Bell and Ronald J. Ostrow, *Taking Care of the Law* (New York: Morrow, 1982), 41. But Lipshutz and

Carter was personally committed to affirmative action and was concerned that it play out well, particularly for appeals court appointments, which clearly were tied to Carter's innovative merit selection commission. For example, Theodore McMillian, an African American, was one of five people recommended by the Eighth Circuit commission to fill a vacancy. Bell favored McMillian. Five days later, Lipshutz seconded that recommendation, noting to Carter that "Frank Moore and Tim Kraft concur in this nomination." Carter wrote on this memo: "OK — Tell Jody and Jerry [Rafshoon, media adviser] to do a good job on this."[12]

During the first two years in office, Carter himself rarely became involved in choosing among individuals for appeals court positions. He accepted the advice of his attorney general and his White House staff. On a few occasions when Lipshutz disagreed with Bell's preference of a white male over a qualified woman or minority, he brought matters to the attention of the president, as in the case of Phyllis Kravitch and Nathaniel Jones. But Carter eventually became frustrated by being brought in at the end of the selection process to ratify decisions made by subordinates. In late October 1978, Carter indicated that he wanted to be informed of prospective nominees *before* the ABA and FBI ran their checks. Several months later, he directed Lipshutz: "In future on Court of Appeals judges at least, give me a written memo before my meeting with Griffin, listing all final nominees [those recommended by the commissions] so that I'll know what's going on."[13]

Judicial selection assumed even greater importance with the deliberations and eventual passage of the largest expansion of the federal judiciary in United States history — the Omnibus Judgeship Act of 1978. This legislation was designed to address the significant increase in cases brought before the federal courts. To a large extent this increase mirrored the expansion of federal government activities, but it also was a reflection of the federalization of criminal law, in part as a result of the criminal procedures decisions of the Warren Court.[c] There were also considerations purely of political patronage, as representatives and senators jockeyed to add judgeships for their states.[14] The judgeships bill began its way in the legislative process in 1977. When it was

---

McKenna prevailed. In mid-1979, Carter specifically asked Lipshutz to have "Margaret McKenna search out women early on in the selection process." Lipshutz to McKenna, July 16, 1979, Lipshutz Papers.

c. In fiscal 1967, there were 102,845 civil and criminal cases filed in the federal district courts; by 1975 the number commenced was 158,428, a 54 percent increase in only eight years. The rate of increase on the appeals courts was even greater. In fiscal 1968, 9,116 cases were filed; in fiscal 1973 the number jumped to 15,629, a 71 percent increase in only five years. By 1980, there would be 188,487 cases filed in the district courts and 23,200 in the appeals courts. Reports of the Administrative Office of the United States Courts.

finally enacted and signed into law on October 20, 1978, 117 new federal district court judgeships and thirty-five new appeals court judgeships were created. These new positions provided an excellent opportunity to place women and minorities on the bench.

The House version of the bill directed the president to establish procedures and guidelines for selection of nominees for district court judgeships "on the basis of merit." Furthermore, the House bill took notice of the exceedingly small proportion of women and minorities on the federal bench and recommended that in selecting judges the president "give due consideration to qualified women, blacks, hispanics, and other minority individuals." The Senate's version of the bill, however, contained no such implicit restrictions on traditional senatorial prerogatives in the selection of district court judges.

At about the time that both houses of Congress had passed their versions of the judgeships bill, but before they had agreed on the final language, White House aides Lipshutz, Moore, and Hamilton Jordan, after consultation with Justice Department officials, submitted a memo to the president recommending "certain principles to follow in the appointment process" and more immediate steps to take. Carter read the memo and jotted on it some brief comments.

The memo recognized that the appointment of the record number of new judges created by the legislation "will constitute a critical part of the legacy of your Administration. Equally important, the process of filling these judgeships provides an instrument to redress an injustice: of the 525 active Federal judges, only twenty are black or hispanic and only six are women. By using the Omnibus Judgeship Act to appoint a substantial number of qualified minority and female lawyers, as well as capable white males, the Administration will begin to bring some balance into this area."[15] The principles in the appointment process which Carter checked off as approving included "Effective consultation with Senators." The memo recommended that

> [b]efore the Administration says anything public about appointing more minority and female judges, Frank Moore's staff should advise all Senators of your intention to direct the Circuit Court Nominating Commission to attempt to identify qualified minority and female nominees for Circuit Court positions.[d]

---

d. Note that this was accomplished by Executive Order 12059, signed May 11, 1978, revising the United States Circuit Judge Nominating Commission. Section 4d of the revised executive order stated, "Each panel is encouraged to make special efforts to seek out and identify well qualified women and members of minority groups as potential nominees."

In addition, we should let them know that their support concerning the new District Court openings in their states is particularly needed. We should also advise the Senators that Justice and the White House will be available to assist them, e.g., by suggesting names of qualified minority and female lawyers from their states.

The second principle was that "[a]t the District Court level, we should concentrate on those states having multiple vacancies. . . . If there is only one opening in a state, it is likely that a Senator may have a candidate who is not a minority or female lawyer. If there is more than one vacancy, however — and that will be the situation in about 25 states — we can fairly ask the Senators in question to assist us and help themselves politically by agreeing to the nomination of some minority or female lawyers. (Those Senators who have commissions can be asked to pass the word along.)"

The third principle was that nominations for particular circuit or district judgeships in a specified state should not be sent to the Senate until all of the potential nominees have been identified for all the positions to be filled in that circuit or state. The reason given Carter was that "[t]his will enable you to get a proper number of women and minorities nominated and confirmed." The president's aides stressed that such a package arrangement will "ensure that we do not inadvertently, through a series of ad hoc decisions, send only a few minority or female nominees to the Senate." The memo pointed out to Carter that of the 31 judges confirmed in little more than Carter's first year "only two are black and only one is a woman." Furthermore, the two blacks were elevations from the district to circuit bench; thus "there has been no net increase in the number of black judges." And in an oblique criticism of Bell and Egan, the memo noted, "We believe these numbers would have been higher if selections had not been made on an ad hoc basis."

The fourth principle was that adequate resources must be devoted to the selection of all the new judgeships and that the White House and Justice Department officials "will be cooperating closely. . . . They will also actively solicit names of qualified minority and female candidates and — in conjunction with Frank Moore's staff [congressional liaison] — pass these names on to interested Senators." The memo continued: "Before beginning consultation with the Senators, we need your approval of the basic objective of attempting to increase the number of minority and female judges, as well as the general principles outlined. The Attorney General concurs with this approach."

Carter checked his approval of the objective and principles. Then the memo called for "certain specific steps" to be taken to implement it. The first major step "is to amend the Executive Order establishing the Circuit Judge Nominating Commission" so that panels would be encouraged "to make special efforts

244 Carter Reforms Judicial Selection

to seek out and identify well qualified women and members of minority groups as potential nominees." Carter wrote, "OK." Attached to the memo was the proposed revised executive order that used the above language. There were other proposed changes in the executive order:

1. Insert a provision explicitly permitting the public release of the names of candidates recommended by a panel. To this, Carter responded, "don't encourage." As a result, the revised executive order that dropped the requirement of confidentiality did not explicitly authorize public release of names.
2. Clarify the panel's authority to submit a single list of more than five names where there were multiple vacancies. Carter wrote, "OK."
3. Specify that at least one lawyer from each state serve on each panel and that lawyers constitute a majority of each panel. Carter underlined the language that a majority be attorneys and wrote, "Why?" The new executive order, as a result, simply stated that at least one lawyer from each state serve on each panel. There was no mandate that lawyers constitute a majority. However, it deleted from the original executive order a provision that approximately equal numbers of lawyers and nonlawyers should serve on each panel.
4. Permit the president to designate someone, "probably the Attorney General or Associate Attorney General," to notify the panels to start their task. Carter responded, "OK."

Some three weeks after Carter signed off on these recommendations, he delivered a speech before the Los Angeles County Bar Association which touched on a number of law-related topics, including judicial selection. Carter emphasized his commitment to merit selection and noted that House and Senate conferees on the Omnibus Judgeship Act "have recently agreed that the President should set standards and guidelines governing the selection of district judges, and I intend to use this authority to encourage the establishment of more merit panels and to open the selection process."[16]

Indeed, as recounted by Bell, Carter in his first year of office "personally wrote a longhand letter to every Democratic senator urging that the senators establish commissions for the selection of candidates for federal district judge positions." Before 1977, senators from only two states (Florida in 1974 and Kentucky in 1976) had commissions. In 1977, commissions were established by senators in ten states. By 1980, senatorial commissions would be operating in thirty-one, with the big push for establishing them coming after passage of the new judgeships law.[17]

In his Los Angeles speech, Carter also addressed affirmative action for the judiciary, noting the nation's "abominable record" of minority and women judicial appointments. He emphasized that the new judgeships act "offers a unique opportunity to make our judiciary more fully representative of our population." Carter pointed out that his "Executive order on the Circuit Court Nominating Commission specifically requires special efforts to identify qualified minority and female candidates."[18] One week later, on May 11, 1978, the revised executive order, 12059, was issued.

The White House had anticipated that the House and Senate conferees on the judgeships bill would reach agreement sometime in late April or early May. But the conferees got bogged down over a proposal to split the Fifth Circuit, a move bitterly opposed by civil rights groups because it would mean that the Deep South would be dominated by conservative judges relatively unsympathetic to civil rights but actively supported by, among others, Senate Judiciary Committee chair Senator James O. Eastland. The controversy over the proposal had already held up the judgeships bill for almost a year.[19] By late summer, the deadlock was broken. The Fifth Circuit remained intact, and its membership was increased from fifteen to twenty-six judges. The judgeships bill passed the House on October 4 and the Senate on October 7.

Carter asked Bell to prepare a memorandum outlining how nominations under the new law would be processed. Bell's memo reflected the new reality that he would have to involve key White House staff members Bob Lipshutz, Hamilton Jordan, and Frank Moore. For the courts of appeals, Bell proposed: "When a panel submits its report to us, I will make a tentative selection in consultation with Hamilton, Bob and Frank, have the routine ABA and FBI checks run, and prepare a nomination for you." Carter, in his desire to be informed earlier, rewrote this proposal to read: "When a panel submits its report to us, I will make a tentative selection in consultation with Hamilton, Bob and Frank, prepare a nomination for you and *then* have the routine ABA and FBI checks run."[20]

Carter was even more explicit in the section Bell prepared on district court judges. Bell wrote: "A tentative selection of nominees will be made by me in consultation with Hamilton, Bob and Frank, and the ABA and FBI checks will be run." Carter handwrote "submit to me" in Bell's sentence before "and the ABA and FBI checks will be run."

In his memo to the president concerning district court judges, Bell noted that the new legislation required the president to issue "standards and guidelines" for filling the new judgeships. Bell wrote: "We will prepare and submit to you proposed standards and guidelines before the end of October." He went on to propose: "We will contact all Senators reaffirming your support of merit selection commissions. . . . We will impress upon the Senators your desire that there be greater representation of women and minorities on the federal judiciary. We will forward . . . all names which have come to our attention as potential district judges." He concluded: "This process will provide the maximum insulation for you from the judicial selection process" — a curious statement in light of Carter's wish to be involved earlier in the process. Bell went on: "You will know that any name presented to you for nomination has been approved by me, Hamilton, Bob and Frank. White House participation in the process will be by Hamilton, Bob and Frank only[e], with the Department of Justice handling the matter entirely except for the participation of those three and, of course, for your final approval. In order to eliminate the paper flow and ensuing delays, I will meet with Hamilton, Bob and Frank on an informal basis in seeking approval of nominees." This was the beginning of what during the Reagan administration became a joint Justice Department–White House committee to make final recommendations to the president.

Hamilton Jordan added his handwritten comments to the memo: "I think this process will work. . . . Tim Kraft [assistant to the president for political affairs and personnel] needs to be heard/involved either unilaterally or through me. The system suggested here is good, practical — will work." Carter responded, "Ham — O.K."

Carter was actively involved in the wording of the standards and guidelines for the selection of judges created by the Omnibus Judgeship Act. Lipshutz had prepared a draft, which Bell rejected. Lipshutz revised his draft and submitted it to Carter along with the Justice Department draft.[21] In his cover memo Lipshutz spelled out the differences between the two drafts and argued for his draft. Carter sided with Lipshutz but, perhaps to lessen the blow to Bell, rewrote some of Lipshutz's language and kept that part of Bell's language not disputed by Lipshutz. Lipshutz outlined three issues of disagreement.

First, in Bell's draft the emphasis was on the attorney general as bearing the responsibility for selecting judges. Lipshutz argued that the emphasis should be on the president's responsibility for selection. In Bell's draft Carter underlined phrases that he wished to alter, either by rewriting or by substituting Lipshutz's language: "1–101. Whenever a vacancy occurs in a district court of the United States, <u>the Attorney General shall recommend to the President for nomination as a district court judge to fill that vacancy one or more persons</u> whose character, experience, ability and commitment to equal justice under law qualify them to serve in the federal judiciary."[22] Carter accepted Lipshutz's substitution: "the President shall nominate as district judge to fill that vacancy a person."

---

e. Bell evidently sought to exclude Lipshutz's aggressive associates Margaret McKenna and Douglas Huron.

Bell's draft continued: "1–102. <u>The Attorney General shall seek to identify persons well qualified</u> to be federal district court judges and shall receive recommendations of such persons from any person, commission or organization." Carter rejected Bell's draft of this section, accepting some of Lipshutz's language but rewriting other portions (what Carter wrote in longhand is italicized): "1–102. The Attorney General shall assist the President *by recommending to the President persons to be considered for appointment who are qualified to be district judges and by evaluating potential nominees.* The Attorney General shall receive recommendations of such persons from any person, commission or organization."

In section 1–104 Bell wrote and Carter underlined: "<u>Before transmitting recommendations to the President, the Attorney General shall consider whether:</u> . . ." Carter accepted some of Bell's and some of Lipshutz's language, so that the revised section read:

> 1–104. Before making recommendations, the Attorney General shall consider whether:
> (a) Public notice of the vacancy has been given and that an affirmative effort has been made, in the case of each vacancy, to identify qualified candidates, including women and members of minority groups;
> (b) The selection process was fair and reasonable;
> (c) The person or persons recommended meet the standards for evaluation set forth in Section 1–2 of this Order.

In his cover memo, Lipshutz explained that Bell's emphasis on the attorney general's role in selection over the president's reflected Bell's "legitimate concern that the entire White House not become involved in judicial selection." Lipshutz advised Carter: "For that reason Hamilton, Frank and I have agreed that any and all contacts with Justice on this issue will be made through my office." Lipshutz then noted that he would coordinate with Jordan, Kraft, and Moore "to make sure that all White House interests are considered."

The second point of disagreement with Bell's draft was over Bell's use in section 1–102 of the term "well qualified" to describe those sought by the administration to fill judgeships. Lipshutz pointed out that "[w]hile the phrase seems innocuous, it is a term of art within the legal profession," being one of the four ratings used by the ABA. Lipshutz indicated he did not believe Bell was intending to adopt the ABA rating system but that because of the special meaning of the term, to include it "could prove confusing." But even more to the point, any greater standard than "qualified" "could have an adverse effect on affirmative action." As we saw, Carter eliminated the phrase "well qualified." In Bell's draft he wrote alongside it "Not imp.[ortant]" and instead used the term "qualified."

The third point of disagreement was that Bell wanted the president to sign the executive order immediately and Lipshutz wanted key senators, particularly Edward Kennedy (the incoming head of the Senate Judiciary Committee) to review the draft. Carter agreed with Lipshutz that senators should be consulted, and he handwrote, "Let Griffin handle this" and "Let AG [attorney general] check with Senators."

Carter himself made an important change in section 1–103 of the Lipshutz draft, which with the exception of one additional word—"publicly," was identical to Bell's phrasing. The Lipshutz/Bell draft read: "1–103. The use of commissions to advise persons making recommendations for district judge is encouraged. The Attorney General shall make publicly available suggested guidelines for such commissions." Carter revised the section to read (Carter's changes in italics): "1–103. The use of commissions to *notify the public of vacancies and to make* recommendations for district judge is encouraged. The Attorney General shall make *public the* suggested guidelines for such commissions." Carter was dedicated to open government and casting a wide net for affirmative action. These changes reflected that commitment.

On the first page of Lipshutz's memo Carter directed: "Bob—Type this as edited. See marginal notes." With the deletion of one paragraph at the behest of Senator Kennedy,[f] the executive order was issued as Carter rewrote it. Carter signed the order on November 8, 1978.

Bell devised a questionnaire for the senators or their selection commissions to complete when recommending one or more persons for a district court judgeship. He reported to Carter that he had tested the questionnaire on senators Kennedy, Morgan, and Bumpers and was "satisfied that we have a workable system." Bell told Carter that once the executive order was signed he would "proceed to contact all Senators by letter and most by telephone to explain the system and to urge the use of selection commissions."[23]

Most Democratic senators, however, at first refused to listen to the message on affirmative action. Only four of the first fifty-nine recommendations from

---

f. According to Griffin Bell, Senator Kennedy "likes everything about [the proposed executive order] except paragraph 1-201 (h)," which stated that one of the standards to be considered in the appointment of district judges is whether the appointment would help "meet a perceived need of the district court in which the vacancy exists, including the need for a certain professional background or legal expertise, or geographical distribution." Bell noted that Kennedy "believes this should be deleted or that we should add an affirmative action factor to it." Bell recommended that the paragraph be deleted because "[i]t really adds nothing as a standard that would not be considered as a matter of course." Bell to Carter, November 6, 1978, Judgeships (Active): Executive Order (District Court Standards and Guidelines), Lipshutz Papers, Carter Library.

senators were women (including two who were nonwhite). Four were nonwhite males. Margaret McKenna, in a passionate plea to Lipshutz, Jordan, and Moore, urged that the White House do something about this. She warned that "the end result as opposed to the process, will be what the [women's and civil rights] groups look at." She added, "They will not question why the Senate did not nominate women and minorities; they will just question why the President did not nominate women and minorities." Doug Huron complained to Hamilton Jordan that because he and McKenna, at the behest of the attorney general, were eliminated "from any ongoing participation in the selection process . . . no one at the White House even had the basic statistical data to know that this problem was coming."[24]

The president responded to these developments by writing to each Democratic senator urging that they recruit women and minorities for the new judgeships and other vacancies. "Fairness requires that we seize the opportunity. . . . I am deeply concerned by the small number of women and members of minorities recommended to date for district judgeships. Please redouble your efforts, whether personal or through a nominating commission, to find qualified lawyers in these categories."[25]

Carter, as mentioned previously, wanted to be involved in the selection process earlier and finally, on March 30, 1979, asked Lipshutz for a memo listing the final cut of prospective nominees "so that I'll know what's going on" before the meetings with Bell. In response, Lipshutz sent Carter a summary of the leading candidates for appeals court positions recommended by the merit selection commissions. For example, for one vacancy on the Tenth Circuit, Lipshutz listed Stephanie Seymour with the notation: "(white female) — private practice, first female partner in a major Oklahoma firm; first woman to serve as an Oklahoma Bar examiner; experience in complex litigation."[26] Three other individuals, all white males, were also listed with capsule biographies. Carter indicated his interest in Seymour on the memo, and she was subsequently appointed.

For a Fourth Circuit vacancy, one white female, one black male, and three white males were listed. Carter indicated his interest in the person who later received the appointment: "James Sprouse (white male) — Extensive career in private practice, where the State AFL-CIO has been a client; served on State Supreme Court 1972–1975."

For vacancies on the Ninth Circuit, Carter showed interest in two men. Otto Skopil was a white U.S. district judge since 1972 who was also a Republican. Carter had him in mind for the Oregon slot, noting: "Repubs want him [and] (to be replaced by woman)." Jerome Farris was an African American serving on the Washington Court of Appeals since 1969, about whom Carter wrote "excellent." Skopil got the job (and was replaced by Helen J. Frye), which meant that the administration passed over the distinguished Oregon Supreme Court justice Hans Linde. Farris, too, was appointed, filling the Washington slot.

In his cover memo Lipshutz noted that Carter was scheduled to meet with him and Bell to discuss their recommendations. He informed Carter, however, that "the Senators are submitting only their final recommendations," in other words, just one name. Thus, Lipshutz could not provide Carter with a list of district court candidates. Carter wrote "OK" on the memo and initialed it. Lipshutz prepared other such memos for further conferences with the attorney general.

Carter apparently had little involvement with the selection of individual district court judges but somewhat more with the selection of appeals court judges, particularly after tensions surfaced between the Justice Department and the White House counsel's office over the pace of affirmative action. Griffin Bell, himself a former federal appeals court judge, no doubt had influenced Carter's thinking on merit selection. Robert Lipshutz was a tireless supporter of affirmative action. Bell resigned from the attorney generalship in mid-August 1979 and his deputy, Benjamin Civiletti, became attorney general. Lipshutz left the White House counsel's office on October 1, 1979, and was succeeded by Lloyd Cutler. The change in personnel seemed to produce somewhat less tension between the Justice Department and the White House staff,[27] and in any event there is much less evidence of Carter's active involvement in the selection process once Bell and Lipshutz left the administration.

The Policy Agenda and Selection

Carter's economic and social welfare programs were generally not issues before the federal courts. There is no evidence that Carter or any key official saw the federal courts as an obstacle to the administration's policy initiatives or viewed judicial appointments as a means to support its policy agenda. Neither Bell, Lipshutz, or Carter criticized the federal courts for being soft on crime or too activist in the expansion of rights or too imperial in the assertion of hegemony over areas of public policy once considered the sole prerogative of elected officials—themes that Nixon developed and Reagan would later expand. To be sure, during the third presidential debate of the 1976 election campaign, Carter had made clear that all other factors being equal, he would prefer the appointment of a person "who would most accurately reflect my own political philosophy."[28] At the very least, this meant individuals firmly committed to civil rights and affirmative action.

There is some indication in the presidential papers of attention paid to the general civil liberties orientation of candidates. For example, the First Circuit panel chairman, Harvard Law School professor Paul A. Freund, in a report to the president, described Hugh H. Bownes, who was then sitting on the federal district bench in New Hampshire, as a "courageous judge, frequently a target, because of his support of civil liberties, of the [right wing conservative] publisher William Loeb." Freund went on to note that in tort cases Bownes, who was subsequently appointed, tended to take a more "liberal" or "plaintiff-oriented" view of law than did the Court of Appeals.[29]

In another memo to Carter, Lipshutz assessed the president's appointments to the Sixth Circuit. Damon Keith, an African American, had been appointed, "but more recently [you] have nominated two individuals who are perceived as being conservative on civil rights issues" — Bailey Brown of Tennessee, who was elevated from the federal district bench and replaced by an African American, Odell Horton, and Cornelia Kennedy of Michigan, a conservative Republican federal district judge. "Appointing Nate [Nathaniel] Jones, now General Counsel of the national NAACP, will restore the balance in the Sixth Circuit."[30]

There was considerable concern in Lipshutz's office over the impact that dividing the Fifth Circuit would have on judicial decisionmaking. In one of the analyses, the memo writer concluded that in the western states of the Fifth Circuit a majority of the judges voted for the civil rights plaintiffs, while in the eastern states a majority voted for the civil rights defendant. The memo also analyzed the "effect of the division of the Fifth Circuit on 50 recent en banc decisions." Another analysis looked at the impact on labor litigation. The judges of the Fifth Circuit were categorized as either pro-employer or pro-union. While conflict over dividing the Fifth stalled the Omnibus Judgeship Bill for more than a year, the Fifth was eventually split in 1980. Opposition eased largely because Carter had appointed enough liberals to address the concerns of the civil rights forces and Mississippi was kept in the Fifth with the "western" states, Texas and Louisiana (leaving the new Eleventh Circuit to consist of Alabama, Georgia, and Florida).[31]

There was one instance in which the administration was seriously embarrassed by not paying enough attention to the civil rights views of a district court appointee. David Belew was recommended to the administration by Texas Democratic senator Lloyd Bentsen for a position on the federal district court for the Northern District of Texas. Bentsen had cooperated with the administration's affirmative action policy by recommending ten individuals of whom four were nontraditional nominees. Belew, a white male, seemed to check out. He had support from local blacks. Attorney General Bell's formal recommendation of Belew to the president contained the typical language of such letters: "He bears an excellent reputation as to character and integrity, has judicial temperament, and is, I believe, worthy of appointment as a United States District Judge."[32]

Once Belew was confirmed and his commission signed by the president, he was quoted in an interview published in a Fort Worth newspaper using a racial epithet several times. When this was picked up by the wire services, the administration was stunned and civil rights groups were angry. Although Belew later apologized, a Justice Department official told a reporter for the *New York Times* that if Belew had spoken in such a racist manner *before* the president had signed the commission, Carter "could have withdrawn his appointment,"[33] a questionable assertion but surely indicative of the strong feelings of the administration including the Justice Department, whose screening procedures had failed.

The policy agenda of the Carter administration relevant to the federal courts concerned the president's personal commitment to reform the process of judicial selection *and* to increase the number of women and minorities on the bench. Increasing women and minorities also furthered the partisan agenda. Evidence of the administration's concern for affirmative action, in addition to what we have seen, includes the following:

- In February 1977, at Lipshutz's direction, associate counsel Huron worked with Hamilton Jordan to select the panel members of the Circuit Judge Nominating Commission. Huron initially drew up the guidelines that "membership is . . . to be representative of minorities and females. There should be five or six women on each [eleven member] panel, with minority representation based loosely on population percentage." Huron's guidelines specified the number of lawyers, nonlawyers, blacks, hispanics, Asians, and women for each circuit panel. Twenty-one months later, Huron reported to Lipshutz: "I believe that our office's participation is largely responsible for the fact that on the first nine panels selected — a total of 99 members — 44 were women, 27 were members of minority groups and a large number were Carter supporters." Lipshutz himself met with Susan Ness of the Judicial Selection Project, who helped choose members of judicial selection panels. The commissions may have engaged in policy- and partisan-agenda screening to the extent that candidates inconsistent with the Carter agenda were unlikely to make the list of recommended candidates.[34]
- When the standards and guidelines for the selection of district judges were being formulated, Lipshutz met with Georgetown University law professor Charles R. Halpern and his colleagues associated with the Judicial Selection Project, along with representatives of the ABA committee and Common

Cause. They "were permitted to review the draft standards and guidelines and to give their oral reaction."[35]

- Lipshutz was continually formulating strategies to increase the number of women and minorities on the bench. For example, in one handwritten note to himself, Lipshutz wrote: "for 6th Circuit Ct. of Appeals (Tenn.) 5 nominated — Bailey Brown (U.S. Dist. Ct.) — 3 blacks in Memphis — definitely 1 to replace Brown. Pres. to talk with [Tennessee Senator] Sasser first." In another note Lipshutz wrote:

North Carolina — 3 U.S. Dist. Ct. [positions] Winberry + 2 others — A.G. to continue [negotiations with North Carolina Senator Morgan for an African American appointment which were ultimately successful]. . . . Hold Illinois — no commission but screening by jury of lawyers — recommends 3 white males — *no* women on bench! . . . Texas — 10 U.S. Dist. Ct. — M.A. [Mexican American]; 2 women (1 black) — 7 white males + M.A. U.S. Dist. Ct. Judge to 5th Circuit & replace him with M.A.[g] . . . O.K. Michigan — 5 U.S. Dist. Ct., black woman, black man, 3 white males per Sen. Riegle.[36]

- On November 15, 1978, Huron met with representatives from Common Cause, the Judicial Selection Project, the NAACP, the Women's Legal Defense Fund, the Coalition for Women's Appointments, the National Council of LaPaza, the National Women's Political Caucus, and some private individuals, urging those present to "try to solicit names as quickly as possible" for federal judgeships. They were asked to send the names and background data to Margaret McKenna or Huron himself at the White House and to Michael Egan or Philip Modlin at the Justice Department. "Names of minority and female candidates should [also] be sent to Drew Days and Barbara Babcock respectively [at the Justice Department]."[37]

The policy goal of achieving affirmative action for the judiciary took much effort. Behind the scenes, the White House counsel's office pushed and prodded the Justice Department and, when necessary, brought the president in. Griffin Bell and Associate Attorney General Michael Egan were sympathetic to affirmative action, up to a point. They defended it in public and were responsible for several appointments of women and blacks. Yet the counsel's office sometimes thought the Justice Department was dragging its feet, unwilling to take the initiative, going too easy on some senators, and in general not placing affirmative action as the highest priority in the selection of judges. A growing tension emerged between the Justice Department and the counsel's

g. A Mexican-American, U.S. District Judge Reynaldo G. Garza, was elevated to the Fifth Circuit, and Mexican-American Filemon B. Vela replaced him on the district court bench.

office that resulted in muted but pointed disagreements between Bell and Lipshutz, which reached the president.

Dissatisfaction began brewing in the counsel's office early on. Just six weeks into the new administration Lipshutz and McKenna complained to the president of the "lack of minority and women candidates" among district judges, United States attorneys, and United States marshals. On March 8, Margaret McKenna met with Michael Egan, Philip Modlin, and two other Justice officials to discuss the selection process for these positions. The conferees agreed that a letter from the president to senators, representatives, Democratic governors, and party chairmen — "those who make recommendations" — would effectively inform these people of the president's interest in meritorious recommendations, particularly of minorities and women. McKenna reported, however, "Such a letter was written for Griffin Bell, but he decided not to sign it." When she suggested that someone from the White House contact senators or representatives "to suggest names of early Carter supporters and/or minority and women candidates," the response was that "[t]he Justice Department does not want to be involved in this kind of suggestion process."[38]

Margaret McKenna learned in the summer of 1977 that the Justice Department had neglected to instruct the selection commission panels for appeals courts to practice affirmative action. And the results showed. The first year of judicial appointments yielded few minorities and women. The White House counsel's office urged a more aggressive posture for affirmative action, but the Justice Department position, as reflected in a memo from the associate attorney general to the associate White House counsel, was that affirmative action should be achieved "in a less rigid manner."[39]

Griffin Bell did not want to share responsibility for judicial selection with the White House counsel's office. Bell resented the pressure from Lipshutz and his associates to move on affirmative action and felt he was doing his best to honor the president's commitment.[40]

Adding to the tension between Bell and Lipshutz was Bell's support of the controversial proposal to divide the Fifth Circuit. In mid-1978, Lipshutz prepared a memorandum for the president suggesting that the administration oppose the division. Lipshutz sent a copy to Bell, who responded with controlled fury. Bell in his response made it clear that he "consistently favored" dividing the Fifth Circuit and that such a course of action had been recommended by a national study commission. Then Bell came to the heart of his dispute with Lipshutz: "I am having some trouble with your office over just who is in charge of clearing judges and making recommendations to the President after having conferred with Senators. To date I have had fairly good luck in my relations with the Senate, and the President has never mentioned to me that this activity was in your charge or was to be transferred to you. I do not believe that I can handle my responsibilities with the Senate on a joint basis with you and your staff."[41]

Lipshutz gave Bell's memo to Huron and McKenna for their reactions, and they responded: "Bell's criticism is unwarranted. We have previously agreed that both offices should work cooperatively on judicial selection under the Omnibus Judgeships Act. The President has approved this arrangement. It is too late for him [Bell] unilaterally to decide otherwise."[42]

Huron and McKenna pointed out that they were specifically designated by Lipshutz to work on judicial selection with the Justice Department. They recounted: "Since that time we have met with Mike Egan and others at Justice to discuss recruitment of minority and female judges and consultation with Senators. The meetings have been both amiable and productive, and we would like for them to continue."

Nevertheless, when the deadlock in the House-Senate conference committee over division of the Fifth was broken by a compromise[h] and final passage of the Omnibus Judgeship bill was at hand, the Justice Department proposed a reduced role for the White House in judicial selection. The department proposed assuming principal or exclusive responsibility for selecting members of the circuit court nominating panels, maintaining contact with the panels, preparing standards and guidelines for merit selection at the district level, contacting senators to push for merit selection and affirmative action and subsequent negotiations with senators, and selecting a nominee when more than one candidate was submitted to fill a vacancy.[43]

Huron and McKenna complained to Lipshutz "that Justice's proposal leaves too little substantive responsibility in the White House. . . . It is the White House's function . . . to examine the pool of competent candidates and to factor in political considerations and affirmative action requirements. Justice should not have final authority, on paper or in reality, to select judges. . . . A substantial White House role here is imperative." Furthermore, in terms of selecting panel members on the circuit court selection commission, "[i]t has been the White House, not Justice, which has pushed successfully to have representative numbers of minorities and women on the panels. . . . Justice has also been indifferent to political considerations. Again, it has been the White House that has insisted that qualified Carter supporters be included on the panels."[44]

h. The Fifth would not be split into two new circuits, but the circuit was authorized to divide for administrative purposes. The circuit's membership was increased to twenty-six judges.

The day after Huron and McKenna wrote to Lipshutz, the director of the Presidential Personnel Office and another White House staffer wrote to Tim Kraft to enlist his support for a White House role in the selection of district judges. They suggested that White House pressure on senators was needed. For example, Missouri senator Eagleton had recommended three white males for three new judgeships in Missouri, and Senator Harry Byrd's commission had recommended nine white males as candidates for four Virginia judgeships. The staffers wrote that they "do not see the Justice Department taking a lead role in insuring that the president's affirmative action goals are actualized" and that "if there is no sector which actively works towards the President's goals . . . we will fall short of his stated ambitions." They urged Kraft's support for the attempt of the White House counsel's office "to place themselves in a position to effectively monitor recommendations and work to see that the President's goals are realized."[45]

That same day, Margaret McKenna wrote to Lipshutz suggesting that he call the attorney general and "tell him that you have talked to Hamilton, Tim, and Frank, and you have designated me as the White House contact for the judges on all of these issues, including nominating panels and judicial selection, as well as matters such as standards and guidelines. It will then be my responsibility to coordinate within the White House with Tim and Frank."[46]

Bell's reaction was to go directly to the president with a memorandum without giving Lipshutz, Moore, or Kraft the opportunity to respond. Lipshutz, in a memo to Jordan and Moore, was evidently furious:

> This is totally inconsistent with the very "good faith" relationship which I have thought we had with the Department of Justice relative to this matter. . . . Since the enactment of this Omnibus Judgeship Act became probable during the Spring of this year, our office has worked closely with Mike Egan, representing the Attorney General, in order to work out a satisfactory procedure for the handling of this very important and voluminous matter. There were numerous discussions between Mike Egan and Margaret McKenna and Doug Huron, and the Department of Justice worked with us in the preparation of the April 12, 1978, memorandum, from Hamilton, Frank and me. . . . In order to carry out the wishes and intent of the President . . . and reach his goals as expressed during the campaign and since being in office — it is extremely important that we have a real (and not superficial) involvement of the key personnel at the White House.[47]

Lipshutz urged that White House staffer Frank Moore be responsible for liaison with senators, that Jordan and Kraft consider other political aspects of appointments, and that reaching "the President's objectives relative to affirmative action . . . be the principal responsibility of the office of White House Counsel."

Lipshutz also argued that the counsel's office coordinate all White House actions and that the White House should be involved in selecting circuit court nomination panels as well as all judges. The Justice Department, on the other hand, "should have primary responsibility for administering this selection process and also for assuring the competence of persons who are recommended to the President for nomination. However, I suggest that it would be inappropriate for the Department of Justice to get itself involved in the political aspects of this process."

Lipshutz was surely right about the need for the White House to push for affirmative action in the judicial selection process, and he was supported in that view by Charles Halpern of the Judicial Selection Project. Halpern wrote to Lipshutz objecting to the Justice Department's selecting judges because of what he considered to be its unsatisfactory affirmative action record and its continued use of criteria that made it more difficult for women and minorities to be chosen.[48]

Lipshutz also seemed to be acknowledging that affirmative action was part of the "political aspects of this process." As recounted earlier, Carter essentially sided with Lipshutz. Bell got the affirmative action message from the president and agreed to cooperate with the White House staff including the counsel's office.[49] The impetus for aggressive affirmative action had come from the White House and not the Justice Department, and it was appropriate that affirmative action be actively promoted by the White House counsel's office.

The disagreements between Bell and Lipshutz apparently did not spill over into their personal relationship, and once the president made clear his support for a more aggressive White House role in affirmative action, Bell graciously bowed to the new reality. For example, Lipshutz wrote of a meeting with Bell, Hamilton Jordan, Frank Moore, and Tim Kraft held on November 28, 1978, to decide on recommendations to the president for judicial appointments. He described the meeting as "very good" and one that reflected a more coordinated approach to selection, with a heavy emphasis on affirmative action. Lipshutz supplied Bell with names and biographical sketches; for example, in a memo of December 13, 1978, Lipshutz wrote Bell: "Attached is some additional information concerning prospective black judges for the District Courts and Circuit Courts. . . . I would appreciate your putting it into the Justice Department 'inventory' and forwarding it to the appropriate senators and commissions."[50]

But all was not well within the White House when the National Women's

Political Caucus released statistics in early January 1979 that fifty-one of the fifty-nine recommendations from Democratic senators for the new judgeships were white males. Doug Huron placed the blame on Bell and, in a memo to Hamilton Jordan, argued: "It should be apparent by now that the attorney general does not adequately represent either the President's views or his interests in judicial selection. The White House should be monitoring the process on a day to day basis."[51]

Huron likely overstated the case against Bell. Others had some responsibility for the slow pace of affirmative action nominations. In at least one instance, the chairman of a judicial selection panel (the Eastern Fifth Circuit) failed to give the members of the selection commission panel the revised executive order and to inform the panel of the need to make special efforts to recruit minority and women candidates. Bell, however, was to make a case to Carter that the administration would be in a position to claim victory insofar as the appointment of blacks to southern federal courts was concerned. On May 17, 1979, Bell wrote to Carter: "It now appears that . . . you will have corrected the imbalance through the use of just your appointments." The implicit message was that there would no longer be any need for affirmative action. Lipshutz, who received a copy of the memo, immediately wrote Carter and noted:

> I think it would be a mistake publicly to conclude that we have overcome historical discrimination simply because the percentage of black judges is equal to or greater than the percentage of black lawyers in a given southern state. Civil rights groups would argue that this premise perpetuates discrimination, since until recently blacks were discriminatorily denied access to the legal profession itself in the South. The conclusion also suggests that it is sufficient to place one black judge in each of the district courts in the South. In some states that may be enough; in others there may be more qualified blacks available, and we should continue to search them out. We should emphasize that a good start has been made in the South and across the country — not that we have reached the end of the road.[52]

An additional indicator that Justice Department officials were not as sensitive to racial concerns as they might have been was over the issue of whether judicial candidates should be asked to resign from clubs that discriminate on the basis of race. Members of the Senate Judiciary Committee were insisting that judicial nominees resign from such clubs, but the associate attorney general was apparently "inclined against advising nominees" to resign from them.[53]

By September 1979, Doug Huron could report that of 130 individuals confirmed or tentatively selected for the district bench, forty-three (or one third) were women or minorities. Of thirty-seven individuals confirmed or tentatively selected for the circuit bench, eighteen (or just under half) were women or members of minority groups.[54]

Griffin Bell left the Justice Department in August 1979, and Robert Lipshutz left the White House counsel's office at the beginning of October. Institutional tension nevertheless continued between the Justice Department and the counsel's office over White House participation in judicial selection.[55] However, Carter's policy of affirmative action for the judiciary was vigorously embraced by his new attorney general, Benjamin Civiletti. In at least one instance the tables appeared to have turned: the new attorney general complained to the White House counsel of a White House delay in the processing of the nomination of an African American woman to the federal district bench in the District of Columbia.[i]

For the Carter administration, the policy and partisan agendas regarding judicial appointments were inextricably intertwined. Affirmative action was indeed a Carter policy, but the appointment of women and minorities significantly furthered the partisan agenda. The implicit assumption may have been that women and minorities would support government affirmative action programs, thus to that extent such appointments would further the policy agenda. But there is little evidence in the presidential papers of any deliberate attempt to use judicial appointments to affect the law in affirmative action or any other policy domain important for the president's agenda.

When we consider appointments to the appeals courts, if we view the appointment of women and minorities without explicit regard to their political or judicial philosophies as primarily partisan-agenda appointments, the available evidence in the presidential papers suggests that almost all of the Carter appointments can be classified as partisan-agenda appointments. There are very few references to political or judicial philosophy or views on policy issues such as civil rights or gender equality. At best there may have been three policy-agenda appointments where such concerns were explicit. Of course it is

---

i. The nominee was Norma Holloway Johnson. Attorney General Civiletti wrote to White House Counsel Lloyd Cutler: "It is my understanding that someone now questions whether to proceed with her nomination. Unless the President has changed his mind, her nomination should be processed promptly or there will be a serious problem as to the perception of our commitment to equal opportunity for Blacks and women and the Administration's effort to increase their representation on the federal bench. I don't think a contrary view from some members of the Bar or one faction or another within the District of Columbia should be a ground for serious reconsideration at this stage." Civiletti to Cutler, January 17, 1980, Judges 1–5/80, Cutler Papers, Carter Library. Johnson was nominated on February 28, 1980, and subsequently confirmed.

likely, given the large representation of women and minorities (as well as Democrats) on the commissions, that implicit if not explicit policy screening took place at least occasionally at the commission level. There is no evidence that Carter made any personal-agenda appointments. Indeed there is no evidence that Carter himself suggested possible judicial candidates, consistent with his view that selection should not be driven by patronage.

The tension between the Justice Department and the counsel's office was not just over turf. Bell was a moderate conservative, as was Associate Attorney General Michael J. Egan, a Georgia Republican. Lipshutz and his staff were considerably more liberal. Had policy-agenda considerations been a major factor, the appointment process would likely have broken down. Bell's focusing on "merit" and not "politics" or "policy" lessened the latent tensions which nevertheless surfaced from time to time over affirmative action and led to a more institutionalized involvement of the White House in the selection process.

That more traditional partisan concerns were not overlooked is revealed by the simple fact that when Carter took office, more than half the federal judges were Republicans. When he left office, more than 60 percent were Democrats.[56]

Senators and Selection

President Carter's attempt to change judicial selection from a patronage-driven system to a merit selection system and at the same time diversify the bench with women and minorities met with some obstacles from senators. Some Democratic senators resisted establishing judicial selection commissions. Senator Bentsen was quoted as saying, "I am the merit commission for Texas," although he later claimed that he could not recall having said that.[57]

But even with merit selection commissions, Democratic senators would have strong preferences that they would actively promote. For example, the commission established in Ohio by Democratic senators Howard Metzenbaum and John Glenn gave the senators a list of people the commission found qualified to fill a district court vacancy. Glenn made one recommendation from the list, Metzenbaum another. Metzenbaum contacted Attorney General Civiletti with his recommendation of Arthur Spiegel for the position and showed "great interest in Spiegel's progress within the Department of Justice and has even been calling the FBI in an attempt to speed up its investigation."[58] Spiegel was appointed.

Democratic North Carolina senator Sam J. Ervin, Jr., wrote to the president recommending his son, Samuel J. Ervin III, for a Fourth Circuit judgeship.[59]

The senator's son was not on the Fourth Circuit commission's list and did not receive that particular appointment. The next time around, however, Ervin was on the list, and he received the judgeship.

The Omnibus Judgeship Act created a new position on the First Circuit that some observers thought would go to Massachusetts, the largest state in the circuit and the home of the incoming chairman of the Senate Judiciary Committee, Senator Kennedy. The *New York Times* reported in late November 1978 that Kennedy's choice for the new circuit judgeship "is expected to be Archibald Cox, the Harvard Law School professor and former Watergate prosecutor."[60][j] But Cox was close to sixty-seven years old and, under the ABA criteria in use at the time, would have been rated "not qualified" because of age. The administration resisted when Kennedy openly pushed for Cox once the Judicial Selection Commission panel for the First Circuit included Cox on its list and unanimously named him its first choice. Neither side budged, and the First Circuit seat remained vacant for almost two years. That Kennedy challenged Carter for the presidential nomination in 1980 did not improve matters.

Once Carter won renomination, he began negotiations with Kennedy to obtain his support in the general election campaign. One of Kennedy's conditions, which Carter accepted, was that the First Circuit slot be filled by Kennedy's choice, the chief counsel to the Senate Judiciary Committee, Stephen G. Breyer, who was on leave from Harvard Law School.[61] Kennedy won support for Breyer from the ranking Republican member of the committee, Strom Thurmond. After the election Carter nominated Breyer, whose name was one of three on a list forwarded to Carter by the nominating commission. Thurmond, the incoming chairman of the Senate Judiciary Committee, kept the Republicans in line. Breyer was confirmed, thus launching a judicial career that would take him to the Supreme Court in 1994. However, since both Cox and Breyer were Kennedy choices before the merit selection commission even met, it appeared that the commission had become window dressing for a more traditional process, although clearly Cox was distinguished and Breyer was certainly "qualified" (also his ABA rating).

The administration was obliged to negotiate with senators to achieve racial

j. What the *New York Times* did not know was that on the very day its story appeared, Bob Lipshutz, Griffin Bell, Hamilton Jordan, Frank Moore, and Tim Kraft had met to consider judgeship recommendations to Carter and had decided to request the Circuit Court Commission "to consider possible nominees" from Massachusetts *and* Rhode Island for the new opening on the First Circuit. Lipshutz, Memorandum for the File, November 28, 1978, p. 1, Lipshutz Papers.

and gender diversification among the nominees for the new judgeships. For example, an account of a high-level, Justice Department–White House meeting on November 28, 1978, noted that Virginia senator Harry Byrd had created his own commissions, which had recommended only white males to fill four vacancies on the district bench. At the meeting it was decided that "[p]ending further efforts by the Attorney General, action is withheld on the recommendations of Senator Harry Byrd."[k] As for North Carolina, the group "agreed that Senator [Robert] Morgan's very close friend [Charles B.] Winberry [Jr.], should be recommended, but the recommendation should be withheld until the Attorney General has discussed with Senator Morgan the two other vacancies, with the expectation that at least one of the two vacancies will be filled by a black."[l] The Georgia senators, Sam Nunn and Herman Talmadge, recommended six males, five white and one black, for six positions, and the administration officials agreed that "[t]he Attorney General is going to discuss [with the senators] a modification in their recommendations . . . so as to include a woman in the group."[m] The group noted that Illinois Senator Adlai Stevenson was recommending three white males and that no women were serving on the federal district court bench in Illinois. It agreed that "[t]he Attorney General is going to follow up on this matter with Senator Stevenson, but only after he has negotiated the appointments in Georgia with Senators Nunn and Talmadge. In the meantime recommendations are being withheld."[n] The new Missouri slots would be "held up at the present time, but it is understood that Senator [Thomas] Eagleton is reviewing his original recommendation of three white males and may very well include one black among the three recommendations."[62][o]

k. Senator Byrd proved to be intractable. See *Washington Post,* December 8, 1978, A1. The administration eventually went ahead with three of those recommended by Byrd and on its own nominated an African American, state judge James Sheffield, who ran into trouble with the Senate Judiciary Committee.

l. An African American, Richard C. Erwin, was nominated on June 11, 1980, for a North Carolina seat. Winberry, however, had been nominated more than fourteen months before Erwin (on March 29, 1979) but was not approved by the Senate Judiciary Committee.

m. A woman, Orinda D. Evans, was nominated on June 5, 1979.

n. Stevenson proved cooperative. Susan Getzendanner was nominated on June 4, 1980, for a position on the federal bench in Illinois.

o. Three white males were in fact nominated, but the next vacancy was filled by an African American, Clyde S. Cahill, who was nominated on April 2, 1980. Senator Eagleton had previously supported the appointment of African American state judge Theodore McMillian from St. Louis for the Eighth Circuit, thus demonstrating his cooperation with the administration's affirmative action goals. He later sponsored Professor Joan

The Senate confirmation process changed when Senator Kennedy assumed the chairmanship of the Senate Judiciary Committee at the start of the Ninety-sixth Congress in 1979. Kennedy made it clear that senators who withheld the "blue slips" of persons nominated for judgeships from their states could no longer rely on the chairman to kill those nominations. Every nomination would be discussed by the full committee, and the committee would determine whether or not to proceed with the nomination by holding a hearing. This change gave the administration some more leeway in its dealings with obstinate senators. In fact, Kennedy quietly informed the administration that he would support it if it bucked Senator Byrd in Virginia in order to nominate a woman or minority candidate.[63]

Kennedy introduced several innovations. At his urging, the committee adopted a questionnaire (including items of financial disclosure) that all nominees were to complete and, with the exception of a limited number of questions, was to become available to the public. The committee also began to routinely publish its nomination hearings. Kennedy invited various groups to testify before the Senate committee and to rate judicial nominees. One of Kennedy's major innovations was the establishment of the committee's own investigatory staff to examine the backgrounds of the nominees independent of the Justice Department.

The Senate committee staff investigations became of crucial importance for two southern nominations, those of Charles B. Winberry, Jr., and James Sheffield. Winberry was nominated to the federal district bench in North Carolina at the behest of Senator Robert Morgan, for whom Winberry had once served as campaign manager. Winberry was rated "qualified" by the ABA by a closely divided vote. The investigatory staff turned up evidence of questionable conduct by Winberry and alerted the ABA, which changed its rating to "not qualified." On March 4, 1980, the Senate Judiciary Committee voted 9 to 6 not to approve Winberry, the first time in modern history that the committee had rejected a judicial nominee sponsored by a senator of the president's party from the state in which the vacancy was to be filled. The administration withdrew the nomination on August 26.[64]

James Sheffield was the first African American ever to be nominated to a federal district judgeship in Virginia. He was a state court judge and was rated "qualified" by the ABA. The administration recruited Sheffield and nominated him despite Senator Byrd's opposition. The investigatory staff of the Senate Judiciary Committee, however, came up with damaging allegations concern-

Krauskopf to fill another vacancy on the Eighth Circuit, a candidacy that was derailed by the ABA, as discussed later in this chapter.

ing Sheffield's financial dealings that the Justice Department had already investigated and found to be without merit. But the investigation by the senate committee delayed the process. By the time the confirmation hearing was held, little more than two months remained before the presidential election. Informed of the allegations at the hearing, Judge Sheffield asked for a postponement so that he could prepare a response. Further investigation of the allegations traced them to an "erroneous inference" made by an Internal Revenue Service agent. A specialist in legal ethics pronounced Judge Sheffield's actions "completely proper."[65] On October 9, Sheffield requested a new hearing, but it was too late. Once Ronald Reagan was elected, Sheffield and fifteen others with pending nominations saw their ambitions doomed as the Republicans were determined that the new administration should fill those judgeships. Only the Breyer nomination was saved, thanks to the efforts of Kennedy.[p]

Other Considerations in the Appointment Process

PARTY CONCERNS

In the effort to emphasize merit selection and to downplay party considerations, starting about April 1978, Griffin Bell stopped including party affiliation on the resumes of persons he recommended to the president. There is little evidence in the presidential papers that party organizations played a role in judicial selection. It is likely, however, that where the organizations were relatively strong, their influence was through senators. The Democratic National Committee was not asked by the Carter administration to clear judicial (and even other) nominees. Yet the White House was occasionally interested in a nominee's party affiliation. For example, two women were the leading candi-

---

p. But even this nomination did not go smoothly. Senator Morgan, smarting over the Winberry defeat and wanting another nominee he was backing to move out of the Senate Judiciary Committee, blocked Breyer's nomination on the floor of the Senate. He was able to do so because the Senate Judiciary Committee had approved Breyer by a telephone poll vote. That procedure is subject to objection by any senator on the floor on the ground that the Senate rules require that members of the committee be physically present when a vote is taken. The nomination could not be sent back to the committee for another vote because Morgan was blocking such a move by a filibuster. With the assistance of the administration, however, Breyer was confirmed. See Cutler to Carter, November 24, 1980, Judges, 9–11/80, Cutler Papers, Carter Library. Also see Ruth Marcus, "The Smoke Clears: A Judge Appears," *National Law Journal,* December 29, 1980, pp. 3, 22. In one of the final ironies of the entire episode to fill the First Circuit vacancy and the subsequent confrontation over Cox's age, the ABA committee abandoned its age criteria on November 30, 1980.

dates for a district judgeship in Pennsylvania. Margaret McKenna, in a memo to Lipshutz, urged that the nomination go to Lisa Richette, a Democrat, over "the other woman candidate . . . a Republican."[66] After Richette took herself out of the running, however, the appointment went to the Republican, Norma Shapiro.

Party was also, on occasion, a factor in filling circuit court positions. Lipshutz urged Carter to elevate U.S. district judge Patrick Higginbotham, a Texas Republican, to one of four Texas seats to be filled on the Fifth Circuit. Lipshutz noted that Higginbotham "is strongly supported by black and Hispanic groups because of his record as a private attorney and as a judge."[67] But, Lipshutz continued, "the principal concern voiced about him is that he is a Republican . . . and one of the other nominees from Texas, Carolyn Randall, was also thought to be a GOP member . . . [and] it would be politically harmful to appoint two Republicans from Texas." However, "the chairman of the Texas nominating panel informed the Attorney General [yesterday] that Randall is *not* a Republican." Lipshutz pointed out that Higginbotham was strongly supported by traditionally Democratic constituencies, by the Democratic leadership in Dallas and Fort Worth, and by other prominent Texas Democrats. In the end, Randall was appointed, but not Higginbotham.[q]

THE AMERICAN BAR ASSOCIATION

The Carter administration sought to have a good relationship with the ABA Standing Committee on Federal Judiciary. The president met with the committee in the cabinet room in the White House on November 17, 1978, and asked for its help in selecting judges in light of the passage of the new judgeships bill. Afterward, one member of the committee wrote to Carter: "It is extremely gratifying to us that you will continue the relationship that this committee has had with various administrations for the past twenty-five years."[68] But that relationship had its strains, and on five occasions the administration went ahead and formally nominated individuals rated "not qualified." There were other instances where the attorney general was able to persuade the committee to reverse itself and to change a negative rating into a "qualified" rating. In still other instances the rating of "not qualified" was

---

q. The appointees from Texas to the Fifth Circuit in addition to Randall were Reynaldo G. Garza, elevated from the district bench; Samuel D. Johnson, Jr., elevated from the Texas Supreme Court; and Thomas M. Reavley, who came to the bench from an Austin law firm. All three had at one time been active Democrats. Two were white; Garza was hispanic. Patrick Higginbotham was eventually elevated to the Fifth Circuit by Ronald Reagan, who nominated him on July 1, 1982.

enough to dissuade the administration from going ahead with the nomination. In one case, concerning Winberry, the ABA changed its rating from "qualified" to "not qualified" after the Senate Judiciary Committee investigators came up with new information.

Carin Ann Clauss was recruited by the District of Columbia Screening Commission and was one of seven persons whose names were submitted to the president as being qualified for the district bench. Clauss, the top lawyer for the Department of Labor, was nominated on September 19, 1978. Despite her excellent qualifications, she was given a negative rating because she allegedly lacked trial experience. That rating caused the Senate Judiciary Committee to delay acting on her nomination. Early the following January, she asked that her name be withdrawn. Another individual nominated, despite a unanimous negative rating, was Donald E. O'Brien to an Iowa judgeship. O'Brien had strong party backing, had been recommended by the Democratic senators' merit selection commission, and had the strong support of the Iowa State Bar Association.[69] Although the nomination caused some controversy because it was alleged that he had acted improperly as a county prosecutor in a 1955 murder case, he was confirmed by the Senate. William Matthew Kidd was nominated for the federal district bench in West Virginia. He was given a negative rating because of his age (sixty-one), but he was confirmed without much fuss.

Two African Americans, U. W. Clemon (an Alabama state senator) and Fred Gray, were rated "not qualified" for positions on the Alabama federal district bench. The votes by the ABA committee, were split, with a minority voting "qualified." The administration, however, was committed to naming blacks it considered to be qualified, particularly to southern judgeships. More than two years earlier, on June 29, 1977, Carter and Bell had met with the Committee for the Appointment of Blacks to the Federal Judiciary in the United States Fifth Circuit, a black group headed by Coretta Scott King. Carter assured the group that he was committed to appoint blacks in the south and that "he would not be guided by lack of endorsement by the American Bar Association." Clemon and Gray, two civil rights activists in Alabama — Gray had represented Rosa Parks and Martin Luther King, Jr., in the legal actions stemming from the historic bus boycott in Montgomery in 1955 — saw opposition to their nominations stemming from what appeared to be disguised hostility to their activist records. The basis for Clemon's negative rating was that on the questionnaire he had completed for the Alabama nominating commission he had neglected to note that he had had two tax liens (since removed) and that he had once filed a late tax return. Clemon argued that not mentioning this information was a secretarial oversight. The Senate Judiciary Committee accepted that explanation and unanimously voted to recommend his nomination to the full Senate, and he was subsequently confirmed. The negative rating for Gray was based on allegations that he had solicited clients and that as city attorney for Tuskegee he had behaved imprudently in an instance in which a bond issue had collapsed, resulting in losses to investors.[70] Gray denied the accusations, but his nomination languished in committee. In August 1980, Alabama senator Howell Heflin withdrew his support. Gray subsequently decided to back out so that a younger, less controversial African American—the thirty-three-year-old, Yale-educated Myron Thompson, rated "qualified" by the ABA—could take his place. Thompson was rapidly confirmed.

There were at least two instances in which the attorney general succeeded in getting the ABA to reconsider negative ratings. In both cases the candidates were women. Diana Murphy was first rated "not qualified" for a district court position in Minnesota, but upon reevaluation the committee rated her "qualified." Stephanie Seymour won out for the nomination to the Tenth Circuit to occupy an Oklahoma seat. Seymour was in private practice and, as Lipshutz described to Carter, had the distinction of being the "first female partner in a major Oklahoma firm" and the "first woman to serve as an Oklahoma Bar examiner." One of those who had been in contention for the nomination was Lee West, a white male, a former state court judge, and, according, to Margaret McKenna, "personal friends" with "supporters" Robert D. Raven, chairman of the ABA committee, and Mike Egan, the associate attorney general. The ABA initially gave Seymour a negative rating. After the attorney general made a personal appeal to the committee, the ABA reconsidered and gave her a rating of "qualified." Seymour was confirmed, and West was appointed to one of the four slots on the federal district bench in Oklahoma.[71]

The Justice Department sometimes decided not to proceed with a candidate after requesting an informal, preliminary rating that turned out to be "not qualified." In at least one instance, the decision was made by Carter himself. Missouri law professor Joan Krauskopf was named on the list of candidates recommended by the judicial selection commission for a slot on the Eighth Circuit Court of Appeals. Nevertheless, she received a "not qualified" rating because of an alleged lack of experience. A White House staffer discovered that "judges on the circuit have expressed the view that her teaching responsibilities have given her the requisite experience to handle the job." The staffer found that "rumors within the ABA state that the ABA rejected Ms. Krauskopf not because she lacks experience, but because she is too liberal."[72]

When the American Bar Association met in Texas, Griffin Bell went there to meet with the ABA committee to press the case for Krauskopf and some others who had been rated "not qualified" (including Stephanie Seymour). The committee did an about-face on Seymour but not Krauskopf. Although Krauskopf had the backing of Missouri senator Thomas Eagleton and appeared to have broad support in the state, Carter, on Bell's recommendation, decided not to buck the ABA. By backing down on Krauskopf, the administration could elevate U.S. district judge Richard Arnold from Arkansas, who was also on the commission's recommended list, to fill the Eighth Circuit position. As Doug Huron pointed out, "If Judge Arnold from Arkansas is elevated, Senator [Dale] Bumpers has agreed to fill the resulting district court vacancy with a black." This is in fact what occurred, as the administration named George Howard, Jr., to replace Arnold, although it took some flak from Missouri newspapers as well as from Senator Eagleton and women's groups for backing down on Krauskopf.[73]

As we earlier saw, Archibald Cox was recommended by the selection commission to fill the new position on the First Circuit. Cox, who would be automatically (under ABA policy) rated "not qualified" because of his age, was finally rejected by Carter himself. Although there was newspaper speculation that political antagonisms between Carter and Senator Kennedy motivated the impasse, there is not a single hint in the presidential papers that this was the case. Jody Powell in his memoirs insisted that only Cox's advanced age stood between him and the judgeship.[74]

The administration asked the ABA for a preliminary report on another person recommended on the First Circuit commission list, a female law professor in Puerto Rico. The rating was "not qualified," and the administration dropped her from consideration, although had she been appointed she would have been the first woman and the first hispanic to serve on the First Circuit. Indeed, Doug Huron suspected that a disproportionate number of women and minority candidates had received the "not qualified" rating, and subsequent scholarly analyses by Elliot Slotnick confirmed what Huron suspected. Women and minorities tended to receive lower ratings, in part because their career paths differed from white males and they tended to lack the visibility that white males often achieved within the legal community. They also tended to be younger, thus their judicial appointments came earlier in their legal careers than the appointments of white males.[75]

Overall, the Carter administration had a record of cooperation with the ABA committee. The bottom line was that the administration went along with over 98 percent of the ABA's ratings. In only five instances did Carter defy the ABA by naming someone who was rated "not qualified," and in only three of these was the administration successful in achieving confirmation.

ETHNICITY

The Carter administration promoted affirmative action for ethnic groups that had long been denied access to federal judgeships. Internally, it added the category "Ethnic Group" to the resumes of leading candidates prepared by the Justice Department, designating candidates as "Hispanic," "Black," "Asian," or "White."

The appointment of African Americans will be looked at later in this chapter. As for the appointment of hispanics or latinos, the administration placed a record number on the district and appeals courts, including Jose A. Cabranes, the first federal judge of Puerto Rican extraction to be appointed to a federal district court in the continental United States; Arthur L. Alarcon (who was also a Republican), to the Ninth Circuit; and Reynaldo G. Garza, to the Fifth Circuit. In total, Carter named fourteen hispanics to the district courts and two to the appeals courts.

Carter named three Asian Americans to federal courts: Thomas Tang, to the Ninth Circuit; A. Wallace Tashima, to the Central District of California; and Walter M. Heen, to the federal district court in Hawaii. Heen's was a recess appointment at the end of the Carter administration. Ronald Reagan did not resubmit the nomination, and Heen was forced to vacate the bench.

During the 1980 presidential campaign, there was some evidence of a concern with ethnicity involving other groups. For example, the White House staff prepared a list of judges of Italian descent for apparent use in the campaign.[76]

Women and Judgeships

We have seen earlier the struggle within the administration and with the administration and senators to name women to federal judgeships. It was generally not easy and usually not a rapid process to bring about the appointment of women. For example, as early as July 1977, Griffin Bell and Frank Moore began pursuing "the feasibility of recommending [the] appointment of United States District Court Judge [Cornelia] Kennedy to the [Sixth] Circuit Court."[77] That Kennedy was a conservative Republican complicated matters, but nevertheless it took close to two years to bring forward her nomination, on April 9, 1979. She was confirmed on September 25.

The nomination of Phyllis Kravitch to the Fifth Circuit assumed epic proportions, as we saw earlier. Bell had ranked U.S. district judge Albert Henderson first and Kravitch second, and Lipshutz and his staff were beside themselves. If still another opportunity for naming a qualified woman to the circuit bench were lost, the administration would be in for well-deserved criticism from women's groups, and the president's talk of opening up the judiciary would appear to be hollow rhetoric. None of the twelve circuit judges nominated up to that time (October 1978) were women. Lipshutz and his colleagues lobbied Carter to select Kravitch, as did the president's wife, Rosalyn Carter, who wrote: "Jimmy, I hope you can appoint Phyllis Kravitch."[78]

Both Cornelia Kennedy and Phyllis Kravitch were recommended by judicial selection commissions. If no woman were to appear on a list, it would be impossible for a woman to be nominated for a circuit judgeship. Lipshutz and his associates in the counsel's office wanted the chairs of the selection commissions to be sympathetic to the recruitment of women and minorities. In November 1978, after passage of the Omnibus Judgeship Act, former federal district judge and deputy attorney general (in the Eisenhower administration) Lawrence E. Walsh was designated to chair the nominating panel for the Second Circuit. The National Women's Political Caucus wrote to Carter arguing that Walsh should be disqualified because in 1975 he had actively opposed an ABA resolution calling on the president to appoint women to the federal bench. Lipshutz wrote Bell that "if it is true . . . and if his position on this issue has not changed, it would seem to be inconsistent with the President's views." In his reply, Bell asserted, "I have no doubt that Judge Walsh is a fair person." He conceded that Walsh may have opposed the ABA resolution, but said this was "a slim basis, indeed, for accusing a distinguished American of being prejudiced."[79] Walsh chaired the selection commission, which recommended, among others, a highly qualified African American woman, Amalya Kearse who received an appointment.

The judicial selection commission for the Eastern Fifth Circuit caused some controversy when the list of twenty names for six new seats was submitted and not one woman was on it. Margaret McKenna, in a memo to Lipshutz, noted that "[a]pparently, members of the panel were not given the revised Executive Order or any directions on the need to locate minority and women candidates and [there are] a number of complaints that women were treated differently."[80]

The prospective nomination of Professor Joan Krauskopf of Missouri to the Eighth Circuit was derailed by a controversial "not qualified" rating from the ABA committee, as discussed earlier. Bell, at the end of his tenure as attorney general, could not bring himself to defy the ABA over an appointment to a circuit court. But where were other voices in the administration, for after all one rationale for the judicial selection commission was that it would independently and fairly assess the candidates who applied for the position and make a determination as to the five who were best qualified. Carter's commission said Krauskopf was qualified. The ABA disagreed. Carter took on the ABA with

O'Brien, Clemon, and Kidd for the district bench and had won (but had lost with Clauss and Gray). Why not put up a fight for Krauskopf? Why didn't the White House counsel's office enter the struggle? The reason may have been simply that the ABA had shown some reasonableness in reevaluating Stephanie Seymour for the Tenth Circuit and that there were other reevaluations being conducted. Unless the administration were simply to break with the ABA committee (but that would not do because "not qualified" ratings from the ABA helped the administration ward off senatorially sponsored candidates it did not wish to appoint), the administration would have to back down. That is exactly what happened.

Other nominations of women went more smoothly. For example, Lipshutz reported to Carter that "[w]ith reference to the Ninth Circuit, all of us [including Bell] are recommending the appointment of Ms. Betty Fletcher of the State of Washington." Indeed, for the first time in the history of the nation, the Justice Department and the White House were committed to placing substantial numbers of women on the federal bench. Bell was ready and able to do his part in this historic transformation, although the counsel's office wanted to move faster and to nominate even more women. In the event of a Supreme Court vacancy, Bell was prepared to recommend Shirley Hufstedler to become the first woman justice (Hufstedler had left her position on the Ninth Circuit to become Carter's secretary of education). Bell said publicly and bluntly, "We have to get more women" on the federal bench.[81] The end result of the struggles and efforts was the placement of twenty-nine women in lifetime positions on the federal district courts and eleven on appeals courts of general jurisdiction. A major breakthrough had occurred.

African Americans and Judgeships

The administration was under a political and moral imperative to name qualified African Americans to judgeships. The first president from the Deep South in over a century, elected with the active help of African Americans and himself personally committed to racial equality, could do no less. Whereas during the first two years of his presidency no women were nominated to the circuit courts, Carter named three African Americans. Two were federal district court judges who first had been appointed to the bench by Lyndon Johnson. These well-deserved promotions went to A. Leon Higginbotham (Third Circuit) and Damon J. Keith (Sixth Circuit). The third African American was Theodore McMillian, a Missouri state court of appeals judge, appointed by Carter to the Eighth Circuit.

But there were obstacles to naming blacks, some of them self-imposed by

Bell and his associates. For example, within six weeks after Carter took office, Justice Department officials indicated in a meeting with Margaret McKenna from the counsel's office that they were reluctant to suggest names of minority and women candidates to senators and representatives. Without an aggressive recruiting mechanism, the administration was faced with the response that Mississippi senator John Stennis gave when asked by congressional liaison Frank Moore about the appointment of blacks to the bench in Mississippi. Moore paraphrased Stennis's reply: "there are no black lawyers of judicial timber in Mississippi . . . the good ones leave."[82]

The White House staff, however, did undertake to gather information on prospective black judges for the district and circuit courts. Lipshutz gave this information to Bell to forward "to the appropriate senators and commissions."[83] But often nothing happened. For example, Lipshutz's office identified an African American administrative law judge for a vacancy on the Oregon federal district court. Although both senators were Republican and the administration had some leeway, neither this candidate nor any other black was nominated for the Oregon bench. It would take fifteen more years for Oregon to have its first African American on the federal bench.

There were some occasions when African Americans appeared on circuit commission lists as being qualified for an appointment but Bell did not support their selection. One concerned Fred Gray, a candidate for the Fifth Circuit. Gray, a Montgomery, Alabama, attorney who played a leading role in the civil rights movement, had the support of Coretta Scott King and other civil rights leaders for a federal judgeship. He was one of five candidates found qualified for the circuit judgeship by the commission. Yet Bell rank-ordered Gray last of the five. As Bell put it in a memorandum to Carter, "Gray is black. I am aware, of course, of your desire that we make every effort to appoint blacks to the federal courts in the South, but I cannot recommend him for the Court of Appeals."[84] Bell suggested that the president consider appointing Gray to one of the new judgeships to be created by the Omnibus Judgeship Bill, "if he is found qualified after investigation." Bell also pointed out that he was told by the commission chairman "that there is a black Justice of the Florida Supreme Court who would be an excellent choice for one of the new seats on the Court of Appeals."[r]

Ironically, it was the person that Bell ranked fourth, Robert Vance, who

r. The person to whom Bell was referring, although not mentioned by name in the memorandum to Carter, was Joseph W. Hatchett, a justice on the Florida Supreme Court, who was in fact named to the Fifth Circuit in 1979.

eventually received the nomination.[s] Gray was nominated in early 1980 to a district judgeship and, as recounted in the discussion of the ABA, was found "not qualified." The rival African American– dominated law association, the National Bar Association, found Gray qualified, as did the Bar Association of the Fifth Circuit. After Alabama senator Howell Heflin withdrew his support, Gray asked Carter to withdraw his nomination so that another black could be appointed.[85] African American Myron Thompson, in place of Fred Gray, became one of the last Carter nominees to be confirmed by the Senate before the administration ended.

The administration passed up the opportunity to name another leading civil rights figure to a southern circuit. Julius Chambers, according to Lipshutz, was "an exceptionally talented lawyer" and "a partner in what is probably the finest integrated law firm in the country." Lipshutz noted in his memo to Carter that "Chambers and his firm have long been identified with civil rights litigation both in his native North Carolina and throughout the South."[86] Chambers was graduated first in his class at the University of North Carolina Law School (he was the first African American to attend). He was also on the Fourth Circuit commission list as one of five qualified individuals for the circuit position that became vacant with the unexpected death in May 1977 of Judge J. Braxton Craven of North Carolina. Another name on the list was that of U.S. district judge James B. McMillan, who had ordered busing to desegregate the Charlotte school system. The remaining three names were of law professors at Duke and the University of North Carolina.

Democratic North Carolina senator Robert Morgan opposed both Chambers and McMillan, apparently because they were too liberal. Republican senator Jesse Helms also opposed Chambers and McMillan, but there is no evidence that this played a part in the selection process, given Helms's extreme conservatism and anti-civil rights posture. But Senator Morgan's vote was needed for the ratification of the Panama Canal treaties. As Lipshutz later noted to the president, "we acceded to Morgan's wishes . . . by appointing neither Chambers nor Judge James McMillan."[87][t]

s. Vance was chairman of the Alabama State Democratic Committee and had powerful political backing. He was rated "well qualified" by the ABA. He was to play an important role in forging consensus among his colleagues on the bench for a proposal to divide the Fifth Circuit. See Deborah J. Barrow and Thomas G. Walker, *A Court Divided: The Fifth Circuit Court of Appeals and the Politics of Judicial Reform* (New Haven: Yale University Press, 1988), 234–38. Tragically, he was assassinated by a letter bomb on December 17, 1989.

t. Carter named University of North Carolina law professor James D. Phillips, Jr. to fill

A second position on the Fourth Circuit, created by the new judgeships act, was slated for North Carolina. The commission came up with a new set of names, all white males. Lipshutz argued in several memos that since the same commission had found Chambers qualified for the first position, Carter would be justified in bypassing the second list for the new position and in naming Chambers.[88] Senator Morgan, however, was still opposed to Chambers. Stalemate ensued, and finally State Judge Samuel James Ervin III was nominated in April 1980. Ervin, the son of former North Carolina senator Sam Ervin, had appeared before the same Fourth Circuit commission in 1978 that had selected Chambers. Ervin was not on the list in 1978 but made it in 1979. Rated "exceptionally well qualified" by the ABA, Ervin took a seat on the all-white U.S. Court of Appeals for the Fourth Circuit that as late as 1996 was still not racially integrated (although President Bill Clinton nominated an African American for elevation from the district bench who went unconfirmed by the Republican-controlled Senate).

Lipshutz and his allies, as previously discussed, were successful in persuading Carter to overrule Bell by naming Nathaniel R. Jones, the General Counsel for the NAACP, to the Sixth Circuit. But there was resistance, and in fact Jones's nomination was not made until Griffin Bell was about to leave office at the end of August 1979, some eleven months *after* Carter had given the go-ahead for the appointment of Jones. Bell had seen no urgency in nominating Jones because, as paraphrased by Lipshutz, "the Sixth Circuit already has one black judge sitting, among the total of eleven."[89]

Bell, of course, played an important role in integrating the federal judiciary, as did his successor in office, Benjamin Civiletti. Likewise Lipshutz and his associates at the White House counsel's office and Lipshutz's successor, Lloyd Cutler, maintained the administration commitment. When the Carter presidency ended, the administration had succeeded in placing twenty-eight African Americans on federal district courts in nineteen states and the District of Columbia. In fourteen (including eleven southern and border states), Carter named the first African Americans ever to serve. He named nine African Americans to positions on the Second, Third, Fifth, Sixth, Eighth, Ninth, and District of Columbia circuit courts. Three of the circuits were racially integrated for the first time.

---

the position. Phillips, politically connected (a former law partner of Governor Terry Sanford), was also rated "well qualified" by the ABA. For a discussion of how this position was filled, see Peter G. Fish, "Merit Selection and Politics: Choosing a Judge of the United States Court of Appeals for the Fourth Circuit," *Wake Forest Law Review,* 15 (1979): 635–54.

The Demographic Portrait of Carter's Judges

Jimmy Carter had an extraordinary opportunity to name more judges to the lower federal courts than any previous president. Table 7.1 compares the demographic portrait of the Carter appointees during the first half of his presidency, before passage of the Omnibus Judgeship Act, to that of the second half, after passage. The Carter appointees from the first half of his presidency, which includes all those confirmed by the Ninety-fifth Congress, are identified as Carter I appointees. Those appointed during the second half, including all those confirmed by the Ninety-sixth Congress, are called Carter II appointees.[u]

AGE

The average age of the Carter II district court appointees was lower than that of the Carter I district court appointees. On the other hand, the average age of the Carter I appeals court appointees was a half-year younger than that of the Carter II appeals court appointees. There is, however, no evidence that the Carter administration made a deliberate attempt to appoint younger judges. But the administration *was* wary of appointing elderly judges, as we saw in the case of Archibald Cox. The Senate had its say on April 1, 1980, over the age issue by unanimously passing a resolution urging the standing committee of the American Bar Association and the attorney general to "immediately take all measures necessary to end discrimination against potential lifetime Federal judges who do not qualify solely as a result of arbitrary age barriers."[90]

u. The figures in table 7.1 do not include the nominations of Carin Ann Clauss, Charles B. Winberry, Jr., and Fred D. Gray, which were withdrawn, and the nomination of Len J. Paletta, who died some six weeks after having been nominated but before the Senate had acted. The figures also do not include sixteen nominees who were not acted upon by the Senate after Jimmy Carter lost to Ronald Reagan in 1980. These include twelve nominees to the district courts and four to the appeals courts. On December 29, 1980, Carter made a recess appointment of one of the sixteen, Walter Meheula Heen, an Asian American, to a district court position in Hawaii. President Reagan withdrew the nomination on January 21, 1981, as soon as he took office. Heen's recess appointment would be the last judicial recess appointment made by a president because of questions raised in litigation as to whether recess appointees lack the essential attributes of Article III judges. A Ninth Circuit panel said they lack the attributes and thus may not exercise the judicial power of the United States. *United States* v. *Woodley,* 726 F.2d 1328 (1983). An en banc decision of the Ninth Circuit reversed and ruled that a recess appointee can constitutionally exercise judicial power. The en banc vote was 7 to 4. *United States* v. *Woodley,* 751 F.2d 1008 (1985). The Supreme Court chose not to decide this issue when it denied certiorari in *Woodley* v. *United States,* 475 U.S. 1048 (1986).

Table 7.1. Selected Backgrounds of Lifetime Carter Appointees to the Federal District and Appeals Courts of General Jurisdiction

	District Court Appointees		Appeals Court Appointees	
	1977–1978 Appointees	*1979–1980 Appointees*	*1977–1978 Appointees*	*1979–1980 Appointees*
Average age at time of appointment	50.2	49.4	51.4	51.9
Undergraduate Education				
Public	47.9%	59.1%	41.7%	27.3%
	(23)	(91)	(5)	(12)
Private not Ivy	35.4%	33.1%	41.7%	54.5%
	(17)	(51)	(5)	(24)
Ivy League	16.7%	7.8%	16.7%	18.2%
	(8)	(12)	(2)	(8)
Law School Education				
Public	39.6%	53.9%	41.7%	38.6%
	(19)	(83)	(5)	(17)
Private not Ivy	33.3%	32.5%	33.3%	15.9%
	(16)	(50)	(4)	(7)
Ivy League	27.1%	13.6%	25.0%	45.4%
	(13)	(21)	(3)	(20)
Experience				
Judicial	47.9%	55.8%	58.3%	52.3%
	(23)	(86)	(7)	(23)
Prosecutorial	35.4%	39.0%	41.7%	29.5%
	(17)	(60)	(5)	(13)
Neither	33.3%	29.9%	33.3%	40.9%
	(16)	(46)	(4)	(18)
Occupation				
Politics — Government	4.2%	1.3%	—	2.3%
	(2)	(2)	—	(1)
Government Lawyer	2.1%	3.2%	—	4.5%
	(1)	(5)	—	(2)
Judiciary	41.7%	45.4%	41.7%	47.7%
	(20)	(70)	(5)	(21)
Large Law Firm*	18.8%	12.3%	—	13.6%
	(9)	(19)	—	(6)
Medium-Size Law Firm†	18.8%	20.1%	25.0%	13.6%
	(9)	(31)	(3)	(6)

Table 7.1. Continued

	District Court Appointees		Appeals Court Appointees	
	1977–1978 *Appointees*	*1979–1980* *Appointees*	*1977–1978* *Appointees*	*1979–1980* *Appointees*
Small Law Firm‡	8.3%	11.7%	16.7%	—
	(4)	(18)	(2)	—
Solo Practice	4.2%	1.9%	—	2.3%
	(2)	(3)	—	(1)
Professor of Law	2.1%	3.2%	16.7%	13.6%
	(1)	(5)	(2)	(6)
Other	—	0.6%	—	2.3%
	—	(1)	—	(1)
ABA Rating				
Exceptionally	6.2%	3.2%	16.7%	15.9%
Well Qualified	(3)	(5)	(2)	(7)
Well Qualified	58.3%	43.5%	58.3%	59.1%
	(28)	(67)	(7)	(26)
Qualified	33.3%	52.0%	25.0%	25.0%
	(16)	(80)	(3)	(11)
Not Qualified	2.1%	1.3%	—	—
	(1)	(2)	—	—
Party				
Democratic	93.8%	89.6%	100.0%	77.3%
	(45)	(138)	(12)	(34)
Republican	4.2%	4.5%	—	9.1%
	(2)	(7)	—	(4)
None	2.1%	5.8%	—	13.6%
	(1)	(9)	—	(6)
Prominent Party Activism				
	60.4%	61.0%	83.3%	70.4
	(29)	(94)	(10)	(31)
Prior or Current Members of Congress				
	—	1.3%	—	2.3%
	—	(2)	—	(1)
Religion				
Protestant	43.8%	55.2%	58.3%	47.7%
	(21)	(85)	(7)	(21)
Catholic	35.4%	25.3%	25.0%	27.3%
	(17)	(39)	(3)	(12)

continued

Table 7.1. Continued

	District Court Appointees		Appeals Court Appointees	
	1977–1978 *Appointees*	*1979–1980* *Appointees*	*1977–1978* *Appointees*	*1979–1980* *Appointees*
Jewish	8.3%	12.3%	8.3%	20.4%
	(4)	(19)	(1)	(9)
Other§	4.2%	3.2%	8.3%	2.3%
	(2)	(5)	(1)	(1)
None	—	1.3%	—	—
	—	(2)	—	—
Unknown	8.3%	2.6%	—	2.3%
	(4)	(4)	—	(1)
Gender				
Male	87.5%	85.1%	100.0%	75.0%
	(42)	(131)	(12)	(33)
Female	12.5%	14.9%	—	25.0%
	(6)	(23)	—	(11)
Ethnicity/race				
White	85.4%	76.6%	66.7%	81.8%
	(41)	(118)	(8)	(36)
Black	10.4%	14.9%	25.0%	13.6%
	(5)	(23)	(3)	(6)
Hispanic	4.2%	7.8%	—	4.6%
	(2)	(12)	—	(2)
Asian	—	0.6%	8.3%	—
	—	(1)	(1)	—
Total Number of Appointees				
	48	154	12	44

* A large law firm was defined as consisting of twenty-five or more partners and associates.

† A medium-size law firm was defined as consisting of from five to twenty-four partners and associates.

‡ A small law firm was defined as consisting of fewer than five partners and associates.

§ Includes four Mormons, two Greek Orthodox, and one Christian Scientist to the district bench and one Mormon and one Bahai to the appeals bench.

EDUCATION

The educational backgrounds of the Carter I and Carter II district court appointees are different. A considerably larger proportion of the Carter II appointees were educated at publicly supported colleges and law schools. About twice the proportion of Carter I than Carter II appointees had an Ivy League education. The Carter II appointees were composed of more women and minorities, and this may have accounted for much of the differences.[91]

The small number of Carter I appeals court appointees requires us to be cautious when comparing percentages with the Carter II appointees. The most striking finding is that close to half the Carter II appointees attended an Ivy League law school. This was the largest proportion of any administration examined in this book. Assuming that the Ivy League law schools are among the best in the nation (of course there are distinguished non-Ivy law schools), Carter's appointees had received a high-quality legal education.

EXPERIENCE

About half the Carter appointees had judicial experience, but a considerably smaller proportion had prosecutorial experience. This held true for the Carter I and Carter II appointees to both the district and appeals courts. Previous administrations' appointees to the district courts had more prosecutorial than judicial experience. An even higher proportion of Carter II district court appointees showed previous judicial experience than Carter I district court appointees, although there was also a somewhat higher proportion of Carter II than Carter I appointees with prosecutorial backgrounds.

The emphasis on judicial experience marks a turning point in the backgrounds of those selected for federal district court judgeships. From the Carter administration to the present, a larger proportion of those selected have had more judicial experience than prosecutorial experience. The Carter administration, with its concern for merit selection, was responsible for a major step in the direction of the professionalization of the judiciary. Looking to the judiciary as a source for recruitment helps an administration seek those with demonstrated judicial temperament. It may also help evaluate the judicial philosophy of the candidates and indeed was used this way by the Reagan administration.

About three in ten Carter district court appointees had neither judicial nor prosecutorial experience. This was about the proportion for the Ford appointees. But about two out of five Carter II appeals court appointees failed to have judicial and prosecutorial experience. However, almost 45 percent of the Carter II appointees without judicial and prosecutorial experience were women. To state it somewhat differently, eight of the eleven women appointees had neither judicial nor prosecutorial experience (73 percent), while only about one-fourth of the white males lacked such experience.

OCCUPATION

The Carter administration appointed very few persons to the district courts who held political or governmental positions (excluding judges and government lawyers) at the time of appointment. The Nixon and Ford administrations had appointed close to three times the proportion of those holding such positions (although the proportion was under 6 percent). The proportion of Carter's district court appointees who were government lawyers was also small—and also well below the proportion of the Nixon and Ford appointees. Only one of the Carter appointees held the position of United States attorney.

Close to 45 percent of the Carter appointees to the district courts were serving as judges at the time of their appointment. The proportion for the district court appointees was higher than that of the Kennedy through Ford administrations. About 3.5 percent (seven appointees) were United States magistrates, and 1.5 percent (three appointees) were referees in bankruptcy.

Almost half the Carter district court appointees were in private practice at the time of their judicial appointments. This was about the same proportion as the Ford appointees but lower than that of the Nixon appointees. A smaller proportion of Carter II than Carter I appointees were employed in large law firms but also in solo practice, whereas a somewhat larger proportion of Carter II appointees were in medium-size and small law firms. The proportion of Carter appointees from large law firms was smaller than that for the Nixon and Ford appointees. About 20 percent of the Carter appointees were in medium-size law firms, a larger proportion than that of the Nixon and Ford appointees. About 11 percent of the Carter appointees were employed in a small law firm, and under 3 percent were in solo practice. About 3 percent of the appointees were law professors.

The major difference between the Carter I and Carter II appeals court appointees is that there were somewhat more Carter II than Carter I appointees in private practice. Considering all the Carter appeals court appointees, over 14 percent were law professors (a total of eight) at the time of appointment, a modern record. At the other extreme, the proportion who were on the state bench or who were federal district court judges was lower than that found for previous administrations. This latter finding appears inconsistent with the suggestion made earlier that the Carter administration was advancing the professionalization of the judiciary. If the women appointees are removed from the figures, however, the proportion of sitting judges elevated to the appeals courts rises to over half, which is comparable to the Nixon and Johnson administrations. When women are eliminated from the figures, the proportion of appointees with judicial experience in their backgrounds rises to 60 percent. Of the twenty-six Carter appointees who were judges at the time of their appointments to the appeals courts, eleven (or 42 percent) were sitting on a state bench and fifteen (or 58 percent) were elevations from the federal district bench. Six of the eleven elevated from a state bench were women or minority males. This was in marked contrast to the Nixon and Ford elevations, almost all of whom were on the federal district bench.

AMERICAN BAR ASSOCIATION RATINGS

About 51 percent of the Carter district court appointees received the two highest ABA ratings. This was higher than the figures for the Johnson, Nixon, and Ford district court appointees. Only the Kennedy appointees had a higher proportion. There was a dramatic difference, however, between the Carter I and Carter II appointees. About 65 percent of the Carter I appointees received the two highest ABA ratings, as compared to about 47 percent of the Carter II appointees, which included more women and minorities.

The ratings of the Carter I and Carter II appeals court appointees were virtually identical. Three-fourths received the two highest ratings, a record comparable to that of the Nixon and Johnson appeals court appointees and higher than that of the Ford appointees.

PARTY

About nine out of ten district court appointees were Democrats, over 4 percent were Republicans, and about 5 percent were independents. About three out of five had a record of prominent party activism, a proportion larger than that of the preceding three administrations. Women appointees, however, did not fit this pattern. Only eight of the twenty-nine women appointed to the district bench by Carter had a record of prominent partisan activism. Thus only 28 percent of the women but about 65 percent or higher of the men had a background of party activism.

There was a marked difference between the Carter I and Carter II appeals court appointees. All the Carter I appointees were Democrats, but over one-fifth of the Carter II appointees were Republicans or independents. The proportion of Carter II appointees with a background of partisan activism was lower than that for the Carter I appointees. Overall, however, a higher proportion of Carter appointees demonstrated a record of prominent partisan activism some time in their backgrounds than was evident in the three previous administrations. But just as with the district court appointees, the large majority of women appointed by Carter to the appeals courts did not have a record of prominent party activism. Thus 91 percent of the white males had partisan activism in their backgrounds, compared to only 36 percent of the women appointees and one-third of the black appointees. In their quest to recruit qualified women and blacks, the Carter administration departed from the political criteria that traditionally played such an important role in the selection process.

Three Carter II appointees (two district and one appeals court) had a background of congressional service. This was a low number. Carter was the first president since Eisenhower not to have served in Congress.

RELIGIOUS ORIGIN OR AFFILIATION

The Carter administration appointed Catholics to over 25 percent of the judicial positions it filled, a proportion similar to that of the Democratic Kennedy and Johnson administrations. The percentage of Jewish judges was also akin to the Johnson record. These proportions were higher than that of previous Republican presidents.

GENDER, RACE, AND ETHNICITY

Carter remarked on December 8, 1978 (before the new judgeships created in 1978 were filled): "If I didn't have to get Senate confirmation of appointees, I could tell you flatly that 12 percent of all my judicial appointments would be black, 3 percent would be Spanish-speaking, and 40 percent would be women, and so forth."[92] As we have seen, his administration indeed made the most deliberate effort in the history of federal judicial selection to place women, African Americans, and hispanics on the federal bench. Women were appointed to federal district judgeships in twenty states, the District of Columbia, and Puerto Rico and to seven of the eleven appeals courts.[v] All the women appointed to the appeals courts were Carter II appointees. By the end of the Carter administration, the proportion of women judges in active service on the federal bench had risen from 1.4 percent to 6.9 percent.

---

v. Women were appointed to the federal district bench in Arkansas, California, Colorado, Connecticut, Florida, Georgia, Illinois, Louisiana, Maryland, Massachusetts, Michigan, Minnesota, New Jersey, New York, Ohio, Oregon, Pennsylvania, Texas, Washington, and Wisconsin. Women were named to the courts of appeals for the Second, Third, Fifth, Sixth, Ninth, Tenth, and District of Columbia circuits. Carter also named Helen W. Nies in 1980 to the Court of Customs and Patent Appeals, which in 1982 became the U.S. Court of Appeals for the Federal Circuit. Because this is a court of specialized jurisdiction, Nies is not counted in the tabulation of lifetime women appointees to courts of general jurisdiction.

Carter nominated at least one African American to the federal district courts of each of ten southern and two border states — although the nomination of James Sheffield to a position in Virginia was not confirmed. Only Mississippi, of the states of the former Confederacy, did not have an African American nominated to the district court bench, because of a lack of cooperation from the Mississippi Democratic senators. Carter appointed nine African Americans (including one woman) to seven appeals courts.[w] A tenth nomination, that of Houston attorney Andrew L. Jefferson, Jr., to the Fifth Circuit, was not acted upon by the Senate before the Carter administration ended.

Carter named fourteen hispanics to the federal district bench in six states and Puerto Rico.[x] He named two to appeals courts. Like his appointments of women and blacks, these were breakthrough appointments that transcended tokenism. In contrast, the two appointments of Asian Americans, A. Wallace Tashima to a California district judgeship and Thomas Tang to a position on the appeals court for the Ninth Circuit, were token appointments.

Carter's presidency brought about major change in the judicial selection process primarily as a result of the creation and use of merit-type nominating commissions. For district court nominations, at the urging of the administration, senators created nominating commissions in thirty states. For appeals court nominations, Carter himself created the U.S. Circuit Judge Nominating Commission. Because Carter had no opportunity to name a Supreme Court justice, no commission was created for that purpose. Although the use of commissions did not mean a sharp break from traditional concerns of party, they succeeded in opening up the selection process so that individuals were considered for nomination who otherwise might never have had a chance for a judgeship, particularly women and minorities. The Carter administration had set the tone with its avowed objective of actively recruiting women and minorities, although there had been some tension between the Justice Department and the White House counsel's office over the pace of affirmative action. That very tension, however, led the counsel's office to become more involved in judicial selection than in previous administrations, a development that accelerated in the Reagan administration and continued in the Bush and Clinton presidencies.[93]

The Senate confirmation process changed when Senator Edward Kennedy assumed the chairmanship of the Senate Judiciary Committee at the start of the

w. Those courts were the appeals courts for the Second, Third, Fifth, Sixth, Eighth, Ninth, and District of Columbia circuits.

x. Hispanics were named to the bench in Arizona, California, Connecticut, Florida, New Mexico, and Texas.

Ninety-sixth Congress. Among other innovations, Kennedy modified the practice of senatorial courtesy by having the committee itself make a decision whether or not to consider a candidate opposed by a senator from the nominee's state. The panels of the circuit judge nominating commissions and the commissions created by senators offered their own professional evaluations of the candidates, and this appeared to lessen the influence of the ABA committee.

The fall of 1980 saw Jimmy Carter fighting to win reelection after having staved off a challenge to renomination by Senator Edward Kennedy. The hostage crisis in Iran continued unabated, and the economy was an issue with inflation a serious concern among voters. Carter with his austere sincerity was up against an affable, charismatic Ronald Reagan. The Republican Party was captured by its right wing, and Reagan put a benign face on the conservative social agenda. Reagan won the presidency, and Republicans won control of the U.S. Senate. Judicial selection would be profoundly affected.

But Ronald Reagan faced a lower-court judiciary in which Democrats constituted more than a 60 percent majority. He also faced the widespread expectations of women and minorities that they would receive more than token numbers of appointments. Indeed, during the presidential campaign, candidate Reagan had acknowledged the new reality at least insofar as women were concerned when he pledged that "one of the first Supreme Court vacancies in my administration will be filled by the most qualified woman I can find, one who meets the high standards I will demand for all my appointments." He also pledged to "seek out women to appoint to other federal courts in an effort to bring about a better balance on the federal bench."[94] How Reagan kept his pledge and how judicial selection changed will be seen in the next chapter.

8

Reaganizing the Judiciary

Ronald Reagan's two terms as president marked a sharp political turn to the right in American politics. In some respects, the Reagan presidency was the mirror image of the Roosevelt presidency. Both Reagan and Roosevelt were enormously popular with the majority of Americans, but their policies and philosophies were opposed and even denigrated by a vocal minority. Reagan, like Roosevelt, was reelected to a second term by a landslide — a victory that was widely interpreted as a mandate to continue along the course set in the first term. Reagan, like Roosevelt, spent the first term dealing with economic crises, and both used Keynesian economics (without credit to Keynes in Reagan's case) to nurse the economy back to health. Both presidents had a view of the role of government, including the courts, that was radically different from their immediate predecessors'.[1]

Both Reagan and Roosevelt sought to change the direction of government, and both saw the federal courts as frustrating their policy agendas. Both self-consciously attempted to use the power of judicial appointment to place on the bench judges who shared their general philosophy. Reagan left office in 1989 with a public opinion approval rating exceeding that of every president since Roosevelt.[2]

In the first two years of the Reagan presidency, an economic program was enacted that included a major tax reduction. The economy, however, faltered, plunging the country into the worst economic crisis since the Great Depression. But massive infusions of federal funds into the economy, particularly through the defense budget, helped launch a dramatic economic rebound. Despite periodic foreign crises, and during the second term a scent of scandal over the funding of the Nicaraguan insurgents by the illegal sale of arms to Iran and also an emerging scandal surrounding the savings and loans industry, the Reagan presidency appeared reasonably well coordinated and orderly.[3]

Ronald Reagan was elected in 1980 by 50.7 percent of the popular vote, but by an electoral college landslide of 489 votes (91 percent). His reelection victory in 1984 was by 58.8 percent of the popular vote and an even greater electoral college landslide (525 votes, 98 percent). In the 1980 election, Republicans gained 33 seats in the House, still short of a numerical majority, but joining with conservative Democrats, mainly from the southern and border states, Republicans for most purposes had a working majority. In the Senate, Republicans gained twelve seats and won control, which they retained for the next six years. Hence judicial selection for three-fourths of the Reagan presidency was in friendly hands on Capitol Hill.

When Reagan became president, there were many questions concerning how the new administration would handle judicial selection. What would happen to the changes in the federal judicial selection process initiated during the Carter administration? What would happen to the policy of affirmative action for the judiciary? What sorts of people would the new administration choose to serve on the bench? How involved would Reagan himself be in the selection process? How would Republican control of the Senate affect judicial selection?

Presidential Involvement and the Selection Process

Ronald Reagan came to the presidency with a political ideology or belief system in place. He was determined to promote his economic and social policy agenda as well as his partisan agenda to establish the Republican Party as the nation's majority party. Reagan and his backers made it no secret that judicial selection would be geared to carrying out these agendas. Indeed, the Republican platform of 1980 included a pledge to direct judicial positions to those sharing conservative values.[4] But how would Ronald Reagan conduct judicial selection and to what extent would he involve himself in the process?

Reagan already had a track record for selecting judges in California during his two terms as governor. He appointed 645 state judges using a merit selection method of county screening committees consisting of lay persons, lawyers, and judges that rated potential nominees on a scale similar to that of the

ABA's Standing Committee on Federal Judiciary. He had tried but failed to persuade the California legislature to enact merit selection. When questioned during the presidential campaign about how he had chosen judges as governor, he described the committees he set up and continued: "I then received a rating [for each candidate] that ranged from NQ, not qualified, to EWQ, exceptionally well qualified, and all the gradations in between, and made my appointments from that list. And without exception in eight years I took my appointees from those who were rated exceptionally well qualified."[5]

This last assertion notwithstanding, there was at least one well-known example when Governor Reagan bypassed the commission system. That occurred when he named his executive secretary and friend William P. Clark, first to a superior court judgeship, then to a position on the court of appeal, and in 1973 to the California supreme court. Clark's nomination to the California supreme court had been heavily criticized because of his lack of distinction in the legal profession. The Clark appointments were the only known instances of Governor Reagan's personal initiative in selection. In general, Governor Reagan emphasized merit, although judicial philosophy was not ignored. As Paul Haerle, the governor's first legal-affairs secretary and the person responsible for handling judicial selection, noted: "A lot of people were judged not qualified [by the selection committee] and we didn't appoint them. . . . [Those appointed] didn't have to be Republicans but we made sure they weren't liberals."[6]

Given this background, it seemed highly significant that in an interview with the editors of the *New York Times* on September 27, 1980, during the height of the presidential campaign, Reagan pledged that as president "he would try to apply the California system for judicial selection." At an October 14 news conference he explained that he would neither announce nor submit Supreme Court nominees to the Senate "until I have conducted a comprehensive search and have received the recommendations of an advisory committee of eminent legal and judicial experts. The procedures they will be asked to follow are the same procedures I intend to establish for *all* judicial appointments." At another point in the news conference he stated flatly, "I will do what I did in California."[7]

But Ronald Reagan as president did not select federal judges the way he selected state judges as governor. Like Carter, he faced the reality of senatorial prerogatives in the selection of district judges. President Reagan's first attorney general, William French Smith, and deputy attorney general, Edward C. Schmults, negotiated a selection process with Senate majority leader Howard H. Baker, Jr., and Senate Judiciary Committee chairman Strom Thurmond that was designed to give the administration more flexibility in naming district judges while retaining senatorial influence.[a] In a cover letter to Senator Baker accompanying the memorandum describing the new process, Attorney General Smith wrote: "Based upon our discussion at lunch on Wednesday, we have prepared a memorandum, a copy of which is enclosed, which sets forth the points that we believe are pertinent to the judicial selection process. Ed [Schmults] and I feel that the meeting was very useful, and we both look forward to a close and cooperative relationship in the months ahead."[8]

The memorandum was notable in several respects.[b] It was a bold move to

a. Jonathan C. Rose, the assistant attorney general for legal policy, revealed in an interview: "Very early in the Administration, the Attorney General and the Deputy Attorney General met with Senator Baker and Senator Thurmond to determine how they wished to have the judicial selection process perceived. We took the position at this early meeting that for district court vacancies, Republican senators should provide the President with a list of three to five names. At that time it was agreed that this procedure would be followed." *Legal Times,* November 8, 1982, p. 6.

Attorney General William French Smith referred to the meeting in his memoirs as follows: "Early in the administration, Ed Schmults and I met with key members of the Senate leadership to discuss the question of judicial selection, and the understanding we reached was memorialized in a letter." *Law and Justice in the Reagan Administration: The Memoirs of an Attorney General* (Stanford, Calif.: Hoover Institution Press, 1991), 72.

b. The memorandum was as follows:

In the process of judicial selection, the Department of Justice will work closely and cooperatively with the Senate leadership, the Judiciary Committee Chairman and individual members. Both the Attorney General, on behalf of the President, and the Senate leadership are firmly committed to the principle that federal judges should be chosen on the basis of merit and quality.

By virtue of the Senators' familiarity with the members of the Bar in their respective States, the Attorney General, in making recommendations to the President for judicial appointments, will invite Republican members to identify prospective candidates for federal district judgeships. Senators are strongly encouraged to submit the names of several candidates, preferably from three to five names, to the Attorney General for a particular vacancy. This information should be shared at the earliest practicable time with the Attorney General's designated representative so that any questions or reservations as to merit or appropriateness of the proposed candidates can be identified sufficiently early to allow meaningful consultation.

Members are encouraged to utilize screening mechanisms to ensure that highly qualified candidates are identified and recommended. Those mechanisms include, but of course are not limited to, advisory groups or commissions charged with the responsibility of assisting in the evaluation and selection of highly capable and

ask Republican senators to give the administration more discretion in the selection process of district judges by submitting to the attorney general from three to five names for each vacancy. The memorandum also encouraged Republican senators to utilize merit selection screening procedures, including commissions (this was similar to the Carter administration's approach). Senators were put on notice that on occasion they would be asked to consider individuals suggested by the Justice Department. This provision of the memorandum signaled an activist stance by the administration on selection.

The memorandum also recognized that Democratic senators, particularly in states without Republican senators, would have to be consulted. It did not, however, address the situation when one senator from a state was a Republican and the other a Democrat. The memorandum also indicated uncertainty about the process to be used for nominations to the courts of appeals, although it suggested that Republican senators would have a say.[c]

Finally, and most significantly, by the absence of any reference to gender or race the memorandum suggested an end to affirmative action for the judiciary. Unlike the Carter procedures for judicial selection, gender and race were no

----

experienced candidates. The Attorney General may, when appropriate, make recommendations to Senators with regard to specific judicial candidates.

With respect to States with no Senators from the majority party, the Attorney General will solicit suggestions and recommendations from the Republican members of the Congressional delegation, who will act in such instances as a group, in lieu of Senate members from their respective States. It is presumed that Congressional members in such cases would consult with the Democratic Senators from their respective States.

The Attorney General also desires to receive suggestions with respect to Court of Appeals nominations to be made by the President. The precise means by which such candidates for appointment will be identified by the Department are currently being formulated, but the President's mechanism for judicial selection at the Circuit Court level will include provisions for receiving the recommendations of members of the Senate (or of the appropriate Congressional delegation, in the case of a State with no Republican Senator).

This memorandum can be found in *The Performance of the Reagan Administration in Nominating Women and Minorities to the Federal Bench,* Hearing, Committee on the Judiciary, United States Senate, 100th Congress, 2nd Session, February 2, 1988, Serial J-100-47 (Washington, D.C.: Government Printing Office, 1990), 122–23.

c. Speaking for the Justice Department, Thomas P. DeCair elaborated on this part of the memorandum and told the *New York Times* that the administration "might retain" the selection commissions instituted by Carter. *New York Times,* March 7, 1981, p. 11. The administration, however, abandoned the commission.

longer considered to be valid considerations for appointment. As Jonathan C. Rose, the assistant attorney general for legal policy, later explained: "I think when we came into office, we found that the level of diversity, given the demographics of the legal profession at this point, was about as successfully achieved as possible, without straining the quality of people to serve on the federal bench. . . . It seems to us to force-feed people who really don't have the substantive background would be a mistake."⁹ Furthermore, Rose pointed out: "The President is unwilling to put someone on the court that does not share his view on the role of the courts in our society, just because that person belongs to a particular group." The administration thus was apparently taking the position that the really qualified women and minorities already had been appointed given the relatively small pool from where they were drawn. But even if there were qualified women and minorities still available, if they did not share the administration's judicial philosophy, they would not be placed on the bench. The contrast between the Reagan administration and the Carter administration, which appointed some politically conservative women and minorities, could not have been greater.

Most Republican senators at first went along with the administration's request that three to five names be submitted to the Justice Department. But soon some Republican senators, according to Rose, "began to buck at that." They insisted on returning to the old ways, whereby the senator would submit only one name, and that individual, unless found unqualified, would receive the nomination. As Rose lamented, "The total result of all of this is that we haven't had a lot of flexibility at the district court level."

Ronald Reagan disbanded the U.S. Circuit Judge Nominating Commission and returned to the pre-Carter method of selection, with senators and others making their recommendations to the Justice Department. Why did Reagan do this? Considering his past use of commissions to select judges in California and his public commitment during the election campaign to continue the practice at the federal level, his actions were unexpected. The answer is suggested by Jonathan Rose, who admitted, "I really was the one who recommended against it [to continue the circuit court commissions], because I was confronted by a very practical problem." When Rose came to the Justice Department in May 1981, there were a number of judgeships to fill. Establishing the commissions, he claimed, would make it impossible to appoint people promptly. Furthermore, Rose asserted, the Carter commissions "were not designed to find high-quality capable people to go on the bench." He acknowledged that the Carter commissions achieved "a much greater diversity of types of people to go on the bench, and that in and of itself was a desirable thing."

Rose's explanation for Reagan's abandonment of the commissions is unconvincing. A likely reason why commissions were not used was that the circuit commissions were too closely identified with the Carter administration. A second, even more compelling reason is that Reagan's desire to appoint conservatives, particularly to the courts of appeals, could best be achieved by tight administration control over the screening process. When he was governor of California, Reagan's staff suggested names of reliable conservatives as potential judicial candidates to the county screening commissions. This would not be easy to do with an independent circuit court nominating commission and would leave the administration open to charges of political meddling. Even though it would have been the Reagan administration that would have chosen the membership of the commission panels, Rose apparently convinced his superiors in the Justice Department that the administration needed to establish its own identity and break with the Carter past as well as retain tight in-house control of the selection of these all-important judgeships. The White House staff evidently was won over, as was the president.

For judicial selection, Ronald Reagan relied primarily on three men: Attorney General William French Smith, who had been Reagan's personal attorney; Edwin Meese III, who in the first term served as a presidential counselor and during the second term replaced Smith as attorney general; and the White House counsel, who until mid-1986 was Fred F. Fielding (later followed by Peter J. Wallison, who served for fifteen months and was then replaced by A. B. Culvahouse, who remained to the end of the Reagan presidency). There is little indication that Reagan took the initiative or was actively involved in the establishment and conduct of the judicial selection process during his presidency. Reagan seems to have routinely approved what a consensus of his advisers recommended. This also appears to have been the case with specific judicial appointments and was consistent with Reagan's presidential management style.[10]

The Reagan administration formalized the judicial selection process by institutionalizing interaction patterns and job tasks that, as we have seen, in previous administrations were more informal and fluid. Before Reagan, the center of judicial selection activity had been the deputy attorney general's office, with an assistant to the deputy responsible for the details and, at times negotiations associated with the selection process. In the Carter administration the attorney general and associate attorney general oversaw selection. During the Reagan administration these responsibilities shifted to the newly created Office of Legal Policy.

The Justice Department's Office of Legal Policy was headed by an assistant attorney general for legal policy, who reported to the deputy attorney general. Jonathan Rose was the first person to hold that position, and he served until

August 1984, when he was replaced by Harold J. Lezar, Jr. When Lezar left a little more than one year later, Stephen J. Markman took the job. The Office of Legal Policy, among its other concerns, became the center of the screening process for judicial selection at the Justice Department. The attorney general, the deputy attorney general, the assistant attorney general for legal policy, and the special counsel for judicial selection (another position established by the Reagan administration), along with some of their assistants, met regularly within the Justice Department to make specific recommendations for judgeships to the President's Federal Judicial Selection Committee, still another major Reagan administration innovation.

The Federal Judicial Selection Committee or Working Group on Appointments, as it became known (because it also dealt with filling United States attorney and United States marshal positions) institutionalized and formalized an active White House role in judicial selection. During Reagan's first term, the committee was chaired by White House counsel Fred Fielding and included presidential counselor Edwin Meese III, the White House chief of staff, the assistant to the president for presidential personnel, the assistant to the president for political affairs, and the assistant to the president for legislative affairs. From the Justice Department, members of the committee during the first term included the attorney general, the deputy attorney general, the associate attorney general, the special counsel for judicial selection, and the assistant attorney general for legal policy.

The highest levels of the White House staff thus played an ongoing, active role in the selection of judges. Legislative, patronage, political, and policy considerations were systematically scrutinized for each judicial nomination to an extent never before seen. This assured policy coordination between the White House and the Justice Department, as well as White House staff supervision of judicial appointments. The president was thus presented with a consensus recommendation for judicial nominations.

The committee did not merely react to the Justice Department's recommendations; it was also a source of names of potential candidates and a vehicle for the exchange of relevant information. For example, the assistant to the president for presidential personnel informally checked out each prospective candidate for a judgeship as to political acceptability to party officials in the candidate's home state.[11] This and other background on the candidates informed the discussion. The committee, like the Justice Department, was determined to place on the bench, insofar as it was possible to do so, those compatible with the administration's overall ideological and judicial-philosophical perspective. Thus the formal mechanism of the committee permitted consistent screening of judicial candidates.

During Reagan's second term the White House counsel continued to chair the committee, but committee membership changed somewhat. The White House chief of staff was still nominally a member, although he ordinarily did not attend due to the press of other business.[12] Ed Meese, no longer a presidential counselor, attended in his capacity as attorney general. The associate attorney general no longer was a member. The special counsel for judicial selection was moved to the attorney general's office, and the title was changed to deputy assistant attorney general (reporting directly to the attorney general); the occupant of that office remained a member of the committee. Otherwise the membership stayed the same as during Reagan's first term.

Throughout the Reagan presidency the committee held meetings (usually weekly) at the White House. Although this certainly was convenient given the larger number of committee members from the White House, it also symbolized White House primacy in the selection process and the importance the Reagan administration placed on judicial selection and its central role in furthering the president's agenda.

For each judicial nomination, the White House counsel sent a memorandum to the president with the formal nomination papers attached for his signature. The cover memo contained the recommendation that the president nominate the individual and that he telephone to ask the prospective nominee to serve as a federal judge. Here was the president's most active personal involvement. For example, the memorandum for the president concerning the nomination of Richard J. Cardamone to be a Second Circuit judge read in part:

> The Attorney General, Deputy Attorney General, Edwin Meese [presidential counselor], James Baker [White House chief of staff], Max Friedersdorf [assistant to the president for legislative affairs], E. Pendleton James [assistant to the president for personnel], Lyn Nofziger [assistant to the president for political affairs] and I [Fred F. Fielding] recommend that you nominate Richard J. Cardamone of New York, to be United States Circuit Judge, United States Court of Appeals for the Second Circuit. Justice Cardamone is presently serving on the New York State Supreme Court. . . . He is 56 years old, married, and has ten children. His biography is attached at Tab A. . . .
> Recommendation:
> 1. That you call Judge Cardamone (telephone memorandum attached at Tab B).
> 2. That you sign the attached nomination at Tab C.[13]

The president made the call, and on the bottom of Fielding's memorandum he wrote, "He says yes," and initialed it "RR."

Typically, Reagan made some notation on the telephone memorandum. The memorandum itself was very specific. For example, the telephone memorandum that recommended to the president that he make a call to offer a judge-ship to Israel Leo Glasser specified the date to call, named those who recom-mended Glasser (the same senior officials who were mentioned in the cover letter), and stated the purpose of the call, which in this case was "[t]o ask him to serve as United States District Judge for the Eastern District of New York." The memo then specified the "Topics of Discussion," basic professional back-ground information about Glasser. Unlike telephone calls to senators (as we shall see later in this chapter), these were not scripted word for word. On the memo, Reagan wrote "O.K.," indicating that he had made the call and that Glasser had accepted.[14]

   The practice of the president himself making telephone calls officially asking individuals to accept judicial nominations was an innovation that the Reagan administration instituted in the late summer of 1981. Certainly the president's personal involvement in this manner underscored the importance the admin-istration placed on judicial selection and no doubt impressed upon the ap-pointees that they were indeed *Reagan* appointees.[d] On some of the cover memos or telephone memos, the president wrote "yes" or "call made" to indicate that he made the call and that the individual accepted. On some of the cover memos he signed his full name, suggesting that this process was so routine that he mistakenly signed the memos as well as the formal nomination papers.

   There is some evidence that hints that on a few occasions Reagan might have played an active role, aside from an occasional meeting with a senator to discuss a nomination. In one instance, the working group recommended New Jersey state judge John Bissell to a federal district judgeship. Bissell had been recommended by a newly appointed Republican senator, Nicholas F. Brady, who had replaced Democratic senator Harrison A. Williams, Jr., who had resigned. Secretary of Labor Raymond J. Donovan, however, had previously

d. There is evidence that personal phone calls from the president were deeply valued by the nominees. Fred Fielding wrote to Reagan: "these telephone calls to your judicial candidates have been very much appreciated. . . . This task . . . has been most worthwhile in communicating the importance you place on these lifetime appointments." Memoran-dum for the President, January 25, 1984, WHORM, PR 7-02 (Presidential Telephone Calls, 172000–187099), #187006, Ronald Reagan Library.

   Nominees themselves wrote to Reagan. For example, Judge Jesse E. Eschbach wrote to "express my deep appreciation for your kindness and consideration in calling me. It was an experience our family will never forget." Eschbach to Reagan, October 21, 1981, WHORM, FG 52 (037000–048499), #044966. Another appointee put it simply, "I shall treasure that action forever." Joel Flaum to Reagan, April 19, 1983, WHORM, FG 52 (126000–138999), #138360.

been the patronage link with New Jersey Republicans, and he reportedly asked Reagan to hold off on nominating Bissell "until he could do further checking."[15] Apparently Donovan and other New Jersey Republicans had their own candidates for the judgeship. But the president refused to delay the Bissell nomination.

In another instance, some conservative business people opposed the prospective nomination of the general counsel of the Central Intelligence Agency, Stanley Sporkin, to a federal district judgeship in the District of Columbia. Sporkin had once headed the Securities and Exchange Commission and had strictly enforced the law. His longtime friend and colleague William J. Casey, head of the Central Intelligence Agency, personally intervened with the president on behalf of Sporkin.[16] Sporkin, recommended by the working group, was nominated by Reagan.[e]

There is one instance in which the available evidence suggests that Reagan likely made the decision not to proceed with a nomination. Benjamin C. Toledano, a conservative Republican lawyer from New Orleans, was recommended for a position on the Court of Appeals for the Fifth Circuit by the Louisiana Republican leadership, including Governor David C. Treen.[17] As a young man in his twenties, Toledano had been a public and active supporter of racial segregation and had spent five months traveling around Louisiana trying to organize the segregationist States' Rights Party of Louisiana. Toledano had renounced his past and for several years had courted black support. Toledano had unsuccessfully run for mayor of New Orleans and United States senator in the early 1970s. Now his past caught up with him, as the local and state chapters of the NAACP and a local group of black attorneys opposed Toledano's candidacy, although Toledano had some black and Democratic support. Toledano also ran into difficulty with the ABA Standing Committee on Federal Judiciary. A member of the committee, the distinguished former secretary of transportation, Republican William T. Coleman, an African

---

e. Sporkin's critics, who feared that he was consumer-oriented and too tough on business, apparently had a better take on him than did the committee. The *Almanac of the Federal Judiciary*, based upon its survey of lawyers who practiced before Sporkin, characterized him as a civil libertarian who was also for the consumer and the underdog. *Almanac of the Federal Judiciary* (Englewood Cliffs, N.J.: Aspen Publishers, 1995), vol. 1, D.C. Circuit, p. 23. Sporkin's consumer activism was prominently commented upon when a panel of judges (one Carter and two Reagan appointees) of the U.S. Court of Appeals for the District of Columbia Circuit overturned a Sporkin decision that negated an agreement made by the Clinton Justice Department and Microsoft Corporation. They criticized Sporkin for trying "to assume the role of attorney general" and removed him from the case. *Washington Post*, June 17, 1995, A1.

American, was reported as mobilizing opposition to Toledano. The ABA appeared poised to rate Toledano "not qualified."

All this was spelled out in a memo to Reagan from Fred Fielding on December 3, 1982. Fielding noted that the joint White House–Justice Department working group "has identified Benjamin C. Toledano . . . as a well-qualified candidate for nomination to the existing vacancy on the 5th Circuit Court of Appeals. However, we believe the facts described below should be brought to your personal attention before further action occurs on this prospective nomination." Fielding described Toledano's past and the opposition within the ABA committee. He also mentioned the likely opposition of Democratic senators to Toledano and anticipated active opposition from national civil rights organizations, who "will undoubtedly claim this nomination is an example of the administration's supposed 'insensitivity' to blacks in general and civil rights in particular."[18]

Reagan apparently decided not to proceed with the nomination. Toledano was informed of the decision on December 7 by Jonathan Rose. But Toledano and his main sponsor, Governor Treen, unaware that Reagan himself decided against proceeding with Toledano, tried to turn the decision around. Fielding finally explained to Treen that Toledano's nomination "had been discussed at the highest level where the decision had been made to not go forward." This "final decision rests exclusively in the President." The prospect of a vigorous protest by civil rights groups, the absence of ABA support, and the likelihood that some Republican senators would join Democratic colleagues in challenging and possibly defeating Toledano was undoubtedly worrisome to the administration.[19]

Reagan's strongest suit was his effective communication with the public. Reagan, as I shall discuss in the next section, went public to articulate his vision of how he wished to shape the judiciary through his appointments. On other occasions Reagan defended embattled nominees, the most prominent of which was Supreme Court nominee Robert Bork, but he also devoted a weekly radio address defending two lower-court nominees who had run into trouble in the Senate (Jefferson Sessions and Daniel Manion).[20] Sessions and Manion are discussed at greater length later in the chapter.

The Policy Agenda and Selection

The Republican Party platform of 1980 contained a plank concerning judicial selection that reflected the importance of the judiciary for the Republican policy agenda. The platform read:

We pledge . . . the appointment of women and men who respect and reflect the values of the American people, and whose judicial philosophy is characterized by the highest regard for protecting the rights of law-abiding citizens, and is consistent with the belief in the decentralization of the federal government and efforts to return decisionmaking power to state and local elected officials. We will work for the appointment of judges at all levels of the judiciary who respect traditional family values and the sanctity of innocent human life.[21]

The president's domestic policy agenda, aside from economic and government regulatory concerns, was shaped by opposition to civil libertarian decisions of the Supreme Court. Those decisions included the establishment of the right of a woman to abort a nonviable fetus, the use of remedies such as busing to bring about desegregation of the public schools, the exclusionary rule (barring the use in court of evidence seized in violation of the Fourth Amendment), generous readings of the Bill of Rights to provide for the rights of the accused, prohibitions on prayer rituals in the public schools, and affirmative action in employment and education.[22] In terms of judicial philosophy, the Reagan administration was looking for those who believed in "judicial restraint." Such judges would likely share Reagan's conservative political beliefs and therefore be opposed to these and similar policy positions in court decisions. A political conservative, Reagan no doubt believed, would read the Constitution narrowly. By framing his appointment goals in terms of the judicial philosophy he believed would accomplish his political purposes, Reagan placed a more legitimate public and professional face on his policy agenda for the judiciary.

Some nine months into Reagan's first term, William French Smith, in a widely publicized speech before the Federal Legal Council (a group of high-ranking attorneys for various federal government agencies), severely criticized the federal courts for their liberal activism in creating rights not mentioned in the Constitution and for unwarranted intrusion in the affairs of state and local government. He singled out a group of rights "only implied by the Constitution" which "has become a real base for expanding Federal court activity." Included among those rights, he asserted, were

the right to marry, the right to procreate, the right of interstate travel, and the right of sexual privacy that among other things, may have spawned a right, with certain limitations, to have an abortion. We do not disagree with the results in all of these cases. We do, however, believe that the application of these principles has led to some constitutionally dubious and unwise intrusions upon the legislative domain. The very arbitrariness with which some rights have been discerned and preferred, while others have not, reveals a process of subjective judicial policymaking as opposed to reasoned legal interpretation.[23]

Smith went on to challenge the federal courts' use of equitable remedies and intrusions in areas in which he asserted they have no expertise: "Federal courts have attempted to restructure entire school systems in desegregation cases and to maintain continuing review over basic administrative decisions. They have asserted similar control over entire prison systems and public housing projects. They have restructured . . . employment criteria even to the extent of mandating numerical results based upon race or gender." Smith pointedly suggested that "the Department of Justice intends to play an active role in effecting the principles upon which Ronald Reagan campaigned." He pointed out that the Justice Department has "opposed the distortion of the meaning of equal protection by courts that mandate counterproductive busing and quotas." And most significantly, Smith pointed out, "We have helped to select appointees to the Federal bench who understand the meaning of judicial restraint." The emphasis on judicial selection was indeed becoming an important component of Reagan administration policy.

The immediate response to the Smith speech from liberal groups was, as expected, negative. But the speech also elicited the concern of the president of the American Bar Association, who told the *New York Times* that Smith's charges "tend to undermine public confidence in our system of justice" and to invite legislative interference with the ability of the courts to protect "the rights of all our citizens against the changing policies of a transient majority."[24] Smith seemed to back off: for the remainder of his tenure as attorney general he refrained from publicly attacking the federal courts.

The president addressed the American Bar Association on August 1, 1983, and his talk in part dealt with judicial selection. He observed that "we've sought judicial nominees who support the limited policymaking role for the Federal courts envisioned by the Constitution." And this was true. Indeed, the administration at the outset of the Reagan presidency focused attention on the selection of conservatives, particularly at the appeals court level. Conservative Republican senators were happy to cooperate. For example, Wisconsin Republican senator Robert W. Kasten, Jr., recommended John L. Coffey to fill a vacancy on the Seventh Circuit that traditionally was filled by a Wisconsin resident. Kasten noted that Coffey's "judicial philosophy is consistent with my own and that of the president."[25] Coffey was appointed.[f]

---

f. Coffey has been seen by practitioners before him as a "very conservative" judge. See the comments of lawyers surveyed by the *Almanac of the Federal Judiciary* (Englewood Cliffs, N.J.: Aspen Publishers, 1995), vol. 2, 7th Circuit, p. 9.

The administration turned to well-known conservative legal scholars for some early appeals court appointments. Robert Bork, Richard Posner, and Ralph Winter were nominated in Reagan's first year, and the attorney general told the *New York Times* that the nominees were "examples of the Administration's determination to use the power of judicial appointment to further President Reagan's views on judicial restraint." That determination was reflected in the internal screening processes of the Justice Department. For example, in Jonathan Rose's memo to his superiors recommending Winter for the Second Circuit, he noted that the selection method was "[r]eview of available philosophically compatible law school faculty members." Those already on the bench who were being considered for elevation had their records reviewed, as, for example, noted in another internal memo from Rose to Schmults and Smith recommending U.S. district judge Jesse E. Eschbach: "Judge Eschbach's opinions were reviewed and found to reflect the positions of this Administration. He is well qualified. He is also a Republican."[26]

There is also some evidence that the administration was responsive to the concerns of extreme conservatives. In 1981, Judith Whittaker, a Republican attorney from Kansas City, was on a list of candidates recommended by Missouri Republican senator John Danforth to fill a slot on the Eighth Circuit. The administration was about to nominate her, but intense right-wing opposition persuaded officials to drop her candidacy. (A detailed discussion of the derailed Whittaker nomination is provided later in this chapter.)

Another example also concerned a prospective woman appointee. The administration had decided that one of two vacant district judgeships in Ohio should go to a woman. Republicans in Ohio recommended Lizabeth A. Moody, whose legal accomplishments included becoming the first woman to become a partner in a Cleveland law firm. Right-wing conservatives, however, mounted a campaign against her, charging her with being pro-abortion (a charge she denied) and holding against her the fact that she had been a partner in the law firm of liberal Democratic senator Howard Metzenbaum. The Ohio Republican congressional delegation recommended the choice of the party's right wing, Alice M. Batchelder, the wife of Reagan's Ohio campaign chairman in 1980.[27] She received the appointment.[g]

A characteristic of judicial selection during Reagan's first term was the apparent reluctance to engage in a confirmation fight in the Senate even if it

---

g. Judge Batchelder was elevated to the U.S. Court of Appeals for the Sixth Circuit by George Bush in 1991. A survey of lawyers practicing before her found that her rulings and decisional predispositions were "quite conservative." *Almanac of the Federal Judiciary* (Englewood Cliffs, N.J.: Aspen Publishers, 1995), vol. 2, 6th Circuit, p. 5.

meant sacrificing a philosophically desirable candidate, as we saw happened with Toledano. But the administration during the first term could rightly claim that they had great success in appointing conservatives to the lower federal courts. The Center for Judicial Studies examined every decision published by every Reagan appointee during the first two years of Reagan's first term and concluded that the overwhelming majority of appointees demonstrated judicial restraint along the lines favored by the administration. Jonathan Rose was quoted as being "tremendously pleased" with the records of the law professors chosen by the administration for the appeals courts. An extensive analysis of Robert Bork's record and accounts of other appointees seemed to offer other evidence to justify this satisfaction.[28]

The 1984 Republican Party platform summarized the judicial selection goals and accomplishments of Reagan's administration: "Judicial power must be exercised with deference towards state and local officials. . . . It is not a judicial function to reorder the economic, political, and social priorities of our nation. . . . We commend the President for appointing federal judges committed to the rights of law-abiding citizens and traditional family values. . . . In his second term, President Reagan will continue to appoint Supreme Court and other federal judges who share our commitment to judicial restraint."[29]

During the first term, the administration utilized its new President's Federal Judicial Selection Committee (working group) not only to determine whom to recommend to Reagan for each judicial vacancy but as a source of generating prospects, particularly for the courts of appeals. A data bank of potential candidates was established which drew upon each committee member's own network of contacts. White House counsel Fielding was reported to have even approached the predominantly black National Bar Association and women's groups for suggestions, although he was quoted as adding a caveat: "Don't send me names of people you know we won't select," referring unmistakably to liberals.[30]

As Reagan's second term got under way, William French Smith stepped down as attorney general and was replaced by presidential counselor Edwin Meese III. Meese was an aggressive and outspoken attorney general, whose style contrasted sharply with Smith's. Although Smith had gone public in his criticism of the federal courts during Reagan's first year, he did not subsequently press his critique. Smith's public face was gentlemanly, even aristocratic, in contrast to Meese's feisty and confrontational persona. Indeed, Meese took the lead, in an address before the American Bar Association in July 1985, in initiating a public debate about the role of judges in interpreting the Constitution.[31]

About three and a half months after Meese's address, Reagan spoke to a group of United States attorneys, and his remarks were front-page news. He pledged to focus his judicial appointments on those who would practice "judicial restraint" and "who understand the danger of shortcircuiting the electoral process and disenfranchising the people through judicial activism." The president declared that the Founding Fathers "never intended, for example, that the courts pre-empt legislative prerogatives or become vehicles for political action or social experimentation." He reminded his audience: "[D]uring the last two Presidential elections, I've made it clear to the American public that I felt the courts had sometimes gone too far in interfering with the constitutional prerogatives of other branches of government, even while they neglected their constitutional duty of protecting society from those who prey on the innocent. Well, this is still my belief." Administration officials reported that Reagan increasingly appreciated that his judicial appointments would likely be his most enduring legacy.[32] The president's remarks seemed to reflect Meese's influence in his new role as attorney general.

Meese approached his new job with gusto. He was originally nominated in February 1984, but charges surfaced that he had obtained government jobs for three individuals who had helped him financially. Attorney General Smith then appointed a special prosecutor, and although Meese was clearly an election-year liability, Ronald Reagan stood by his friend. Meese, however, was eventually cleared of any criminal wrongdoing, and he took office in March 1985.

Meese and Reagan were close. (Meese had served as Reagan's chief of staff when Reagan was governor of California.) Fielding observed: "His [Meese's] instincts are Ronald Reagan's instincts." Meese himself revealed that when Reagan was not traveling, he saw the president several times a day: "Often, just privately, I'll see him for a few minutes here, or a few minutes there. Sometimes I'll ride in the car with him to someplace. . . . We have worked together closely for almost 20 years. We are good friends. And we are people who, by and large, without any real effort on my part to do this, come up with the same viewpoint on most issues, pretty much totally independent of each other."[33]

In April 1985, President Reagan established the Domestic Policy Council, consisting of eight cabinet officials who had the task of making domestic and social policy recommendations. Meese was chair of the council and was seen as carrying great weight in determining and coordinating the domestic policy agenda of the administration. No doubt Meese viewed the selection of those sharing Reagan's judicial philosophy as interrelated with domestic policy. To better supervise judicial selection, particularly of judges to the courts of appeals, Meese brought into the Justice Department a special assistant whose task it would be to examine the judicial philosophy of candidates and report directly to him. That assistant was a young law professor, Grover Rees III, whose office was located across the hall from the attorney general.[34h] Rees actively participated in the interview process, which will be described shortly.

The connection between judicial appointments and the administration's policy agenda surfaced dramatically during the congressional campaign in the fall of 1986. Reagan actively campaigned for Republican senatorial candidates in an effort to prevent the Senate from returning to Democratic control. In a speech in North Carolina, he made that connection: "The proliferation of drugs has been part of a crime epidemic that can be traced to, among other things, liberal judges who are unwilling to get tough with the criminal element in this society. We don't need a bunch of sociology majors on the bench. What we need are strong judges who will aggressively use their authority to protect our families, communities, and our way of life; judges who understand that punishing wrongdoers is our way of protecting the innocent; and judges who do not hesitate to put criminals where they belong — behind bars." Reagan went on to stress that "we've been appointing" the "strong judges" that are needed, and that "[i]t's already beginning to have an effect."[35]

Reagan accurately reflected the administration's concern with appointing "strong judges." One example of this was the unsuccessful attempt of New York Republican senator Alfonse D'Amato to have William E. Hellerstein, a public defender, appointed to a federal district court judgeship in New York City. Hellerstein was actually recommended by Democratic senator Daniel Patrick Moynihan under an arrangement that had begun in the 1970s with D'Amato's Republican predecessor, Senator Jacob Javits, that the senator whose party was not in the White House would recommend the individual to fill every fourth district court vacancy on the federal bench in New York. Moynihan recommended Hellerstein, and Senator D'Amato then endorsed and forwarded that recommendation.[36]

Hellerstein, a Democrat, headed the Criminal Appeals Bureau of the New York Legal Aid Society. His agency was responsible for representing indigent defendants in appeals of their convictions. Before working for the Legal Aid Society, Hellerstein had been a staff attorney for the United States Commission on Civil Rights. Hellerstein had achieved prominence in the New York legal community. He had served as vice president of the Association of the Bar of the City of New York and chaired that bar's executive committee. But the Justice

---

h. Rees served for about one year before being appointed chief justice of the High Court of American Samoa. His successor, Steve A. Matthews, saw his job title change to deputy assistant attorney general.

Department soon discovered that in 1979 Hellerstein had written an article on court congestion which suggested that the criminal justice system would be better off not imprisoning those convicted of relatively minor offenses such as prostitution, gambling, and possession of small amounts of narcotics. Roy Cohn, the notorious right-wing lawyer who had achieved prominence as chief counsel for Senator Joseph R. McCarthy's investigatory committee in the 1950s, was reported as having contacted his friends in the White House urging the rejection of Hellerstein. Cohn told a reporter that Hellerstein was not qualified because he was too liberal.[37]

About four months after Senator D'Amato sent Hellerstein's name to the administration, two former United States attorneys for the Southern District of New York (Manhattan), along with twenty-five assistant United States attorneys, wrote to Attorney General Smith urging him to move on the Hellerstein nomination. They strongly endorsed him, praising him as "an outstandingly able lawyer." But the administration stood firm, and about a year after his name was first submitted, disclosed that it had determined that Hellerstein's views were not consistent with those of the president. In an interview with National Public Radio some months later, Fred Fielding said simply that a candidate "active for defendant's rights" would be eliminated from consideration. Hellerstein was quoted as being "disappointed" and suggested that no one in the administration had spoken to him about his judicial philosophy. Indeed, "[n]o one at the Justice Department or the White House interviewed me."[38] [i]

Justice Department officials were undoubtedly convinced that Hellerstein was a liberal Democrat and that an interview would accomplish little. Interviewing, however, played a central role in selection. There are a number of accounts as to how the process worked. For example, Michigan Supreme Court judge James L. Ryan, nominated to be a judge on the U.S. Court of Appeals for the Sixth Circuit, was asked at his confirmation hearing to describe his experience. He responded that he "was asked to come to Wash-

---

i. On July 25, 1985, Senator D'Amato forwarded the name of Senator Moynihan's choice, Miriam Goldman Cederbaum, to replace Hellerstein. *New York Times*, July 26, 1985, B3. Cederbaum, a Wall Street lawyer with impeccable credentials and also a Democrat, had been a member of the Board of Directors of the New York Civil Liberties Union in 1969 and 1970. Nevertheless, the administration decided not to challenge Senator Moynihan's recommendation of a woman with outstanding credentials and strong support from the organized bar (she was to receive a "well qualified" rating from the ABA; her law partner, Robert B. Fiske, Jr., was chairman of the ABA committee, although he recused himself from consideration of her rating). Cederbaum was nominated on December 4, 1985. Her nomination was resubmitted to the new session of the Senate on February 3, 1986, and she was confirmed one month later.

ington for a half-day of interviews . . . and I was interviewed by four or five lawyers in the Justice Department. . . . By some, I was asked little or nothing; by one or two lawyers in the Justice Department I was given the benefit of their judgment and their views about matters philosophical. . . . I was asked questions of the most general sort, about my philosophy, about what is the sweep of judicial decisionmaking. There was a discussion about general areas of judicial self-restraint, some of which were touched on in the questionnaire which the Senate submitted." When pointedly asked by Democratic senator Paul Simon, "Did anyone ask you how you would rule on any given case?" Ryan responded, "Absolutely not."[39]

One appeals court nominee, Emmett R. Cox, nominated for the Eleventh Circuit, described his interview: "I was asked questions about my personal background, my legal background, and my interest in the position. I was also asked general questions relative to judicial philosophy, how I as a judge would approach cases of various types, etc."[40]

Stephen J. Markman, assistant attorney general for legal policy, described the interview process that his office coordinated with attorneys in the Justice Department:

> Each interview generally ran between 30 minutes and one hour, and candidates generally averaged between four and five hours of interviews during their visit to the Department. . . . These interviews supplemented our analysis of the candidate's written record and our communications with individuals in the state or district who could speak to the candidate's reputation and abilities. . . . Department interviewers sought to learn more about a candidate's background and professional experience and to determine whether he or she appreciated that the source of law for a self-governing citizenry is the consent of the people themselves as expressed in the Constitution and legislatively-enacted statutes and not the judiciary; in other words, whether a candidate reasoned from constitutional premises. Candidates who evinced an intention to impose their policy preferences from the bench, whether liberal or conservative, were not selected.[41]

Markman went on to argue that "[w]e were not interested so much, for example, in the conclusions reached by candidates in hypothetical discussions but in how and why they seemed to be getting there." He stressed that a wide variety of issues were considered, including "federalism, the separation of powers, statutory interpretation, constitutional interpretation, criminal justice, and a candidate's reasons for wanting to go on the federal bench." Markman also claimed that candidates were not asked "their perspectives on contemporary issues of controversy such as abortion or school prayer."

Grover Rees revealed, however, that the constitutional issues involved in

Roe v. *Wade* were topics of discussion in the interviews with which he was familiar. A National Public Radio report found that several women candidates for judgeships "were asked directly about their views on abortion. One female State court judge said she was asked repeatedly, how she would rule on an abortion case if it came before her."[42] Perhaps it was an impossible feat for Justice Department interviewers to get at the reasoning process the candidate would use in handling an issue such as abortion without touching on the substantive results that were part of the Reagan social agenda. As might be expected, no successful candidate claimed that the interview process was improper or that "litmus test" questions were asked. Some unsuccessful candidates apparently did complain, but clearly they were not disinterested parties either.

The Reagan administration did not proceed with a judicial nomination, particularly to the appeals courts, unless it felt assured that the nominee shared the administration's judicial philosophy. When a potential nominee had strong political backing but doubts were raised about the candidate's philosophical reliability, the burden was on the candidate's backers to demonstrate that the doubts were unfounded.

An example of this occurred with the filling of an Illinois seat on the Seventh Circuit. In 1981, Republican senator Charles Percy and Republican governor Jim Thompson, of Illinois, strongly recommended the elevation of Judge Joel M. Flaum.[j] Before Flaum had been appointed to the federal district bench by Gerald Ford, he had been first assistant United States attorney under Thompson, who was then United States attorney. Flaum had the strong support of the organized bar as well. But the vacancy was filled by Professor Richard Posner of the University of Chicago Law School. Senator Percy, by his own account, agreed to support Posner with the understanding that Flaum would be considered for the next vacancy.[43] When Seventh Circuit judge Robert Sprecher died in May 1982, another Illinois seat on the Seventh came open. Once again Senator Percy and Governor Thompson strongly recommended Flaum.

When it became known that Judge Flaum was being seriously considered, a number of letters from far-right conservatives were sent to administration officials. For example, an Illinois state senator sent a "Dear Ed" letter to then presidential counselor Ed Meese in early July 1982: "Several members of the

---

j. Governor Thompson was so enthusiastic about Flaum that he told the administration that Flaum was Supreme Court caliber. Fielding's handwritten note read, "Jim Thompson: Flaum — Supreme Court." Fred F. Fielding files, CFOA Box 426, President's Federal Judicial Selection Committee Meeting — July 23, 1981 (1), Ronald Reagan Library.

Chicago Bar have talked to me regarding the Flaum appointment. They express concern with Mr. Flaum's "bleeding heart" philosophy. I have received similar comments from people more knowledgeable about Mr. Flaum than myself."[44] Even more perilous for the Flaum candidacy was the "Dear Ed" letter from Paul M. Weyrich, the president of the ultra-conservative Coalition for America:

> Our own examination of Flaum's opinions has convinced me that his judicial tendencies are worrisome. Specifically, he seems to have a predilection for "class action" suits. In addition, at least one of his rulings raises questions as to how he would interpret the recently passed Voting Rights Act Amendments. He has also shown a tendency to intervene in clearly local or state matters, such as the academic decision making process. In sum, he is not the sort of judge we would expect from this Administration. . . . We would oppose the elevation of Judge Flaum to the Circuit seat.[45]

The Flaum candidacy seemed to stall, and Senator Percy met with Meese in late September. Realizing that Flaum had been unfairly labeled a judicial activist, Percy asked the dean of the Loyola University School of Law, Charles W. Murdock, who was known as a conservative, to analyze Flaum's decisions and comment on Flaum's judicial philosophy. Percy sent Murdock's eighteen-page analysis to Meese, which concluded that Flaum's decisionmaking "is a model of judicial restraint." Unbeknownst to Percy, the Justice Department in 1981 had undertaken its own review of Flaum's record, which apparently cast doubt on Flaum's commitment to judicial restraint.[46]

To get the Flaum candidacy back on track, Governor Thompson personally met with Justice Department officials to review *every* published decision of Judge Flaum's. As Senator Percy recounted to Reagan, "I am told that at the end of that session there were only *two cases* that were cited as causing concern, out of his over 250 published opinions."[47] Percy continued in his letter: "Governor Thompson and I would not urge someone on you who we believed would be a discredit to you or your own beliefs. We believe that the record shows that Judge Flaum has exhibited a philosophy of judicial restraint during his eight years on the bench and that he would contribute to your desire to see additional restraint in the decisions being made by our federal courts."

Flaum, unanimously rated "exceptionally well qualified" by the ABA, was nominated on April 14, 1983, and the following May 4 was confirmed.[k] Meese apparently had hoped to fill the position caused by Judge Sprecher's

---

k. Years later, lawyers surveyed were divided over whether Flaum's leanings were liberal or conservative. *Almanac of the Federal Judiciary* (Englewood Cliffs, N.J.: Aspen Publishers, 1995), vol. 2, 7th Circuit, p. 16.

death with the brilliant young conservative professor from the University of Chicago, Frank H. Easterbrook.[l] Easterbrook in fact was named to the next vacancy on the Seventh Circuit.[m]

Judicial selection was a high-stakes activity for the Reagan administration. There was a genuine commitment to reverse the course of judicial policymaking through the appointment of those sharing the president's judicial philosophy. That philosophy was consistent with the conservative policy positions of the social agenda; thus, in effect, philosophical screening was ideological screening. Available evidence in the presidential papers lends support to this view of the Reagan appointment process. Although many of the presidential papers relating to appointments have yet to be processed, from the information that is available it appears that at least 75 percent of appeals court judges were policy-agenda appointments (thirty-eight out of forty-nine for whom a determination could be reasonably made). The balance probably can be considered partisan-agenda appointments. There is no evidence of the personal agenda coming into play. But the administration never had a free ride in its journey to reshape the judiciary. The Senate played an increasingly important role both before and after the election of 1986, in which the Democrats regained control of the Senate.

Senators and Selection

During Reagan's first term, relations between the administration and Republican senators appeared to be reasonably cordial. Senator Strom Thurmond chaired the Senate Judiciary Committee, and he shared the administration's policy agenda. The reforms instituted when Senator Kennedy headed the committee, however, were retained, which meant that the committee would not be a rubber stamp. Indeed, it continued to investigate nominees independently.

The agreement between Attorney General Smith and the Senate leadership that Republican senators would submit several names for each district court vacancy did not always work in practice.[n] When a Republican senator submit-

l. Easterbrook, finding out that he lost to Flaum, wrote Meese expressing his appreciation that Meese had seriously considered his candidacy. Easterbrook to Meese, March 14, 1983, WHORM, FG 52 (126000–138999), #130873, Ronald Reagan Library.

m. The lawyers surveyed for the *Almanac of the Federal Judiciary* were agreed that Frank Easterbrook was indeed "conservative." *Almanac of the Federal Judiciary* (Englewood Cliffs, N.J.: Aspen Publishers, 1995), vol. 2, 7th Circuit, p. 14.

n. But submission of several names did not preclude a Republican senator from indicating a strong preference. For example, Schmults wrote to the attorney general, "Senator

ted the name of someone who was found not to share the president's judicial philosophy, long delays could occur, as we saw in the case of Senator D'Amato's recommendation of William E. Hellerstein. D'Amato was one of the senators who did not abide by the agreement and persisted in putting forward one name for each judicial vacancy. Senatorial recommendations were made to the administration and then announced to the press, as if it were a foregone conclusion that the person would be nominated. But Hellerstein and several others announced by D'Amato as being in line for judgeships wound up being passed over.[48]

The administration ran into problems in the Senate with some nominees. There were far fewer such problems when William French Smith was attorney general than when Ed Meese held that office. Nevertheless, during Smith's time in office, John P. Vukasin, Jr., was nominated for a district judgeship in the Northern District of California. California's liberal Democratic senator Alan Cranston, however, was opposed to Vukasin on the grounds that he was too right-wing and biased. Cranston registered his opposition and was able to delay the nomination from coming up for a confirmation vote for over six months. Cranston did not, however, invoke the formula "personally obnoxious," which would have triggered senatorial courtesy. Vukasin was not a personal political enemy of Cranston's, and he was eventually confirmed.

Morton R. Galane was nominated for a federal district judgeship in Nevada on July 21, 1983, and his name was resubmitted after the summer recess on September 13. Damaging allegations were raised concerning his behavior in a legal malpractice suit, and on October 18 Galane requested that his nomination be withdrawn.[49]

Major controversy in the Senate over some nominations occurred during Reagan's second term with Ed Meese at the helm in the Justice Department. In part the controversy was fueled by the active participation of such interest groups as People for the American Way. That group mounted a major campaign against two nominees — Jefferson B. Sessions III, nominated to a federal

---

Thurmond sent the Department nine candidates, but expressed a strong preference for Mr. [William W.] Wilkins [Jr.]." Schmults to Smith, April 13, 1981, Fred F. Fielding files, CFOA Box 425, President's Federal Judicial Selection Committee Meeting — April 30, 1981 (1), Ronald Reagan Library. Schmults also wrote that "Senator Gorton recommended four nominees for the vacancy, and voiced unequivocal preference for Mr. Coughenour, whose legal credentials are unexceptionable." Schmults to Smith, April 6, 1981, Fred F. Fielding files, CFOA Box 425, President's Federal Judicial Selection Committee Meeting — April 30, 1981 (1). Both Wilkins and Coughenour were nominated and confirmed.

district judgeship in Alabama, and Daniel A. Manion, nominated to the U.S. Court of Appeals for the Seventh Circuit. This was the first instance of a major national media campaign to defeat lower-court nominations.

Sessions had been serving as the United States attorney for the Southern District of Alabama since 1981 and was actively backed by Alabama's Republican senator Jeremiah Denton. The Sessions nomination was first sent to the Senate on October 23, 1985, and was resubmitted on January 29, 1986. The ABA committee gave Sessions a substantial majority vote of "qualified," with a minority of the committee voting "not qualified." Although the split rating in itself did not seriously undermine nominations during the Reagan presidency, the opposition of African Americans in Alabama did. In 1985, Sessions had prosecuted three black civil rights leaders on voting fraud charges, but the trial ended in acquittals. African Americans in Alabama saw Sessions as insensitive, if not hostile, to their rights. Evidence of racial insensitivity produced unfavorable publicity for Sessions, the administration, and Senator Denton.° Sessions was asked to return to the Senate for further hearings, where he argued that the damaging remarks attributed to him had been said in jest or taken out of context. He denied that he was racially prejudiced. The administration claimed that opposition to Sessions was political and based on his conservative views. Finally, on June 5, 1986, the Senate Judiciary Committee voted 10 to 8 against recommending the nomination and split 9 to 9 on a motion to send the nomination to the full Senate without recommendation, thus defeating the motion.[50] Alabama's other senator, Democrat Howell Heflin, voted against Sessions. The committee vote essentially killed the nomination, and it was formally withdrawn on July 31. The following November, Senator Denton was narrowly defeated for reelection. His defeat was attributed to the heavy African American vote against him. In an ironic postscript ten years later Sessions was elected to the Senate replacing Heflin, who did not run for reelection.

The fate of the Manion nomination was different, but only after a bitter

o. When asked in a Senate hearing by Senator Biden whether he had called the NAACP "un-American" and "Communist," Sessions replied, "I'm often loose with my tongue. I may have said something about the NAACP being un-American or Communist but I meant no harm by it." A Justice Department civil rights division attorney, in a sworn statement, said that Sessions had referred to a white civil rights lawyer as "a disgrace to his race." A black attorney who had worked with Sessions swore that when discussing the murder of a black man by the Ku Klux Klan, Sessions had joked that he had once thought the Klan "was O.K. until I found out they smoked pot." *New York Times,* March 14, 1986, A36.

national debate in which Reagan himself vigorously defended the nomination and campaigned for senatorial votes — unusual for a lower-court nomination. Manion's supporters argued that opposition to his nomination was based on his conservative views and his activities with his late father, Clarence Manion, dean of the University of Notre Dame Law School and a founder of the right-wing fringe group the John Birch Society. Although not a member of the society himself, Daniel Manion, according to supporters, was being smeared with guilt by association.

Manion's opponents argued that he lacked the record of distinction and achievement that was expected of appointees to the courts of appeals. They questioned his ability to be an unbiased judge. Furthermore, they doubted his legal competence on the basis of briefs that he had submitted to the judiciary committee as representative of his legal ability.[p]

Manion, like Sessions, received a split vote from the ABA, with a substantial majority voting "qualified" and a minority voting "not qualified." On May 9, 1986, the Senate Judiciary Committee was evenly divided on the vote to approve the Manion nomination. A second vote, however, produced a majority in favor of sending the nomination to the floor of the Senate without recommendation. This was the opportunity the administration needed, and it made the most of it. A Justice Department official declared, "There is a top-level determination to make sure this thing goes through."[51]

The president was brought into the fight, and the first item of business was to mobilize and energize Republicans in the Senate. On June 17, Reagan made a phone call to Senate majority leader Bob Dole. In the Recommended Telephone Call memorandum submitted to Reagan, under the heading "Purpose" was the following: "To impress upon the Senate Majority Leader your personal interest in the nomination of Daniel Manion to the Seventh Circuit Court of Appeals." In a paragraph briefing Reagan on the background for the call, the memo continued:

> The Democrats have decided to make the Manion nomination their "test case." Although they argue points to the contrary this is a contest of political philosophy. With the threat of a filibuster it will be necessary to garner sixty votes to invoke cloture before proceeding to a simple majority vote on the nomination itself. It is recommended that you call Bob Dole to impress upon

p. The Chicago Council of Lawyers reviewed five of Manion's legal briefs, finding numerous spelling errors as well as poor writing and organization. The group's verdict was that Manion "has not demonstrated the level of legal skill necessary for appointment for the 7th Circuit." *Congressional Quarterly Weekly Report* 44 (June 21, 1986): 1413.

him your own personal interest in the Manion nomination. You should ask Senator Dole to announce at this Tuesday's Policy Luncheon that you had called him to urge that he call for Party unity.

Attached to the memo were the "talking points" for the telephone conversation. The script read as follows:

Bob, I want to talk to you about Dan Manion's nomination to the Seventh circuit. As I mentioned at our abbreviated leadership meeting last week, this nomination is of vital importance to me. The opposition is plainly fighting Dan Manion's confirmation on purely political grounds. If they succeed, all nominations to the Federal courts are in jeopardy for the remainder of this session. I would appreciate your assistance in winning this fight and would be personally grateful if you would tell your colleagues at the Policy Luncheon that this is of personal interest and importance to me. We need every single Republican vote.

I know you have a full agenda, such as tax reform, and other items of vital importance to the country before the Senate at this time, but I consider this matter just as urgent. Thanks Bob for your continued support.

On the memo, Reagan handwrote: "Call made. He'll go to work on it."[52]

Lobbying by the administration was intense. The administration was ready to make deals with Republican senators who had indicated opposition to Manion. Republican Slade Gorton of Washington switched from a Manion opponent to a supporter after the administration agreed to nominate Democrat William Dwyer, Gorton's choice for a judgeship in Seattle. Senator David Durenberger of Minnesota committed himself to support Manion after the administration decided to move on his candidate, David Doty, for the Minnesota bench. Reagan actively lobbied for Manion and devoted a Saturday radio address on June 21 to counteracting the negative campaign waged by the People for the American Way.[53]

June 26, 1986, was a dramatic day in the Senate.[54] Senate Democratic minority leader Robert C. Byrd and the ranking Democrat on the Senate Judiciary Committee, Joseph R. Biden, Jr., thought they had the votes to defeat the nomination. To the surprise of the Republicans who had expected a filibuster, the Democrats offered to proceed directly to a vote on the nomination. Initially Dole did not agree to this move, because two Republican senators, Paula Hawkins of Florida and Bob Packwood of Oregon, whom Dole believed were likely to support Manion, were away. But after Biden and Hawaii senator Daniel K. Inouye, two Democratic opponents of Manion, agreed to pair their votes, thus abstaining, the vote proceeded. When the roll call was already under way, one Republican opponent of Manion, Kansas senator Nancy L.

Kassebaum, was prevailed upon by Indiana senator Dan Quayle, Manion's chief sponsor, to withdraw her vote and be paired with Arizona Republican senator Barry Goldwater, who was not on the floor.[q]

The vote was a tie, 47 to 47. Vice President George Bush was ready to break the tie by voting for Manion. But in a parliamentary maneuver, Senator Byrd switched his vote from a vote against to a vote *for* confirmation. This made the vote 48 to 46 but gave Byrd the opportunity, which he immediately took, to move for reconsideration, which meant that sometime after the July 4 recess the Senate would vote again.

Technically, Manion had been confirmed, but there was doubt because the Senate had on its table the vote to reconsider. Finally, after weeks of political jockeying and continued national media coverage, the Senate voted on July 23 on whether to reconsider the Manion confirmation. Senator Barry Goldwater, who had harbored serious doubts about Manion and chose to stay away from the Senate chamber on the first vote, this time was prevailed upon to oppose reconsideration. But early on July 23, Goldwater was suddenly hospitalized. His fellow Arizona senator, Democrat Dennis DeConcini, an opponent of Manion, when asked by Goldwater agreed to abstain, thus pairing his vote with Goldwater's. The final tally was 49 votes to reconsider to 49 votes against reconsideration, and the vice president provided the fiftieth vote against reconsideration. (Bush's tie-breaking vote was purely a flourish, for the tie meant that the motion to reconsider had already failed for lack of a majority.)

After the vote, Reagan made a phone call to Senator DeConcini. In the telephone memorandum to the president, White House assistant William L. Ball III noted that the purpose of the call was to thank Senator DeConcini for

q. Senator Kassebaum later revealed that she subsequently discovered that Senator Goldwater had *not* authorized a pairing and that there was evidence that Goldwater had had serious doubts about Manion's legal ability. At the time of the vote on Manion, Goldwater had been on Capitol Hill, had known that the voting was taking place, but had chosen not to go to the Senate floor and vote. Furthermore, Senator Packwood later claimed that Senator Dole had no authority to pair his vote, and in fact Packwood later voted against Manion. When Dole said on the Senate floor on June 26, "It is my impression he [Packwood] would vote for the nominee, for confirmation," that was clearly a misleading statement. *Congressional Record*, June 26, 1986, p. S8572. Although Dole said he was willing to telephone Packwood in Oregon to confirm his position, Biden was impatient to get on with the vote, apparently convinced that with Kassebaum's vote not to confirm there would be a one-vote margin to defeat Manion. It was obvious that those opposed to Manion's confirmation were outfoxed. See *New York Times*, June 28, 1986, p. 28; *New York Times*, July 24, 1986, B9; *Congressional Quarterly Weekly Report* 44 (June 28, 1986): 1508–9.

pairing his vote and thus paving the way for the defeat of the motion to reconsider. Attached to the memorandum were the "talking points" for the phone call:

> Dennis, I just wanted to let you know how much I appreciate your willingness to pair with Barry Goldwater on the recent vote to reconsider the Manion nomination. I followed this debate carefully, and was deeply disturbed by the charges that Dan Manion is unqualified to serve on the Circuit Court. Dan has an excellent reputation among those who know him and have first hand knowledge of his work. I am convinced he will do a fine job on the Seventh Circuit. On many occasions during my years in the White House, I have had the benefit of your guidance and support, and I appreciate this. Your vote last week was crucial, and again you have my deep gratitude.

On the first page of the memo, Reagan dutifully handwrote: "call made."[55]

Manion was home free, and he took his seat on the Seventh Circuit.[r] The administration had won, but at the cost of a bruising battle. Senator Gorton was hurt politically in his home state of Washington, where he had been favored to win reelection, and the following November he was narrowly defeated.[s] The administration, keeping its end of the bargain with Gorton, nominated William Dwyer in September. The ABA rated Dwyer "exceptionally well qualified." The nomination, however, was not acted upon by the Senate Judiciary Committee, after Democrats on the committee exacted revenge on Gorton by blocking consideration of Dwyer (despite Dwyer's being a Democrat and a civil libertarian).[56] But with the vigorous backing of Washington's remaining Republican senator, Dan Evans, and after some hesitation by the administration, Dwyer was renominated in the next session of Congress and was unanimously confirmed.[t]

---

r. In light of the severe criticism of Manion's legal ability, his subsequent performance on the bench proved to be a surprise. A survey conducted for the *Almanac of the Federal Judiciary* of lawyers practicing before him rated Manion "average-to-good" and also noted that he "has a good grasp of legal issues." He was labeled "conservative." *Almanac of the Federal Judiciary* (Englewood Cliffs, N.J.: Aspen Publishers, 1995), vol. 2, 7th Circuit, p. 19.

s. Following Gorton's defeat, forty-five Republican senators petitioned the president to name Gorton to a vacancy on the Ninth Circuit. Dole et al. to Reagan, November 20, 1986, WHORM, FG 52, #456111, Ronald Reagan Library. Nothing came of this. Gorton, however, ran again for the Senate two years later, in 1988, winning a seat that had been given up by fellow Republican senator Dan Evans.

t. The administration had received complaints from conservatives in the state of Washington that Dwyer was too liberal. See, for example, Petition to the President, September 8, 1986, WHORM, PR 13 (Petitions, Resolutions, Multiple Signatures, 451198–

There were three other second-term lower-court nominations, aside from Manion's, whose controversy led to debate and roll-call votes in the Senate. One was for the federal district bench in Texas, and the nominee was thirty-two-year-old state judge Sidney A. Fitzwater. Before ascending the state bench, Fitzwater had been very active politically. His opponents accused him of having behaved improperly during one election campaign by discouraging blacks from voting. They also argued that he had relatively little experience. The ABA gave him a split rating, with the majority voting "qualified" and a minority "not qualified." The Senate Judiciary Committee approved the nomination by a vote of 10 to 5 and sent it to the floor, where it was heatedly debated before a motion to end debate passed 64 to 33. The vote on the nomination was fifty-two votes to confirm and forty-two against. Fitzwater became the youngest sitting federal district court judge in the nation.[57]

There was vigorous senate debate over two appeals court nominees prior to roll-call votes on confirmation. Alex Kozinski, nominated to the Ninth Circuit, graduated first in his class at the UCLA Law School, had clerked for Chief Justice Warren E. Burger, and was a rising legal star. He was appointed to the U.S. Court of Claims when he was thirty-two and was only thirty-four when nominated to the Ninth Circuit. Kozinski received a split ABA rating, with a majority voting him "qualified" but a minority deeming him "not qualified." During Kozinski's confirmation hearing, questions were raised about his judicial temperament based upon a number of allegations concerning his behavior when he served as special counsel to the Merit Systems Protection Board. As a result, the committee held further hearings but then voted to recommend the nomination to the full Senate.[58] After debate, the Senate confirmed Kozinski by a vote of 54 to 43.[u]

James L. Buckley, a Republican who had been elected to the Senate from New York in 1970 on the Conservative Party line, was nominated in 1985 to the U.S. Court of Appeals for the District of Columbia. At first, the administration wanted to appoint Buckley to the Second Circuit, but the New York

4539999), #451344, Ronald Reagan Library. However, Dwyer had broad-based support at home, perhaps in part because of the prominent role he had played as a lawyer for a group that had successfully sued the major league baseball owners and won a franchise for Seattle that brought about the establishment of the Seattle Mariners. Senator Evans reportedly warned the Justice Department that if Dwyer were not renominated, he would block all judicial nominations to fill vacancies on the West Coast. *New York Times,* December 3, 1987, A36.

u. The lawyer survey for the *Almanac of the Federal Judiciary* found Kozinski to be "conservative" but also "libertarian." *Almanac of the Federal Judiciary* (Englewood Cliffs, N.J.: Aspen Publishers, 1995), vol. 2, 9th Circuit, p. 21.

bar strongly objected and Republican senator Lowell Weicker of Connecticut, in whose state Buckley now claimed legal residence, was also opposed. The ABA was split on Buckley's rating, with a substantial majority calling him "qualified" and a minority "not qualified." Although no one doubted Buckley's intelligence, wit, and accomplishments, his opponents questioned his judicial temperament and his lack of experience in the practice of law. At the time of his nomination, he was president of Radio Free Europe. Buckley nonetheless was approved by the Senate Judiciary Committee, and the Senate confirmed his nomination on December 17, 1985, by a vote of 84 to 11.[59]

The nomination of Albert I. Moon, Jr., to a judgeship in Hawaii foundered on the strenuous opposition of Democratic senator Daniel Inouye, which was not based on Moon's credentials but on what Moon did to receive the nomination. Inouye argued in the hearings held on November 22, 1985, that in 1978 Moon, a leading Honolulu attorney, had persuaded Inouye to establish a bipartisan judicial selection panel to recommend candidates for federal district judgeships. But in 1985, Inouye claimed, Moon bypassed the panel to secure the nomination for himself.[60] Inouye's unrelenting stance eventually led the White House to withdraw the nomination.

Another Reagan nominee, Joseph H. Rodriguez, met with a skeptical reception on the part of three conservative Republican senators on the Senate Judiciary Committee: John East of North Carolina, Jeremiah Denton of Alabama, and Orrin Hatch of Utah. Rodriguez was nominated in 1984 for a federal district court judgeship in New Jersey. He was recommended by the Republican governor, Thomas Kean, and would be the first hispanic to serve on the federal bench in New Jersey. Although Rodriguez was nominally a Democrat, he had taken a leadership role in Kean's election campaign. Rodriguez had a distinguished legal career, was a former president of the New Jersey Bar Association, was serving as public advocate of New Jersey at the time of his nomination, and was unanimously rated "exceptionally well qualified" by the ABA. Apparently East, Denton, and Hatch feared that the administration's rigorous screening process to sift out liberal judicial activists had failed with the Rodriguez nomination. These three senators devised an eight-page questionnaire, which they sent to Rodriguez, containing twenty-six questions designed to elicit in detail the nominee's views on a wide variety of issues, including abortion, affirmative action, equal rights for women, prayer in the public schools, the death penalty, various criminal-procedural guarantees, and school busing for the purpose of desegregating the public schools. In his answers Rodriguez cited Supreme Court decisions and pointedly noted, "A district judge is bound by oath to respect the authority of the Supreme Court and its interpretation of the Constitution."[61]

This questionnaire was sent apparently without the knowledge of Senate Judiciary Committee chairman Strom Thurmond. Members of the committee were angered. The administration was clearly embarrassed and claimed no advance knowledge of the questionnaire. The publicity was unfavorable, for the questionnaire seemed to give substance to the charge that nominees for federal judgeships were being given litmus tests of their views on matters of public policy. Hatch and his colleagues said that they were satisfied with the answers and understood that they could no longer use such a questionnaire. Later that year, at the confirmation hearing of Stephen Markman for assistant attorney general for legal policy, the nominee, who had been Hatch's chief counsel, conceded that the questionnaire had been inappropriate and that he regretted not having advised Hatch to disassociate himself from it.[62]

The administration's experience with Supreme Court nominations until 1987 had not prepared it for the explosive events surrounding the nomination of Robert Bork, who in 1982 had achieved easy confirmation to the Court of Appeals for the District of Columbia. Reagan's first Supreme Court nominee, Sandra Day O'Connor, had generated minimal opposition, and she was confirmed unanimously on September 21, 1981.[v] In 1986, Chief Justice Warren E. Burger announced his intent to retire at the end of the Court term. Reagan named Associate Justice William H. Rehnquist to succeed Burger and court of appeals judge Antonin Scalia to fill the associate justiceship to be made vacant by Rehnquist's elevation. There was some opposition to Rehnquist among Senate Democrats, and while the votes for confirmation were in hand, there was a Democratic filibuster to overcome. The filibuster, however, was broken by a vote of 68 to 31, and Rehnquist was confirmed on September 17, 1986, by a vote of 65 to 33. The president was appreciative and telephoned key supporters of Rehnquist.[w] Scalia's confirmation was smoother, and the confir-

v. Reagan had provided cover for Republican senators who needed it so that they could defend their support for O'Connor against the pressure from the right-to-life lobby. For example, Reagan wrote to Senator D'Amato about Sandra Day O'Connor: "May I assure you that your support for the nomination of Judge Sandra Day O'Connor . . . will not in any way be inconsistent with the [anti-abortion] commitments both of us made during our successful campaigns in 1980. . . . I am satisfied with her views on judicial philosophy and with her position with respect to the right-to-life issue." Ronald Reagan to Alfonse D'Amato, September 15, 1981, WHORM, FG 51, #033433, Ronald Reagan Library.

w. Reagan, following the advice of an aide, telephoned Senator Hatch to thank him "for his extraordinary efforts in the confirmation of the Chief Justice of the United States, William Rehnquist." The talking points included the following: "Orrin, I didn't want the day to go by without thanking you for your outstanding efforts in getting Justice Rehnquist confirmed last evening. . . . Thank you my friend." William L. Ball, III, to the

mation vote was unanimous. But the Bork nomination, coming after the Democrats had regained control of the Senate in 1986, was a different story.

Robert H. Bork had been a well-known Yale Law School professor, solicitor general from 1973 to 1977, and acting attorney general under President Nixon — at whose behest he had fired Watergate prosecutor Archibald Cox. He was serving on the District of Columbia appeals court when nominated for elevation. Bork had gained a reputation as an intellectually forceful judge who aggressively championed the judicial philosophy he shared with the Reagan administration. It is likely that Reagan chose Bork because he saw the judge as a conservative intellectual leader who with Scalia, O'Connor, and Rehnquist would provide a critical intellectual mass to push the Court down the path the president favored.

The events that followed Bork's nomination have been ably told by others.[63] The end result was that on October 23, 1987, the nomination went down to defeat on the floor of the Senate by a vote of 42 to 58. Reagan subsequently announced that he would name another conservative judge from the District of Columbia circuit, Douglas H. Ginsburg. The president began mobilizing support. In an extraordinary meeting, he gave the marching orders to his Cabinet.[x] But Ginsburg's nomination was never sent to the Senate, because support for the nominee quickly eroded when it was revealed that he had smoked marijuana while a professor at Harvard Law School. Anthony Kennedy, a Ninth Circuit judge, was subsequently nominated and, on February 3, 1988, unanimously confirmed.

The Bork defeat highlighted the new reality concerning judicial selection — that with the Democrats in control of the Senate Judiciary Committee, controversial nominees could run into trouble fatal to their nominations. This was brought home at the lower-court level with the relatively unpublicized nomination on February 2, 1987, of Bernard H. Siegan to the U.S. Court of Appeals

President, Recommended Telephone Call, September 18, 1986, WHORM, PR 7-02 (406300–406429), #406400, Ronald Reagan Library.

x. The suggested talking points for Reagan to make at the cabinet meeting to be held on November 2, 1987, included the following: "I'm going to need each and every one of you — in every possible forum — to find opportunities to counter the partisan political obstacles that the Democrats will throw at us. You will be given materials to add to your speeches; You will be asked to do op-ed pieces; and to look for television and radio opportunities. . . . But if the print news doesn't carry our side of the story, and if the managers of the congressional clock put our witnesses on at the end of the day, one way to beat them is to take every opportunity available to us to speak *personally* to people — here and around the country." Nancy J. Risque to the President, Cabinet Meeting, October 30, 1987, WHORM, FG 10-01 (506500–523599), #523592, Ronald Reagan Library.

for the Ninth Circuit. Siegan, a law professor at the University of San Diego, had written two provocative books whose constitutional views were deemed by his opponents as extremist, representing a selective activism in its advocacy of vigorous judicial protection of property rights but not civil rights and liberties.[64] His senatorial opponents failed to be satisfied by the answers Siegan gave during his confirmation hearing on November 5, 1987, and a follow-up hearing on February 25, 1988. Siegan told the committee that he would follow the Supreme Court and that his own views would be irrelevant to his judicial decisionmaking. Siegan's senatorial supporters claimed that once again a brilliant legal mind was being opposed because of politics. Close to a year and a half after he had been nominated, Siegan's nomination was rejected (on July 14, 1988) by the Senate Judiciary Committee by a vote of 8 to 6. The committee then decided, by a vote of 7 to 7, not to report the nomination to the full Senate. On September 16, the nomination was officially withdrawn.

One other appeals court nomination made in 1987 was subsequently withdrawn. Former Louisiana governor David C. Treen was nominated to the Fifth Circuit on July 22. The ABA unanimously rated him "qualified." But he proved to be controversial in part because of his past participation, like Ben Toledano's, in the Louisiana segregationist States' Rights Party.[65] Treen's nomination was withdrawn on May 10, 1988.

Six other people were nominated but not confirmed for positions on the appeals courts during Reagan's last two years in office. One nominee, New Yorker Stuart A. Summit, for the Second Circuit, came tantalizingly close to confirmation, having been cleared by the Senate Judiciary Committee on August 11, 1988. But Senator D'Amato apparently put a hold on the nomination, and it was not included in the last batch of nominees confirmed before the end of the 100th Congress. The hold on Summit may have been a form of payback to Summit's chief sponsor, Deputy Attorney General Arnold Burns (a former law partner of Summit's), who had left the Justice Department the previous April 23 and had let it be known that his resignation was in protest of the attorney general's unethical behavior.[66] The publicity surrounding the resignation (and for the same reason that of William Weld, the assistant attorney general for the criminal division) was intensely embarrassing for the administration and for the Republican Party in a presidential election year. It is plausible that Meese loyalists might have passed the word to D'Amato and other Republican senators.[y] Other appeals court nominations died because

y. Note that Meese announced on July 5, 1988, that by early August he would resign from the attorney generalship. He made this announcement after the independent counsel, James C. McKay, declined to prosecute him, although conceding that Meese "probably violated" the criminal law. *Congressional Quarterly Weekly Report* 46 (July 23, 1988): 2034.

Democrats wanted to wait for the presidential election results. After George Bush took office in 1989, he did not renominate Summit. (The slot went instead to Bush's first cousin, U.S. district judge John M. Walker.)

There were three nominations to the district courts in 1987 that went nowhere essentially because of senatorial opposition and were subsequently withdrawn. Robert N. Miller was nominated to a judgeship in Colorado on February 5, 1987, but one year later his nomination was withdrawn. Robert Roberto, Jr., was nominated on November 24, 1987, to a judgeship in the Eastern District of New York, but after damaging revelations his name was withdrawn on the following July 26.[z] Alfred C. Schmutzer was named on December 18, 1987, to the Eastern District of Tennessee, but three months later his nomination was withdrawn.

Nine nominations to the district bench during Reagan's last two years went unconfirmed and died with the end of the 100th Congress. One nominee, Vaughn R. Walker, was opposed by gay rights groups because he had successfully represented the United States Olympic Committee in its suit to prevent the use of the term *olympics* in the "Gay Olympics." California Democratic senator Alan Cranston opposed the nomination and during the 100th Congress, it was not voted on in the Senate Judiciary Committee. (Walker was renominated by Bush and confirmed in 1989.) Still another nominee, Pennsylvania state court judge James R. McGregor, slated for the Western District of Pennsylvania, went unconfirmed because he was too liberal for Republican senator Gordon J. Humphrey of New Hampshire, who obstructed the nomination.[67] This particular judgeship had been vacant since July 2, 1985, and it had taken the Reagan administration two and a half years of negotiation with the Pennsylvania senators (Republicans John Heinz and Arlen Specter) to achieve McGregor's nomination. The other nominees who did not make it were opposed for either political or ideological reasons.

Other Considerations in the Appointment Process

STATE REPRESENTATION

State claims to representation or to a particular position on the courts of appeals were made through Republican senators. Administration officials

---

z. Roberto was opposed for alleged political favoritism in one particular ruling as a judge. It was also revealed that in 1971, as chief of the vice squad in the Nassau County district attorney's office, and as part of an investigation, he followed orders to visit a massage parlor undercover. This was part of the evidence gathered against that establishment, but Roberto's participation now proved to be an embarrassment to him and the Reagan administration. *New York Times,* April 24, 1988, p. 31, and June 26, 1988, p. 24.

generally had little problem accommodating senators from the larger states, but a state with a small population was another matter. The saga of Republican senators Larry Pressler and James Abdnor of South Dakota to have a South Dakota native named to the Eighth Circuit illustrates this disparity.

On June 23, 1981, Senator Pressler wrote to President Reagan, pointing out that every state within the Eighth Circuit with the exception of South Dakota was represented on the bench. For more than two decades, no one from South Dakota had served on the court. In 1981, two states (Arkansas and Nebraska) within the circuit were each represented by two judges, and the other states (Iowa, Minnesota, Missouri, and North Dakota) were each represented by one. There was now a vacancy, and Pressler urged the president to select a nominee from South Dakota so as to "rectify its longstanding lack of representation and bring a proper geographic balance to this Court."[68]

White House aide Max L. Friedersdorf responded with a letter of acknowledgement on July 8, but clearly a more substantive reply was warranted. A response was worked out by Fielding and sent to Friedersdorf, who then replied to Pressler, pointing out that the existing vacancy was created by the retirement of a Missouri judge, Floyd Gibson: "While there is no requirement that the next individual appointed to the Eighth Circuit be from Missouri, geographic representation is an important consideration in reviewing these appointments. This is particularly so as a growing percentage of cases in the Eighth Circuit originate in the Missouri District Courts. At the same time your letter struck a responsive chord." Friedersdorf promised that "your request will be given serious consideration in filling future vacancies on the Eighth Circuit."[69]

What Pressler did not know was that the administration had decided to move ahead with a highly qualified woman from Missouri, Judith Whittaker. But when Whittaker's name surfaced as the likely nominee, right-wing groups mobilized to oppose her. When Pressler got wind of these developments, he wrote to the president on December 2: "I am informed by knowledgeable individuals in my state and elsewhere in the circuit that questions as to judicial philosophy and courtroom experience are being raised as to the nomination currently under consideration." Pressler did not mention Whittaker by name or acknowledge that she was a woman. He then went on to make a pitch for a South Dakotan to fill the circuit vacancy and suggested the names of eighteen *men*, including federal district court judges, state court judges, and even the governor of South Dakota. Pressler in a subsequent letter to Reagan offered the name of a woman attorney from South Dakota.[70] The vacancy, however, was filled by a Missourian, John R. Gibson.

On March 15, 1982, Eighth Circuit judge J. Smith Henley informed Reagan of his intention to retire from active service at the end of May. Henley noted in his letter that at the end of February he had informally advised the deputy attorney general and selected members of the Arkansas congressional delegation of his plans, and that he urged them to replace him with someone from Arkansas. Four days earlier, U.S. district judge Henry Woods of Arkansas wrote a letter ("Dear Ed") to Meese apprising him of Henley's plans and noting that "it would seem logical that his [Henley's] replacement might well come from our state."[71] Woods recommended the chief judge for the Eastern District of Arkansas, G. Thomas Eisele. Arkansas, however, had two Democratic senators, so the administration had much more flexibility in choosing the state from which to make the appointment.[aa]

The South Dakota senators found out about Henley's plans even before Henley had written to Reagan. They recognized an opportunity and wrote a joint letter to Reagan on March 10 in which they reminded the president that they had "received assurances from the Justice Department that when another vacancy occurred in the Circuit, South Dakota candidates would be included in the selection process."[72] They emphasized that "South Dakota is long overdue for representation."

But again, the South Dakota senators were disappointed. The administration set its sights on Pasco M. Bowman II, dean of the University of Missouri–Kansas City School of Law, a recently transplanted southerner (former dean of the Wake Forest School of Law) and an extremely conservative Republican. His appointment would mean that Missouri would have a third representative on the circuit. This distressed Senator Pressler, and he wrote to Reagan, "I have been very frustrated by the lack of consideration we have been given by this Administration."[73] Pressler ended by appealing to Reagan to appoint someone from South Dakota, and he offered to provide names of qualified South Dakotans.

---

aa. About this same time, another vacancy arose on the Eighth Circuit. Iowa's Republican senators Charles E. Grassley and Roger W. Jepsen wrote to Meese ("Dear Ed") advising him that the Iowa representative on the Eighth Circuit, Judge Roy Stephenson, would be taking senior status effective on April 1. The senators attached a memo in which they emphasized their strong desire to replace an Iowan with an Iowan. They revealed that they had contacted the Iowa Bar Association for its help in reviewing the applications of individuals who were interested in filling the position. The senators ended their memo by noting, "We look forward to working with the White House in selecting a qualified Iowan for this vacancy." Grassley and Jepsen to Meese, March 19, 1982, with attached memo, WHORM, FG 52 (06330–074477), #067045, Ronald Reagan Library. Indeed, the position was filled by an Iowan, state judge George G. Fagg, who was nominated on September 22, 1982, and confirmed ten days later.

Senator Abdnor also wrote to Reagan, but he was more blunt:

> I object strenuously to this nomination [of Bowman] and want you to know that several of my colleagues and I will be placing a "hold" on it should it come before the Senate for confirmation.
>
> South Dakota has not been represented on this court for 22 years. . . . When the last vacancy occurred about 18 months ago, South Dakota argued its case vigorously, but the appointment went to another Missourian. The South Dakota law profession, its representatives in Congress and the people of our state find it unacceptable that another Missourian is slated to fill the latest vacancy.[74]

Abdnor noted that the Justice Department had submitted to the White House (he presumably meant the Federal Judicial Selection Committee) a list of five acceptable candidates, including two from South Dakota, but the White House had selected Bowman. Abdnor concluded by urging Reagan to overturn the recommendation of Bowman as the nominee "because it is quite likely that he will never be confirmed by the Senate."

Abdnor's threat was taken very seriously by the administration, and it responded in two ways. First, the Republican leadership in the Senate changed the rules so that (as Senator Abdnor told one of the rejected South Dakota candidates) "one no longer can place a 'hold' on a member of the Judiciary from another state."[75] Second, the administration promised the South Dakota senators that "South Dakota will get the next vacancy." After the rule change, Bowman was nominated and, on July 18, 1983, confirmed.

In 1984, a new judgeships bill was enacted that provided for twenty-four new circuit court positions, including a new position for the Eighth Circuit. After some prodding, the administration kept its word, and Roger L. Wollman, a justice on the South Dakota supreme court rated "exceptionally well qualified" by the ABA, was nominated on June 25, 1985, and confirmed July 19.

State representation was also a serious matter for senators in regard to the distribution of new judgeships. With twenty-four new circuit judgeships created in 1984, the potential for battling over the spoils was great. For example, the Fifth Circuit, consisting of Texas, Louisiana, and Mississippi, gained two new judgeships. Almost immediately after enactment of the new law, Mississippi Republican senator Thad Cochran wrote to Reagan, claiming one of the new positions for Mississippi and arguing that Texas, which already held eight of the fourteen old judgeships, dominated the circuit and should not be allotted even one of the new seats: "The allocation of the two new positions to the States of Mississippi and Louisiana . . . would create a more regionally balanced Court and assure that the administration of justice in the Fifth Circuit continues to be free of the taint of local interests."[76]

The Louisiana senators, both Democrats, wrote to the president, arguing that since Louisiana was responsible for more than one third of the caseload of the Fifth Circuit, it should have at least one third of the seats on the court. That would mean at least one of the new judgeships.[77] What happened, however, was that the administration determined that both seats should go to Texas! Edith H. Jones was nominated on September 17, 1984, and resubmitted to the new Congress on February 27, 1985. She was confirmed the following April 3. But the second new seat on the Fifth proved more troublesome to fill with the administration's preferred candidate, Lino Graglia, to be discussed later in the chapter. The judgeship was not filled until June 2, 1987, when Texan Jerry E. Smith was nominated. More than six months later he was finally confirmed.

The potency of state representation, and the expectation that the state from which a vacancy arises will be the one from which the replacement will be chosen, is attested to by the fact that of the forty-seven circuit judges on the numbered circuits (excluding the District of Columbia Circuit) who were appointed by Reagan to fill a vacancy created by death or retirement, forty-two (89 percent) were from the same state as the person the new judge replaced.

AMERICAN BAR ASSOCIATION

The American Bar Association Standing Committee on Federal Judiciary was a part of the judicial selection process of the Reagan administration but, just as in the Carter administration, it was kept at arm's length. Only one name at a time was given to the ABA committee for evaluation. The name given was the one agreed upon by the working group.[78] The ABA committee was asked first to make an informal report, which had the benefit of alerting the administration to any potential problem with the candidate that the administration's own screening process had not uncovered. The FBI investigation likewise took place during this time. Assuming that nothing unexpectedly negative surfaced from either the ABA's informal report or the FBI's investigation, the ABA was then asked for a formal report.

Unlike previous administrations, the Reagan administration did not always wait for the ABA's formal report before the attorney general sent over the official recommendation and nomination documents. For example, in the official letter of recommendation to President Reagan concerning Richard J. Cardamone for a Second Circuit judgeship, Attorney General Smith wrote: "The Standing Committee on Federal Judiciary of the American Bar Association has submitted an informal report which states the Committee's opinion that Justice Cardamone is well qualified for appointment to this position."[79]

Sometimes the administration did not even wait for an informal report from the ABA. On July 27 and 28, 1984, Acting Attorney General Carol E. Dinkins, apparently with the go-ahead from Smith and Fielding, sent letters and nomination documents to the president in the absence of ABA reports for six appeals court nominees. The wording relating to the ABA in each letter was identical. For example, the letter to the president for Emory M. Sneeden for a position on the Fourth Circuit read: "The Standing Committee on Federal Judiciary of the American Bar Association is expected to furnish, in the very near future, its report on the qualifications of General Sneeden for appointment to this position. We will inform you immediately upon its receipt."[80] Although soon each of these nominees received a positive rating by the ABA, about a year and a half earlier the administration had gone ahead and nominated someone in the absence of an ABA rating who then received a negative rating.

Sherman E. Unger, general counsel for the Department of Commerce, was recommended to serve on the U.S. Court of Appeals for the Federal Circuit, a court of specialized jurisdiction. The letter from Attorney General Smith to President Reagan did not include the ABA rating, and by way of explanation Smith wrote in words identical to those the acting attorney general would later use.[81]

Unger was nominated on December 15, 1982, two days after the letter from the attorney general's office was dated. The ABA unanimously rated Unger "not qualified." The nomination died at the end of the Ninety-seventh Congress, but the administration renominated Unger on April 21, 1983. The hesitancy no doubt reflected some administration concern whether to buck the ABA. Nevertheless, the Republican-controlled Senate Judiciary Committee and Senate Democrats conducted their own investigations of Unger, and extensive hearings were held on five days over a three-month period. Brooksley Born, the chair of the ABA committee, and William T. Coleman, Jr., the member of the committee with responsibility for investigating Unger, testified that Unger was not qualified "because he lacked the personal integrity and judicial temperament required of a federal judge." They offered concrete examples that allegedly supported the committee's rating. Unger, however, had many supporters who attested to his personal integrity, including Democrats from the Carter administration — former White House counsel Lloyd Cutler and former attorney general Griffin Bell.[82] The Senate Judiciary Committee took no action on the nomination, undoubtedly because the senators were informed that Unger had been diagnosed as terminally ill with cancer. Unger died on December 3, 1983, close to a year from the day he was first nominated.

Unger is the only example of the administration's nominating an individual rated "not qualified" by the ABA. The administration clearly was concerned with winning ABA approval, particularly for appeals court nominees who would likely be controversial.

One example concerns J. Harvie Wilkinson III, first nominated on November 10, 1983, to be a judge on the Fourth Circuit. He was renominated January 30, 1984, during the first weeks of the new session of Congress. Wilkinson, a thirty-nine-year-old law professor at the University of Virginia, had begun an academic career at Virginia, taken three years off to serve as editorial-page editor of the *Norfolk Virginia-Pilot,* served in 1982 and 1983 as a deputy assistant attorney general in the Civil Rights Division of the Justice Department, and returned to the University of Virginia in the fall of 1983. Wilkinson's family was close to Justice Lewis Powell, for whom Wilkinson had clerked during the 1972–1973 term; he later wrote a well-received book about Justice Powell and his own experience as a law clerk. The Wilkinson candidacy originated with the Justice Department. Wilkinson was not among the persons suggested to the administration by Virginia's Republican senator, John Warner, although Warner agreed to support the nomination.[83]

The problem with Wilkinson was that he had never had a private client and never tried a case in a court of law (although he once had argued a motion before a court). Furthermore, he was clearly not in the legal profession during the three years in which he worked as an editorial writer; thus he had only eight years of legal practice, well below the criterion of twelve years of trial experience that the ABA committee considered necessary to earn a "qualified" rating. Yet a majority of the ABA committee voted to rate Wilkinson "qualified," although a minority found him "not qualified."

Justice Powell revealed that one of the members of the ABA committee had asked him to call another member to convey his strong backing of Wilkinson. Powell had made the call, later telling a reporter, "I have no apologies whatsoever." Deputy Attorney General Schmults and Assistant Attorney General Rose had also contacted members of the committee before the ABA committee vote was taken. Representatives of minority and women's groups were outraged at what they saw as the double standard of the ABA by which women and minorities with more trial experience than Wilkinson but fewer than twelve years of legal practice had been rated "not qualified" by the ABA, and these groups so testified at the confirmation hearing for Wilkinson on February 22, 1984. They also questioned Wilkinson's commitment to civil rights and equal opportunity.[84] Senator Edward M. Kennedy led the attack on the ABA and on Wilkinson. Conservative Republican senators supported Wilkinson but also lashed out at the ABA, recalling ABA opposition to Sherman Unger.

On March 15, the Senate Judiciary Committee, by a vote of 12 to 4, recommended Wilkinson to the Senate for confirmation. The following August, Senator Kennedy conducted a filibuster, hoping to kill the nomination. Cloture, however, was invoked, and Wilkinson was confirmed on August 9 by a vote of 58 to 39.

Clearly, had the administration (with the help of Justice Powell) not successfully lobbied for a "qualified" rating for Wilkinson, the nomination would have been doomed. Another law professor, Lino Graglia of the University of Texas Law School, did not fare as well. His candidacy, despite the persistent efforts of the administration, failed to win ABA approval, and ultimately Graglia was dropped from consideration.

Graglia had actively opposed school busing for the purpose of desegregation. In 1979, in response to a federal court order requiring busing, he suggested that there be no voluntary compliance and that Texas officials should "publicly take the position that they [court orders] ought not to be enforced." Graglia was also the author of a book that severely criticized the Supreme Court's public-school desegregation decisions. The ABA told the administration that Graglia would be found "not qualified" for a position on the Fifth Circuit. There were many similarities to the Toledano candidacy (also for a Fifth Circuit judgeship). But Attorney General Meese was unwilling to let go of the Graglia candidacy and instead asked former attorney general Griffin Bell to investigate Graglia and report back to the Justice Department. Bell agreed and eventually submitted a report, after which Graglia was dropped from consideration.[85]

The ABA committee had angered liberals by, among other actions, giving "qualified" ratings to Manion and Wilkinson. The committee had annoyed the administration and Republicans in the Senate with its opposition to Sherman Unger and to several other candidates for judgeships, including Lino Graglia. Republican displeasure reached a peak when the ABA committee failed to unanimously recommend Robert Bork as "well qualified" for the Supreme Court, with four members of the committee finding Bork "not qualified." Liberals and conservatives in the Senate were thus joined in their opposition to the ABA committee, and the Senate Judiciary Committee decided that it would hold a hearing devoted to the ABA committee and its role in the confirmation process.[bb] Liberal and conservative interest groups also joined forces in a suit

---

bb. The hearing was held early in the Bush administration. See, *The ABA Role in the Judicial Nomination Process,* Hearing Before the Senate Judiciary Committee, 101st Congress, 1st Session, June 2, 1989, Serial No. J-101-20 (Washington, D.C.: Government

against the Justice Department and the ABA for violating the Federal Advisory Committee Act, which requires advisory committees to the federal government to hold meetings open to the public and to maintain records available for public inspection. The suit was eventually decided in favor of the ABA by the Supreme Court.^{cc}

ETHNICITY

The Reagan presidential papers suggest that the administration was aware of ethnicity in the selection process. Italian Americans on a number of occasions pressed for the appointment of Italian Americans to the federal bench. For example, Antonin Scalia was pushed for consideration for a circuit court position on the District of Columbia Circuit by the president of the National Italian American Foundation. New Mexico Republican senator Pete V. Domenici also wrote to Reagan recommending Scalia and pointedly noted that "the selection of Mr. Scalia, an Italian American, would result in significant approval by the Italian-American community of this Nation." Scalia was appointed, although his ethnic background was probably a plus rather than a determining factor. After nominating Scalia to the Supreme Court four years

---

Printing Office, 1991). During the hearing, Attorney General Dick Thornburgh revealed that after negotiations, the ABA had agreed to "delete any reference to consideration of *political or ideological philosophy* from its description of the Committee's role and would henceforth confine the Committee's role to evaluation of *professional qualifications — integrity, competence, and judicial temperament.*" *ABA Role,* 8. The president of the ABA also told the Senate Judiciary Committee that in deference to Senate concerns and to those of the Bush administration, the ABA would no longer use the "exceptionally well qualified" rating. The only ratings to be used would be "well qualified," "qualified," and "not qualified." *ABA Role,* 114.

cc. The decision was rendered in *Public Citizen* v. *U.S. Dept. of Justice,* 491 U.S. 440 (1989). The Court determined that the Federal Advisory Committee Act (FACA, the so-called "open meeting" law) does not apply to the Justice Department's solicitation of the ABA committee's views on prospective judicial nominees. The Court found that Congress did not intend to subject to the requirements of FACA a group such as the ABA committee, which was not formed by or at the instigation of the federal government and which does not receive government funds. Furthermore, construing FACA to apply to the Justice Department's relationship with the ABA committee would present formidable constitutional problems, including infringing on the president's Article II power to nominate federal judges, thus violating the separation-of-powers doctrine. Since it was plausible to interpret the intent of Congress as not meaning to apply FACA to the ABA committee, the Court chose that alternative rather than reach the constitutional issues. There was no dissent.

later, Reagan publicly took credit, in his words, for "the first Italian-American to be nominated to the Supreme Court in history."[86]

When Italian Americans were appointed to the lower courts, it was not unusual for the telephone memorandum for Reagan to mention this. For example, the telephone memo concerning Judge Leroy J. Contie, Jr., noted: "Judge Contie was enthusiastically endorsed by many Italian organizations and is a member of the Sons of Italy." And the nominees themselves were not without ethnic consciousness. For example, when Richard I. Cardamone was appointed to the Second Circuit, he wrote to the president: "I . . . happen to be the first person of Italian ancestry to serve as a member of the 180-year-old Second Circuit."[87]

The resumes prepared by the Justice Department that accompanied the nomination documents sent by the attorney general to the president contained the category "Ethnic Group" (following the Carter administration's practice of including such designations as "hispanic," "black," "Asian," and "white"). For example, the resume for Juan R. Torruella listed his ethnic group as "hispanic." Judge Torruella was named to the First Circuit. Among those who recommended him was Luis A. Ferre, the Republican state chairman for Puerto Rico and the member for Puerto Rico on the Republican National Committee. In his letter to Reagan, Ferre noted that the appointment of Torruella would provide the "unique opportunity" to name someone "intellectually supportive of the administration and at the same time would allow you to appoint the first Hispanic to the [First Circuit] bench."[88]

The administration had an active interest in the appointment of hispanics. For example, Meese received a letter from a friend recommending a state judge of hispanic ethnicity for a federal district court position in California. Meese handwrote on the copy of the reply to which he attached the original letter: "John Herrington [assistant to the president for personnel] Hispanic — What do you know/think?"[89] The candidate, Edward Garcia, was in fact appointed to the California federal bench.

During the two terms of Reagan's presidency, fifteen hispanics were named to the bench (fourteen to the district courts and one to the appeals bench).[dd] In absolute numbers, Reagan's record was just one appointment shy of the Carter record of sixteen hispanics appointed to the lower federal courts.

Reagan named two Asian Americans to the district bench (in Hawaii and California) but none to the appeals courts.

---

dd. Hispanics were named to the bench in Puerto Rico and California, Florida, Indiana, Michigan, New Jersey, Rhode Island, and Texas.

Women and Judgeships

The Reagan administration was at cross-purposes when it came to the appointment of women as well as minorities. Reagan was philosophically opposed to affirmative action, yet he also wanted to remove barriers and open opportunities to groups of Americans long denied entry to the federal judiciary. This contradiction came across in his address to the American Bar Association convention on August 1, 1983. In his talk, Reagan stressed: "[W]e will never select individuals just because they are men or women, whites or blacks, Jews, Catholics or whatever. I don't look at people as members of groups; I look at them as individuals and as Americans." But then Reagan pointed to his having placed Sandra Day O'Connor on the Supreme Court: "When an opening appeared on this nation's highest court, I selected the person I believed the most outstanding candidate. I'm proud that for the first time in our history, a woman, named Sandra Day O'Connor, now sits on the Supreme Court of the United States. But I'm proudest of this appointment not because Justice O'Connor is a woman, but because she is so well qualified."[90]

At the time of her appointment, Sandra Day O'Connor was known in her home state of Arizona but few outside her home state had heard of her. It would be difficult to demonstrate that she was "the most outstanding" man or woman available in the entire country, or even that she was one of the many legal stars of the nation. Other women jurists were better known, but she clearly was bright and talented. O'Connor's appointment was obviously due to affirmative action. Reagan went on to state what was fundamentally an affirmative action position: "We're committed to appointing outstanding blacks, Hispanics, and women to judicial and top-level policymaking positions in our administration."

The administration's schizophrenic attitude concerning women played itself out frequently. The administration was publicly committed to gender equality. The president signed Executive Order 12336 on December 21, 1981, establishing the Task Force on Legal Equity for Women. Its stated purpose was "to provide for the systematic elimination of regulatory and procedural barriers which have unfairly precluded women from receiving equal treatment from Federal activities."[ee] The president made good on his campaign promise to

ee. The Task Force members, drawn from each of the Cabinet-level departments and major federal agencies, were charged with "coordinating and facilitating in their respective agencies, under the direction of the head of their agency, the implementation of changes ordered by the President in sex-discriminatory Federal regulations, policies, and practices."

Reagan's Executive Order revoked Jimmy Carter's Executive Order 12135 that had

appoint a woman to the Supreme Court. Furthermore, the administration on other occasions actively sought out women for judgeships. For example, in response to a June 23, 1982, letter from the Ohio Republican congressional delegation to Reagan concerning a vacancy in their state, presidential assistant Ken Duberstein wrote each of the Ohio members of Congress a letter in which he reminded them: "As White House Counsel Fred Fielding indicated in his June 15 letter to you, we have asked for your help in identifying qualified candidates who share the President's judicial philosophy. With regard to the vacancy on the Northern Ohio District Court, we have also indicated that *we are particularly interested in the Delegation's recommendation of women candidates for the President to consider.*"[91] Alice Batchelder received the appointment.

Another instance of the administration's interest in women candidates occurred with the nomination of U.S. Tax Court judge Cynthia Holcolm Hall to the federal district bench in California. Hall had been strongly recommended by Elizabeth H. Dole, a member of the White House staff (assistant to the president for public liaison) and wife of Senate majority leader Bob Dole. As Jonathan Rose noted in a memo: "Department of Justice received letters of recommendation for Judge Hall's appointment to the District Court from Elizabeth H. Dole, Darrell Trent, and Carla Hills." Hall had not yet been cleared by California Republican senator S. I. Hayakawa, but Elizabeth Dole had written to him that "Judge Hall is a conservative judge who believes in judicial restraint—interpreting the laws, not making them."[92] Senator Hayakawa eventually came on board, and Hall was nominated and confirmed. She was later elevated to the Ninth Circuit by George Bush.

One of the most troubling episodes concerning the Reagan administration and the selection of women to the judiciary involved the candidacy of Judith Whittaker to the Eighth Circuit. Whittaker, associate general counsel of Hall-

---

established the President's Advisory Committee for Women that had a much broader mandate "to promote equality for women in the cultural, social, economic, and political life" of the country. Press Release, May 9, 1979, *Public Papers of the Presidents: Jimmy Carter, 1979*, vol. 1 (Washington, D.C.: Government Printing Office, 1980), 826. In some respects, Reagan's executive order seemed to be a retreat on women's rights, but from the perspective of the administration it eliminated the wide-ranging feminist agenda and focused on achievable short-range goals—ensuring that federal regulations present and future do not discriminate on the basis of gender. The Task Force on Legal Equity for Women in fact reported to the Cabinet Council on Legal Policy, and the reports were on the agendas of council meetings, which at times were presided over by the President. See, for example, WHORM, FG 10-02, #077506 (9/30/82), #077792 (2/10/83), #168885 (1/16/84), #168909 (2/14/84), #255047 (8/30/84), Ronald Reagan Library.

mark Cards in Kansas City, came from a prominent Republican family—her father-in-law was former Supreme Court justice Charles E. Whittaker. She was one of five persons from Missouri recommended by Republican senator John Danforth to the administration in the spring of 1981.

At first, Whittaker seemed to be on track to a nomination. Jonathan Rose recommended that she be named to the Eighth Circuit seat. In a memo dated July 14 he noted: "I have personally interviewed her and found her to possess common sense, be aware of women's issues but not radical, and feel she is one of the best qualified women available for our consideration." Rose also observed, "She is a Republican."[93]

Reagan's judicial selection committee discussed Whittaker at its July 23 meeting and decided that more work had to be done before going ahead with the nomination. As Fielding wrote in his notes, Whittaker's nomination was to "continue 1 wk." Apparently, consultation within the White House, probably with Meese, convinced Fielding that Whittaker's name should be eliminated, and at the July 30 meeting the committee agreed to drop her as a candidate.[94]

Supporters of Whittaker then mounted an intense campaign on her behalf. Her candidacy was embraced by prominent women. In a letter to Reagan, Republican congresswoman Claudine Schneider from Rhode Island pointed out that Whittaker had been graduated first in her class at the University of Missouri Law School and was a distinguished member of the legal profession. "Further," wrote Schneider, "she possesses a strong background as a Republican . . . [and] has long engaged in Party activities in Kansas City."[95]

Whittaker was considered again by the working group, but there was hesitation within the administration, with opponents of Whittaker calling into question her Republican credentials. On August 18, Rose wrote a strongly supportive memo in which he pointed out: "There have been some questions raised concerning Ms. Whittaker's party affiliation but Ms. Whittaker has the support of Senator Danforth, Mayor Berkley of Kansas City, and several prominent Republican businessmen in Missouri."[96]

In late August, Fielding was alerted that "there has been a large increase in conservative Republican support in Missouri for this appointment" and that Fielding's office had received some thirty letters from leading lawyers in Missouri supporting Whittaker. Finally, at its September 3 meeting, the working group decided to go ahead with Whittaker. They authorized FBI and ABA investigations, with the presumption that Whittaker would be nominated in the absence of unexpected negative and disqualifying results. To answer the charge that she was not really a Republican, the committee agreed that an aide would check on her voter registration and report back to the Justice Department. As one informed individual later put it, "they [the FBI and ABA] found

Mrs. Whittaker to have exemplary qualifications." [ff] Indeed, the ABA reported Whittaker to be "well qualified." The nomination papers were prepared and sent to the White House in early November, and Whittaker was told by the Justice Department that her appointment would be announced in a matter of days. But Whittaker was never nominated.[97]

What had happened was that as the FBI and ABA were conducting their investigations, extremely conservative Republicans within and outside of Missouri mounted an intense campaign to keep Whittaker from being nominated. Richard Viguerie, a right-wing activist, attacked Whittaker in his newsletter, *New Right,* as a pro-abortion "strong feminist." [98] Viguerie and other New Right leaders orchestrated a letter-writing campaign in opposition to Whittaker. The nature and scope of the anti-Whittaker campaign come through in a letter that Terry E. Branstad, the lieutenant governor of Iowa, wrote to Reagan on October 14:

> It has just been called to my attention that there is a possibility of you appointing Judith Whitaker [*sic*] to the Eighth District [*sic*] Court of Appeals. I have been told that she is a liberal democrat and a pro-abortionist. A number of my constituents are very concerned and upset about this possibility. I certainly hope that Judith Whitaker will not be appointed to this position as it would be a real blow to some of your most ardent and active supporters here in the states covered by the Eighth Circuit.[99][gg]

ff. That informed individual was the chief judge of the Eighth Circuit, Donald P. Lay, who was alarmed by the fact that it had taken so long to fill the vacancy on the bench (over two years). He was upset that the position was just about to be filled by Whittaker when sudden, intense right-wing opposition emerged, causing Whittaker to be dropped. The quotation is from a letter Lay wrote to Senator Edward Zorinsky, which Lay widely distributed, recounting the problems of filling the vacancy and imploring all concerned to expedite the filling of vacancies. Donald P. Lay to Edward Zorinsky, December 29, 1981, WHORM, FG 52 (054000–057999), #055046, p. 2, Ronald Reagan Library. In that letter the judge also wrote, "Mrs. Whittaker has appeared before our court, and is an outstanding lawyer possessing the qualities to become a great and gifted judge."

gg. Not only did Branstad misspell Whittaker's name and misname the court to which she was about to be nominated; he was also seriously misinformed about the candidate. Whittaker was not a member of the Democratic Party, nor was she known to be "liberal." It is true that she had supported the Equal Rights Amendment, but she had never taken a public position on abortion. *New York Times,* December 24, 1981, B4. Her position on the Equal Rights Amendment was identical to that of the Republican Party platform of 1976 and earlier years. The 1976 platform stated unequivocally: "The Republican Party affirms its support for the ratification of the Equal Rights Amendment. Our Party was the first national party to endorse the E.R.A. in 1940. We continue to believe its ratification is

Branstad's letter was brought to the attention of White House chief of staff James A. Baker III, who was informed by a White House aide: "You should also know that [Republican Iowa] Senator Roger W. Jepsen met with [White House aide] Max Friedersdorf on Friday, October 23rd regarding Judge Whitaker's [sic] candidacy. In addition to the concerns raised above [in Branstad's letter], the Senator indicated that history and tradition dictate that this vacancy on the Court of Appeals go to an Iowan."[100]

In November, the administration put the Whittaker nomination on hold. Within weeks, the prospective nomination was dropped because, in the words of the deputy attorney general, she lacked enough "broad-based support." Jonathan Rose later looked back on the Whittaker affair: "We all thought Whittaker was a fully qualified and excellent lawyer, and we recommended her. She was found *well qualified* by the ABA, but she ran into considerable political opposition in the home state. I never fully knew where that opposition came from, or why it was as strong as it was."[101]

Eighth Circuit chief judge Donald Lay, referring to the right-wing attack on Whittaker, wrote: "It is incredible to me and my colleagues [on the Eighth Circuit] that such an attack can be effective so late in the day." Newspaper editorials deplored the administration's decision. The *Kansas City Star's* editorial was entitled "Shabby Assault on Judicial Nominee." The *New York Times* had as its headline "Political Snipers and a Good Judge."[102]

Attempts were made to have the administration reconsider the Whittaker nomination. The bipartisan congresswomen's caucus wrote to Reagan urging that the Whittaker nomination be revived. The letter stressed that "[t]he opposition to the appointment is based largely on rumor and innuendo." Reagan was reminded that only one woman had been nominated to a lower-court judgeship during his first year in office. Republicans from the National Women's Political Caucus attempted a last-minute campaign on behalf of Whittaker, but it came too late.[103]

There is some evidence that the administration was "interested in receiving recommendations of qualified women to fill the vacancy," as Senator Pressler put it in his letter recommending a South Dakota woman for the position. But the reality was that there was not enough time to start from scratch, and it was necessary to move quickly to prevent the situation from deteriorating further. In mid-January, the Justice Department recommended John R. Gibson. Barely a half year earlier, Gibson had been named to the federal district bench in

essential to insure equal rights for all Americans." *Congressional Quarterly Almanac 94th Congress, 2nd Session, 1976* (Washington, D.C.: Congressional Quarterly, 1976), 908.

Missouri, although he had also been on Senator Danforth's list as a possible Eighth Circuit appointment. That meant that Gibson had recently passed FBI and ABA scrutiny, already had the backing of Senator Danforth, and was clearly someone who could be confirmed rapidly. Gibson's nomination was sent to the Senate on February 2, and he was confirmed on March 4. Fielding, in response to a member of Congress's inquiry on behalf of a constituent about Judith Whittaker, wrote: "Please be assured that the administration remains committed to the appointment of qualified women to positions on the Federal Bench."[104]

When the Reagan presidency came to an end, his record with regard to the appointment of women to lifetime positions on federal courts of general jurisdiction stood at one woman to the Supreme Court, four to the appeals courts (one each to the Third and Ninth circuits, which were elevations of Reagan-appointed district judges, and one each to the Fifth and Tenth circuits), and twenty-four to the district bench. This represented a considerable drop from the record of the Carter administration but was superior to that of every president before Carter.[hh] The Reagan administration appointed women to the lower federal bench from sixteen states.[ii]

AFRICAN AMERICANS AND JUDGESHIPS

The Reagan administration was conscious of race. It continued the Carter administration practice of indicating racial background on the biographical resumes of judicial candidates. When at the beginning of his fourth year in office Reagan nominated John R. Hargrove, his first appointment of an African American to the district bench, the telephone memorandum pointed out: "Judge Hargrove will be your first nomination of a Black to a *District* Court seat; you have only appointed one other Black to the Federal bench and that was Lawrence Pierce to serve on the Second *Circuit* Court of Appeals."[105] The Reagan administration appointed the first African Americans ever to serve in the southern states of Mississippi and Virginia, thus completing the task begun by Carter of desegregating the federal district bench in the south.

hh. Note that Reagan appointed two women to the U.S. Court of Appeals for the Federal Circuit and one each to the Court of International Trade and the U.S. Claims Court, lifetime positions on courts of specialized jurisdiction. Nominations of four other women (one to the district bench, two to appeals courts of general jurisdiction, and one to the Federal Circuit) were not acted upon by the Senate.

ii. Women were appointed to the federal district bench in California, Delaware, Florida, Illinois, Indiana, Michigan, New Jersey, New York, Ohio, Pennsylvania, South Carolina, Tennessee, Washington, and West Virginia.

Overall, however, the Reagan record of appointing blacks was the worst since the Eisenhower administration. In eight years Reagan named seven African Americans to the federal bench.[jj] Nixon and Ford in their eight years had named nine. Carter surpassed every president until Bill Clinton and made thirty-seven appointments of African Americans to the federal bench.

Reagan's record of relatively few appointments of women and minorities was the subject of a Senate Judiciary Committee hearing in 1988, when the committee had returned to Democratic control. Senator Kennedy, presiding over the February 2 hearing, pointed out that every one of the fourteen persons named by Reagan to the federal bench in the District of Columbia was a white male, even though there were over ten thousand women attorneys and three thousand black and hispanic attorneys practicing in the district. He particularly emphasized the administration's overall poor record of appointing African Americans. Stephen J. Markman, assistant attorney general for legal policy, responded in testimony: "Nothing would please us more to find more qualified black and minority candidates in this process. It is not easy, however. There simply is not the pool. . . . [T]here is just not even a respectably small pool of black lawyers of suitable age, in suitable career positions, with any kind of Republican background, with some affinity for the President's philosophy."[106]

The hurdles the administration placed on appointing blacks, which were also the same hurdles placed on others, virtually guaranteed that few would be selected. But there was at least one instance when a black who would seem to have met the administration's criteria was nevertheless not chosen.[kk] Whatever the reasons may have been, actions did not follow from good intentions when it came to the appointment of African Americans. Clearly the appointment of African Americans was not seen as furthering the partisan agenda.

jj. African Americans were appointed to federal district judgeships in Illinois, Maryland, Mississippi, Pennsylvania, Texas, and Virginia.

kk. African American Stephen Lloyd Maxwell applied for a federal district court position in Minnesota. He was a state judge who had previously been an assistant county attorney and later corporation counsel for the city of St. Paul. He had been active in Republican politics, had run for Congress in 1966 and had been a member of the Minnesota Republican State Central Committee and the Republican National Committee's Negro Advisory Group. Maxwell was one of five persons recommended by a Minnesota merit selection panel. Fred F. Fielding files, CFOA Box 425, President's Federal Judicial Selection Committee Meeting—June 18, 1981 (2), Ronald Reagan Library. He was considered but then rejected by the judicial selection committee at its June 18 meeting. United States District Judges, Candidates Not Selected, Fred F. Fielding files, CFOA Box 425, President's Federal Judicial Selection Committee Meeting—June 18, 1981 (2).

The Demographic Portrait of Reagan's Judges

Ronald Reagan in his two terms of office appointed three associate justices and one chief justice of the United States Supreme Court, seventy-eight appeals court judges, and 290 district court judges.[ll] In total, Reagan filled 372 out of 736 lifetime positions on federal courts of general jurisdiction, an historic record. The 372 appointments, however, included eighteen elevations to the appeals courts of district judges originally appointed by Reagan,[mm] one elevation to the Supreme Court of an appeals judge (Antonin Scalia) earlier appointed by Reagan, and seven judges who either retired, resigned, or died during the Reagan years. When Ronald Reagan left office in 1989, his judicial legacy was 346, or 47 percent of the judges in active service on Article III courts of general jurisdiction. The record number of Reagan appointments was helped by the enactment in 1984 of the Judgeships Bill, which created eighty-five new positions (twenty-four to the appeals courts and sixty-one to the district bench). Table 8.1 offers the demographic profile of the Reagan appointees during his first term, when William French Smith was attorney general, as compared to the appointees during his second term, during most of which Ed Meese served in that post.

AGE

The average age of the Reagan appointees decreased from the first to the second term. The proportion of those appointed under the age of forty to the district bench rose from about 7 percent for the first term to over 12 percent for the second term. The proportion of district court appointees under the age of forty-five was 37 percent for the second term, compared to 26 percent in the first term and about 20 percent for the Carter district court appointees.

ll. There were others who were nominated but were not confirmed — most notably, at the Supreme Court level, Robert H. Bork and Douglas Ginsburg (whose nomination was dropped before it was officially sent to the Senate). At the Court of Appeals level (excluding the Federal Circuit), three nominations were subsequently withdrawn and six nominations were not acted upon by the Senate. At the district court level, seven nominations were withdrawn by the administration and nine nominations were not acted upon by the Senate.

mm. Reagan-appointed district judges elevated by Reagan to the appeals bench included Frank X. Altimari, Bobby R. Baldock, Clarence A. Beam, Robert E. Cowen, Emmett R. Cox, John M. Duhe, John R. Gibson, Cynthia H. Hall, Michael S. Kanne, Edward Leavy, Carol Los Mansmann, H. Ted Milburn, Roger G. Miner, John P. Moore, Anthony J. Scirica, Bruce M. Selya, David B. Sentelle, and William W. Wilkins, Jr.

The Reagan appeals court appointees were about two years younger than the Carter, Ford, and Johnson appointees and close to four years younger than the Nixon appointees. On the whole, it appears that there was a tendency to select younger judges, which reflected a desire to prolong the Reagan legacy on the bench. As Schmults put it when rejecting the candidacy of the sixty-nine-year-old judge Edward R. Neaher for elevation to the Second Circuit, selecting judges who could serve for a long time was "a very important factor." Fielding was even more blunt in a memo to Meese and Baker summarizing the views of the working group on appointments: "In view of Judge Neaher's age, appointment runs counter to President's desire to appoint younger judges who will have lasting impact on the judiciary."[107]

EDUCATION

Table 8.1 reveals that a majority of the Reagan first- and second-term appointees to the district courts attended private schools, including the Ivy League schools. Somewhat more than one-third of the Reagan appointees attended a public university for their undergraduate work, as compared to over 56 percent of the Carter appointees. This was perhaps a reflection of the poorer socioeconomic roots of a substantial segment of the Carter judges. The majority of the Reagan district court appointees attended private law schools, while a bare majority of the Carter appointees attended public-supported law schools. The proportion of Reagan district court appointees with an Ivy League law school education was the lowest of all the administrations studied in this book. Even if such prestigious non–Ivy League law schools as Berkeley, Chicago, Duke, Michigan, New York University, Stanford, and Virginia are considered, the proportion of Reagan appointees with a prestigious legal education rises to only about 29 percent of the first- and second-term appointees combined.

The majority of the Reagan appointees to the appeals courts attended private schools for both their undergraduate and their law school training. About one in four appointees had an Ivy League undergraduate education, the highest proportion of appointees since the Eisenhower administration. In contrast, the proportion of first-term appointees with an Ivy League law school education was the lowest since the Truman administration, and the proportion for the second-term appointees was considerably lower than that for the Carter and Nixon appeals court appointees. When prestigious non–Ivy League law schools are included, the proportion of Reagan appeals court appointees (both terms combined) with a high-quality legal education comes to about 45 percent.

Table 8.1. Selected Backgrounds of Lifetime Reagan Appointees to the Federal District and Appeals Courts

	District Court Appointees		Appeals Court Appointees	
	First Term	*Second Term*	*First Term*	*Second Term*
Average age at time of appointment	49.6	47.9	51.5	49.0
Undergraduate Education				
Public	34.9%	37.9%	29.0%	21.3%
	(45)	(61)	(9)	(10)
Private not Ivy	48.8%	50.3%	45.2%	55.3%
	(63)	(81)	(14)	(26)
Ivy League	16.3%	11.8%	25.8%	23.4%
	(21)	(19)	(8)	(11)
Law School Education				
Public	43.4%	41.6%	35.5%	44.7%
	(56)	(67)	(11)	(21)
Private not Ivy	48.1%	44.1%	48.4%	27.7%
	(62)	(71)	(15)	(13)
Ivy League	8.5%	14.3%	16.1%	27.7%
	(11)	(23)	(5)	(13)
Experience				
Judicial	49.6%	43.5%	70.9%	53.2%
	(64)	(70)	(22)	(25)
Prosecutorial	43.4%	44.7%	19.3%	34.0%
	(56)	(72)	(6)	(16)
Neither	28.7%	28.6%	25.8%	40.4%
	(37)	(46)	(8)	(19)
Occupation				
Politics — Government	2.3%	4.4%	—	6.4%
	(3)	(7)	—	(3)
Government Lawyer	6.2%	13.0%	3.2%	2.1%
	(8)	(21)	(1)	(1)
Judiciary	39.5%	34.8%	61.3%	51.1%
	(51)	(56)	(19)	(24)
Large Law Firm*	11.6%	23.0%	12.9%	14.9%
	(15)	(37)	(4)	(7)
Medium-Size Law Firm†	25.6%	13.7%	6.5%	10.7%
	(33)	(22)	(2)	(5)

Table 8.1. Continued

	District Court Appointees		Appeals Court Appointees	
	First Term	*Second Term*	*First Term*	*Second Term*
Small Law Firm[‡]	8.5%	6.2%	—	2.1%
	(11)	(10)	—	(1)
Solo Practice	2.3%	3.1%	—	—
	(3)	(5)	—	—
Professor of Law	2.3%	1.9%	16.1%	10.6%
	(3)	(3)	(5)	(5)
Other	1.6%	—	—	2.1%
	(2)	—	—	(1)
ABA Rating				
Exceptionally Well Qualified	7.0%	2.5%	22.6%	12.8%
	(9)	(4)	(7)	(6)
Well Qualified	43.4%	53.4%	41.9%	42.6%
	(56)	(86)	(13)	(20)
Qualified	49.6%	44.1%	35.5%	44.7%
	(64)	(71)	(11)	(21)
Party				
Democratic	3.1%	6.2%	—	—
	(4)	(10)	—	—
Republican	95.3%	88.8%	96.8%	95.7%
	(123)	(143)	(30)	(45)
Other	—	—	—	2.1%
	—	—	—	(1)
None	1.6%	5.0%	3.2%	2.1%
	(2)	(8)	(1)	(1)
Prominent Party Activism				
	62.0%	56.5%	51.6%	74.5%
	(80)	(91)	(16)	(35)
Prior or Current Members of Congress				
	—	0.6%	3.2%	2.1%
	—	(1)	(1)	(1)
Religion				
Protestant	51.2%	51.6%	58.1%	44.7%
	(66)	(83)	(18)	(21)
Catholic	32.6%	23.6%	25.8%	31.9%
	(42)	(38)	(8)	(15)

continued

Table 8.1. Continued

	District Court Appointees		Appeals Court Appointees	
	First Term	Second Term	First Term	Second Term
Jewish	7.0%	11.2%	9.7%	17.0%
	(9)	(18)	(3)	(8)
Other§	1.6%	3.1%	—	—
	(2)	(5)	—	—
Nondenominational or none	—	1.2%	—	—
	—	(2)	—	—
Unknown	7.8%	9.3%	6.4%	6.4%
	(10)	(15)	(2)	(3)
Gender				
Male	90.7%	92.5%	96.8%	93.6%
	(117)	(149)	(30)	(44)
Female	9.3%	7.4%	3.2%	6.4%
	(12)	(12)	(1)	(3)
Ethnicity/Race				
White	93.0%	91.9%	93.5%	100.0%
	(120)	(148)	(29)	(47)
Black	0.8%	3.1%	3.2%	—
	(1)	(5)	(1)	—
Hispanic	5.4%	4.3%	3.2%	—
	(7)	(7)	(1)	—
Asian	0.8%	0.6%	—	—
	(1)	(1)	—	—
Total Number of Appointees				
	129	161	31	47

* A large law firm was defined as consisting of twenty-five or more partners and associates.

† A medium-size law firm was defined as consisting of from five to twenty-four partners and associates.

‡ A small law firm was defined as consisting of fewer than five partners and associates.

§ Includes three Greek or Eastern Orthodox and four Mormons.

EXPERIENCE

Over 70 percent of Reagan's district court appointees had either judicial or prosecutorial experience (or both), comparable to the appointees of the Carter administration. Of special interest is that the proportion of those with judicial experience exceeded the proportion of those with prosecutorial experience (this was only true for the first-term appointees and when the first- and second-term appointees are combined), a trend begun only in the Carter administration. Judicial experience provides an administration with a track record with which to evaluate judicial nominees, and the Reagan administration examined such records to determine if the candidates shared the president's judicial philosophy.[108]

Just as with the district court appointees, the proportion of appeals court appointees with judicial experience was higher than the proportion with prosecutorial experience. The proportion of those with neither judicial nor prosecutorial experience, however, jumped from about one-fourth in the first term to two-fifths in the second term, perhaps reflecting Meese's somewhat lesser concern than Smith's with judicial experience. The second-term appointees also had a higher proportion than the first-term appointees of those with prosecutorial experience.

OCCUPATION

The occupational profile at the time of appointment of the first-term district court appointees is somewhat different from that for the second-term appointees. A larger proportion of first-term appointees was recruited directly from the judiciary (primarily the state bench, but in several instances United States magistrates or bankruptcy judges), and a smaller proportion was drawn from the large law firms. Under 5 percent were chosen from the offices of the United States attorneys during the first term, compared to about 11 percent in the second term. Private law practice was the occupation at the time of appointment for close to half the Reagan appointees. During his last two years, Reagan did not appoint any law professors, in contrast to the record for the preceding six years. Considering the importance placed by the administration on judicial philosophy, its low overall rate of appointment of law professors was unexpected. The Carter, Nixon, and Johnson administrations all appointed higher proportions of law professors to the district bench.

Three out of five first-term Reagan appointees to the appeals courts were recruited from lower courts. Of the nineteen Reagan appointments who were judges at the time of appointment, sixteen were promoted from the federal district bench and the remaining three came from the state bench. A somewhat smaller proportion (but still a majority) of second-term appointees also came directly from the judiciary and, like the first-term appointees, most were elevated from federal district courts. (Seventeen of the twenty-four were such elevations, and of these, fifteen had first been appointed by Reagan to the district bench.)

The first-term proportion of law professors appointed to the appeals courts is striking. Because Robert Bork had left his professorship at Yale Law School some six months before he was named to the District of Columbia Circuit and at the time of appointment was a senior partner in a Washington, D.C., law firm, he was not counted as a professor of law. Had Bork been counted, the proportion of professors appointed to the appeals courts during Reagan's first term would have been about one in five, the highest of all administrations considered in this book. Bork as well as the five other law professors were all known as conservative thinkers and had a track record of published works that enabled the evaluation of their candidacies in terms of their compatibility with the administration's vision of the role of courts. The appointment of academics was expected to provide intellectual leadership on the circuits and a potential pool of candidates for future vacancies on the Supreme Court. During the first half of Reagan's second term, five law professors were selected for the appeals courts. The second half of the second term, however, saw no law professors confirmed to the appeals bench, although the administration had nominated Bernard Siegan and had considered appointing several others but was stymied by Democrats, who controlled the Senate Judiciary Committee.

AMERICAN BAR ASSOCIATION RATINGS

About 7 percent of the Reagan first-term appointees to the district courts received the highest ABA rating, "exceptionally well qualified." The next-highest rating, "well qualified," was received by about 43 percent, which meant that half the Reagan first-term appointees were in the top two categories, comparable to the record for the Carter appointees. During the second term the proportion of those receiving the highest rating was lower, but the proportion receiving the "well qualified" rating was considerably higher, and as a result the proportion of Reagan appointees in the highest two categories was the greatest since the Kennedy administration. However, the proportion given a split "qualified" rating, with one or more committee members voting "not qualified," was greater during the second term, when about one-fourth had such a split rating. Of all second-term appointees, about 11 percent had such split ratings, as compared to only about 2 percent of the first-term appointees.

The proportion of Reagan's first-term appeals court appointees with the highest ABA rating was considerably greater than the proportion for the second-term appointees. This was the highest proportion since the Johnson administration. The Reagan first-and second-term appeals court appointees, however, had the highest proportion since the ratings began of those with the lowest "qualified" rating. Significantly, nine of the ten who were professors of law at the time of their nominations were only rated "qualified," despite their scholarly achievements. And five of the nine had a split rating, the majority voting "qualified" and the minority voting "not qualified," reflecting what appears to have been a committee bias against academics. But there were non-academics, particularly during the second term, who also received such split ratings (more than half those receiving the "qualified" rating), including a member of the judiciary (from the state bench).

PARTY

Approximately 95 percent of the first-term Reagan appointees to the district courts were identified as Republicans, the highest level of partisanship since Eisenhower's first term. The figures for previous prominent party activism suggest that the first-term Reagan district court appointees had a level of political activism comparable to that of the Carter appointees. The second-term appointees, however, reflected somewhat less partisanship and party activism. The proportion of Democrats appointed, though small, was double that of the first term.

The findings for the courts of appeals are startling. No Democrat was appointed by Reagan during his eight years in office. And during the second term, three out of four appeals court appointees had a background of prominent partisan activism. The absence of any appointee affiliated with the opposition political party had last occurred in the Kennedy administration. Apparently, the Reagan administration considered the appeals courts far too important to risk appointing a Democrat, who might not fully share the judicial philosophy of the administration.

Three Reagan appointees (one to a district court and two to appeals courts) had a background of congressional service. Like Carter, Reagan had never served in Congress, and his administration did not look to Congress as a source of nominees.

RELIGIOUS ORIGIN OR AFFILIATION

In religious origin or affiliation the Reagan first-term district court appointees differed markedly from the appointees of previous Republican administrations. Reagan appointed more Catholics and fewer Protestants — proportions similar to those of Democratic administrations. In fact, the first-term proportion was very close to Truman's first-term proportion, which was a record. In the past, Republican administrations had appointed more Protestants and fewer Catholics and Jews than had Democratic administrations. This could be attributed to the fact that the religious composition or mix of the parties was different and thus, to a large extent, so was the pool of potential judicial candidates from both parties. This finding for the Reagan administration does not necessarily mean that the administration gave preference to Catholics because of their religion but rather that more Catholics had entered the potential pool from which Republican judicial nominees emerged, thus increasing the proportion of Catholics chosen. This is consistent with the relatively heavy Catholic vote for Reagan in 1980 and especially 1984. The second-term proportion of Catholics was down for the district courts but up for the appeals courts. The second-term proportion of Catholics was approximately the same as for the Carter administration. In the second term the proportion of appeals court appointees who were Catholic or Jewish was larger than in the first term.

GENDER, RACE, AND ETHNICITY

The record of the Reagan administration's first-term district court appointments in regard to gender, ethnicity, and race was mixed. Although Reagan's record of appointing women was second only to Carter's, it did not match the Carter record. The second-term proportion of women appointed to the district courts was even lower than the first term's. But the record of appointing women was far superior to that of appointing blacks. Only one African American was appointed during the first term and five during the second. The proportion and number (14) of hispanics appointed to the district courts, however, was considerably higher than that of blacks. It was no secret that the Republican Party sought to woo hispanic voters in the 1984 election, and it clearly better served the partisan agenda to appoint Hispanic Americans than African Americans.

Of the thirty-one appeals court appointees during the first term, there was only one woman, one black, and one hispanic. Of the forty-seven second-term appeals court appointees, three were women and none were minorities. During the last two years of the Reagan presidency, two women received nominations that were not acted upon by the Senate. The overall Reagan record for the appeals courts was a poor second to Carter's in regard to women and much worse in regard to African Americans.

In remarks to the Knights of Columbus on August 5, 1986, President Reagan asserted: "In many areas — abortion, crime, pornography, and others — progress will take place when the Federal judiciary is made up of judges who believe in law and order and a strict interpretation of the Constitution. I'm pleased to be able to tell you that I've already appointed 284 Federal judges, men and women who share the fundamental values that you and I so cherish."[109] Indeed, Ronald Reagan's presidency was significant in reshaping the judiciary. His administration was intent upon selecting judges who shared the president's vision. The decisions and precedents of the federal judiciary that greeted the new administration in 1981 were most troubling, and the administration was intent upon changing politically liberal judicial policy by changing the judges—through the focused use of the power to make judicial appointments. To this extent, Reagan came full circle to the president with whom we began this inquiry into judicial selection—Franklin Roosevelt.

Both Reagan and Roosevelt were concerned with appointing judges who shared their philosophy of judicial restraint. Both presidents saw their policy agendas affected by the actions of the courts. Roosevelt was concerned about the judiciary's restrictions on government's use of its economic regulatory powers. Reagan was concerned about the judiciary's restrictions on government's use of its police powers in the regulation of civil liberties. Judicial selection was a prominent feature of both administrations and the source, at times, of public controversy.

But the selection process utilized by Reagan differed somewhat from Roosevelt's. Reagan built upon and added to the existing process. His administration took the next logical step from the Carter administration's heavy involvement of the White House counsel's office in judicial selection by institutionalizing that involvement through the creation of a joint White House–Justice Department committee to make the final recommendations of judicial candidates to the president.

The Reagan presidency had to contend with the rising expectations of women and minorities that they would receive a share of judicial appointments. Carter was a tough act to follow, and Reagan could not or would not match Carter's record. Reagan, however, did appoint more women than any president with the exception of Carter, and he named the first woman to the Supreme Court. Reagan likewise appointed more hispanics than any president other than Carter. But African American appointees were scarce, as ideological and political concerns stopped the momentum begun by Carter toward racial diversity on the bench.

To what extent has the judicial process changed since Roosevelt's presidency? To what extent has the demographic and professional profile of those selected to serve on the lower federal courts changed? How do we evaluate the federal judicial selection process and the need or prospects for change? To these questions we turn our attention in the concluding chapter.

9

Summing Up over Fifty-Six Years

We have seen the selection process at work from the Roosevelt through the Reagan administrations. We have also examined the demographic portraits of each administration with attention to comparisons between and (with some presidencies) within terms. Now it is appropriate to compare the overall demographic trends over the fifty-six-year period spanned by this book before considering more general conclusions about the selection process. Table 9.1 looks at district court appointments, table 9.2 at appeals court appointments. The total number of district judge appointments over the fifty-six-year period was 1,308. The total number of appeals court appointments was 373.

Portrait of the District Court Appointees

In table 9.1 we see fluctuations in the average age at the time of appointment of district court judges. The difference between the youngest and oldest average age was 3.6 years. The Reagan administration had the youngest judges, the Eisenhower administration the oldest. (The same was true for the average age at time of appointment of appeals court appointments.) The Reagan administration was most concerned with its policy agenda and judicial legacy, while the Eisenhower administration was relatively unconcerned with the judiciary as a tool for achieving its policy agenda. Also since Eisenhower was the first Republican president in twenty years, the pool of Republicans for judicial posts was likely to have consisted of older people who had been waiting the longest. Since the Eisenhower administration, the trend has been for relatively younger judges to be appointed.

Table 9.1 also reveals a trend in the increase in formal education. Almost one in three Roosevelt appointments to the district courts had no undergraduate education. By the time of the Nixon administration all district court appointees had had an undergraduate education. The same was true for law school education: about one in seven Roosevelt district court appointees had no law school education, but by the time of the Nixon administration all district court appointees had had a law school education.

The proportions of district court appointees who had gone to an Ivy League law school reached a high point with the Eisenhower administration and showed a steady decline through the Reagan administration, whose proportions of Ivy League law school graduates were about the same as for the Roosevelt appointees. In the intervening years, however, several public and private law schools have achieved distinction and prestige equal to the Ivy League schools; thus a decrease in the proportions of Ivy League law school graduates does not necessarily mean a decline in the quality of law school education.

There is no clear trend as to the proportions of district court appointees who graduated form state-supported law schools. The majority of all administrations' district court appointees, with the exception of Carter's, attended non-public-supported law schools.

In terms of professional experience, the trend has been for appointees to come to the federal district court bench with previous judicial experience. There were variations among the administrations, with the Carter appointees having the most judicial experience (54 percent) and the Eisenhower appointees the least (32.5 percent). In contrast, the Eisenhower appointees had the highest proportion with prosecutorial experience (52.4 percent) and the Carter administration the least (38.1 percent). The proportions with neither judicial nor prosecutorial experience varied by administration, the Nixon and Ford administrations having had the highest proportion of appointees with neither judicial nor prosecutorial experience (37.2 percent) and the Reagan administration the lowest (28.6 percent). Before the Carter administration there was a larger proportion of district court appointees with prosecutorial than with judicial experience. Starting with the Carter administration the balance shifted, and the proportion with judicial experience has been higher

Table 9.1. Selected Backgrounds of Lifetime Appointees to the Federal District Courts, Roosevelt through Reagan

	FDR	HST	DDE	JFK/LBJ	RMN/GF	JC	RR
Average age at time of appointment	49.9	51.4	52.3	51.4	49.1	49.6	48.7
Undergraduate Education							
Public	28.6%	22.7%	34.9%	43.2%	42.9%	56.4%	36.6%
	(38)	(22)	(44)	(99)	(99)	(114)	(106)
Private	34.6%	42.3%	34.9%	35.8%	38.5%	33.7%	49.7%
	(46)	(41)	(44)	(82)	(89)	(68)	(144)
Ivy League	6.0%	8.2%	17.5%	13.1%	18.6%	9.9%	13.8%
	(8)	(8)	(22)	(30)	(43)	(20)	(40)
None	30.8%	26.8%	12.7%	7.9%	—	—	—
	(41)	(26)	(16)	(18)	—	—	—
Law School Education							
Public	31.6%	29.9%	39.7%	40.6%	43.3%	50.5%	42.4%
	(42)	(29)	(50)	(93)	(100)	(102)	(123)
Private	42.1%	53.6%	35.7%	38.0%	36.4%	32.7%	45.9%
	(56)	(52)	(45)	(87)	(84)	(66)	(133)
Ivy League	12.0%	13.4%	23.0%	20.5%	20.3%	16.8%	11.7%
	(16)	(13)	(29)	(47)	(47)	(34)	(34)
None	14.3%	3.1%	1.6%	0.9%	—	—	—
	(19)	(3)	(2)	(2)	—	—	—
Experience							
Judicial	36.8%	35.0%	32.5%	40.6%	37.2%	54.0%	46.2%
	(49)	(34)	(41)	(93)	(86)	(109)	(134)
Prosecutorial	48.9%	48.4%	52.4%	41.5%	42.4%	38.1%	44.1%
	(65)	(47)	(66)	(95)	(98)	(77)	(128)
Neither	33.1%	33.0%	36.5%	34.1%	37.2%	30.7%	28.6%
	(44)	(32)	(46)	(78)	(86)	(62)	(83)
Occupation							
Politics — Government	18.8%	20.6%	4.8%	10.0%	4.3%	2.0%	3.4%
	(25)	(20)	(6)	(23)	(10)	(4)	(10)
Government Lawyer	21.8%	16.5%	8.7%	7.9%	9.1%	3.0%	10.0%
	(29)	(16)	(11)	(18)	(21)	(6)	(29)
Judiciary	20.3%	18.6%	21.4%	31.4%	30.7%	44.6%	36.9%
	(27)	(18)	(27)	(72)	(71)	(90)	(107)
Large Law Firm	1.5%	1.0%	12.7%	3.5%	10.8%	13.9%	17.9%
	(2)	(1)	(16)	(8)	(25)	(28)	(52)

Table 9.1. Continued

	FDR	HST	DDE	JFK/LBJ	RMN/GF	JC	RR
Medium-Size	7.5%	9.3%	13.5%	25.3%	26.8%	19.8%	19.0%
Law Firm	(10)	(9)	(17)	(58)	(62)	(40)	(55)
Small Law Firm	20.3%	16.5%	26.2%	17.9%	11.7%	10.9%	7.2%
	(27)	(16)	(33)	(41)	(27)	(22)	(21)
Solo Practice	9.0%	12.4%	12.7%	1.8%	4.8%	2.5%	2.8%
	(12)	(12)	(16)	(4)	(11)	(5)	(8)
Law Professor	0.8%	2.1%	—	2.2%	1.7%	3.0%	2.1%
	(1)	(2)	—	(5)	(4)	(6)	(6)
Other	—	3.1%	—	—	—	0.5%	0.7%
	—	(3)	—	—	—	(1)	(2)
ABA Rating							
Exceptionally	—	—	8.7%	10.0%	2.6%	4.0%	4.5%
Well Qualified	—	—	(11)	(23)	(6)	(8)	(13)
Well Qualified	—	—	42.9%	45.9%	41.6%	47.0%	49.0%
	—	—	(54)	(105)	(96)	(95)	(142)
Qualified	—	—	34.9%	39.3%	55.8%	47.5%	46.6%
	—	—	(44)	(90)	(129)	(96)	(135)
Not Qualified	—	—	6.4%	4.4%	—	1.5%	—
	—	—	(8)	(10)	—	(3)	—
Unrated or	—	—	7.1%	0.4%	—	—	—
Unknown	—	—	(9)	(1)	—	—	—
Party							
Democratic	98.5%	93.8%	4.8%	92.1%	10.0%	90.6%	4.8%
	(131)	(91)	(6)	(211)	(23)	(183)	(14)
Republican	1.5%	6.2%	95.2%	7.9%	89.6%	4.5%	91.7%
	(2)	(6)	(120)	(18)	(207)	(9)	(266)
None	—	—	—	—	0.4%	5.0%	3.4%
	—	—	—	—	(1)	(10)	(10)
Prominent Party Activism							
	61.7%	58.8%	62.7%	57.2%	55.4%	60.9%	59.0%
	(82)	(57)	(79)	(131)	(128)	(123)	(171)
Prior or Current Members of Congress							
	12.8%	7.2%	2.4%	3.1%	1.7%	1.0%	0.3%
	(17)	(7)	(3)	(7)	(4)	(2)	(1)
Religion							
Protestant	65.4%	53.6%	73.0%	60.3%	67.5%	52.5%	51.4%
	(87)	(52)	(92)	(138)	(156)	(106)	(149)

continued

Table 9.1. Continued

	FDR	HST	DDE	JFK/LBJ	RMN/GF	JC	RR
Catholic	30.1%	33.0%	19.0%	27.1%	16.4%	27.7%	27.6%
	(40)	(32)	(24)	(62)	(38)	(56)	(80)
Jewish	4.5%	11.3%	6.4%	10.0%	7.8%	11.4%	9.3%
	(6)	(11)	(8)	(23)	(18)	(23)	(27)
Other	—	2.1%	1.6%	0.9%	3.0%	3.5%	2.4%
	—	(2)	(2)	(2)	(7)	(7)	(7)
None	—	—	—	0.4%	0.9%	1.0%	0.7%
	—	—	—	(1)	(2)	(2)	(2)
Unknown	—	—	—	1.3%	4.3%	4.0%	8.6%
	—	—	—	(3)	(10)	(8)	(25)
Gender							
Male	100.0%	99.0%	100.0%	98.7%	99.1%	85.6%	91.7%
	(133)	(96)	(126)	(226)	(229)	(173)	(266)
Female	—	1.0%	—	1.3%	0.9%	14.4%	8.3%
	—	(1)	—	(3)	(2)	(29)	(24)
Ethnicity/Race							
White	100.0%	100.0%	100.0%	93.9%	93.9%	78.7%	92.4%
	(133)	(97)	(126)	(215)	(217)	(159)	(268)
Black	—	—	—	3.9%	3.9%	13.9%	2.1%
	—	—	—	(9)	(9)	(28)	(6)
Hispanic	—	—	—	1.8%	1.3%	6.9%	4.8%
	—	—	—	(4)	(3)	(14)	(14)
Asian	—	—	—	0.4%	0.9%	0.5%	0.7%
	—	—	—	(1)	(2)	(1)	(2)
% White Male							
	100.0%	99.0%	100.0%	93.0%	93.1%	68.3%	84.8%
	(133)	(96)	(126)	(213)	(215)	(138)	(246)
Total Number of Appointees							
	133	97	126	229	231	202	290

than the proportion with prosecutorial experience. Whether intended or not, this reflects a growing professionalization of the federal judiciary, a trend that continued with the Bush and Clinton administrations.[1]

The trend toward the professionalization of the federal judiciary is more clearly seen in the statistics for occupation at time of appointment. The proportion of federal district court appointees promoted primarily from the state judiciaries increased from the Roosevelt, Truman, and Eisenhower administrations to the high point in the Carter administration (44.6 percent). The proportion for the Reagan administration was about 37 percent, a significant rise from the approximately 20 percent for the Roosevelt, Truman, and Eisenhower appointees.[a]

The proportion of appointees whose occupation at time of appointment was in political or governmental office (excluding judicial and prosecutorial positions) showed a marked decrease from the about one in five Roosevelt and Truman appointees to one in fifty for the Carter administration and one in thirty for the Reagan administration. Similarly, the proportion of appointees drawn from prosecutorial office at the time of appointment has shown a major decrease since the Roosevelt and Truman years.

The proportion of Roosevelt and Truman district court appointees who were in large law firms at the time of appointment was negligible. That proportion jumped about twelvefold with the Eisenhower administration, dropped significantly for Kennedy and Johnson appointees, rose threefold during the Nixon and Ford administrations, went up a more modest proportion for the Carter judges, and then rose again during Reagan's presidency. Republican administrations appeared to draw from the large law firms to a greater extent than Democratic administrations. But the converse was not necessarily true. The proportions of the Truman and Eisenhower appointees drawn from a solo law practice were approximately the same — 12 percent, the high point over the fifty-six-year period. There was a marked decrease in subsequent administrations, reflecting in large part the changing nature of legal practice. But even at the high point the proportion was significantly lower than the well-over-half the nation's lawyers who were individual practitioners.

The ABA ratings for district court appointees from the Eisenhower through Reagan administrations show the Eisenhower and the Kennedy-Johnson appointees with the highest proportion of the top "exceptionally well qualified" rating. If that rating and the next-highest rating, "well qualified," are combined, the Kennedy-Johnson proportion is highest, followed by those for the Reagan, Eisenhower, and Carter appointees. The lowest proportion, for the Nixon-Ford appointees, was about 9 percentage points lower than that for the Reagan appointees. The Eisenhower administration had the highest proportion rated "not qualified." The Nixon-Ford and Reagan administrations made no district court appointments to anyone deemed unqualified by the ABA.

Politically, over the fifty-six-year period, about nine out of ten appointees were members of the president's political party, a statistic in line with the

---

a. The proportion of Bush appointees was 41.9 percent and of Clinton appointees during his first term 44.4 percent.

historical trend.[2] Roosevelt appointed the lowest proportion of opposition party members (1.5 percent), while Nixon and Ford appointed the highest (10 percent). Appointees unaffiliated with a political party began appearing in the post-Watergate period, but the numbers and proportions were small.

There was no clear trend as to the level of previous political activity on the part of appointees. Approximately three out of five appointees have been politically active, with little change from Roosevelt through Reagan. There was, however, a change in the proportion of those who had at some point in their careers served in Congress. Close to 13 percent of Roosevelt's district court appointees had served in Congress. About 7 percent of Truman's appointees also had congressional service experience. But the proportion dropped markedly in subsequent administrations and was virtually negligible among the Reagan appointees. This aspect of selection to further the partisan agenda is almost extinct. The path to the federal bench is not through Congress.

Religious origin or affiliation is of interest because it to some extent mirrors the different religious compositions of the two major political parties. About 30 percent of the Roosevelt and one-third of the Truman appointees were Catholic, and until the Reagan years Democratic administrations appointed more Catholics than did Republican administrations. That changed with Reagan, as pro-life Catholics flocked to the Republican Party and were "rewarded" with about 28 percent of district court judgeships, a proportion close to Roosevelt's and in absolute numbers setting a new historic record. (Recall also that two of Reagan's four Supreme Court appointments were Catholic.)

The proportions of Jewish appointees reached high points with Truman and Carter. Reagan's proportion was in excess of 9 percent and in absolute numbers set a new record. Because Jews were not a major component of Reagan's political support, the relatively high proportion suggests that religious origin or affiliation was no barrier to consideration for appointment. The small numbers and proportion for Roosevelt, the lowest for the entire fifty-six-year period, suggest that this was not necessarily true for his administration.

Table 9.1 shows that the Kennedy and Johnson administrations broke the racial barrier on the federal district courts, and that Nixon and Ford sustained the pace. The big breakthrough quantitatively came with Carter, but Reagan sounded a dramatic retreat on the appointment of African Americans.

The findings for gender also show similarities to that for race. The gender barrier for the district court bench, however, was broken by Truman. Kennedy and Johnson continued tokenism, as did Nixon and Ford. Again, the major quantitative breakthrough came with Carter, when over 14 percent of appointments went to women. Although the Reagan proportion of women appointments was lower than Carter's, it was significantly higher than every other president's, and in absolute numbers Reagan's twenty-four women appointees represented an important continuation of the momentum toward gender diversification of the district court bench. The proportion of white male appointees dropped from almost 100 percent for Roosevelt and Truman to 93 percent for Kennedy and Johnson and also Nixon and Ford, to about 68 percent for Carter and rising to about 85 percent for Reagan.

Portrait of the Appeals Court Appointees

Table 9.2 shows the spread between the highest and lowest average age at time of appointment to the appeals courts to have been almost six years. The highest average age was for Eisenhower's judges (55.9 years), the lowest for Reagan's (50.0 years).

As with district court appointees, the trend has been for an increase in formal education. By the time of the Carter administration, all appeals court appointees had had an undergraduate education. Nonpublic undergraduate education predominated over public-supported education. The proportions of appointees with an Ivy League undergraduate education reached high points with the Eisenhower and Reagan appointees.

By the time of the Kennedy administration, all appointees had attended law school. The majority went to non–public-supported law schools. Over one-third of the Roosevelt appointees had an Ivy League law school education. The highest proportion of appeals court appointees with an Ivy League law school education was under Carter (over 40 percent) and the lowest was for Truman and for Reagan (about 23 percent).

Over half of the appointees of each administration had had previous judicial experience, and the proportion with judicial experience was larger than the proportion with prosecutorial experience. Here, as with the district courts, we can see the professionalization of the judiciary, except that this professionalization spanned the entire fifty-six-year period. The proportion with neither judicial nor prosecutorial experience fluctuated, and the spread was more than 17 percentage points. The lowest proportion was for the Roosevelt and Eisenhower appointees and the highest for Carter's and Reagan's.

One in five Roosevelt appointees to the appeals courts held political office (excluding judicial and prosecutorial positions) at the time of appointment. This was the high point for the fifty-six-year period. There was some fluctuation between 44 percent (for Roosevelt's judges) and almost 58 percent (Nixon and Ford judges) who were elevated from lower courts to the appeals

Table 9.2. *Selected Backgrounds of Lifetime Appointees to the Courts of Appeals of General Jurisdiction, Roosevelt through Reagan*

	FDR	HST	DDE	JFK/LBJ	RMN/GF	JC	RR
Average age at time of appointment	52.9	55.1	55.9	52.7	53.4	51.8	50.0
Undergraduate Education							
Public	34.0%	26.9%	28.9%	32.8%	40.4%	30.4%	24.4%
	(17)	(7)	(13)	(20)	(23)	(17)	(19)
Private	34.0%	34.6%	17.8%	39.3%	38.6%	51.8%	51.3%
	(17)	(9)	(8)	(24)	(22)	(29)	(40)
Ivy League	18.0%	15.4%	24.4%	16.4%	17.5%	17.9%	24.4%
	(9)	(4)	(11)	(10)	(10)	(10)	(19)
None	14.0%	23.1%	28.9%	11.5%	3.5%	—	—
	(7)	(6)	(13)	(7)	(2)	—	—
Law School Education							
Public	24.0%	15.4%	31.1%	39.3%	40.4%	39.3%	41.0%
	(12)	(4)	(14)	(24)	(23)	(22)	(32)
Private	30.0%	42.3%	37.8%	36.1%	26.3%	19.6%	35.9%
	(15)	(11)	(17)	(22)	(15)	(11)	(28)
Ivy League	34.0%	23.1%	28.9%	24.6%	33.3%	41.1%	23.1%
	(17)	(6)	(13)	(15)	(19)	(23)	(18)
None	12.0%	19.2%	2.2%	—	—	—	—
	(6)	(5)	(1)	—	—	—	—
Experience							
Judicial	54.0%	61.5%	64.4%	60.7%	61.4%	53.6%	60.3%
	(27)	(16)	(29)	(37)	(35)	(30)	(47)
Prosecutorial	40.0%	38.5%	37.8%	37.7%	28.1%	32.1%	28.2%
	(20)	(10)	(17)	(23)	(16)	(18)	(22)
Neither	22.0%	26.9%	22.2%	27.9%	28.1%	39.3%	34.6%
	(11)	(7)	(10)	(17)	(16)	(22)	(27)
Occupation							
Politics — Government	20.0%	11.5%	6.7%	8.2%	5.3%	1.8%	3.9%
	(10)	(3)	(3)	(5)	(3)	(1)	(3)
Government Lawyer	6.0%	7.7%	8.9%	3.3%	—	3.6%	2.6%
	(3)	(2)	(4)	(2)	—	(2)	(2)
Judiciary	44.0%	50.0%	55.6%	54.1%	57.9%	46.4%	55.1%
	(22)	(13)	(25)	(33)	(33)	(26)	(43)
Large Law Firm	2.0%	—	11.1%	4.9%	5.3%	10.7%	14.1%
	(1)	—	(5)	(3)	(3)	(6)	(11)

Table 9.2. Continued

	FDR	HST	DDE	JFK/LBJ	RMN/GF	JC	RR
Medium-Size	6.0%	7.7%	4.4%	19.7%	19.3%	16.1%	9.0%
Law Firm	(3)	(2)	(2)	(12)	(11)	(9)	(7)
Small Law Firm	12.0%	15.4%	8.9%	1.6%	5.3%	3.6%	1.3%
	(6)	(4)	(4)	(1)	(3)	(2)	(1)
Solo Practice	—	7.7%	2.2%	4.9%	—	1.8%	—
	—	(2)	(1)	(3)	—	(1)	—
Law Professor	10.0%	—	—	1.6%	1.8%	14.3%	12.8%
	(5)	—	—	(1)	(1)	(8)	(10)
Other	—	—	2.2%	1.6%	5.3%	1.8%	1.3%
	—	—	(1)	(1)	(3)	(1)	(1)
ABA Rating							
Exceptionally	—	—	35.6%	24.6%	15.8%	16.1%	16.7%
Well Qualified	—	—	(16)	(15)	(9)	(9)	(13)
Well Qualified	—	—	42.2%	45.9%	54.4%	58.9%	42.3%
	—	—	(19)	(28)	(31)	(33)	(33)
Qualified	—	—	15.6%	24.6%	28.1%	25.0%	41.0%
	—	—	(7)	(15)	(16)	(14)	(32)
Not Qualified	—	—	2.2%	3.3%	1.8%	—	—
	—	—	(1)	(2)	(1)	—	—
Unrated	—	—	4.4%	1.6%	—	—	—
	—	—	(2)	(1)	—	—	—
Party							
Democratic	96.0%	88.5%	6.7%	95.1%	7.0%	82.1%	—
	(48)	(23)	(3)	(58)	(4)	(46)	—
Republican	4.0%	11.5%	93.3%	3.3%	93.0%	7.1%	96.2%
	(2)	(3)	(42)	(2)	(53)	(4)	(75)
Other	—	—	—	1.6%	—	—	1.3%
	—	—	—	(1)	—	—	(1)
None	—	—	—	—	—	10.7%	2.6%
	—	—	—	—	—	(6)	(2)
Prominent Party Activism							
	66.0%	61.5%	68.9%	70.5%	59.7%	73.2%	65.4%
	(33)	(16)	(31)	(43)	(34)	(41)	(51)
Prior or Current Members of Congress							
	12.0%	7.7%	4.4%	4.9%	5.3%	1.8%	2.6%
	(6)	(2)	(2)	(3)	(3)	(1)	(2)

continued

Table 9.2. Continued

	FDR	HST	DDE	JFK/LBJ	RMN/GF	JC	RR
Religion							
Protestant	86.0%	69.2%	80.0%	63.9%	68.4%	50.0%	50.0%
	(43)	(18)	(36)	(39)	(39)	(28)	(39)
Catholic	12.0%	23.1%	13.3%	24.6%	19.3%	26.8%	29.5%
	(6)	(6)	(6)	(15)	(11)	(15)	(23)
Jewish	2.0%	7.7%	6.7%	11.5%	8.8%	17.9%	14.1%
	(1)	(2)	(3)	(7)	(5)	(10)	(11)
Other	—	—	—	—	3.5%	3.6%	—
	—	—	—	—	(2)	(2)	—
Unknown	—	—	—	—	—	1.8%	6.4%
	—	—	—	—	—	(1)	(5)
Gender							
Male	98.0%	100.0%	100.0%	98.4%	100.0%	80.4%	94.9%
	(49)	(26)	(45)	(60)	(57)	(45)	(74)
Female	2.0%	—	—	1.6%	—	19.6%	5.1%
	(1)	—	—	(1)	—	(11)	(4)
Ethnicity/Race							
White	100.0%	96.1%	100.0%	95.1%	98.2%	78.6%	97.4%
	(50)	(25)	(45)	(58)	(56)	(44)	(76)
Black	—	3.9%	—	4.9%	—	16.1%	1.3%
	—	(1)	—	(3)	—	(9)	(1)
Hispanic	—	—	—	—	—	3.6%	1.3%
	—	—	—	—	—	(2)	(1)
Asian	—	—	—	—	1.8%	1.8%	—
	—	—	—	—	(1)	(1)	—
% White Male							
	98.0%	96.1%	100.0%	93.4%	98.2%	60.7%	92.3%
	(49)	(25)	(45)	(57)	(56)	(34)	(72)
Total Number of Appointees							
	50	26	45	61	57	56	78

courts. But clearly at the appeals court level there is a substantial career judiciary.[b] The large law firms were a source of appeals court judges for over 10

b. The large majority of lower-court elevations were from the federal district bench. Of
the Roosevelt appointees whose occupation at time of appointment was the judiciary,
sixteen of twenty-two (72.7 percent) were promoted from the federal district bench. The
figures for Truman appointees were eleven of thirteen (84.6 percent); for the Eisenhower

percent of the Eisenhower, Carter, and Reagan appointees. Lawyers who practiced in small law firms and solo practitioners were more evident among the Roosevelt, Truman, and Eisenhower appointees than in the appointments made by subsequent presidents. Ten percent of Roosevelt's appeals court appointments went to law professors, a record exceeded only by Carter and Reagan.

The Eisenhower administration had the highest proportion of appeals court appointees receiving the "exceptionally well qualified" ABA rating, Nixon and Ford the lowest. Combining the two highest categories, the Eisenhower administration remained at the top, with more than three out of four receiving the highest ratings. The Reagan administration, with 59 percent in the two highest ratings, had the lowest proportion.

There was no change in the level of partisanship in appointments to the appeals courts. With the exception of the Carter appointees, at least nine out of ten were members of the president's political party. All administrations with the exception of Reagan's and Kennedy's named token members of the major opposition party.[c] Between six and seven out of ten had some background of prominent party activism. Each administration appointed at least one former member of Congress. The Roosevelt numbers and proportion were the highest, Carter's the lowest.

Table 9.2 shows a distribution of religious origins or affiliations by administration similar to that found for the district court appointees. Until Reagan, Democratic administrations appointed a larger proportion of Catholics than did Republican administrations.

In terms of gender, after Roosevelt's token appointment of Florence Allen, no woman was appointed to the appeals bench until Johnson appointed Shirley Hufstedler. No other woman came to the appeals bench after her until Carter's breakthrough administration, when eleven women were appointed — about one in five Carter appointees. Reagan's numbers and proportions were a dramatic drop from Carter's, but Reagan was the first Republican president to name women to the appeals courts, and he was responsible for appointing the first woman to the U.S. Supreme Court.

The figures for race and ethnicity are comparable to those for gender. Tru-

appointees, eighteen of twenty-five (72.0 percent); for the Kennedy-Johnson appointees, twenty-seven of thirty-three (81.8 percent); for the Nixon-Ford appointees, thirty-one of thirty-three (93.9 percent); for the Carter appointees, fifteen of twenty-six (57.7 percent); and for the Reagan appointees, thirty-three of forty-three (76.7 percent) were promoted from the federal district bench.

c. Lyndon Johnson named two Republicans, and that accounts for the Kennedy-Johnson figures in table 9.2.

man made the first appointment of an African American to the appeals bench, William Henry Hastie. Not until the Kennedy and Johnson administrations were other African Americans appointed. Ethnic diversity was most in evidence among the Carter appointments, while Reagan reverted to the pre-Carter pattern.

Structural Changes in the Selection Process

Over the fifty-six years from Roosevelt's first inauguration to the end of the Reagan presidency, there have been changes in the judicial selection process which likely have had some impact on the changing portrait of the judiciary. The judicial selection apparatus in the executive as well as in the Senate has undergone changes in part due to the significant increase in the numbers of federal judicial positions that are filled. Roosevelt made 183 lifetime lower-court appointments to courts of general jurisdiction over a twelve-year period. Reagan appointed more than twice that number (368) in eight years. Carter, in only four years, filled 258 judgeships. Increased opportunities for judicial appointments were a result of new positions created by Congress at the behest of the Judicial Conference of the United States in various judgeship bills over the fifty-six-year period as federal caseloads grew. Judicial pork barrel politics, however, were also at work, as Deborah Barrow, Gary Zuk, and Gerard Gryski have shown, particularly between 1933 and 1968, as "Congress exceeded the number requested, authorizing additional judgeships well beyond what caseload figures would support."[3]

During the administrations of Roosevelt through Reagan there was a degree of rivalry and sometimes tension between the Justice Department and the White House over selection. Roosevelt was the most engaged in selection activity, furthering his partisan, personal, and policy agendas. Other presidents and their staffs had occasional forays onto the selection battlefield, but not until the Carter presidency did the White House counsel's office assert a major role. It took the Reagan administration to institutionalize the White House role with White House domination symbolized by the White House counsel (*not* the attorney general or deputy attorney general) chairing the President's Committee on Federal Judicial Selection.

The American Bar Association's entry into the selection process strengthened the forces within each administration favoring the professionalization of the judiciary, particularly at the district court level, whose appointees primarily were products of senatorial patronage. (Table 9.1 showed a significant increase from Eisenhower to Kennedy-Johnson in the proportion of appointees coming to the federal district bench from other judicial positions.) The

Carter administration's use of selection commissions for appointments to the courts of appeal, as well as senatorial use of selection commissions or advisory committees to fill district court positions, helped open up the judiciary to women and minorities and to some extent transformed judicial selection into a less closed, patronage-based process.

At the same time that the ABA entered the process during the Eisenhower administration, the national party organizations were losing their place in selection. By the time of the Carter administration, the national party organizations no longer routinely cleared judgeships.

Although policy-agenda considerations were behind the Reagan administration's abandonment of the selection commissions for appeals court appointments, senatorial selection committees continued to operate to fill many positions. Policy-agenda considerations no doubt underlay the creation of the joint White House–Justice Department selection committee chaired by the White House counsel, which essentially made judicial selection decisions.

Structural changes at the senatorial level began with the use of senatorial commissions encouraged by the Carter administration (although not all senators used them). There were changes in the workings of the Senate Judiciary Committee when Edward Kennedy became chairman in 1979. Innovations included the diminution of the de facto blue-slip veto power of individual senators and the creation of an investigatory staff for the committee to check on the qualifications of nominees independent of the White House, the FBI, and the ABA. This autonomous investigatory capacity of the Senate Judiciary Committee would in later years feature prominently in the handling of Supreme Court nominations such as those of Robert Bork and Clarence Thomas, but also on occasion at the lower court level.

To sum up, judicial selection had changed incrementally from 1933 to 1989, so that by 1989 the structures and processes of selection and confirmation were distinctive as compared to the earlier era, although there were commonalities in the mechanics of selection throughout the period, as we have also seen.

Presidential Agendas and Selection

There has been a constant tension between patronage, merit, and policy-ideology considerations in the appointment process. The balance that is struck has differed from administration to administration. In part, as I argued at the outset of this book, this is a function of the state of the political system. The Roosevelt, Nixon, and Reagan administrations were associated with fundamental changes in the American political landscape. And indeed we saw the

Roosevelt and Reagan administrations strike a balance where the presidential policy agenda achieved prominence (well over half their appeals court appointees were of the policy-agenda type). For Nixon the intent to focus on the policy agenda was there, but with the important exception of his Supreme Court appointments and a few instances at the appeals court level there seemed to be little systematic follow-through. Nixon's typical lack of personal involvement and direction in the lower-court selection process is probably responsible for this even before Watergate consumed his time and then his presidency.

For Roosevelt, the partisan, personal, and policy agendas were typically interwoven. Roosevelt's unusually active personal involvement in selection points up the complexity of presidential motivations and the difficulties of trying to unravel them, although we can be reasonably confident that the policy agenda loomed large. Reagan, on the other hand, remained uninvolved in the selection of individual judges, but he clearly trumpeted his presidential motivation, that of furthering his policy agenda. True, Reagan read from a script, but it was *his* script — that is, he promoted his own ideas. Reagan, the consummate actor, played both Edgar Bergen and Charley McCarthy.

For the Carter administration the opening up of the judiciary to women and minorities, although based on conviction, helped further his partisan agenda. There is little evidence of policy-agenda screening by his administration, although such screening may have been done by the selection commissions. Carter, as a Deep South politician, could not have won the nomination and the presidential election without the overwhelming support of African Americans and Hispanic Americans. African American and hispanic groups looked to Carter to desegregate the federal bench, and Carter's partisan agenda required more than token judicial appointments of minorities. Similarly, women's groups looked to Carter to sexually integrate the bench and to remove barriers to the advancement of women. The racial desegregation and sexual integration of the federal bench by the breakthrough Carter appointments not only furthered an important facet of Carter's affirmative-action policy agenda but also, as I have argued, largely satisfied his partisan agenda. Reagan, on the other hand, owed little to minorities and women's groups. After fulfilling his campaign pledge to appoint a woman to the Supreme Court, his record on women appointees and especially minority appointees was in marked contrast to Carter's.

For Truman and Eisenhower, the partisan agenda appeared to have dominated selection, being the primary concern in at least three out of four appeals court appointments. This was also largely true for Kennedy and Johnson (for at least four out of five appeals court appointments). The few Kennedy and

Johnson appointments of African Americans to the lower courts, and then Thurgood Marshall to the Supreme Court, represented political recognition by these Democratic presidents of the group most consistently identified with the Democratic Party. That Kennedy and Johnson believed it was the right thing to do does not diminish the partisan benefits accruing from those appointments.

In short, the evidence presented in this book at the least suggests that presidential agendas and judicial selection are intimately tied and that the policy agenda tends to predominate in times of political realignment. As David O'Brien has observed, "The increase in caseloads, changes in the business coming before the federal courts, and the growth both of the federal bench and of the role of courts in implementing national public policy make judicial appointments a critical policy tool—especially for presidents who want to influence the direction of the judiciary and the course of public law and policy long after they have left office."[4] Franklin Roosevelt realized this toward the end of his first term. Ronald Reagan knew it when he took office.

Evaluation of Judicial Selection

In evaluating modern judicial selection we must ask ourselves what sorts of judges we want to populate the federal bench and what type of selection process is best suited to achieve the quality and mix we desire. These are questions far easier to ask than answer.

Assume that our goal is to place on the bench professionally accomplished men and women of all races who have demonstrated that they have judicial temperament—that is, a reputation as even-tempered and fair-minded and, if already on the bench, a track record as a fair and impartial lower-level judge.[5] Assume also that we want our lower-court judges to exercise their discretion so as not to be obviously biased at either end of the ideological spectrum. Does an essentially political process, now laden with numerous clearance stations (FBI, ABA, and Senate Judiciary Committee investigations, on top of the original White House and Justice Department examinations), accomplish or have the potential for accomplishing these goals? Is there a method of judicial selection better suited to meet them?

There are other methods—for example, those used by the states to choose judges. Methods used by states to select judges include gubernatorial appointment with the advice and consent of an elected body (analogous to federal judicial selection), partisan and nonpartisan elections, merit selection, and selection by the entire legislature. State electoral methods in practice often involve a governor's making the initial appointment to replace a judge who has died, resigned, retired, or been elevated to a higher court. The person appointed by the governor to serve in the interim subsequently runs for judicial election as an incumbent, often unopposed.[6] Merit selection, the preferred method of the American Judicature Society, places heavy reliance on bar associations, particularly with statutory or constitutional provisions requiring the associations to select some members of the merit commissions. The governor, under merit selection, is obliged to select from the list of names certified to be qualified to fill the particular judicial vacancy. It is difficult, however, to determine objectively that any particular selection process is superior to the others, although gubernatorial appointment has been found to produce the most diverse bench.[7]

Jimmy Carter's selection commissions created to recruit and screen appeals court appointees came closer to merit selection than any other method used by previous administrations. Carter, however, chose all the members of the commissions, and this added a partisan bias to the commission process. Had Carter's selection commissions had their membership chosen equally by the administration, the ABA and/or other bar groups, and the Judicial Councils of each circuit, they likely would have been comparable to merit selection in the states, and that might have defused attacks on the commissions. Nevertheless, the commissions appeared to do their work well, expanding the recruitment net and, with the encouragement of the administration, recommending women and minorities at an unprecedented rate. The professional credentials of the Carter appeals court appointees were comparable to those of previous administrations, and most appeared to be moderate to liberal on the political spectrum.

Selection commissions have the potential for bringing about a diverse and highly qualified judiciary, but ultimately it is the president and the president's administration as well as senators of the president's party that must have the commitment and will to accomplish this. Institutional structures can help, but the will must be there. Arguably, there is no constitutional bar from the establishment under statutory law of the merit selection method to choose lower-court judges in order to achieve the minimal selection goals posited earlier.[8] It is, however, unrealistic to expect that the Senate will relinquish its hold on the process.

Despite occasional dissatisfaction with how a particular nomination is handled, or charges that excessive partisanship or ideological litmus tests are being applied, our current judicial selection process, with the checks and balances envisioned by the framers (and even with some that were not, such as the role of the ABA), appears under most circumstances (with the possible exception of presidential election years) to be working reasonably well. There will always be a tension between patronage, merit, and ideological considerations, and how that tension is resolved will differ from administration to administration. It will depend upon the point in political time in which an administration is functioning.[9] It will depend upon the particular personality of the president and style of presidential management. It will depend upon the personalities and the nature of the interactions within and between the White House and the Justice Department and between the executive branch and the Senate. But on the basis of the evidence reviewed in this book it appears that the goal of a professionally accomplished, politically balanced and diverse federal judiciary can potentially be served by our evolving judicial selection process.

This does not mean, however, that problems or potential problems with the process and its results are lacking. As Barrow, Zuk, and Gryski have documented, "Since the turn of the century, the party capturing the White House ultimately controls the federal bench." They have shown that this is not only facilitated by the filling of newly created judgeships (that occurs with regularity when the president and congressional majority are of the same party), but also by politically timed retirements of members of the president's party that enable the president to fill vacancies. From 1933 to 1989, the judiciary has been partisanly transformed six times (by Roosevelt, Eisenhower, Kennedy-Johnson, Nixon-Ford, Carter, and Reagan). There are decisional implications of this partisan transformation that have been shown by Robert Carp and C. K. Rowland and others.[10] If the process of selection and confirmation is increasingly seen as a politicized one, and partisan transformation of the bench is recognized as a political fact of life, will the decisional tendencies of a president's appointees be viewed as too political, thus eroding the legitimacy and authority of the federal judiciary? Would a requirement of bipartisan appointments, last proposed by the Eisenhower administration in its waning months and then championed by the ABA at the time of an evenly politically divided bench, ever be able to be enacted and overcome the traditional winner-take-all (or almost-all) mindset?

But partisan transformation of the bench, which after all is an American tradition, may pose more of a potential than a pressing problem. A more immediate concern may be the swelling of the ranks of the judiciary and high turnover, which not only makes it more difficult to socialize and integrate new members within each circuit but also can lead "to a breakdown of cohesiveness, uniformity, and certainty in national law and legal policy."[11] Should the Judicial Conference continue to recommend the creation of new positions, and should Congress follow through? Will the creation of a federal judiciary reaching or exceeding one thousand judges devalue the prestige of a federal judgeship and lead to the breakdown just suggested?

As we have seen, there has been a trend toward a more professionalized judiciary and it is reasonable to ask whether a continuation of this trend, even without a major expansion of the bench, will lead to a more technocratic, bureaucratic, bloodless judiciary, relegating the courts to the outer margins of public policy? Or will the political nature of the appointment process assure that a career judiciary will continue to exercise discretion in a policy-oriented direction?

This book has examined the diversification of the judiciary. Are the barriers and biases that worked against women and racial minorities gaining access to judicial office now evils of the past, or will the struggle be ongoing in the context of partisan agendas? This, too, like other questions I have posed, cannot be answered with certainty, although it is surely too late in the day to return to a gender- and racially biased selection process that produces mere tokenism. Yet the 1996 report of the ABA Commission on Women in the Profession, concluding that bias against women remains entrenched in the legal profession, suggests that diversification will be a continuing challenge.[12]

Because the selection process is a political process, it is amenable to change. Dissatisfaction with the confirmation process in the Senate, particularly for Supreme Court appointments following the notorious hearings concerning Clarence Thomas, has made it more likely that sensational charges against a nominee will first be heard behind closed doors rather than in full view of the media and the public. Delays in filling vacancies from nomination through confirmation, an ongoing concern of the federal judiciary, may inspire some structural changes in the process if sufficient pressure is brought to bear. A bipartisan commission on judicial selection sponsored by the Miller Center of Public Affairs at the University of Virginia, including former federal judges and former government officials involved in selection, concluded that the nomination and confirmation process has become too prolonged and un-wieldy. It recommended required timetables to shorten the timeline between a vacancy and confirmation and urged that if the Senate takes too long in con-firming judgeships, the president should make recess appointments.[13] It is uncertain as of this writing whether such changes (in terms of recess appoint-ments that would be a return of an occasional practice last used by President Carter) will find sufficient backing from the Judicial Conference and from the organized bar to be taken seriously by the Senate and the president.[d]

d. Bill Clinton's reelection in 1996 along with a Republican Congress, the first time in American political history that a Democrat has won the White House at the same time that a Republican Congress was elected, produced an unusual turn of events for lower court judicial selection. Some Republican senators succeeded in, for the most part, stop-ping the confirmation process so that by the spring of 1997 only 2 nominees out of 29

The judiciary of the twenty-first century is likely to be staffed by well-trained professionals, with substantial numbers drawn from the lower-level judiciaries. Although some judges will have had some political experience, judgeships as patronage may well become the exception rather than the rule. Women and minorities will likely make up a larger proportion of the judiciary, but unless women and minorities become a majority of the legal profession, white males can be expected to continue to hold a substantial majority of federal judgeships.

Each administration will have to balance the conflicting pull of patronage, merit, and ideology and the extent to which the partisan, policy, and personal agendas prevail. The personal participation of the president will depend upon his or her own interests in partisan and policy politics and the extent to which a president's managerial style leads toward micromanaging selection. But one facet of the appointment process will be ongoing. Each filling of a judicial vacancy is a minidrama of individual ambitions, backstage maneuverings, mobilization of support, and occasional double-dealing, and is affected by the values of those involved in the process. There is human drama as political forces, events, and personalities intersect.[14] And the end result is the staffing of the third branch of government, which by its actions — or inactions — has a profound effect on American lives.

---

nominations had been voted on by the Senate. Some Republican senators were insisting on an ideological veto over Clinton's nominees while others were demanding a share of judicial patronage. The Republican senatorial conference narrowly rejected proposals that would have permitted the exercise of such a veto. See Neil A. Lewis, "Move to Limit Clinton's Judicial Choices Fails," *New York Times*, April 30, 1997, A20 (New England edition). These court-blocking tactics posed a challenge to the president's constitutional nomination power.

Appendix: A Note on Sources and the Data Base

In preparing this book I relied principally on the presidential papers of the presidents under study. Biographical information on the appointees found in the papers was used to construct the data base and was considered definitive. Another authoritative source for those appointed in 1979 and beyond was the questionnaires completed by the nominees for the Senate Judiciary Committee. The original questionnaire was published in *Selection and Confirmation of Federal Judges,* Hearing Before the Committee on the Judiciary, U.S. Senate, 96th Congress, 1st Session, 1979, Serial No. 96–21, Part I, pp. 123–32. During the Ninety-seventh Congress a shortened and modified questionnaire was substituted. A discussion of some of those changes was presented in Sheldon Goldman, "Judicial Selection and the Qualities That Make a 'Good' Judge," *The Annals* 462 (July 1982): 117–18. Personal interviews with appointees or responses to written queries from the author were also considered definitive sources.

Biographical information supplied by the judges is also contained in *Judges of the United States,* 2d ed. (Washington, D.C.: Government Printing Office, 1983). The information published in that volume was derived for many of the judges from questionnaires sent to them from the Federal Judicial Center. Those questionnaires, located in the Federal Judicial History Office, were also examined.

For appointees to the courts of appeals, an especially useful source of data on party affiliation and religion is the 1972 publication of the Senate Judiciary Committee, 92nd Congress, 2nd Session, *Legislative History of the United States Circuit*

Courts of Appeals and the Judges Who Served during the Period 1801 through May 1972.

Before 1979, hearings by the Senate Judiciary Committee on lower-court nominations were ordinarily not published. Published and unpublished hearings were consulted.

Several commercially published biographical directories are useful sources of information: *The American Bench* (various editions), *The Federal Judiciary Almanac, Who's Who* (national and regional editions), *Who's Who in American Law, Who's Who in American Politics,* and the *Judicial Staff Directory* (annual editions). The annual editions of *Martindale-Hubbell Law Directory* were used to determine size of law firms.

The annual *Congressional Quarterly Almanac,* state legislative handbooks, newspaper articles about the appointees published in home state newspapers, and Senate Judiciary Committee and administration staff, along with several academic colleagues, were all additional data sources. So was Harold W. Chase, Samuel Krislov, Keith O. Boyum, and Jerry N. Clark, *Biographical Dictionary of the Federal Judiciary* (Detroit: Gale Research Company, 1976).

Coding the Variables for the Data Base

Age at the time of appointment was the age of the nominee when first nominated. If the individual was renominated, the date of the first nomination was used. If the nominee was within thirty days of his or her birthday, the age used was that of the closest birthday.

Judges who attended an undergraduate institution even if not receiving a degree were counted as having an undergraduate education. The same was true for law school education.

Any type of judicial and prosecutorial experience, regardless of duration, was counted in the experience variable.

Occupation was classified according to principal activity. Thus, for example, an elected state or federal official who also maintained an interest in a law firm was classified as "politics-government" and not as being in the private practice of law. A member of a law firm who also taught part-time in a law school was categorized by size of firm and not as a professor of law. There were two different criteria for size of firm—one for the Roosevelt through the Eisenhower appointees and one for the Kennedy through the Reagan appointees. (These criteria are described in the tables within the chapters). The changing criteria sought to capture the change in the private practice of law in what is considered a large, medium-size, or small firm.

The ABA ratings were obtained from the files and reports of the American Bar Association, from the files of the Senate Judiciary Committee in the National Archives, and from administration personnel.

Political party affiliation was for the most part readily determined in the presidential papers until early in the Carter administration, when the Justice Department stopped listing party affiliation in the resumes of nominees. Other biographical sources, as mentioned previously, were used to determine party affiliation.

Prominent party activism was defined as any public partisan activity. Thus, for example, a financial contribution by itself would not qualify as prominent party activism. But being a co-treasurer of a campaign or listing active party work on behalf of a party candidate, at whatever governmental level, would be classified under prominent party activism.

Religion was a difficult variable to code for judges who did not indicate religious origin or affiliation in the various questionnaires or volunteer that information to the publishers of biographical directories. In some instances religion was revealed in newspaper stories, including obituaries. In others, inferences were drawn based on family name in combination with other background information. In my published *Judicature* articles I was more liberal than I am here in drawing such inferences. Thus there are some appointees whose religion I now classify as "unknown."

There are some minor differences in the statistics in this book as compared with those found in my *Judicature* articles and other writings that relied on my original data base. These differences are a result of my having recoded the data base with the presidential papers as the definitive source. Also, in some instances, more authoritative information became available and replaced less reliable data. Coding or data-processing errors and reconsideration of conflicting data sources were responsible for a few other differences. None of the changes, however, appear to affect the interpretation or conclusions of my overall findings in this and my other work.

Notes

Chapter One: Judicial Selection in Theoretical and Historical Perspective

1. On the Fortas nomination to the chief justiceship see Bruce Allen Murphy, *Fortas: The Rise and Ruin of a Supreme Court Justice* (New York: Morrow, 1988), chaps. 11–22, and Laura Kalman, *Abe Fortas: A Biography* (New Haven: Yale University Press, 1990), 327–58. On the Bork nomination, see Ethan Bronner, *Battle for Justice: How the Bork Nomination Shook America* (New York: Norton, 1989), and Mark Gitenstein, *Matters of Principle: An Insider's Account of America's Rejection of Robert Bork's Nomination to the Supreme Court* (New York: Simon & Schuster, 1992). On the Thomas nomination, see Timothy M. Phelps and Helen Winternitz, *Capitol Games: Clarence Thomas, Anita Hill, and the Story of a Supreme Court Nomination* (New York: Hyperion, 1992) and Jane Mayer and Jill Abramson, *Strange Justice: The Selling of Clarence Thomas* (Boston: Houghton Mifflin, 1994). On the battle over Taney, see Carl B. Swisher, *Roger B. Taney* (New York: MacMillan, 1936), chaps. 15–17, and Walker Lewis, *Without Fear or Favor* (Boston: Houghton Mifflin, 1965), 238–49. On Brandeis, see A. L. Todd, *Justice on Trial: The Case of Louis D. Brandeis* (New York: McGraw-Hill, 1964), and Alpheus T. Mason, *Brandeis: A Free Man's Life* (New York: Viking, 1946), chaps. 30 and 31. See also Stephen L. Carter, *The Confirmation Mess: Cleaning up the Federal Appointments Process* (New York: Basic Books, 1994); John Anthony Maltese, *The Selling of Supreme Court Nominees* (Baltimore: Johns Hopkins University Press, 1995), and Mark Silverstein, *Judicious Choices: The New Politics of Supreme Court Confirmation* (New York: W. W. Norton, 1994).

2. Some scholars, however, have paid attention to lower-court appointments. See Joel B. Grossman, *Lawyers and Judges* (New York: Wiley, 1965); Harold W. Chase, *Federal Judges: The Appointing Process* (Minneapolis: University of Minnesota Press, 1972); J. Woodford Howard, Jr., *Courts of Appeals in the Federal Judicial System* (Princeton, N.J.: Princeton University Press, 1981); David M. O'Brien, *Judicial Roulette* (New York: Priority Press, 1988); Sheldon Goldman, "Federal Judicial Recruitment," in John B. Gates and Charles A. Johnson, eds., *The American Courts: A Critical Assessment* (Washington, D.C.: CQ Press, 1991), 189–210; Deborah J. Barrow, Gary Zuk, and Gerard S. Gryski, *The Federal Judiciary and Institutional Change* (Ann Arbor: University of Michigan Press, 1996); and C. K. Rowland and Robert A. Carp, *Politics and Judgment in Federal District Courts* (Lawrence: University Press of Kansas, 1996). See also Elliot E. Slotnick, "Federal Judicial Recruitment and Selection Research: A Review Essay," *Judicature* 71 (1988): 317–24; Walter F. Murphy, "Reagan's Judicial Strategy," in Larry Berman, ed., *Looking Back on the Reagan Presidency* (Baltimore: Johns Hopkins University Press, 1990), 207–37.

3. *The Status of Federalism in America: A Report of the Working Group on Federalism of the Domestic Policy Council* (Washington, D.C.: Justice Department, Office of Legal Counsel, November 1986).

4. See Stephen Labaton, "Presidents' Judicial Appointments: Diverse, but Well in the Mainstream," *New York Times,* October 17, 1994, A15.

5. The concept of agenda is developed in John W. Kingdon, *Agendas, Alternatives, and Public Policies,* 2d ed. (New York: HarperCollins, 1995), and Paul C. Light, *The President's Agenda: Domestic Policy Choice from Kennedy to Reagan,* rev. ed. (Baltimore: Johns Hopkins University Press, 1991).

6. Sheldon Goldman, "Judicial Appointments and the Presidential Agenda," in Paul Brace, Christine B. Harrington, and Gary King, eds., *The Presidency in American Politics* (New York: New York University Press, 1989), 22.

7. See Thomas P. Jahnige, "Critical Elections and Social Change: Towards a Dynamic Explanation of National Party Competition in the United States," *Polity* 3 (1971): 465–500; Walter Dean Burnham, *Critical Elections and the Mainsprings of American Politics* (New York: Norton, 1970); Walter Dean Burnham, *The Current Crisis in American Politics* (New York: Oxford University Press, 1982), 251–320; Bruce A. Campbell and Richard J. Trilling, eds., *Realignment in American Politics: Toward a Theory* (Austin: University of Texas Press, 1980); and James L. Sundquist, *Dynamics of the Party System: Alignment and Realignment of Political Parties in the United States,* rev. ed. (Washington, D.C.: Brookings, 1983).

8. The concept of a deviating election was first suggested in Angus Campbell, Philip E. Converse, Warren E. Miller, and Donald E. Stokes, *The American Voter* (New York: Wiley, 1960), 532–33.

9. Max Farrand, ed., *The Records of the Federal Convention of 1787* (New Haven: Yale University Press, 1911), Virginia Plan: 1:21; Rutledge: 1:119; Madison: 1:120.

10. Wilson: Farrand, *Records,* 2:41; Mason: Ibid., 2:83; The convention reaffirmed: Ibid., 2:83.

11. September 4: Ibid., 2:495; September 7: Ibid., 2:539.

12. Ibid., 2:659–60.

13. Alexander Hamilton, *Federalist 76*, in Jacob E. Cooke, ed., *The Federalist* (Cleveland: Meridian Books, 1961), 512, 513.

14. See Julius Goebel, Jr., *Antecedents and Beginnings to 1801*, vol. 1, *History of the Supreme Court of the United States* (New York: Macmillan, 1971), 457–508, and Maeva Marcus, ed., *Origins of the Federal Judiciary: Essays on the Judiciary Act of 1789* (New York: Oxford University Press, 1992).

15. As quoted in Benjamin F. Wright, *The Growth of American Constitutional Law* (Chicago: University of Chicago Press, 1967), 31.

16. Kermit L. Hall, *The Politics of Justice* (Lincoln: University of Nebraska Press, 1979), chap. 1.

17. Ibid., 5.

18. Ibid., 29.

19. Ibid., 62.

20. Ibid., 90.

21. Ibid., 131–50. Buchanan named forty-two men to the lower courts.

22. An example of this is the decision in *The Prize Cases*, 2 Black 635 (1863).

23. Daniel S. McHargue, "President Taft's Appointments to the Supreme Court," *Journal of Politics* 12 (1950): 509.

24. Judicial selection in: Henry J. Abraham, *Justices and Presidents: A Political History of Appointments to the Supreme Court*, 2d ed. (New York: Oxford University Press, 1985), 178–83, and Rayman L. Solomon, "The Politics of Appointment and the Federal Courts' Role in Regulating America: U.S. Courts of Appeals Judgeships from T.R. to F.D.R.," *American Bar Foundation Research Journal* (1984): 314–23; This resulted in: Joseph P. Harris, *The Advice and Consent of the Senate: A Study of the Confirmation of Appointments by the United States Senate* (Berkeley: University of California Press, 1953), 317–20.

25. Memorandum to My Successor, November 26, 1968, EX FG 50 The Judicial Branch [1969–70], WHCF, Nixon Materials Project.

26. Ibid., 1.

27. Ibid., 5.

28. Ibid., 6.

29. Ibid., 6, 7.

30. Ibid., 7.

31. Ibid., 8.

32. Ibid., 9.

33. Ibid., 10.

34. Ibid., 11.

Chapter Two: Roosevelt Remakes the Courts

1. There are several outstanding biographies of Roosevelt that capture his imprint on the presidency. Among them are James MacGregor Burns, *Roosevelt: The Lion and the Fox* (New York: Harcourt, Brace, 1956); Frank Freidel, *Franklin D. Roosevelt: A Rendezvous with Destiny* (Boston: Little, Brown, 1990); and Arthur M. Schlesinger, Jr.,

The Age of Roosevelt, 3 vols. (Boston: Houghton Mifflin, 1957–1960). Roosevelt's impact on the presidency is also considered by William E. Leuchtenburg, *In the Shadow of FDR,* rev. ed. (Ithaca, N.Y.: Cornell University Press, 1989). Leading studies of the presidency with relevant material on Roosevelt include James D. Barber, *Presidential Character,* 3d ed. (Englewood Cliffs, N.J.: Prentice-Hall, 1985), and Richard Neustadt, *Presidential Power: The Politics of Leadership,* rev. ed. (New York: Wiley, 1964).

2. The material in this and the following four paragraphs is drawn from Sheldon Goldman, *Constitutional Law and Supreme Court Decision-Making* (New York: Harper & Row, 1982), 248–50.

3. OF 208 n South Carolina 1934–1939. Unless otherwise noted, all references in this chapter are to papers found in the Franklin D. Roosevelt Library, Hyde Park, New York.

4. OF 208 s Missouri 1933–1942.

5. Roosevelt memo to Cummings and letter to Connally in OF 208 l Texas 1933–1945.

6. OF 208 t Rhode Island 1933–1945.

7. Corcoran to Roosevelt, April 29, 1935, OF 208 t Rhode Island 1933–1945.

8. OF 209 a 1st Circuit 1935–1939.

9. For a discussion of the court-packing plan and the unsuccessful battle to enact it, see Burns, *Roosevelt,* 291–315, and Freidel, *Franklin D. Roosevelt,* 221–39. Also see James A. Farley, *Jim Farley's Story: The Roosevelt Years* (New York: McGraw-Hill, 1948), 77–99.

10. OF 208 ee Mississippi 1933–1945.

11. See Francis Biddle, *In Brief Authority* (Westport, Conn.: Greenwood, 1976), 182–83.

12. OF 208 x Oregon 1933–1945.

13. OF 208 c New York 1937–1939.

14. OF 209 g 7th Circuit 1933–1945.

15. Roosevelt to Jackson, August 5, 1940, in OF 208 l California Aug.–Dec. 1940.

16. All memos relating to Duncan are found in OF 208 s Missouri 1943–1945; Biddle wrote: Biddle, *In Brief Authority,* 204.

17. *New York Times,* February 21, 1939, p. 12.

18. All letters and memos concerning the Meaney nomination are found in OF 208 ll New Jersey 1940–1945; letter from Walker to Roosevelt, October 2, 1941; see the column by Arthur Krock, *New York Times,* May 7, 1942, p. 18, decrying the Meaney nomination as propping up the Hague machine. Also see the *New York Times* news story on Meaney and Walker on May 5, 1942, p. 38.

19. All the memos in this section concerning Brennan are found in OF 208 c New York 1942–1945.

20. See *New York Times,* March 25, 1934, sec. 4, p. 7.

21. OF 209 i 9th Circuit 1933–1935.

22. Bert E. Haney to Roosevelt, Sept. 4, 1935, OF 209 i 9th Circuit 1933–1935.

23. OF 51 s Court of Appeals for D.C. 1933–1945.

24. See Marvin Schick, *Learned Hand's Court* (Baltimore: Johns Hopkins University Press, 1970), chap. 8. Also see the empirical evidence showing Clark to be a leading

liberal on the circuit in Sheldon Goldman, "Conflict and Consensus in the United States Courts of Appeals," *Wisconsin Law Review,* 1968: 467–71.

25. OF 51 s Court of Appeals for D.C. 1933–1945.

26. See Francis Biddle, *A Casual Past* (Garden City, N.Y.: Doubleday, 1961), 168–69, 279.

27. OF 209 c 3rd Circuit Oct.–Dec. 1938.

28. Biddle, *In Brief Authority,* 80.

29. OF 209 c 3rd Circuit 1939.

30. See Burns, *Roosevelt,* 358–80, Freidel, *Franklin D. Roosevelt,* 280–88, and Farley, *Jim Farley's Story,* 120–50.

31. Dean Acheson, *Morning and Noon* (Boston: Houghton Mifflin, 1965), 212, as quoted in Harold W. Chase, *Federal Judges: The Appointing Process* (Minneapolis: University of Minnesota Press, 1972), 12. Also see *New York Times,* February 9, 1939, p. 10.

32. Figures on the number of injunctions and the proportion of Republican judges are from Schlesinger, 3:447–48.

33. OF 209 f 6th Circuit 1934–1938.

34. Senators Robinson and Caraway to Roosevelt, May 4, 1933, in OF 208 a Arkansas 1933–1945.

35. OF 208 k Montana 1933–1945.

36. OF 208 r Alabama 1933–1945.

37. Albert B. Maris to Roosevelt, June 22, 1936, OF 208 hh Pennsylvania 1933–1935.

38. William Denman to Roosevelt, November 7, 1936, OF 208 U.S. District Judgeships 1933–1945.

39. Keenan to Mac, June 18, 1937, OF 208 h California 1933–1937.

40. Henry Wallace to Roosevelt, March 30, 1937, OF 208 o Florida 1933–1939.

41. Lloyd L. Black: Mon C. Wallgren to Roosevelt, June 15, 1938, OF 208 d Washington 1933–1938; Bankhead: Bankhead to Roosevelt, September 6, 1939, OF 208 d Washington 1938–1945; John Miller praised: Clyde Ellis to Roosevelt, September 23, 1940, OF 208 a Arkansas 1933–1945.

42. Moses praising Vogel: OF 208 qq North Dakota 1933–1940; Wickard letter: Claude Wickard to Roosevelt, April 15, 1941, OF 208 qq North Dakota March–Dec. 1941.

43. Kentucky Federation of Labor quote: *Cincinnati Enquirer,* January 28, 1939; Linton M. Collins to Frank Murphy, February 15, 1939, OF 208 q Kentucky 1933–1945; Senators Barkley and Logan to Frank Murphy, January 30, 1939, in Department of Justice file on Shackelford Miller.

44. Roosevelt to James Rowe, March 13, 1941, OF 208 h California 1941–1945.

45. Clark to Roosevelt, June 29, 1934, OF 209, U.S. Circuit Court of Appeal 1933–1945.

46. Cummings to Roosevelt, October 9, 1937, OF 51 s END U.S. Court of Appeals for District of Columbia 1933–1945.

47. Murray to Roosevelt, May 27, 1937, OF 209 i 9th Circuit 1936–1939; James Roosevelt to Roosevelt, June 1, 1937, OF 209 i 9th Circuit 1936–1939.

48. Pope to Senator Murray, August 8, 1937, OF 51 s END, U.S. Court of Appeals for District of Columbia 1933–1945.

49. "very much in sympathy": Justice Department File of John Biggs, Jr.; John Biggs, Jr., to Roosevelt, February 19, 1937, OF 209 c 3rd Circuit 1937–July 1938.

50. Mac to Roosevelt, March 13, 1937, and Roosevelt to Mac, March 17, 1937, OF 209 j 10th Circuit 1933–1939. These and all other memos relating to the promotion of Judge Williams are found in OF 209 j 10th Circuit 1933–1939.

51. *Guinn* v. *United States,* 238 U.S. 347.

52. OF 209 j 10th Circuit 1933–1939.

53. Biddle to Rowe, March 8, 1943, Justice Department file of Gerald Michael Francis McLaughlin.

54. Raymond B. Stevens [chairman of the U.S. Tariff Commission] to Roosevelt, September 27, 1939, OF 209 a 1st Circuit 1935–1939.

55. Roosevelt to Murphy, December 28, 1939, OF 209 a 1st Circuit 1935–1939.

56. Perkins to Jackson, April 25, 1940, Justice Department file of Peter Woodbury.

57. Justice Department file of Peter Woodbury. The memo and letters cited in the next paragraph are also from this source.

58. OF 209 a 1st Circuit June–Dec. 1940.

59. Smathers to Keenan, June 10, 1938, OF 208 ll New Jersey 1938.

60. OF 208 ff Ohio 1938.

61. Cummings prepared: OF 208 ff Ohio 1938; Donahey to Mac, January 19, 1939, OF 208 ff Ohio Jan.–Feb. 1939.

62. Roosevelt to Biddle, December 22, 1941, OF 208 l Texas 1933–1945.

63. OF 208 s Missouri 1933–1942.

64. Roosevelt to Mac, July 7, 1942, OF 208 l Texas 1933–1945.

65. Mac to Roosevelt, July 13, 1942, OF 208 l Texas 1933–1945.

66. OF 208 m Georgia 1941–1945.

67. OF 209 e 5th Circuit 1933–1945.

68. Douglas to Roosevelt, August 31, 1942, OF 209 e 5th Circuit 1933–1945; Lyndon Johnson: memo from James Rowe, Jr., to Grace Tully, September 4, 1942, OF 209 e 5th Circuit 1933–1945; Biddle to Roosevelt, April 2, 1943, OF 209 e 5th Circuit 1933–1945.

69. See the account of the Roberts affair in Joseph P. Harris, *The Advice and Consent of the Senate* (Berkeley: University of California Press, 1953), 231–34. Also see the following stories that appeared in the *New York Times,* July 12, 1938, p. 4; January 10, 1939, p. 7; February 2, 1939, p. 1; February 7, 1939, p. 1; February 8, 1939, p. 1.

70. OF 208 z Virginia (Roberts Folder 1933–1938). Other memos and letters related to Roberts are found here.

71. Roosevelt to Dobie, May 31, 1939, OF 208 U.S. District Judgeships 1933–1945.

72. Farley, *Jim Farley's Story,* 35.

73. Handwritten notation: OF 208 m Georgia 1941–1945; Rowe to Mac, October 13, 1941, James Rowe Papers, Box 17, Justice Appts., Roosevelt Library.

74. OF 41 c 1943–1945 District Court of Washington D.C.–End.

75. Rowe to Roosevelt, September 24, 1941, James Rowe Papers, Box 18, Justice Appts., U.S. District Courts.

76. Brown to Roosevelt, February 8, 1941, OF 209 f 6th Circuit Jan.–Feb. 1941.

77. Garrett Whiteside to Marvin H. McIntyre, October 20, 1941, OF 209 h 8th Circuit April 1941–1945.

78. Cummings to Roosevelt, August 9, 1937, OF 209 g 7th Circuit 1933–1945.

79. Cummings to Roosevelt, December 7, 1937, OF 209 g 7th Circuit 1933–1945; Rowe to Roosevelt, April 28, 1941, OF 209 g 7th Circuit 1933–1945.

80. Cummings to Roosevelt, June 11, 1938, OF 209 f 6th Circuit 1934–1938.

81. OF 208 d Washington 1938–1945.

82. Biddle, *In Brief Authority,* 83–84.

83. Clark to Roosevelt, August 13, 1941, PPF 576 Clark, William.

84. Watson to Clark, August 21, 1941, in PPF 576 Clark, William.

85. See *New York Times,* March 18, 1942, p. 4; and March 25, 1942, p. 24.

86. William O. Douglas, *Go East, Young Man* (New York: Random House, 1974), 334.

87. OF 209 c 3rd Circuit 1940–1945.

88. Biddle to Roosevelt, December 19, 1944, OF 209 c 3rd Circuit 1940–1945; Biddle to Roosevelt, January 17, 1945, OF 209 c 3rd Circuit 1940–1945.

89. Allen's political support: Florence Ellinwood Allen, *To Do Justly* (Cleveland: Press of Western Reserve University, 1965), 93–95; on Dewson and Eleanor Roosevelt's support, see Beverly B. Cook, "The First Woman Candidate for the Supreme Court— Florence E. Allen," *Yearbook 1981, Supreme Court Historical Society,* 26.

90. Roosevelt to Mac, October 29, 1943, OF 209 i 9th Circuit 1940–1945.

91. OF 208 h California 1941–1945.

92. OF 208 h California 1941–1945.

93. OF 208 h California 1938–Mar. 1939; April–July 1939.

94. Roosevelt to Rowe, September 25, 1941, OF 208 j Massachusetts 1940–Sept. 1941.

95. Mary Connor Myers: OF 41 c J-Z 1938–1939 District Court of Washington, D.C. END; Murphy quote, emphasis added: J. Woodford Howard, *Mr. Justice Murphy* (Princeton: Princeton University Press, 1968), 192. Also see Murphy to Roosevelt, December 7, 1944, OF 208 cc Michigan 1939–1945; Roosevelt quote, emphasis added: *New York Times,* December 30, 1936, p. 2. Also see *New York Times,* June 8, 1938, p. 19.

96. Susan Brandeis: OF 208 c New York 1937–1939; Some months later: Materials concerning the filling of the vacancy are found in OF 208 c New York 1940.

97. OF 208 ff Ohio 1933–1937.

98. OF 208 bb Virgin Islands 1936–1944.

99. Biddle to Roosevelt, December 12, 1944, OF 41 c 1943–1945 District Court of Washington D.C. END.

100. *Smith v. Allwright:* 321 U.S. 649 (1944); Roosevelt to Biddle, December 17, 1944, OF 41 c 1943–1945 District Court of Washington D.C. END.

101. OF 41 c 1938–1939 A-I District Court of Washington, D.C. END.

102. "For your information": Roosevelt to Jackson, April 11, 1940, OF 208 c New York 1940; Chicago branch NAACP: OF 208 e Illinois 1933–1945; So, too, in 1940: OF 208 hh Pennsylvania 1933–1945.

103. OF 208 c New York 1937–1939.

104. Biddle to Roosevelt, December 29, 1941, OF 208 b Nebraska 1933–1945.

105. Memorandum for the Attorney General, November 27, 1942, Francis Biddle Papers, Box 2, Judicial Appts.

106. See, for example, Lawrence Baum, Sheldon Goldman, and Austin Sarat, "The Evolution of Litigation in the Federal Courts of Appeals, 1895–1975," *Law & Society Review* 16 (1981–82): 291–309. For a history of changes in judicial bureaucratic structures, see Peter G. Fish, *The Politics of Federal Judicial Administration* (Princeton: Princeton University Press, 1973).

Chapter Three: Truman Carries On

1. Two major biographies of Harry Truman that also contain extensive bibliographies are David McCullough, *Truman* (New York: Simon and Schuster, 1992) and Alonzo L. Hamby, *Man of the People: A Life of Harry S. Truman* (New York: Oxford University Press, 1995). An older but more detailed exploration of the Truman presidency is the two-volume work by Robert J. Donovan, *Conflict and Crisis: The Presidency of Harry S. Truman, 1945–1948* (New York: Norton, 1977) and *Tumultuous Years: The Presidency of Harry S. Truman, 1949–1953* (New York: Norton, 1982). Also see the biography written by Truman's daughter, Margaret Truman, *Harry S. Truman* (New York: Morrow, 1973).

2. The material in this section draws from Sheldon Goldman, *Constitutional Law and Supreme Court Decision-Making* (New York: Harper and Row, 1982), 400–402.

3. First letter from senators: Josiah W. Bailey and Clyde R. Hoey to Truman, OF 208 a Endorsements A–Z Eastern District; follow-up letter: Bailey and Hoey to Truman, April 20, 1945, OF 208 a Endorsements A–Z Eastern District. Unless otherwise noted, all references in this chapter are to papers found in the Harry S. Truman Presidential Library, Independence, Mo.

4. Joseph H. Ball to Truman, OF 208 b Endorsements; Truman to Joseph H. Ball, OF 208 b Endorsements.

5. Truman elevated his friend: OF 209 g Seventh Circuit; Democratic leaders in Vermont: OF 208 p Vermont.

6. Keech continued playing: Robert H. Ferrell, ed., *Truman in the White House: The Diary of Eben A. Ayers* (Columbia: University of Missouri Press, 1991), 166, 178, 312; Truman's Supreme Court appointments: Henry J. Abraham, *Justices and Presidents,* 2d ed. (New York: Oxford University Press, 1985), 237–47.

7. Clark to Truman, November 9, 1945, OF 208 k Kansas.

8. Memorandum from the President for Tom C. Clark, April 7, 1947, OF 208 ff Eastern District.

9. Joseph Keenan to Donald Dawson, n.d., OF 208 ii Endorsements — Eastern District A–S; Becker's support: William T. Evjue to Truman, March 24, 1949, OF 208 ii Endorsements — Eastern District A–S.

10. Zablocki to Truman, March 30, 1949, OF 208 ii Endorsements — Eastern District W–Z.

11. Labor backs Tehan: Reuther to Truman, March 25, 1949, OF 208 ii Endorsements-Eastern District A–S; Humphrey to Connelly, March 30, 1949, OF 208 ii Endorsements-Eastern District T–V; Vaughan to Dawson, March 31, 1949, OF 208 ii Endorsements-Eastern District A–S.

12. Zablocki to Truman, April 13, 1949, OF 208 ii Eastern District (Wisconsin).

13. This account is drawn from the documents in OF 208 n Northern District and OF 208 n Endorsements A–Z.

14. Oliver Carter to Truman, August 20, 1949, OF 208 O Endorsements-Northern District O–Z.

15. Mrs. Edward H. Heller to Truman, January 16, 1950, OF 208 o Endorsements-Northern District A–F.

16. Sabath had previously: Sabath to Truman, October 18, 1949, OF 208 t Northern District A–D; Truman wrote on sketch: OF 208 t Northern District A–D; Truman informed Sabath: A.J. Sabath to J. Earl Major, June 15, 1951, OF 208 t Illinois.

17. Joseph P. Harris, *The Advice and Consent of the Senate* (Berkeley: University of California Press, 1953), 321.

18. Irv Kupcinet, "Kup's Column," *Chicago Sun-Times,* August 12, 1951, p. 32.

19. OF 208 t Northern District A–D.

20. Douglas asks Chicago bar: Harris, 322; results of poll: Cushman B. Bissell to Truman, July 30, 1951, OF t Endorsements-Northern District E–Z; Illinois Bar: Harris, 322, and *New York Times,* July 25, 1951, p. 16; American Bar Association: *New York Times,* August 3, 1951, p. 9.

21. *New York Times,* October 10, 1951, p. 15.

22. Administration attacked: See Andrew J. Dunar, *The Truman Scandals and the Politics of Morality* (Columbia: University of Missouri Press, 1984); Arvey did note: Arvey to Connelly, March 15, 1952, OF 208 t Northern District Endorsements Miscellaneous.

23. Truman to William M. Byrne, October 19, 1950, OF 208 o Southern District.

24. *Youngstown Sheet & Tube Co. v. Sawyer,* 343 U.S. 579 (1952).

25. Vaughan to the Attorney General, September 7, 1945, OF 209 c Endorsements A–Z.

26. OF 209 c Endorsements A–Z.

27. OF 208 d Western District. The letter was misfiled and should have been with the Eastern District file.

28. OF 208 d Michigan-Eastern District.

29. Solomon was backed: Sweetland to Dawson, October 6, 1949, OF 208 c Endorsements Q–Z; A newspaper editor wrote: Ben Buisman to Truman, July 29, 1949, OF 208 c Oregon; Ritter attacked: See letters in OF 208 e Endorsements A–Z.

30. Stevenson to Truman, October 3, 1949, Justice Department File on Charles Fahy.

31. Gillette considered him: Jake Moore to Donald Dawson, April 29, 1950, OF 208 nn Endorsements A–Z; Gillette charged: *New York Times,* June 12, 1949, p. 43. For a detailed examination of the filling of this vacancy, see Robert A. Carp, "The Function, Impact, and Political Relevance of the Federal District Courts: A Case Study," Ph.D. diss., University of Iowa, 1969.

32. Gillette announced: *New York Times,* June 26, 1949, p. 38; *New York Times* claimed: *New York Times,* August 10, 1949, p. 18; Truman responded to telegram: Truman to Switzer, August 16, 1949, OF 208 nn Endorsements A–Z; Truman on September 8: *New York Times,* September 9, 1949, p. 21.

33. *New York Times,* August 10, 1950, p. 1.

34. McCarran wanted a Nevadan: McCarran to Truman, April 16, 1946, OF 209 i

Endorsements A–L.; Clark advised Truman: Clark to Truman, July 20, 1945, OF 209 i Ninth.

35. Wiley announced: *New York Times,* December 2, 1946, p. 26; Wanted a political balance: *New York Times,* January 6, 1947, p. 1; He also proclaimed: *New York Times,* January 10, 1947, p. 12.

36. OF 208 m Pennsylvania Western District.

37. Boyle to Connelly, January 13, 1950, OF 208 l New Jersey.

38. See *New York Times,* March 2, 1950, p. 4.

39. *New York Times,* July 15, 1951, sec. 4, p. 7.

40. Hannegan urged Truman: Hannegan to Truman, May 18, 1945, OF 41 g District Court of the U.S. for the District of Columbia; Truman replied: OF 41 g District Court of the U.S. for the District of Columbia.

41. Boyle to Ford, February 7, 1951, OF 208 m Endorsements Western District A–Z.

42. Truman to Mike Mansfield, February 1, 1949, OF 209 i Endorsements M–Z.

43. Minton to Truman, November 26, 1948, OF 209 g Endorsements A–F.

44. Truman to Dawson, November 30, 1948, OF 209 g Endorsements A–F.

45. Richard K. Burke, *The Path to the Court: A Study of Federal Judicial Appointments,* Ph.D. diss., Vanderbilt University (1959), 229.

46. Letter from Collet: Collet to Truman, December 20, 1950, OF 208 l Endorsements A–Z; Truman memo: Truman to McGrath, October 27, 1951, OF 208 l New Jersey.

47. Truman to Taft, November 16, 1949, OF 208 z Northern District of Ohio.

48. Taft to Truman, December 5, 1949, OF 208 z Northern District of Ohio.

49. ABA created: *New York Times,* July 4, 1946, p. 17. Also see Joel B. Grossman, *Lawyers and Judges* (New York: Wiley, 1965), pp. 60–69; Wiley announced: *New York Times,* February 3, 1947, p. 14; delayed consideration: *New York Times,* July 9, 1947, p. 11; opposed the nomination: *New York Times,* July 16, 1947, p. 16.

50. Keenan to Truman, January 18, 1950, OF 208 z Northern District of Ohio; Truman to Keenan, January 21, 1950, OF 208 z Northern District of Ohio; Truman to Dawson, January 21, 1950, OF z Northern District of Ohio.

51. Burns to Dawson, February 12, 1951, OF z Northern District of Ohio.

52. Burns to McGrath, February 29, 1952, OF 208 mm Endorsements of Eastern District A–V.

53. ABA on Hennock: *New York Times,* June 28, 1951, p. 16; ABA on Drucker and Harrington: *New York Times,* August 3, 1951, p. 9; Truman remarked: *New York Times,* October 26, 1951, p. 17.

54. For background to the events that led up to McGrath's firing, see, Dunar, *Truman Scandals,* 96–120; arrangement with ABA: Grossman, *Lawyers and Judges,* 70–71.

55. See the correspondence in OF 208 bb Endorsements A–Z.

56. Patterson also noted: Patterson to McGrath, April 17, 1951, OF 209 b Second Circuit; Fitzpatrick noted: Fitzpatrick to Dawson, June 7, 1951, OF 209 b Endorsements Miscellaneous.

57. See OF 208 o Endorsements Southern District D–Z.

58. Mansfield to Truman, January 30, 1949, OF 209 i Endorsements M–Z.

59. The memo is found in the papers of J. Howard McGrath, Box 57, Additional Judgeships folder, in the Harry S. Truman Library.

60. Fitzpatrick meeting with Truman: *New York Times,* July 28, 1949, p. 24; The four men: Robert P. Patterson to Truman, September 22, 1949, OF 208 i Southern District Endorsements, Miscellaneous.

61. *Truman in the White House: The Diary of Eben A. Ayers,* ed. Robert H. Ferrell (Columbia: University of Missouri Press, 1991), 78. Ayers was assistant press secretary to Truman and usually met with the president daily.

62. Truman to Senator Edwin C. Johnson, October 14, 1949, OF 208 v Colorado (emphasis added); letter released to the public: *New York Times,* August 9, 1950, p. 54 (emphasis added).

63. Influential supporters: Memorandum for the President, January 14, 1947, OF 208 i Endorsements Southern District A–C; editorial writers on Medina: see, for example, *New York Times,* May 17, 1947, p. 14. For a detailed examination of Medina's appointment, see J. Woodford Howard, Jr., "The Amateurs Win: Harold R. Medina's Appointment as a Federal District Judge," *New York State Bar Journal* (October 1989): 14–22; two other women lawyers: see the letters sent on behalf of Shientag in OF 208 i Endorsements Southern District S–Z and for Kross in OF 208 i Endorsements Southern District K, Folder 2.

64. Telegram to Truman, September 17, 1948, OF 208 ll Endorsements Miscel.

65. Dawson to Truman, January 6, 1949, OF 208 m Endorsements Western District A–Z (emphasis in original).

66. Mrs. Roosevelt to Truman, February 3, 1949, OF 208 m Endorsements Western District A–Z.

67. Truman to Eleanor Roosevelt, February 7, 1949, OF 208 m Endorsements Western District A–Z.

68. Shientag won endorsement: *New York Times,* September 18, 1949, p. 48; Celler backing: *New York Times,* September 22, 1949, p. 37; O'Dwyer to Truman, August 12, 1949, OF 208 i New York, Southern District; O'Dwyer released letter: *New York Times,* August 15, 1949, p. 14.

69. Frank endorsed Hennock: Frank to Truman, May 8, 1951, OF 208 i Endorsements Southern District D–J; New York City bar opposition: *New York Times,* June 13, 1951, p. 17; ABA opposition: *New York Times,* June 28, 1951, p. 16; Truman refused to back down: *New York Times,* June 29, 1951, p. 23; Women's groups rallied: *New York Times,* July 12, 1951, p. 28; Federal Bar Association backed Hennock: *New York Times,* September 28, 1951, p. 24; McGrath before Senate committee: *New York Times,* October 14, 1951, p. 58; India Edwards, *Pulling No Punches: Memoirs of a Woman in Politics* (New York: Putnam, 1977), 190; ABA allegations: Grossman, *Lawyers and Judges,* 65; McCarran killed nomination: *New York Times,* October 16, 1951, p. 36.

70. Edwards to Don Dawson, January 17, 1951, OF t Northern District A–D.

71. See OF 41 g District Court of the U.S. for the District of Columbia.

72. Letters in OF 41 g Endorsements H–Z.

73. Edwards to Truman, October 14, 1949, OF 41 g Endorsements H–Z; Edwards brings Matthews to White House: Edwards, *Pulling No Punches,* 186.

74. See *New York Times,* October 4, 1945, p. 40.

75. National Bar Association president: C. W. Anderson, Jr., to Truman, September 14, 1945, OF 41 g Endorsements H–Z; Charles H. Houston: Telegram to Truman, September 1, 1945, OF 41 g Endorsements H–Z.

76. *New York Times,* January 31, 1947, p. 2.

77. Tweed to Truman, February 1, 1947, OF i Southern District Endorsements Miscellaneous.

78. *New York Times,* March 11, 1947, p. 30.

79. Alexander Wiley: *New York Times,* February 3, 1947, p. 14; Medina received nomination: Howard, "Amateurs Win," 14–22.

80. *New York Times,* September 18, 1949, p. 75.

81. Papers of J. Howard McGrath, Box 57, Additional Judgeships, Truman Library.

82. O'Dwyer to Truman, August 12, 1949, OF 208 i New York Southern District.

83. Meeting with Niles: *New York Times,* August 16, 1949, p. 4; also see OF 208 i New York and OF 208 i Southern District Endorsements Miscellaneous; Liberal Party pressure: *New York Times,* September 1, 1949, p. 16.

84. Barrett to Truman, August 24, 1949, OF 208 m Eastern District Endorsements Miscellaneous; Lilienthal to Truman, September 7, 1949, OF 208 m Endorsements Eastern District A–Z; Alexander to Niles, September 2, 1949, OF 208 m Eastern District Endorsements Miscellaneous.

85. Biddle to Truman, September 30, 1949, OF 209 c Endorsements A–Z; Truman to Biddle, October 5, 1949, OF 209 c Endorsements A–Z.

86. White House responded: Stephen J. Spingarn, Administrative Assistant to the President, to the Vice President, May 12, 1950, OF 209 c Third Circuit; committee held hearings: *New York Times,* June 29, 1950, p. 27, and July 14, 1950, p. 15; committee finally approved: *New York Times,* July 18, 1950, p. 48; Senate voted unanimously: *New York Times,* July 20, 1950, p. 50; Biggs to Truman, November 17, 1949, OF 209 c Third Circuit.

87. Files of Martin L. Friedman, Box 4, Endorsements, Letters A–E, Truman Library.

Chapter Four: Eisenhower Takes Charge

1. Among the useful works on Eisenhower and his presidency are Stephen E. Ambrose, *Eisenhower: Soldier, General of the Army, President-Elect 1890–1952,* vol. 1 (New York: Simon & Schuster, 1983) and *Eisenhower: The President,* vol. 2 (New York: Simon & Schuster, 1984); Fred I. Greenstein, *The Hidden-Hand Presidency: Eisenhower as Leader* (New York: Basic Books, 1982); Piers Brandon, *Ike: His Life and Times* (New York: Harper & Row, 1986); and Chester J. Pach, Jr., and Elmo Richardson, *The Presidency of Dwight D. Eisenhower,* rev. ed. (Lawrence: University Press of Kansas, 1991). Also see Herbert Brownell, with John P. Burke, *Advising Ike: The Memoirs of Attorney General Herbert Brownell* (Lawrence: University Press of Kansas, 1993).

2. Richard E. Neustadt, *Presidential Power: The Politics of Leadership* (New York: Science Editions, 1962), 9.

3. In general, see Greenstein, *Hidden-Hand Presidency.*

4. Supplementary Notes, Legislative Leadership Meeting, January 10, 1956, in Dwight David Eisenhower Diary Series, January 1956 Misc. (5). Unless otherwise noted, all references in this chapter are to papers found in the Dwight David Eisenhower Presidential Library, Abilene, Kansas.

5. Eisenhower to Arn, March 28, 1957, OF 100 B-10 Tenth Judicial Circuit.

6. Nomination cleared through chairman: Memorandum for Governor Adams from

William J. Hopkins, April 24, 1953, OF 100 c Illinois Northern; Eisenhower to Adams: March 9, 1955, OF 100 c District Courts of the U.S.

7. March 5, 1958, William Rogers Papers, Box 4, Pres. Eisenhower March 1955–1958.

8. Emphases in the original. Eisenhower to Rogers, February 12, 1959, Ann Whitman Administration Papers, Rogers, William P. 1959 (4).

9. Thursday, February 12, 1959, Ann Whitman Diary Series, February 1959 (1).

10. Dwight D. Eisenhower, *Mandate for Change* (Garden City, N.Y.: Doubleday, 1963), 226–27.

11. Interested in nominees: Eisenhower to Rogers, February 12, 1959, Ann Whitman Administration Papers, Rogers, William P. 1959 (4). Also see Supplementary Notes, Legislative Leadership Meeting, January 10, 1956, in Dwight David Eisenhower Diary Series, January 1956 Misc. (5); ABA rating in formal letter to president: Rogers to Robert K. Gray, June 7, 1956, OF 100 c Illinois, Eastern; Eisenhower recounted: Diary, February 5, 1957, Ann Whitman Administration Papers, Brownell, Herbert 1957 (4).

12. Eisenhower demonstrated concern: Diary, February 5, 1957, Ann Whitman Administration Papers, Brownell, Herbert 1957 (4); Eisenhower wrote to Cooper: February 18, 1959, OF 100 B-6 Sixth Judicial Circuit.

13. Capehart backed Hastings: *Chicago Tribune,* March 16, 1956, sec. 1, p. 23. Hastings was on a list of seven men from Indiana whom Capehart recommended to the president. Capehart to Eisenhower, March 30, 1956, GF 4 C-7 Seventh Circuit; president signed nomination paper: Hopkins to Adams, March 14, 1957, OF 100 B-7 Seventh Judicial Circuit.

14. Meyner to Eisenhower, October 28, 1958, OF 100 B-3 Third Judicial Circuit (emphasis in original).

15. Eisenhower to Brownell, March 8, 1955, Ann Whitman Administration Papers, Brownell, Herbert, 1955–56 (3).

16. Eisenhower to Brownell, January 30, 1953, Ann Whitman Administration Papers, Brownell, Herbert, 1952–4 (6).

17. Memorandum for the Attorney General, December 4, 1954, Ann Whitman Administration Papers, Brownell, Herbert, 1954–4 (1).

18. "Judicial Performance in the Fifth Circuit," *Yale Law Journal* 73 (1963): 120–21n156. Also see J. W. Peltason, *Fifty-Eight Lonely Men* (Urbana: University of Illinois Press, 1971), 26.

19. Memorandum for Whitman from Martin, July 7, 1954, Ann Whitman Diary Series, July 1954 (5).

20. Shanley contacted Brownell: see acknowledgement from Brownell to Shanley, February 13, 1953, GF 4 d Pa. E.D.; when the nomination papers came: Memorandum for Adams from Charles F. Willis, Jr., March 24, 1954, OF 100 c Pennsylvania Eastern.

21. Sherman Adams said: Memorandum for Adams from Charles F. Willis, Jr., January 18, 1955, OF 100 c Pennsylvania Eastern; deal with Pennsylvania senators: Richard K. Burke, *The Path to the Court,* Ph.D. diss., Vanderbilt University, 1959, p. 312.

22. Eisenhower to Brownell, January 31, 1955, OF 100 c Florida, Southern.

23. Hopkins to Eisenhower, October 24, 1958, OF 100 c Arkansas, Eastern.

24. Roberts to Eisenhower, January 29, 1959, Ann Whitman Administration Papers, Rogers, William P. 1959 (4).

25. Jack Porter: Burke, 308; Eisenhower to Porter, February 5, 1960, OF 100 c Texas, Southern; Porter to Eisenhower, May 31, 1960, OF 100 c Texas, Southern.

26. McCarthy to Eisenhower, October 14, 1959, OF 100 c Virginia, Eastern.

27. Eisenhower to McCarthy, March 21, 1960, OF 100 c Virginia, Eastern.

28. Arn to Eisenhower and Eisenhower memo: OF 100 B-10 Tenth Judicial Circuit.

29. Arn to Eisenhower, March 23, 1957, OF 100 B-10 Tenth Judicial Circuit; Eisenhower to Arn, March 28, 1957, OF 100 B-10 Tenth Judicial Circuit.

30. Justice Department file of Jean Sala Breitenstein.

31. Memorandum for the Acting Attorney General, August 19, 1957, OF 100 B-10 Tenth Judicial Circuit.

32. Eisenhower to Arn, January 10, 1958, 100 c Kansas.

33. Eisenhower to Warren, June 21, 1957, OF 100 A Supreme Court (2).

34. When Eisenhower had to fill: Eisenhower to Rogers, September 17, 1958, William Rogers Papers, President Eisenhower May 1958–December 1958; This was also Eisenhower's goal: Interview with Lawrence E. Walsh, May 27, 1964; In his memoirs: Eisenhower, *Mandate for Change,* 227.

35. Lumbard to Walsh, April 30, 1959, Justice Department file of J. Joseph Smith.

36. Letter on behalf of Haynsworth: Daniel to Brownell, June 11, 1955, Justice Department file of Clement F. Haynsworth, Jr.; Flanders to Rogers, November 23, 1954, in Justice Department file of Sterry R. Waterman.

37. Interview with Judge John Minor Wisdom, July 17, 1964.

38. Eisenhower to Rogers, May 12, 1958, William P. Rogers Papers, President Eisenhower May 1958–December 1958.

39. Ann Whitman Administration Papers, Rogers, William P., 1958 (4).

40. Harold W. Chase, *Federal Judges: The Appointing Process* (Minneapolis: University of Minnesota Press, 1972), 102.

41. Victor Friedman to Walsh, January 30, 1959, Justice Department file of Philip Forman.

42. David Klingsberg to Walsh, January 27, 1959, Justice Department file of Philip Forman.

43. Eisenhower privately: Arthur Larson, *Eisenhower: The President Nobody Knew* (New York: Charles Scribner's Sons, 1968), 124; remove from a draft: Telephone Call from Eisenhower to the Attorney General, August 19, 1956, Ann Whitman Diary Series, August 1956 ACW Diary (1).

44. The five were: Peltason, *Fifty-eight Lonely Men,* 11–12, 77, 113–15, 127–28; Peltason criticized: ibid., 84, 87, 115, 133, 140–44.

45. Support for Richard Butler: GF 4 d Arkansas Eastern; A letter: J. R. Booker to Val Washington (Republican National Committee), May 15, 1959, GF 4 d Arkansas Eastern; Cobb, however: Bernard G. Segal to Rogers, June 17, 1957, William P. Rogers papers, Segal, B.–Sey (Misc.).

46. Peltason, 26. Also see "Judicial Performance in the Fifth Circuit," 120–21n156.

47. Known southern liberal: Interview with Judge Tuttle, July 14, 1964; Interview with Judge Wisdom, July 17, 1964.

48. Rogers in an interview: Chase, *Federal Judges,* 102; Tuttle to Brownell, November 4, 1954, Justice Department file of Warren L. Jones.

49. Byrnes to Eisenhower, February 23, 1956, OF 100 B-4 Fourth Judicial Cir-

cuit; Brownell telephoned Byrnes: Memorandum for L. A. Minnich, Jr. from Rogers, March 15, 1956, with attached suggested reply for the President to the Honorable James F. Byrnes, OF 100 B-4 Fourth Judicial Circuit.

50. For a description of the Justice Department files, see Sheldon Goldman, "Judicial Appointments to the United States Courts of Appeals," *Wisconsin Law Review* (1967): 187n3.

51. Run interference: Interview with Lawrence E. Walsh, May 27, 1964; One former Justice Department official: Interview with Judge Stanley N. Barnes, July 29, 1964; were willing to stand their ground: Chase, 102–3.

52. Memo to General Persons from Max Rabb, June 10, 1953, OF 100 C Washington, Western.

53. Gray to Seaton, May 18, 1956, OF 100 c New York, Southern.

54. Memorandum for the Files, March 14, 1957, OF 100 B-2 Second Judicial Circuit.

55. See the materials in GF 4 d Maine and Rogers to Smith, June 17, 1957, William Rogers Papers, Daily Correspondence, 6/57–12/57.

56. Homer H. Gruenther to Edward A. McCabe, March 17, 1959, OF 100 c New York, Eastern.

57. Memorandum for Mr. McCabe, June 7, 1960, OF 100 c Hawaii.

58. Tucker asked the administration: *New York Times,* August 4, 1959, p. 25; ABA committee: Walsh to Hampton, September 6, 1959, OF 100 c, Texas, Eastern.

59. Rogers to Eisenhower, September 6, 1959, OF 100 c, Texas, Eastern.

60. Justice Department file of Paul C. Weick.

61. Shanley to Brownell, October 15, 1953, GF 4 d Rhode Island Endorsement.

62. Shanley to Adams, May 1, 1953, OF 100 c Louisiana.

63. Interview with Judge John Minor Wisdom, July 17, 1964.

64. Eisenhower wanted: see, for example, Hopkins to Adams, April 24, 1953, OF 100 c Illinois, Northern; there was the notation: OF 100 c Alaska (emphasis in original); not cleared: Memorandum for Governor Adams, May 12, 1955, OF 100 c Wisconsin, Eastern.

65. Flanders to Rogers, November 23, 1954, in Justice Department file of Sterry R. Waterman.

66. Shoop to Rogers, January 30, 1956, Rogers Papers, Shio-Sla.

67. All references and quotations in this and the preceding paragraph are from Memo re vacancy on Ninth Circuit Court of Appeals, GF 4 C-9 Endorsements.

68. Conducted a campaign: Interview with Judge Koelsch, July 30, 1964; ABA cleared him: Kendall to Eisenhower, September 12, 1959, OF 100 B-9 Ninth Judicial Circuit.

69. See Joel B. Grossman, *Lawyers and Judges* (New York: Wiley, 1965), 70–71, and Chase, 125–28.

70. Eisenhower specifically asked: Memorandum from Robert Gray to Sherman Adams, June 7, 1956, OF 100 (2); Gray then related: Memorandum for the File, June 8, 1956, OF 100 (2).

71. As quoted in Bernard Segal, "Federal Judicial Selection—Progress and the Promise of the Future," *Massachusetts Law Quarterly* 46 (1961): 144.

72. In his memoirs: Eisenhower, *Mandate for Change,* 226; Schnackenberg report: Fox to Rogers, December 5, 1953, in Justice Department File of Elmer J. Schnackenberg;

Given the position: Fox to Rogers, January 20, 1954, in Justice Department File of Elmer J. Schnackenberg.

73. Eighth Circuit Court of Appeals, no date, GF 4 C-8 Endorsements.

74. All quotations are from the memorandum entitled "Eighth Circuit Court of Appeals," no date, GF 4 C-8 Endorsements.

75. Segal responded: Segal to Walsh, May 25, 1959, in Justice Department File of Harry A. Blackmun; Segal suggested: Segal to Roy Willy, May 20, 1959, in Justice Department File of Harry A. Blackmun.

76. Segal had spoken with the editor: Segal to Walsh, September 14, 1959, in Justice Department File of Harry A. Blackmun; Segal informed Blackmun: Segal to Blackmun, September 17, 1959, in Justice Department File of Harry A. Blackmun.

77. Rogers wrote to the president: Rogers to Eisenhower, June 25, 1959, Ann Whitman Administration Papers, Rogers, William P. 1959 (2); Rogers promised: *New York Times,* August 28, 1959, p. 1; Rogers added another incentive: *New York Times,* May 30, 1960, p. 24.

78. Ambrose, *Eisenhower: The President,* 28; A record of a briefing: Pre-press conference briefing, April 25, 1956, Ann Whitman Diary Series, April '56 Diary ACW (1).

79. Rogers to Harold J. Gallagher, October 3, 1958, Rogers Papers, White House Correspondence, vol. 2, July–Oct. 1958 (emphasis added); Eisenhower to Wright, November 22, 1954, OF 100 a Supreme Court (1) (emphasis added).

80. Governor of Oklahoma: Murray to Eisenhower, July 22, 1954, GF 4 d Hayse, Mrs. Joseph M., Kentucky Western District Endorsement; Dean of her law school: Russell to Eisenhower, August 11, 1954, GF 4 d Hayse, Mrs. Joseph M., Kentucky Western District Endorsement.

81. In 1956: GF 4 d Illinois, Eastern; Gray to Palmer, November 2, 1957, GF 4 d Illinois, Northern District Endorsements.

82. GF 4 d New York, Southern District and Southern District Endorsements.

83. GF 4 C-9 Ninth Circuit.

84. *New York Times,* May 27, 1955, p. 27.

85. Chase, *Federal Judges,* 93.

86. Memorandum for Honorable Sherman Adams, July 13, 1956, GF 4 d Missouri, Eastern District.

87. *St. Louis Globe-Democrat,* December 26, 1956, p. 6a. Also see *New York Times,* October 5, 1956, p. 8; Many racist letters: GF 4 d Missouri.

88. Cooper to Eisenhower, August 20, 1958, OF 100 Judiciary (2).

89. Brown to Eisenhower, April 25, 1960, OF 100 c District of Columbia.

90. Gatling to Shanley, February 6, 1954, GF 4 d Pennsylvania, Eastern District Endorsements.

91. Powell and other letters to administration: GF 4 d New York, Southern District Endorsements; Denman recommended Hastie: *New York Times,* October 12, 1954, p. 19, and *New York Times,* September 12, 1956, p. 33.

92. White to Eisenhower, July 27, 1954, GF 4 c District of Columbia Endorsements.

93. *New York Times,* March 3, 1958, p. 1. Also see Memo re Vacancy on Ninth Circuit Court of Appeals, GF 4 C-9 Ninth Circuit Endorsements.

Chapter Five: *The New Frontier/Great Society Judiciary*

1. John F. Kennedy, *Profiles in Courage* (New York: Harper, 1956).

2. See the classic study of the 1960 election by Theodore H. White, *The Making of the President, 1960* (New York: Atheneum, 1961).

3. See, for example, William R. Manchester, *The Death of a President* (New York: Harper & Row, 1967).

4. A particularly harsh and unflattering look at Kennedy and his family, focusing on Kennedy's life until his first election to Congress, can be found in Nigel Hamilton, *JFK: Reckless Youth* (New York: Random House, 1992). The book has been repudiated by the Kennedy family but is the most scholarly of the works critical of Kennedy.

5. The material in this and following paragraphs in this section is drawn from Sheldon Goldman, *Constitutional Law and Supreme Court Decision-Making* (New York: Harper & Row, 1982), 404–6.

6. Among the many works on Kennedy and his presidency are Arthur M. Schlesinger, Jr., *A Thousand Days: John F. Kennedy in the White House* (Boston: Houghton Mifflin, 1965); Theodore C. Sorenson, *Kennedy* (New York: Harper & Row, 1965); Herbert S. Parmet, *JFK: The Presidency of John F. Kennedy* (New York: Dial Press, 1983); and Paul Harper and Joann P. Krieg, eds., *John F. Kennedy: The Promise Revisited* (New York: Greenwood Press, 1988). Among the works on Johnson and his presidency are Eric F. Goldman, *The Tragedy of Lyndon Johnson* (New York: Knopf, 1969); Doris Kearns, *Lyndon Johnson and the American Dream* (New York: Harper & Row, 1976); and George Reedy, *Lyndon B. Johnson: A Memoir* (New York: Andrews & McMeel, 1982). Johnson's own account of his presidency is given in his memoirs, *The Vantage Point: Perspectives of the President, 1963–1969* (New York: Holt, Rinehart and Winston, 1971). Scholarly accounts of Johnson before his White House years can be found in the first two volumes of a planned multi-volume life of Johnson by Robert A. Caro, *The Path to Power* (New York: Knopf, 1982), and *Means of Ascent* (New York: Knopf, 1990), and also can be found in Robert Dallek, *Lone Star Rising: Lyndon Johnson and his Times 1908–1960* (New York: Oxford, 1991). An excellent account of judicial selection by Johnson's administration can be found in Neil D. McFeeley, *Appointment of Judges: The Johnson Presidency* (Austin: University of Texas Press, 1987).

7. Harold W. Chase, *Federal Judges: The Appointing Process* (Minneapolis: University of Minnesota Press, 1972), 55.

8. Joseph F. Dolan, recorded interview by Charles T. Morrissey, December 4, 1964, pp. 91, 117, John F. Kennedy Library Oral History Program.

9. Dolan, 92, 117.

10. Dolan, 79.

11. Robert Kennedy claimed: Robert F. Kennedy, recorded interview by John Barlow Martin, April 13, 1964, p. 132, John F. Kennedy Library Oral History Program; "raised a fuss": Robert F. Kennedy, recorded interview by Anthony Lewis, December 4, 1964, p. 410, John F. Kennedy Library Oral History Program; He estimated: Kennedy, April 13, 1964, p. 133.

12. Kennedy, December 4, 1964, pp. 403, 404. Also see the account in Arthur M. Schlesinger, Jr., *Robert Kennedy and His Times* (Boston: Houghton Mifflin, 1978), 374–75.

13. Kennedy, recorded interview by John Barlow Martin, February 29, 1964, p. 12.

14. Justice Department file of J. Spencer Bell.

15. O'Brien to O'Donnell, January 18, 1962, FG 500 The Judicial Branch, WHCF, John F. Kennedy Library.

16. Transcript, John W. Macy, Jr., Oral History Interview, April 26, 1969, by David McComb, p. 13, tape 3, Johnson Library.

17. Katzenbach assured Johnson: Memo, Katzenbach to Johnson, February 3, 1965, FG 500 The Judicial Branch 11/23/63–3/16/67, WHCF, Johnson Library; Johnson relied on Macy: see, for example, memo, John Macy to Johnson, February 15, 1965, FG 530/FG 216/A, WHCF.

18. Notation, October 16, 1965, Ex & Gen FG 505/#1–A, WHCF, Johnson Library.

19. Johnson checked the "no" boxes: Memo, Clark to Johnson, August 20, 1965, p. 4, FG 505/#6–#10, WHCF, Johnson Library; Johnson handwrote: notation on letter from Hickey to Johnson (no date but probably January 1966), FG 505/#6–#10; WHCF; Johnson replied: Memo from Watson to Johnson, January 20, 1966, FG 505/#6–#10, WHCF.

20. Notation on memo from Marvin [Watson] to Johnson, June 23, 1966, FG 500 The Judicial Branch 11/23/63–3/16/67, WHCF, Johnson Library.

21. Notation on memo from Marvin [Watson] to Johnson, May 27, 1966, CF FG 505 Circuit Courts of Appeals, WHCF, Johnson Library.

22. Johnson dictated note attached to memo from Liz [Carpenter] to Johnson, March 23, 1967, FG 505/#1–#5, WHCF, Johnson Library.

23. Notation on memo from Marvin [Watson] to Johnson, June 27, 1966, ExGen FG 530/ST 5/A, WHCF, Johnson Library.

24. Notation on memo from Temple to Johnson, May 10, 1968, ExGen FG 530/ST 6-ST 9, WHCF, Johnson Library.

25. See, for example, Christopher to Temple, March 13, 1968, ExGen FG 505/#6–#10, WHCF, Johnson Library.

26. Katzenbach interview with author, February 18, 1964; Dolan interview with author, February 18, 1964.

27. Willis W. Ritter to Robert F. Kennedy, July 3, 1961, in Justice Department file of Delmas C. Hill.

28. Mike Mansfield and Lee Metcalf to Robert Kennedy, March 13, 1961, in the Justice Department file of James R. Browning; Metcalf to White, February 22, 1961, Justice Department file of James R. Browning.

29. James Rowe to Robert Kennedy, June 17, 1961, James Rowe Papers, Box 86, Browning, James, in the Franklin D. Roosevelt Library, Hyde Park, New York.

30. Rowe to Browning, June 22, 1961, James Rowe Papers, Box 86, Browning, James, Roosevelt Library; Robert Kennedy to Rowe, no date, James Rowe Papers, Box 86, Browning, James, Roosevelt Library.

31. Robert Kennedy to the President, August 25, 1961, FG 505A, WHCF, John F. Kennedy Library.

32. "a helluva impact" and "I went to see Warren": Robert F. Kennedy, recorded interview by John Barlow Martin, April 13, 1964, p. 135; "you'd put him up there": Kennedy, recorded interview by Anthony Lewis, December 4, 1964, p. 412.

33. Cox's racism: *New York Times*, March 9, 1964, p. 42. Also see "Judicial Perfor-

mance in the Fifth Circuit," *Yale Law Journal* 73 (1963): 93, 101n, 102n, 106n, 107; Victor S. Navasky, *Kennedy Justice* (New York: Atheneum, 1971), 244, 245, 247, 248–53; Gerald E. Stern, "Judge William Harold Cox and the Right to Vote in Clarke County, Mississippi," in Leon Friedman, ed., *Southern Justice* (Cleveland: World, 1967), 165–86, and Leon Friedman, "The Federal Courts of the South," in ibid., 188–89. Robert Kennedy to the President, June 15, 1961, FG 530/ST 21–30/A, WHCF, John F. Kennedy Library.

34. Kennedy, recorded interview by Anthony Lewis, December 4, 1964, pp. 402, 406.

35. "Judicial Performance in the Fifth Circuit," 96–97, 101n, 106n; Navasky, *Kennedy Justice*, 247, 256–57; Friedman, *Southern Justice*, 191–92.

36. Dolan interview, February 18, 1964.

37. Kathleen Devine to Dolan, July 2, 1963, Justice Department file of Pat Mehaffy.

38. Dolan to Robert Kennedy, June 25, 1963, in the Justice Department file of Harry Phillips.

39. Hill and Sparkman actively backed Gewin: Memo in Justice Department file of Walter P. Gewin; Gewin unsympathetic to civil rights: see Sheldon Goldman, "Conflict and Consensus in the United States Courts of Appeals," *Wisconsin Law Review* (1968): 467, 471, and Sheldon Goldman, "Conflict on the U.S. Courts of Appeals 1965–1971: A Quantitative Analysis," *University of Cincinnati Law Review*, 42 (1973): 648, 655; Navasky, *Kennedy Justice*, 247; per curiam opinion, *McClung* v. *Katzenbach*, 233 F. Supp. 815 (1964), overturned by *Katzenbach* v. *McClung*, 379 U.S. 294 (1964); Bell sought to find a middle ground: interview with Griffin Bell, July 14, 1964; Bell's voting record: Goldman, "Conflict and Consensus," 467, 471, and Goldman, "Conflict on the U.S. Courts of Appeals," 648, 655.

40. Goldman, "Conflict on the U.S. Courts of Appeals," 647, 655.

41. Notation on memo from Marvin [Watson] to Johnson, June 23, 1966, ExGen FG 500 The Judicial Branch, 11/23/63–3/16/67, WHCF, Johnson Library.

42. Notation on memo from Macy to Johnson, August 13, 1966, ExGen FG 505/#4A–#5A, WHCF, Johnson Library.

43. Clark on Atkins: Clark to Watson, June 22, 1966, ExGen FG 530/ST 9/A, WHCF, Johnson Library; Wisdom on Ainsworth: Clark to Watson, June 23, 1966, ExGen FG 505/#4–A, WHCF, Johnson Library; NAACP on Scott: Clark to Johnson, October 10, 1966, ExGen FG 530/ST 9/A, WHCF; Macy on Comiskey: Macy to Johnson, January 10, 1967, ExGen FG 505/#1–#3A, WHCF; Clayton "fair and just": Sanders to Johnson, October 7, 1967, ExGen FG 505/#4–A, WHCF.

44. Clark on Heebe: Clark to Johnson, February 16, 1966, ExGen 530/ST 15/A–ST 21/A, WHCF, Johnson Library; Russell "quite satisfactory": John W. Macy, Jr., memo attached to nomination papers of Dan M. Russell, Jr., September 24, 1965, ExGen FG 530/ST 22/A–ST 26/A, WHCF; Keady endorsed: Larry Temple memo attached to nomination papers of William C. Keady, March 26, 1968, ExGen FG 530/ST 22/A–ST 26/A, WHCF; Smith "moderate on race relations": Christopher to Temple, July 17, 1968, ExGen FG 530/ST 22/A–ST 26/A, WHCF; Evers to Johnson, July 27, 1968, ExGen FG 530/ST 22/A–ST 26/A, WHCF.

45. Johnson instructed Watson: notation on memo from Watson to Johnson, April 21, 1965, ExGen FG 505/#4–A, WHCF, Johnson Library; Humphrey to Johnson, July 8, 1965, ExGen FG 505/#4–#5, WHCF. Also see Chase, *Federal Judges*, 170–73.

46. *Charlotte Observer,* February 25, 1967, 4A; "strongly opposed": Sanders to Johnson, May 15, 1967, Ex FG 530/ST 33/A–ST 37/A, WHCF, Johnson Library; Sanders to Johnson, June 3, 1967, Ex FG 505/#1–#5, WHCF; Jones confirmed before NAACP convention: Sanders to Watson, June 26, 1967, Gen FG 500 3/17/67–7/24/68, WHCF.

47. On the part that the Lawrence nomination played in ending Abe Fortas's nomination to be chief justice, see Bruce Allen Murphy, *Fortas* (New York: Morrow, 1988), 337–59; Lawrence recommended by McGill: Tom Johnson to Johnson, June 11, 1968, ExGen FG 530/ST 10, WHCF, Johnson Library; Clark tried to prevent nomination: Clark to Johnson, May 13, 1968, ExGen FG 530/ST 10, WHCF; ABA rating: Jenner to Clark, July 10, 1968, ExGen FG 530/ST 10–ST 12/A, WHCF; Lawrence wrote a letter: Lawrence to Mills B. Lane, Jr., June 19, 1969, ExGen FG 530/ST 10, WHCF; Fortas responded: Jim [Jones] to Johnson, June 24, 1968, ExGen FG 530/ST 10, WHCF; Russell joined Republican senators: Murphy, *Fortas,* 359; Lawrence enforced desegregation: Murphy, *Fortas,* 358.

48. "An all-out J-man": notation on memo from Watson to Johnson, September 12, 1966, Ex FG 530/ST 40–ST 42, WHCF, Johnson Library; Gordon "clearly the Johnson man": cover memorandum with appointment papers of Myron L. Gordon, January 16, 1967, Ex FG 530/ST 49, WHCF; Curtin nomination: Sanders to Johnson, November 18, 1967, Ex FG 530/ST 27/A–ST 32/A, WHCF; Lasker nomination: Watson to Johnson, November 22, 1967, Ex FG 530/ST 27/A–ST 32/A, WHCF; "Barefoot and I": Temple to Johnson, April 3, 1968, Ex FG 530/FG 216/A, WHCF; "both possess": Temple to Johnson, April 8, 1968, EX FG 530/FG 216/A, WHCF.

49. Robert F. Kennedy, recorded interview by John Barlow Martin, April 13, 1964, p. 133.

50. "Tell Ramsey": notation on memo from Clark to Johnson, February 11, 1965, Ex FG 530/ST 44–ST 51/4, WHCF, Johnson Library; "Senators make the choice": notation on memo from Moyers to Johnson, August 9, 1965, Ex FG 530/ST 33–ST 39, WHCF; "If both senators": notation on memo from Clark to Watson, September 28, 1966, Ex FG 530/ST 44–ST 51–4, WHCF; Johnson sought to accommodate Dirksen: Jim J. [Jones] to Johnson, May 5, 1967, Ex FG 530/ST 13–ST 14/A, WHCF; As Johnson explained: Johnson to Jones, May 5, 1967, Ex FG 530/ST 13–ST 14/A, WHCF.

51. In general, see White, *Making of the President,* and Thomas J. Weko, *The Politicizing Presidency: The White House Personnel Office 1948–1994* (Lawrence: University Press of Kansas, 1995), 20–31.

52. Bratton nomination: Davies to O'Donnell, February 20, 1964, Ex FG 530/ST 27/A–ST 32/A, WHCF, Johnson Library; New York judgeships: Sanders to Johnson, November 18, 1967, Ex FG 530/ST 27/A–ST 32/A, WHCF.

53. Meyner to Kennedy, April 5, 1961, FG 505 Circuit Courts of Appeals, WHCF, John F. Kennedy Library; Daley to Robert Kennedy, March 13, 1961, Justice Department file of Roger J. Kiley; Johnson respectful of local party: see, for example, Sprague to Watson, October 31, 1967, Ex FG 505/#6A, and Watson to Johnson, May 4, 1967, Ex FG 530/ST 13–ST 14/A, WHCF, Johnson Library.

54. Robert Kennedy, recorded interview by John Barlow Martin, April 13, 1964, p. 134; Republicans appointed from states with Republican senators: Joseph F. Dolan, recorded interview by Charles T. Morrissey, December 4, 1964, p. 83, John F. Kennedy

Library Oral History Program. Also see Chase, *Federal Judges,* 78; Michigan Democratic senators blocked Feikens: Chase, *Federal Judges,* 76.

55. Breeding was especially active: Justice Department file of Delmas C. Hill; Kansas Democrats opposed: White to Breeding, December 1, 1961, FG 500 The Judicial Branch, WHCF, John F. Kennedy Library; Dolan to O'Donnell, February 6, 1962, FG 530/ST 11 through 20/A, WHCF, John F. Kennedy Library; White responding to criticism: *New York Times,* February 20, 1962, p. 21.

56. Dolan to Katzenbach, June 14, 1963, Justice Department file of George C. Edwards, Jr.; Katzenbach to Dolan, June 19, 1963, Justice Department file of George C. Edwards, Jr.

57. Johnson told his staff: Macy to Johnson, February 11, 1966, Ex FG 505/#1–A, WHCF, Johnson Library; Johnson wanted to appoint Kuchel: Clark to Johnson, June 28, 1968, FG 505/#6–#10, WHCF.

58. Scott claimed: Manatos to Watson, April 17, 1967, Ex FG 500 3/17/67–7/24/68, WHCF, Johnson Library; Lawrence bitterly opposed: Lawrence to Johnson, August 19, 1966, FG 505/#1–#5, WHCF; "will break the deadlock": Sanders to Johnson, April 17, 1967, Ex FG 530/ST 38/A–ST 42/A, WHCF.

59. Christopher to Temple, April 10, 1968, Ex FG 530/ST 27/A–ST 32/A, WHCF, Johnson Library.

60. Bell to Robert Kennedy, February 27, 1961, in Justice Department file of Griffin B. Bell; sensitive to state representation claims: see, for example, Valenti to Johnson, September 15, 1965, FG 505/#6–#10; Clark to Johnson, September 2, 1966, Ex FG 505/#6A; Clark to Watson, January 9, 1967, Ex FG 505/#1–A; Christopher to Temple, June 19, 1968, Ex FG 505/#4–A; Temple to Johnson, July 10, 1968, FG 505/#6–#10, WHCF, Johnson Library.

61. Robert Kennedy met with ABA: *New York Times,* January 12, 1961, p. 30; Segal pushed for bipartisan selection: *New York Times,* February 18, 1961, p. 20; Justice officials responded: *New York Times,* May 20, 1961, p. 8; Kennedy thanked ABA: *New York Times,* August 7, 1961, p. 23; Segal praised appointments: *New York Times,* August 10, 1961, p. 15.

62. ABA decries imbalance: *New York Times,* February 20, 1962, p. 21; 150 rated "not qualified": 87 A.B.A. Reports 606 (1962), as cited in Chase, *Federal Judges,* 136–37. Also see *New York Times,* August 8, 1962, p. 17.

63. Cooper nomination: see Joel B. Grossman, *Lawyers and Judges* (New York: Wiley, 1965), 181–95; Democratic Party establishment: *New York Times,* September 1, 1961, p. 1; New York Criminal and Civil Courts Bar: *New York Times,* September 30, 1961, p. 13; "emotionally unstable": *New York Times,* March 20, 1962, p. 1.

64. Kennedy to Johnson, September 2, 1964, Ex FG 530/ST 20–ST 24, WHCF, Johnson Library; Watson to Johnson, September 13, 1965, Ex FG 530/ST 15/A–ST 21/A, WHCF. Also see Chase, *Federal Judges,* 173–77.

65. Morrissey to Johnson, November 3, 1965, Ex FG 530/ST 15/A–ST 21/A, WHCF, Johnson Library.

66. Relationship improved markedly: Jenner to Weisl, May 23, 1966, CF FG 500 The Judicial Branch, WHCF, Johnson Library; ABA committee commended: Jenner to Johnson, January 16, 1969, Gen FG 500 7/25/68, WHCF.

67. Dolan, recorded interview by Charles T. Morrissey, December 4, 1964, pp. 84–86.

68. Kennedy, recorded interview by John Barlow Martin, April 30, 1964, pp. 214–15.

69. Katzenbach saw the political importance: Katzenbach to O'Donnell, January 23, 1964, FG 505/FG 216, WHCF, Johnson Library; Valenti stressed: Valenti to Johnson, August 30, 1965, Ex PE 2 7/27/65–8/31/65, WHCF; Belloni not Italian: Califano to Johnson, March 12, 1967, Ex FG 530/ST 33–ST 39, WHCF; efforts to appoint Italian-Americans: Dent to Johnson, January 16, 1968, FG 505/#1–#5; Califano to Annunzio, March 12, 1968, Gen FG 500 3/17/67–7/24/68; Califano to Johnson, July 23, 1968, Gen FG 500 3/17/67–7/24/68, WHCF; administration aware of Jewish candidates: Clark to Watson, January 19, 1967, Ex FG 505/#1–A, WHCF; significance of appointing second hispanic: Macy to Johnson, September 26, 1966, Ex FG 530/ST 5/A, WHCF.

70. Kennedy pledged: *New York Times,* May 20, 1961, p. 8; Kennedy asked by women's groups: see, for example, Pat Noble Lundy to Kennedy, July 20, 1961, in FG 500 The Judicial Branch, WHCF, John F. Kennedy Library; O'Brien's response: O'Brien to Celler, September 20, 1961, FG 500 The Judicial Branch, WHCF.

71. Agger approached by Johnson: Johnson to [Justice] Douglas, March 2, 1964, Ex FG 520-2 District of Col. Court of Appeals, WHCF, Johnson Library; Macy recalled lists: Macy, interviewed by David McComb, April 26, 1969, pp. 15, 16, Johnson Library; Temple's recollection: Emphasis added. Larry Temple, transcript of Oral History, interviewed by Joe B. Frantz, June 11, 1970, Tape 2, p. 3, Johnson Library; "why not a good man": notation on memo from Clark to Johnson, August 20, 1965, FG 505/#6–#10, WHCF.

72. Edwards to Johnson, March 13, 1967, Ex FG 500 The Judicial Branch, 11/23/63–3/16/67, WHCF, Johnson Library; Johnson to Edwards, March 16, 1967, Ex FG 500 The Judicial Branch, 11/23/63–3/16/67, WHCF; Johnson marked "yes": Watson to Johnson, February 14, 1967, Ex FG 530/ST 5, WHCF.

73. Clark to Johnson, February 16, 1968, Ex FG 520 Courts of the District of Columbia, WHCF, Johnson Library.

74. Temple to Johnson, April 3, 1968, Ex FG 530/FG 216/A, WHCF, Johnson Library.

75. Clark on Hufstedler: Clark to Johnson, June 17, 1968, FG 505/#6–#10, WHCF, Johnson Library; Lillie active Democrat: Lillie to Watson, July 2, 1968, FG 505, WHCF; Johnson was told: Sprague to Temple attached to memo from Temple to Johnson, July 13, 1968, Ex FG 505/#6A, WHCF; Hufstedler recommended: Christopher to Temple, July 9, 1968, Ex FG 505/#6A, WHCF.

76. Friedan: (New York: Norton, 1963); over 6000 women: *Statistical Abstract of the United States 1959,* p. 220.

77. Kennedy to Elmer C. Jackson, Jr., March 16, 1961, FG 500 The Judicial Branch, WHCF, John F. Kennedy Library.

78. Celler to Robert Kennedy, May 24, 1961, in the Justice Department file of Thurgood Marshall.

79. Carter on the list: *New York Times,* August 11, 1961, p. 11; did not want two NAACP lawyers: *New York Times,* September 15, 1961, p. 22.

80. Marshall would only accept: interview with Joseph Dolan, February 18, 1964; racist opposition: letters in Marshall's Justice Department file.

81. Kennedy, recorded interview with John Barlow Martin, May 14, 1964, p. 304.

82. See, for example, Philadelphia Baptist Ministers Conference to Kennedy, July 30, 1961, FG 530/ST, WHCF, John F. Kennedy Library.

83. Katzenbach to O'Donnell, September 12, 1963, FG 530/FA, WHCF, John F. Kennedy Library.

84. Green strenuously objected: Katzenbach to O'Donnell, December 27, 1963, FG 505/FG 216, WHCF, Johnson Library; proceed with Coleman: notation on memo from Clark to Watson, August 3, 1965, FG 505/#1–#5, WHCF; Coleman declined: Coleman to Johnson, September 2, 1966, FG 505/#1–#5, WHCF.

85. Johnson briefly considered Hastie: Macy to Johnson, May 24, 1967, FG 505/#1–#5, WHCF, Johnson Library; Johnson ordered: instruction to unnamed assistant, September 21, 1967, Ex FG 530/ST 15/A–ST 21/A, WHCF.

86. Humphrey to Johnson, May 9, 1966, FG 505/#1–#5, WHCF, Johnson Library.

87. Memorandum for the Record by Clifford L. Alexander, Jr., April 8, 1967, FG 505/#1–#5, WHCF, Johnson Library.

88. "Would go along": Tom Johnson to the President, June 27, 1968, Ex FG 500 3/17/67–7/24/68, WHCF, Johnson Library; Temple reported conversation: Temple to Johnson, July 13, 1968, FG 505/#1–#5, WHCF.

89. Macy, interviewed by David McComb, April 26, 1969, p. 12.

90. This figure is derived from *The 1971 Lawyer Statistical Report,* pp. 6, 10 (tables 2, 5).

91. See Sheldon Goldman, "Bush's Judicial Legacy: The Final Imprint," *Judicature* 76 (1993), p. 287 (table 2).

92. In general, see Diego R. Figueroa, *The Selection of the Federal District Judges in Puerto Rico: An Extension of Puerto Rican Politics,* honors thesis, 1996, on file at the University of Massachusetts at Amherst, University Honors Office.

Chapter Six: Picking Judges in the Shadow of Watergate

1. The most extensive biography of Nixon is Stephen E. Ambrose's three-volume *Nixon* (New York: Simon and Schuster, 1987, 1989, 1991). Also see Herbert S. Parmet, *Richard Nixon and His America* (Boston: Little, Brown, 1990); Leon Friedman and William F. Levantrosser, eds., *Richard M. Nixon: Politician, President, Administrator* (New York: Greenwood, 1991); and Richard M. Nixon, *The Memoirs of Richard Nixon* (New York: Grosset & Dunlap, 1978).

2. This section draws on material from Sheldon Goldman, *Constitutional Law and Supreme Court Decision-Making* (New York: Harper & Row, 1982), 527–33.

3. For accounts of the Fortas resignation, see Robert Shogan, *A Question of Judgement: The Fortas Case and the Struggle for the Supreme Court* (Indianapolis: Bobbs-Merrill, 1972), and Bruce Allen Murphy, *Fortas: The Rise and Ruin of a Supreme Court Justice* (New York: William Morrow, 1988), 545–77.

4. On the Watergate scandal, see Stanley I. Kutler, *The Wars of Watergate: The Last Crisis of Richard Nixon* (New York: Knopf, 1990). Also see J. Anthony Lukas, *Nightmare: The Underside of the Nixon Years* (New York: Viking, 1976). Watergate is also thoroughly covered in Ambrose, *Nixon,* volumes 2 and 3. Nixon's version of the events that toppled his presidency can be found in his *Memoirs.*

5. Nixon named unindicted co-conspirator: Ambrose, *Nixon,* 3:337, 345; Agnew resignation: Ambrose, *Nixon,* 3:207–8, 231.

6. *United States* v. *Nixon,* 418 U.S. 683 (1974).

7. On the Ford presidency, see Bernard J. Firestone and Alexej Ugrinsky, eds., *Gerald R. Ford and the Politics of Post-Watergate America,* 2 vols. (Westport, Conn.: Greenwood, 1993); John R. Greene, *The Presidency of Gerald R. Ford* (Lawrence: University Press of Kansas, 1995). Also see Gerald R. Ford, *A Time to Heal* (New York: Harper & Row, 1979).

8. Dent to Nixon, July 9, 1969, Ex FG 53/ST 30–FG 53/ST 39 [1969–1970], WHCF, Nixon Materials Project.

9. Nelsen backed Alsop: Vern Loen to William E. Timmons and Max Friedersdorf, March 8, 1974, Ex FG 53/ST 16–ST 30 [1-1-73–8-9-74], WHCF, Nixon Materials Project; Nixon to MacGregor, March 13, 1974, Ex FG 53/ST 16–ST 30 [1-1-73–8-9-74], WHCF.

10. Nixon to Meskill, June 24, 1974, CF FG 52 [1971–1974], WHSF, Nixon Materials Project.

11. Memorandum for the Attorney General, July 13, 1974, Ex FG 50 The Judicial Branch 1/1/73–, WHCF, Nixon Materials Project.

12. For the Deputy Attorney General, September 18, 1969, Ex FG 53/ST 1–FG 53/ST 9 [1968–70], WHCF, Nixon Materials Project.

13. Memorandum for the Attorney General, January 16, 1973, Ex FG 53/ST 1–ST 15 1/1/73–[8-9-74], WHCF, Nixon Materials Project.

14. Wright to Ehrlichman, January 13, 1969, Gen FG 52/#9 [1969–70], WHCF, Nixon Materials Project; Ehrlichman to Wright, January 25, 1969, Gen FG 52/#9 [1969–70], WHCF; Wright's commission: see documents in Gen FG 52/#9 [1969–70], WHCF.

15. Hullin wrote: For the Record, December 10, 1970, Ex FG 53 United States District Courts [1969–70], WHCF, Nixon Materials Project. Also see Ehrlichman to Kleindienst, December 10, 1970, in same file; Ehrlichman engineered: see, for example, Ehrlichman to Boldt, October 13, 1971, and Hullin to Boldt, November 2, 1971, in Ex FG 53/ST 47/A 1/1/71–[1972], WHCF; Sharp acknowledged: Sharp to Ehrlichman, December 16, 1971, Ex FG 53/ST 47/A 1/1/71–[1972], WHCF.

16. Kleindienst to Ehrlichman, Feb. 14, 1972, Ex FG 53/ST 47/A 1/1/71–[1972], WHCF, Nixon Materials Project; McGovern to Ehrlichman, March 17, 1972, Ex FG 53 United States District Courts 1/1/71–[1972], WHCF.

17. Ogden to Ehrlichman, November 20, 1971, Ex FG 52/#9 1/1/71–[1972], WHCF, Nixon Materials Project; Ehrlichman to Ogden, December 1, 1971, Ex FG 52/#9 1/1/71–[1972], WHCF.

18. Ehrlichman to Kleindienst, December 1, 1971, Ex FG 52/#9 1/1/71–[1972], WHCF, Nixon Materials Project.

19. See, for example, Bennett to Ford, July 16, 1975, FG 53/ST 46—, WHCF, Ford Library.

20. Meeting with Attorney General Edward H. Levi from James E. Connor, February 28, 1975, FG 17 2/28/75 pp. 1, 4, WHCF, Ford Library.

21. See, for example, Meeting with Attorney General Edward H. Levi from Jim Cannon, May 24, 1975, FG 17 5/21/75–6/30/75, WHCF, Ford Library.

22. Ford on Cook: Ford to Walker, n.d., FG The Judicial Branch (1), President's Hand-

writing File, Ford Library; Ford on Fay: April 12, 1976, FG The Judicial Branch (2), President's Handwriting File. Emphasis in original.

23. June 17, 1976, FG The Judicial Branch (2), President's Handwriting File, Ford Library.

24. From Connor to Bennett, February 9, 1976, FG The Judicial Branch (1), President's Handwriting File, Ford Library. Emphasis in original.

25. Memorandum for the President, March 25, 1969, p. 1, Ex FG 50 The Judicial Branch [1969–70], WHCF, Nixon Materials Project.

26. Emphasis in original, ibid., p. 2.

27. Ibid., p. 6.

28. Emphases in original, ibid., p. 7.

29. Emphasis in original on cover memo from Ehrlichman to the Staff Secretary, March 27, 1969, News Summaries (March 1969), Box 30, President's Office Files, Nixon Materials Project.

30. Ehrlichman to Nixon, March 5, 1969, Ex FG 50 The Judicial Branch [1969–70], WHCF, Nixon Materials Project.

31. Memorandum for the President, May 24, 1969, Staff Members & Office Files, Frederic V. Malek, Subject Files, 1970–73, Box 2, WHSF, Nixon Materials Project.

32. Letter recommending Erikson: Louis B. Nichols to Nixon, November 2, 1973, Ex FG 50 The Judicial Branch 1/1/73–, WHCF, Nixon Materials Project; letter praising Coffey: Philip E. Casper to Haig, June 3, 1974, Ex FG 53/ST 31–ST 50 1/1/73–[8-9-74], WHCF.

33. *New York Times,* June 15, 1969, p. 51. Bane was a former Rhodes Scholar, was rated "well qualified" by the ABA, and was a member of a prestigious Chicago law firm. Ex FG 52/A [1969–70], WHCF, Nixon Materials Project.

34. For Bill Timmons, December 15, 1972, Ex FG 50 The Judicial Branch [1971–1972], WHCF, Nixon Materials Project.

35. Handwritten notation by Geoff Shepard on memo from Warren Hendricks to Geoff Shepard, October 30, 1974, FG 53/ST 21-34, WHCF, Ford Library.

36. Levi described Stevens: Levi to Ford, November 10, 1975, p. 5, Cheney collection, Ford Library; "views on environmental questions": Buchen to Cheney, November 25, 1975, Cheney collection.

37. BeLieu to Byrd, August 1, 1971, Ex FG 52/A [1971–72], WHCF, Nixon Materials Project.

38. Hullin to Kleindienst, October 28, 1971, Ex FG 53/ST 47/A 1/1/71–[1972], WHCF, Nixon Materials Project.

39. Ehrlichman was counseled: Clinton to Ehrlichman, April 17, 1973, Gen FG 53/ST 47, WHCF, Nixon Materials Project; Ehrlichman responded: Ehrlichman to Clinton, April 25, 1973, Gen FG 53/ST 47, WHCF.

40. Ford in his memoirs: Ford, *A Time to Heal,* 92; Scott "vigorously" backed: Marsh to Bennett and Buchen, February 28, 1976, Judicial Appointments — Virginia, Buchen collection; Ford preferred Poff: Friedersdorf to Cheney, February 25, 1976, Judicial Appointments — Virginia, Buchen collection; Poff rated "qualified": From Bennett to Ford, January 6, 1976, FG 50 12/1/75–3/31/76, WHCF; Poff to Ford, May 27, 1976, FG 53/ST 46–49/A, WHCF.

41. Dalton urged the administration: Donna to Marsh, May 7, 1976, Williams, Glen, Marsh collection, Ford Library; Buchen vetoed: note in files, n.d., Ex FG 53/ST 46–, WHCF; advisers recommended: Buchen to Ford, September 2, 1976, FG The Judicial Branch (2), President's Handwriting File.

42. Senators would withhold endorsement: Connor to Ford, February 28, 1975, p. 3, FG 17 2/28/75, WHCF, Ford Library; administration's preferred Republican candidate: Buchen memo, February 12, 1976, Judicial Appointments — Florida, Buchen collection.

43. Bennett to Ford, August 3, 1976, District Judges (1), Connor collection, Ford Library.

44. Cauble to Nixon, July 23, 1970, Gen FG 53/ST [1969–70], WHCF, Nixon Materials Project; Dent to Cauble, July 28, 1970, Gen FG 53/ST [1969–70], WHCF.

45. Dent to Ehrlichman, December 12, 1969, Frederic V. Malek, Subject Files 1970–73, Box 2, WHSF, Nixon Materials Project; Flanigan to Mitchell, January 2, 1970, Frederic V. Malek, Subject Files 1970–73, Box 2, WHSF.

46. Names submitted to Republican national committee: see, for example, Bennett to Ford, July 16, 1975, FG 53/ST 46–, WHCF, Ford Library; Arch Moore: Marsh to Buchen, November 30, 1974, Judicial Appointments — West Virginia, Buchen collection; Wisconsin and California recommendations: Williams to Buchen, November 11, 1974, p. 2, Judicial Appointments — General (1), Buchen collection; Reagan recommends Kennedy: Walker to Ford, February 4, 1975, Circuit Judges, Connor collection.

47. Telegram to Nixon: Coker to Nixon, February 4, 1971, Gen FG 53 United States District Courts 1/1/71–[1972], WHCF, Nixon Materials Project; Dent reply: Dent to Coker, February 5, 1971, Gen FG 53 United States District Courts 1/1/71–[1972], WHCF.

48. Flanigan to Kleindienst, April 21, 1969, Gen FG 53/ST [1969–70], WHCF, Nixon Materials Project.

49. Case to Rumsfeld, October 23, 1974, FG 53/ST 19–30/A, WHCF, Ford Library.

50. Buckley supported Broderick: Bennett to Ford, August 16, 1976, FG 53/ST 21–34, WHCF, Ford Library; package deal: Bennett to Ford, August 20, 1976, FG 52/#4, WHCF.

51. Kleindienst announced: *New York Times,* August 11, 1969, p. 18; "the basic principles": Laporte to Mitchell, June 5, 1969, Judicial Appointments — General (1), Buchen collection, Ford Library. All quotations in the following four paragraphs in the text are from this letter.

52. Mitchell to Laporte, June 18, 1969, Judicial Appointments — General (1), Buchen collection, Ford Library.

53. ABA found Donaldson: Eugene S. Cowen to Harlow, October 14, 1969, Ex FG 53/ST 30–FG 53/ST 39 [1969–70], WHCF, Nixon Materials Project; Scott protested: Scott to Harlow, October 9, 1969, Ex FG 53/ST 30–FG 53/ST 39 [1969–70], WHCF.

54. *New York Times,* July 28, 1970, p. 1.

55. See Donald Dale Jackson, *Judges* (New York: Atheneum, 1974), 352–53.

56. Bork to Nixon, November 29, 1973, Ex FG 53/ST 13A–ST 30/A [1/1/73–8/9/74], WHCF, Nixon Materials Project.

57. Saxbe to Nixon, February 7, 1974, Ex FG 53/ST 13A–ST 30/A [1/1/73–8/9/74], WHCF, Nixon Materials Project.

58. Timbers to Ford, May 28, 1974, Meskill, Thomas J., Hartmann collection, Ford Library; Ford to Timbers, June 12, 1974, Meskill, Thomas J., Hartmann collection.

59. Leading law professors: *New York Times,* September 15, 1974, p. 22; editorial: *New York Times,* September 18, 1974, p. 40.

60. *New York Times,* October 12, 1973, p. 37.

61. Falk to Ford, December 18, 1974, FG 52 United States Courts of Appeals, WHCF, Ford Library.

62. Lazarus to Buchen, March 19, 1975, American Bar Association (1), Buchen collection, Ford Library.

63. *New York Times,* April 23, 1975, p. 1.

64. Baker called the White House: Marsh to Buchen, July 26, 1976, Judicial Appointments—Courts of Appeals, Buchen collection, Ford Library; Lazarus reported back: Lazarus to Marsh, July 28, 1976, Judicial Appointments—Courts of Appeals, Buchen collection.

65. Malek to Mitchell, June 9, 1971, Frederic V. Malek, Subject Files, 1970–1973, Box 2, WHSF, Nixon Materials Project.

66. Strachan to Malek, December 16, 1971, Frederic V. Malek, Subject Files, 1970–1973, Box 2, WHSF, Nixon Materials Project.

67. Malek to Kleindienst, December 20, 1971, Frederic V. Malek, Subject Files, 1970–1973, Box 2, WHSF, Nixon Materials Project.

68. Malek to Kleindienst, January 10, 1972, Frederic V. Malek, Subject Files, 1970–1973, Box 2, WHSF, Nixon Materials Project.

69. Deputy attorney general expressed willingness: Kleindienst to Virginia Kerr, November 11, 1971, Gen FG 50 The Judicial Branch 1/1/71–[1972], WHCF, Nixon Materials Project; Hruska talked up Kovachevich: Hruska to A.B. Hermann, March 23, 1973, Ex FG 52/#[1–10] [1973–74], WHCF, Nixon Materials Project; administration officials believed: Lazarus to Buchen, June 15, 1976, Judicial Appointments—Florida, Buchen collection, Ford Library.

70. Armstrong planned a meeting: Armstrong to Judge Cornelia G. Kennedy, July 13, 1973, Ex FG 53/ST 16–ST 30 1/1/73–[8-9-74], WHCF, Nixon Materials Project; a few instances: see, e.g., Loen to Johnson, March 5, 1974, and Wimer to El Paso County Women's Bar Association, June 26, 1974. Both letters in Gen FG 53/ST 31–ST 50 1/1/73–[8-9-74], WHCF.

71. Armstrong to LaFontant, September 13, 1974, FG 17 Dept. of Justice 8-9-74–9-30-74, WHCF, Ford Library.

72. Judicial Status Report, January 6, 1976, Judicial Appointments—General (2), Buchen collection, Ford Library.

73. Lindh to Bennett, November 14, 1975, FG 51 Supreme Court 8/9/74–11/19/75, WHCF, Ford Library.

74. Williams to Haldeman, March 10, 1969, Gen FG 53/ST [1969–70], WHCF, Nixon Materials Project.

75. Haldeman to Williams, March 13, 1969, Gen FG 53/ST [1969–70], WHCF, Nixon Materials Project.

76. Young to Mitchell, February 2, 1971, Gen FG 52/#3 1/1/71–[1972], WHCF, Nixon Materials Project.

77. Ferguson too liberal: *New York Times,* May 14, 1971, p. 13; Ortique was considered: Judges/Tab D, January 6, 1976, Judicial Appointments — General (2), and Johnston to Ford, March 2, 1976, Judicial Appointments — Louisiana, Buchen collection, Ford Library.

78. Ehrlichman to Gautier, December 1, 1971, Ex FG 53/ST 47 1/1/71–[1972], WHCF, Nixon Materials Project.

79. Dent to the Attorney General, January 3, 1972, [CF] FG 52 [1971–74], WHSF, Nixon Materials Project. For a profile of Judge Alexander, see Jackson, *Judges,* 110–11, 112, 114, 117, 123–32, 133–34.

80. Malek to Haldeman, January 12, 1972, Staff Member & Office Files, Frederic V. Malek, Subject Files, 1970–1973, Box 2, WHSF, Nixon Materials Project.

81. Malek to Haldeman, January 12, 1972, p. 2, Staff Member & Office Files, Frederic V. Malek, Subject Files, 1970–1973, Box 2, WHSF, Nixon Materials Project.

82. Malek to Kingsley, February 28, 1972, Staff Member & Office Files, Frederic V. Malek, Subject Files, 1970–1973, Box 2, WHSF, Nixon Materials Project.

83. Jackson, *Judges,* p. 124; *The Boston Globe,* June 12, 1973, p. 46.

84. Long and Johnston to Ford, May 19, 1975, FG 53/ST 16–20, WHCF, Ford Library.

85. Long and Johnston to Ford, February 24, 1976, Judicial Appointments — Louisiana, Buchen collection, Ford Library.

86. In general, see Barbara A. Perry, *A "Representative" Supreme Court?* (New York: Greenwood, 1991).

87. "Strict constructionists": *New York Times,* October 16, 1972, p. 1; over half the judiciary Republicans: Deborah J. Barrow, Gary Zuk, and Gerard S. Gryski, *The Federal Judiciary and Institutional Change* (Ann Arbor: University of Michigan Press, 1996), 62, 84.

88. Ford, *A Time to Heal,* 41.

Chapter Seven: Carter Reforms Judicial Selection

1. See Charles O. Jones, *The Trusteeship Presidency: Jimmy Carter and the United States Congress* (Baton Rouge: Louisiana State University Press, 1988); Erwin C. Hargrove, *Jimmy Carter as President: Leadership and the Politics of the Public Good* (Baton Rouge: Louisiana State University Press, 1988); Kenneth W. Thompson, ed., *The Carter Presidency: Fourteen Intimate Perspectives of Jimmy Carter* (Lanham, Md.: University Press of America, 1990). Also see Jimmy Carter, *Keeping Faith: Memoirs of a President* (New York: Bantam Books, 1982). For a political biography of Carter extending through most but not all of his presidency, see Betty Glad, *Jimmy Carter* (New York: Norton, 1980). For an account of how Carter won the presidency in 1976, see Jules Witcover, *Marathon: The Pursuit of the Presidency 1972–1976* (New York: Viking Press, 1977).

2. Witcover, *Marathon,* 541.

3. Inflation number one problem: Gallup Opinion Index Report No. 164, March 1979, p. 4; moralistic taskmaster: Glad, pp. 446–47. Carter's major address to the nation on the energy crisis was given on July 15, 1979.

4. As a candidate, he promised: "The Candidates Answer," *American Bar Association*

Journal 62 (1976): 1270; Sidney Kraus, ed., *The Great Debates: Carter vs. Ford 1976* (Bloomington: Indiana University Press, 1979), 534; Senator Eastland insisted: Griffin B. Bell, "Merit Selection and Political Reality," *Washington Post,* February 25, 1978, A15.

5. Five panels failed: Larry C. Berkson and Susan B. Carbon, *The United States Circuit Judge Nominating Commissions: Its Members, Procedures and Candidates* (Chicago: American Judicature Society, 1980), 143; These results were unexpected: ibid., 45.

6. Doug Huron, Memorandum for the File, November 7, 1978, Lipshutz Papers.

7. Lipshutz, Kraft and Moore to Carter, October 10, 1978, p. 1, FG 52/#5 1/20/77–1/20/81, WHCF, Carter Library. Emphasis in original.

8. Ibid., p. 2.

9. Ibid., p. 1.

10. Huron complained: Doug Huron, Memorandum for the File, November 7, 1978, Lipshutz Papers; Bell told of despair: Griffin B. Bell and Ronald J. Ostrow, *Taking Care of the Law* (New York: Morrow, 1982), 41–42.

11. Lipshutz's staffers had urged: McKenna, Huron & Dyke to Lipshutz, January 17, 1978, Judgeships (Active): Omnibus Judgeship Bill, 6/77–10/78 [CF, O/A 438], Lipshutz Papers, Carter Library; became more aggressive: Bell and Ostrow, *Taking Care of the Law,* 41.

12. Bell favored McMillian: Bell to Carter, June 22, 1978, FG 52/#8 1/20/77–1/20/81, WHCF, Carter Library; Carter wrote on this memo: Lipshutz to Carter, June 27, 1978, FG 52/#8 1/20/77–1/20/81, WHCF.

13. Carter indicated: see Carter's notations on memorandum for the President from the Attorney General, n.d., Judgeships (Active): Miscellaneous Closed, 1–12/78, Lipshutz Papers, Carter Library; Carter directed Lipshutz: Carter to Lipshutz, March 30, 1979, Lipshutz Papers.

14. See Deborah J. Barrow, Gary Zuk, and Gerard S. Gryski, *The Federal Judiciary and Institutional Change* (Ann Arbor: University of Michigan Press, 1996), 70–72. For a discussion of the congressional politics involved, see Deborah J. Barrow and Thomas G. Walker, *A Court Divided: The Fifth Circuit Court of Appeals and the Politics of Judicial Reform* (New Haven: Yale University Press, 1988), 192–94, 199–217.

15. Jordan, Lipshutz, and Moore to Carter, April 12, 1978, p. 1, Judgeships (Active): Miscellaneous Closed, 1–12/78, Lipshutz Papers, Carter Library. All quotations and references are from this memo and can be found within pages 1–4.

16. The speech was delivered on May 4, 1978. *Public Papers of the Presidents of the United States, Jimmy Carter 1978,* vol. 1 (Washington, D.C.: Government Printing Office, 1979), 838.

17. Carter "personally wrote": Griffin B. Bell, "Merit Selection and Political Reality," *Washington Post,* February 25, 1978, A15; By 1980: Alan Neff, *The United States District Judge Nominating Commissions: Their Members, Procedures and Candidates* (Chicago: American Judicature Society, 1981), 56.

18. Los Angeles speech: *Public Papers of the Presidents of the United States, Jimmy Carter 1978,* vol. 1 (Washington, D.C.: Government Printing Office, 1979), 838–39.

19. For details, see Barrow and Walker, *A Court Divided,* 184–218.

20. Carter's notation on memorandum for the President from Bell, n.d., but internal

evidence indicates sometime in October, 1978, p. 1, Lipshutz Papers, Judgeships (Active): Miscellaneous Closed, 1–12/78, Carter Library. Emphasis added. References in the next several paragraphs are from this source on pages 1 and 2.

21. Lipshutz to Carter, October 27, 1978, Lipshutz Papers, Judgeships (Active): Executive Order (District Court Standards and Guidelines) 2/78–1/79, Carter Library.

22. The Bell and Lipshutz drafts on which Carter wrote are attached to the memo, Lipshutz to Carter, October 27, 1978, Lipshutz Papers, Judgeships (Active): Executive Order (District Court Standards and Guidelines) 2/78–1/79, Carter Library.

23. Bell to Carter, November 6, 1978, Judgeships (Active): Executive Order (District Court Standards and Guidelines), Lipshutz Papers, Carter Library.

24. She warned: McKenna to Lipshutz, Jordan, and Moore, January 11, 1979, Judgeships (Active): Miscellaneous Closed, 1–5/79, Lipshutz Papers, Carter Library; Doug Huron complained: Huron to Jordan, January 12, 1979, Judgeships (Active): Miscellaneous Closed, 1–5/79, Lipshutz Papers.

25. Carter to individual Democratic Senators, February 5, 1979, FG 53 1/20/77–1/20/81, WHCF, Carter Library.

26. Lipshutz to Carter, April 7, 1979, Lipshutz Papers. The quotations in the next two paragraphs are also from this source.

27. But see Cardozo to Cutler, February 7, 1980, Judges 1–5/80, Cutler Papers, Carter Library.

28. Kraus, *The Great Debates,* 534.

29. Freund to Carter, June 20, 1977, FG 52/#1 1/20/77–1/20/81, WHCF, Carter Library.

30. Lipshutz to Carter, May 2, 1979, Lipshutz Papers.

31. In one of the analyses: "Dividing the Fifth," n.d., Judgeships (Active): Omnibus Judgeship Bill, 6/77–10/78 [CF, O/A 438], Lipshutz Papers, Carter Library; Opposition eased largely: see Barrow and Walker, *A Court Divided,* 219–45.

32. Bell to Carter, February 2, 1979, FG 53/ST 43A, WHCF, Carter Library.

33. *New York Times,* July 14, 1979, p. 5. Also see *New York Times,* May 8, 1979, p. 16, and May 13, 1979, E7.

34. Huron's guidelines: Huron to Hamilton, February 22, 1977, Judgeships (Active): Exec. Order (Circuit Court Selection Panels) 2/77–11/78, Lipshutz Papers, Carter Library; Huron to Lipshutz, November 6, 1978, Judgeships (Active): Exec. Order (Circuit Court Selection Panels) 2/77–11/78, Lipshutz Papers; Ness helped choose members: Lipshutz to Huron, February 24, 1978, Judgeships (Active): Exec. Order (District Court Standards and Guidelines), 2/78–1/79 [CF O/A 438], Lipshutz Papers; The commissions engaged: in general, see Peter G. Fish, "Merit Selection and Politics: Choosing a Judge of the United States Court of Appeals for the Fourth Circuit," *Wake Forest Law Review,* 15 (1979): 635–54, and Peter G. Fish, "Questioning Judicial Candidates: What Can Merit Selectors Ask?" *Judicature* 62 (1978): 8.

35. Lipshutz to Bell and Jordan, October 23, 1978, Judgeships (Active): Exec. Order (District Court Standards and Guidelines), 2/78–1/79 [CF O/A 438], Lipshutz Papers, Carter Library.

36. In one handwritten note: November 8, 1978, Judgeships (Active): Exec. Order

(Circuit Court Selection Panels) 2/77–11/78, Lipshutz Papers, Carter Library, emphasis in original; In another note: November 20, 1978, Judgeships (Active): Miscellaneous Closed, 1–12/78, Lipshutz Papers.

37. Memorandum for the File, November 15, 1978, Lipshutz Papers.

38. Lipshutz and McKenna complained: Lipshutz and McKenna to Carter, March 3, 1977, FG 53 1/20/77–1/20/81, WHCF, Carter Library; McKenna reported: Memorandum for the File from Margaret McKenna, March 9, 1977, FG 53 1/20/77–1/20/81, WHCF.

39. McKenna learned: Memorandum for the File, From Doug Huron, November 7, 1978, Lipshutz Papers; "in a less rigid manner": Egan to Huron, April 12, 1978, File: Judgeships (Active): Miscellaneous Closed, 1–12/78 [CF O/A 438], Lipshutz Papers, Carter Library.

40. Bell and Ostrow, *Taking Care of the Law,* 40–42.

41. Bell to Lipshutz, July 7, 1978, Judgeships (Active): Omnibus Judgeship Bill 6/77–10/78, Lipshutz Papers, Carter Library.

42. Huron and McKenna to Lipshutz, July 19, 1978, Judgeships (Active): Omnibus Judgeship Bill 6/77–10/78, Lipshutz Papers, Carter Library. The next paragraph is also from this source.

43. Huron and McKenna to Lipshutz, October 12, 1978, Judgeships (Active): Miscellaneous Closed, 1–12/78, Lipshutz Papers, Carter Library.

44. Ibid.

45. Arnie Miller and Michael Grant to Tim Kraft, October 13, 1978, FG 53 1/20/77–1/20/81, WHCF, Carter Library.

46. McKenna to Lipshutz, October 13, 1978, Judgeships (Active): Miscellaneous Closed 1–12/78, Lipshutz Papers, Carter Library.

47. Lipshutz to Jordan and Moore, October 16, 1978, Judgeships (Active): Miscellaneous Closed 1–12/78, Lipshutz Papers, Carter Library.

48. Halpern to Lipshutz, October 20, 1978, Judgeships (Active): Executive Order (District Court Standards and Guidelines), 2/78–1/79, Lipshutz Papers, Carter Library.

49. Carter essentially sided: Lipshutz to Carter, October 27, 1978, Judgeships (Active): Executive Order (District Court Standards and Guidelines), 2/78–1/79, Lipshutz Papers, Carter Library; Bell agreed to cooperate: Bell to Carter, November 6, 1978, Judgeships (Active): Executive Order (District Court Standards and Guidelines), 2/78–1/79, Lipshutz Papers.

50. He described the meeting: Lipshutz Memorandum for the File, November 28, 1978, Lipshutz Papers; Lipshutz to Bell, December 13, 1978, Lipshutz Papers.

51. Huron to Jordan, January 12, 1979, Judgeships (Active): Miscellaneous Closed, 1–5/79, Lipshutz Papers, Carter Library.

52. In at least one instance: McKenna to Lipshutz, March 15, 1979, Lipshutz Papers; Bell to Carter, May 17, 1979, FG 53 1/20/77–1/20/81, WHCF; Lipshutz to Carter, May 17, 1979, FG 53 1/20/77–1/20/81, WHCF.

53. Huron, Memorandum to File, June 29, 1979, Lipshutz Papers.

54. Huron, Memorandum for the File, September 14, 1979, Lipshutz Papers.

55. See, e.g., Cardozo and Huron to Cutler, October 24, 1979, Judges 5/78–12/79,

Cutler Papers, Carter Library, and Cardozo to Cutler, February 7, 1980, Judges 1–5/80, Cutler Papers.

56. Barrow, Zuk, and Gryski, *Federal Judiciary,* 84.

57. "I am the merit commission": *Washington Post,* November 7, 1978, p. 5; could not recall: *New York Times,* November 9, 1978, A18.

58. Cardozo to Cutler, January 28, 1980, Judges 1–5/80, Cutler Papers, Carter Library.

59. Ervin to Carter, September 2, 1977, FG/#4 1/20/77–1/20/81, WHCF, Carter Library.

60. *New York Times,* November 28, 1978, A16.

61. *Boston Globe,* November 12, 1980, p. 3.

62. All quotations in this paragraph from Lipshutz, Memorandum for the File, November 28, 1978, Lipshutz Papers.

63. Every nomination: see Neff, *Nominating Commissions,* 42–44; Kennedy quietly informed: Huron, Memorandum for the File, December 13, 1978, Lipshutz Papers.

64. Winberry was rated "qualified": *New York Times,* March 5, 1980, A18; changed its rating: see *Congressional Quarterly Weekly Report* 38 (March 8, 1980): 674. Also see *New York Times,* March 5, 1980, A18.

65. Justice Department had already investigated: Interview with Philip Modlin, Office of the Deputy Attorney General, U.S. Department of Justice, December 19, 1980; Sheffield's actions "completely proper": *New York Times,* October 10, 1980, A18. Also see *Richmond Times-Dispatch,* December 14, 1980, B1.

66. Judicial (and even other) nominees: Thomas J. Weko, *The Politicizing Presidency* (Lawrence: University Press of Kansas, 1995), 85ff.; McKenna to Lipshutz, May 3, 1978, FG 53/ST 38, WHCF, Carter Library.

67. Lipshutz to Carter, May 2, 1979, Lipshutz Papers. All quotations in this paragraph are from this source. Emphasis in original.

68. Frank C. Jones to Carter, November 21, 1978, FG 50 1/1/78–12/31/78, WHCF, Carter Library. Also see Robert D. Raven to Carter, November 21, 1978, Judgeships (Active): American Bar Association Judiciary Committee, 11/78 [CF O/A 438], Lipshutz Papers, Carter Library.

69. Hearings on the Nomination of Donald E. O'Brien before the Senate Judiciary Committee, 95th Congress, 2nd Sess., October 4, 1978, pp. 4, 10.

70. Carter assured the group: *New York Times,* September 4, 1977, p. 16; a secretarial oversight: *New York Times,* January 20, 1980, p. 14; allegations that he had solicited: *New York Times,* February 8, 1980, A15.

71. Lipshutz to Carter, April 7, 1979, Lipshutz Papers; McKenna to Lipshutz, March 15, 1979, Lipshutz Papers; ABA reconsidered: Huron, Memorandum for the File, September 14, 1979, Lipshutz Papers.

72. Cardozo to Lipshutz, August 27, 1979, p. 2, Lipshutz Papers.

73. "Bumpers has agreed": Huron, Memorandum for the File, September 14, 1979, Lipshutz Papers; took some flak: Cardozo to Lipshutz, August 27, 1979, Lipshutz Papers.

74. Cox rejected by Carter himself: Huron, Memorandum for the File, August 30, 1979, Lipshutz Papers; newspaper speculation: see, e.g., *New York Times,* June 3, 1979,

p. 26; only Cox's advanced age: Jody Powell, *The Other Side of the Story* (New York: Morrow, 1984), 186–88.

75. Huron suspected: Huron, Memorandum for the File, September 14, 1979, Lipshutz Papers; analyses by Slotnick: see Elliot E. Slotnick, "The A.B.A. Standing Committee on Federal Judiciary: A Contemporary Assessment," *Judicature* 66 (1983): 348–62, 385–93, and Elliot E. Slotnick, "The Paths to the Federal Bench: Gender, Race and Judicial Recruitment Variation," *Judicature* 67 (1984): 370–88; career paths differed: Slotnick, "Paths to the Federal Bench," 380–81 and passim; younger than white males: Slotnick, "Paths to the Federal Bench," 375–76.

76. Cardozo to Cutler, October 24, 1980, Judges, 9–11/80, Cutler Papers, Carter Library.

77. Lipshutz to Bell, July 27, 1977, FG 52 1/20/77–1/20/81, WHCF, Carter Library.

78. Carter to Carter, September 14, 1978, Judicial Appointments, 4–10/78 [O/A 7498], Lipshutz Papers, Carter Library. Also see FG 52/#5 1/20/77–1/20/81, WHCF, Carter Library.

79. Lipshutz to Bell, November 7, 1978, Lipshutz Papers; Bell to Lipshutz, November 13, 1978, Lipshutz Papers.

80. McKenna to Lipshutz, March 15, 1979, Lipshutz Papers.

81. Lipshutz to Carter, May 9, 1979, Lipshutz Papers; Bell prepared to recommend Hufstedler: conversation with author on June 1, 1981, Washington, D.C.; "we have to get more women": *Springfield Daily News,* January 26, 1979, p. 6.

82. Justice Department officials indicated: Margaret McKenna, Memorandum for the File, March 9, 1977, FG 53 1/20/77–1/20/81, WHCF, Carter Library; Stennis's reply: Moore to Lipshutz, April 10, 1978, Judicial Appointments 4–10/78 [O/A 7498], Lipshutz Papers, Carter Library.

83. Lipshutz to Bell, December 13, 1978, Lipshutz Papers.

84. Gray had the support: *New York Times,* September 4, 1977, p. 16; Bell to Carter, July 14, 1977, FG 52/#5 1/20/77–1/20/81, WHCF, Carter Library.

85. Gray to Carter, September 16, 1980, FG 53/ST 1A 1/20/77–1/20/81, WHCF, Carter Library.

86. Lipshutz to Carter, May 2, 1979, Lipshutz Papers.

87. Morgan opposed both Chambers and McMillan: Sanford Levinson, "How Not to Pick a Judge," *The Nation,* September 23, 1978, p. 262; Lipshutz to Carter, May 2, 1979, Lipshutz Papers.

88. See Lipshutz to Carter, May 2, 1979, Lipshutz Papers, and Lipshutz to Carter, May 17, 1979, FG 53 1/20/77–1/20/81, WHCF, Carter Library.

89. Lipshutz to Carter, December 27, 1978, FG#6 1/20/77–1/20/81, WHCF, Carter Library.

90. Senate Resolution 374. *Congressional Record,* April 1, 1980, p. 7278.

91. See the discussion in Slotnick, "Paths to the Federal Bench," 377–78.

92. As quoted in Griffin Bell, Walter Berns, Sheldon Goldman, and Orrin G. Hatch, *Whom Do Judges Represent* (Washington, D.C.: American Enterprise Institute, 1981), 24.

93. Carter administration's avowed objective: see, in general, Robert Lipshutz and Douglas Huron, "Achieving a More Representative Federal Judiciary," *Judicature* 62

(1979): 483ff.; continued with Bush and Clinton: Sheldon Goldman, "Bush's Judicial Legacy: The Final Imprint," *Judicature* 76 (1993): 282–97, and Sheldon Goldman, "Judicial Selection under Clinton: A Midterm Examination," *Judicature* 78 (1995): 276–91.

94. *New York Times,* October 15, 1980, A24.

Chapter Eight: Reaganizing the Judiciary

1. On the Reagan presidency, see Martin Anderson, *Revolution: The Reagan Legacy* (Stanford, Calif.: Hoover Institution Press, 1990); Larry Berman, ed., *Looking Back on the Reagan Presidency* (Baltimore: The Johns Hopkins University Press, 1990); Lou Cannon, *President Reagan: The Role of a Lifetime* (New York: Simon & Schuster, 1991); Michael Deaver, *Behind the Scenes* (New York: Morrow, 1987); Dilys M. Hill, Raymond A. Moore, and Phil Williams, *The Reagan Presidency: An Incomplete Revolution?* (New York: St. Martin's Press, 1990); Donald T. Regan, *For the Record: From Wall Street to Washington* (San Diego: Harcourt Brace Jovanovich, 1988); George P. Shultz, *Turmoil and Triumph: My Years as Secretary of State* (New York: Scribner's, 1993). Also see Ronald Reagan's autobiography, *An American Life* (New York: Simon and Schuster, 1990).

2. George Gallup, Jr., *The Gallup Poll: Public Opinion 1989* (Wilmington, Delaware: Scholarly Resources, 1990), 7. Reagan's approval rating was 63 percent. Roosevelt's had been 66 percent.

3. On the Iran-Contra affair, see Theodore Draper, *A Very Thin Line: The Iran-Contra Affairs* (New York: Simon & Schuster, 1992); Michael A. Ledeen, *Perilous Statecraft: An Insider's Account of the Iran-Contra Affair* (New York: Scribner, 1988); Robert C. McFarlane, *Special Trust* (New York: Cadell & Davies, 1994); and Lawrence E. Walsh, *Iran-Contra: The Final Report* (New York: Times Books, 1994). On the savings and loan scandal, see Cannon, *President Reagan,* 824–28; Robert Emmet Long, ed., *Banking Scandals: The S&Ls and BCCI* (New York: H. W. Wilson, 1993); Stephen Pizzo, Mary Fricker, and Paul Muolo, *Inside Job: The Looting of America's Savings and Loans* (New York: HarperPerennial, 1991); and Lewis William Seidman, *Full Faith and Credit: The Great S&L Debacle and other Washington Sagas* (New York: Times Books, 1993).

4. Reagan came to the presidency: William French Smith, *Law and Justice in the Reagan Administration: The Memoirs of an Attorney General* (Stanford, Calif.: Hoover Institution Press, 1991), xv–xvii. Also see Reagan, *An American Life,* 196–99; pledge to direct judicial positions: *Congressional Quarterly Weekly Report* 38 (July 19, 1980): 2046.

5. Failed to persuade legislature: *Congressional Quarterly Weekly Report* 38 (July 19, 1980): 2013; he described the committees: *New York Times,* October 15, 1980, A24.

6. Clark's lack of distinction: *New York Times,* October 2, 1980, B14; Paul Haerle noted: *Newsweek,* September 8, 1980, pp. 78, 79.

7. Reagan pledged: *New York Times,* October 2, 1980, B14; October 14 news conference: *New York Times,* October 15, 1980, A24.

8. William French Smith to Howard H. Baker, Jr., March 2, 1981, Justice Department Files.

9. All quotes from Rose in this and the next four paragraphs are from *Legal Times,* November 8, 1982, p. 6.

10. For Reagan's management style, see Hill, Moore, and Williams, *The Reagan Presidency,* chaps. 1, 3; Cannon, *President Reagan,* passim; Deaver, *Behind the Scenes,* 28–29, 174; Regan, *For the Record,* passim; Shultz, *Turmoil and Triumph,* passim.

11. Interview with Jane Swift, special counsel for judicial selection, office of legal policy, Department of Justice, December 18, 1984; interview with Stephen J. Markman, assistant attorney general for legal policy, Department of Justice, December 23, 1986.

12. Interview with Markman, December 23, 1986.

13. Fielding to Reagan, September 22, 1981, WHORM, FG 052 (037000–048499), #042110, Ronald Reagan Library. Unless otherwise noted, all references to letters and memoranda are from the Ronald Reagan Library, Simi Valley, California.

14. Fielding to Reagan, Recommended Telephone Call, November 16, 1981, WHORM, FG 53, #033963, p. 2, misfiled with FG 52 (033000–034999).

15. For a reference to meeting with a senator, see, for example, Thad Cochran to Reagan, October 15, 1981, WHORM, FG 52 (037000–048499), #043144; "until he could do": *New York Times,* September 27, 1982, B2.

16. William J. Casey to the President, January 7, 1984, WHORM, FG 52 (166000–171799), #168652. Also see *New York Times,* June 12, 1984, A24.

17. David C. Treen to the President, May 31, 1982, WHORM, FG 52 (078900–086999), #081816. This account draws from the presidential papers and from Christopher Drew, "Toledano's Past Haunts His Ambition to be Federal Judge," *The Times-Picayune* (New Orleans), February 6, 1983, pp. 1, 4.

18. Fielding to Reagan, December 3, 1982, WHORM, FG 52 (095608–099999), #098491.

19. Toledano was informed: Toledano to Meese, July 13, 1983, WHORM, FG 52 (149267–158899), #154918; tried to turn the decision around; Fielding to James A. Baker III, March 22, 1983, WHORM, FG 52 (183468–191999), #190199, and Treen to Meese, March 30, 1983, WHORM, FG 52 (126000–138999), #131945; "final decision rests exclusively": Fielding to Treen, April 25, 1983, WHORM, FG 52 (139000–149265), #141861.

20. Reagan went public: see, e.g., *New York Times,* October 22, 1985, p. 1; *New York Times,* August 6, 1986, A13; Reagan also devoted: *New York Times,* June 22, 1986, p. 1.

21. *Congressional Quarterly Weekly Report* 38 (July 19, 1980): 2046.

22. See William French Smith, *Law and Justice,* xv–xvii; Charles Fried, *Order and Law: Arguing the Reagan Revolution, A Firsthand Account* (New York: Simon & Schuster, 1991). Also see Bruce Fein, "A Reagan Court Would Overturn Past Errors," *Human Events* (July 6, 1983), cited in Herman Schwartz, *Packing the Courts: The Conservative Campaign to Rewrite the Constitution* (New York: Scribner's, 1988), 6, 206.

23. All quotations from the Smith speech are taken from the text as reprinted in *New York Times,* October 30, 1981, A22.

24. *New York Times,* October 31, 1981, p. 15.

25. He observed: *Public Papers of the Presidents of the United States: Ronald Reagan 1983,* book 2 (Washington, D.C.: Government Printing Office, 1985), 1112; Kasten noted: *Milwaukee Journal,* June 10, 1981, p. 1.

26. "examples of the Administration's determination": *New York Times,* December 8, 1981, A27; "[r]eview of available": Rose to Schmults and Smith, May 26, 1981, Fred F. Fielding files, CFOA Box 425, President's Federal Judicial Selection Committee Meeting—May 21, 1981 (1); "Judge Eschbach's opinions": Rose to Schmults and Smith, July 7, 1981, Fred F. Fielding files, CFOA Box 426, President's Federal Judicial Selection Committee Meeting—July 9, 1981 (2).

27. The administration had decided: Duberstein to Latta, July 12, 1982, WHORM, FG 52 (087000–095607), #084738; congressional delegation recommended: *New York Times,* August 3, 1982, A14.

28. The Center for Judicial Studies: "With or Without Supreme Court Changes, Reagan Will Reshape the Federal Bench," *National Journal* 16 (December 8, 1984): 2341; "tremendously pleased": *Legal Times of Washington,* October 22, 1984, p. 15; extensive analysis: *Legal Times of Washington,* October 22, 1984, pp. 1, 10–15; *New York Times,* August 23, 1984, B8; and *Boston Globe,* July 29, 1984, A28.

29. *Congressional Quarterly Weekly Report* 42 (August 25, 1984): 2110.

30. Graeme Browning, "Reagan Molds the Federal Court in His Own Image," *ABA Journal* 71 (August 1985): 62.

31. The address was published. Edwin Meese III, "The Attorney General's View of the Supreme Court: Toward a Jurisprudence of Original Intention," *Public Administration Review* 45 (1985): 701.

32. All quotations in this paragraph are from *Public Papers of the Presidents of the United States: Ronald Reagan 1985,* book 2 (Washington, D.C.: Government Printing Office, 1988), 1270; Reagan increasingly appreciated: "Reagan Says He'll Use Vacancies to Discourage Judicial Activism," *New York Times,* October 22, 1985, A1, A29.

33. Fielding observed: John A. Jenkins, "Mr. Power: Attorney General Meese Is Reagan's Man to Lead the Conservative Charge," *New York Times Magazine,* October 12, 1986, p. 19; Meese himself revealed: Jenkins, pp. 19, 96.

34. Carrying great weight: "Meese Playing Central Role in Domestic Policy Now," *New York Times,* September 17, 1986, B8; Grover Rees: see *Newsweek,* October 14, 1985, p. 73, and *Dallas Morning News,* November 24, 1985, 1A.

35. *Public Papers of the Presidents of the United States: Ronald Reagan 1986,* book 2 (Washington, D.C.: Government Printing Office, 1989), 1348.

36. D'Amato to Reagan, February 27, 1984, WHORM, FG 53 (203939–203943), #203939.

37. Hellerstein had written an article: Schwartz, *Packing the Courts,* 81–82; because he was too liberal: *New York Times,* April 2, 1985, B2.

38. "an outstandingly able lawyer": *New York Times,* July 1, 1984, p. 22; Fielding said: as quoted in Schwartz, *Packing the Courts,* 83; "[n]o one . . . interviewed me": *New York Times,* April 1, 1985, A15.

39. *Confirmation Hearings on Federal Appointments, Hearings Before the Committee on the Judiciary,* 99th Congress, 1st Session, Serial No. J-99-7, part 2 (Washington, D.C.: Government Printing Office, 1986), p. 291 (Hearings on September 25, 1985). All quotations are from this source.

40. Senate Judiciary Committee Questionnaire completed by Emmett R. Cox, p. 43, Senate Judiciary Committee file on Emmett R. Cox, 100th Congress.

41. Stephen J. Markman, "Judicial Selection: The Reagan Years," in *Judicial Selec-*

tion: Merit, Ideology, and Politics (Washington, D.C.: National Legal Center for the Public Interest, 1990), 38–39. All quotations from Markman are from this source.

42. Grover Rees revealed: *Dallas Morning News,* November 24, 1985, 22A; "how she would rule": *Confirmation Hearings on Federal Appointments,* 99th Congress, part 2, September 25, 1985, p. 430.

43. Percy to Reagan, February 4, 1983, WHORM, FG 52 (113000–125999), #123643.

44. Totten to Meese, July 7, 1982, WHORM, FG 52 (087000–095607), #087441.

45. Weyrich to Meese, July 21, 1982, WHORM, FG 52 (087000–095607), #089270.

46. Percy met with Meese: Percy to Meese, September 30, 1982, WHORM, FG 52 (103000–112999), #103429; "a model of judicial restraint": Murdock to Percy, October 11, 1982, WHORM, FG 52 (103000–112999), #108661, p. 18; apparently cast doubt: Mullins to Rose, attachment to Rose to Cicconi, January 11, 1983, WHORM, FG 52 (221000–231999), #221989.

47. Percy to Reagan, February 4, 1983, WHORM, FG 52 (113000–125999), #123643. Emphasis in the original. All quotations from Senator Percy are from this source.

48. The agreement between Smith: Smith, *Law and Justice,* 72; wound up being passed over: see, e.g., D'Amato to Reagan, March 28, 1984, WHORM, FG 53, #205121 (concerning Nicholas Tsoucalas); D'Amato to Herrington, January 28, 1985, WHORM, FG 53, #306827 (Elizabeth F. Defeis); D'Amato to Baker, February 12, 1988, WHORM, FG 53, #552820 (John Carro); D'Amato to Meese, March 28, 1988, WHORM, FG 53, #558827 (Reginald H. Dodds).

49. *Legal Times,* December 26, 1983–January 2, 1984, p. 1.

50. *Congressional Quarterly Weekly Report* 44 (June 7, 1986): 1297.

51. *New York Times,* May 28, 1986, A16.

52. Ball to Reagan, Recommended Telephone Call memorandum, June 16, 1986, WHORM, PR 7-02 (390270–390349), #390327, p. 1. All quotations from the memo are from this source.

53. Gorton switched: *New York Times,* June 27, 1986, p. 1ff.; *Congressional Quarterly Weekly Report* 44 (June 28, 1986): 1509; Durenberger committed himself: *New York Times,* June 26, 1986, A17; Saturday radio address: *Public Papers of the Presidents of the United States: Ronald Reagan 1986,* book 1 (Washington, D.C.: Government Printing Office, 1988), 818–20.

54. This account draws upon *New York Times,* June 27, 1986, pp. 1ff.; *Congressional Record,* June 26, 1986, S8541–S8573; and *Congressional Quarterly Weekly Report* 44 (June 28, 1986): 1508–9.

55. Ball to Reagan, Recommended Telephone Call, July 25, 1986, WHORM, PR 7-02 (406100–406199), #406138.

56. Gorton was hurt politically: *Washington Post,* July 11, 1986, A18; *New York Times,* December 3, 1987, A36; Democrats exacted revenge: *New York Times,* October 15, 1986, B14; *New York Times,* December 3, 1987, A36.

57. His opponents accused: *New York Times,* March 19, 1986, A24; heatedly debated: see *Congressional Record,* March 11, 1986, pp. S2387–S2393. The votes were

taken on March 18. *New York Times,* March 19, 1986, A24. Also see *Congressional Quarterly Weekly Report* 44 (March 22, 1986): 670.

58. *Congressional Quarterly Weekly Report* 43 (November 9, 1985): 2308.

59. See the debate in *Congressional Record,* December 17, 1985, pp. S17737–S17743.

60. *Confirmation Hearings on Federal Appointments,* Hearings Before the Senate Judiciary Committee, 99th Congress, 1st Session, Part 2, Serial No. J-99-7 (Washington, D.C.: Government Printing Office, 1986), 1149–53.

61. *New York Times,* April 18, 1985, B4. The questionnaire and responses are in *Confirmation Hearings on Federal Appointments,* Hearings Before the Senate Judiciary Committee, 99th Congress, 1st Session, Part 1, Serial No. J-99-7 (Washington, D.C.: Government Printing Office, 1986), 90–101.

62. Members of the committee were angered: *Hearings,* 87–89, 102; regretted not having advised Hatch: *Hearings,* 426.

63. See, for example, Ethan Bronner, *Battle for Justice: How the Bork Nomination Shook America* (New York: Norton, 1989); Mark Gitenstein, *Matters of Principle: An Insider's Account of America's Rejection of Robert Bork's Nomination to the Supreme Court* (New York: Simon & Schuster, 1992); Patrick B. McGuigan, *Ninth Justice: The Fight for Bork* (Washington, D.C.: Free Congress Research and Education Foundation, 1990); and Paul Simon, *Advice and Consent: Clarence Thomas, Robert Bork and the Intriguing History of the Supreme Court's Nomination Battles* (Washington, D.C.: National Press Books, 1992). For Bork's perspective, see Robert H. Bork, *The Tempting of America: The Political Seduction of the Law* (New York: Free Press, 1990).

64. Bernard H. Siegan, *Economic Liberties and the Constitution* (Chicago: University of Chicago Press, 1980), and *The Supreme Court's Constitution: An Inquiry into Judicial Review and Its Impact on Society* (New Brunswick, N.J.: Transaction Books, 1987).

65. Fielding to Reagan, December 3, 1982, WHORM, FG 52 (095608–099999), #098491, p. 3.

66. Cannon, *President Reagan,* 800–801. Also see *New York Times,* October 19, 1988, A22.

67. *New York Times,* October 19, 1988, A22.

68. Pressler to Reagan, June 23, 1981, WHORM, FG 52 (026000–031599), #029940.

69. Friedersdorf to Pressler, September 4, 1981, WHORM, FG 52 (026000–031599), #029940.

70. Suggested the names: Pressler to Reagan, December 2, 1981, WHORM, FG 52 (048500–053999), #051468; woman attorney: Pressler to Reagan, January 20, 1982, WHORM, FG 52 (054000–057999), #056920.

71. Replace him with someone from Arkansas: Henley to Reagan, March 15, 1982, WHORM, FG 52 (063300–074477), #066578; "it would seem logical": Woods to Meese, March 11, 1982, WHORM, FG 52 (063300–074477), #066046.

72. Pressler and Abdnor to Reagan, March 10, 1982, WHORM, FG 52 (063300–074477), #065981.

73. Pressler to Reagan, December 21, 1982, WHORM, FG 52 (113000–125999), #115944.

74. Abdnor to Reagan, December 22, 1982, WHORM, FG 52 (113000–125999), #116023.

75. Abdnor to Nelson, March 31, 1983, WHORM FG 52 (139000–149265), #143784.

76. Cochran to Reagan, July 12, 1984, WHORM, FG 52 (232000–233799), #232790.

77. Long and Johnston to Reagan, July 27, 1984, WHORM, FG 52 (233800–234399), #233801.

78. Markman, "Judicial Selection," 41.

79. Smith to Reagan, September 17, 1981, WHORM, FG 52 (037000–048499), #042110. Other examples include Smith to Reagan, July 27, 1981, Fred F. Fielding files, CFOA Box 426, President's Federal Judicial Selection Committee Meeting — July 30, 1981 (1) (concerning Roger J. Miner to the district bench for the Northern District of New York); Smith to Reagan, February 11, 1982, WHORM, FG 52 (058000–063299), #062450 (concerning John L. Coffey to the Seventh Circuit); Smith to Reagan, April 4, 1983, WHORM, FG 52 (113000–125999), #124904 (concerning Joel M. Flaum to the Seventh Circuit); Smith to Reagan, February 28, 1984, WHORM, FG 52 (195800–199999), #195898 (concerning Robert R. Beezer to the Ninth Circuit).

80. Dinkins to Reagan, July 27, 1984, WHORM, FG 52 (216000–216999), #216693.

81. Smith to Reagan, December 13, 1982, WHORM, FG 52 (095608–099999), #098586.

82. Born and Coleman testified: *Hearings,* September 29, 1983, p. 47, unpublished transcript; Unger had many supporters: see the six folders in WHORM, FG 52 #183467, esp. folder 5.

83. Wilkinson's own experience as a law clerk: J. Harvie Wilkinson, *Serving Justice: A Supreme Court Clerk's View* (New York: Charterhouse, 1974); Warner agreed to support: *New York Times,* April 1, 1984, p. 22.

84. "I have no apologies whatsoever": *Washington Post,* March 8, 1984, C4; Schmults and Rose had also contacted: *Washington Post,* March 15, 1984, A17; They also questioned: *Confirmation Hearings on Federal Appointments,* Hearings Before the Senate Judiciary Committee, 98th Congress, 2nd Session, Part 3, Serial No. J-98-6 (Washington, D.C.: Government Printing Office, 1985), 17–69. Also see *Washington Post,* February 23, 1984, A14.

85. "Publicly take the position": *Dallas Morning News,* November 24, 1985, 22A; Lino A. Graglia, *Disaster By Decree: The Supreme Court Decisions on Race and the Schools* (Ithaca, N.Y.: Cornell University Press, 1976); Bell submitted a report: *New York Times,* August 7, 1986, p. 1.

86. Scalia was pushed for consideration: Stella to Reagan, July 21, 1981, WHORM, FG 52 (031600–032999), #032838; Domenici to Reagan, August 3, 1981, WHORM, FG 52 (035000–036999), #035957; "the first Italian-American": *Public Papers of the Presidents of the United States: Ronald Reagan 1986,* book 2 (Washington, D.C.: Government Printing Office, 1989), 1055.

87. "Judge Contie was": Memorandum for the President, January 11, 1982,

WHORM, FG 52 (058000–063299), #063109; "I . . . happen to be": Cardamone to Reagan, November 9, 1981, WHORM, FG 52 (037000–048499), #047790.

88. Listed his ethnic group: Resume Sheet for Juan R. Torruella, WHORM, FG 52 (216000–216999), #216690; "would allow you to appoint": Luis A. Ferre to Ronald Reagan, July 10, 1984, WHORM, FG 52 (232000–233799), #232801.

89. The note was handwritten on the copy of the reply from Meese to Puglia, July 5, 1983, WHORM, FG 52 (149267–158899), #151210, misfiled, should be with FG 53.

90. All quotations from the Reagan address are taken from *Public Papers of the Presidents of the United States: Ronald Reagan 1983*, book 2 (Washington, D.C.: Government Printing Office, 1985), 1112.

91. Emphasis added. Duberstein to Latta, July 12, 1982, WHORM, FG 52 (078900–086999), #084738.

92. Rose to Schmults and Smith, June, 1981, Fred F. Fielding files, CFOA Box 426, President's Federal Judicial Selection Committee Meeting—June 25, 1981 (2); "Judge Hall is a conservative": Dole to Hayakawa, May 19, 1981, Fred F. Fielding files, CFOA Box 426, President's Federal Judicial Selection Committee Meeting—June 25, 1981 (2).

93. Rose to Schmults and Smith, July 14, 1981, Fred F. Fielding files, CFOA Box 426, President's Federal Judicial Selection Committee Meeting—July 16, 1981 (1).

94. Fielding wrote in his notes: Candidates in "Hold" Status Following July 23, 1981, Meeting, Fred F. Fielding files, CFOA Box 426, President's Federal Judicial Selection Committee Meeting—July 23, 1981 (1); consultation convinced Fielding: Candidates in "Hold" Status Following July 23, 1981, Meeting, Fred F. Fielding files, CFOA Box 426, President's Federal Judicial Selection Committee Meeting—July 30, 1981 (1); committee agreed to drop her: Candidates in "Hold" Status Following July 30, 1981, Meeting, Fred F. Fielding files, CFOA Box 426, President's Federal Judicial Selection Committee Meeting—August 5, 1981 (1).

95. Schneider to Reagan, August 6, 1981, WHORM, FG 52 (035000–036999), #036285.

96. Rose to Schmults and Smith, August 18, 1981, Fred F. Fielding files, CFOA Box 426, President's Federal Judicial Selection Committee Meeting—August 27, 1981 (2).

97. "There has been a large increase": Wilson to Fielding, August 27, 1981, Fred F. Fielding files, CFOA Box 426, President's Federal Judicial Selection Committee Meeting—August 27, 1981 (1); at its September 3 meeting: Summary List of Candidates for U.S. Circuit/District Judge, U.S. Attorney and U.S. Marshal Approved for Pre-Nomination Process at the September 3, 1981, Meeting, Fred F. Fielding files, CFOA Box 426, President's Federal Judicial Selection Committee Meeting—September 10, 1981 (1); aide would check: Fielding notes, September 3, 1981, Fred F. Fielding files, CFOA Box 426, President's Federal Judicial Selection Committee Meeting—September 3, 1981 (1); ABA "well qualified": *Los Angeles Times,* December 25, 1981, B1; *Legal Times,* November 8, 1982, p. 8; Whittaker was told: Lay to Zorinsky, December 29, 1981, WHORM, FG 52 (054000–057999), #055046, p. 2.

98. *New York Times,* December 24, 1981, B4.

99. Branstad to Reagan, October 14, 1981, WHORM, FG 52 (037000–048499), #043282.

100. Williamson to Baker, October 26, 1981, WHORM, FG 52 (037000–048499), #043282.

101. She lacked enough "broad-based support": *New York Times,* December 24, 1981, B4; Jonathan Rose observed: *Legal Times,* November 8, 1982, p. 8.

102. "It is incredible to me": Lay to Zorinsky, December 29, 1981, WHORM, FG 52 (054000–057999), #055046, p. 2; "Shabby assault": *Kansas City Star,* December 27, 1981, 2B; "Political snipers": *New York Times,* January 7, 1982, A26.

103. "The opposition to the appointment": Heckler and Schroeder to Reagan, January 7, 1982, WHORM, FG 52 (054000–057999), #055046; attempted a last-minute campaign: National Women's Political Caucus Republicans, Action Alert, FG 52 (054000–057999).

104. "interested in receiving recommendations": Pressler to Reagan, January 20, 1982, WHORM, FG 52 (054000–057999), #056920; on Danforth's list: Advisory Status Report for the Attorney General and Deputy Attorney General, Fred F. Fielding files, CFOA Box 426, President's Federal Judicial Selection Committee Meeting—July 2, 1981 (4); "Please be assured": Fielding to Walker, March 30, 1982, WHORM, FG 52 (054000–057999).

105. Indicating racial background: for example, the resume of Lawrence W. Pierce stated, "Ethnic Group: Black." WHORM, FG 52 (033000–034999), #033338. The resume of Richard A. Posner read, "Ethnic Group: Caucasian." WHORM, FG 52 (033000–034999), #033728; "Judge Hargrove will be": emphases in original. Memorandum for the President, January 27, 1984, WHORM, PR 7-02 Presidential Telephone Calls (172000–187099), #187006.

106. Every one of the fourteen persons: *The Performance of the Reagan Administration in Nominating Women and Minorities to the Federal Bench,* Hearing Before the Committee on the Judiciary, United States Senate, 100th Congress, 2nd Session, February 2, 1988 (Washington, D.C.: Government Printing Office, 1990), 4; responded in testimony: ibid., 25–26.

107. "A very important factor": *New York Times,* July 26, 1981, p. 23; "President's desire to appoint": Fielding to Meese and Baker, June 15, 1981, Fred F. Fielding files, CFOA Box 425, President's Federal Judicial Selection Committee Meeting—June 11, 1981 (1).

108. Interview with Jane Swift, special counsel for judicial selection, Office of Legal Policy, Department of Justice, December 18, 1984.

109. *Public Papers of the Presidents of the United States: Ronald Reagan, 1986* book 2 (Washington, D.C.: Government Printing Office, 1989), 1055.

Chapter Nine: Summing Up over Fifty-Six Years

1. See Sheldon Goldman, "Judicial Selection under Clinton: A Midterm Examination," *Judicature* 78 (1995): 281.

2. Evan A. Evans, "Political Influences in the Selection of Federal Judges," *Wisconsin Law Review* (May 1948): 330–51.

3. Judicial Conference: see, in general, Peter G. Fish, *The Politics of Federal Judicial Administration* (Princeton, N.J.: Princeton University Press, 1973); judicial pork barrel

politics: Deborah J. Barrow, Gary Zuk, and Gerard S. Gryski, *The Federal Judiciary and Institutional Change* (Ann Arbor: University of Michigan Press, 1996), 54, and Jon R. Bond, "The Politics of Court Structure: The Addition of New Federal Judges, 1949–1978," *Law and Politics Quarterly* 2 (1980): 181–88; "Congress exceeded": Barrow, Zuk, and Gryski, *Federal Judiciary,* 56.

4. David M. O'Brien, *Judicial Roulette* (New York: Priority Press, 1988), 19.

5. For a more detailed list of qualities that make for a good judge, see Henry J. Abraham, *Justices and Presidents: A Political History of Appointments to the Supreme Court,* 2d ed. (New York: Oxford University Press, 1985), 4, and Sheldon Goldman, "Judicial Selection and the Qualities That Make a Good Judge," *Annals of the American Academy of Political and Social Science* (July 1982): 112–24.

6. See, in general, Philip L. Dubois, *From Ballot to Bench: Judicial Elections and the Quest for Accountability* (Austin: University of Texas Press, 1980); Lawrence Baum, *American Courts: Process and Policy,* 3d ed. (Boston: Houghton Mifflin, 1994), 114–29; and Robert A. Carp and Ronald Stidham, *Judicial Process in America,* 3d ed. (Washington, D.C.: CQ Press, 1996), 256–61.

7. See Barbara Luck Graham, "Do Judicial Selection Systems Matter? A Study of Black Representation on State Courts," *American Politics Quarterly,* 18 (1990): 316–36.

8. Harold W. Chase, *Federal Judges: The Appointing Process* (Minneapolis: University of Minnesota Press, 1972), 4–6, 205–8.

9. See, in general, Stephen Skowronek, *The Politics Presidents Make: Leadership from John Adams to George Bush* (Cambridge, Mass.: Harvard University Press, Belknap Press, 1993).

10. "Since the turn": Barrow, Zuk, and Gryski, *Federal Judiciary,* 62; decisional implications: see, for example, Robert A. Carp and C. K. Rowland, *Policymaking and Politics in the Federal District Courts* (Knoxville: University of Tennessee Press, 1983), C. K. Rowland and Robert A. Carp, *Politics and Judgment in Federal District Courts* (Lawrence: University Press of Kansas, 1996), and the literature and findings discussed in Carp and Stidham, *Judicial Process,* 291–369.

11. O'Brien, *Judicial Roulette,* 19. Also see Barrow, Zuk, and Gryski, *Federal Judiciary,* 101.

12. *New York Times,* January 8, 1996, p. 9.

13. *Improving the Process of Appointing Federal Judges: A Report of the Miller Center Commission on the Selection of Federal Judges* (Charlottesville: Miller Center at the University of Virginia, 1996). Also see *New York Times,* May 16, 1996, B9; *The Third Branch* (June 1996), 7.

14. A classic study of a Supreme Court appointment focusing on these facets is David J. Danelski, *A Supreme Court Justice Is Appointed* (New York: Random House, 1964).

Index

ABA, 10, 11, 358–359; enters selection process 1946–1952, 86–88; opposes Frieda Hennock, 96; Eisenhower interested in, 115; rating Eisenhower's nominees, 120–123, 128–130, 133–135, 137–141, 148, 151; pushes Kennedy for bipartisan appointments, 157, 175, 177; rating Kennedy-Johnson nominees, 159, 165, 167–169, 171, 177–180, 183–184, 186–187, 190, 194; rating Nixon-Ford nominees, 201, 205, 210–211, 213–218, 221, 223–225, 228, 231, 234; rating system, 247, 261, 326–327n; rating Carter nominees, 263–268, 270–271, 277, 281; rating Reagan nominees, 295–296, 303, 306, 309–310, 313–315, 318, 322–327, 332, 339, 342–343; president of ABA responds to Att'y Gen'l Smith, 298; trends in ratings, 349, 351, 355, 357

Abdnor, James, 320–322
Abraham, Henry J., 123, 372, 377, 411
Acheson, Dean, 30
Adams, Ida May, 95
Adams, John, 7
Adams, John Quincy, 7
Adams, Sherman, 113, 119, 131, 132, 135, 144
affirmative action, judges, 244–245, 253–260, 269, 290, 329
AFL-CIO, 240
African Americans, as candidates for judgeships: Roosevelt admin., 54–57; Truman admin., 98–101; Eisenhower admin., 143–146; Kennedy-Johnson admin.,182–187, 191, 195–196; Nixon-Ford admin., 222–226, 229, 233–234; Carter admin., 258–259, 271–274, 278, 282–283; Reagan admin., 334–335, 340; trends, 340, 352, 356, 358

Hills, Carla, 220, 221, 330
Hispanics, as candidates for judgeships:
 Harold Medina, 196n; Kennedy-
 Johnson admin., 191, 196; Nixon-
 Ford admin., 218–220, 229, 233;
 Carter admin., 269, 278, 282–283;
 Reagan admin., 328, 340, 344;
 trends, 350, 356
Hodge, Walter H., 136
Hoffman, Walter E., 128
Holder, Cale, 117
Holland, John W., 32
Hollowell, Donald, 186
Holtzoff, Alexander, 37, 83
Hooper, Frank A., 71, 91
Hoover, Herbert, 9, 15
Horton, Odell, 251
Houston, Charles, 56, 98
Howard, George, Jr., 268
Howard, J. Woodford, 371, 376, 380,
 381
Hufstedler, Shirley, 181–182, 271, 357
Hughes, Sarah T., 180
Hughes, William J., Jr., 90
Hullin, Tod R., 203
Humphrey, Gordon J., 319
Humphrey, Hubert H., 71, 82, 171, 185,
 197
Hurley, George, 18, 19
Huron, Douglas, 239, 240, 246, 249,
 252, 253, 255, 256, 258, 268
Huston, Tom Charles, memo, 205–207
Huxman, Walter A., 36

Ibanez, Richard, 219–220
Ickes, Harold, 20, 45, 55
Inouye, Daniel K., 311, 315
interest groups, 308, 326–327

Jackson, Andrew, 1, 4, 7, 8
Jackson, Donald Dale, 182, 395, 397
Jackson, Henry M., 209, 210
Jackson, Robert, 21, 24, 28, 29
James, E. Pendelton, 293
Javits, Jacob, 132, 133, 177, 208, 302

Jefferson, Andrew L., Jr., 283
Jefferson, Thomas, 4, 7
Jenner, William, 116, 117
Jenney, Ralph E., 32
Jepsen, Roger W., 321, 333
Jews, as candidates for judgeships:
 Roosevelt admin., 59, 62–63; Tru-
 man admin., 105, 107; Eisenhower
 admin., 149, 152; Kennedy-Johnson
 admin., 179–180, 191, 195; Nixon-
 Ford admin., 229, 232–233; Carter
 admin., 278, 282; Reagan admin.,
 340, 344; trends, 350, 352, 356
Johnsen, Harvey M., 36
Johnson, Frank M., 128
Johnson, Lyndon B., 1, 42, 80, 133–34,
 154–197, 360–361
Johnson, Norma Holloway, 259
Johnson, Samuel D., Jr., 265
Jones, Catesby L., 23, 24
Jones, Charles Alvin, 28
Jones, Charles O., 397
Jones, Edith H., 323
Jones, Nathaniel, 239, 240, 251, 274
Jones, Warren L., 129–130
Jones, Woodrow Wilson, 171
Jordan, Hamilton, 242, 245, 246, 247,
 249, 252, 256, 257, 261
Judd, Orrin, 177
Judd, Walter, 139
judicial selection commission, 140, 210,
 238, 239, 244
judicial selection, mechanics of, 9–13
Judicial Conference of the United States,
 358, 363
Judicial Selection Project, 252, 253, 257

Kalbfleisch, Girard Edward, 135
Kalman, Laura, 370
Kanne, Michael S., 336
Kassebaum, Nancy L., 312
Kasten, Robert, W., Jr., 298
Katzenbach, Nicholas deB., 158, 161,
 163, 178, 179, 184
Kaufman, Irving R., 92, 132, 133